GREEK EPIGRAM IN RECEPTION

CLASSICAL PRESENCES

General Editors

Lorna Hardwick   James I. Porter

CLASSICAL PRESENCES

Attempts to receive the texts, images, and material culture of ancient Greece and Rome inevitably run the risk of appropriating the past in order to authenticate the present. Exploring the ways in which the classical past has been mapped over the centuries allows us to trace the avowal and disavowal of values and identities, old and new. Classical Presences brings the latest scholarship to bear on the contexts, theory, and practice of such use, and abuse, of the classical past.

Greek Epigram
in Reception

*J. A. Symonds, Oscar Wilde, and the Invention
of Desire, 1805–1929*

GIDEON NISBET

OXFORD
UNIVERSITY PRESS

OXFORD

UNIVERSITY PRESS

Great Clarendon Street, Oxford, OX2 6DP,
United Kingdom

Oxford University Press is a department of the University of Oxford.
It furthers the University's objective of excellence in research, scholarship,
and education by publishing worldwide. Oxford is a registered trade mark of
Oxford University Press in the UK and in certain other countries

First Edition published in 2013

Impression: 1

Published in the United States of America by Oxford University Press
198 Madison Avenue, New York, NY 10016, United States of America

British Library Cataloguing in Publication Data
Data available

ISBN 978-0-19-966249-4

As printed and bound by
CPI Group (UK) Ltd, Croydon, CR0 4YY

Acknowledgements

Written in the academic year 2011–12, this book has been in gestation since 2005, and has benefited from plenty of help in the busy years in between. I am grateful to colleagues, academic hosts, and seminar participants in Manchester, Glasgow, St Andrews, Oxford, and Durham, for their sympathetic responses to my early attempts to make sense of the material presented here, and particularly to Paul McKechnie at Macquarie. Colleagues in Classics and Ancient History here at Birmingham have been especially generous with their time in those last few days of tying loose ends together.

It is a pleasure, too, to acknowledge the pleasant and helpful staffs of the Pierpont Morgan Library in New York and Cambridge University Library; the support of Ken Dowden and Michael Whitby; and particularly the kind encouragement of Chris Stray, who generously read two of the chapters in draft and gave me some invaluable pointers. At Oxford University Press, I would like to thank Hilary O'Shea (Senior Commissioning Editor), Taryn Das Neves (Senior Assistant Commissioning Editor), and Mary Morton (proofreader). I thank also the Press's anonymous and very gracious reader.

This book is for Diana, always; and for Katherine Rose.

Birmingham
November 2012

Contents

'We are never free from the consciousness of a long past'

(John Addington Symonds, *Studies of the Greek Poets*,
Second Series (1876), 352; the phrase is underlined
in the copy owned by his attentive contemporary
reader, the young Oscar Wilde)

Introduction

1. GREECE AND THE VICTORIANS: HERITAGE, MEMORY, TRAUMA

> What you call vice...is not vice...It is as good to me as it was to Caesar, Alexander, Michelangelo, and Shakespeare. It was first of all made sin by monasticism...It may be a malady, but, if so, it appears only to attack the highest natures.
>
> (Oscar in court, 1895)[1]

> Which is the more effective in keeping the peace: blunt censorship of 'dangerous' texts, or safe interpretations of supposedly 'respectable' ones?[2]

The one thing we can say with certainty about the past is that it is not there any more. For the postmodern historian, the past is ontologically absent. To believe that we can know its reality from the present, let alone that hindsight grants epistemological privilege, is wishful fantasy, no matter how ingeniously argued.[3]

Paradoxically, however, the past *only* exists in the present—the one place we can experience it, feel its presence (it is 'here' for us by being 'now'), and make it work for us. We might say: the past exists *for*, and is a function *of*, the present. Like Oedipus—the lifelong obsession of that eminent Victorian, Freud—we look to what lies beyond our own conscious memories to dig out the truth of ourselves.[4] History is our Sphinx,

---

[1] Quoted from Hyde (1972: 312–13).

[2] Dollimore (2001: 95).

[3] e.g. K. Jenkins (1995: 10): 'the pretence that they can engage in a "real" dialogue with the "reality" of a (somehow) non-historiographically-constituted-past-as-history...modernist renditions are now naive: their historical moment has passed. What are therefore required today are guides who, accepting not so much the "end of history" per se but the "end of modernist renditions of history", can face this with equanimity and even optimism.'

[4] Armstrong (2005) digs into how Freud grappled with ancient myth to produce his new psychiatric paradigm. He was also a keen but not atypical bourgeois collector of small

and the riddle it poses has the same solution Oedipus puzzled out: ourselves. What is the truth of human nature, made evident through history and its patterns? What is our own particular identity, as the current generation of a family, tribe, city, or nation? *How did we get here* (and why 'us' in particular)? These are the questions that keep the past perpetually *in* the present.

This book takes as its theme the perception, representation, and occasional outright invention of the classical Greek past in one peculiarly revealing aspect. It follows a single and ostensibly 'minor' ancient literary genre, epigram, through a connected sequence of historically recent moments in Anglophone literary culture and the British public sphere—moments in which the shadow of Greece loomed larger than ever before or since.[5] In order to establish context for this reception history, its narrative necessarily casts both backwards and forwards in time from the notional span of 120-odd years marked out in its title (1805–1929); but the heart of its action is Victorian and Edwardian, a phase of classical reception that is now attracting intense critical scrutiny in specialist aspects.[6]

The Victorians have been ridiculed for romantically construing ancient Greece as the sunny childhood of humanity, but to do so made compelling sense to them.[7] This was *their* past, their collective early childhood, which merged imperceptibly and by way of a succession of other, complementary invented traditions (Anglo-Saxonism, Merrie England, mock-Tudor and Good Queen Bess, with a side order of Celtic Twilight) into the past they *could* remember—their collective 'adulthood'

antiquities, which now seem numinous in the light cast back on them by his famous theories; on his collecting habits see, inter alia, Forrester (1994) and the several contributors to Barker (1996).

[5] I use the latter term in the sense defined by Collini's important monograph of 1991. Vance (1997: 17) cautions his reader against being misled by Pater et al. into thinking the Victorians were fixated on Greece and forgot about Rome ('The Hellenists have misled us for too long'), but no one is suggesting they did; these two visions of the ancient world were complementary, and addressed different social uses and reception contexts.

[6] Notable recent instances include Barrow (2007) (classical literary allusion in art); Hurst (2006) and Fiske (2008) (women writers and the classics); Evangelista (2009a) (the Aesthetic movement); Dowling (1994), Blanshard (2010), and Orrells (2011a) ('Greek' sexuality, on which Dowling is deservedly influential); and the prodigious output of Christopher Stray, most famously (1998a) (education). Bradley (2010c) is invaluable on the uses of Classics in the British Empire; Vandiver (2010) brings the curtain down on Edwardian classical reception with her fine study of classical motifs in the poets of the First World War. Goldhill (2011) blends diverse enthusiasms, some carried over from Goldhill (2002); older works by, among others, Liversidge and Edwards (1996) (art) and Hingley (2000) (imperialism, and cf. Smiles 1994) are still valuable.

[7] e.g. Jenkyns (1980: 172), with characteristic impatience.

as a modern, technocratic, forward- and outward-looking Power in the world. They looked for the truth of themselves in the fragmented memories of their own collective infancy.[8]

Rome's military-*cum*-civil engineers and hard-headed provincial administrators played a clearly defined role in this stirring parade of ancestor masks, dignifying Britain's present exercise of military force as the patrimonially bequeathed work of civilization. Simultaneously, curating the archaeological record of the Romans as Britain's own conquerors (under 'bad' emperors, no less) emphatically declared 'their' ethical distance from 'us', delivering a woad-drenched parallel origin story that underwrote Britain's moral high ground in perpetuity as a nation of plucky underdogs.[9] Augustus's stable of on-message poets and historians—Vergil, Horace, Livy, et al., all of them fixtures of the Victorian classroom—supplied the obvious soundtrack to the new *imperium sine fine* alongside the assertively nativist (yet sneakily also classicizing) *Rule Britannia*. Yet it was the supposed Hellenic spirit of fearless rational enquiry that tied it all together as an ethically and philosophically acceptable package for the polite classes, turning the whole colonial enterprise into more than just lawcourts, garrisons, and railroads.

Greece also handily explained the new superpower's industrial, technological, and consequent economic edge. A scientified vision of Greek philosophy was semi-explicitly construed as the seed from which Britain's own modern Empire had grown:

> it was Ionia that gave birth to an idea, which was foreign to the East, but has become the starting-point of modern science,—the idea that Nature works by fixed laws. A fragment of Euripides speaks of him as 'happy who has learned to search for causes'... and the Greek precocity of mind in this direction, *unlike that of the Orientals*, had in it the promise of uninterrupted advance *in the future*—of great discoveries in mathematics, geometry, experimental physics, in medicine also and physiology.[10]

---

[8] On invented traditions as a symptomatic response to rapid cultural change in the modern nation-state, see the influential edited collection of Hobsbawm and Ranger (1983), invaluably complemented by Anderson (2006); specifically on the Ancient Britons, Smiles (1994); on non-English 'Ancient British' traditions, Morgan (1983) and Trevor-Roper (1983). Besides Jenkyns (1980), important general treatments of Greece as nineteenth-century British 'heritage' include F. M. Turner (1981), (intermittently) Lloyd-Jones (1982), and Clarke (1989). Collectively these established the framework within and against which more focused studies have been emerging from the 1990s onwards. On Victorian reception of ancient Rome, see in particular Vance (1997) (predominantly literary) and now Sachs (2010); Malamud (2009) surveys the American scene.

[9] The dedicated monograph is Hingley (2000); Bradley (2010b) is wide-ranging and thoughtful.

[10] Butcher (1893: 10; emphasis added).

This 'Greek precocity of mind' in the direction of technological progress is but one of many mid- to late Victorian formulations based squarely on the famous opposition drawn by Matthew Arnold's *Culture and Anarchy* (1869) between fearlessly rational 'Hellenism' and religiously obedient 'Hebraism'. It is fairly obvious that neither Arnold's Hellenism nor his Hebraism had much if anything to do with the social practice and cultural production of ancient Greece or Israel, insofar as we can reconstruct those cultures from the textual and material sources available to us; they were never really supposed to.[11] Where modern critics may err is in presuming that the Victorians were somehow collectively fooled by Arnold into taking this fantastic caricature of a schema, packaged as it was within an entertainingly quirky and digressive tractarian diatribe, as a sober historiographic proposition. Arnold was having fun with his material, and declared himself in two minds as to whether there was any real opposition there at all.

In the wake of *Culture and Anarchy*, however, and with less consistent self-aware good humour and irony, the Hellenism–Hebraism binary was expropriated and exaggerated as a useful rhetorical tool for talking through social questions and concerns—thinking and more particularly *feeling* them through. With melodrama as its predominant aesthetic, Victorian popular culture was already in the habit of taxonomizing its world into polar opposites—good and evil, purity and danger; rote Arnoldianism slotted seamlessly into this affective structure. Antiquity became a stage on which the emotionally loaded moral questions of the day could be played out in heightened form.[12]

Hellenism–Hebraism established a synergy with related binaries that shared with it melodrama's powerful emotive appeal to an emblematic scenario of confrontation between opposing or incompatible principles—Greece–Rome, pagan–Christian, East–West (a peculiarly toxic combination of Classics and Orientalism by supporters of the classical status quo will be addressed in Chapter 5). These buzzword binaries were already circulating in the public sphere as common coin, and their

---

[11] 'Arnold's discussion of Hebraism and Hellenism was brilliantly executed and proved rhetorically convincing... Yet double meanings and an almost disingenuous concealment of purpose characterized the entire chapter' (F. M. Turner 1981: 21). As Turner goes on to explain (pp. 23–4), Arnold developed his so-called Hellenism in dialogue, not with the Greek literary sources, but with the eighteenth- and early nineteenth-century German Romantic tradition, which, beginning with Herder, took the Greek spirit as its theme.

[12] In the later nineteenth century, melodrama became intricately wound up in popular reception of classical antiquity through bestselling novels and the spectacular 'toga plays' presented and discussed by Mayer (1994). There is a wealth of scholarship on melodrama as a theatrical mode and a habit of thought; Crosby (1991) is something of a classic.

culturally loaded evocation of the key moments in the *Bildungsroman* of Western Civilization made them ideal for bypassing scepticism and bluffing hecklers. By flipping or juggling these coins, or simply by switching one for another at the right moment, the astute participant in discourse could re-parse a contentious proposition into temporary and qualified acceptability, and potentially thus alter by tiny degrees the tone of the culture's conversation about itself and its relation to its past(s). Or—and inevitably this was the more usual recourse—the familiar tropes could be strengthened through minor variation and near-endless iteration.

Either way, these skilled participants in public discourse knew exactly what they were about, and knew that contemporary readers with the 'right' social background would be on their wavelength. A shared education and social base brought these readers into community with present and past authors whose complex relation to antiquity, at the same time passionate and ironic, was also their own.[13] Generations of schoolboys had groaned through the 'gerund grind' only to mine their shared ordeal for billiard-room witticisms and campaign-tent *mots justes* in later life; one new irony that became available post-*Culture and Anarchy* was that Arnold's gospel of the instinctive antipathy of the Hellenic genius to dogma and cliché was now itself being peddled as dogma and cliché.[14] Readers who had not yet established a 'right' relation with classical culture—the young, and the aspiring working and lower-middle classes to whom in the later part of the century Classics was marketed as a gateway to social mobility and self-betterment—were perceived as needing some extra and markedly un-ironic coaching in how to put Greece to work for (and on) themselves in the present moment. Interpretation and use were equated with what may now seem startling frankness:

no one can now be a pure Hellene, nor, if he could, would it be desirable... [but] The Greek influence has acted upon modern life and literature even more widely as a pervading and quickening spirit than as an exemplar of form... by its spirit, it supplies a medicine for diseases of the modern mind, a correction for aberrations of modern taste, a discipline, no less than a delight, for the modern imagination...[15]

The author of these remarks, Sir Richard Claverhouse Jebb, was one of the leading lights of the several generations of British Victorian and Edwardian

[13] Invoking relevant theory, in Ch. 1 I bring to bear the perspective of contemporary media fandom studies on the residual, post-eighteenth-century cultural formation of Classics as a social network.

[14] On the social uses of classical learning and especially verse composition in underpinning male camaraderie and class solidarity, see, of course, Stray (1998a: 57, 65–80).

[15] Jebb (1893: 271, 273, 279).

classicists of whom it has been dismissively remarked that 'the literary men set the tone, and the professional scholars followed tamely behind them', but his commentaries on Sophocles still command respect, whereas scholars hailed as 'originals' by a discipline's self-appointed talent-spotters not infrequently turn out to have been one-hit wonders.[16] What the ancient world of the Victorians needed was team players, both to put their shoulders to the subject's uniquely debilitating teaching load (intellectually as well as physically—Oxbridge Classics was as much a grind as school Classics; indeed it was effectively the same grind in grown-up clothes), and to promote and defend a coherent, Humanistic vision of the role of the ancient world in addressing modern social challenges. Authors such as Jebb, here as elsewhere writing for the largest possible general audience, are actively and above all *collaboratively* engaged in the mass manufacture of cultural memory. Whatever we may now think of the ancient Greece of the Victorians—and here, as in other aspects of their *imaginaire*, it is all too easy (and intrinsically '*not very interesting*') to play to the crowd, projecting our own maps of social reality backwards in order to find our forebears wanting—it was a fantasy of the past made powerful in the present by active consensus.[17] While we can never know the exact extent to which these readerships internalized exhortations such as Jebb's and took his judgements on trust, we can say with confidence of this didactic discourse that, through frequent iteration by authoritative cultural figureheads, its coherence and cumulative rhetorical force lent serious momentum to its consistent core message of a Hellas defined by untroubled serenity and marble-white purity.[18]

---

[16] Jenkyns (1980: 173).

[17] '*Not very interesting*' (emphasis added) is Sinfield (1994b: p. vi), on reasons not to patronize the nineteenth century by assuming our own categories of sexual identity objectively unmask what was 'really' going on in people's heads or in the (sub)culture at large. These terms and the categories of experience and identity implied by them continue to meet resistance to this day in developing-world cultures, which present a fluid array of alternate sexual classifications, hierarchies, and scenarios, much as did early modern Britain (Sinfield 1994a: 13); see, soberingly, McKenna (1995). Nor should we presume that our current formulations of gay/lesbian identity (coming-out narratives; Plato, Symonds, etc., as 'gay history' forefathers) will arouse any reaction beyond benign condescension a hundred years from now—if not sooner, at least within the pockets of middle-class privilege we tend to inhabit as academics and students (Abelove 1995). All the while bearing in mind these chastening caveats, I sometimes use the terms 'gay' and 'homosexual' in what follows as convenient shorthands. The key work on collective memory is by Maurice Halbwachs (collected in translation in 1992); within collective memory, 'cultural memory' distinguishes the forms of collective memory made durable through text and material culture, and is associated with the Egyptologist Jan Assmann (2006).

[18] Relevant here is Donoghue (1995), on the creeping ideological 'colonization' of sub-elite readerships by genteel periodical publications that sold them Establishment values as

'Serenity'—the facility to rise calm and untroubled above the storms of life—cut Greece off from the modern politics of protest; purity made implicit statements about mutual compatibility of racial heritage ('Genius') and about British cultural ownership of Hellas as a key enabler of national destiny, as well as the obvious lessons to be drawn in sexual propriety. These implicit truth-claims were all of a piece, because sex and the nation state were discursively closely linked. Regulating continence was as much an issue of public hygiene as one of private morality, and late-nineteenth-century writers on medical and social issues foresaw dire consequences for Britain's global position if its racial stock were to be weakened or contaminated as a consequence of improperly directed and inadequately disciplined sexual desires. Running alongside this public discourse of civic hygiene, a predilection for viewing disease as an outward sign of character or as a concretization (we might almost say a personification) of social issues made it hard to keep figurative and literal diseases separate in one's head.[19] Applied to a heretofore little-known backwater of ancient Greek literature, this toxic association between sex, disease, and empire was nastily to inflect the backlash against dissident Hellas in the 1890s (Chapter 5) and into the twentieth century (Chapter 6).

This is not a simple case of the 'uses and abuses' of classical antiquity for propagandistic ends by a society's lords and masters; the Victorians got the Greece most of them *wanted*. (It is tempting but, I will argue, a little too optimistic to suggest pluralistically that between them they got *all* the Greeces they wanted, severally and individually: as Stephen Greenblatt observes of an earlier era, individual liberty to remake and re-present the self is always constrained by the range of cultural materials and shared meanings that come to hand in a particular time and place; but certainly optimism about the possibilities of Hellenism's many adaptive mutations was in the ascendant, right up to the moment the Wilde trials dragged it down into the journalistic gutter.[20]) 'Uses and

the road to self-betterment; convenient for comparison is Marchand (1996: pp. xiii–xix), outlining a prevailing nineteenth-century German sales package that, although differently developed in detail and tied more explicitly to the mechanisms of civil authority, similarly asserted and built on a nationally specific model of Hellenic identification as an aspirational class identifier.

[19] See usefully Mort (2000: 12–15 (on 'moral environmentalism') and 23–5), and, from a literary-critical perspective, Fletcher (1979b). The rhetoric of moral panic (a formulation from Cohen 1972, subsequently much used elsewhere) was even more feverish in the United States: Beisel (1997). On the pernicious effects of turning illness into metaphor, see classically Sontag (1978).

[20] 'When I first conceived this book several years ago, I intended to explore the ways in which major English writers of the sixteenth century created their own performances, to

abuses', embedded in the title of Wyke and Biddiss (1999b) and bullishly talked up in their co-authored introduction, was an early formulation of classical reception methodology and priorities, focusing on overt propaganda imposed on societies from above by history's more colourful villains (Mussolini and his Fascists featured prominently).

The enduring tendency of modern popular discourse to caricature and trivialize the Victorians as pious hypocrites and jingoistic bunglers (bracingly debunked by Sweet 2001) encourages the too-hasty application of 'uses and abuses' to anything written before the First World War (as, for example, at Jenkyns 1980: 292, in these very words); but cultural responses to classical heritage are always more complex and polyphonic than stereotypes would allow. Invariably, and in a strong sense for which the 'uses' model leaves no conceptual space, they are actively and continually (re-) *negotiated* within historically located interpretive communities (the term is Stanley Fish's), within which alternative and dissident perspectives may bubble under and occasionally erupt into the mainstream. The terminology of community risks confusion with the uniform and ideologically closural 'world picture' of old-school Eng. Lit., a viewpoint latterly assaulted by the 1990s critical project of Cultural Materialism, but Fish's phrasing is too apt to disregard, chiming as it does with the useful insights of Jaussian *Receptionsästhetik* on how interpretation is negotiated within historically located readerships. Where I would move on from both is in viewing interpretation and particularly the negotiation of 'heritage' as the means by which an interpretive community is forever *constituting itself as* a 'community'—that is to say, presenting an evolving proposition about identity in the present.[21]

analyze the choices they made in representing themselves and in fashioning characters ... It seemed to me the very hallmark of the Renaissance that middle-class and aristocratic males began to feel that they possessed such shaping power over their lives ... But, as my work progressed ... the human subject began to seem remarkably unfree' (Greenblatt 1980: 256; his chapter of 1994 revisits the concerns of the monograph, which established 'self-fashioning' as a critical vogue). See evocatively Fiske (2008: 22) on 'the rich, passionate heterodoxy of Victorian Hellenism ... unstable [and] malleable'; the many available flavours of Hellas made for a heady blend, and even more so once the fast churn rate of mass culture is factored in.

[21] The term 'interpretive community' originates with Fish (1980: 147–74). Anderson (2006) is extremely useful here, but see also Sinfield (1994a, b) on how dissident reading styles help articulate sexual-minority subcultures, and the active-audience model of fan studies pioneered by H. Jenkins (1992) and subsequently Hills (2002) (see Ch. 1). 'World picture' has a headline role in Tillyard (1948); the *locus classicus* of Cultural Materialist critique is Dollimore and Sinfield (1994), by which I am deeply influenced. Mieke Bal's introduction to Jauss (1982) is by far the clearest and most compelling statement of the Jaussian approach. Darnton (2001) is good on both the importance and the difficulty of digging into who was reading what, when, and why.

Viewed in this light, Richard Jenkyns's dismissal of an ancient Greece 'used and abused to suit the convenience of the moment' by, in particular, members of a nascent urban homosexual subculture—interpretation is what an implicitly heterosexual 'we' do to the text as good scholars, (ab)use is the signature behaviour of a caricatured Other—presents far too simplistic a map of the production and especially the consumption of textual culture as discourse.[22] Works such as *Greek Literature* or Jebb's later *Growth and Influence of Classical Greek Poetry* (1893) are, as Cary Nelson writes of a rather different instance of invention of tradition, 'almost impossible to think about only as discrete texts': they make sense and achieve their powerful cumulative effect within 'a kind of reflexive...cantata', collectively sung by an indefinite but certainly very large number of harmonious voices across different genres and, not infrequently, across multiple media.[23] These were not always the only voices out there—subcultural and dissident readings of Hellas have a long pedigree, aspects of which this book will explore—but strength and depth in number could make it hard to pick up on dissonant notes in the polyphony, unless with an attuned ear.

What prompts so many voices to take up the same song-sheet and chant its socially resonant lyrics (often with minimal variation from one instance to the next) is the need to repair collective memory, to renew or re-manufacture a negotiated and communally viable vision of the past in the wake of trauma.[24] Here the terminology of cultural memory usefully complements the politically engaged readings and categories of Cultural Materialism, the 1980s–1990s bible of which was Dollimore and Sinfield's edited volume *Political Shakespeare* (1994). The ever more miscellaneous portfolio of ideological work that 'Classics' has historically been required to perform, and the ever-growing weight of the residual past meanings that it must bear on its back, together entail that the culturally powerful messages it delivers always carry the potential of their own deconstruction. Construed by Marxist critics as monolithic, ideology is actually a never-ending process of containment, made necessary (but also, as Dollimore et al. reveal, fuelled) by subversion.[25] Viewed from a

---

[22] Jenkyns (1980: 292, and cf., e.g., 297). His account pigeonholes homosexuality as a social formation pure and simple—by nature a passing phase, turned into a bad habit for life by a certain kind of school (1980: 286–7).

[23] Nelson (1996: 91, cf. 71); and cf. again the congenial approach advocated by Marchand (1996).

[24] For rounded consideration of memory in its relation to trauma and rupture, see Bal, Crewe, and Spitzer (1999); specifically applied to Classics, Parker and Mathews (2001).

[25] For a classic Marxist formulation of ideology as all-crushing juggernaut, see the essay 'Ideology and ideological state apparatuses' in Althusser (1971: 127–88).

Cultural Materialist point of view in which ideology is a project forever in progress, classical heritage stands revealed as the original faultline of 'Western Civilization', a place where the production of mainstream ideology through culture sometimes feels the ground shifting uncertainly beneath its feet, and insists in a voice too loud for complete credibility on its secure and confident footing.

At these moments, other meanings leak out, and the dominant ideology must hurry to contradict, exclude, marginalize, explain away, or (its best outcome) modify and subsume them into its strengthened consensus. This containment of subversion leaves semantic scars— as Thucydides long ago noted in his account of the *stasis* in Corcyra (3.82–4), shared meaning is the first casualty when a culture calls time on its unresolved tensions—and it generates a 'long tail' of residual media noise. In an age of cheap print and rapid proliferation of factoids this may easily build into a full-blown moral panic, but for much of the period considered here the churn rate is less frantic—media storms attach only to 'sensational' topics and certainly never to Classics, the public aura of which as the stolid high-culture bedrock of the Establishment is only entrenched by creeping populism. When Classics confronts trauma in the Victorian age, ranks close; the response is all the more effective for being muted, considered, discreet. Nonetheless, the strain shows.

2. CONTESTING MEMORY: THE GREEK ANTHOLOGY AND RADICAL CLASSICS

One such trauma, magisterially analysed by Christopher Stray (1992, 1997, 1998a), is the (partial, gradual, hotly contested) retooling of Classics in (fitful, grudging, belated) response to a series of dramatic social, institutional, and intellectual changes throughout the nineteenth century and into the twentieth. As Stray shows, this long, slow train wreck elicited an ongoing defensiveness and, by the end, a siege mentality. The initially non-urgent perception of a challenge to the predominance of Classics, developing over time into a sense of existential threat not merely to the discipline's undisturbed operation in schools and universities but to the survival of the humane values for which Greece now stood (in its proponents' eyes at least) as the necessary and sole rallying-point—thereby spiritually underwriting Britain's 'Roman' civilizing mission of empire—is the background buzz against which play out the particular and localized traumas explored in this book.[26]

Through the medium of Greek epigram, a previously 'minor' genre about which the British public initially knew very little, a dissident strand of Classics upset the apple cart of Victorian Hellenism. The broad thrust of *Greek Epigram in Reception* is that these traumas fall into three clear phases: first, the transgressive appropriation of the Victorian ideal of ancient Greece within an elite epistolary network and urban subculture of male same-sex desire, enabling a new kind of homophile identity dignified by the classical past and setting off occasional and muted conservative alarm bells (1860s, subtly and compellingly unpicked by Dowling 1994); second, the dissemination of this appropriation, barely disguised, in a publicly available and durable print format (1870s); and, third, the unanticipated opening-up of this key modern text of homosexual apologetics to what was by now a genuinely mass public readership, in a reordered format that by overwhelming narrative logic installed the work's most passionate encomia and glowing exempla of homophile desire as the glorious *telos* and climax of Hellenic art, life, and thought. This final phase was by far the most publicly visible, despite coming nearly two decades on from the book's first publication (1890s), and as such it provoked the most concerted and urgent response.

The text in question is John Addington Symonds's *Studies of the Greek Poets* (first series 1873), by far the most important book on classical literature of which most professional classicists today have never heard; and it achieved this extraordinary feat of apologetics in its unprecedentedly long and bold essay on epigram. This was the first and is still in some ways the best account of the genre ever to be made available to the non-specialist reader in English, but it was packed with subtle and not so subtle apologetics for 'Uranian' homosexual love. An analytic account of Symonds's representation and enthusiastic promotion of epigram, the relation of his account to existing subculture, and its immediate reception (1870s), occupies the central part of this book (Chapters 3 and 4).

---

[26] A cogent example recently documented by Christopher Hagerman (2009) is the integration of a benevolently construed Alexander the Great into the imaginative logic of British imperialism: Aristotle's pupil supplied an ethical prototype for bringing the benefits of civilization to 'darkest' India with whatever force necessary. The Platonic pedagogy of Benjamin Jowett, Oxford's own Aristotle (1860s and onwards), had empire-building in every sense explicitly on its agenda: see Dowling (1994: 70). Traditionally minded dons, public-school masters, and concerned parents uniformly viewed with horror the proposal to remove Greek as a compulsory entrance requirement for Oxford, seeing this as the first step in turning it into a glorified trade school; between August 1890 and January 1891 *The Times* was crammed with letters and petitions against the selling of the pass, and the protest flared up again in October and November. Arthur Sidgwick and Richard Jebb were among the big names weighing in, on 27 and 28 October 1891 respectively.

The third phase (1890s and onwards), explored through the backlash against *Studies of the Greek Poets* in the years and indeed decades after its author's death, is the subject of this book's final movement (Chapters 5 and 6). It is here (1895) that we see Oscar Wilde, an assiduous reader of Symonds in his formative years at Oxford, holding forth in court on what by now is a slightly old-fashioned and even fogeyish Greek pederastic ideal. His encomium of Uranian love is straight out of *Studies*—a work that is now for the first time available to a genuinely mass reading public, in a new and dangerously improved third edition (1893). In the years running up to the Wilde trials—years in which no one inside or outside of gay subculture seems to have anticipated a coming storm that in tragic retrospect historians of the gay community experience as inevitable—the moral threat of *Studies* in its new guise as a standard literary-historical handbook is met and countered by a Leonidean phalanx of the great and good of Classics, Jebb among them. This was not merely a conservative reaction in defence of conventional sexual politics (although Jebb himself was as Establishment as they came). As declared progressives within the mainstream, Liberals had if anything an even larger stake in disassociating ancient Greece from modern Decadent contagion and social disease, so as to keep it in play as a rhetorical ploy in arguing for political reform.[27]

The distinctiveness of Symonds's intervention, and the profound threat it was seen to pose, can be properly understood only in the context of the interpretative tradition against which he writes. The first part of this book (Chapters 1–2), therefore, establishes the underlying trends in the gradual emergence of Greek epigram into the periphery of the public sphere in the early and mid-nineteenth century. Before this can begin, it is necessary to lay some groundwork regarding the ancient genre of epigram and the transmission and publication histories of its text. Readers familiar with epigram may wish to skip ahead, at the small risk of missing some particular emphases that set the scene in readiness for the six main chapters.

3. THE ANCIENT GENRE, ITS TRANSMISSION, AND ITS PUBLICATION

Semantically, the Greek ἐπίγραμμα is straightforwardly a text or other meaningful mark written or incised upon (ἐπί) the surface of an object.

---

[27] Schultz (2004: 457). On the early 1890s as an ever-widening window for homophile self-expression and self-representation, see usefully Dellamora (1990: 209) and Sinfield (1994b) (for whom this is a principal theme).

The obvious rendition of the root meaning, and its usual sense in Greek literary sources of the 'classical' fifth and fourth centuries, is thus 'inscription'; specialist meanings include a written tally or 'mark-up' of costs (LSJ ἐπίγραμμα 4) and the brand on the forehead that identified a slave (LSJ ἐπίγραμμα 5). Within the field of inscriptionality, ἐπίγραμμα came to carry the specialized meaning of an inscriptional text composed in verse, a feature uncommon enough to be worth singling out for comment. The presumption would be that most such texts were short—as were inscriptional prose texts when their content allowed, given the labour and expense of precision stonecutting.

By extension and drift in meaning, ἐπίγραμμα in the Hellenistic age shifted to include short literary texts that *resembled* verse inscriptions in their formal characteristics and choice of topics. The bivalency of the Greek ἐπί, a word/prefix equally at home being applied figuratively (composed 'on' a topic) as literally (incised 'on' a monument), will have made this an easy and natural expansion of sense. The thematic range of literary epigram then broadened from obvious (pseudo- or meta-) inscriptional topics—dedications of offerings, the erection of a statue to a successful athlete, or commemoration of the departed—to topics associated with the symposium: wine and love, whether of courtesans or handsome boys. Here, too, an inscriptional aura may have lingered, since for a lover to declare his passion by carving it into a tree had already become a cliché of ancient erotics, but the discovery in the 1990s of a papyrus book-roll of epigrams by the famous Posidippus points to a rapid diversification and proliferation of topics during the Hellenistic period.[28]

Genuinely inscriptional epigrams from the old Greek heartland had themselves become the subject of antiquarian connoisseurship and collection into organized handbooks, a practice that may well have inspired the Hellenistic poets who authored the first books of literary epigram.[29] Building on this, and towards the close of the Hellenistic era if not before—the evidence is shaky—scholars and poets began to select individual poems by diverse authors on grounds of thematic interest and quality, and to arrange their gleanings into edited anthologies.[30] Like the

---

[28] Gutzwiller (2005) is thorough and informative on this papyrus. The latest edition of its text, which reports the recent scholarship, is Seidensticker, Staehli, and Wessels (2012); I thank my anonymous reader for bringing it to my attention.

[29] Gutzwiller (1998: 5).

[30] Prior to Meleager's Garland (on which see below), a 'Sōros' is attested containing epigrams by Posidippus and perhaps others; summarizing the scholarship, Gutzwiller (2005: 7) advises caution. Other hints come from papyri excavated at Oxyrhynchus, but this is all inconclusive. For discussion, see Cameron (1993), whose account (pp. 3–12) reacts against earlier scholarship in emphasizing the originality and ambition of Meleager's project.

authored books that preceded them—and here the discovery of the Milan papyrus usefully confirms the scholarly consensus—these were almost invariably organized by thematic category. The first such anthology of which we have secure knowledge, compiled by the poet Meleager of Gadara (first century BCE) and including many poems of his own, was divided into four categories that (with Tarán 1979, an early classic of the field) we may reasonably surmise to have been the firm favourites of the Hellenistic epigrammatic tradition up until his day: anathematic (offerings), sepulchral (tombs), epideictic (objects), and erotic.

Meleager's title, 'Garland' (Greek Στέφανος), aligns epigrams with flowers, influentially defining the anthologist (literally 'flower-gatherer') as a skilled weaver of blooms from many different species. His substantial verse preface, preserved in book 4 of the Anthology, rhetorically amplifies an essentially meta-sympotic flower discourse already at home within the genre into a full-blown literary connoisseurship in which the poetic voice of each author is wittily matched to its appropriate bloom: lilies for Anyte and Nossis, roses for Sappho, and so on. That Meleager has fun weaving non-floral plants into his garland as well, making it playfully multi-textured, not to mention an unlikely headpiece for the ancient party-goer—Leonidas is swarming ivy, Mnasalcas spiky pine—strongly suggests that in his day the figurative equation was already well established, a topos on which the inventive poet and collector of poets could ring the changes.

Varieties of flower supplied one of the two figurative languages available within ancient and late antique epigram for reflexive comment on poetics; the other is types of precious stone. We know that the latter was deployed meta-poetically at least as early as Posidippus (early third century BCE). Each of these typologies is suggested by the small scale of the epigram as a discrete text, and dignifies what might be taken as a shortcoming by emphasizing the beauty of the finished poem—for gems, a combination of inherent brilliance and artful polish, cutting, and setting; for flowers, the delicacy and unstudied perfection of a freshly plucked bloom. The nature of each class of comparison also advertised the enhanced aesthetic effect that could be achieved by the artful arranger of epigrams in antiquity, whether original author or later anthologist. Only when the garland was woven, or the stone set harmoniously with others in a ring or diadem, did the latent beauty of the individual epigram fully reveal itself.

Of the two, and perhaps in large part due to the success of Meleager's collection, the language of flowers was much the more popular and influential, as the ubiquity of the term 'anthology' attests. Through their association with declarations of love at the symposium, these flowers of meta-poetic flourish additionally accrued a strong homoerotic shading, prominent in the Anthology's Stratonian twelfth book. Poems could be flowers, but so could pretty boys, and the poet might choose to make it difficult to draw a firm line between the two.[31] These figurative registers of gemstones and flora will turn out to have significant afterlives in the sophisticated and ever-shifting discourse of epigram reception in the nineteenth century and after, when the roses and lilies of purity and health could be hard to tell apart from Decadent *fleurs du mal* (Chapters 3, 5–6; an Appendix probes Symonds's use of precious stones to convey figurative meanings).

If we leave aside occasional individual practitioners (foremost among them Piso's friend Philodemus (second century BCE) but also including the Archias defended by Cicero), Meleager's Garland was where Roman literary culture first encountered epigram, a genre that it never fully made its own despite the best efforts of key individuals (notably Catullus and Martial, the latter of whom belatedly inspired a minor third- and fourth-century boom in Latin epigram). Instead, epigram continued to prosper through the Second Sophistic and beyond as a characteristically Greek authorial exercise, with Roman admirers of Greek culture often composing in the senior language.[32] The practice of epigram-composition in Greek continued without serious interruption into the Byzantine era and was thus a *living* tradition to the genre's great compiler, Constantine Cephalas (tenth century CE); indeed, it continued well beyond his day.[33]

Cephalas's gigantic anthology is our one great source for the Greek literary epigram tradition in all its breadth and depth. It built on the practice of its several predecessors, none of which survives except as more or less faint traces in its arrangement, and particularly on the large anthology of Diogenianus (fourth century CE), the basic scheme of which (scaled up from Meleager's so that each thematic category occupied one whole book) it took over along with its content.[34] To these were prefaced Christian epigrams and miscellanea, and the collection closed with books of puzzles and other miscellaneous material. Erotic epigram was now divided into two separate books, 5 and 12, declaring desire for women

---

[31] As, e.g., at AP 12.4, 91, etc. (the erōmenos as a flower of desire); 12.32, 39–40, 234 (the bloom of youth is a flower that dies and falls). At AP 12.256 Meleager playfully weaves pretty boys into a Garland that echoes his own literary creation; we touch on this again in Ch. 4.

[32] Bowie (1990: 55, 61–7); Livingstone and Nisbet (2010: 103–5).

[33] Livingstone and Nisbet (2010: 137–9).

[34] The tortuous manuscript tradition of epigram, from Meleager to Cephalas and beyond, is addressed with daunting confidence by Cameron (1993).

and boys respectively, where Meleager's Garland had drawn no typological or ethical distinction. The latter book, AP 12, was built around the armature of a collection of pederastic verse by a single major author, Strato of Sardis (second century CE).

The Greek Anthology we read today is founded on Cephalas. Its intermediary source is the so-called 'Anthologia Palatina'—'AP' for short. A manuscript with an exciting history well worth exploring (Symonds tells it very well), this sizable parchment quarto is an essentially faithful version of Cephalas's work, made near the original date of composition, but with some lacunae, almost certainly including one entire book on works of art.[35] We are aware that these lacunae exist because some of the missing material is preserved in an inferior later redaction and rearrangement of Cephalas's work by a fourteenth-century monk, Maximus Planudes. For completeness's sake, all modern editions end with a 'Planudean Appendix' incorporating all the poems found in Planudes but not in the Palatine MS.

While Planudes's abridgement established a strong manuscript tradition, the Cephalan anthology lay forgotten: its sole known exemplar, the Palatine MS, was not rediscovered until 1606, long after the coming of print. Until then, no one had even known that Planudes's version *was* an abridgement. Even then, more than a century was to pass before the Palatine Anthology was edited and published, at first only through an imperfect intermediary copy (Brunck 1772–6), and a version that respected the structure and ordering of the manuscript did not appear until well into the nineteenth century (Jacobs 1813–17).[36] In the meantime, the censored, reordered, and abridged anthology of Planudes had established itself as *the* Greek Anthology in the world of Greek letters.

4. CHUNKING THE ARCHIVE: EPIGRAM BETWEEN READERSHIPS

No critic has ever had a good word to say for Planudes's acumen as an editor; in the nineteenth century, his assiduity as a censor only seriously

---

[35] J. A. Symonds (1873: 344–6 = 1920: 500–2). For ease of reference, the version of *Studies* most often referred to in this book is the most commonly available, viz, the 1920 repagination of the third edition of 1893.

[36] On Brunck's reliance on the incomplete apograph of Jean Bouhier, see Hutton (1946: 8–12), with useful context.

became an issue when Symonds made one of it (1873), and (as we will see) could be a cause for either regret or celebration depending on point of view. The enduring popularity of editions of his redaction well into the nineteenth century, however, when the near-complete and far superior text of his source author was finally available (and soon relatively affordable in a new Tauschnitz), suggests that few readers were feeling short-changed by not getting all the available poems. This was perfectly understandable: the Palatine Anthology is huge. Commercially this will have made it a difficult proposition for the non-specialist market, especially while the Planudean version remained a steady seller and could be economically reissued using printer's plates already in hand.[37]

Even if we set aside considerations of length, the Anthology made very little sense as a reading experience. A leading light of the 1890s backlash (Chapter 5), the prolific literary critic and classical popularizer John William Mackail, declares:

> There is no doubt a certain charm in the very confusion of the order, which gives great variety and unexpectedness; but for practical purposes a more accurate classification is desirable...

> some sort of arrangement by subject is plainly demanded... [but the arrangement of the AP] is not a natural division, and is not satisfactory in its results.[38]

As we will come to see, Mackail's agenda is close to the surface here: he is downplaying the value of Symonds's account of the Anthology, which (with one significant lie-by-omission) had taken the Cephalan scheme as its road map, and he is building up to the moment when he will declare his own editorial authority through the unveiling of his preferred thematic categories—categories that in turn perform ideological containment and that repurpose the Anthology as a tool of empire. All the same, from a readerly perspective his point cannot be denied. Whether in its Planudean or (even more so) its more authentic Palatine form, the Anthology is decidedly not a page-turner. Its individual books display no editorial personality or intelligence in their ordering of poems, except on rare occasions where traces of the poems' pre-Byzantine sequencing are preserved; even printed in a small typeface, the physical

---

[37] The Planudean Anthology had an extensive publication history. One of the first Greek texts to be printed (by Henricus Stephanus in 1566), it continued to be republished in new editions as well as reissues well into the nineteenth century, decades after the Codex Palatinus finally saw print (Livingstone and Nisbet 2010: 13). Indeed, as the century turned, the error-riddled text of Stephanus's sixteenth-century *editio princeps* was being republished with lavish illustrations and a facing translation into Latin verse, with copious volumes of notes to follow (de Bosch and van Lennep 1795–1822).

[38] Mackail (1890: 28–9).

bulk of the text must make any edition heavy and awkward in use; and its chronologically disturbed and thematically disconnected sequence of categories refuses any attempt to read the total work as narrative. These last two points are even more true of the heftier and more miscellaneous Palatine than of the then familiar and accepted Planudean version.

Perhaps worst of all for readerships raised in the wake of Romanticism to expect originality of feeling and expression in their poets, ancient epigram is predicated on imitation and 'capping' of predecessors' efforts. Creative variation is a virtue within the genre, and this makes the content of the Anthology highly repetitive, based as it is on a limited repertoire of viewpoints and tropes. Inscriptional epigram had always been formulaic because it responded to a limited and ritually bounded spectrum of occasions and material contexts: victory, dedication, and burial.[39] Hellenistic literary epigram then built this archaic and classical inscriptional heritage into its working methods alongside the 'capping' behaviour of symposiasts at play, again within a rule-bounded context in which only a limited range of sentiments could be expressed. The result is numerous 'families' of epigrams that ring the changes (albeit often playfully and with a meta-poetic edge) on a limited set of themes; Mackail's declaration of 'great variety' applies only in the long view, not as one turns the pages.[40] We should be glad the Greek Anthology is there, but it is simply too big and too full of clutter for any single reader. Not even specialists read it from cover to cover.

To 'use and abuse' the Anthology (using the formulation with all due irony) was thus a natural and reasonable recourse for all but the driest scholar, and nineteenth-century scholarship was on the whole *not* dry. Even in the 1870s and 1880s, the era of Symonds, there was no hard-and-fast divide in Classics between professional academics and interested enthusiasts. Disciplinary specialization was a work in progress, and progress was at best intermittent, because the *status quo ante* had clear

---

[39] These formulae were so well known that in later literary epigram they lend themselves to parody: see Robert (1968), an indispensable classic of modern epigram studies, on paradoxical meta-inscriptionality in Lucillius.

[40] Cameron (1995: 71–103), vigorously argued, places the Hellenistic epigrammatists in an elite symposiac context; the editors' introduction to Bing and Bruss (2007: 12–14) suggests some caveats. On the literary genre in relation to epigraphic tropes, see Fantuzzi and Hunter (2005: 291–37). On Hellenistic literary epigram's development of tropes that reflexively simulate inscriptional identities and spaces for the reader-as-viewer, see respectively the monographs of Bruss (2005) and Tueller (2008). On thematic families, the foundational study is Tarán (1979), complemented by the more sophisticated Gutzwiller (1998); for a case study (the AP 9 cycle on Myron's Cow) see Livingstone and Nisbet (2010: 7–12, 131–4 (Ausonius)).

advantages for individuals already in the system. Scholars could range freely between authors and fields of study, and the new German model of secular and scientific *Altertumswissenschaft* was making very little headway against the monastic collegiality of the ancient universities and a sporting partiality for the gentleman amateur. Oxford and Cambridge saw every reason to encourage this amateur spirit, and indeed vigorously defended it on occasions when it was called into question—occasions that appear as moves towards professionalization only in hindsight.[41] Individuals might move repeatedly towards and away from full-time classical pedagogy as they progressed through an academic–ecclesiastical *cursus honorum*, not discriminating overmuch between Oxford and public-school common rooms as they did so—the personnel of each were interchangeable, both in social standing and in the kind of classical curriculum they made it their business to deliver. Oxford's Fellowships retained their monastic aura, and *Literae Humaniores* its historic remit of educating churchmen. In the course of a successful career a Greek scholar might hop strategically between college post, country living, and the headmastership of a public school, finally landing the cherished plum of a bishopric. Meanwhile, his ex-pupils would form a growing network of influence and mutual advantage in the interconnecting worlds of politics, commerce, diplomacy, and the civil and colonial services.[42]

What in the early twenty-first century appears a fixed and 'natural' opposition between academic writing and writing to be read by the public (and/or by society's influential movers and shakers) was only beginning to firm up. There was still space (although admittedly it was narrowing) for individuals to define their research *and* public roles as they went along. The emergence of learned societies and discipline-specific journals was a sign of change that again appears clearly as such only in retrospect: their early members aimed at 'something of a cross between a club and a special-interest pressure group rather than a professional testing and licensing body', and they were often politically engaged in the public sphere rather than purely academic. Indeed, the use of 'academic' to mean something not intended for application in the

---

[41] Collini (1991: 201–9), congenially invoking as a case study the research career of Symonds's great friend and lifelong correspondent from college days, Arthur Sidgwick. On the importance of this friendship to Symonds, see Schultz (2004: 401); on Sidgwick's conscious suppression of his own homophile urges, Schultz (2004: 415).

[42] 'Positions of considerable emolument', all more or less interchangeable: Stray (1998a: 60–4). R. Symonds (1986: 27–9, 186–8) gives compelling detail on Benjamin Jowett's string-pulling to corner the market in liberal (and, in his case at least, colour-blind) imperialism for Balliol, laying groundwork that started paying off for Oxford as a whole in the 1890s (p. 189). On Jowett, see also briefly Stray (1998a: 122).

world of affairs was itself new in these years.[43] One consequence for a writer such as Symonds is that communication and argument about antiquity is *either* through intimate networks (face to face and epistolary) *or* in the full light of the public sphere. Without an academic press in the modern sense, there was no available halfway house, no middle ground.[44] What we would term a subcultural writerly perspective could be expressed either publicly; intimately in correspondence, with the creeping fear that a shared secret might at any time be made public or semi-public knowledge, whether through ill will or simple mischance; purely privately, in a diary intended never to meet other eyes in the author's lifetime; or not at all.

A privately commissioned and strictly limited edition, run up by a discreet printer and circulated within a closed network of known individuals, was the only conceivable middle ground between personal communication and the public sphere, and this ran a yet greater risk that incautiously phrased personal views might be publicly exposed, albeit perhaps far enough away that scandal at home might be deferred. The United States market was a byword for indiscriminate breach of copyright. Publishers such as Thomas Bird Mosher piratically expropriated hundreds of British small-press works associated with the fashionable and newsworthy Aesthetic movement. Various works by Symonds quickly fell prey to these unlicensed presses, thankfully far enough away that they created no ripples at home. The two sexological treatises (1883 and 1891) for which he is now famous were intended to observe strict information hygiene. *A Problem in Greek Ethics* was limited in its original run to 10 copies, each of which Symonds did his best to track as they circulated among his correspondents years after the fact; the later *A Problem in Modern Ethics*, to 100. Despite his precautions, they enjoyed only a few years' grace before they too began to circulate as unauthorized cash-ins.[45]

For a writer such as Symonds, committed as he was (on our best estimation) to making a socially provocative statement by going back to the key sources for Hellenism and already a confirmed devotee of reading against the grain to dig out the truth of a writer's sexual being (Chapter 3), it might well appear actually *safer* to pitch his wares in the full light of the

---

[43] Collini (1991: 213).   [44] Stray (1997: 366).

[45] An 1896 pirated edition of *Greek Ethics* is obscurely attested; better known is the unauthorized edition of 100 copies printed in 1901 by Leonard Smithers, publisher of the *Savoy*; but in any case *Greek Ethics* had already appeared as part of Havelock Ellis's *Sexual Inversion*, which was pirated hot off the press on its first appearance (1883, in German translation). On Mosher, his methods and milieu, see Bishop (1998).

public gaze, under the cover of keywords that flagged up subcultural perspectives for those in the know while enabling a wider readership to enjoy an engaging and illuminative surface narrative; and, of course, there were huge potential benefits in taking the word to the largest possible readership. Experiencing Hellenic sweetness and light through a sexually dissident subtextual filter—deniable, easy to miss, but always subtly *there*—might in time relax the preconceptions of this wider reading public, clearing the way for eventual legislative reform. Indeed, in later life, and with the Labouchère amendment of 1885 specifically in mind—'a disgrace to legislation, because of its vague terminology & plain incitement to false allegations'—Symonds felt able to prioritize making the case for legal reform above influencing public opinion, precisely because he thought this shift was already under way. Asking around among his contacts, he had come round to the view that decriminalization would not now create a public outcry and that in fact the public would be indifferent and perhaps even sympathetic, provided only that a media circus could be avoided.[46] Two years after his death, alas, the Wilde trials would turn that optimistic prospect on its head.

5. FRAGMENTARY LIVES: DOMESTICATING THE ANTHOLOGY

The social uses and readerly habits relating to Greek epigram in the nineteenth century, which subsequent chapters will unpack, need to be understood against the context of a general tendency in the reception of the ancient world in nineteenth-century Britain. We have seen that the Anthology was invariably dealt with in part rather than as a whole, for sensible reasons. Already at the start of the nineteenth century (Chapter 1), the epigram's social uses tended toward the piecemeal; in print, radical excerption and reordering were as much the rule at the century's end as at its beginning. One might imagine that the Anthology's gappy and ramshackle character would have made it an increasingly obvious if inexact synecdoche for the parlous state of the classical literary canon, and therefore inspired heroic attempts at conservation and reconstruction—but no; the new science of papyrology had yet to give the lie to the providentialist presumption that all the great books of lasting value had made it safely through to the modern age.

---

[46] Grosskurth (1964: 282–3); J. A. Symonds (1967–9: iii. 554, 792).

What we will instead see promoted in the post-Symonds backlash (Chapters 5–6), again aggressively reversing the rhetorical strategies of *Studies*, is a point of view in which the bulk of the Anthology in its transmitted state (the Palatine MS) is written off as valueless and weed-infested rubble—a ruin from which, against the odds, a handful of pretty flowers struggle to bloom. (Often these green shoots of recovery centre on a rediscovered 'Meleager' whose career and work are so heavily rewritten as in effect to turn him into a fictional character.) But this conception of the Anthology as a mess of detritus in turn reacts against a crowd-pleasing formulation by Symonds himself, who sold the tattered Anthology as a unique experiential window into the real lives of ordinary ancient people—not the heroes of history or the giants of literature, but people just like 'us' (Chapter 3).

The emergent mass reading public of the later nineteenth century wanted to know its classical heritage, up close and personal, but their window on it was frustratingly narrow. The classical literary canon might have had a stranglehold on pedagogy, but it had disappointingly little to say about the ancient world as it was lived from day to day by anyone other than a Cicero or a Seneca. The incompleteness and disorder of the material culture, meanwhile, told no one clear story; only by being read off against canon text could it furnish classical lessons for modern life, but canon text was not playing along.

The rest was speculation: the inherited eighteenth-century Romantic cult of the fragment, filtering the heritage industry of the Grand Tour through a Piranesian aesthetic that made a fetish of ivy-smothered ruin, was an open invitation to try one's hand at filling in the gaps in contemporary understanding of the lived past through sympathetic dialogue with the shades of long-dead authors who had instinctively distilled the intrinsic and historically unique 'Genius' of the vanished culture. This national character was in turn construed with increasing directness and emphasis as racial, rooted in blood (shared descent, which could be more or less 'pure') and soil (the landscape and climate of the motherland, a physical rootedness in the past, the savour of the air the ancients breathed).

In the later nineteenth century we see a shift in this reconstructive urge towards what we may term the bourgeois domestic scene. The dilettanti had hacked across the Levant to adore heroic marbles and ivy-clad pediments; their grandchildren preferred the cult of the domestic fragment. While grand sculpture filled out the national collections, the heroic age of archaeology (and of tomb-robbing) fed a thriving market in more modestly scaled antiquities—statuettes, lamps, amulets, and so on. These accessorized the home interiors of those many nineteenth-century consumers who possessed (or wished to possess) the social distinction

conferred by intimate familiarity with classical culture. Through imaginative sympathy, these domestic collectibles promised access to an ancient
daily life of families who were very much like the Victorians' own, united
by the bonds of affection and a shared love of shopping for knick-knacks.
The tendency to imagine life stories for them was very strong.[47] The
classical genre paintings of Symonds's older contemporary Lawrence
Alma-Tadema were famously criticized for presenting 'Victorians in
togas', but were loved for that very reason. Meticulously stocked with
ancient household *objets* from the artist's own extensive photographic
reference library, these tasteful Roman interiors invited contemporaries
to dip into an ancient world that flatteringly mirrored the contemporary
ideal of harmonious family life, comfortingly everyday but also aspirational in its foregrounding of leisure and materialism.[48]

This, then, is the well of desire that Symonds tapped when he
announced the Anthology as the forgotten key that alone could unlock
the cipher text of the material record of everyday Greek life, unpacking
the buried memories and emotions that lay encoded in the silent stones.

6. SEX, ART, AND DEATH: GREEK EPIGRAM IN AND OUT OF POMPEII

Alma-Tadema's tableaux of Roman interiors also, of course, teased with
sex. Pale female flesh allured through flimsy gauze, bathtime ripples, or
the fronds of an ostrich feather. This escape into a playground of sensual
experimentation came pre-loaded with unimpeachable moral closure on
at least two fronts. First, Pagan Rome was preordained to be brought
low by its sins as a necessary step in ushering in the new religious
dispensation—a scenario more or less literal-mindedly enacted in the
artist's most famous work, *The Roses of Heliogabalus* (1888), in which
pagan vice unwittingly faces extinction under the suffocating press of its
own excesses. Second, the masterworks of the Greek sculptural canon—
at least as sampled and imitated by the Rome of the Alma-Tadema
universe—made it clear that nudity had engendered no sense of sin
within a culture born too early to know God's will as revealed by Christ
and the Gospels (Good News that the depraved Rome of the Emperors

---

[47] For a slightly different emphasis, see Jenkyns (1980: 81) on 'Boswellism'.

[48] On Alma-Tadema as an enthusiastic and purposeful collector of antiquity through
photographs commissioned on-site, see Barrow (2003: 28–31); this was an artist who even
painted his own studios in 'Pompeian' shades to get him in the mood (p. 72).

had then chosen to ignore). Dipping one's toe into the Rome of Victorian popular culture thus became a popular mode of virtual sex tourism.[49]

In print, Symonds's subculturally informed commentary on sex and sexuality would necessarily be much less blatant than this. We will see that, like the comparatively few Greek genre paintings of Alma-Tadema, his textual tableaux de-sexualize the nude body—or, at least, make its sexual availability conveniently deniable—by abstracting it into the Edenic 'innocence' of a pastoral scene of semi-wild Mediterranean nature. In this symbolically rich countryside, the desirable Greek physique can be glossed as pure Art. Symonds's peer-directed subtext may have played on the shared homosexual rite of passage of getting one's classically themed sex tourism for real, on the Bay of Naples (on which theme, see Aldrich 1993), but the message on the surface of his epigram narrative—a message that later writers would exaggerate and inflate to the point of rupture— aimed at careful decorum in its evocation of private life. In Chapter 3 we will see him treading carefully to keep his preferred model of 'Greek' homosexual identity at a safe distance from 'Rome' in its popular aspect as a fantasy world of uninhibited sensuality, and thus from the teleologic- ally inevitable pay-off once the orgy has wound down.

This task was further complicated by Alma-Tadema's incessant resort to floral motifs. Meleager had established flowers as the fundamental critical and meta-poetic language of his genre, but during Symonds's active writing career popular art was turning them into an iconographic shorthand for a classical antiquity specifically coded as Roman, flagging up feminine refinement but also an Empire choking on Bacchanalian excess (again encapsulated in *The Roses of Heliogabalus*). We may have here one motive for Symonds's penchant for an alternate language of epigram connoisseurship, based on gemstones (Chapter 3 and Appendix).

One further fragmentary complication merits identification at the outset. Impatient of the slow pace and complex causality of Gibbonian decline and fall, the Victorian melodramatic imagination boiled down this general Roman doom into what could be played as a classic wrath- of-God moment (as well as boilerplate melodramatic closure on a 'bad' character): the fiery immolation of that secular Sodom of the Vesuvian plain, Pompeii.[50] Visiting the disappointingly tame (because thoroughly

---

[49] As, e.g., in *A Sculptor's Model* (1877), and *In the Tepidarium* (1881); Judith Harris (2007: 203–5) is stimulating and enjoyable.

[50] This pop-culture presumption has proved extraordinary durable, as evidenced by the anecdote that gave Arthur Pomeroy the title for his book on the ancient world in film, *Then it was Destroyed by the Volcano* (London: Duckworth, 2008).

bowdlerized) archaeological site as part of the standard itinerary overseas and primed by Bulwer-Lytton's *The Last Days of Pompeii* (1834), sensation-hungry Anglophone culture pilgrims experienced the ruins through the filter of a shared fantasy of doomed sexual licence; if they craved more, a peek behind the curtain of the discreetly renowned Museo Segreto promised to reveal a mind-blowing sexual reality utterly unlike and outperforming their own.[51]

As a wealthy mercantile seaport of Magna Graecia and subsequently a Roman colony, Pompeii was additionally and influentially construed as a melting-pot where the pure Greek lifeblood came under threat from two directions at once—a Rome of rapacious consumers, and a sensual and villainous Orient that pandered to the worst urges of the new Western superpower.[52] Following Symonds through his essay on epigram and watching him subtextually unpack his meticulous schema of 'good' and 'bad' sexual identities, we will see this nationally popular *lieu de mémoire* invoked in these several aspects as a grisly stalking horse, with rhetorically startling implications (Chapter 3).[53]

7. EPIGRAM AS SOCIAL PRACTICE AND POLITICAL STATEMENT

As explained in Section 3 of this Introduction, the Palatine MS is our most faithful version of Cephalas, and Cephalas stands in retrospect as our most comprehensive repository of the ancient epigram tradition; but retrospective archival curation and antiquarian fidelity were no more the principal driving forces of Greek epigram in the nineteenth century than they had been in the tenth. Epigram-composition in Greek was once again

---

[51] Bridges (2011) is excellent on Bulwer-Lytton's novel. Fisher and Langlands (2011) read the 'secrecy' of the Museo Secreto as more strip-tease than genuine prohibition.

[52] Taking as its focus the rhetorical inscription of Greco-Egyptian mummy portraits into Hellenic and Orientalist stereotypes in nineteenth-century reception, Montserrat (1998) is both a page-turner and a valuable analytic tool. Pompeii and its reception are now the subject of an excellent edited volume, Hales and Paul (2011); on Pompeii as cultural crossroads, see in passing their Introduction, Hales and Paul (2011: 2). Like Pompeii, the Eastern villains of the melodramatic historical novel (and the youthful subjects of Montserrat's 'Eastern' mummy portraits) must, of course, meet wretched ends so that the audience can experience the catharsis and sentimental reaffirmation of values so intrinsic to the melodramatic mode (and, subsequently, *film noir*).

[53] The term is Pierre Nora's (1984–92).

a *living* tradition, just as it had been for Cephalas and his garland-weaving predecessors all the way back to Meleager. Until at least the mid-century Greek epigram was as much written as read, by an upper class whose advanced education in Greek—an education in which epigram occupied an important niche—signalled and underwrote their socially privileged status. It enlivened epistolary exchanges within friendship networks, and filled figurative and literal gaps in the periodical journals that circulated cultural capital and extended the reach of polite values. Authentically ancient Greek epigrams, too, were versatile in their literary–social applications (Chapter 1).[54]

As the century progressed, to detect and approve a national taste for Greek over Latin epigram became an expression of the speaker's sound taste, in contemporary politics as well as in literary classics—indeed, like sex and racial vigour, taste and politics became inseparable partners in an elite discourse of the distinctive rightness of the British nation state. For the readers of certain periodicals, a systemic failure to 'get' Greek epigram became emblematic of how Britain's constant enemies, the French, had become aberrant in their relation to the common European heritage of the ancient world. Revolutionary and imperial France had created difficulties for the British not merely on the world stage, but also by compromising their formerly secure hotline to the classical past. A sense of spiritual continuity with a genially conceived Roman Republicanism had formerly confirmed Britain's eighteenth-century elite in the constitutionality and 'liberty' of squirearchical rule-by-consent, but the French had put this affirming self-identification beyond use by becoming Republicans for real in the here and now.[55] Their Republic (1792–) flaunted the antique trappings of Rome's magistracies, and quickly enacted the fate of its antique predecessor by imploding politically, to be reconstituted as an Empire that pursued Roman paradigms every bit as thoroughly (1804–). Within a few years (1811) tens of millions of continental Europeans lived under the Eagles of a terrifying new Caesar, Napoleon Bonaparte, a history that would later (and after a turbulent intervening period) be replayed as farce under his nephew, Napoleon III (1852–70).[56]

---

[54] On this breadth of use of Greek epigram in nineteenth-century reception, see briefly Haynes (2007: 566).

[55] Dowling (1994: 16): 'All the familiar civic categories and expressive language, British writers antagonistic to the French Revolution were to find, had been hideously usurped and contaminated by the Jacobins.'

[56] On French Republican receptions of Roman antiquity and the British reaction, see Vance (1997: 24–38); on Napoleonic Augustanism, Huet (1999).

France's supposed predilection for Martial's pungent and frequently obscene satirical punchlines, and its near-proverbial impatience with the simplicity of *épigramme à la Grecque*, were now held up as the signs of an unhealthy national hunger for sensation and novelty. The ancient author whom they were held to have adopted as their main model was thus damned by association.[57] For correlation of this national character, one needed look no further than their recent and continuing history, for what were revolution, regicide, the Terror, and its shabby aftermath, if not the natural and obvious consequences of a hunger for *political* novelty and sensation? Again, Chapter 1 will show this astounding rhetorical association in action. Nineteenth-century Britain remembered that eighteenth-century Britain had been fond of Martial in its way,[58] but the two national versions of the Roman poet were chalk and cheese. (Again—and this will be a recurring theme, perhaps *the* recurring theme, of this book—the power of selectivity from an over-large corpus of *opuscula* asserts itself in massaging away an inconvenient self-inconsistency.[59]) The Martial the French loved was a Martial who was trying too hard, straining to deliver a showy rhetorical effect that betrayed its own artificiality and pandered to the jaded palate of a politically servile readership. No wonder the enemy across the Channel found him so congenial; but Greek epigram was spontaneous, unforced, organic, and, above all, serene.

A Britain in sympathy with the genre's ancient Greek spirit could, therefore, claim a politics that shared those qualities. As part of a much broader, politically inspired shift from Roman to Greek authors, the choice of an idealized Meleager over a Martial condemned for his servile flattery of the tyrant Domitian made a very specific statement of Britain's instinctive antipathy to generalissimos and despots.[60]

---

[57] Yes, this is crazily circular, but it really did play out like this; for a close and pointed parallel, see Nisbet (2012a: 497–8), on how nineteenth-century educational and translation discourse rhetorically constructed a French–British polarity between 'bad' Persius and 'good' Juvenal. On the ubiquity of *à la Grecque* (often cited within an anecdote of French high society that explicitly reveals national character) in discussion of epigram by British authors of the earlier nineteenth century, see usefully Haynes (2007: 571–2).

[58] As, e.g., at Dodd (1870: p. vii).

[59] 'When dealing with collections of epigrams, selection (or deselection) is the most obvious method of censorship' (Leary 2012: 130, specifically on school editions of Martial).

[60] Greek over Latin: Jenkyns (1980: 155–63), and for context F. M. Turner (1989); Martial unstintingly condemned as Domitian's toady at, e.g., Westcott (1894: p. vi) and Post (1908: 11–13), two late examples (both incidentally published in America), which usefully illustrate just how long the residual afterlives of these rhetorical polarities can be in the slow-moving schoolbook market; on this point see Nisbet (2012a: 491, 493–4), and this book's Conclusion.

8. CONTROVERSY AND DISCIPLINE: A STATEMENT OF METHOD

> Disciplines are defined not only by their shared methods, theories,
> and objects of study, but by their controversies.[61]

These censorious voices of a bygone era may seem silly now, but they 'must remain significant precisely because they once seemed obviously right and sensible'.[62] We would do well not to become complicit in an ever-renewing culture of critical self-congratulation. In retrospect, we see male chauvinism and homophobia, heavy-handed censorship and crude nationalism, anti-Semitism and Orientalist fantasy; but, in telling ourselves we view the errors of our predecessors from a position of enlightenment and objectivity, we assume a superiority that they too felt in their moment.[63] Yes, the classical antiquity of the nineteenth century was (in the words of a scholar of German intellectual history) 'a fantasy world of their own devising, a world less true to the past than it was a utopian sublimation of classicist desire—classicists who were themselves entirely unsatisfied with the "modern" world in which they lived';[64] but in long retrospect it may become equally obvious that *our* ancient world(s) respond to our desires too, the desires that got us collectively and individually into Classics to begin with, and that will perhaps offer up to a future reader every bit as blatant a subtext, in work that, if read at all, may (like the Victorians' today) be valued mainly as a historical curiosity.

As classicists and ancient historians of the twenty-first century, we would doubtless like to think and may well have good grounds for arguing that 'our' ancient world is less crudely and absolutely a mirror of our society's concerns; that what we have gained procedurally in technical specialisms, and are now gaining in our ability to reflect critically on our disciplinary heritage through reception studies, makes for a supple and diverse ancient world which can bend with the times.[65] But there have been losses as well as gains, including a schooled facility in

---

[61] Graff (1997: 389).

[62] Dollimore (2001: 96), and see, entertainingly, Sweet (2001: 210), a fine polemicist: 'There are some British academics who have made entire careers out of reading aloud misogynist passages from Victorian medical texts in a sarcastic voice.'

[63] Anti-Semitism: Flaig (2003); elitist homophobia: DeJean (1989b), both regarding the nineteenth century's Sappho.

[64] Ruprecht (1996: 30).

[65] On the personal voice and auto-critique in Classics, see Hallett and van Nortwick (1997), with critical review by Nisbet (1997). On the ability of Classics to take on board external criticism and generate its own, see Kaster (1997), reflecting on a disciplinary history of productive controversy; less optimistically, DuBois (2001: 4–5).

switching between the languages, and not least in our collective capacity to speak meaningfully to and be heard by society and its leaders. It is a long while since Greek epigram has beguiled the leisure of prime ministers and the governors of provinces, as for a while it seemed natural that it should.

I therefore propose to take these historic voices seriously, not as objective scholarship (if indeed such a thing exists; the reader must make up his or her own mind on that score) but as primary texts, and thus as part of a privileged cultural domain that produces, contests, and reaffirms the ideology of their place(s) and time(s). Even the most 'purely' aesthetic declarations about classical heritage are inescapably political, if only with a small 'p' (and in the nineteenth century the 'p' is often very large)—there is nothing timeless about 'timeless' aesthetic ideals, or indeed about asserting that such ideals even exist.[66] This book will explore the rich rhetorical culture of epigram-discourse through a series of close readings that will unpack the ideological strategies underlying the genre's representation in public print.

My underlying approach places comparatively little weight on biography and personal anecdote. The life of the author does not explain his text. (Or *her* text; but, in reception of epigram in the nineteenth century and thereafter, preponderantly 'his'. Chapter 1 should leave the reader with a sense of why this was.[67]) Academically at least, I am not particularly interested in, for instance, who slept with whom, when, and how. Some tidbits are too juicy not to share, and I am unabashedly an heir to Symonds's urge to use epigram to tell good stories. On the whole, though, and to the extent to which it is knowable, the truth tends in any case to underwhelm—when Symonds wrote his great paeans of Uranian desire in *Studies*, his homosexual experience amounted to not much more than heavy petting. Following the author's experiences through diaries and correspondence does not deliver the last word on the meaning of the published text by revealing his secret self as a hidden whole, mere aspects of which were ever seen by the public at large—rashly presuming, of course, that such a concept of selfhood could be taken as read: as subjects we are formed within culture and wear its masks; this is a fairly standard Cultural Materialist position, but also, when phrased a little differently, one of the basic presumptions of postmodernism.

However, I *am* deeply concerned with how these authors present themselves to their public(s), and in how others represent them. Consequently,

---

[66] Mukarovsky (1979: 62); cf. p. 64: aesthetic value 'is a process and not a state'.

[67] On the underlying issues in studying the masculinization of nineteenth-century Classics, see concisely Bristow (1995: 9) and Fiske (2008: 16–17).

I am interested in how these writers explained their life experiences and perspectives to themselves and to their intimate correspondents—through letters, dedications, private poetry—in so far as this lays groundwork for their strategies of public utterance or helps constitute (whether through public journalism or elite network gossip) the authorial *personae* that contemporary and/or subsequent audiences subsequently read into these public utterances. It is above all in the persuasive force of what *was* put before that public—in the long conversation that played out within its hearing—that my interest lies. By picking apart how the rhetoric works, I want to reconstruct how the initial intended readership(s), and in some cases (especially that of Symonds) also subsequent and unintended readerships, experienced the ancient Greece that was being mediated to them by these authors, and also how changing social and political contexts must have added new layers to these mediations.[68] I aim to develop a sense of how Symonds and the rest came across as *characters* at different points in the long-running and increasingly popular serial drama that was epigram's reception history in the later nineteenth and early twentieth centuries.

A recurring concern of *Greek Epigram in Reception* is to trace how public voices interact and reinforce each other to construct a discourse of inevitability about how the past should be read in, and for, a present with which it is represented as being virtually interchangeable. The construction of an ideological edifice on the scale of that studied in this book represents a truly impressive effort in sustained rhetorical collaboration, and this brings us full circle to the concerns of heritage, memory, and trauma with which this Introduction opened, and to Cary Nelson's notion of the 'reflexive cantata'. The context he has in mind is the collective and inevitably socially engaged role of poets in negotiating in retrospect an agreed cultural memory of the internationally contentious Spanish Civil War: 'The poems, prose poems, and statements that make up this extended international wake are almost impossible to think about only as discrete texts, for they make up a kind of reflexive Lorca cantata . . . [characterized by] distinctive and sometimes uncanny continuities.'[69] These 'uncanny continuities' are, for a Cultural Materialist critic, precisely the points of pressure at which ideological tension is breaking through, provoking panicked efforts to stem the leak; we will see numerous examples in the backlash against *Studies* (Chapters 5–6),

---

[68] Julia Gaisser (2002: 387) formulates this wonderfully: texts are 'pliable and sticky artifacts gripped, molded, and stamped with new meaning by every generation of readers and they come to us irreversibly altered by their experience'. Her discussion is of classical literature, but why not apply it to modern exegesis as well?

[69] Nelson (1996: 91, and cf. 70–1).

in the form of too-insistent repetitions, endorsements, and circles of citation. In Nelson's account, Lorca's crucial poetic account swiftly became the inescapable intertext against which all subsequent writers on the war needed to situate their own perspectives, and, again, the later chapters of this book will make it clear that the same is true in the epigram-discourse of those who wrote after, around, and against Symonds's *Studies*. Indeed, one of the main objectives of this explanatory cabal was to dethrone Symonds from his position of foundational influence and to install a substitute 'Lorca' in his place. Also congenial is Nelson's emphasis on reading 'the poems themselves' as part of a continuity of explanatory discourse: in the case of epigram (as for other ancient genres in the nineteenth century) this includes commentary, editorializing, and journalistic and educational exegesis.[70]

Engagement with these notionally more peripheral sources will throw light on the key role of explanatory paratext in setting up the non-expert's reading experience in advance, shutting down ambiguities and tensions both within the text and (often) in how it relates to its initial and subsequent reception contexts. Paratext of this kind often efficiently delivers an ideology of the obvious by asserting the existence of disciplinary consensus within a community of scholarly experts.[71] Healthily for the project as a whole, taking this range of sources into account also entails that we assign due importance to the material form of the text, and how it interacts with economic forces and with the social and physical environment in which it circulates. From cradle (or at least schoolroom) to grave (the genre was swiftly repurposed to deliver decorous *memento mori*), during times of peace and war, and—a particular rhetorical point of emphasis—in country at least as much as in town (Chapter 6), epigram was 'there' for readers in numerous formats and applications. It was sold to them as their most user-friendly but also their most comprehensive point of access to the spirit of Hellenic antiquity, now available in a material format convenient for consumption on the go: ancient Greece in a can. This made it all the more crucial to ensure that the formula was right.

---

[70] The irony quotes around 'the poems themselves' are mine, and reflect my scepticism regarding any critical account that treats these socially (hyper-)interactive texts as unitary and self-sufficient works of literary art; cf., on slightly different grounds, Nisbet (2006: 85, 88, 113), deconstructing 'the film itself'. For a model of scholarship that integrates these diverse forms as the basis of a joined-up, ideologically aware reading of Latin satire in nineteenth-century translation, see Nisbet (2012a).

[71] Leitch (2004: 377–8), reflecting on his own practice as editor of a major teaching anthology, notes the 'monumentalizing' character of the editorial headnote to an anthologized text and teases out its implications.

The work of ideological closure, and the faultlines towards which it points even as it endeavours to paper them over, are not set aside as one enters the cultural domain of academe—a domain to which the nineteenth century assigns privilege but not, as we have seen, clear boundaries. Academic disciplines are formed and reformed through contestations in which the personal quickly becomes academic–political. Individual players get burned, and their personal legacies fall into neglect, but the dialectic between outlying personal and interest-group agendas and established power bases is what powers the dynamic of adaptation that enables collective professional survival and disciplinary renewal. Nowhere is this seen more clearly than in Classics. Shanyn Fiske suggests that we might well not be here as a discipline, doing what we do, without the biases, passions, and compulsions of numerous nineteenth-century individuals who fought tenaciously to promote the several and peculiar versions of antiquity in which they were personally invested, and I suggest that reappraisal of Symonds as a paradigmatic case in classical studies is long overdue.[72]

At the level of macrocosm, *Greek Epigram in Reception* respects Stefan Collini's call to interrogate past and current controversies in discipline formation for social subtext. In debates over the meaning and remit of Classics, ownership of a particular kind of cultural capital was being contested; redrawn positions or reframed terminology in what was notionally a purely 'academic' controversy can lay bare significant faultlines with the public sphere.[73] Discipline formation is always about cultural forgetting as well as cultural memory: it entails exclusion of viewpoints, materials, and whole eras and canons that do not fit the needs of the moment at which the discipline is talking and writing itself into being, through public articulation of its core interests and values.[74] This in turn helps explain how Classics has chosen to forget Symonds (and, largely, Pater), very much as did English Literature—very emphatically, if not for all of the same reasons—in the early twentieth century.[75] However, these disavowed interpretative formations do not simply vanish into thin air. As the example of Symonds and the backlash will show, they leave behind traces that continue to inflect the disciplinary subconscious (Chapter 6 and Conclusion).

As a site where Romantic author cult meets para-scientific rigour, Classics has long been particularly rich in controversies—controversies that, in the discipline's old capacity as guardians of high-culture capital,

---

[72] Fiske (2008: 22).   [73] Collini (1991: 217–20, 223–4).
[74] I am indebted here to Nelson (1996: 96).
[75] On the Eng. Lit. side, see Booth (2000).

it has attempted to downplay, and from which it has done its best to distract the attention of outsiders. Its conservative collegialism favours a slow-food model of intellectual work, and views with disfavour the outsiders, chancers, and disrespecters of convention who are the likeliest short-term winners in a culture of argument by sound bite and public stunts.[76] What we see in *Studies* and its aftermath is a special case. For once, the discipline breaks cover and, on behalf of (its conception of) the humane culture it serves, puts a deviant view of antiquity on what amounts to trial in the court of public opinion. It does not specify the charges (it dares not speak their name, because to do so might help make them real in the world of discourse), but there is never any doubt as to the identity of the unnamed defendant—Symonds, on epigram.

That this figurative trial falls into a close temporal orbit around the late nineteenth century's most sensational trial-by-media (and, lost somewhere in the middle of it, the actual courtroom appearances of a modestly successful Irish playwright) suggests that our close attention to the speeches of the defence and prosecution will be rewarded, as we trace the impact of their rhetoric on the crowd in court.[77] For epigram and Symonds, this meant everyone who cared about classical Greek heritage and its value as a road map of present realities. With a new version of the map open on the table, we needed to be told whether North was still 'up', which was the same as knowing—since we all knew that classical Greece made us what we were—whether we were still going to be the same people from now on.

The publicly staged contestation of the values of Hellenism that coalesced around epigram in the wake of *Studies* is thus, in the formulation of Robert Hariman,

a form of social knowing in that it is the means by which we hold what we know. It is a symbolic container *allowing symbolic material to be collected and affirmed as social goods*—that is, as substantive knowledge. It is a means by which we create, disseminate, judge, and ratify as facts those assumptions about the world and those values of the community that together are supposed to be informing the laws.... [popular trials are typically] *staging knowledge that is explicitly or implicitly implicated in social control.*[78]

It is an in-house settling of scores that also increasingly attempts to tamp down an elite–subcultural counter-discourse of Hellenic self-knowledge

---

[76] See Kaster (1997: 345–6) and Most (1997b: 361), thoughtful participants in a complementary dialogue which also draws in (inter alia) Stray (1997); a recent noteworthy example of the closing of academic ranks in a good cause is supplied by the *Black Athena* controversy of the 1990s, ongoing at the time Kaster et al. were writing.

[77] Helpful in conceptualizing the 'popular trial' is Hariman (1990: 19–20).

[78] Hariman (1990: 21–2; emphasis added).

and self-actualization in the public sphere. In an age that took it as axiomatic that reading formed character, dissident reading of classical literary heritage gave particular cause for concern.[79] Counter-cultural Hellenism was hydra-headed, assuming many intermingling forms that it could be hard for the outsider to tell apart,[80] but its crystallization around the nexus formed by Symonds's encomium of epigram and Wilde's trial-by-media seemed not only to make it dangerously public but also to offer an opportunity to cauterize many of its stumps. Chapters 5 and 6 chart the methods tried out by successive champions of decency in this collective and public act of monster-slaying.

9. SURVIVAL OF THE FITTEST: HOW THE ANTHOLOGY WAS FRAMED

why are we being asked to sample so many poets of little or no lasting value? Anthologists may now be extending a too general welcome. Selectivity has been condemned as 'elitism', and a hundred flowers are invited to bloom.[81]

Just like discipline-formation, a process from which it is increasingly inseparable in modern Humanities pedagogy, anthologization is an act of cultural memorialization that is predicated upon exclusion and forget-ting—a *damnatio memoriae* as powerful in its consequences as it is (seemingly) passive in its method and objective in its necessity. Since every inclusion is simultaneously an exclusion, the making of an anthol-ogy is inescapably an act of would-be canon-formation. Indeed, the prospect of forming future minds within a preferred version of the discipline's core literature is the lure that, whether through personal vanity or a sense of duty, attracts the ambitious scholar or critic to undertake what can be strenuous intellectual work.[82] Excerpting the highlights of a literary tradition both helps to *create* that tradition for a new generation by asserting its coherence, and *excludes* the non-expert

---

[79] 'Beginnings and endings hang or fall together' (Ruprecht 1996: 31). On the Victorian conception of character-formation through reading, see Mays (1995: 180); a modern parallel is the panic over 'media effect' in young people's access to internet pornography or violent content in videogames, on which see invaluably H. Jenkins (2006: 208–21).

[80] Livesey (2007: 6); and cf. again Fiske's 'rich, passionate heterodoxy' (2008: 22).

[81] Helen Vendler, 'Are These the Poems to Remember?', *New York Review of Books*, 24 November 2011: 19, reviewing Rita Dove (ed.), *The Penguin Anthology of Twentieth-Century American Poetry* (New York: Penguin, 2011).

[82] Johnson (2004: 385).

reader from those parts of the corpus that now become invisible through their failure to make the cut. Real-world pressures of time, energy, access to texts, and individual reading expertise typically combine to discourage independent and open-ended exploration of the corpus as a whole, shutting readers off from a larger corpus that can be made visible again only through tools requiring specialist expertise.[83]

The Greek Anthology stands as a *mise-en-abîme* within Classics, a canon within (although simultaneously *outside*) the Canon, and puts at centre stage the role of the translator and anthologist as a *mediator of value* within as well as between national cultures.[84] In the Anthology's particular case as in no other, attempts at canon formation are inseparable from translation history. Throughout almost all of the period under consideration, non-specialist access to the whole text was in most cases an impossibility. For the minority who knew Greek, editions of the Palatine exemplar did gradually emerge around the start of the nineteenth century, and became more usable and affordable as time went on. For the common reader dependent on translations, no possibility existed of reading independently in the Anthology in order to reach a personal view of the genre of epigram (and thus, they kept getting told, of Greek identity in the round).

That this changed in the years of the First World War is entirely due to the facing-text edition of W. R. Paton (1916–18) for the Loeb Classical Library, in the service of that estimable series' mission of complete coverage of the extant Greek and Latin authors (the Loeb is still the only complete translation, albeit not always *into English*).[85] A shrewd editor and sensitive translator, Paton inherits the concerns of the 1890s backlash critics and sees danger in unrestricted public access to the whole text, going so far in his preface as to 'beg any possible, but improbable, reader who desires to peruse the Anthology as a whole' to do no such thing, but instead to be guided by him in reading only the 'best' epigrams by the earliest and purest authors. Only by putting on Paton's blinders will the modern reader arrive safely at the 'right' view of Hellenism's essence, uncontaminated by later misunderstandings and misrepresentations.[86]

---

[83] See Leitch (2004: 380) and Schrift (2004: 192), the latter reflecting from personal experience on the contradictory pedagogic priorities of anthology-editing for college students and the temptations of editorial fiat.

[84] Nelson (1996: 72–4).

[85] Paton translates some sexually explicit epigrams in AP 5 into Latin, a move not without parallel in the early years of the Loeb series, notably the old Martial of Walter Ker (1919–20), which transposed the naughty bits into Italian; we pick up on this briefly in Ch. 5. Green (1998: 243) serves up a delicious anecdote.

[86] Paton (1916–18: i, p. viii).

Although its narrative will revisit this extraordinary moment—a translator going down on his knees to entreat his public *not to read* the majority of what he has so painstakingly produced, for the good of their souls—only in passing (Conclusion), my hope is that my own readers will come away from *Greek Epigram in Reception* equipped to make sense of it; to ascertain the shape of the deep structure that underlies it. We will tease out the lingering and contradictory agendas that inform the rhetoric of an early twentieth-century writer such as Paton, seeing between the lines the after-effects of a moment of crisis in the continuing emergence of a modern Western Self produced through sexual self-knowledge as (in the first instance) gay or straight. Why did these writers take such pains to draw a line between 'Greek epigram', on the one hand, and mere actual epigrams by ancient Greeks, on the other? Identity politics starts here.[87]

---

[87] 'I have a suspicion that the quest for the moment at which the modern homosexual subject is constituted is misguided...that what we call gay identity *has for a long time been in the process of getting* constituted' (Sinfield 1994a: 14; emphases added); gay identity continues to be a work in progress, now as part of an open-ended portfolio of queer identities, and straight identity has evolved right alongside it, originally as its byproduct.

Part I

The Descent from Olympus

1

The Miscellanies of Bland
and Merivale

1. 'BE MINE TO WREATHE': FROM ANTHOLOGY TO MISCELLANY

> Poetry is now a drug; all the European markets are overstocked;
> there is a universal glut; prices have fallen far below prime cost...[1]

The story of *Greek Epigram in Reception* has no one beginning, but its first publication of note (1806) makes for a suitable point of departure: *Translations Chiefly from the Greek Anthology: With Tales and Miscellaneous Poems*. This small octavo volume was published anonymously, but the names of its several authors are known; for reasons that a later section of this chapter will make clear, parts of their originally intended readership will already have been in on the secret, or else in a good position to guess. The largest share of the labour was undertaken by the Revd Robert Bland, the son of an eminent London physician. He was assisted by two good friends who shared his Cambridge background: the barrister John Herman Merivale, an assiduous collaborator who was to assume the editorship in the volume's final incarnation, and in a more casual capacity the Revd Francis 'Frank' Hodgson, who was simultaneously working on the translation of Juvenal, with commentary, that would come out the following year. The two subsequent versions of *Translations*, both clearly distinguished from the first by their billing (*Collections from...*), abandoned circumspection and admitted what was in any case the open secret of the identities of those involved.[2]

This gentleman–amateur production attained lasting popularity, and individual translations by Bland and Merivale in particular were much cited by later anthologists and literary critics (Chapters 4–5), particularly

---

[1] Anon (1833c: 865), playfully introducing a wholly positive review of Merivale (1833).
[2] Bland (1813); Merivale (1833).

Lord Charles Neaves (1874), the first writer to take a stand against the
new understanding of Greek epigram promulgated by John Addington
Symonds (1873). In his satire 'English Bards and Scotch Reviewers'
(1809), Byron, a personal friend of Hodgson and Merivale, places the
first edition at the climax of his notably short catalogue of signs of poetic
genius in the modern age. *Translations* augurs a literary renaissance, of
which its editor and collaborators will be the leading lights:

> And you, associate bards! who snatch'd to light
> Those gems too long withheld from modern sight;
> Whose mingling taste combined to cull the wreath
> Where Attic flowers Aonian odours breathe,
> And all their renovated fragrance flung
> To grace the beauties of your native tongue;
> Now let those minds that nobly could transfuse
> The glorious spirit of the Grecian muse,
> Though soft the echo, scorn a borrow'd tone:
> Resign Achaia's lyre, and strike your own.
> Let these, or such as these with just applause,
> Restore the muse's violated laws ...[3]

Translations and the two versions of *Collections* are demonstrably the
stimulus for nineteenth-century Britain's literary interest in translating
Greek epigram.

By the end (Merivale 1833), the roll call of contributors bore witness to
a new generation's recruitment into the family firm, with Merivale's son
Charles (like his father a Cambridge man) turning his hand to the genre
in dutiful memory of his father's much-missed friend; the declared aim
of this final edition of 1833 was to generate a college fund for the eldest
son of Bland, who had died in 1825 while still in his forties.[4] This
intergenerational *pietas*, praised as such in the conservative press and
usefully indicative of close-knit loyalties within this early epigrammatic

[3] Twenty-some years later, Merivale (1833: p. v) is still making copy out of this. Less
happily, a sniffy reviewer of that volume insinuates that the efforts of Merivale and his
deceased collaborator would have been long forgotten were it not for Byron's endorsement,
made incontrovertible by his romantic end in the cause of Greek freedom: Anon. (1833f:
536). Byron knew both men from his time at Harrow, where Bland had attempted to teach
him Latin; *Translations* confirmed him as an admirer of Bland's literary talents and he
subsequently attempted to secure for him at least one literary commission.

[4] Merivale (1833: p. xi) on Charles, who contributed several translations and moreover
'whom I am proud to name on the present occasion as having afforded me the most
material assistance in the arrangement of the Work'. Unlike his father, Charles Merivale
was what we would call a proper classicist: he had netted a Browne Medal for verse
composition, and the fourth-highest First in his year; in 1833 he won a Fellowship at St
John's. Reviewers praised the volume's charitable impulse, whether or not they thought the
latest version was any good: Anon. (1833e: 194 ('noblest motives')), Anon. (1833f: 536).

peer group, will turn out later in our story (Chapter 3) to have set an advantageous precedent.[5]

A precedent of a different kind had been established by the composition of the friends' first version of 1806, to which its portmanteau title ('Translations *Chiefly*, etc.') honestly attests: the reader will find therein a medley of epigrams from the Anthology together with other ancient poetry, and more besides ('Tales and Miscellaneous Poems'). Numerous future 'Greek Anthologies' will follow the lead set by Merivale and Bland in assembling their miscellanies from mixed fare, without displaying any of the scruple of these early authors: in later chapters (Chapters 5–6), we will meet some very peculiar concoctions passed off under a title, 'The Greek Anthology', that is at best inexact and often actively misleading.

In its first version (1803), following some comic fragments and numerous explanatory notes on the text up to that point, *Translations* continues with Bland's own substantial narrative compositions in blank verse. These are the 'Tales' of the title: the classically themed 'Paris and Oenone' (pp. 171–83); 'The Abbot of Dol: A Legendary Tale' of ghost-haunted mediaeval Brittany (pp. 184–95); 'The Wraith: A Scottish Tale' (pp. 196–202), and several more in a similarly Gothic vein of antiquarian amateur dramatics. Then come some pleasant metrical versions of Horace (pp. 222–30), a rather lovely sonnet (p. 231), and, of all things, some Ossian (pp. 232–3), the Homer of the Celts, a notorious literary fake of the previous century but one whose claim to authenticity was still being asserted by the romantically inclined.[6] The chosen excerpt delivers unambiguous closure to *Translations'* miscellaneity through a sombre motif suggestive of *memento mori*—and, in so doing, sets another important precedent for Anthology-makers and -fakers to come. The lines are addressed to Malvina, the radiant betrothed of Ossian's now dead son Oscar, and Bland's choice to translate into elegiacs (connoting love but also death and mourning) complements the mood:

> We sit around the rock—but there no more
>   Thy Voice remains to soothe, thy light to cheer:
> Soon hast thou set on our deserted shore,
>   And left us all in gloomy darkness here!

THE END

---

[5] Epigram as family business and homage to a departed friend, with approving notice of Merivale's 'paternal pride': Anon. (1833c: 869), reviewing for *Blackwood's Edinburgh Magazine*, a major player in what follows.

[6] Readers intrigued by Ossian and the long-drawn-out controversy over the provenance of his text will find a comprehensive resource in Moore (2004).

Bland's splendid eclecticism places this first English translation of the Greek Anthology squarely within a thriving tradition of miscellanies billed as 'anthologies' and composed of multiple shorter works (for example, essays) and extracts from longer ones (for example, novels), generally miscellaneous in theme and *ad hoc* in internal arrangement. The small-'a' anthology format had a long history as a reliable money-maker in the English book trade, since books of this kind maximized publisher–booksellers' return on their investment in copyrighted authors. Their variety and brevity of content made them ideal for what Barbara Benedict has dubbed 'dip, sip and skip' reading—the kind of miscellany that keen readers might today mentally pigeonhole as a bathroom book.[7]

The charming and stimulating higgledy-pigglediness of the anthology format also aligned these books structurally and experientially with the hand-copied commonplace books of private individuals, flattering the reader by proffering inclusion in the public sphere.[8] Rather like the eighteenth-century democratization of the collecting impulse, the literary miscellanies forged consensus—and 'forged' is the right term in more senses than one; hammering out a *status quaestionis* entailed dicey assertions of personal *auctoritas*. Their mode of dialectic sociability brought readers into the debate, at least in simulation—or more charitably, prosthesis at a distance—and invited them to bring their judgements into dialogue with those of the editor, selecting favourites as browsing consumers much as he had in his role of proxy 'author'.[9]

Thus it is that, with his prose introduction out of the way, Bland prefaces his selection of epigrams with a verse prologue that invites his readers to become active participants in the Anthology's continuing tradition. This brings Meleager (praised earlier as 'tender and affecting', p. xiv) into play though emulation—famously, he had begun his Garland in just this way—while emphasizing that *Translations* will depart from his ancient precedent by incorporating more than one genre of ancient verse. Bland's evocation of the epigram's withering—the genre garden fallen to ruin through long neglect, choked by weeds—was to furnish tropes for the critics of the backlash against Symonds, eighty or ninety years later (n.p.):

---

[7] Benedict (2003: 232–3).

[8] The concept of the 'public sphere', a term much bandied since, is developed by Habermas (1988).

[9] Benedict (2003: 236–7) is evocative here: the miscellany format 'enable[d] readers to bridge public and private, aesthetic and sentimental meanings...the touted multiplicity and free organization of the items ensure each reader a private experience, since each is invited to construct his/her own hierarchy of merit'.

> Be mine to wreathe, these sweets among
> (Menander, prince of comic song),
> Some honours spar'd by age and clime,
> That live to grace an after-time,
> Pluck'd from thy many garlands bright,
> So charming once and new to sight.
> Our unavailing sorrows mourn
> Thy roses pale, thy lilies torn,
> Thy garden rifled of its bloom...
> And now some sad and wint'ry plant,
> Some wither'd shrub, of pow'r malign
> (Of all that grace thy garden fine),
> Remains of thee, or sickly yew...

And yet 'here and there a rose is found', defying all odds, or a lily, poking its head through the snow of epigram's long winter. The prologue ends with a series of open questions that put the onus on the reader to decide the genre's future:

> For zephyrs soft that fann'd thy youth,
> How wilt thou meet the gale uncouth?
> Torn from a genial Summer's smile,
> How wilt thou bear a northern isle?
> Far from thy home and native sky,
> Meek stranger, wilt thou live or die?

This plaintive Ciceronian tricolon puts us under pressure to determine not so much whether Greek epigram is *likely* to die but whether it *ought* to, and the weight of the rhetoric is heavily slanted towards rejecting the death of the 'meek stranger'. Bland and his collaborators are committing a vulnerable orphan into the hands of a community of readers who can actively save it through collective cultivation. The authors do not need to fill in the blanks: in context, as we will shortly discover, it will have been obvious to their readers by what means they were to preserve Greek epigram from extinction. First, however, we will follow the reader's journey through the front matter and opening pages of Bland's miscellany, to see how the 'meek stranger' is introduced to its new public.

2. 'SOME WITHER'D SHRUB, OF POW'R MALIGN': PREFACE AND PROLOGUE

The opening page of Bland's preface, quoted below in its entirety, establishes two rhetorical characterizations that will be of crucial importance to the reception of epigram later in the century. First, the epigram of the Greeks is simple, organic, harmonious, and graceful. The genre thus encompasses in miniature the canonic qualities of the best period in Greek sculpture, as influentially defined by the pioneering art criticism of Johann Joachim Winckelmann (1717–68), and specifically his *Geschichte der Kunst des Alterthums* of 1764.[10]

The merit to which the poems in the Greek Anthology have a claim consists generally in the justness of a single thought conveyed in harmonious language. Very little can be done in the space of a few couplets, and it only remains for the writer to do that little with grace. The eye is fatigued with being raised too long to gaze on rocks and precipices, and delights to repose itself on the refreshing verdure and gentle slopes of scenery less bold and daring. In the same manner, the lover of poetry will sometimes find a grateful pause from grandeur and elevation, in the milder excellence of suavity and softness.[11]

Implicit in this vision of statuesque serenity is a contrast with Martial, the busy sensation-monger of the big city, and this is brought to the surface a few pages later in a discussion of how the meaning of the word 'epigram' has been debased by the popularity of the Roman authors.[12] Already a British investment in the Greek form is being explicitly asserted, or rather at this early date proposed, as a collective project. Bland's vision is of a genre fundamentally in sympathy with the character of his nation; naturalizing it for Britain will deliver cultural ownership of a precious 'natural' resource that heretofore has been all but untapped by modern civilization: 'The Greek Anthology opens a wide and almost an untried field for further exertions . . . We have those whose taste may enable them to pluck a few flowers that grow by the way side, *and preserve them to their country.*'[13]

Second, Greek epigram is a foothill, not a mountain. This image requires a little unpacking, and once again the work and particularly the legacy of Winckelmann supply the necessary context. His long study of the ancient masterpieces in the Vatican collections had led the founder of art history to propose for Greek sculpture an overarching schema of

---

[10] For a stimulating general introduction to Winckelmann's ideas and influence, see Beard and Henderson (2001: 68–74); Curtis (2000) is a personal favourite.

[11] Bland 1806: p. i; repeated verbatim (1813: p. i), and reproduced as a supplement to his own newly written preface by Merivale (1833: p. xv).

[12] Bland (1806: p. v), citing Martial and the third-century epigrammatist Ausonius, on whom see concisely Livingstone and Nisbet (2010: 131–5).

[13] Bland (1806: p. ii) (emphasis added), and cf. pp. ii–iv on proofs of national sympathy in older poets.

growth, maturity, and decline. This was in effect the life cycle of an artistic medium viewed as a single living organism. Furthermore, the organic birth, life, and death of the medium kept pace with and directly expressed changes in the civilization of Greece itself. Art had grown to and declined from greatness in symbiosis with the social and political life of the race. The latter term is used advisedly; Winckelmann viewed the Greeks as a distinct *Volk*, bound together by ties of blood and language that determined their national character or 'Genius'. Following Winckelmann, one could read off the ancient Greek cultural climate at any period in its history from the masterworks of its art, forensic close readings of which invariably revealed an authorial style perfectly in keeping with the mood of its day, be that classical serenity or Hellenistic fervour and disarray.

Winckelmann's stylistic schema—effectively, art history as bell curve—offered a distinct new vision of ancient art, with immediately obvious applications to the art of later periods as well; and yoking to it a parallel schema of national destiny was a brilliantly provocative masterstroke. Who was to say what might be revealed about our own societies by interpreting the art of yesterday, today, and tomorrow? This linked pair of key concepts was immediately, profoundly, and lastingly influential. Quickly translated into other languages, *Geschichte der Kunst des Alterthums* permanently redirected the European cultural imagination along new channels whose ends could not then be foreseen. Within his own national culture Winckelmann's influence became colossal.[14] One early and local effect (among many) is well known: Winckelmann's notion of a national mood particular to a chronologically bounded era is expanded upon in the idea of *Zeitgeist* propounded after his death by his younger contemporary Herder (1744–1803).

Specifically in relation to ancient Greece and its reception in Britain, we may note the following. Not only Greek art, but Greek literature (at least in its preferred incarnation as verse), soon came to be viewed as displaying a Winckelmann bell curve of rise, peak, and decline. Individual genres could be picked out as occupying particular places on the curve. Within a national mode of Classics predicated on literary appreciation, tragedy thus came to be viewed as the apex of the historical Greek achievement in literature. Because art and society ran in parallel, the greatness of tragedy and the greatness of fifth-century Athens were discursively welded into an inseparable unity: each stood for, mirrored, and authenticated the other.

---

[14] The title of Butler (1935), while polemical in tone, is indicative: *The Tyranny of Greece over Germany*.

The bell curve could also be scaled down. Individual genres came to be seen as displaying their own micro-histories, again embodying what soon came to seem a natural law of all human production—rise, peak, and decline. There were now curves within curves. Again, tragedy (the Victorians' great fixation because it topped the curve of Greek literary history) offered up its own diachronic parabola of rough-hewn early greatness (Aeschylus), serene maturity (Sophocles), and decline into either sophistic cynicism or irrational superstition, depending on one's point of view (Euripides)—a story whose gaping plot holes and inconsistencies have in retrospect been thoroughly trounced by Richard Jenkyns, but that at the time made perfect sense at an emotional gut level as well as intellectually. This then is why the Victorians made a cult of Sophocles, or why they told themselves they did.[15] Even the career of the individual poet might be viewed in Winckelmanian terms, generating curves within curves within curves—early vigour, mature grandeur, and a tailing-off of creative powers in old age. The model generated satisfying complexity across every level of organization, all of them connected by the same underlying dynamic to form a total literary–cultural system. It was chaos theory as imagined by a Stoic.

Reading art, literature, and the world through a Winckelmanian prism came to seem second nature, which is a sign that it was heavily ideological. There could now be no such thing as politically innocent aesthetics, because art always told on the health and strength of the culture that produced it. While the discovery of a natural 'law' of stylistic development implied the semantic weight of scientific objectivity, the whole box of tricks stands in retrospect as an obvious and massively circular zero-sum game. The hermeneutics of a still nascent art-critical discourse gave free play to personal subjectivity—in the case of its own founder, passionately so; Winckelmann's evaluations and taxonomies were as much as anything an encoded sublimation of his homosexual desires, which forever after bubbled just below the surface of his culturally indispensable text.[16] This was to have important consequences later on in our story, with Symonds (Chapter 3).

Returning to the programmatic claims of Bland's preface, the influence of the Winckelmann curve is immediately evident in his 'rocks and precipices ... bold and daring'. The peak achievements of classical Greek literature are here defined figuratively as peaks of cultural achievement, as though by force of habit, but also visualized as physical high places

---

[15] Jenkyns (1980: 92–3, 106–7), and cf. Stray (2007a).

[16] Orrells (2011a: 18–22) sensitively unpacks the issues surrounding one statue of particular significance in his art-historical scheme, the Apollo Belvedere, complementing the discussion at Beard and Henderson (2001: 107–11).

within a concretized literary landscape. This extrapolation of Winckelmanian elevation into three-dimensional space acknowledges the majesty of the great works (and already many readers would think first of
tragedy, although in a different context later on Bland adds the historians
and Attic orators, viewed as 'documents' of the great period of Greece's
history).[17] But it also suggests that getting to grips with these jagged
masterpieces entails arduous labour and perhaps also risk; indeed, they
are tiring even to look at from below. The high wild places of the canon
are thus configured as sites of Sublimity, the pleasurable, vertiginous
terror of confronting the uncaring Absolute. The Sublime began its life as
an English literary topos in the published journals of Grand Tourists
whose itineraries took them into Italy through the Alps, and became
thoroughly naturalized in eighteenth-century Romanticism.

As a trope of horror, the Sublime is antithetical to conventional beauty
in the world of Nature; its sites are arid death zones. The domain of life is
the 'gentle slopes' below—gentle in gradient, but also to Nature in sympathy with humanity ('refreshing verdure'). And it is here in the foothills
and valleys that epigram, in its own characteristic 'milder excellence', is
to be found—an Alpine flower meadow, placed in a landscape human
in scale and lying within the reach of the ordinary culture tourist.
Wandering in this meadow, we may pluck a posy of 'private lives and
domestic occurrences' that put us in touch with the lived experience of
yesteryear.[18] This vivid formulation will be revisited many years later
when Symonds presents epigram to its new readership in the 1870s. The
phrasing will be much the same, but the implied meanings will have
acquired new topicality for his public (Chapter 3), and, as the century
draws towards its close amid widespread fears of British racial decline,
still further layers of implication will accrue (Chapter 5).

A final consequence of Bland's presentation of epigram through the
prism of Winckelmann is that from now on the chronological progression of genre history acquired strong potential importance in determining which poets were worth reading—worth singling out within the
Anthology's 'mighty wreck' for individual attention.[19] It also presented
knotty difficulties and ambiguities that interested critics later in the
century were to exploit. As a literary genre within the body of Greek
verse literature, epigram was expected to display its own micro-history,
its curve within a curve (we may at this point feel grateful that no body of
ancient biography or testimonia survived to inspire the fabrication of
career trajectories for individual epigrammatists, but we will shortly see

---

[17] Bland (1806: p. xi).   [18] Bland (1806: p. xi).   [19] Bland (1806: p. xi).

that this is no obstacle to Bland once he gets going). The 'best' authors would naturally find their place at its 'highest' point, preceded by hearty pioneers and followed by decadent latecomers. In its literary manifestation, however, epigram was problematically late. In the 'best' period of Greek poetry, fifth-century Athens, the genre did not yet exist: it was still wholly an inscriptional form. This bothered its nineteenth-century readers, some of whom went so far as to place epigram at the Athenian symposium through imaginative fakery.[20] As we have seen, though, literary epigram began only in the Hellenistic age, and in terms of both quantity and polish there is a strong case for placing its *floruit* under the Roman Empire of the early centuries CE.[21]

This lateness created tensions with which any subsequent explanation of epigram would have to grapple. Within the overall arc of Greek literary history, the earliest non-inscriptional epigrammatists (of whom the best known are Callimachus and Asclepiades) ought to be the best, because they are the closest to poetry's universally acknowledged golden age—and they still ought not to be authors of the first rank, because as Hellenistic poets they are already 'late'. Within the micro-history of epigram, however, and in order to deliver a suitably shaped curve, these same poets ought to be counted as crude forebears, with the sunny peak of the genre occurring somewhat later—but this pushes epigram's 'best' poets yet further into the age of decline. Something would always have to give, and in subsequent chapters (Chapters 3, 5–6) we will see critics working with these tensions in ways that suit the particular stories they wish to tell.

3. 'A GUILTY EXCESS': REDEEMING MELEAGER IN THE PREFACE

> The sweetest buds that deck'd the land
> Were pluck'ed by Meleager's hand ... (prologue, n.p.)

For his own part, Bland opts for a positive spin on the lateness of the Hellenistic period: it is Greece's 'green old age', a vibrant characterization

---

[20] The faked-up epigrams of Becker's didactic historical novel *Charicles*, a work much read in English translation, are used as an opening gambit in Livingstone and Nisbet (2010: 1–4); see also briefly Jenkyns (1980: 83). Bland attests to the practice in his own time at (1806: p. liii), citing as the publication context the *Observer* and indicating use of the same materials that Becker would subsequently raid (the fragmentary comic poets).

[21] Livingstone and Nisbet (2010: 118).

that by association posits epigram in its 'verdure' as the natural poetic voice of the era. Meleager thus inhabits a still-healthy Greek world in which 'the features of [Greece's] youth were discernible, and the spirit with which it was animated burst forth in irregular and partial gleams, that evinced her not yet to be exhausted by the efforts of former days'. There is life in the old culture yet.[22] Meleager's own date is late even by Hellenistic standards (the modern consensus is c.100 BCE), but Bland keeps this as vague as he can.[23] Under the cover of telling apart Meleager the anthologist from Meleager the Cynic, he goes to great lengths to disassociate the former from the 'coarseness' of the satirical mode—a keyword that we will later see recurring as a synonym for the spiritual contamination of Greece's literary life under Roman influence. (To the best of my knowledge, this bifurcation of Meleager's attested literary career to create two separate Meleagers is Bland's own invention, perhaps inspired by the two Sapphos of the ancient biographical tradition.[24]) The poetic Meleager's creative period is anchored by 'the fall of Corinth'. Later in the book we get a couple of nicely resonant versions from epitaphs to the Corinthian slaughter by Antipater of Sidon—

> Where has thy grandeur, Corinth, shrunk from sight,
> Thy antient treasures, and thy rampart's height? ...

—but the uninformed reader would never guess that this fall had anything to do with Greece becoming a Roman province.[25]

Instead, the coming of the new Mediterranean superpower is associated with the following century and Philip, a collector who we are explicitly told worked under very different conditions, and the inferiority of whose Garland reflects a dramatically altered political landscape. 'Perfection is no longer to be found', as by implication it had been in Meleager's day. Instead, all that Philip can do is to gather up the falling leaves of Greece's 'Autumn', leaves 'interesting even to *their latest decay*' (emphasis added; another characterization to which later critics will add topical new twists).[26] After Philip, and in blanket denial of much of the Anthology's content, Bland tells us that there is nothing until the sixth century and Agathias—a 'silent lapse of more than five hundred years', covering what we now term the Second Sophistic and the high and late

[22] Bland (1806: p. xx).
[23] On the dating of the Garland, see Cameron (1993: 19–33). Bland is aware of this, but buries the data in a technical footnote (p. xiv).
[24] Bland (1806: p. xvi); on Sappho and the ancient biographers, see Lefkowitz (1981: 36–7); DeJean (1989a: 16–17) sums up tidily.
[25] Bland (1806: pp. xix, 44–5).   [26] Bland (1806: pp. xxi–ii).

Empire.[27] Even when epigram returns with Agathias in the sixth century, its gleanings are not leaves—the organic outcrop of a still-living tree of Hellas—but dead scraps, 'raked together' by the anthologist as the detritus of a Greece declining into its final senility. The epigrams of Agathias's contemporary Paul the Silentiary are taken as indicative of a nation steeped in vice, a 'polluted imagination' addicted to 'debasing pleasures'. This is clearly the tail end of the genre's micro-history.[28] ('And now some sad and wint'ry plant, | Some wither'd shrub, of pow'r malign...'—or, we may recall from the book's prologue, a yew, the poisonous death-tree of graveyards throughout Britain.)

This misdirection keeps Bland's readership focused on Meleager's late Hellenistic Garland as the only 'Greek Anthology' worth getting to know, underwriting the scholar–poet's position as the designated spokesman of the 'green old age' of Hellas. That being said, Bland's Meleager is only marginally Greek himself. To be 'tender and affecting' implies Romantic sentiment, not classical Hellenic serenity, and the explanation for this is found in Meleager's ethnicity. At his first appearance he is 'Meleager, the Syrian'. His Eastern temperament informs a supine and emotionally 'soft' character, dedicated to exploring and celebrating sensuality, and inclined to fatalism—'by turns a slave to love and melancholy'.[29] Buried in a note on Menander we later find Meleager invoked as exemplar in an explicit 'comparison between the Oriental and Grecian systems of poetical morality', the former identifiable by its 'voluptuous precepts'; India is invoked, albeit in an antiquarian interest.[30]

Later in the century (Chapter 5) we will see this character sketch spelled out in greater detail, expanded, and politicized: Eastern servility will no longer be simply a matter of lack of self-control, but also predestines subordination as a colonial subject, on whom control must be imposed for his own good. Meleager's Orientalism changes its aspect to mirror the newly dominant ideology of Empire. This agenda of the later nineteenth century is not part of Bland's scheme: his Meleager does not need to be whipped into shape, but is a poet to be cherished for his 'records of affection, tenderness, and sorrow'. To that extent at least, he is

---

[27] Bland (1806: p. xxii).

[28] Bland (1806: xxiii), and cf. p. xxvi, 'decrepitude'; Paul's prostituted muse, p. xxiv. Symonds will find advantage in reactivating Bland's characterization of Paul the Silentiary for *Studies*, albeit within a tweaked chronological bell curve (Ch. 3); the writers who react against Symonds strive to recuperate Paul as a neglected late classic (Ch. 5).

[29] Bland (1806: pp. xiv–v), and cf. eloquently p. xvii, 'a mind woven of the finest texture, [but] soft and pliable to a guilty excess'.

[30] Bland (1806: 163–5).

a poet of Romanticism in the eighteenth-century English taste, transcribing the emotional truth of suffering and love.[31]

Under the sign of Romanticism, Bland appears actively indignant at attempts to muzzle his sighing ancient poet. The first wave of the assault on Meleager belongs, we learn, to a safely distant but also topically available past: with 'gloomy and unrelenting zeal', the Church of the fourth to sixth centuries 'persecuted every work of ingenuity and fancy'.[32] This conforms to a peculiarly British literary stereotype, of which the paradigm example interrogated in modern criticism is Kingsley's *Hypatia: or, New Foes with an Old Face* (1853). In *Hypatia*, which adds to the mix the contemporary English cult of muscular Christianity, the Mediterranean Church of the late Empire is a debased death-cult of hysteria, hypocrisy, and bloody fanaticism, in thrall to an effete clerisy. Only the infusion of hardy northern European blood can cleanse and redeem it at some future date (and note how Kingsley's title makes this all about Protestantism versus the Church of Rome, in about the least subtle way conceivable).[33]

Immediately after Bland's excoriation of the censor's fanaticism, to which the 'ingenuity and fancy' of a tender poet have fallen prey, there follows a paragraph worth quoting in full. It puts what Bland has just been saying in a very different light, but is careful not to throw too much illumination on its own real topic:

The first of Meleager's collections was necessarily exposed to their fury. The specimens of that work which yet remain too abundantly justify the persecution. It was written for the express purpose of celebrating Eastern sensuality; and it is said to have contained nothing but the *divitias miseras* of a mind pregnant with ideas wasted in the embellishment of vice. But unfortunately its undiscriminating enemies appear to have been actuated by a rage no less furious against those beautiful relics of affection and sorrow by which the poet endeavoured to make amends to an insulted world for the extravagance of his youth.[34]

'The first of Meleager's collections' is pure fancy on Bland's part, but the reader is strongly encouraged to buy into the logic that underlies it: the only way to make sense of and redeem Meleager as 'one of us' is to confine part of his work to a period of poetic and personal immaturity. By implication this is his homosexual verse, which we are urged to dismiss as youthful folly—really just a silly phase, during which his talent was for a time sadly misdirected ('wasted', and so on), and for which he

---

[31] Bland (1806: p. xvii).   [32] Bland (1806: p. xxviii).

[33] On *Hypatia* as sectarian agitprop, see usefully Dorman (1979); the impact of muscular Christianity is pithily addressed by Jenkyns (1980: 169–71).

[34] Bland (1806: p. xxviii).

later attempted to atone ('make amends'). 'The specimens... which yet remain' must be Meleager's many epigrams in AP 12, a book that by lucky coincidence—or, more likely, deliberate design—Bland has already excluded, by shaping the life cycle of his genre to tail off into coma in the first century CE (Strato is a second-century poet; nothing happened in epigram in the second century) before expiring with a final death rattle in the sixth.

Bland now reimagines these *divitias miseras* ('pitiful wealth') as the extant fragments of an imaginary lost book of juvenilia, and shrouds that book in fabricated rumour as to its vile content ('is said to have ...'), the nature of which he decorously avoids specifying. 'Vice' is so handy a catch-all; it can cover so much or so little. *Divitias miseras* is itself a tag from Horace's *Cena Nasidienis* (Satires 2.8.18); Horace's theme there is very different, so this is a handy bit of misdirection. Also, Horace was nationally favoured as a plain-sense moralist who took an indulgent view, unlike the stern Juvenal, so was a handy author to invoke in excusing youthful folly and giving a fellow a second chance.[35]

Some readers with Greek—and the constitution of his readership (shortly to be addressed) will have included many such—may have known exactly what Bland meant by 'vice' here. Then again, if they did not, finding the answer will have been hard work even for a Hellenist. There was still no edition that presented the poems of the Palatine Anthology according to Cephalas's own arrangement of thematic categories, so no one could go and read book 12 as a unit, except conceivably by consulting the manuscript itself in Paris, where it had resided since 1797 along with many other Vatican treasures surrendered by the Papal States after their defeat by the rising young general Napoleon Bonaparte.[36] Since France and Britain were at war (Trafalgar had been fought the year before the Cambridge trio brought their book to press), this was unlikely to occur.

Bland berates Planudes for ruining the scheme of the Anthology through clumsy reorganization, but leaves his own readers no better off, and utterly unable to check his story.[37] The editions of the Palatine Anthology available at the time were arranged alphabetically by author, so his contemporaries could go and look up Strato if they had heard of him; but Bland keeps Strato's name out of the discussion. So the reader is

---

[35] On the rhetorical opposition between Horace and Juvenal in British discourse of translation and pedagogy during this period, see briefly Nisbet (2012a: 504–5), with further bibliography.

[36] Huet (1999: 61–3), on Napoleon's expropriations from the Borghese Collection, is useful as context.

[37] Bland (1806: p. xxxiii) casts Planudes as a product of 'his tasteless times'.

left to guess, or to take 'vice' as a warn-off—just knowing that these practices (whatever they are) exist could be permanently harmful to the moral character of the reader. (We will see numerous latter-day zealots grapple with the unspeakability of 'vice' when we turn to epigram's reception history in the later nineteenth century (Chapters 4 and 5).) Book and poem numbers are not included, even in the notes. The reader has to take everything on trust.

Without ever quite saying as much, *Translations* constructs a readerly perspective in which Meleager's pederastic epigrams had objectively demanded ('too abundantly justified') censorship, on the basis of a public morality presumed to be unchanging through time. Expressions of heterosexual desire are romantic, and have lasting artistic value; expressions of homosexual desire are pornographic, and do not deserve to exist. If only the fanatics of late antiquity had called it a day after destroying the latter, they would have done the world a service; Bland's great regret is that they failed to discriminate, attacking also the heterosexual poems of AP 5 (parsed as respectably conjugal 'affection') and the literary epitaphs of AP 7 (decorous 'sorrow'), by means of which a repentant Meleager attempted to make his peace with 'an insulted world'. The insult is not to any one society or nation, but to the universal order of things ('world'); effectively, though not in so many words, to God's Creation. Read in the correct sequence—AP 12 first, then AP 5, and finally AP 7—the Meleagrian elements of the Anthology offer up a life story that can be reconstructed on the basis of unchanging human nature and moral continuity: Meleager *must* have regretted these poems in the wisdom of his mature years, because any of 'us' would. The self-evident sequel to a misspent youth is that he came to his senses, looked to his end, and settled down with a nice girl.

No other life choice was available to him. Bland's imaginative biography of Meleager creates an ancient Hellas in which same-sex desire was emphatically not accepted. Like the modern Britons with whom they stand in sympathy, Bland's ancient Greeks would never have stood for sexually deviant behaviour, or even for smutty talk. Instead, Meleager's youthful phase of pederastic enthusiasm bears witness to a specifically Oriental cultural contagion for which the poems of AP 12 are insidious propaganda ('written for the express purpose of celebrating Eastern sensuality'). That this diseased sexuality had been seen by its ancient adherents as needing propagandistic 'embellishment' is itself further proof of its antipathy to a human nature now construed in explicitly Western terms.

The initial characterization of 'Meleager, the Syrian' as a soft sensualist is now thrown into sharp relief, and the sense of a throwaway phrase there, 'few of [his fellow creatures] were half so prone to weakness and error as himself',[38] is now clarified—for those few contemporary readers who knew the Anthology thoroughly *despite* the editions then available. Censorship has been endorsed without ever being named as such— indeed, while notionally being rejected as the aberrant behaviour of a fanatical Other. Bland's treatment of Planudes is revealing in this regard; while taking him to task for editorial wrong-headedness regarding arrangement, he reveals his enthusiastic bowdlerization of the corpus only indirectly through hand-me-down quotation, and in the decent obscurity of a dead language at that: 'and, as Lascaris says of him in his preface, "Non magis disposuit, quam mutilavit, et, ut ita dicam, castravit hunc librum, detractis lascivioribus epigrammatis; ut ipse gloriatur."'[39] Bland may regret the depredations of the monks of late antiquity, but his portrait of Meleager has plugged the gap with ample 'ingenuity and fancy' of his own.

One final point deserves our attention before we move on to the *Translations* proper. Reducing the Anthology's millennium of epigrams to its Hellenistic core delivers a welcome thematic concentration. We have already seen how the homoerotic poems of AP 12 are implicitly excluded on grounds of the date of its key author, Strato, but Bland's rhetorical emphasis on the poets of Meleager's *Garland* also has a constructive agenda. It sets up for a concentration in the *Translations* on two themes characteristic of Meleager's collection, though not exclusively so: the elegiac topoi of love and death. Heavy emphasis is placed in the preface on the pessimism of the Greek character in the face of death's inevitability:

The short observations on human life, couched in Greek Epigrams, are ever of a melancholy cast: a complaint on the ills of age, sickness or poverty; or a beacon set up to light us on our road, and to warn us against pride, perfidy, ingratitude, envy... Gloomy and uncomfortable reflections on the shortness and misery of life seem equally to have inspired the philosopher and the voluptuary...

To those, whose notions of a future state were perplexed, dark, and uncertain; whose belief in retribution was unsettled and wavering, and rather an object of speculation than a ground of hope or satisfaction, this present life must have appeared the boundary of all human desires and fears... These ideas followed them in solitude, and crept in upon their banquets...[40]

Born too early to hear Christ's message of everlasting life for the virtuous (and self-righteously to gloat at the presumptive eternal torment of the wicked), the Greeks of the Garland offer up decorous pagan *memento*

---

[38] Bland (1806: p. xv).   [39] Bland (1806: p. xxxiv).
[40] Bland (1806: pp. ix–xi).

mori to a future that, from its position of superior knowledge of the divine dispensation, can interpret their sentiments better than they could themselves. Latent in Bland's phrasing is a Herculean choice. Born too soon to be saved by Gospel truth, those pagan Hellenes cursed with the clear-sightedness to know their condition have only two options open to them: the stony (Western) path of philosophic self-mastery, or the easy (Eastern) road of sensual indulgence. Raised in the East but reborn to painful self-knowledge in his mature years, Meleager is thus the consummate all-round pagan poet. His subtle melancholy[41] makes him the perfect curator of the *tristesse* of an ageing and careworn nation, dimly aware that it was missing something vital as it grappled with its own looming mortality—here cast fairly literally as the skeleton at the feast.[42]

When we turn the pages and enter the *Translations* proper, however, we may notice that its content does not match the sales pitch. It is a truism that bears repeating that what translators say they are doing is not what they actually do.[43] This is not Meleager's Garland at all: far from it.

4. 'POOR LOST ELIZA!': THE ANTHOLOGY
IN ENGLISH DRESS

The title has promised 'Translations *Chiefly* from the Greek Anthology', and that is what Bland and his collaborators deliver. We may note that the promise does not specify 'Epigrams'. Thus we begin with some Meleager, freely rendered and with much expansion, typically twelve lines for four in the original (pp. 3–6); then some Archilochus, Sappho, Erinna, and Anyte. These are all poets excerpted by Meleager for inclusion in his Garland, though (Anyte excepted) they are not technically epigrammatists (pp. 7–10). Then we get the early lyricist Mimnermus (pp. 11–12); Theognis (pp. 13–14); Ibycus (p. 15); and in short order a selection of skolia, or drinking songs (pp. 24–7).

What we are seeing here is an extension of the Meleagrian ploy of including token non-epigrammatic poets of a bygone age. For Meleager, whether in a spirit of literary play or simply because the evident generic

---

[41] Bland (1806: p. xvii).

[42] In a later note, even the purer romantic feelings of the Greeks are cast into question as unsustainable without knowledge of Christian doctrine: lifelong fidelity presupposes awareness of a Heaven in which the lovers' matrimonial bond will be resumed for all eternity: Bland (1806: 137).

[43] Hayes (2009: 214), consistently insightful.

affiliations of a literary text may change with changing times, the archaic lyricists staked out a time-honoured tradition for non-inscriptional epigram.[44] For Bland and his collaborators to follow in his footsteps (and go much further down the same path) is a little peculiar, since they have the whole of the Anthology to choose from, as obviously Meleager did not.[45] If we set aside as unknowable their several personal tastes in poetry (and perhaps many of these selections were indeed personal favourites), the effect aimed at—and certainly the effect created—must be the bulking-up of Meleager's catalogue of archaic pseudo- or proto-epigrammatists. This gives the right kind of shape to the genre's micro-history: however unevenly, it lends the appearance of a fatter curve as epigram ascends towards its Hellenistic peak.

In fact much of the content is much later than Meleager. Following the precedent set by the first published editions of the Palatine Anthology, those of Brunck (1772–6) and Jacobs (1794–8), Bland arranges his authors in what he takes to be their chronological sequence; and, forty pages in, we meet a footnote to the effect that we are passing beyond the period of the Garland.[46] Another fourteen later, and less than two-thirds of our way through the epigrams and pseudo-epigrams, we are advised that we are leaving behind us the collection of Philip. That is to say, we move in the third act of Bland's Anthology into the 'silent' second century and beyond.[47] We meet here poems by Lucian (pp. 57–8); satirical poems by the Roman-named Lucillius and his imitator Nicarchus (pp. 58–63), just the kind of satire the editor has denounced in his preface as 'coarse'; and so on. Agathias, and the despised Paul the Silentiary, get a good showing—indeed, they fill more pages than are allotted to beautiful Meleager (pp. 71–7). There is even a poem, although unsurprisingly not a pederastic one, from Strato (p. 79)—placed sequentially almost at the end of the epigrams by named authors, and thus implicitly made extremely 'late' in period and outlook.

The spirit of these translations is, as mentioned, free. There is considerable expansion, everything is made to rhyme, and the metres are

---

[44] Acosta-Hughes (2010) explores how Hellenistic authors experienced Archaic lyric within the literary horizon of expectations of their own era.

[45] In a muddled section added to the preface for the 1813 version of *Collections*, Bland (p. xli) justifies these recruitments with reference to the precedent for 'arbitrary' generic expansion set by Brunck and Jacobs—a 'they started it' defence worthy of a primary-school playground. Diana Spencer points out to me that it is odd that he does not think to invoke Meleager as an authentically classical precedent for just this kind of behaviour. A disturbing thought: did he not *know* that Sappho, Anyte, et al. had not been *bona fide* epigrammatists but had been retrospectively recruited by Meleager to dignify the pedigree of his genre?

[46] Merivale (1833: pp. iv–v) confirms that the friends took Brunck and Jacobs as their organizational model in the first edition.

[47] Bland (1806: 40, 54).

miscellaneous, although with a preference for the English iambic pentameter. Occasionally this is laid out on the page so as to resemble the Anthology's characteristic elegiacs, as in this example from Callimachus:

> Oh had no venturous keel defied the deep!
> Then had not Lycid floated on the brine... (p. 38)

Truncating Lycidas to 'Lycid' is the least of the liberties taken with proper names, as the editor frankly admits in his preface: 'This latter liberty the structure of our language induces, or rather compels me to take; for the Greek names, if admitted, would not only impede the rhyme, but would give a foreign air to what should appear familiar' (pp. iv–v).[48] And appear familiar they should, since we have just been told (pp. ii–iv) how our own island poets have found in their ancient forebears such congenial inspiration. Giving English names to '*e.g.* Clearista, Heliodora, Zenophile' (p. v) will naturalize them within what is now construed as in effect a living, Anglo-Hellenic epigrammatic tradition. Sometimes this creates a pleasing prospective intertextuality. In elegiac translation, this epigram directed at a woman who once coldly rejected the poet's wooing picks up flavour from *Romeo and Juliet*:

> Did I not warn thee, Rosaline, that Time
> Would soon divide thee from the youthful throng,
> Feed on the blooming damask of thy prime... (p. 67)

'Rosalind' (p. 54) gets the same treatment, and Antipater of Thessalonica berates the lark in terms that recall Romeo's: 'O hateful bird of Morn, whose harsh alarms | Drive me thus early from Chrysilla's arms, Forc'd from th'embrace so newly tried to fly, | With bitter soul, to curs'd society' (p. 48). Bland's note on the poem eagerly draws attention to the similarity in case we should miss it (p. 136).

There are adjustments of social custom and geography as well, which occasionally create charming incongruity, as in this rather splendid version of an epigram by Nicarchus, AP 11.162:

> Tom prudently thinking his labour ill spar'd
> If e'er, unadvised, for his plans he prepar'd,
> Consulted a witch on his passage to Dover...

The seer's reply:

> 'You may sail there and back without danger or fear
> —Unless you are caught by a French privateer.'[49]

---

[48] 'Lycid' recurs at p. 83. Cf. 'Diomed' (p. 25), the standard rendering of Diomedes in translation and in English literature generally prior to the twentieth century.
[49] Bland (1806: 63).

Greek gods and goddesses are rendered in their Anglicized Roman guise for the same reason of poetic naturalization, as these were the versions then much better known—'Minerva's adverse fane' (24), 'Grim Pluto' (p. 60), 'When Bacchus fights on Cupid's side' (p. 67), 'great Jove' (p. 78), 'Juno's royal dome' (p. 84). Mythological reference is occasionally transposed between cultural registers: as a figure for old age, Deucalion appropriately becomes 'Noah' (p. 62), whose myth he shares. Of one particularly allusive epigram on a bunch of grapes torn unripe from the vine, we are told in an endnote that 'the aim here has been to Anglicize the Epigram, and to leave out all allusions as far as possible to antient fables. The turn of idea remains unaltered' (p. 163).

The overall drift of these revisions is to turn the Anthology into a byway of English poetry, even at the cost of taking on features denounced by Bland as characteristic of debased modern pretension:

An English lover has seldom contented himself with the picture of his Amanda, until he has rifled the rose of its bloom and sweetness for her cheek and breath; beds of coral for the redness of her lips . . . A Greek lover never labours at a picture for which the colours must be so far fetched. Indeed he seldom gives any picture at all.[50]

The friends' enthusiasm for poetic expansion sometimes undoes this classical simplicity:

> Cold on the wild wave floats thy virgin form,
> *Drench'd are thy auburn tresses by the storm,*
> Poor lost Eliza! . . .[51]

The friends' policy with proper names and local colour was not to go unchallenged. It flagged up a larger issue: just how 'English' should the Anthology be, on the printed page? This was a question to which subsequent translators and other interested parties were to develop some very different answers.

5. REVIEWING THE ANTHOLOGY

More often than not . . . what is under review [in the *Edinburgh*] is less a book than a policy, an institution or a prevailing opinion on a topic or issue taken to be worth discussing, regardless of who wrote it . . .

---

[50] Bland (1806: pp. viii–ix).
[51] Bland (1806: 55) (emphasis added).

Even the reviewer who did remain attentive to the book was always liable to digress.[52]

'A "Prologue" follows, in which the too obvious metaphor of a "wreath of flowers", already woefully jaded in the preface, is absolutely ridden to death': Bland, Merivale, and Hodgson must have hoped for a more positive early notice.[53] Their anonymous assailant for the *Edinburgh Review* finds particular fault with the Englishing of names, although not for any reason of fidelity:

> we must decline all share in a practice which our judgement condemns as very strange and unwarrantable ... we are of the opinion, that if a chance is to be made [to comply with English versification], the *costume* ought at any rate to be so far respected, that no English names should be substituted that are not of Greek origin. When Erinne laments the death of a virtuous companion, we confess our disappointment at finding that the adopted name of 'Julia' makes it possible to confound her with the abandoned daughter of Augustus.[54]

The reference is to a version of an epitaph from Erinna: 'I mark the spot where Julia's ashes lie ...'.[55] The substituted name of 'Rosalind' is one of those singled out for opprobrium, although not so much as 'Thyrza'— 'on what principle of justice are our starting tears to be intercepted, and sprinkled over the grave of Cain's wife?'[56] This is unduly harsh—'Thyrza' in the 1780s had been the harem sweetheart of John Adams's Orientalist sensation, the short story 'Pirnaz and Mirvan: An Eastern Tale', and the exoticism of her name made her the addressee of passionate elegies including Byron's 'On Thyrza' a few years down the line (1811)—but the anonymous reviewer is not in the business of literary criticism in a modern sense.[57] Similarly, and for the sake of a cheap barb, his cutting remark on Bland's prologue affects not to know that the 'too obvious metaphor' is Meleager's own. Some of this professed ignorance is probably genuine: the review opens with an account of 'the several anthologies' that appears to believe that they are all extant, and that Cephalas

---

[52] Christie (2009: 25–6).   [53] Anon. (1807: 325).

[54] Anon. (1807: 325–6) (emphasis in original).

[55] Bland (1806: 9). Subsequent translators of epigram into English tended to agree that names should not be replaced with cute Latin-pastoral cut-outs: 'Baucis should appear as Baucis. To dwindle Anaxagoras into Corydon, and Philaenion into Chloe is not desirable' (Macgregor 1864: p. xiv).

[56] Anon. (1807: 326).

[57] 'Pirnaz and Mirvan' is collected at Adams (1791: 256–62), which contains several similarly exploitative tales of the lustful East; previously it had been published in periodicals on both sides of the Atlantic.

was merely a predecessor to Planudes, represented as the culmination of the Anthology tradition.[58] At other times, though, the reviewer actively misrepresents the content of the volume, as in the rejection of another substitute name: 'We should be loath to object to the celebration of Janet, a lively countrywoman of our own, we presume, who has captivated our author in a tour to the Highlands, with the national graces of rosy arms, sandy hair, and far-projecting cheeks.'[59]

The implicit criticism of trite expansion in the physical description of the beloved (and here we must recall Bland's preface and poor lost Eliza) is undeniably just, and is righteously driven home four pages later in the excoriation of an 'ingenious idea laboriously expanded into eight lines' from a single pithy couplet, but this is pure hypocrisy: Janet's 'rosy arms...and far-projecting cheeks' are the reviewer's own ekphrastic amplification around the 'golden hair' of Janet in *Translations*.[60] Similarly, Bland's undeniable penchant for imaginative biography is justly dismissed as arrant fantasy—but the Scottish holiday pulled out of thin air in the quotation above is no less fanciful.[61] There is some faint praise ('felicity'), but also condemnation ('far duller than the dull original'); the motive of the unnamed author is admitted to be pure ('pious care'), but the closing words write off the whole volume as manifest juvenilia.[62]

For an anonymous review of an anonymous book, this attack feels violently *ad personam*. Small wonder that the young Byron felt compelled to defend their honour as well as his own in his 'English Bards and Scotch Reviewers' two years later, a polemical reply to the *Edinburgh*'s hostile reviewers (according to him, an 'oat-fed phalanx' of drunken anti-intellectuals, enemies of taste, who prefer any drivel so long as it is local).

Why such ire? Part of the explanation for the tone of this review is that its author has his own hobby-horse to exercise, on a largely unrelated topic (and the remark by Christie quoted as the incipit to this section indicates how par for the course this was with *Edinburgh* contributors). This particular reviewer's *idée fixe* takes the form of a partisan view on Planudes as the wholesale forger of Aesop's fables; he is incensed that this important fact (in which few seriously believed even then) has not been taken on board, for it strongly suggests that much of the *Anthology* as well is likely to be a Planudean fake.[63] But we might look for a further and less ostensibly personal motive in the respective politics of the *Edinburgh* and of the journal in which Bland and his collaborators had extensively tested the waters through serial publication, Richard

---

[58] Anon (1807: 319–20).   [59] Anon (1807: 326).
[60] Bland (1806: 71).   [61] Anon (1807: 330).
[62] Anon (1807: 325, 330–1).   [63] Yes, really; Anon (1807: 321).

Phillips's *Monthly Magazine and British Register*.[64] The *Monthly* was radical in its editorial agenda (and 'downmarket' in its brisk publishing schedule); the *Edinburgh*, staunchly Whig, within what was becoming a two-party publishing domain to which the *Monthly* stood as an unfancied outsider and minor irritant.[65]

Although it was happy to pick a fight with anyone, the most constant enemy for the *Edinburgh* was its neighbouring Other, *Blackwood's Magazine*, a rival quarterly Review also based in Edinburgh and familiar to the Tory faithful as 'Maga'.[66] When the *Edinburgh* came out against Merivale and Bland, Maga naturally became the pair's biggest fans, and thus acquired its own stake in the representation of Greek epigram to the British public—the consequences of which will be explored in Chapter 4. Maga, for instance, is much more supportive of their practice of loose translation tending towards adaptation: 'the felicity of the execution being such as that the deviation from the original is not felt to be a flaw, but an even better bringing out of the thought or feeling that constitutes its pervading and prevailing character'. This was a decidedly sunny view; Bland's blithe re-castings were felt by a less partisan critic to be all the more regrettable given his patchy grasp of the ancient literary context.[67]

Often published quarterly, the Review periodicals were a new literary species of the later eighteenth century. Their market share was to decline from the 1860s under competition from new, cheaper monthly magazines, at a time when cheap newspapers were also rapidly growing their readerships following the 1855 abolition of newspaper tax; this process would culminate in the foundation of the *Daily Mail* in 1896 and with it the birth of mass journalism in its modern sense.[68]

Like letter-writing but open, the Reviews facilitated the social networking of a highly educated elite while also making available to a wider readership, through their dissemination of society gossip, the fantasy of participation in urbane society (the ideological potency of this virtual salon was addressed in the Introduction). Journalism and other forms of

---

[64] Bland and Merivale (1805–6), a dozen installments.

[65] Haywood (2004: 83).

[66] On the Edinburgh's spat with the *Quarterly Review*, see Stray (2007b).

[67] Christie (2009: 39–40, 148–9, 161); Anon (1833c (quoted here at p. 868), 1833d). The notional stimulus for Maga's championing of Merivale (1833) is a negative review of the previous edition by Charles Blomfield, now Bishop of London, twenty years before—a blink of an eye as Maga measured grudge time, but they had no quarrel with Blomfield (quite the opposite) and I think *Edinburgh* must be the real target. We meet Blomfield again very briefly in Ch. 2. Bland too loose a paraphraser and an unperceptive reader: Anon (1826: 268–9), much preferring Hodgson.

[68] Donoghue (1995: 55, 57–8) gives a chronology of the various Reviews. On their decline, see Brake (1995: 292); the rise of the cheap newspaper is surveyed by Wiener (1988).

ephemeral publication (broadsheets, ballads) were as important as were the newly popular durable genres (novels, works of reference) to Habermas's public sphere of 'enlightened' secular discourse. Periodicals in particular were vital, broadcasting and annotating as they did the Big Conversation of the urban scene's clubs and coffee houses, but also reporting on more structured and progressive debate within single-issue special-interest groups on causes such as female emancipation. Journals whose ambit was 'Review' were frequent conduits for edgy political agitation, and not just in the explicit opinion pieces that they interspersed with notional exercises in literary criticism.[69]

Editors and contributors generated sequels to their magazines' published 'conversations', both through letter-writing and face to face, within their elite friendship networks; these conversations stimulated written follow-up pieces, and explicitly chewed over the limits of (while simultaneously going far beyond) what could be said in print.[70] These ongoing threads of discourse were cosmopolitan in outlook, and receptive to the latest events and trends in continental Europe. That Greek epigram got its first British foothold in the Reviews, and from there became a preferred genre for nineteenth-century Britain, must in large part reflect the fashionability within these urbane networks at the century's turn of German Romanticism—and specifically the interest expressed in the Greek Anthology by Johann Gottfried Herder. From the 1780s onwards, the British monthlies followed with enthusiasm Herder's project of translating poems from the Anthology, and kept their readers up to date on his critical thoughts on Greek epigram.[71]

Playing around with epigram was in any case a practice ideally suited to the maintenance and extension of social networks. As Baudrillard

---

[69] Klein (1995: 233–4) nicely summarizes the role of the periodical; Rosenberg (2005) reveals how the *Westminster Review* core team overlapped with the feminist Men and Women's Club.

[70] Rosenberg (2005) gives concrete examples from participants' personal correspondence, diaries, and autobiographies. Havelock Ellis, the great sexological writer who collaborated with Symonds (Ellis and Symonds 1897), came up through just such a network and learned there how to pitch his material so as not to frighten the horses: Rosenberg (2005: 124–6).

[71] Anon (1793), reviewing the fourth instalment of Herder's *Zerstraute Blätter* ('Scattered Leaves'), usefully tabulates how his translations from and two-part critical essay on the Anthology (1785) fitted into the overall scheme, and samples his original epigrams in German (pp. 506–7); Anon (1804), a posthumous retrospective, applauds the essay's 'sagacity and taste' (p. 134). For a brief account of Herder's translations of Anthology poems, and his own original compositions in the genre, see Sauder (2009: 310–11). Hirsch (2007: 76–80) has a particularly nice account of Herder's fascination with Greek epigram and how his translation process influenced Goethe; see also briefly Riikonen (2008: 183).

observes, the culture of collecting pushes individuals into increased collegiality and peer exchange, because in the eyes of its owner each collection is forever full of gaps that will one day need to be filled—and, with so many to choose from, the epigrams of the Anthology are the last word in literary collectibles.[72] They are also quick to translate and conveniently portable.

A letter from Bland himself illustrates the usefulness of epigram to enliven personal correspondences that keep social networks ticking over in the individual's absence, and that could then, in turn, feed back into public print. Writing to Merivale from Amsterdam in 1810, Bland announces that his income is now secure—a 'sinecure' of £100 a year—and that his prospects of attracting a patron are excellent on his return from French-occupied territory (he escapes back to England in disguise in 1811):[73]

Thus, between ourselves, Merry, I shall not be again the outcast that I have been. No; no more writing. Our 'Anthology', our dear 'Anthology', shall receive our united efforts. If you apply to William Harness (Berkeley Street) you may get dozens of my new pieces; Yatman has one or two; Mrs Burnley has a great number; my sister a few; Denman (to whom I wrote two months ago a very long letter) a few; Dr Drury (to whom I wrote an almost endless letter) has one or two. Have you read my 'Origin of Snoring'? No, no more reviewing for me, my friend. In short, no more scribbling of any kind except in the way of a clergyman, and conjointly with you a finish to the 'Anthology,' and by myself a thorough revisal of my last romance . . .'[74]

Harness had been befriended by Byron from his Harrow days; Henry Joseph Drury had taught Byron there, and thereafter was his friend and correspondent; Drury's father, the school's former Headmaster, later married Hodgson's sister. By the time Merivale and Son were putting together the final iteration of the friends' Anthology, Thomas Denman, another contemporary at Cambridge and an eminent barrister, had been raised to the bench as Lord Chief Justice; he was another epigram fan, having contributed three unsigned versions to *Translations*.[75]

Short poetry was also recited from memory when dining and socialising with friends. An earlier letter to Merivale, exuberantly dated '9 August 1805, St Alban's Street, Wednesday, *midnight*', reveals the three friends as poetically interdependent at table as well as on the printed page:

Mrs—— recited several beautiful scraps of poems; I retaliated with your 'Clarissa,' your 'O'er the Smooth Main', and Hodgson's 'Moderate Wishes', The sensation was so great, that, drunk as I was with pleasure at hearing my

---

[72] Baudrillard (1994: 2).   [73] Hodgson (1878: i. 231).
[74] Hodgson (1878: i. 239–40).   [75] Merivale (1833: p. v).

friends applauded, I was on the verge of reciting something of my own and should have done so—but (luckily) I forgot everything, and so was saved the disgrace of being hissed off the stage.[76]

Epigram is not mentioned, but this is the year before they published *Translations* and it is extremely tempting to imagine the three friends trying out memorized snippets of Meleager and pseudo-Plato within their circles of acquaintances in just this kind of context; waiting to gauge face-to-face reactions to each new version, before offering it to the editor of the *Monthly* to be put before its public. This is a social world in which the ideology of the amateur is paramount; where producers and consumers of niche culture are often the same people; and where textual production and exchange is an enabler of face-to-face networking and shared identification. Reviews, and readers' responses to them, therefore repay analysis as a form of participatory culture.[77] Several decades later, a sympathetic reviewer closed his account of Merivale's final *Collections* with the fond wish that he, the late Bland, the pair's collaborators, and other epigram-workers before and since might all come together for a pleasant evening in which the erudite yet playful spirit of the classical symposium (the comparator evoked is Aulus Gellius's *Attic Nights*) might be reborn. In this attractive fantasy, the ancient genre lives again in mutually respecting performance:

Would that Merivale, and Hodgson, and Wrangham, and Denman, and Sandford, and Elton, and the Adelphi, and young Bland, and H. N. Coleridge, and Keene, and 'the rest' were here; then might we indeed have a Noctes; *and while all our brows were bound with roses, each mouth would be an Anthology, and however various our utterance,* 'twould be all one in the Greek.[78]

In the world outside the printed text, these responses are effectively impossible to pin down. Our knowledge of the actual composition of the readerships of the different Reviews is next to non-existent: the nitty-gritty of publication history is at best largely inaccessible (and at worst chimerical), leaving the specialist scholarship with no clear idea of how many copies were produced or of how they were distributed, still less of the demographic profile associated with any publication. Even if circulation data were available, we would have no firm sense of through how many pairs of hands each copy had typically passed, or of how long it might have continued to be circulated informally and read second-hand.[79]

---

[76] Quoted at Hodgson (1878: i. 233).

[77] For some opening moves in this direction within the ambit of periodical studies, see Brake and Codell (2005).

[78] Anon (1833d: 140) (emphasis added).

[79] On the fundamental unknowability of the historic readerships of the Reviews, see bracingly Brake (2005: 1), and cf. Jordan and Patten (1995: 1). On the dangers of equating circulation with influence, see Rose (1995: 205). Rose is an isolated and polemical voice

Close reading, a traditional tool of the classical scholar, must instead be our recourse. As the example of this chapter will have shown, the model of reader-response I propose for the Reviews—and consequently for the reception of Greek epigram in nineteenth-century print media— is one peculiarly alive to subtext and to the unpicking of underlying controversy. The Reviews, and the social world in which they circulated and which they enabled, thus bear productive comparison to, on the one hand, the textual and material cultural forms produced by modern media fandom, and, on the other hand, the face-to-face (and now also virtual) social spaces that fans come together to construct, which define them *as* fans, and through which these cultural forms circulate. Like the social world of the Reviews, these spaces consist of numerous overlapping networks—many fandoms, collectively constituting a bounded public sphere ('fandom' as collective totality). Each fandom is defined by a particular interest shared by its members (*Doctor Who* and *Star Trek* fandoms are much-studied examples), and each is centred around an evolving textual discourse that both lubricates it and glues it together. The textual discourse includes fiction written by fans and set within a shared fictional universe ('fanfic'), and fan-edited magazines ('zines'). Through these participatory forms, as well as face to face at conventions ('cons'), fans can offer their creative work to their peers.

The division between media consumers and producers is thus blurred, although a top-down, trickle-down hierarchy of relation to 'canon' remains operative.[80] As small and largely closed social worlds of diverse people brought together by (and in the first instance only by) a single interest, and within which degrees of personal closeness and privacy of communication can easily be misconstrued, fandoms are also notorious sites of internal controversy and *ad personam* invective ('flamewars').[81] The social worlds of the early eighteenth-century Reviews and their reader-contributors are every bit as small and closed, and sometimes two such worlds collide.

This, I suggest, is the third available part of the answer to the riddle of why the *Edinburgh* is so savage in reviewing Bland: the review is personal because it is tribal. *Translations* smells of a rival magazine. Simply by

---

against the textualist, reader-response consensus (a consensus with which obviously I am in full sympathy), and instead favours archival research into the diaries of individual readers; but this cannot produce meaningful results except on the smallest of scales, and in any case diaries are themselves texts in which identities are tried on and performed.

[80] The classic study is H. Jenkins (1992), highly recommended, as is H. Jenkins (2006); Nisbet (2006) applies the ideas of fan studies to parts of Classics.

[81] The first serious study of this phenomenon is Hills (2002).

appearing to be the property of one Review rather than another, Greek epigram might be seen to have picked a side in contemporary political disagreements. The big split in Review politics in the nineteenth century was, as noted above, Whig versus Tory, with the *Edinburgh* and Maga the main players on each side. The rhetoric was typically fierce. To Maga, a great nurser of grudges, their progressive rival was 'a great organ and receptacle of infidelity' to the Crown, the established aristocracy, and conventional religion—in other words, a hotbed of closet Republicans and atheists (which was probably two ways of saying the same thing).[82]

Literary criticism was thus construed as inescapably political, and hermeneutic style became legible as a sign of party affiliation. The Whig–Tory fissure in the Reviews was as much about *who* should read, and *how*, as what they would be best advised to be reading; Whiggism was discursively tied to the legacy of Nonconformism, the theology of which encouraged individual believers (typically non-elite in social background and further marginalized by their dissident faith) to adopt a critically engaged and active mode of reading and interpreting what they read, from the Bible on downwards. Its Tory opponents made of this association a soapbox for panic-mongering insinuations of sedition against Church and Crown authority, at a time when Nonconformist congregations were still mistrusted by the Establishment and subjected to legal discrimination.[83] That excluded Others were being incited to read *at all* was bad enough; that turbulent priests were urging them to read against the grain, a good deal worse.

This is not just a story about the Review magazines—British print culture as a whole in the late eighteenth and the early nineteenth centuries is dramatized by recent scholarship as a tug-of-war between progressive and reactionary politics for the hearts and minds of the common reader—but it is nonetheless a story in which the Reviews play a pivotal role, each vying to be the upmarket analytical brand the public could trust as it ranged freely over the big issues of the day.[84] Maga and the *Edinburgh* did not merely reflect factional policy; their tight-knit circles of friendship and influence actively drove it, generating an internal consensus or 'party line' with which the party at Westminster

---

[82] '[A] great organ', etc: a regular contributor, quoted at Christie (2009: 158). As his account makes clear, 'infidelity' was a regular Maga buzzword when doing down the *Edinburgh*. Maga was capable of nursing grudges for decades; the *Edinburgh* largely ignored all this, doubtless to their rivals' annoyance: Christie (2009: 154, 158, 160). For a separate Edinburgh literary feud, revealingly similar in its overheated rhetoric, see (entertainingly) Morris (2007) on the 'battle of the grammars' of 1849–50.

[83] Donoghue (1995: 59–60, 63).   [84] Haywood (2004: 83, 240–1).

did well to touch base if it hoped to please its constituents. Many opinion pieces in the *Edinburgh* are demonstrably the product of a collaborative writing or brainstorming process; its op-ed agitation famously kicked off the parliamentary initiative to make Oxford University mend its ways, an important context for Chapter 2.[85]

The old factional split in the quality press between Liberalism and Conservatism must then be borne in mind as an informing backdrop for the Greek epigram culture wars of the later nineteenth century; Chapter 4 in particular will show us that the faultline has not gone away, with Maga once more rearing its hoary head, and liberal uses will vie with conservative to the century's end and beyond (Chapters 5–6).

6. ANTHOLOGIZING THE REVIEWS

Epigram in translation was a no-brainer for inclusion in Review-style magazines, given their miscellaneous content and their blurring of the line between consumer and producer. For an editor with six inches of column to fill at the close of a page, a handful of epigrams made for a great gap-filler. The string of epigrams listed in the Bibliography as 'Anon. (1833b)' nicely illustrate this—note the complexity of the reference, with short sequences of epigrams by (presumably) a single contributor dropped in at the bottom right of odd pages in successive numbers. The occasionality of epigram in this form of publication played to its received image as a symposiac form, and its variety and brevity— simulating for this readership the overheard snippets of ancient gossip— must have enhanced their experience of mediated engagement in a 'live' public sphere. A shared figurative rhetoric brought the genre into sympathy with the ephemeral nature of the serial magazine format, and created an aura of equivalency between the writer on topical issues and the translator of ancient couplets: Review essays were 'fugitive periodical literature', and epigrams assimilated to a native tradition in short occasional poetry as 'fugitive verses'.[86] The genre encouraged occasional

---

[85] Co-authoring the *Edinburgh*: Christie (2009: 42, 53–4).

[86] 'Fugitive' essays: Anon (1875: 378); 'fugitive' as applied to epigrams is so ubiquitous as to preclude a tally. It is ironic that the interpretation of Greek epigrams as self-evidently occasional poems, seen throughout these early publications, probably derives from the perception of the *Latin* epigrams of Martial as witty reportage on his actual, day-to-day life experiences. See, for instance, Byron's letters and journals (standard edition 1973–82), in which dashing off an epigram in response to something just heard in conversation or seen in the street is seen as a prototype of Tweeting—the default response of the literate

dabbling, which indeed is how Bland and his collaborators ended up a few years down the road with enough new bits and pieces to make them consider a second edition, the first of the *Collections* volumes, and how Merivale in turn pieced together its successor.[87]

Within this ephemeral milieu, the veiling of authorial identity behind anonymity or a *nom de plume* takes on a special significance. Part of the fun within the social worlds of the Reviews must have lain in knowing, affecting to know, or making an educated guess at the flesh-and-blood author (or often, collaborative authors) behind a particular unsigned or pseudonymous piece. Much later in the century, this same fascination with degrees of veiling is experienced by Symonds—and played upon knowingly by Wilde to draw in his audience ('the public like an open secret').[88] The closer the reader was to the author socially, the more likely he or she was to know the material already or to identify a familiar style; degrees of de-anonymization could thus function as a gauge of the extent and character of a personal network. Being in on the secret while others were not—self-identifying, we might say, as the model reader against the naive reader—delivered its own pleasures of mastery.

Or occasionally chagrin, as at this moment of secret embarrassment for Byron. As a half-open secret, anonymity can cut both ways:

To-day Campbell called, and while sitting here in came Merivale. During our colloquy, C. (ignorant that Merivale was the writer) abused the 'mawkishness of the *Quarterly Review* of Grimm's *Correspondence*'. I (knowing the secret) changed the conversation as soon as I could; and C. went away, quite convinced of having made the most favourable impression on his new acquaintance. Merivale is luckily a very good-natured fellow, or God he only knows what might have been engendered from such a malaprop. I did not look at him

---

trend-watcher, feeding sound bites of cultural observation to a circle of similarly interested friends.

[87] For a dry run of some new material for that latter occasion, see Anon. (1833b). Merivale (1833: p. vi) recalls how he and Bland 'had continued to contribute occasionally to the periodicals of the day—first to the *Monthly Magazine* (as before), and afterwards to Dr Aikin's *Athenaeum*—some of the fruits of their respective gleanings' from the Anthology and other 'minor poets'. (Dr John Aikin had previously edited the *Monthly* for Phillips, and started the *Athenaeum* when that folded; his new magazine was short-lived, 1807–9.)

[88] Sinfield (1994b: 125) riffs on Wilde's *bon mot* (emphases added): 'Of course, the authorship [of *Reading Gaol*] would become known, *but anonymity would allow readers not to notice it,* and hence not to take the unacceptable risk of becoming involved with "Oscar Wilde". Even more strikingly, Wilde saw that this indirection would work positively; that it would constitute *an attraction, as well as an alibi.* "The public like an open secret", he wrote—intuiting, in precisely the theoretical terms of the 1990s, the prurient fascination that the oblique image of the queer was to produce.'

while this was going on, but I felt like a coal—for I like Merivale, as well as the article in question.[89]

Nonetheless, anonymous authorship had attractions beyond the obvious allure of a half-open secret. Deniability created an emotional outlet that did not upset the smooth running of polite society. The reviewer for the *Edinburgh* may well have known what names lay behind the anonymous *Translations*. At a minimum, he knew in what journal many of these poems had previously been published, and thus the politics and likely milieu of their translator(s). (A sizeable part of the preface, too, had been tried out in the *Monthly*, setting the scene for those first translations.[90]) In turn, and with their networks surely including individuals who were close to the inner circles of other periodicals, Bland, Merivale, and Hodgson may well have had a good idea of who the reviewer was. All four (or more?) operated within an urbane literary culture in which the reviewers and authors of books were each others' peers and often swapped roles, last week's victim becoming this week's perpetrator. Anonymity and pseudonymity can never reliably have concealed writers' identities within such a socially tight milieu.[91] Conceivably they even knew each other socially. But at no stage had anyone been insulted by name, and thus to their fully public face.

Pseudonymity offered similar advantages but also something more, at least for Bland, Merivale, and Hodgson in their initial forays into epigram in the *Monthly*: it placed epigram within a lush realm of fantasy shared between authors and their readers. Versions of Greek epigrams to which in *Translations* no authorship was ascribed had already appeared in the Monthly, as had much of the preface, under a memorable *nom de plume*: 'Narva'.

These first efforts had included wry metapoetic comment on the creative process that was generating them:

> When Narva asks a friend to dine,
> He gives a pint of tavern wine,
> A musty loaf and stinking ham,
> Then overwhelms with epigram . . . [92]

[89] Journal entry of 7 March 1814 (Byron 1973–82: iii. 247).

[90] Bland and Merivale (1805–6). For a fairly full and lively retrospective account of this preliminary publication history, see Merivale (1833: p. iv).

[91] Donoghue (1995: 56). Anonymity, deniability, and information hygiene were to become a recurring concern for Symonds; see Ch. 3.

[92] Bland (1806: 60), a version of Lucillius 11.137, later revealed to be by Merivale; Narva is 'Heliodorus' in the original.

In later life, Merivale recalled (in a conversation written up by Hodgson) how he and Bland had settled on the name. 'Narva' was 'an appellative borrowed (as I well remember) from a poem of Chatterton's'—a poem which their friend Hodgson had been quoting aloud and (perhaps too) frequently to them—and was chosen by them '*euphoniae gratia* [for its nice sound], for I think it possessed no other merit'. Merivale and Bland then used the name as a shared cover for the versions they individually and collectively devised.[93] The Chatterton poem is 'Narva and Mored. An African Eclogue' (1770), which Hodgson surely encountered in the still quite new edition of the poet's works by Robert Southey and J. Cottle (1803). This was the first time the poems had been offered to the public as originals by Chatterton, rather than (as Chatterton had put about) merely his transcriptions of the work of his fictional fifteenth-century mask, 'Thomas Rowley':

> 'Recite the loves of Narva and Mored',
> The priest of Chalma's triple idol said ... (ll. 1–2)[94]

'Narva and Mored' was a fever dream of Afro-Orientalist eroto-mysticism, glorying in the objectification of black African flesh and muscle:

> Tall, as the house of Chalma's dark retreat;
> Compact and firm, as Rhadal Ynca's fleet.
> Completely beauteous, as a summer's sun,
> Was Narva, by his excellence undone.... (ll. 83–6)

Narva here stands as the rampant black warrior *kouros*, at once ideal ('Completely beauteous') and fiercely physical. Whatever may have been in the minds of Bland and Merivale when they picked it, his name will thus have conjured up associations of exotic Otherness for contemporary readers of these Greek epigrams in the *Monthly Magazine*. That this Orientalist thrill-ride is utterly suppositious, a dark mirror only to the audience's own desires and fears (and fears of desires), comes as no surprise.[95] Through the hand-me-down practice of versioning epigram

---

[93] Hodgson (1878: i. 226). Merivale addressed Hodgson in an occasional poem of 1806 as 'my Narva', surely with a gently mocking edge: Hodgson (1878: i. 40–3). When Merivale (1833: 4) credits Bland with authorship of the Narva poems, he is being generous to the memory of his dear friend; it was never much of a mystery who had written what (see Ch. 2).

[94] Originally, of course, with Ye Olde Spellingge, since it was presented as a poem by Rowley: 'Recyte the loves of Narva and Mored, | The preeste of Chalmas trypell ydolle sayde', etc.

[95] The classic polemic on Western objectification of an imaginary non-European Other is Said (1978).

(see Chapter 2), the Harrovian grammar grind now courts savage passions too strong for the civilized world to bear, and into which the ostensible serenity of Greek epigram offers an unexpected point of entry.

7. 'A *SIFTING* COLLECTION': EPIGRAM'S CHANGING WORLD

> I have so all-to-be-Greeked myself, that I am yet more stupid than of old—an inconvenience somehow attached to the study of the finest language in the world, and from which none, without exception, who know anything about it, can possibly escape.[96]

Writing to Merivale from Kenilworth (where he is now set up for life as curate, with a wife and growing family), and demurring from his friend's kind suggestion of writing more for the magazines, Bland declares himself burned out—ruined for lesser work by his labours on the Anthology, the most recent fruits of which lie six years in their shared past. Bland died young, six years on (1825), and Merivale's second version of *Collections* (1833) faces an already very different world. This version concentrates on the 'early', 'good' poets: its chronological progression ends with Meleager, maker of the first Garland, thus fulfilling what we are told is the editor's long-term ambition of offering 'a *more correct and classical* representation of the original Anthology, by a more abundant infusion of the best specimens'.[97]

'Correctness' is here redeemed from association with accuracy or proportionality in representing the mass of what in fact survives of Greek epigram, and implicitly re-parsed as the correct standard *for* the genre: the best authors, displayed to edifying effect. The poets of that first Garland are the only ones who count: they provide a template for the genre that is 'classical' not merely in date (well, almost) but in the example it sets for future poets. But this standard is impossible for any poet after them to achieve. Even by the most optimistic admissible reading, the Hellenistic poets already totter on the cusp of the long, steep, slippery slope of their culture's Winckelmann curve. The poets of the first Garland are thus *sui generis*, their achievement unrepeatable, not so much a rising curve as a sudden surge of brilliance: 'original' is 'best'. To smooth out the bell curve, the title (*Collections from the Greek*

---

[96] Hodgson (1878: i. 246, a letter dated 2 April 1819).
[97] Merivale (1833: p. viii) (emphasis added).

Anthology... Comprising...) now enlists the fragmentary Lyric poets into 'the Anthology' in a double act with Meleager's Garland. They are early, so their presence must be 'correct'.

Note also the sleight of hand in 'the original Anthology', recalling the anonymous reviewer's theme of several successive Anthologies, all contemporaneously available to a modernity that can decide for itself which one matters. Turning the Garland of Meleager into an 'Anthology' loads it with connotations particular to this reading culture. As the century pressed on, the role of the editor was gaining a new cultural authority; and the term 'Anthology' itself had come to connote that the book so labelled was the *only* book one needed for a working (that is, culturally validated and socially enabling) knowledge of the subject in question.[98] Ownership of a volume with this title on its spine negated any troublesome requirement to read around and form an opinion:

> even in this post-literary age, vestigial traces are still visible of an older culture in which the possession of a general anthology of English poetry—perhaps obtained as a school prize—was felt to be, along with a good dictionary, the complete works of Shakespeare, and a copy of the Authorized Version of the Bible, a *sine qua non* for any civilised household.[99]

Calling the Garland of Meleager a 'Greek Anthology' thus accords to it totemic status as the *only* book one needs to read in order to know the ancient Greeks—their lives, loves, hopes, and fears. That the poets of Meleager's selection write on a limited range of themes, spun by modernity as the elegiac commonplaces of love and death, makes the ancient Greece on which they report so much more *manageable*. Merivale is not going so far as to say that his selections *are* the Greek Anthology—but after him, the titles chosen by or for each successive scholar-translator-editor-*cum*-pundit were to declare to the British public that all human life lay between the covers of the book newly in their hands, crystallized through the directly reported daily experiences of the classical culture that stood to their own as a timeless paradigm and bright beacon. In any case, if the example of Byron is at all indicative, Bland's contemporaries naturally shortened the title to 'Greek Anthology' in use, awarding to it an authority its editors notionally refused—and the short form was already there for them to see, embossed on the book's spine, where there was no room for anything longer.

All human life is therein—which is to say, all the parts that count; if an experience is *not* here, it is not Greek, not for 'us', and not to be specified.

---

[98] On the increasing cultural weightiness of the role of anthology editor, see again Benedict (2003: 206–7).

[99] Hopkins (2008: 285–6).

As a genuinely mass reading public begins to emerge at mid-century, the role of the editor as gatekeeper and censor will come to seem all the more vital. Already in 1807 the anonymous reviewer complains that Bland's miscellany includes poems that mean it cannot be recommended to ladies: 'what we should call a *sifting* collection, would have admitted our fair countrywomen to the enjoyment of many exquisite productions.'[100] The reviewer is especially put out that the collection fails to censor impropriety while also being so limited in coverage—Bland's selection falls between two stools. This *could* have been a Pompeii, albeit a gated site off-limits to all but the gentleman scholar: 'A complete and indiscriminate version...would supply such a gratification *to the antiquarian of Grecian customs and habits of thinking*, as Pompeii has afforded to the traveller regarding the Roman equivalents.' By this account, *Translations* is both too inclusive and not inclusive enough; it is all a matter of audiences.[101]

By the later nineteenth century, it will be the duty of the editor to protect not only women and the young (whose 'innocence' and vulnerability are increasingly fetishized), but especially the working classes, from socially dangerous ideas—ideas that can never be voiced, and that must at all cost remain disassociated from the prestigious ancient cultural template against which Britain in the nineteenth century is increasingly measuring itself. To 'all-to-be-Greek ourselves' became increasingly vital to British social identities and prospects, collectively and as individuals—all the more important, then, that Britons model themselves on the right *kinds* of 'Greek'. And the Anthology was not about to go away; Bland as quoted above is ruefully spot-on regarding its insidiousness as a cultural infection (one that he and his collaborators bear the main responsibility for spreading around).

This perception of dangerous new reading constituencies, on whose behalf and for whose well-being the Book of Greek Life must be winnowed, was not always to correspond neatly to social reality as lived by the majority population. Indeed, by the 1830s, the era of Merivale's definitive version, writers in the elite periodicals were already looking out with tangible moral concern over a 'mass' market in books—but the reality was still a long way off. Cheap reprint series were on the ascendant, but cheapness was relative: working-class wages were at a low ebb, cheaper printing techniques were a decade and more in the future, and the 'mass' market was really just the middle class. In Altick's vivid

---

[100] Anon. (1807: 319) (emphasis in original).
[101] Anon. (1807: 319) (emphasis added).

illustration, 'five shillings—the price of a reprinted novel—would buy five pounds of butter, or ten pounds of meat'—and Merivale's chunky (438-page) octavo will have cost rather more than five shillings.[102]

The middle-class market is still small, but it is starting to grow, and by mid-century publishers will need to factor it in if they are to survive. Our next chapter will take us to the 1850s, and three attempts at a 'Greek Anthology' for a broadening readership; but the schemes, fantasies, habits of thought, and significant silences of Bland, Merivale, and their social worlds will continue to reverberate through the mid-century and beyond. For the moment, this is essentially an internal conversation within the charmed circles of the Reviews and their high-end constituencies—but right now, these are the people whose opinions are held to matter. This is where politics is made, and each of these three versions of the Greek Anthology carries political weight within its own cultural moment.

When Byron, later to achieve immortality as the great overseas martyr of the Greek War of Independence, visited Greece as part of his idiosyncratic version of the Grand Tour in his early twenties, the one book he regretted having omitted to bring with him was not Homer or Pausanias, but Bland's *Translations* of 1806—his indispensable *vade mecum* to the immortal spirit of Hellas. It left a gap in his experience he regretted bitterly.[103]

When Bland brought out the first version of *Collections* in 1813, he appended to his verse prologue an epilogue that reread Greek epigram as the unsilenced voice recalling an enslaved contemporary Greece to its ancient liberty:

> 'Tis past—and o'er her laurels torn
> The Queen of Nations bends to mourn,
> The Nurse of heroes crouches low,
> Slave to a base ignoble foe . . .
> Dead are the bards, but living lays
> Resound and tell of early days,
> And still the trembling chords prolong
> Untouch'd the power of ancient song;
> Dear is their minstrelsy, that floats
> In solemn, sweet, and liquid notes,
> That registers the orphan's sigh,

---

[102] Altick (1957: 274–8, 276, 286).
[103] A letter to Hodgson of 29 June 1811, written at sea a year or two after his Greek jaunt: 'I regretted very much in Greece having omitted to carry the Anthology with me—I mean Bland and Merivale's' (Byron 1973–82: ii. 55).

The plighted lover's perjury,
The pride of riches and of power,
The mirthful, and the mournful hour;
That paints the virgin in her bloom,
The triumph, banquet, and the tomb,
The deeds of mighty chiefs, who broke
The tyrant's chain, and spurn'd his yoke...[104]

The elegiac themes already amplified by the rhetoric of the preface (mournful orphan and faithless lover), and the convivial occasionality of epigram as 'fugitive verse' (the banquet and happy hour), are here interwoven with 'pride...of power', rhetorically making inevitable pride's future fall. Bland invokes the two defining moments of ancient Greek emancipation from tyranny: the Persian Wars ('spurn'd his yoke' conjures the shade of Leonidas), and the violent self-sacrifice of Harmodius and Aristogeiton, glossed since antiquity as tyrannicide ('broke | the tyrant's chain'). Ever since the first *Translations* of 1806, the friends' Anthology had included an epitaph by Simonides on Megistias, a seer who went knowingly to his death in battle against the Persians; and two versions of a drinking-song in honour of Harmodius and Aristogeiton, glossed in Bland's note as a 'most noble ode of Callistratus, on the illustrious action of the two Athenian patriots' (who were also lover and beloved, a fact that supplies the motivation for their suicide mission but unsurprisingly does not impact on Bland's account). Now these ancient celebrations of self-sacrifice are repurposed as a call to patriotic Greek nationalism in the present age, as one voice—and quite an early one—in the supportive groundswell of idealizing Philhellene cultural production into which so many British radicals and romantic liberals poured their progressive urges, and which inspired the foundation in the following year (1814) of the first Greek-nationalist underground network, Filike Eteria.[105] In closing, Bland passionately urges us to 'in the past descry | The visions of futurity'; the only fit master for Hellenes is the eternal abstraction with which Winckelmann's legacy has now forever paired them, 'Beauty'.[106]

Two decades on, with the war won and Greece newly independent as a sovereign state, the second version of *Collections* (1833) brought Byron's love affair with the Anthology full circle, by prefacing Merivale's chosen

---

[104] Merivale (1833: pp. lxiv–v) (emphases added).

[105] On the cause of Hellenic liberty as a liberal–progressive displacement activity, see in passing, pithily, Boime (2004: 191); further bibliography at Potter (2004: 183), recommended. Reflecting scholarly consensus, Potter (2004: 188) places the main phase of British Philhellenism in the 1820s.

[106] Merivale (1833: p. lxv).

epigrams with stanzas familiar to any classicist or lover of poetry. Lent additional poignancy by elegiac retrospect, these lines mourn the imprint of a tyranny since defeated, at a cost that had turned out to include the poet's own life. Through citation here, Byron becomes Megistias. Foreseeing his own demise, he nonetheless marches willingly—and directly from epigram's sympotic scene (with a Romantic twist of defiant fatalism—'Dash down yon cup . . . !')—to battle against the invader from the East. Sappho is, of course, an Anthology author, in Bland as in Meleager:[107]

> The isles of Greece, the isles of Greece!
>   Where burning Sappho lov'd and sung . . .
>
> Place me on Sunium's marbled steep,
>   Where nothing, save the waves and I,
> May hear our mutual murmurs sweep:
>   There, swan-like, let me sing and die:
> A land of slaves shall ne'er be mine—
>   —Dash down yon cup of Samian wine!

Bland's 'triumph, banquet, and the tomb' all combine here; Merivale's convivial Anthology is Byron's memorial, and a victory-monument for the Greek nation now being reborn.

---

[107] Merivale (1833: pp. xvlvii–viii) (emphasis added).

2

Three Mid-Century 'Anthologies'

1. 'A FAULTY AND INJUDICIOUS ARRANGEMENT': SIZES AND SCHEMES

The chronological position of the poems [of Bland 1806], according to the era of their respective authors, (which is however exceedingly incorrect), we also disapprove, and should have thought the form much more attractive, had they been ranged according to their subjects...[1]

This new work [Bland 1813] ... was constructed on the principle of an entirely new arrangement; being divided into distinct heads or subjects—the Amatory—the Convivial—the Moral—the Sepulchral—the Descriptive—the Dedicatory—and the Humorous, or Satirical—together with a pretty copious infusion, in the midst of one of these departments, of irrelevant matter, consisting of metrical versions of passages from the Grecian drama—each division being followed by notes...

The defects of such an arrangement were too glaring to escape the just censure of even the most indulgent critics.[2]

Do what they might, editors and translators of the Greek Anthology in the earlier nineteenth century found it ridiculously hard to bring home as a naturalized classic. Each decision seemed bound to offend at least as many pundits and constituencies as it pleased (a sign that large issues were in play, unvoiced but deeply felt). If one rendering was beautiful and felicitous, the next would be found clumsy or dull; the selection was too narrow or too broad, too small or too large, or (as in the *Edinburgh*'s review of Bland 1806) neither large/broad nor small/narrow enough.[3] And how was it all supposed to be arranged? At the outset (Chapter 1), this seemed naturally an open question, since the received schemata of

---

[1] Anon. (1807: 325).   [2] Merivale (1833: p. vii).
[3] Anon. (1807: 319–20 (neither fish nor fowl), 325, 329–30 (see-sawing quality of versions)).

both the Planudean and the superior Palatine Anthology had been cast aside in the printed editions of the latter then current, and this sense of openness persists after a correctly ordered text becomes available (Jacobs 1813–17)—and indeed to the present day, and not without reason. What shape should the Greek Anthology be, in English dress? What should it *look* like, as a book and on the page?

The three mid-century 'Anthologies' examined in this chapter go about answering these questions in characteristically different ways, and in doing so they inform on contemporary social formations. We will see here how epigram slots into perceptions of cultural ownership, within a discourse of artistic–literary patrimony that has already claimed the raw resource of the Anthology as a national project worth pursuing, but is still figuring out an appropriate range of strategies for naturalizing it and putting it to work.[4] We begin, however, by turning aside to establish a larger context. What shapes were being proposed for Greek poetry as a whole, as the century moved through its mid-point? How was Greek literary history being represented to the middle-class readership that was now occupying so much of publishers' attention, and what changes in representation can we detect over time? This survey will also supply necessary context for the next chapter (Ch. 3), on the new and very much improved version of Greek literary history that Symonds will put before the public in *Studies* a generation later. By neat coincidence, just as there are three mid-century 'Anthologies', we must reckon with three mid-century histories of Greek literature. Like the 'Anthologies', these will be addressed in chronological order.

2. 'FRUSTRATED BY VAGUENESS': THREE MID-CENTURY HISTORIES OF GREEK LITERATURE

Talfourd, Blomfield, et al., *History of Greek Literature* (2nd edn, 1850)

An early and extremely long work of literary appreciation, Talfourd's *History of Greek Literature* is squarely a product of the elite social networks that gave context to the Anthologies of Merivale and Bland, explored in the previous chapter. It is now an extremely rare book, although not a valuable

[4] This claim is staked as soon as the genre goes public: the poets of the Anthology are pegged by even the hostile reviewer of the *Edinburgh* as 'capable of forming a most desirable accession to our national libraries' (Anon. 1807: 319). Intellectual ownership of the Anthology's Greek text will become a rallying point for patriotic classicists in Ch. 5.

one; only five copies are known in British libraries. Called a second edition, it is in fact straightforwardly a reissue, alongside other volumes in its series: the *Encyclopaedia Metropolitana* (1817–45), an ambitious part-work in twenty-eight volumes conceived as a rival to the *Britannica*. It aimed at complete coverage of all the arts and sciences, treated expansively in essay form (within an overarching plan drawn up by Samuel Taylor Coleridge) where *Britannica* preferred multiple short entries.

Talfourd, like Merivale a barrister and a crusading liberal MP, had written prolifically for the Reviews in the 1820s as a way of making ends meet, and the History he puts together for the *Metropolitana* reflects this background.[5] Its 'chapters' are an eclectic assortment, once again demonstrating how material first developed as ephemeral magazine essays could later be recycled into a physically heftier, semiotically more durable, and ideologically more authoritative format. The arrangement is approximately and, we are told, incidentally chronological; but there are gaping holes in the scheme, in period as in genre, and the coverage is eccentric by any later standard:

Chapter 1: Ionic logographers
Chapter 2: Greek historians
Chapter 3: Greek orators
Chapter 4: Greek pastoral poetry

By including pastoral, this scheme takes Greek literature through into the Hellenistic age, a not uncommon cut-off point, although by no means every literary historian would stretch the definition of 'Greek' so far. A fifth essay, on early Greek poetry, was added in the second edition. Both of these topics reflect the interests of Talfourd's main collaborator, Charles Blomfield, a skilled classical linguist known for his early career work on Aeschylus, Callimachus, and the lyric poets.[6] A former contributor to the *Edinburgh Review*, Blomfield had moved out of Classics into a busy and extremely successful church career at the start of the 1810s, so this is very old material indeed.[7] This frankly unsatisfactory History left no impact on posterity.

---

[5] For a succinct and useful character sketch, see Lamb and Lamb (1978: 175–7). Talfourd the politician was interested in the uses of Greek literary heritage in the service of reform: see Hall (1997) on his well-regarded original tragedy, *Ion* (1835).

[6] It can be no more than a piquant coincidence that Blomfield (first encountered in passing in Ch. 1) was a particular target of the *odium scholasticum* of George Burges, the jobbing Hellenist who put together the 'Anthology' of the Bohn series (examined later in this chapter) and a confirmed Aeschylean.

[7] Blomfield wrote copiously for the *Edinburgh* between 1809 and 1813 but broke off relations on account of the 'godlessness' of its editorial line, just as his church career was kicking off; Stray (2007b) gives the background.

Browne, *A History of Classical Literature* (1851–3)

This two-volume handbook divides ancient literature into Greek (vol. 1) and Latin (vol. 2).[8] In this account Greek literature predominantly means Homer, followed in the latter part of the volume by some much more cursory coverage of lyric and iambic, drama, philosophy down to Aristotle, and the historians. While prose takes a back seat, poetry ends with Euripides and Aristophanes. The package clearly sold well; there are plenty of second-hand copies still doing the rounds. Contrary to the slipshod miscellany of Talfourd, Blomfield and friends, Browne's handbook successfully promoted a chronologically narrow vision of Greek literature based around a front-loaded Winckelmann curve. The 'classical' is implicitly ranked by its proximity to Homeric epic. After Aristotle, with the coming of the Hellenistic age, Greece simply stops.

Browne not infrequently quotes epigrams in translation, acknowledging the Anthology as his source. However, his purpose in doing so is invariably to sum up on an Archaic or Classical author in a non-epigrammatic genre. The Anthology for Browne is a convenient repository of literary-critical sound bites and nothing more; its authors (and of course many of the epigrams on canon poets are by anonymous amateurs) do not merit consideration as literature in their own right.

Mure, *A Critical History of the Language and Literature of Antient Greece* (1850–7)

> On arriving at the end of the already published portion of Colonel Mure's colossal work, we look back with something like awe on the region we have traversed, and forward with blank dismay to that which has still to be crossed. We know not what compact the Laird of Caldwell may have made with destiny for enjoying a life beyond that which is usually accorded to man; but, however favoured he may be, his readers will still be exposed to the ordinary infirmities of the race. Nor can we suggest any remedy.[9]

A classic instance of not knowing when to stop, and of dogged perseverance with a project so bloated in scope as to defy the capacity of author

---

[8] The Revd Robert William Browne also wrote a history of Greece, two of Rome, and, as Chaplain to Her Majesty's Forces in London, edited a compilation of *Tracts for Soldiers* (1854), his own contribution to which praises Roman legionary discipline as the bedrock of the Church Militant.

[9] Anon. (1857d: 135).

and readers alike, the exhaustive and digressive *Critical History* of Colonel William Mure of Caldwell (the colonelship was an honorary command in the militia of Renfrewshire, the county that he long served as Member of Parliament) remained unfinished at the time of his death. As his reviewer hints ('compact ... with destiny'), the *History* preoccupied Mure's declining years; born in 1790, he was already 'antient' (a spelling that by mid-century smacked of archaism) in his own right. Of the five laborious volumes completed, an anonymous review identifies the first as a safe if dull choice for school libraries, and it is all downhill from there.[10] 'All his critical discussions ... fall on the mind flat and unconvincing ... [the reader finds] total incapacity to appreciate [the classical Greek authors'] great intellect ... [and] good wishes frustrated by vagueness.'[11] The review quoted above ('with blank dismay') is for volume 4, with many more planned in a grandiose total scheme that committed Mure and his readers to a very long haul indeed, admitting of no downscaling once undertaken ('Nor can we suggest any remedy'). Mure was only just getting round to fifth-century drama when his death called the project to a close that few readers will have felt premature.

Browne, Talfourd, and Mure constitute a failed triumvirate of mid-century 'Histories of Greek Poetry': three syntheses, each in its own way seriously flawed, and in two out of three cases soon discarded. The three mid-century 'Greek Anthologies' run neatly alongside them, paralleling not merely their chronology but their difficulties in determining scope and defining a framework, and largely failing as they do so to find their feet within an increasingly volume-driven literary marketplace that is rapidly transforming itself around them. In the middle of all this W(illiam) H(enry) Smith is opening the first branches (in 1852) in what will become a national chain of rail-station booksellers, pushing the book into the visual culture of public space.[12] These flawed and increasingly forgotten tomes leave the door wide open for Symonds in the 1870s to reinvent Greek poetry as a literary system and canon and,

---

[10] It also made a worthy school leaving present: when John Addington Symonds finished his studies at Harrow, the boys of his house (of which he had been the head boy) clubbed together to buy him a set, 'handsomely bound'. He eventually looked into it when preparing the lectures for Clifton College, which became chapters in the first series of *Studies of the Greek Poets*, the subject of our next chapter: J. A. Symonds (1984: 87, 234).

[11] Anon. (1850b), naturally in the *Edinburgh*; Anon. (1857c: 313–14), for the *Westminster Review*.

[12] On Smith's new business model, and how his more traditionally minded rivals were feeling the pinch of thin margins of profit on individual titles, see evocatively the ever-useful Altick (1957: 301–2, 304–5). Chronology: Talfourd (1850)—Wellesley (1849); Browne (1851-3: i)—Burges (1852); Mure (1850-7)—MacGregor (1855-64).

within it, epigram as a genre. Other than Symonds, there will be no takers for role of literary-cultural chronicler and custodian until Wilde's old tutor Mahaffy gives it a try in 1880; Bowra and Murray are long in the future (and later still Hadas, Lesky, Dover, and so on); if Symonds does not exactly invent the genre of the 'handbook of Greek literature', he certainly gets to *reinvent* it for a new generation.

In the meantime, not one of the three available mid-century literary handbooks has defined a role and context for epigram—one of their rare areas of implicit agreement is that this genre that is so full of Greek life has no place in Greek poetry as they variously define it. Readers of the three mid-century 'Anthologies' will thus come to it as a free-floating genre, devoid of an ancient space in which to operate, and subject to whatever kinds of explanation the translator may see fit to superimpose through commentary, editorializing, paraphrase, and other less obvious forms of paratext.

3. 'A PUBLIC EVIL': WELLESLEY'S *ANTHOLOGIA POLYGLOTTA* (1849)

> It requires but little penetration to see that this work is essentially a labour of love. Even without the knowledge which those who are acquainted with Oxford possess of Dr Wellesley's various accomplishments,—his sympathy with artistic beauty in all its forms,—a chance observer would at once pronounce that the Editor is a man who has taken up his subject from the mere pleasure which a devotion to it inspires, and pursued it with a zeal which could hardly be supplied by any other motive short of a high sense of duty, such as one does not expect to find dictating in a question of belles lettres. This enthusiasm does not manifest itself, as is so often the case now-a-days, in elaborate attention to external decoration . . .[13]

The volume under review was plain in outward appearance, but its price was steep: fifteen shillings for the base model, or twice the daily wage of a skilled engineer, rising to two guineas for the limited-run quarto edition.[14] As this anonymous reviewer conceded, what made it worth paying for (if it *was* worth paying for—but that was a separate question) were the fruits of colossal labour concealed within its workmanlike binding. As its title indicates, *Anthologia Polyglotta* is a translation of

---

[13] Anon. (1850a: 429).
[14] Wage data from <http://www.oldbaileyonline.org/static/Coinage.jsp> (accessed 14 April 2013).

poems from the Anthology into more than one language—a novel departure, under a brazenly flimsy pretext.[15] The editor is Henry Wellesley; his billing on the title page as the Principal of New Inn Hall is the reader's first large clue that the volume is Oxford-centric. Each poem is given in the Greek, followed by three or more translations or adaptations. The first version supplied is always in Latin, and the last in English.[16]

Between these are placed versions in one or more—usually more—modern European languages, predominantly Italian and German, but including also French and Spanish. Old and new versions rub shoulders. Some of the Latin ones go back to late antiquity (Ausonius), while others are newly minted by the editor and his Oxford colleagues—Wellesley was well connected and an excellent academic networker.[17] In between we find Samuel Johnson (who famously sought solace during his final illness in making Latin versions of Anthology epigrams), the poet Thomas Gray, and others. Prominent among the authors in Latin is the Renaissance Italian poet Poliziano, a very early translator of Anthology epigrams who could also boast of having revivified the ancient tradition of original epigram-composition in Greek.[18]

A layout of elegant simplicity encourages browsing and richly repays the attentive reader.[19] But should it be read at all? Did this book even deserve to exist?

The result is a book which, whatever we may have to object against either its design or its execution, must secure many pleasing recollections to those who

---

[15] Misrepresentation topped with abject non sequitur: 'But the mixed nature of the materials in the Greek Anthology seemed to demand the aid of more than one vehicle for due exhibition, and [*sic*] it was thought that the addition of versions in the principal modern languages, whilst it rendered more conspicuous the varied beauties of the Greek originals, would place in an instructive context the genius of the classical and living tongues' (Wellesley 1849: p. v).

[16] Among these last, one find that must have surprised many readers is a sonnet of Shakespeare, Britain's own national bard. Sonnet 154 is presented without comment as a version of Marius Scholasticus AP 9.7 at *Polyglotta* (Wellesley 1849: 63). The connection is compelling, and, given the playwright's familiar troping as classically uneducated, it feeds into modern conspiracy theory around the authorship of Shakespeare's plays: Greenwood makes much of it even in his reduced version (1937: 29–32).

[17] Henry's surname hints strongly at his connection with Wellington: he was the illegitimate son of the elder brother of the first Duke, whose support of his nephew's career included appointing him as Principal of New Inn Hall while Chancellor of the University (Anon. 1866).

[18] Poliziano ('Politianus' in Wellesley) was writing versions of Anthology poems before the Planudean manuscript was even in its *editio princeps*: Hutton (1935: 124–40).

[19] A digitally imaged copy is among the versions linked to from the Internet repository, archive.org: http://archive.org/details/anthologiapolyg01wellgoog (accessed 14 April 2013). I recommend having a look.

have been engaged in it, and afford much scope for agreeable relaxation to all who have a taste for the minor elegances, or as modern parlance would call them, the amenities of literature...

Still, it should be remembered that the praise of having performed a labour of love is not necessarily a very high one. Love, however elevating it may be in itself, (we speak as general moralists), depends for a great part of its worth and dignity on the character of its object...[20]

With several decades' hindsight, it was all too easy to dismiss *Polyglotta* as nothing more than the mutually gratifying vanity project of a club of former public schoolboys made good.[21] Even the title's Latinized Greek might well be offputting to the uninitiated. Nor does the aim declared in its preface automatically secure sympathy today. The book's primary purpose is 'promoting, or rather, reviving the taste for Latin verse composition in the University' at a moment of crux when sweeping reform was in the air.[22] Is this then the last hurrah of the old traditionalists?

Certainly this was an interpretation that the anonymous reviewer was keen his readers should share. *Polyglotta* is, we are told, a blatant exercise in propaganda for the retention of Latin verse composition's full dignity and institutional prestige, which prefers mere 'ornamental scholarship' to the new, scientific philology that is even now beginning to make headway against it.[23] Verse composition is presented here as a relic of bygone centuries, and predominantly the eighteenth, a time when style was favoured over substance. In the new Oxford, it is 'very much on the wane', its former glory 'rather at a discount', and its passing is not to be regretted: its life has run its natural course, and Wellesley's attempt to direct university policy by stealth must therefore be rejected by the right-thinking reader.[24]

This view of verse composition as a relic of Oxford's past has the ring of truth. The exercise is quintessentially eighteenth-century both in its Romanticism (every boy his own poetic genius) and in its narrow pedantry over metre. And certainly verse comp. had held Oxford Classics back for many years, eating up Fellows' time and energies to the active detriment of critical scholarship and humanistic education alike—not

[20] Anon. (1850a: 429–30).
[21] Anon. (1892: 304), interestingly from an American perspective, at a time when the social and intellectual value of maintaining classical studies was hotly debated there: Beisel (1997: 160–4), Winterer (2002: 152–78); and cf. my discussion at pp. 203–6.
[22] Wellesley (1849: p. v).
[23] Anon. (1850a: 430, 434).
[24] Anon. (1850a: 432–3); *Polyglotta* pegged as 'a less obtrusive medium' for achieving goals that would otherwise be pursued through University regulations or 'College countenance' (p. 433).

that prose comp. was any better in that regard.[25] Even if these repetitive and mechanistic exercises made some kind of sense as part of time-honoured pedagogic tradition at the major public schools (a topic to which we shall return in the immediately following section), there was no ready-made justification for continuing with exactly the same type of exercise at University, where common sense said the programme of studies ought to be different in kind. The anonymous reviewer is scathing on this institutionalized system of versification by rote, or more particularly its textual legacy:

the infinitude of mechanical mediocrity, very excellent in its way, which the system inflicts upon the world. We are entitled to speak of it as a public evil... There is scarcely a fine piece in the English language... which is free from the unpleasant association of an admirable version by a first-rate scholar.[26]

The 'public evil' results when the young men formed within this system clog up the public sphere with Latin and Greek renditions of a literature properly enjoyed in its native English (ancient epigram as 'spam'), and Wellesley the seeker of selfish pleasures is to be condemned for glorifying this type of self-indulgent display. 'The evil lies in a want of proper estimation of high ends': personal enjoyment is a 'low standard' for literary writing, which instead should aim at the betterment of society.[27] *Polyglotta* incites thoughtless violence against our national literary canon and stymies forward-minded writers in the here and now. 'Nevertheless, if Dr Wellesley will allow us to accept his gift for its own sake, and not as part of an educational course, we may find it in our hearts to thank him for it'—faint praise indeed, and heavily qualified in terms that effectively accuse the author of academic–political skulduggery.[28]

To begin to see beyond the rhetorical front of this review we may begin with a throwaway statement of revealing brevity. The reviewer declares that he has paid no attention to the polyglot aspect of *Polyglotta*, 'for we have no dealings with modern continental languages'—end of story. This is an astonishing statement, given the nature of the volume under consideration.[29] Instead *Polyglotta* is represented solely in terms of its alleged propaganda purpose, as a reactionary intervention in a (whether real or wishfully imagined) contemporary hot debate over the value of Latin verse comp.[30] What this review does not want us to know, and the

[25] Brink (1986: 126–9); on metre as an eighteenth-century fixation, Stray (1992: 5).
[26] Anon. (1850a: 435–6).
[27] Anon. (1850a: 432).
[28] Anon. (1850a: 435).
[29] Anon. (1850a: 437).
[30] On the heroization of Latin verse comp. throughout the century, see Stray (1998a: 68–72).

reason that it is trying to dissuade us from reading the book, is that the real *Polyglotta* is anything but reactionary. Its editor knows his ancient languages well enough, but he is not a classicist: he is a modern linguist, and, in so far as *Polyglotta* has a cause to promote (and I agree that it does), it is the academically progressive cause of modern language studies at Oxford.

The reason the review can claim to have 'no dealings with modern continental languages' is that it articulates a viewpoint from within the religious wing of the English Establishment. The quarterly journal in which it appears, *The Christian Remembrancer; or, The Churchman's Biblical, Ecclesiastical, and Literary Miscellany*, was doctrinally High Church and thus resistant to liturgical modernization. It kept its clerical readership abreast of developments in classical and ancient near eastern studies in so far as these neighbouring civilizations formed the antique backdrop against which the events of the Old and New Testaments needed to be explained to their parishioners. Pagan antiquity was one area in which the *Remembrancer*'s reviewers were capable of taking a progressive line—the volume for the previous year (vol. 17, 1849) had praised to the skies the early volumes of George Grote's new *History of Greece*, despite the author being a Utilitarian atheist.

That a religious ideology appears to underlie the defamation of Wellesley and of his *Polyglotta* threatens to muddy the waters further, for epigram as the principal vehicle for Greek and indeed Latin verse comp. was very much church property, indeed practically part of its ritual calendar. The exclusively male educational institutions at which it was practised—the major public schools, and the ancient universities—were religiously constituted, effectively on monastic lines.[31] That the pedagogic exercise of versification into the classical languages was in its origins not merely foreign but Jesuitical seems to have bothered nobody; year by year, the prize lists roll out in the 'Ecclesiastical Intelligence' column of *John Bull*, celebrating the latest crop of winning epigrams within a context that is squarely and timelessly C. of E. The format and practice continued without change for decades:

ECCLESIASTICAL INTELLIGENCE.

PREFERMENTS, &C...

OBITUARY...

UNIVERSITY INTELLIGENCE...

[31] Indeed, celibacy was still required of the Fellows of Oxford colleges (although not for too many years longer), and the High Church Oxford Movement of the 1830s–1840s had celebrated its mystique. On the Tractarians and the celibate ideal in late Victorian retrospect, see evocatively Church (1891: 183).

Cambridge, Dec. 23.—Prize Subjects.—the Vice-Chancellor has issued the following notice:–

I. The Most Noble Marquess Camden, Chancellor, being pleased to give annually a third gold medal for the encouragement of English poetry, to such resident Undergraduate as shall compose the best Ode, or the best Poem in heroic verse...[32]

That year, the supplied topic for this Cantabrigian equivalent of the Newdigate was 'The conflagration of Rome in the reign of Nero'. Further prize advertisements follow; two fifteen-guinea prizes are offered in Latin prose composition, two for essays in Latin (each to take as its theme a classical Latin motto), and finally, three five-guinea medals:

1. The best Greek Ode in imitation of Sappho;
2. The best Latin Ode in imitation of Horace;
3. The best Greek Epigram after the model of the Anthologia, and the best Latin epigram after the model of Martial.

Again, any poem entered for the prize had to respond to a classical Latin tag—for the Greek epigram, the Horatian *Nil fuit unquam | Sic impar sibi*. Four decades later (1874), tellingly similar festivities are reported from Harrow's annual shindig: among the medals for Latin prose, hexameters, and elegiacs, and the prizes for Greek prose ('Translation from Burke's Speech on the Nabob of Arcot's Debt') and iambics, we see the Oxenham Prize for Greek Epigram go to a boy named Godley. Inspired by a specified motto from tragedy, he came up with a winner on the theme of 'Napoleon at St Helena'.[33]

Where *Polyglotta* crucially differs from this comfortable tradition—a remnant of which endures to this day—is precisely in its polyglot nature, and in the enlarged sense of literary tradition it thus invites its reader to share.[34] The preface sets out Wellesley's stall, 'the object being to illustrate, even through its minor productions, the extensive connexion of Greek literature with the study of literature in general'.[35] Two separate readerships are anticipated. For 'the Greek scholar' (a phrase that should

---

[32] Anon. (1836a).   [33] Anon. (1874b).
[34] Sir William Browne's Medals are still offered at Cambridge for Greek and Latin odes and epigrams; in recent years the topics stipulated for Greek epigram by the Statutes and Ordinances of the University have included surfing, Girl Power, junk food, the iPod, and tuition fees. They are not always awarded; often no entries are submitted. In 1929, Shane Leslie (1929: 15) remarked patronizingly of Marcus Argentarius that his 'cleverness would have qualified him more than once for the Prize at the modern University'.
[35] Wellesley (1849: p. vi).

be parsed in its widest sense as including all those readers who have attained competence in Greek at school), 'the chief use of this volume will be to remind him of the many favourites of his boyhood, perhaps to make him acquainted with new ones';[36] but while this 'scholarly' reader may enjoy comparing the Greek originals with their Latin and (if his skills are rusty) the English versions, he will get little or nothing out of the polyglot translations that are the volume's main selling point. All this reader can look forward to is a limited exercise in the indulgence of public-school nostalgia. Instead the book is primarily intended to benefit 'the general reader': 'it may help to prove how largely at every period the literature of Europe has been indebted to the language of Greece; to that tongue "which has been held one of the best instruments for training the young mind…"'.[37] And so on for several lines, dutifully parroting the introductory remarks to Liddell and Scott's Greek–English Lexicon after the manner of an apotropaic formula,[38] but the point has been made: this is not about classical Greek epigram *per se*, but about how authors within vernacular European literary traditions have used it as a creative tool in their own writing (hence versions 'including imitations, and adaptations, in the way of parody or paraphrase, and even anticipations').[39] Wellesley's *Anthologia Polyglotta* is a sourcebook in comparative literature glossed as classical tradition.[40] The stock encomium to the beauties of Greek is a long-lived trope among writers reaching out to non-classically trained audiences; we may compare, for instance, Sir Richard Jebb, specifically on the Greek of Homer as 'the most perfect among the forms of human speech'.[41] A contemporary advertisement used to promote the book through the back pages of periodicals makes the point still more emphatic: 'The Greek originals are prefixed throughout, with a view to contrast the genius of the classical and modern languages, to illustrate the principles of translation, and to exhibit the influence of Greek poetry upon literature in general.' The originals are merely 'prefixed', for ease of reference; *Polyglotta* is first and foremost about the versions inspired by them, 'by authors of all countries and all periods, down to the present day; many of them inedited [i.e. previously unpublished], and of these the greater number by living writers'. The originals are included principally to illustrate the creative processes of the later poets who have variously amplified, rewritten, and even

[36] Wellesley (1849: p. vii).　　[37] Wellesley (1849: p. vii).
[38] Wellesley (1849: p. iii).　　[39] Wellesley (1849: p. v).
[40] And is leaned on as such by Hutton (1946: pp. viii, 439, 569).
[41] Jebb (1893: 24–5).

parodied them—and who continue to do so, never more prolifically than at the time of publication.

Western Europe in this view is united by a single, living, and thriving literary tradition, which is amicably shared between its many ethnicities and language groups and can be traced back to a common source of inspiration. Because of its sociable qualities, brevity, and tendency to quick iteration, epigram is chosen as the ideal genre through which to explore this family tree.[42] These qualities have generated a rich back catalogue for Wellesley to explore, and make it easy for him to solicit additional contributions from his fellow Oxonians and contacts further afield. Naturally these two types of source place limits on the volume's focus and potential for narrative; the dead cannot be asked to rewrite in the light of a now improved text, and getting academics to follow a brief is notoriously like herding cats.

Also, both sources were limited in thematic range, in the same way and for the same reason. The relatively few poems from the Anthology that had already attracted a significantly large 'family' of imitations and versions were invariably part of the repertoire of syntactically easy poems used in schools across Western Europe from the Renaissance onwards (see next section). In the light of these difficulties, and rather refreshingly, Wellesley attempts no overarching scheme of thematic or chronological arrangement, instead aiming at variation and miscellany. From the way he structures his opening and closing sequences, however—the two places a classically primed reader is bound to look for meta-poetic commentary—a strong original story does emerge.

Let us look first and very briefly at the book's ending. The penultimate poem, on a bronze portrait image of Alexander by Lysippus, supplies in the concluding couplet of its English translation a welcome note of piety: 'The living metal seems to say with eyes uplift to Jove: | Mine are the realms of earth below, thine be the realms above.'[43] The translator is Goldwin Smith, Wellesley's most industrious and talented Oxford contributor. The last poem of all, the anonymous funerary distich AP 9.40, is presented in four translations and two paraphrases; of these, the last word goes to Wellesley himself. In this context his version does double duty in reflecting on the labours of the modern anthologist, and marking the conclusion of his book—the 'I' is readable as either the editor or his text.

---

[42] Just as one might study transmission of biologically heritable characteristics through fruit flies or mice; or, in the case of the Augustinian friar Gregor Mendel, who was shortly to begin his research into heredity at Brno, peas.
[43] Wellesley (1849: 463).

Fortune and Hope, a long adieu!
I've entered into port:
I've nothing more to do with you;
Make others now your sport.[44]

The book's opening sequence offers up a more particular and challenging contextual message. The two poets in question, Marianus Scholasticus and Thallus of Miletus, are extraordinarily obscure: otherwise unknown, but believed to be widely separated in date, they are represented in the Anthology by a mere five poems apiece. Marianus' poem is substantial, at twelve lines; I give the English, in rhyming couplets by Goldwin Smith. We may usefully note in passing that Smith also composed the Latin versions that accompany both these opening epigrams, thus helping, if not exactly to invent, then at least to shore up a gappy literary timeline and genealogy for the European vernacular tradition.

Turn, Trav'ller, and beneath this wood's deep shade,
Awhile thy way-worn limbs to rest be laid!
Here the fresh native rill the planes between
Bright welling forth from many a source is seen;
Here on the flowery sod in springtime blows
The soft-leav'd violet blended with the rose.
Trail'd o'er the dewy mead with clust'ring leaves
Her lavish tresses lo! the ivy weaves,
While by their shaggy bank the waters shoot,
And undermine the self-sown thickets' root.
'Tis LOVE.—What other name befits the place,
That teems in every part with every grace?[45]

On a first reading this is obviously an excellent choice as an opening gambit, welcoming in the world- or text-weary wayfarer for a pleasant hour of literary relaxation (we may recall Bland on this topic, and it is not the last time we will see it invoked)—notwithstanding that the book is not exactly constructed so as to provide it. The original Greek poem, prefaced to the run of translations and versions, comes from the Anthology with its own explanatory heading already attached—'On a suburb known as Eros, in Amaseia'—but Smith's rendering conjures up a more

---

[44] Wellesley (1849: 464).
[45] The English translation of poem 1 is at Wellesley (1849: 2–3). Unlike some of the Oxford Latin versions berated by the anonymous reviewer, who affects to miss the point of their inclusion (Anon. 1850a: 437), Smith's renditions are artful, and take the originals in yet another direction: his version of the Thallus poem turns it into an anticipation of Vergil's *Eclogues* through careful word choice: *Haec frondens platanus viden! ut bene celat amantum | Delicias patulis officiosa comis . . .* (Wellesley 1849: 3).

proximate and resonant Arcadia. Because of its programmatic situation in the book, this leafy paradise demands in the first instance to be read meta-poetically as an ekphrastic encomium to the Anthology now in the reader's hands.

Wellesley's book of versions finds embodied expression in two intersecting images. The Greek originals are a fount of inspiration, 'Bright welling forth... from many a source' in the Anthology, and the water of this mingled stream brings life to the flower meadow of the later (chronologically 'downstream') adaptations through which it flows.[46] The infusion of these pure classical waters validates their vernacular descendants. That this reception tradition is described in the classic meta-poetic flower language of Meleager ('The soft-leav'd violet blended with the rose', 'clust'ring leaves' of ivy) affirms its legitimacy as a continuous tradition.

This repurposing of Marianus' poem transposes epigram into a leafy riverbank idyll, complete with shady trees—and what trees. The second poem chosen by Wellesley rounds out the picture. Again, I quote the English translation only, a hand-me-down piece (1829) by the Revd William Shepherd:

> Wide-spreading plane-tree, whose thick branches meet
> To form for lovers an obscure retreat,
> Whilst with thy foliage closely intertwine
> The curling tendrils of the cluster'd vine,
> Still mayst thou flourish, in perennial green,
> To shade the vot'ries of the Paphian queen.[47]

The plane-tree is the constant and defining fixture in Greco-Roman literary and pictorial representation of philosophy as being at home in the culturally resonant scene of garden and grove.[48] The tree's explicit presence in these two juxtaposed poems, each of which also invokes mysteries of Eros, inescapably evokes Platonic dialogue as a first point of reference, and with it the ideal of the philosophic lover. Erotodidaxis within this secluded *locus amoenus* takes on particular and pointed significance in the Oxford of 1849, a university whose own Arcadian setting can be read into Smith's creative rephrasing (as a 'fresh *native* rill' the Anthology merges with the Cherwell, where the plantings of Addison's

---

[46] The meta-poetic image of water as poetic production is, of course, Callimachean, as famously developed in the *Hymn to Apollo*, where the god of poetry associates purity with poetic brevity. The topos is taken up by ancient poets, including Parthenius.

[47] Wellesley (1849: 3).

[48] For a nuanced and stimulating discussion of the associations invoked by the presence of plane-trees in suburban and literary scenography alike, see now Spencer (2010: 17, 21, 30, 65–6).

Walk throw dappled shade), and where Plato was beginning to assume
a crucial role within an exciting new kind of tutorial-based Classics
pedagogy, under the inspiration of the dynamic Balliol classicist Benjamin
Jowett.

Like Wellesley and key members of his creative team, Jowett was a
progressive Liberal and an energetic exponent of university reform.[49] His
vision of the Oxford tutorial as an intimate bond between an older and
younger man (the classic philosophic lovers of the *Phaedrus* and *Symposium*, transmuting the dross of desire into the gold of true knowledge)
was essentially a pirated version of the Tractarians' religiously inspired
'confessional' model (1830s–1840s), now aggressively repurposed. Putting Plato at its heart—a classic author already tainted for conservatives
by association with modern Utilitarianism—created what was in effect a
secular alternative to the default clerical–conservative vision of Oxford's
pedagogic mission in the world.

As inflected by *Polyglotta*, this secular and rationalist philosophy of
education was actively outward-focused and cosmopolitan, holding
borders and religious differences at nought—a mode congenial to Jowett
(himself an assiduous empire-builder), but all the more so to modern
linguists. Epigram's European reception history is made to encompass in
microcosm the transnational Republic of Letters.[50]

---

[49] Wellesley's chief co-conspirator Goldwin Smith is a case in point—Eton-educated (so
an accomplished epigram-worker) but from new money (railway stocks), and at that time
Stowell Law Professor at University College, he was already heavily involved in the cause.
He served as assistant secretary to the 1850 Royal Commission, and secretary to the
Commissioners appointed by the Act of 1854. A Liberal friendly to the cause of Labour,
he wrote polemically on the need for reform at Oxford (see in passing Dowling 1994: 71–2),
confirmed his classical credentials by assisting on Conington's Vergil, and was then
poached by the newly founded Cornell University as its Professor of Modern History; a
Hall of Residence there is still named for him, although maybe not for much longer.
Biography: Phillips (2002). Smith is not the only one; cf., e.g., Charles Abraham Elton,
the sixth Baronet Elton of Cleveland Court (e.g. at Wellesley 1849: 4), another old Etonian
Liberal, ex-soldier (one of at least two represented in the opening pages of *Polyglotta*), for
much of his life a Nonconformist, and, like his friends Charles Lamb and Samuel Coleridge,
a regular *Edinburgh* contributor. Volume 1 of his 1814 *Specimens of the Classic Poets*
included several versions from Meleager and one from Rhianus (Elton 1814: i. 387, 435–48).
[50] On classical language literacy as enabler of international communication in the arts
and sciences, see Waquet (2001: 7–12, 33–6, 39–40). The internationalist spirit of *Polyglotta*
is strikingly illustrated by the prominence it assigns to an Italian nobleman then resident in
Oxford: Alessandro, Count Mortara, graciously thanked in the preface (Wellesley 1849:
p. vi). A hero of the First Carlist War of the 1830s (Stephens 1837: i. 130, 185, 290) and 'a
scholar of profound acquirements, both in ancient and modern literature' (Cramer 1841:
p. xxiii), Mortara had been in Oxford since 1842. While maintaining his courtly connection
to the Duke of Lucca, he missed no opportunity to make himself useful in his adoptive
home. Among other activities (which included committee service for the Archaeological

At the same time, and as Linda Dowling has compellingly argued, turning college tutorials into Platonic dialogues left ajar a door that dissident readers of Plato would later force wide open—Symonds and Wilde included; the ghosts of Phaedrus and Alcibiades were always in the room.[51] For the time being, though, Jowett could charismatically gloss the erotics of Plato's text as the mutual enthusiasm of spiritual uplift, leaving the Oxford of *Polyglotta* as an eroto-philosophic Eden, prelapsarian in its innocence.[52] And it is Jowett's progressive Oxford that Wellesley's Anthology bids to represent through synecdoche or figurative equivalency—*Polyglotta*'s groves are Oxford's groves are the groves of Academe, collectively gelling into an eternal *locus amoenus* where free enquiry will always overthrow unexamined orthodoxy and traditional pieties.[53] In this context, and with hero worship of gay Platonist culture-hero Politian thrown in for good measure, perhaps it is small wonder that the *Christian Remembrancer* saw red.[54]

If so, it was over nothing; *Polyglotta* was fondly remembered as a resource on epigram, but the demands it made on its readers were too rigorous to win over many. Wellesley's wished-for 'general reader' is not the casually interested reader, still less the common person in the street; he is instead 'general' in the sense of being an expert generalist, what we

Institute of Great Britain and Ireland), he compiled a catalogue of the Canonici collection of Italian MSS in the Bodleian Library. Before returning to Italy he sold his excellent personal library of 1, 400 volumes to the Bodleian for the princely sum of £1,000: Burton (1837: 12). His contributions, identified by the initial 'M.', begin with the Italian version of the very first poem in *Polyglotta*, at Wellesley (1849: 2).

[51] This is precisely Dowling's 'larger and more significant story of cultural transformation and unintended consequences' (1994: 35), a story for which she brilliantly lays groundwork; on the Decadent appropriation of the philosophic lover in the 1890s, see the equally first-rate Evangelista (2006).

[52] On Jowett's concern to represent Plato to English readers on morally familiar terms, see Dowling (1994: 71). Much later, and particularly in the aftermath of Wilde, Jowett would make repeated attempts to disassociate Plato from Greek love, but the genie was well and truly out of the box: Evangelista (2006: 233–4).

[53] In this light, it is even tempting to read Smith's 'thine be the realms above' spiel (Wellesley 1849: 463), as a policy statement on the separation of spiritual and temporal authority with specific reference to the contemporary Oxford context; certainly the positioning of the poem invites a programmatic (postgrammatic?) reading; but perhaps this is pushing the text too far.

[54] Philosopher, philologist, professor, and poet Angelo Poliziano (1454–94) compounded the above offences by his close relationships with the Neoplatonic Hermeticists Pico della Mirandola and Marsilio Ficino (his tutor in philosophy and the translator of Plato's corpus into Latin); he was also an assertive modernizer in the classical studies of his own time, urging the rejection of ideologically safe gush in favour of forensic close reading: Grafton (1994: 72–3).

might term in today's parlance a Renaissance man. He—and the ideal reader is definitely a 'he'—must know all the languages in which the versions are written (Latin, Italian, German, French, Spanish, English), and must also be competent in Greek, so as to 'test' individual versions 'by a careful reference to the original'.[55] Indeed, this ideal reader is expected to have learned individual Anthology epigrams by heart at school, and still to have them on call. The preface may boast that the text derives from the new edition of Jacobs, but the index gives only the Greek incipit for each poem, arranged in alphabetical sequence, with no clue to where any of them sit in Cephalas' scheme. Taken together, all of this is a lot to ask. Idlers are warned off at the outset—this book is a brain gym, and the *profanum uulgus* can stick with the safe choices of Merivale's Meleagrian *Collections* of 1833:

A more limited selection, comprising nothing but the choicest gems, would doubtless have proved more acceptable to the common-place lounger. But every 'Delectus' formed on that plan has been proved to be comparatively unimproving: it spares the student every exercise of the judgment ... whereas it is only from a selection sufficiently copious and varied to tax his own faculties of observation and criticism that any useful inductions can be drawn.[56]

That is not to say that Merivale's own efforts are excluded; far from it, and he merits inclusion both as a celebrity author and for the superior merit of his renditions when compared to, among others, Bland's.[57] Now positively identified as the work of the former, the 'French privateer' poem makes the cut, as do some of his son's efforts from the 1833 version of *Selections*.[58] The dig at the French is not merely a tip of the hat to the old master. In supplying his own loose rendition of the anonymous source poem, headed in the Anthology 'on Nemesis', Wellesley substitutes a quasi-inscriptional heading of his own:

On the first Stone of Buonaparte's marble column, raised by the Expeditionary army and the flotilla of Boulogne, and afterwards made to commemorate the restoration of the Bourbons:

---

[55] Wellesley (1849: p. vi).

[56] Wellesley (1849: p. vi); I suggest a likely inspiration for his dig at the 'common-place lounger' at Nisbet (2012b: 92 n. 29).

[57] Merivale the celebrity: Wellesley (1849: p. vi).

[58] The index of authors gives twenty-three versions to Merivale senior and four to Merivale junior, the same number as Bland. The French privateer poem: Wellesley (1849: 216). After a decent interval, Merivale had let it be known which versions in *Translations* and *Selections* had been his and which Bland's; the reviewer for *Blackwood's* (Anon. 1833a, b) writes as if none of the versions on which he comments had ever been anonymous in the first place.

Frenchmen! who brought this marble block to stand
A trophy of th'invasion of yon land,
Behold! it marks a Bourbon's restoration,
And tells that you are the invaded nation.[59]

The Column of the Grande Armée, on which construction began in 1804 as a premature monument to Napoleon's successful invasion of Great Britain (a plan abandoned the following year), stands to this day in Wimille near Boulogne; its bronze accoutrements were indeed melted down for a statue of Henry IV, founder of the Bourbon line, but the expropriation of a stone from its base smacks of rhetorical grandstanding rather than material plausibility. The only politics happening here is family politics, through nostalgic retrospect and with present realities resolutely screened out: Wellesley the bastard nephew speaks for Wellesley the lauded First Duke, defeater of the Xerxes of Europe at Waterloo in 1815. Topicality is out of the window here: the restored Bourbons (actually restored twice, briefly in 1814 and then again post-Waterloo) had thoroughly alienated their French subjects and been thrown out in the Revolution of 1848, the year before *Polyglotta*. Indeed, in December of that year Napoleon's nephew Louis had been elected President of the newly installed Second Republic. In the Greek original, as commonly in sepulchral epigram, the inscribed monument (in this instance a statue of Nemesis) addresses the passer-by in the first person; here the identity of the speaking persona is deliberately left ambiguous, but has definitely shifted to align with a victorious British perspective (the stone is now 'it'). For all its progressive instincts, *Polyglotta* is still stuck in the past, refighting old wars and trading on patronage.

In the light of *Polyglotta*'s necessarily limited impact, the *Remembrancer*'s character assassination reads retrospectively as panic-driven overkill. It certainly did Wellesley's book no harm with its smallish core market of omni-capable 'general' Humanists: *Polyglotta* finds itself frequently and approvingly cited by cognoscenti for decades thereafter, is leaned on as a convenient authority for the Greek text of its traditionally favoured poems, and ends its days as a minor source for the compendious genealogies of epigram's European literary tradition compiled by James Hutton in the first half of the twentieth century.[60] It even created

---

[59] Planudean Appendix 263: Πρίν με λίθον Πέρσαι δεῦρ' ἤγαγον | στήσονται νίκας· εἰμὶ δὲ νῦν Νέμεσις. | ἀμφοτέροις δ' ἔστηκα, καὶ Ἑλλήνεσσι τρόπαιον | | νίκας καὶ Πέρσαις τοῦ πολέμου νέμεσις. Wellesley's selection of versions is at (1849: 317).

[60] Approving citation of Wellesley's acumen as editor-contributor at, e.g., Anon. (1865c), on a 'spirited version' of a particular epigram by an 'accomplished editor' (p. 209), known for his 'dexterity and neatness' (p. 217). A quick Internet search throws

its own little stub of literary tradition, appropriately enough, at the international level—Rþorleifur Repp's slender (sixteen-page) homage of 1864, *Epigrömm*, translates a selection from Wellesley's crop of Greek originals into, of all things, Icelandic. Disgusted churchmen were never really part of this book's intended audience to begin with. Nonetheless, the review is significant in the rhetorical shorthand it established. Nearly half a century later, we will see 'enthusiasm' co-opted by the backlash critics as a cover word when attacking queered readings of ancient Greece through epigram in the Decadent *fin de siècle*—but it is already being tried out here, disparaging Wellesley as an Aesthete *avant la lettre*, producing evil art for art's sake.[61]

4. AN ETON MESS: GEORGE BURGES'S *GREEK ANTHOLOGY* (1852)

Britten groaned aloud and every one regarded him. 'Greek epigrams on the fellows' names,' he said. 'Small beer in ancient bottles. Let's get a stuffed broody hen to SIT on the magazine.'

'We might do worse than a Greek epigram', said Cossington. 'One in each number. It—it impresses parents and keeps up our classical tradition. And the masters CAN help. We don't want to antagonise them. Of course—we've got to departmentalise. Writing is only one section of the thing. The ARVONIAN has to stand for the school. There's questions of space and questions of expense. We can't turn out a great chunk of printed prose like—like wet cold toast and call it a magazine.'[62]

The stout and sturdy volume of George Burges (518 pages) pays homage both to its immediate predecessor, *Anthologia Polyglotta*, 'a very beautiful

---

up multiple citations of Wellesley as an authority in *Notes and Queries* through to at least 1890. Honorable mention of *Polyglotta* at e.g. Hutton (1935: p. viii).

[61]   Again, the crucial section of text is Anon. (1850a: 429–30). 'Enthusiasm' as a term for pigeonholing Aesthetic writers carries the sense (*OED* 1b) of poetical over-excitement but also the lingering suspicion (*OED* 2, common in the eighteenth century) of 'ill-regulated or misdirected religious emotion, extravagance of religious speculation'. When applied to the Wildean Aesthete, it will turn Hellenizing Uranism into a socially dangerous 'cult', against which the authority of the Church of Compulsory Heterosexuality must be asserted for the sake of the public good (Ch. 4). Evangelista (2006: 235–6) unpacks how Pater started the hounds by riffing on the ἔνθεος of Plato's *Phaedrus* in his controversy-courting essay 'Winckelmann'.

[62]   Quoted from Wells, *The New Macchiavelli* (1910); at the fictional City Merchants School, the boys plan a new school magazine.

volume... where fidelity and elegance are happily combined', and at greater length to Bland and Merivale, whose *Translations* and *Collections* began it all.[63] Burges's Anthology appeared as an instalment of Bohn's Classical Library, a uniform series of relatively affordable but nonetheless well-produced volumes that ran alongside similar imprints on science, history, archaeology, and theology within the publishing empire of Henry George Bohn. This former bookseller and entrepreneur sold his stable of 'Library' imprints to Bell and Daldy (later George Bell and Sons) in 1864, where they remained in print for many years. Burges himself was another Philhellene who had produced a slew of classical editions in the first three decades of the century.[64]

More transparently than *Polyglotta*, the Bohn *Anthology* betrays its origins in the world of the elite boarding school: indeed, the book's subtitle attempts to parlay its direct link to 'Westminster, Eton, and Other Public Schools' into sales. The connection is if anything over-egged; the only 'Other' school noticeably involved is King Edward's School at Bury St Edmund's. These three sources together supply the majority of the volume's inelegant structure:

> Westminster Selection
> Eton Selection (referred to in the text also as the 'Eton Extracts')
> Edwards's Selection
> Miscellaneous Selections[65]

'Miscellaneous' includes poems from Bland's *Collections* of 1813, including 'When Narva asks a friend to dine', now revealed as one of Merivale's from the latter's *Collections* of 1833; and 'those [poems] contributed by Mr Hay and others to the series of articles writen by Professor Wilson, in Blackwood's Magazine for 1833 and 1835'.[66] A handful of poems are gleaned from other periodicals, and Burges individually thanks as a contributing author 'a lady, who is desirous of concealing her name'

[63] Praise of *Polyglotta*: Burges (1852: p. vi); Bland and Merivale discussed at pp. iv–vi, with extensive quotation on epigram's definition and value.

[64] Cordasco (1951) gives rich detail on the Bohn Libraries; see also Rota (1998: 219–20), with further bibliography. Not to be confused with the Revd George Burges, 'our' Burges had written and privately published a play in five acts, *The Son of Erin, or the Cause of the Greeks* (1823), and was around 70 when he undertook the Bohn volume.

[65] The structure is prefaced to the text at Burges (1852: p. viii). 'Edwards's Selection' is *Epigrammata e purioribus Graecae anthologiae fontibus* (1825), named not for King Edward's School but for its editor, the Revd John Edwards—who (just to keep things nice and complicated) compiled it for the use of King Edward's School. The Eton volume included excerpts from several non-epigrammatic authors, principally Anacreon and Theognis but with a scattering of Hellenistic elegies by Callimachus, Moschus, and Bion.

[66] Burges (1852: p. vi).

under the initials M.A.S. (not the Miss Alma Strettell who will contribute extensively to the 1889 *Selections* of 'Graham Tomson', but a 'Miss Stodart, of Hampstead').[67] He also includes a few versions under his own name.[68]

These school Selections come out of a long tradition in elite pedagogy that throws much light on the early collections we have already encountered, from *Translations* through to *Polyglotta*, and with which we must now engage. Such books had been known in continental Europe from the 1520s onward.[69] They were particularly favoured in the upper years of Jesuit schools, which had borrowed from the humanists the practice of epigram-composition in Latin. Rendering Greek verses into Latin and vice versa helped develop fluency and was pedagogically convenient: the order's *Ratio Studiorum* stipulated it as an improving occupation for pupils while the master was marking papers. The publication of numerous continental European translations from the Anthology into Latin, largely working from the same set of favourite poems, strongly indicates that this practice was widespread, and by the end of the sixteenth century British secondary education had sufficiently taken the practice on board that the schoolbook market would support local productions.[70]

This is hardly surprising: Britain had had a stake in epigram translation from Greek into Latin, if not explicitly with an educational aim, since the mid-fifteenth century.[71] A century and more before Edwards's Selection, the anonymous Westminster Selection (1724) and Johnson's for Eton (1699) thus already looked back on an established national pedagogic tradition, as did similar selections produced at around the same time for the use of rival schools: for Winchester (Anon. 1791, with English verse translations), for the Puritan stronghold of Felsted in Essex (Lydiat's *Stachyologia* of 1696—the Greek *stachys* is an ear of corn or growing grain), and plenty of others besides.[72] Westminster itself had already worn out one previous Anthology schoolbook, the anonymous *Anthologia Deutera* of 1667. For an overview of how Greek epigram was being used in the classroom we may turn to a Tunbridge schoolmaster. The full title of John Stockwood's *Progymnasma Scholasticum* of 1597, a revision of Henri Estienne's much-used *Epigrammata Graeca Selecta* of

---

[67] Burges (1852: p. vi).
[68] Burges (1852: p. vi); 'When Narva asks a friend to dine' (p. 499). This poem lives long in citation: cf., e.g., Dodd (1870: 284).
[69] Hutton (1946: 15).
[70] All this is straight out of the estimable Hutton (1935: 38–9, 44; 1946: 16–18).
[71] Farnaby (1453).
[72] Skelton (1971: p. xi) claims knowledge of over twenty selections of this kind.

1570, is nothing if not detailed (the translation from Stockwood's Latin is my own):

School preliminary exercise, i.e., Grammatical exercise using Greek epigrams, selected from Henri Estienne's Anthology, and explained by means of his twofold interpretation, in a clear and easy-to-follow arrangement, explaining all the important and difficult words which appear in these poems, and elucidating them, to the great reward and alleviation as much of learned as of student readers. By the effort and industry of John Stockwood, former schoolmaster at Tunbridge School. As an added feature, the Greek text is rendered in Latin script between the lines to make it easier to read, as a service to young learners.

There were equivalent volumes for Latin epigram as well. Predominantly of course derived from Martial but also incorporating Neo-Latin compositions and Greek-to-Latin *sententiae*, Eton's *Epigrammatum Delectus* (1659) went through nine editions and a century of imprints; it was the work of the French monk and grammarian Claude Lancelot, once again indicating the international character of epigrammatic pedagogy.[73]

Writing in 1910, H. G. Wells has the narrator of his fictional memoir *The New Macchiavelli* (quoted at the onset of this section), a fallen star of late Victorian Liberal politics, reflect on a childhood formed within a centuries-old pedagogic tradition in which 'Greek epigrams and Latin verse' are effectively the sole academic content.[74] Cloistered from the world of practical commerce, this tradition is enfeebled by long use. The narrating persona, 'Dick Remington', thinly veils Wells's own habitual Fabian-reformist archness:

Here all about me was London, a vast inexplicable being, a vortex of gigantic forces, that filled and overwhelmed me with impressions, that stirred my imagination to a perpetual vague enquiry; and my school not only offered no key to it, but had practically no comment to make upon it at all ... We joined in the earnest acquirement of all that was necessary for Greek epigrams and Latin verse, and for the rest played games. We dipped down into something clear and elegantly proportioned and time-worn and for all its high resolve of stalwart virility a little feeble, like our blackened and decayed portals by Inigo Jones.[75]

---

[73] Described at Maxwell Lyte (1875: 230): 'Martial predominates in it, but the compiler was not exclusive in his views, and found room for several productions of modern Latinists, as Sannazaro, Strozzi, Strada, Beza, Grotius, John Owen, Buchanan, and others. Another portion of the book consists of choice quotations from classical poets, and it ends with a collection of short Greek sentences accompanied by Latin translations.' A literary primer this was not. Eton's successively expanded versions of *Epigrammatum Delectus* were published by the London firm of William Bowyer. To the best of my knowledge, the ninth edition was reprinted for the last time in 1762.
[74] Wells (1910: 67).   [75] Wells (1910: 67).

Provided care was exercised in their selection, epigrams were considered easy to read, and suitable material for early-stage learners who might not yet have fully mastered their Greek alphabet; a later primer, popular through most of the nineteenth century, placed elegiac distichs from the Anthology at the midway point between single sentences and longer passages in prose.[76]

Traces of this long history are legible in the detailed arrangement of Burges's text. The anonymous compiler of the Westminster Selection had been well up with the latest European practice in arranging his poems into separate books (of which there were three, of a hundred epigrams each) by length: distichs first, then four-line poems, then six, and so on. This was all about verse comp. and its cognate exercises in translation from one classical language to the other: 'in verse-writing the simplest exercise, whether in Greek or Latin, was the epigram in elegiac distichs,' and, for the nervous beginner, the fewer distichs the better.[77] Even with some quite loose versions muddying the waters, an underlying difference in length is immediately evident when turning from book 1 of the Westminster material (pp. 1–23) to book 2 (pp. 24–56); book 2 to book 3 (pp. 56–82); and book 3 to book 4 (pp. 82–96).

The old verse-comp. ambit is additionally evident in the individual Selections of each of the public schools, in two distinct ways. The first is duplication from one Selection to another. Burges sensibly declares at the outset that he will not refer back to the same Greek original twice. As a consequence, when the Eton Extracts duplicate the choice of the Westminster Selections (or when Edwards's Selection duplicates choices from either), he omits the sequentially later version. Conscientiously, however, he indicates each excision and supplies the details of where in his volume the poem has already been translated, making the extent of duplication extremely easy to track. (Burges bends his own rule when he comes to Edwards's Selection, sometimes giving additional translations of poems already treated earlier in the book, but he does at least keep up the habit of noting each occasion on which the Greek original is the same as one in a previously treated Selection.) Examples occur right from the start of the Eton Selection. Over a third of the Eton poems are duplicates of Westminster's choices; Edwards's much larger selection is considerably more independent.[78]

---

[76] Valpy (1860), on which see n. 93.

[77] Hutton (1946: 16, 19; cf. 1935: 39). Arrangement by length was characteristic of eighteenth-century Italian school editions in particular: Hutton (1935: 39).

[78] By my count, 80 of Eton's 217 poems are tagged as duplications of Westminster's, including the first 2 poems (Burges 1852: 97); and 204 of Edwards's 808, as duplications of either Westminster's or Eton's.

The other way in which the influence of verse comp. continues to be manifest is in the nature of the poems selected and the dates of their authors. The first book of the Westminster Selection runs to a hundred poems. Of these, a mere two are by Meleager, the first ancient anthologist and Merivale's gold standard. Simonides, he of the patriotic epitaphs for the victorious dead of the Persian Wars, does a little better (four poems). But these early, 'good' poets are lost amid a sea of post-classical voices. Particularly prominent are the skoptic poets of AP 11: Nicarchus, Lucillius, and above all Lucian.[79] These are writers of the Roman era, and Lucillius and Nicarchus in particular come much closer than any other Anthology poet to the witty paradoxes and pointed style of epigram as practised by Martial—as well they might, since they were approximate contemporaries whom the Latin poet frequently imitated.[80]

There is even a pederastic epigram by Strato, which Burges presents in two versions, including one by Wellesley, which might seduce any youthful beau:

> If age thy beauty must impair,
> The fleeting charm impart;
> If it endure, why fear to share
> What never can depart?[81]

Of course, the schoolboy readers will not know that the poem is pederastic, since they have no way of placing it in the *Mousa Paidikē*; but, still, Strato was a name to conjure with as the author of 'poems of an amatory cast, and those too not the most delicate', and one hardly imagines Westminster expected its boys to grow up treating women this way either.[82] Moral instruction is no more a priority in Westminster School's Selection than is perceived literary merit. Instead the poems are solely and aptly chosen for their utility in linguistic pedagogy. The Greek of the originals is straightforward, and the instant gratification attained each time a student got the joke must have been an excellent incentive to persevere with an otherwise dry and repetitive exercise. (Imagine if

---

[79] Lucian: 8 poems; Lucillius: 7 poems; Nicarchus: 3 poems; also one apiece by the second-century minor skoptic poets Ammianus and Pollianus. The skoptic poets are the subject of Nisbet (2003).

[80] Burnikel (1980) is the fundamental study of an evidently extensive relationship of indebtedness, sometimes played down by Martial's modern advocates (briefly noted at Livingstone and Nisbet 2010: 105), and is the source for Holzberg (2002: 100–9).

[81] Burges (1852: 20), and this is not Strato's only appearance in the volume as a whole; Burges includes two of his poems in his own Miscellaneous Selections (1852: 504), one of them in a translation that makes it clear that the beloved is an adolescent boy.

[82] Strato as cad: Burges (1852: p. iii).

beginners were taught English as a foreign language by reading the jokes out of Christmas crackers.)

The remaining books of the Westminster Selection tell a very similar story, as do the Selections of the other schools included. There is frequent recourse to 'late' poets such as Paul the Silentiary (reviled by Bland) and Rufinus, both writers of amatory verse transmitted in AP 5.[83]

This same verse-comp. background echoes only faintly in 'Miscellaneous Selections', Burges's concluding section and the one in which he puts his personal stamp on the Anthology. A few poems by the schoolboy favourites occur late in the Selection (e.g. Lucillius (pp. 489–9), Paul the Silentiary (pp. 501–2)), but the impetus of the Selection is to correct the schoolbooks' implicit portrayal of epigram as a 'late' genre. There is a drastic change of organizational principle, from arrangement by length to arrangement by date—a principle that invariably generates a subtext of genre historiography. Burges bullishly front-loads his Selection with famous 'early' authors to firm up the genre's trajectory. Thus we begin with archaic iambus from Archilochus in quantity (pp. 415–22), and quickly come to an even bigger tranche of patriotic Simonides (pp. 425–38). The combination of Archilochean symposium and Simonidean epitaph also implicitly aligns Burges's authorial voice with a pre-existing explanatory discourse of epigram as the poetry of love, wine, and death (and the Selection wraps up with three anonymous literary epitaphs to close the loop).

Burges's chronological scheme more or less holds together as far as Meleager (pp. 480–92), treated extensively as befits the first and best of anthologists; there are some worrying wobbles thereafter (the very next poem is by Agathias), but the overall narrative of change is clear enough. The post-Meleagrian section (pp. 492–506) is dwarfed by its Archaic, Classical, and Hellenistic run-up. This version of genre history implicitly corrects that of the schoolbooks, moving the curve of its micro-history back into the Classical and thus into the realm of literature proper, and minimizing the appearance of decline under Rome—but at the cost of a broken-backed book that undermines its own credibility through internal contradiction.

The genre's internationally shared history as the basic training tool in verse composition had given Wellesley's contributors, living and dead, their shared facility in re-versioning epigram from one language to the

---

[83]   As, e.g., at Burges (1852: 111, 132, 246, 248), and the unbroken run of epigrams by Paul in Edwards's Selection at pp. 262–8. Bland on Paul: (1806: p. xxiv). Bland's arrangement (1806: 65–7) placed Rufinus in the second century or after. A date in the third or fourth century was academic orthodoxy until quite recently, as, e.g., at Page (1978: 49), against which see persuasively Cameron (1982). Rufinus and Paul are evocatively paired as late antique degenerates in the agenda-driven genre history of Symonds, as we will see in Ch. 3.

next: to do so was practically a conditioned reflex. Now, the educational textbooks that had for centuries facilitated the running of this boot-camp supplied Burges with a ready-made text for three-quarters of his book, requiring only scissors and glue (and a little something extra) to attain a length suitable for the uniform series. This 'lazy' scheme also aimed to lure aspiring middle-class readers with the promise of inclusion in a socially privileged textual milieu. Despite the series's built-in durability, second-hand copies are today rare, suggesting that this gambit was not a notable success. In or out of Burges, the school Selections continued to be cited occasionally and eccentrically as a reference source, but they never made the mainstream as works of literature—quite understandably, as literary merit had never been a consideration at any point in their centuries-long back-story (at no point had any of the various European schoolbooks been a 'set author').[84] Realistically, Burges's Bohn was never going to change that, given its rickety structure, sloppy implementation, and general user-unfriendliness. Again Greek incipits are all we find in the index, or rather the indices—there are three, for the different sections and types of content.[85]

One thing the Bohn Anthology did achieve was to transpose some of the post-Merivale epigram activity of the Reviews—a 'chaos of fugitive pieces, good, bad, and indifferent' in the acerbic view of Wellesley's nameless reviewer—into an organized and permanent form.[86] Specifically, Burges's Anthology is the first foothold in durable print of the *Blackwood's* crowd. Professor Wilson's two articles in Maga establish a preliminary conservative position on epigram, a genre initially staked out by radical and Liberal interests, and this is not the last we shall hear of them.

5. 'A HARD CLOG': ROBERT MACGREGOR'S *GREEK ANTHOLOGY* (1864)

Major Macgregor deserves great credit for the industry and perse-verance he has displayed in the accomplishment of a laborious and

[84] A few years later, MacGregor refers familiarly if not often to all three school collections (e.g. at 1857: 191, 1864: 162); the Westminster and Eton volumes are cited for the epigrams of Lucian at Williams (1888: p. xxi), although, since this is another Bohn Classical Library volume, series loyalty is likely a factor. Anticipating the more thoroughgoing researches of Hutton (1935, 1946), the neo-Latinist Francis Barnard (1922: 110) anticipates a reader who has never heard of this aspect ('barely remembered') of British and continental educational practice in the eighteenth and early nineteenth centuries.

[85] Burges (1852: 507–18). A dying echo of the vanished public-school world of memorization comes in Walter Ker's old two-volume Loeb of Martial (1919–20), which concludes with an index by incipit in full mid-nineteenth-century style.

[86] Anon. (1850a: 429), obviously with an axe to grind.

difficult task. . . . we prefer to give him credit for what he has done, rather than to lay stress upon the points in which he has failed. . . . To turn over the leaves of Major Macgregor's translation is, to anyone who is familiar with the original, about as pleasant an occupation as looking through a case of dried plants after a ramble through meadows rich with living flowers.[87]

This unnamed critic in the *London Review* was not alone in his view; everyone kept telling Robert Guthrie MacGregor to call it a day, but, like his historian counterpart William Mure, he was not one to take a hint.[88] Like Mure the holder of military rank, but in his case a real one (a former artillery officer: the title page of MacGregor (1854) announces its author's enrolment in the Bengal Retired List), MacGregor devoted the leisure hours of many years to epigram translation. He was encouraged along the way by the help and advice of a friend—none other than George Burges, he of the Bohn Anthology, eulogized on his passing.[89] After initial forays in 1855 and 1857, the last a substantial work (700 poems) in its own right, these efforts culminated in the unwieldy and vast (740 pages! 3,707 poems!) *Greek Anthology, with Notes Critical and Explanatory* of 1864. MacGregor dedicated his masterwork to Gladstone, in admiration of his qualities as 'financier, orator, statesman, scholar'— an optimistic dedication but not entirely quixotic, since Gladstone was known as a Hellenist and enjoyed the odd epigram from time to time.[90] Judging by the consistent tone of the reviews and what we can deduce regarding sales, few enjoyed MacGregor's.

That there is no 'The' in MacGregor's title is significant. The absence bespeaks neither modesty of ambition (most of 'the' Anthology is here), nor a failure to grasp nomenclature, but rather the author's conception of epigram as less a corpus than an activity.[91] 'Anthology' is a kind of

---

[87]   Anon. (1864b: 643).

[88]   Cf., e.g., Cracroft (1865: 302), with crushing condescension (Cracroft cannot even be bothered to spell his name right): 'The versification is nervous, sometimes obscure, the inversions are too frequent . . . But on the whole, it is a fine instance of the combined effect of the accumulation of driblets of time spent on a great object.' And cf. Anon. (1857a: 956), on MacGregor (1857): 'Sometimes the Major's echo is musical and soft; often, however, it is harsh and mechanical, and grates on the ear . . . [sometimes] very quaint . . . Many persons will be glad to possess Major Macgregor's volume, with all its defects.'

[89]   MacGregor (1864: p. ix), on his indebtedness to Burges's 'kindness and learning and taste', and cf. (1857: pp. iv–v). A literary biographer might have fun teasing out how the two men became intimate; Burges was born in Bengal.

[90]   Cook (1919: 300), quoting a letter of 1891 by Lord Morley.

[91]   This conception is consistent: cf. MacGregor (1854: 528) (where 'Anthology' covers a multitude of versions from Italian (for the most part), French, German, and Latin—how very *Polyglotta* (also MacGregor 1855).

gerund, a verbal noun that denotes a characteristic activity, like whittling or stamp-collecting. In the author's disarmingly frank account of his process, Anthology is a hobby he is incapable of quitting, a phase he never grew out of:

> Greek Anthology, moreover, has, for years, been a favourite subject with me. In the far East, whenever an old class-fellow came in my way, or some old school-book turned up, or when the perusal of kindred Articles in periodical literature revived in me the thoughts and studies of youth, I would, again, and again, try my hand on its fine things, until many versions accumulated upon me... [92]

The trouble with epigram is that, as the British comedian Harry Hill once said of heroin, it's very more-ish, and the Reviews were clearly not helping MacGregor kick his habit. 'They were for my own amusement merely, the relaxation of a hard-worked life of uncongenial duties'— honestly, he could stop any time he wanted. The charming picture of school pals renewing old ties of friendship by swapping epigrams in barracks or on campaign raises interesting questions about how these old class-fellows were circulating (the public schools as feeders for the outposts of empire), and more intractable ones about how and by what channels the Reviews and (more surprisingly) their old schoolbooks were doing the rounds so far from home—a question that would perhaps repay further archival research onsite; there is also the more basic hermeneutic issue of how directly we take this ideal image to correspond to MacGregor's experiences and activities on the ground. [93] Setting these imponderables aside, MacGregor is the first translator to have at his disposal a body of translations numerically on a near par with the Cephalan original (albeit that not all of them are from that source),

[92] MacGregor (1864: p. ix), and note that the main title of his first foray into Anthology ten years previously (1854) is 'Indian Leisure'. Rationalizing an inability to set limits: 'to *select* is not easy where *all* is valuable' (MacGregor (1864: p. xii) (emphases in original). His 1857 preface gives a little more detail, citing the Maga, *Edinburgh*, and *Quarterly* articles of c.1833–5, additionally specifying 'a new edition of Merivale or of Elton' (on the latter, see n. 49) as a spur to Anthology, and locating schoolday memories in 'the pleasant Forbury and the silver Thames' (1857: p. i).
[93] MacGregor specifies (1857: p. iv) that at Reading the boys were drilled in Greek epigram by 'the venerable and accomplished [Revd Richard] Valpy', a cane-happy grammarian who held the headmastership for half a century from 1781 and whose long-lived and influential language primer of 1815, *Delectus Sententiarum Graecarum*, relied heavily on Greek epigrammatic distichs for intermediate instruction (Valpy 1860: 32–46, in a book running to fifty-one pages plus notes). On the martial ethos of school spirit in the British imperial imagination, see enjoyably Bristow (1991); on the uses of a classical education in India, Vasunia (2013).

and this presents an organizational challenge.[94] How can such a huge collection be presented so as to be both an enjoyable literary translation, and a useful tool for the academically interested student of the Greeks?

MacGregor's solution is twofold. One of his opening moves is to narrow down his intended readership, just as had Wellesley, and the new middle-class leisure readership be damned: 'I write for the few only.' This bluff old soldier's 'faithful and forcible' versions were not written to please 'the ordinary patrons of lighter literature' but to convey the sense of the originals as closely as possible. Women's interests are also excluded: this is *manly* Anthology.[95] With the book's remit resolved, the structure presented is quite like that of the Greek Anthology itself, arranged in this case into nine thematic categories rather than the Anthology's sixteen (and of these only eight to do with the Anthology proper):

1. Amatory and erotic
2. Convivial, humorous, satirical
3. Cyzicene and miscellaneous
4. Dedicatory and votive
5. Descriptive
6. Epitaphs
7. Ethical, prescriptive, sententious
8. Planudean
9. Appendix (i.e. the Appendix of inscriptional epigrams in Jacobs's edition)

The explicit agenda here is to showcase the breadth of topics covered by the Anthology poets, whose range has typically been artificially narrowed in English translation to service the receiving culture's elegiac preoccupation with the topoi of love and death—a fair point on MacGregor's part and one well made.[96] In remedying this shortcoming, however, he feels bound to exclude numerous poems and indeed whole books for various reasons, beginning with the Christian epigrams of AP 1 ('because I did not like to deal, in any light way, with such sacred subjects'), and continuing with AP 2 and AP 4 (neither of which contains raw material for 'Anthology'), AP 8 ('less pure' in period), and anything sexually

---

[94] His 3,707 versions do not represent as much of the Greek Anthology as one might think, since more than one in ten (396 poems) are translations from Jacobs's 'Appendix' of miscellaneous epigrams known through other literary sources (prominent among them Athenaeus) and as inscriptions.

[95] MacGregor (1864: pp. xi–xiii), and cf. at p. xiii: 'I have preferred strength to *mere* sweetness' (emphasis in original).

[96] MacGregor (1864: p. x).

suspect—broad coverage, but not *too* broad.[97] The exclusion of AP 1 on grounds of religious scruple was quickly ridiculed by Cracroft (1865: 302), in terms that must immediately strike the modern reader as bizarre but that Chapter 4 will retrospectively put in the context of Maga's epigrammatic empire: 'The days are past when the translation for literary ends of epigrams, however light in tone, could affect the religious feeling of this country.'

In the actual selection presented, however, death predominates (at 719 versions, 'Epitaphs' takes up more than a fifth of the Anthology content included in categories 1–8). This reflects the material MacGregor had to hand; his previous collection (1857) had after all been sepulchral, and its content is essentially reproduced here. Its pretext is noteworthy: the Greeks were much better at memorializing their dead than we are, because, for them, death really was the end:

In the ΕΠΙΤΥΜΒΙΑ [epitaphs] we are *confessedly* inferior to both Greek and Latin. Do we think *why* this is, and are we sufficiently thankful that it is so? Our Christianity makes the difference... FAITH bars us from encomiums of the departed, however near in blood or dear to friendship, faith dwells not on the love which is past and gone, but fixes on the hope to come, the hope which is certainty, for ours is the Promise, and ours the Beyond, of which the old world knew not.[98]

Classical death is here conceived as a series of exemplary tableaux in the grand Roman style, which by implication convey vibrant ('colourful') moral object lessons in the here and now:

the slain warrior on his shield—the martyr for freedom or faith—the disappointed in love or ambition—the leap of Sappho and the poison-cup of Socrates—Anacreon of the lyre, Leonidas with his 300—the asp of Cleopatra and the sword of Aelius—all, all is Death, yet how distinct and new is each several picture.[99]

The reviewers were on the money about the quality of MacGregor's versions: they are doggerel. Readability and good English come a distant second to scansion, and scansion is often horribly forced (run these examples through in your head a few times before attempting aloud):

> Boldly beneath my breast I bear sharp pain,
> And a hard clog's indissoluble chain...

---

[97] MacGregor (1864: p. x).

[98] MacGregor (1864: p. xiii) (emphases in original); cf. p. xii, 'almighty Death—now no longer almighty, but, through Christ, stingless and swallowed up in victory.'

[99] MacGregor (1864: pp. xi–xii), reproduced from MacGregor (1857: p. ii).

> Tho' ignorant and rustic she, nor such as Sappho sung,
> For dusky Andromede of Ind fierce love Perseus stung.

This in a version in which a cod-Elizabethan Philodemus is also made to praise his beloved's 'clipsome waist'.[100] The phrase had been singled out as unbearably artificial as long ago as 1816, in a generally polite Maga review of Leigh Hunt's *Story of Rimini*; Hunt was a major stylistic influence on Keats, and their linguistically innovative idiom, dubbed 'Cockney' by Maga regulars, was used as a stick with which to beat the latter poet at every opportunity.[101] Proper names are not infrequently mangled in the service of metre:

> My love, Magnesian Heraclite,
> Surpasses natural magnet quite...[102]

6. CONCLUSION

> The cause for learning would be benefited by the translation of the complete Anthology. Surely Major MacGreggor [*sic*] hardly flatters himself that his volume will find its way into the hands of women, children, and mere idlers...[103]

Responding not (as we might expect) to the thorny issue of translating obscenity, but to MacGregor's pious refusal to approach the 'sacred' epigrams of AP 1, this off-hand remark by Cracroft is symptomatic of the discourse surrounding and animating translation from the Greek Anthology around the middle of the nineteenth century. It had been twenty years and more since the elite constituencies serviced and constituted by the Reviews had first looked out in mild alarm and seen the emergence of a mass readership—however phantasmagorical that appearance may in fact have been (see Chapter 1)—yet here we are in 1865 with serene unconcern that the 'wrong' kind of reader may pick this book up and find inappropriate ideas therein. Only men—men of substance and

---

[100] MacGregor (1864: 14); choice of period idiom justified at p. xv.

[101] Kandl (2001: 7–9) sets up the issues nicely. This is not the last we will hear of Keats as a Conservative whipping boy. 'A hard clog' (MacGregor 1864: 66). For examples of tortured diction and sense, as opposed to scansion, see, e.g., 'The evil setting of the wet Arcturus unforeseen, | Thy sailing to a deadly course has, Theotimus! been' (p. 491); 'Who on craz'd iambs so could lure | his poet fire to spend' (p. 515).

[102] MacGregor (1964: 65); cf., e.g., at p. 133 'Magnus' for Maximus, at 137 'Herclides' for Heracleides.

[103] Cracroft (1865: 302), referring specifically to MacGregor's pious refusal to translate AP 1.

worth—will ever peruse these pages. While Cracroft's confidence on this occasion may in part be fuelled by the offputting bulk of MacGregor's production, the supposition behind it is constant, running from Wellesley's dismissal of *déclassé* loafers and swells through Burges's extended exercise in public-school prize-giving. As received through epigram, Classics is not being seen as women's or family reading matter—a striking anomaly in an age when sociable reading was the norm. Nor is it yet being viewed as having the potential to excite a socially inappropriate response from working-class readerships, let alone from within sexual subculture, through dissident reading strategies.

With Wellesley we see the gentlemanly spirit of epigram articulated through elite networking and facility in European high culture; with Mac-Gregor, through the ideology of the amateur, expressed both in the translator's own repeated self-characterizations—'I do not claim to be a Greek SCHOLAR' (capitalization in original)—and in the acquiescence of his reviewers. 'Dealing with classical literature as a dilettante' is a claim first and foremost about class and status entitlement, and only secondarily about academic qualification (not that there was yet any formal system of accreditation to begin with).[104] This claim to amateurism is reinforced by MacGregor's authorial self-fashioning as reliant on non-specialist reference works—'the ordinary sources of information, Potter, Lemprière, Smith, and others'—among them being Becker's educational novel, *Charicles*.[105]

The privileged background of the dilettante—a 'scholar' in the lower case—is also woven into the preferred indexing system of all three translators. For all that Jacobs's improved and reordered edition is their avowed touchstone, these mid-century Anthologists all index by Greek incipit, a practice that limits access to verification to readers from the 'right' social background. (Wellesley additionally indexes by author, but only because, as we have seen, he has a particular point to make about epigram as a European literary tradition.) That Burges supplies explanatory notes to his Selections might seem an aid to the Greek-less reader, until we look at their content:

The expression ἡμέτερος Πὰν seems rather strange here. Perhaps the author wrote-νεβρίδ᾽, ἔμην᾽ ὅτ᾽ ἔρως. Πὰν—'when love had maddened him—'Compare Epigr Inc. 619, ἢ καὶ σὴν Κύπρις ἔμηνε φρένα. . . .

---

[104] MacGregor (1857: p. iv; cf. 1864: p. ix), and noted without adverse comment by his reviewer, Anon. (1857b).
[105] MacGregor (1864: p. x, 'wishing to avoid learned pretensions', and cf. 1857: p. v). Use of *Charicles*: (1864: 76). While it may seem shockingly sloppy, MacGregor is not the only nineteenth-century translator to resort to this richly footnoted novel as a historical sourcebook.

This is the ingenious correction of Jacobs, who saw acutely that in τὸν Λιβάσι κούφαις lay hid Ἄλμασι τὸν κούφοις, similar to ἄλματι κούφῳ in Oppian, and κούφοις ἄλμασιν in Heliodorus. Others, perhaps, will prefer Ὀκλάσεσιν κούφοις: for ὀκλάζω and its derivatives were the proper words, applied to the leap of a frog, as shown by Pseudo-Babrias, Fab. 25. Καὶ βατράχων ὅμιλον εἶδον ἀκταίων, Βαθεῖαν εἰς ἰλὺν ὀκλαστὶ πηδώντων: for so found Suidas in his MS., who quotes the verse in Ὀκλαδίας: but as the Athos MS. reads ὀκλαδιστὶ, perhaps Socrates [sic] wrote—ὀκλάσεσι—[106]

This learned apparatus addresses exclusively the confirmed connoisseur of epigram, a well-schooled gentleman confident in his classical languages. As readers we are expected to share the editors' intimate familiarity with these poems in the original Greek, and with it their gut certainty that imitations and translations are mere faint reflections of 'that tongue "which has been held one of the best instruments for training the young mind" ... '.[107] We must remember these poems from our own schooldays, rose-tinged as for MacGregor through fond memory; and by remembering them may effect a temporary escape from the duties of the present (or, in the case of MacGregor in 1857, from the grief of family bereavements) into a carefree Etonian or Redingensian youth glossed in retrospect as a Hellenic idyll.[108] For MacGregor, the act of translation itself is intrinsically backward facing, an exercise in Merrie English rooted methodologically in the theory wars of the preceding century.[109] For all that his fellow editors may at times be forward-looking (Wellesley's modern languages) or gesture towards some limited form of broader inclusion (Burges's Bohn), the mid-century Anthology is a fantasy activated by privilege.

This is a privilege, too, that naturalizes itself by insisting on the timelessness and the ordinariness of the Anthology in its relation to modern daily life. If the epigrams of the Anthology are repetitive, says MacGregor, this merely foregrounds their occasionality: there is nothing new under the sun, and the Greeks first and best described the gamut of experiences universal to the human condition (the ideological whitewash is slapped on here in thick layers).[110] The claim that everything one could wish to know about ancient life and customs may be found in a literary

---

[106] Burges (1852: 413, 442), the latter on an epigram by ps.-Plato.

[107] Wellesley (1849: p. vii), quoting with enthusiasm the preface to Liddell and Scott.

[108] Epigram translation as amateur bereavement therapy: MacGregor (1857: p. v), a view endorsed by his reviewer: Anon. (1857b). On Victorian assimilation of Hellenic scenography into public-school nostalgia, see acerbically Jenkyns (1980: 212–18); Vandiver (2010: 36–42) thoughtfully sketches the affective patterns that underlay it.

[109] Usefully clear on this is Stark (1999: 67–77).

[110] MacGregor (1864: pp. x–xiii), citing in particular (pp. xii–xiii) the skoptic poets of AP 11; on 'timelessness' and 'human condition' as fundamental tools of conservative

text, making dirt archaeology an irrelevance, is itself an ideologically weighted position within a simmering culture war in nineteenth-century elite pedagogy.[111] Uniquely, by this account, the Anthology lets its socially privileged readers discover a 'real' and eternally *living* ancient Greece without getting their hands dirty.

'Enquire within upon everything' is a discourse still in its infancy at this faltering onset of epigram's reorientation towards the public at large; later writers on the Anthology will develop it much more fully. Mac-Gregor is both its keenest mid-century exponent (by far) and its least successful advocate. On a humorous poem by Macedonius,

> Spread thy wan cheeks with paint, Laodice!—
> So the world's vengeance just and full may be—
> But never ope thy lips—of teeth a row
> Who to fix there by utmost art can know? . . .

he straightfacedly comments, 'Hence it would appear that dentists were not then known.'[112] (This is really not the editor best qualified to be working on AP 11.)

Another discourse is by now much more securely established, to the extent that these mid-century authors take it as read: the soothing simplicity of Greek epigram, as rhetorically opposed to the pointed and paradoxical style of Martial (Chapter 1). MacGregor resorts to 'Anthology' to relieve executive stress because his culture knows that serenity lies therein.[113] What we are now in a position to see is how little this discourse connects with elite writers' and indeed elite readers' own formative immersion in Greek epigram, an experience that we know was traditionally weighted towards the most Martial-like Greek epigrams of all, the skoptic verses of AP 11, favourites of the school Selections. Instead, the translators' rhetoric recuperates and repurposes the French (enemy) negative discourse of insipid epigram 'à la Grecque'. It asserts a national stake in representing the Hellenic past through the Anthology, a

---

ideology, see the Cultural Materialist critics, e.g. Sinfield (1994a: 4): 'The "universal" Shakespeare usually means the one we want to recruit as ratification for our point of view'.

[111] As Beard 2001 shows using nineteenth-century Cambridge as her case study, literary Classics was notably reluctant to factor in any study of ancient history or material culture because these 'easy' subjects might dilute the brand; implicitly this is about mystique cloaking privilege.

[112] MacGregor (1864: 144 (poem), 165 (comment)); for similarly obtuse comment, cf. p. 162.

[113] Again, see MacGregor (1864: p. ix); and more fully: 'the relaxations of hard-worked life of uncongenial duties, which, without such and similar resources, I should certainly never have been able to discharge' (1857: p. iv).

stake that could be strengthened through fuller scholarship ('the cause for learning', above)—but simultaneously weakened, if this meant forfeiting a collective claim to amateur status. This underlying tension between academic authority/ownership and amateur authenticity/connection will recur later in our story, particularly in Chapter 6.

Far less securely pinned down at mid-century is epigram's chronology as an evident 'late' genre with a problematic curve. Merivale had already flagged this up as a matter of concern in 1833, deciding on Meleager as his terminus; Burges fudges the issue, counterbalancing the incidental fidelity of the school Selections (where length had entirely displaced date as a criterion for inclusion) with a 'Miscellaneous' Selection of his own devising, biased heavily towards older authors. MacGregor excludes later poems—but only some of them, and not consistently, since he hates leaving anything out.[114]

In strong contrast, Wellesley frees himself from the spectre of lateness and presents an optimistic genre history by uncoupling epigram from cultural context and Greek genre chronology. His arrangement instead presents a multiply recurring narrative of the progress of specific poems *between* cultures: each poem is its own miniature genre (model plus versions), and its presumptive curve approaches apogee in the present (even if the originals possess a certain inimitable something just by virtue of being in Greek). In Wellesley's hands, each poem describes a rising arc plotted by its moments of cultural transition, as it migrates through space and time from its Hellenic birthplace to Rome, to the Italy of the Renaissance, and onward through a predominantly German Romanticism to claim its place in English literary tradition. The ambition of Wellesley's ambit is such that no later translator will follow his lead, including his optimistic bypassing of the bell curve of inevitability. For now, with the century moving past its mid-point and into the middle of the Victorian era, where to place and how to shape that bell curve remain very much open questions; and the fundamental question of how to read epigram as literature of, and for, the present day has hardly begun to be addressed. This creates room for manœuvre, and the author with whom we will engage in the next two chapters is ready to take full advantage of it.

---

[114] MacGregor (1864: pp. x, xii).

Part II

Wilde's Meleager

3

'The Most Precious Relic'

1. 'THIS WORLD OF PHANTOMS': ET IN ATTICA, EGO

I feel the truth of all I said to you on the downs one afternoon when I discussed my sentence of ostracism. *I am afraid of forming a permanent double consciousness in my own mind, of being related to this world of phantoms, & moving meanwhile in the world of fact. But the phantoms are so beautiful to me & so real.* Last night we had a dinner party, & over our wine I was listening to a certain Dr Marshall droning in a saccharine medical medicinal voice about local politics, when suddenly Myronides appeared before me, as he fell on Theron's neck & the dawn overspread the hills of Attica. *It was too good. I enjoyed my double consciousness; for I talked to Dr Marshall about Lewis Fry & John Myles, & all the while I heard Athenian night breezes shuddering in the myrtle groves of Harmodius.*[1]

The point at which the text falls silent is the point at which its ideological project may be disclosed.[2]

The date is 29 July 1868; the place, Clifton, an affluent suburb of Bristol; and the mode, confessional. The essayist John Addington Symonds, 27 years of age and known for some promising work on Dante, writes a letter to his intimate friend since university days, Henry Graham Dakyns, since 1862 a schoolmaster at the newly established progressive public school Clifton College (where he introduced the playing of rugby) and later to win modest fame as the translator of Xenophon. In five years' time, when the London publishing firm of Smith, Elder brings out the collected First Series of the lectures and essays Symonds is even now beginning to write, Dakyns will be its dedicatee; another twenty years on, and with their author only weeks from death, the third and final edition of *Studies of the Greek Poets* will again address itself to Dakyns as 'a sign of my unalterable

---

[1] J. A. Symonds (1967–9: i. 829) (emphases added).　　[2] Sinfield (1994b: 9).

affection after the lapse of what is counted as a generation in the life of humanity'.[3]

It is no surprise that the 1893 dedication takes the form of a letter from overseas, written in this instance from Venice (19 March). Symonds spent much of his adult life abroad, making his permanent family home in the pretty Swiss Alpine town of Davos for his health (he was a hypochondriac but also genuinely very ill), but making repeated forays to Italy to feed the appetites of spirit and flesh, and Venice held special memories for him on both counts.[4] He did not return from the visit of 1893; a month to the day after his letter to Dakyns about the third edition he was dead. His grave is in the Protestant Cemetery at Rome, within coughing distance of Shelley (about whom in the meantime he had written a well-liked book); the same resting place holds Keats, like him a casualty of tuberculosis.[5]

Symonds and his friends were tireless correspondents, taking advantage of the improved postal service of the 1860s and 1870s to sustain the easy comradeship and frank enthusiasm of their shared undergraduate days into an extended intimacy in which the private self could be unburdened. Initially the bulk of the network traffic was commercial; as with modern LGB identities in the early Internet age (1980s to mid-1990s), an outlaw elite carved out a space for self-articulation in the cracks of a new system that the majority of the population lacked the technological literacy to access. Distance was now no obstacle, and some things were easier to put on paper than to say out loud, making possible new kinds of self-representation within virtual communities defined by common interests; identities could now be written into being through close and sustained dialogue, and an enlarged epistolary habit soon became one of the culturally legible signs of elite gay identity.[6] Symonds

---

[3] J. A. Symonds (1920: p. v), riffing on Horace on the passage of time ('*Eheu Postume*'). For the sake of uniformity and convenience, all citations to the third edition refer to this, its final imprint, for which the text was repaginated for publication in a single volume.

[4] Grosskurth (1964: 236–44) evokes the scene with vivid detail; see also Aldrich (1993: 78–9, 84–5), and cf. the latter's accounts of twentieth-century exiles' love affairs with the city at pp. 92–3 (Corvo), 122–3 (Cocteau).

[5] Shelley is an important figure for Symonds generally—his biography of Shelley aside (J. A. Symonds 1878a), *New Italian Sketches* (1884) is one long love letter to the dead poet—and their combined legacies push the buttons of conservative critics in the worst way; see Ch. 4.

[6] Booth (2002). 'The coming of the railways and the reforms of the Post Office made possible new ways of living. A community could be sustained by those living at a distance...The extension of postal services had particularly important implications for minority groupings; the like-minded could now develop their contacts' (2002: 283). On the make-up of early postal traffic, with the striking observation that even after the 1871 Education Act 'no more than two per cent [of children] were given limited instruction in how to lay out a letter' (2002: 284)—cf.

alone dashed off many hundreds of letters throughout his life. The modern editors of his three fat volumes of correspondence, Herbert Schueller and Robert Peters, clarify the Grecian allusivity in his Clifton letter of 1868 through good old-fashioned archival digging: Theron and Myronides are characters not from a classical canon text but from Symonds's own febrile erotic imagination, as expressed in privately printed verse pamphlets. Posterity has written off Symonds as a poet of any merit, though he felt he had the soul of one, and his verses were rarely discreet; friends with an eye to his social reputation and fragile health pressed him, in the end successfully, to lock away anything explicit enough to be used against him.[7]

At dinner with the unfortunate Dr Marshall, Symonds was not so much seeing double as willing himself into a mental hall of mirrors. The heady scenarios of his private poetry overwrite the material and social realities of the suburban villa—but these poems themselves are already explicitly conceived as dream quests, in which the over-sensitized ego-narrator projects his ghost image into a hyperreal yet forever unattainable fantasy of ancient Greece.[8] Overlaid on mundane existence, 'double consciousness' lets Symonds escape from one world—one life—into an addictively sweeter alternative, while still being present in the moment. In this augmented reality, Dr Marshall's 'droning' becomes a background hum, no more intrusive than the cicada's, mingling with the breezes of Attica as Theron surrenders to his lover in between the starter and the fish course. The Greece of his imagination—in which Myronides and Theron are recurring characters—is more 'beautiful' and (with Keatsian Romanticism available as subtext) *therefore* more 'real' than the lamplit interior of Clifton Hill House. It filters reality and makes it much better—so much so that one might well never want to leave.[9]

again the Internet age, initially the preserve of a libertarian–contrarian 'hacker' culture defined by uncommon technological literacy and subverting a military–scientific information infrastructure. Orrells (2011a: 45) identifies letter-writing and letter-reading as a leitmotif of gay male identity in literary fiction as well as fact between 1870 and 1914. Explicit awareness of epistolarity as subcultural writing at, e.g., J. A. Symonds (1967–9: ii. 991, iii. 544).

[7] On how the renowned philosopher Henry Sidgwick (another lifelong friend from college days) kept Symonds out of potentially very serious trouble, see Schultz (2000); on Symonds as erotic poet, Venables (2000). No modern critic has a good word to say for Symonds's poetry, but as an undergraduate he won Oxford's Newdigate prize, previously held by (among others) the literary titans Ruskin and Arnold; Arnold was on the panel, voted in his favour, and volunteered useful feedback (J. A. Symonds 1984: 118). Eighteen years later, it would be Wilde's.

[8] Booth (2002) is wonderfully productive of thought here.

[9] 'Beauty is truth, truth beauty...': Theron's wooing of Myronides, macabre to my taste (to prove the superiority of his love to that of rival suitors he cuts off his thumb), is the

A life-changing visit to Sorrento in 1864 equipped the young Symonds to flesh out his imaginary Arcadia with memories of its closest available contemporary analogue in real life, the Bay of Naples—a classical landscape populated with 'ardent' young men, the sight of whose heroic physique aroused in him a painful yearning. The parental home to which he would then return (to be trapped by dull conversationalists at parties) was a 'cold' and 'narrow' trap from which willed fantasy seemed his only escape:

> Here might I rest for ever!
>
> .   .   .   .   .
>
> Were not these splendours made for me,
> Who nursed from earliest infancy
> Mid narrow walls, with cramping rules,
> In mist and clinging cold, have freed
> My spirit like a wingéd steed
> To bear me far from tedious fools?[10]

Hellenic hyperreality took him out of himself—exactly the motivation that, as read by the historian of sexuality Daniel Orrells, impelled Michel Foucault to embark on his own much better-known survey of Greek eros a century later.[11]

Greece had been hyperreal to Symonds for some years by now, at least if we believe the juvenile epiphany written up late in life in his *Memoirs*, a

subject of 'The Festival of Harmodius and Aristogeiton, or The Love of Theron', at J. A. Symonds (1878b: ii. 32–41). We meet them again later in the volume's closing poem, 'The Elysium of Greek Lovers', in which Love (Eros conceived as a patron of boy-love) reveals to Symonds in a dream vision the homophile Isle of the Blest (the 'blissful shore' referred to in passing: 1878b: i. 30). Theron has been transformed there into a pomegranate tree, around whose branches Myronides twines himself in the form of a 'moon-white' clematis (1878b: i. 52). The pomegranate is already part of the hyperreal visual fantasy, a landscape fixture freighted with symbolic meaning: at 1878b: i. 24, and at p. 5 of the undated but revealingly titled pamphlet *Genius Amoris Amari Visio*, its fruit signifies the destructive implacability of merely physical lust. The poems had been written a decade earlier, in 1868, at Clifton: J. A. Symonds (1984: 180).

[10] Symonds (1875) (in a poem titled 'Sorrento'), presumably written during his visit there in January–February 1864, the year after his inglorious Magdalen Fellowship. In a letter of February 1864 to his Oxford friend and recent travelling companion A. O. Rutson, he writes admiringly: 'The people are finer and more beautiful than in other parts of Italy...They seem to retain some of the old Greek loveliness of shape...the young men look like Achilles with deep ardent eyes' (J. A. Symonds 1967–9: i. 439). Rutson was a frequent correspondent, particularly in the early years; see Grosskurth (1964: 46, 78–9).

[11] Orrells (2011a: 268), on Foucault's introduction to *The Use of Pleasure* (1977): 'His is a curiosity not to know himself (his sexual self) but to lose the way of himself—indeed to lose the reason and mind of himself...The most famous historian of madness here (rhetorically) flirts with madness, with a wish to lose his senses and to find another self through his essay into antiquity.'

text suppressed for the better part of a century after his death but originally envisaged for widespread publication as propaganda for the cause of homosexual liberation.[12] Down from Harrow to London on a permitted absence ('exeat') during term and at a loose end for the evening, a 17-year-old youth looks into a volume of Plato and finds himself:

> We were reading Plato's *Apology* in the sixth form. I bought Cary's crib, and took it with me to London on an *exeat* in March. My hostess, a Mrs Bain, who lived in Regent's Park, treated me to a comedy one evening at the Haymarket. I forget what the play was ... When we returned from the play, I went to bed and began to read my Cary's Plato. It so happened that I stumbled on the *Phaedrus*. I read on and on, till I reached the end. Then I began the *Symposium*; and the sun was shining on the shrubs outside the ground-floor room in which I slept, before I shut the book up.
>
> I have related these insignificant details because that night was one of the most important nights of my life ... Here in the *Phaedrus* and the *Symposium*—in the myth of the Soul and the speeches of Pausanias, Agathon and Diotima—I discovered the true *liber amoris* at last, the revelation I had been waiting for, the consecration of a long-cherished idealism. It was just as though the voice of my own soul spoke to me through Plato, as though in some antenatal experience I had lived the life of philosophical Greek lover.[13]

The mature Symonds here retrospectively homes in on, dramatizes, and indeed sacralizes the essential narrative crux of any modern coming-out story: the moment of transformative self-realization at which one suddenly 'just knows' the truth of one's sexuality, and thereby (fulfilling the commandment of the Oracle at Delphi) knows oneself. Here is Symonds's personal point of entry into Theron's 'myrtle groves of Harmodius' (a name that instantly cues up for the cognoscenti a patron saint of classical gay heroics). Whatever its truth-value, this confessional performance slots into a standard template of Victorian queer self-fashioning: then

---

[12] The *Memoirs* open (J. A. Symonds 1984: 29–30, written May 1889 at Venice) by invoking a solitary, chance, and posthumous reader, but the 'message in a bottle' gambit is a familiar literary device; Symonds had publication firmly in mind pretty much all the way through working them up from his old diaries and letters, including at this time. In August 1890 he remarks that it is only 'now—when the thing is almost done—[that] I do not see how it could be published', and another year (1891) brings cautious optimism; he now hopes that the work 'may yet be published: if its candour permits publication' (1967–9: iii. 490, 563). A couple of pages from the end of the *Memoirs*, he prospectively lists them among his recent publications (1984: 281).

[13] J. A. Symonds (1984: 99). Three years later he reread the *Phaedrus* in the text-with-commentary edited by Godfrey Stallbaum for D. Nutt's *Bibliotheca Graeca* series (2nd edn, 1857), racing through its Greek in two days plus one evening, as indicated by extant marginalia in his hand; amazingly, the book was a gift from his father.

as now, telling tales on oneself lies at the heart of coming out as a social practice, and the coming-out story as a rule-bounded genre of self-(melo)dramatization is basic to collective as well as to individual identity formation.[14] A few years later, and independently of Symonds's account, Wilde was to frame the crux of his own personal *Bildungsroman* in similarly mythic terms, helping inscribe the moment of self-realization through reading as a mainstay of the gay autobiographic genre.[15]

Prospectively addressing here a broad reading public, the mature Symonds of the early 1890s plays his youthful moment of epiphany for maximum sympathy as well as impact, by pinning it to a classical author who had in the meantime been thoroughly assimilated and vetted—Plato, translated and naturalized for the Victorians by his beloved old tutor Benjamin Jowett.[16] This is more than mere name-dropping of an author whose text offers conveniently upbeat references to love between men, although that is certainly its main motivation. The form of Symonds's anecdote invites a Plato-literate readership (and thanks to Jowett this could now be practically anybody) to piggyback on a formative experience that could have come straight out of the *Republic*. Suddenly recognizing the London apartment as mere material reality, a shadow of the world of Hellenic Forms, Symonds escapes from the Cave of his unexamined early self.

If we look back to the letter to Dakyns with which we opened, even this moment of notionally private experiential self-disclosure turns out to be part of a narrative system structured on allusion. This time, the key text for Symonds's augmented reality is not Plato but Théophile Gautier's notorious novel of polymorphous infatuations, *Mlle de Maupin* (1835), championed by the hardly less notorious Baudelaire and (in tandem with its programmatic introductory essay) a foundational work of nineteenth-century Aestheticism. This is where Wilde, too, draws his inspiration, as reported by his friend and fellow Irishman Frank Harris:

I was nearly sixteen when the wonder and beauty of the old Greek life began to dawn upon me. Suddenly I seemed to see the white figures throwing purple

---

[14] See, in particular, Plummer (1995) and McDermott (2008), and cf. Dollimore (1991: 12); on melodramatic self-narration as a constituent behaviour in Victorian homosexual subculture, see Buckton (1998), with specific references to Symonds at, e.g., pp. 99–106. Blanshard (2010: 145) reads Symonds's Platonic secret-origin story as straight reportage.

[15] 'The erotic revelation is also a cultural initiation': see (brilliantly) Evangelista (2006: 232) on Symonds, Wilde, and sexual self-realization as a shared narrative trope. 'For both Symonds and—as we shall see—Wilde, going Greek offered, in the most basic sense, a deliberate means of self-representation' (McDermott 2008: 24).

[16] 'His translations were small masterpieces of English prose that brought the dialogues into the mainstream of good literature in the same way that Pope's translation had transformed Homer into an English classic' (F. M. Turner 1981: 416).

shadows on the sun-baked palaestra—'bands of nude youths and maidens'—you remember Gautier's words—'moving across a background of deep blue as on the frieze of the Parthenon'.[17]

Harris himself, who shared Wilde's early devotion to this hallucinatory overlay of Hellenic softcore, was later to repent of his seduction into youthful error and repudiate Gautier's influence as atheistical poison. The prodigal son came home: 'Born rebels even have to realize that [Christ's] Love is the way.'[18] Hyperreal and intertextual, these bands of youths and maidens will re-enter our story later in the chapter, with Meleager.

2. SYMONDS AS OXFORD CLASSICIST

> On the contrary, Professor Jowett seems to reserve most of his admiration for the *Symposium* . . . which, however perfect it may be as a work of art, degenerates at last into a drunken orgy, and is filled, at least in the speech of Alcibiades, with sentences of unutterable profligacy . . . for our own part we would rather far that this discussion on Love had ended with the sublime declaration of Socrates which he had heard from Diotima . . .[19]
>
> The doublefacedness of Aphrodite. To me she is Urania & to him Pandemos: but one statue smiles on both.[20]

Symonds may not have been a great poet, but Balliol (1858–62) turned him into a terrific Hellenist. Taken in hand by Jowett (an experience he recalled as transformative), he could quote obscure Greek authors from memory and sometimes dreamed in Latin. Following a First in Greats, the best in his year, he took the Chancellor's Essay Prize for a topic in what we would now call classical reception studies: Platonism, appropriately

---

[17] Harris (1916: ii. 29). For the palaestra as a site of seduction in ancient Greek pederastic discourse, see AP 12.222; I am sure Symonds had.

[18] 'I, too, read Gautier in Paris and pages of his *Mlle de Maupin* still stick in my memory; like [the scandal-courting Irish modernist writer George] Moore I could boast that "the stream which poured from the side of the Crucified One and made a red girdle round the world, never bathed me in its flood". I, too, "love gold and marble and purple and bands of nude youths and maidens swaying on horses without bridle or saddle against a background of deep blue as on the frieze of the Parthenon". But afterwards . . . I came to understand that Jerusalem and not Athens is the sacred city and that one has to love Jesus and his gospel of love and pity or one will never come to full stature' (Harris 1919: 136).

[19] Anon (1871).

[20] From a letter to Dakyns, 26 November 1866 (J. A. Symonds 1967–9: i. 680); 'he' must be Arthur, his infatuation of the moment.

enough, in the Renaissance. That same autumn (1862), and despite having been seriously ill over the summer, he competed for and won an open fellowship at Magdalen, beating a strong field.[21] Although poor health meant he could not hold it for long, his classical expertise continued to make him useful as a book-reviewer, and, when in 1871 his former tutor published his landmark translation of the works of Plato into English, Symonds's rendering of the Presocratics found a place there.[22]

When Symonds came up to Oxford, Classics at the university was beginning to emerge from the long dry spell of introspection and scholarly underachievement that had been brought on in large part by the mania for prose and especially verse comp.[23] Jowett was busy changing all that, and putting Plato at the heart of the reformed Oxford experience in a way that would dramatically raise the public profile of Greek philosophy and give it a new civic role in subsequent nineteenth-century engagement with classical antiquity.[24] This was not cause for universal rejoicing at Oxford or elsewhere. *The Times* was not in the habit of giving long book reviews, but Jowett's subsequent translation of the whole of Plato into English merited a full-page warning (quoted above) of a work fraught with moral dangers, all the more so because 'nearly perfect' in execution. The Devil has all the best tunes, and the translator's idiom made the old pagan philosopher sound as soothingly reasonable as an Oxford don. (The reviewer complains that Jowett should have included Christianizing exegeses to put Plato's doctrines, especially on the immortality of the soul, in their proper place as inferior harbingers of 'Christian revelation'.)

By 1871, this temporary wariness of Plato was unsurprising to anyone in the know: Oxford had become the hub of an important homophile network, and of a whole new way of thinking about masculine identities,

[21] Schultz (2004: 394). As observed by Orrells (2011a: 178–9), Symonds's take on what we would now call classical reception studies was notably supple and sophisticated. He was not nearly as impressed with his achievements as were his contemporaries: in the *Memoirs* he berates himself for laziness both at school and at university, from which he says he 'emerged a wretchedly inadequate scholar' (1984: 220–1). The top First (1984: 121); winning the Magdalen open fellowship (1984: 129).

[22] Symonds (1967–9: ii. 284; i. 683, 689, 633).

[23] See Ch. 2 and Brink (1986: 129–40, 149); the statutory reforms of 1854 are a foundational moment in this process of modernization, but in this context we should view them in concert with the installation of Plato as a Greats author in the reformed examination system of 1853: Dowling (1994: 68).

[24] On the new prominence of Plato and Aristotle, a marked reversal of eighteenth-century habit, see briefly F. M. Turner (1989: 75–6); on Jowett as prime mover of Plato-with-everything at Oxford, Evangelista (2006: 232–3). Dowling (1994) has much of value to say on this—e.g. at pp. 68–9.

rooted in a newly serious and topical reading of Plato as a valid ethical authority independent of Scripture. 'Rival attempts to co-opt the Platonic legacy were everywhere', but Jowett's Oxford was their epicentre, with Pater, Symonds, and (later) Wilde as major players. All three of the latter read Plato against the grain of accepted sexual morality, seeking to uncover the larger truth of his and their identities in his culturally weighty text.[25]

In his *Memoirs*, and with palpable nostalgia for Balliol days spent under the sway of Platonic idealism, Symonds recalls writing torrid undergraduate verse on the dreamily personified 'Genius of Greek Love', a form of Eros conceived as racially characteristic of the ancient Greeks in their own place and time; in Jowett's eroto-philosophic Grove of Academe, that vanished world seemed to live again.[26] These Oxford experiences are important to bear in mind, not so much because biography casts light on the ever-receding phantom of authorial intent, but rather because, although what happens in Oxford stays in Oxford, one's peer group never forgets, and because shared habits of thought formed at university tend to stick: once an Oxford man, always an Oxford man.[27] The secret of the university's sexual subculture in those years was always open for the contemporaries who mattered, most of whom had been there (and if not there then to Cambridge, a university whose own dissident Hellenic enthusiasms have yet to be properly charted).[28] Since the initial publication of *Studies* primarily addressed the Review-reading classes, and many of its essays first saw print in those same journals, the Oxford gossip of Symonds's generation is potentially part of the competence that members of this socially distinctive primary readership will have brought to his text.

The initial Oxford context also gave an airing to material, part of which would later end up in *Studies*, as the essay 'The Genius of Greek Art'. Its genesis as a paper read to 'Old Mortality', an anything-goes

---

[25] The fundamental study of Oxford's role as a seed-bed of modern homosexual identities is, of course, Dowling (1994); see also briefly (e.g.) Dellamora (1990: 102) and, on Plato and identity politics, Evangelista (2006: 231). On the vital interest of Plato to Victorian philosophical debates on ethical norms, see Irwin (1992) in the useful edited collection by Schultz, whose monograph (2004) on Sidgwick is a wonderfully rich resource. 'Rival attempts': Schultz (2004: 106); Oxford as epicentre: (2004: 341). Wilde was an attentive reader of Plato as an undergraduate: e.g. at (1989: 109, 121, 146–7).

[26] J. A. Symonds (1967–9: i. 123); on how transcendental Oxford Hellenism shaped Symonds, Dowling (1994: 76–81).

[27] Schultz (2004: 283); Mikhail (1979) gives ample material to back this up.

[28] On Hellenism at Cambridge, see Schultz (2004: 284). Pemble (2005: 224) picks up on this, and on how the Oxford-centrism of Victorian studies buys into Victorian Oxford's own busy image-packaging.

debating society, will be addressed in the next section, on Symonds and Walter Pater. In the decade or so between Old Mortality and *Studies*, he continued to tinker with a manuscript that would eventually be divided up for publication in two very different types of output: the public-facing *Studies*, and the strictly clandestine *A Problem in Greek Ethics* (henceforth *Greek Ethics*), a short treatise printed privately in a tiny print run for (as we shall see) the consideration of a handful of trusted friends. This treatise, subsequently complemented by the slightly more widely circulated *A Problem in Modern Ethics*, was the first serious study in English of male same-sex attraction in antiquity. In the later twentieth century it was eagerly recuperated as a foundational text by historians of the modern lesbian and gay movement; as such it is much discussed in the scholarly literature, but in its time its impact was negligible.[29]

Calling homosexuality a 'problem in' ancient and modern 'ethics' was tactically vague, but not disingenuous or even really euphemistic; with Oxford as a shared frame of reference, it immediately confirmed the topical relevance of what was being discussed. The linked questions of what Greek ethics had actually been, and how (if at all) they could be applied in the present, were philosophically important and of the moment, with Henry Sidgwick taking a strong stand against T. H. Green within what was very much a 'live' social controversy on the compatibility of the Aristotelian Mean with Christian duty; Symonds was personally close to both men (Green married his sister).[30] Symonds's notionally intended readers, although he never took the plunge and shared it with more than one of them (the sexologist Havelock Ellis), are medical men; this is by now an old pretext for otherwise inadmissible content but may also genuinely address itself to society's main opinion-formers on a topical issue, for the gist of *Greek Ethics* is that the recent medicalization of homosexuality as a systemic pathology susceptible to objective diagnosis does not stand up in the light of the evidence from ancient culture. The biological doomsayers equate homosexuality with psychic and somatic disorder, and scaremonger it as a harbinger of racial degeneration; Symonds counters with comparative anthropology through the lens of Jowett's Plato.[31]

[29] Holliday (2000) sets up the issues nicely.

[30] Irwin (1992). Ethics is a burning concern for the Symonds of the correspondence: '[I] believe that on the method of Ethics will depend the future of the human race. One such discovery as Newton's law of gravitation in the field of morals would advance us aeons forward in all that concerns spiritual life' (J. A. Symonds 1967–9: ii. 322).

[31] 'Plato's writings…historicized male love—that is, they acted as documents which recorded the existence, ethics, and modes of practice of ancient homoeroticism; and they provided a very eminent blueprint that sympathetic modern commentators used to theorize

One crucially helpful point was that same-sex attraction had already been influentially claimed as Greek, and thus as Western and masculine— even hyper-masculine. Specifically, homosexuality was Dorian. Karl Otfried Müller's *Die Dorier*, a monument of scholarship, was an influential work in its English translation and soberly attested the durability of pederastic relations as a Spartan martial virtue. The discussion occupies only a very small part of the book (ii. 306–13) but is eloquently articulated, communicating to a broad readership something of the passionate self-identification with the idealized heroic erastēs prevalent in sections of nineteenth-century German philology, within a national reception culture that already claimed the Dorians (historically cast as warlike invaders of Greece from the North) as racial kin.[32] 'This pure connexion' is justified with reference to the social institutions within which the male citizen–soldier was formed, casting male eros as the necessary precondition to the 'Mental and Bodily Training in Sparta and Other Doric States' outlined in the chapter that immediately follows.[33]

We see Müller's distinctive advocacy of military Dorianism developed and embellished in *Greek Ethics*, attributing to its heroic pairs of Greek lovers a 'fire and valour' in the cause of their nation and at the root of Western identity:

παιδεραστία in Hellas assumed Hellenic characteristics, and cannot be confounded with any merely Asiatic form of luxury...

Greek love was, in its origin and essence, military. Fire and valour, rather than tenderness or tears, were the external outcome of this passion; nor had μαλακία, effeminacy, a place in its vocabulary...

We have seen in the foregoing section that παιδεραστία at Athens was closely associated with liberty, manly sports, severe studies, enthusiasm, self-sacrifice, self-control, and deeds of daring, by those who cared for those things.[34]

And what patriotic reader could not so care? This was potentially useful counter-propaganda. The equation by mainstream culture of male homosexuality with effeminacy was not quite set in stone even as late

<hr/>

about the rehabilitation of an aesthetic of male love, and indeed to argue for social tolerance, in the nineteenth century' (Evangelista 2006: 235).

[32] On the profound influence of Müller on Greek studies in mid-nineteenth-century Britain, see Kennedy (2001: 16). The German homophile context: DeJean (1989b); Davis (1996) helps clarify where Müller is coming from as a systematizer and (through translation) an exporter of an established scholarly discourse. See briefly, too, Challis (2010: 99), on Müller's influential insistence on the North European racial character of his Dorians.

[33] Müller (1830: ii. 313–29).

[34] J. A. Symonds (1883: 8, 12, 59), and cf., e.g., p. 15 on 'hardy' Greek love, p. 16 on Dorian 'martial comradeship'; Müller cited as the standard authority: p. 19.

as 1883, when *Greek Ethics* was at long last printed, but it was definitely there; it built on, and imported unwelcome baggage from, an older political discourse that troped effeminacy as a fifth column or enemy within.[35] In explicit contradiction of this prejudice, Symonds's gay lovers are virile and patriotic. (In a not dissimilar but typically obfuscatory mode, Walter Pater finds the *ne plus ultra* of heroic Dorian self-sacrifice in Harmodius and Aristogeiton, 'young assassins, moving, with more than fraternal unity'—hardly the most logically consistent of illustrations considering where they are from.[36]) With Arnold's all-conquering polarity of Hellenism and Hebraism as its backdrop, it was Oxford Hellenism that gave men such as Pater and Wilde the tools to counter the residual ideological baggage of this small-'R' republican discourse that troped sexual difference as a betrayal of the body politic.[37]

Symonds's theorization of a non-pathological, culturally situated homosexuality had one more trick up its sleeve, and the source was again Plato. In *Greek Ethics*, and calling on the *Symposium* and *Phaedrus* as his principal witnesses, Symonds distinguishes two distinct types of male homosexual love in antiquity: Pandemic and Uranian Eros. While Pandemic pederasty could be found in every historical period, and in any of the great metropolises towards which inverts drifted as though by a homing instinct, Uranian pederasty was characteristic of the Greeks and the Greeks alone:

Resuming the results of the last four sections, we find two separate forms of masculine passion clearly marked in early Hellas—a noble and a base, a spiritual and a sensual. To the distinction between them the Greek conscience was acutely sensitive; and this distinction, in theory at least, subsisted throughout their history. They worshipped Eros, as they worshipped Aphrodite, under the twofold titles of οὐράνιος and πάνδημος; and, while they regarded the one love with the highest approval, as the source of courage and greatness of soul, they never publicly approved the other. It is true, as will appear in the sequel of this essay, that boy-love in its grossest form was tolerated in historic Hellas with an

[35] Bristow (1995: 1–5) surveys constructions of effeminacy in the nineteenth century in relation to inherited prejudices, arguing that the effeminacy–homosexuality link becomes definitive only with the media circus surrounding the Wilde trials; this is when 'homosexuality' is typecast for public consumption as a pathology symptomatic of wider social degeneracy, the latter being a classic *fin de siècle* concern that in the 1870s is simply not yet in play. While public trials of one kind and another are clearly important (see pp. 33–4), the effeminate–homosexual nexus is clearly already circulating in public discourse of the 1870s (J. E. Adams 1995: 150). This should make us wary of identifying neat 'turning points' at which one social paradigm of sexual identity replaces another, a model that elides the complexly negotiated nature of sexualities. There is no one moment at which (say) 'the invert' becomes 'the homosexual' for all parties concerned (Sinfield 1994b: 13; cf. 8).
[36] Pater (1901: 276–9).   [37] Dowling (1994: 78–9).

indulgence which it never found in any Christian country, while heroic comrade-ship remained an ideal hard to realise, and scarcely possible beyond the limits of the strictest Dorian sect. Yet the language of philosophers, historians, poets and orators is unmistakable. All testify alike to the discrimination between vulgar and heroic love in the Greek mind...

With the baser form of παιδεραστία I shall have little to do in this essay. Vice of this kind does not vary to any great extent, whether we observe it in Athens or in Rome, in Florence of the sixteenth or in Paris of the nineteenth century; nor in Hellas was it more noticeable than elsewhere, except for its comparative publicity. The nobler type of masculine love developed by the Greeks is, on the contrary, unique in the history of the human race... I shall use the term *Greek Love*, understanding thereby a passionate and enthusiastic attachment subsisting between man and youth, recognised by society and protected by opinion, which, though it was not free from sensuality, did not degenerate into mere licentiousness.[38]

This polarity had had a long gestation. Years before Arnold preached Culture against Anarchy, Symonds was already deploying a very clear and fully worked-out distinction between Uranian and Pandemic eros, in correspondence that shows how nascent propositions about homosexual identity were being negotiated within elite subcultural networks over distance.[39] In propounding a 'Heavenly' or 'Higher' eros, and by implica-tion making it largely if not exclusively the reserve of homosexual rela-tions, Symonds floats the idea of a culturally positive gay identity—albeit to a microscopically tiny constituency of readers. A mere ten copies of *Greek Ethics* were printed, finally, in 1883, and the quires were not actually bound till 1885 at Davos, by which time Symonds was safely off the British scene; he distributed them with great care among trusted personal contacts, keeping several in hand. Forty years later, when the definitive bibliography was being planned, his literary executors were able to account for each and every one. In Symonds's lifetime and thereafter, its readership thus presumably numbered in single digits.[40]

---

[38] J. A. Symonds (1883: 10–11).

[39] The terminology is explicit at J. A. Symonds (1967–9: i. 677), written to Dakyns in 1866, and he is clearly presuming the same basic distinction in his famous letter earlier that same year on Platonic eros: (i. 614). On the subculturally negotiated character of these attempts at erotic schematization, see Booth (2002: 292).

[40] The distribution and use of *Greek Ethics* thus stands in stark contrast to those of *Modern Ethics* (fifty copies printed), which we are told circulated busily within the 1890s 'homosexual underground' (Kemp 2000: 56–8). Two of the ten copies are now in the Pierpont Morgan Library in New York, one of them Symonds's own working copy, with handwritten revisions towards the version subsequently printed in Havelock Ellis's soon-pulped first imprint of *Sexual Inversion*. A pasted note on the flyleaf written by Symonds (annotated in 1925 with tracking notes) assigns copies to Dakyns, Jowett, Gosse, Burton,

Greek Ethics is not much more than a pamphlet; if we look into its origin, we find that it is only half the treatise it could have been. Where its 'missing' half had ended up in the meantime is, given the hush-hush nature of *Greek Ethics*, utterly surprising: minimally tweaked and by way of an intermediary essay draft, it became the red-rag-to-a-bull concluding chapter of the first series of *Studies*, 'The Genius of Greek Art'.[41]

3. AESTHETICS OF DESIRE: SYMONDS, PATER, AND 'WINCKELMANN'

> Ah me! words fail. I bow my head and seem
> To be but singing in a golden dream.
> I cannot bring again the days of Greece,
> Or raise to life beloved Eudiades:
>
> .   .   .   .   .
>
> In vain. I faint. Yet listen, and endure:
> The men of whom I speak were strong and pure.
> No shame oppressed them: they could fight and fall;
> And the whole earth mourned at their funeral.
>
> (J. A. Symonds, *Eudiades*, written at Clifton
> in July–August 1868)[42]

Calling on myth and literature, aesthetic Platonism takes homosexuality away from the emergent sexological approach and into the wider cultural field.[43]

The essay with which Symonds concluded the First Series of *Studies* in 1873, 'The Genius of Greek Art', began life in a paper delivered to the

and the Uranian poet Charles Sayle, '& keep 5 in stock'; two more are sent later on to Ellis and to Symonds's old college friend Claude Cobham, on whom see briefly Grosskurth (1964: 66).

[41] J. A. Symonds (1984: 173–4) reports that 'an essay on Platonic love', in progress in 1867 (surely from the Old Mortality performance touched on in the next section) but never properly finished, was the source of both the surreptitious pamphlet and the high-profile book chapter: 'This essay remained in ms for a long while. Part of it I used for my chapter, in *Studies of the Greek Poets*, on the Greek spirit. The rest I rewrote at Clifton in 1874, and privately printed under the title of "A Problem in Greek Ethics"' (nine years later!). Cf. Grosskurth (1964: 125).

[42] J. A. Symonds (1878b: i. 20–1); the long delay between composition and publication (of a very limited kind) is not atypical of Symonds. Although I give citation details to the original publications, Symonds's verse is most accessibly sampled through the invaluable John Addington Symonds Pages maintained by Rictor Norton <http://rictornorton.co.uk/symonds/> (accessed 14 April 2013).

[43] Evangelista (2006: 244).

Old Mortality debating society in June 1862. (We saw in the previous section what became of that material in the meantime.) The society had a reputation for fearless disregard of social and religious convention, and Balliol men were prominent in debate throughout its ten-year lifespan, as befitted the college's role as Oxford's intellectual powerhouse.[44] Again the modern scholarship on Victorian sexualities has its favourite passage:

Like a young man newly come from the wrestling-ground, anointed, chapleted, and very calm, the Genius of the Greeks appears before us. Upon his soul there is no burden of the world's pain; the whole creation that groaneth and travaileth together, has touched him with no sense of anguish; nor has he yet felt sin. The pride and the strength of adolescence are his—audacity and endurance, swift passions and exquisite sensibilities, the alternations of sublime repose and boyish noise, grace, pliancy, and stubbornness and power, love of all fair things and splendours of the world, the frank enjoyment of the open air, free merriment, and melancholy well beloved. Of these adolescent qualities of this clear and stainless personality, this conscience whole and pure and reconciled to Nature, what survives among us now? The imagination must be strained to the uttermost before we can begin to sympathize with such a being.[45]

The wistfully erotic 'Genius of the Greeks' of the essay is a minimally deniable clone of the private poetry's 'Genius of Greek Love'; what we get here is effectively an ekphrasis of the Vatican *Apoxyomenos* of Lysippus, an image repurposed by Symonds in the 1860s as an erotic template for his crush on the cathedral chorister Alfred Brooke.[46] A very few pages later we find the statue invoked by name as the physical manifest-ation of the ideal Athenian gymnastic education extolled by the Dikaios Logos in Aristophanes's *Clouds*, and summoned to the mind's eye in markedly similar terms: 'This life rises above us imaged in the sculptor's marble... Upon his features there rests no care or thought, but the delicious languor of momentary fatigue, and the serenity of a nature in harmony with itself.' The speech of the Dikaios Logos is notoriously the pedagogic manifesto of an enthusiastic boy-fancier, but only readers with a good knowledge of the Greek would pick up on that particular twist.[47] The majority would also never know how close this gay Genius of the

---

[44] J. A. Symonds (1967–9: i. 354). This incautious essay was later to land Symonds in hot water; see pp. 193–5. On the society (active from 1856 to 1866) and its membership, see briefly Schultz (2004: 341) and, with much charming detail, Monsman (1970). 'The tone of the Society was, to a large degree, the tone of Balliol... In literature, art, politics, and religion the Society was avowedly "Radical"' (Swinburne had been the life and soul of the party in early years): Monsman (1970: 366).

[45] J. A. Symonds (1873: 399 = 1920: 554–5).

[46] Anticipated at J. A. Symonds (1984: 78).

[47] J. A. Symonds (1873: 407–8 = 1920: 559–60).

Greeks is to Symonds's swooning paradoxography (he calls it a 'prose dithyramb') of Brooke's own qualities, in explicitly carnal terms: 'softness mingled with audacity; lasciviousness beneath the virile bosom; love-languor in the large bold steady eyes...readiness to grant favours; knowledge and appreciation of sensual delight.'[48] The tangible influence of Walter Pater suffuses these two passages, echoing his celebration of oxymoron both in public print and in erotically charged performance before his fellow symposiasts (Symonds among them) in Old Mortality.[49] 'Nor has he yet felt sin' is most obviously a biblical motif: the 'Genius' is an Adam in a pagan Eden, unburdened by fallen humanity's knowledge of Good and Evil—and with no Eve to lead him astray; and there are potential echoes too of the sacrificial Christ of 2 Corinthians 5:21, 'who knew no sin' so that he might carry the weight of ours to the Cross. But for those in the know it is also an explicitly and publicly Paterian riff, the point of departure being the latter's important and controversial essay 'Winckelmann', published in 1867.[50]

A contemporary of Pater at Oxford, Symonds was never personally close to him, but Pater's literary and critical output were always import-ant touchstones for his own development and self-critique as a writer. He considered Pater's opinion the only one that really counted among his reviewers, a habit Wilde was to acquire as well, and continued to wrestle with Paterian topics throughout his career as an essayist.[51] Like Pater, he engaged seriously with the fashionable German prophets of self-cultivation in formulating his own distinctive understanding of the meaning of Hellenism; although the fundamental influence must be Jowett, who had gone out on a limb by bringing in Hegel in the 1850s, his citation of 'Winckelmann' points to an element of conscious dialogue.[52] Congenially for Symonds's purposes, the essay sculpts a

---

[48] J. A. Symonds (1984: 124), additionally crediting the youth with 'thick and sinewy thighs; prominent and lusty testicles'.

[49] On Pater's own epideictic triumph within this radical–elite homosocial space—his essay 'Diaphaneitè', of 1864—see evocatively Dowling (1994: 81–5).

[50] J. A. Symonds (1984: 122–9), a passage I came to through Davis (1999: 192).

[51] Grosskurth (1964: 162). On Pater as stimulus and intertextual backdrop to Symonds's writing in the 1870s, see Evangelista (2009a: 133). Symonds's late essay 'The Philosophy of Evolution' (in J. A. Symonds 1890, critically scorned) seeks to merge Pater's ideas with current scientific thinking.

[52] On his intellectual debts to Winckelmann, Goethe (a profound presence in his essays and correspondence), and Hegel, see Evangelista (2009a: 130). On the German Romantic tradition and British liberal-Utilitarian care of the self, Dowling (1994: 60) is enlightening, as (at p. 70n.) on reactionary Oxonian suspicion of 'Germanism' in the 1850s. On Jowett's Hegelian streak and Pater's more thorough Hegelianism, see F. M. Turner (1981: 68–74, 417–27), a classic treatment.

Winckelmann who achieves self-realization and oneness with his essential nature through physical and spiritual communion with the ideal
male nude of Greek art:[53] 'the absence of any sense of want, or corruption, or shame... He fingers those pagan marbles with unsinged hands,
with no sense of shame or loss. That is to deal with the sensuous side of
art in the pagan manner.' 'Nor has he yet felt sin': the Winckelmann of
Pater is a confirmed Platonist, foreshadowing and borrowing subtext
from the homophile aura of contemporary veneration of Plato in Oxford,
and a shameless/sinless idolater of the adolescent male body. The boys he
loves are glossed as 'youths', but any readers who knew their Plato in
Greek would see right through the veneer of ambiguity.[54] In Symonds's
essay too, soft-focus 'youths' drift alluringly through a sylvan Hellenic
dreamscape: '*Beneath the olive-trees*, among the flowers and ferns, move
stately maidens *and bare-chested youths. Their eyes* are starry-softened or
flash fire, and their lips are parted to drink in the breath of life.'[55] Again
(did Symonds's public but know it), the phrasing recalls the private
poetry, familiar to only a few of the writer's intimate circle, and no
sooner circulated than suppressed:

> Thus by the Love-God's shrine, *beneath the trees,*
> Fragrant with summer, musical with bees,
>
> .   .   .   .   .
>
> These lovers vowed unspoken vows and blent
> Their throbbing souls in love's accomplishment...
>
> Then changed the vision: lo, before me stood
> *Framed in the arches of the olive wood*
> *Another Youth,* still fair and like a god,
> Irradiate; *his fierce eyes were fixed on me;*
> Lust burned within their orbs unquenchably...[56]

Pater turns ambiguity into his own personal art form: his Greece is a
connoisseur's delight, but too studiously ambivalent to change anyone's
mind about issues in the world beyond his slippery text.[57] Symonds's

[53] Dellamora (1990: 112), from whom I also gratefully borrow Pater's 'unsinged hands'
snippet (p. 110).
[54] I am indebted here to Evangelista (2006: 236 ('youths', drawing attention in particular
to the *Lysis*) and 346 (Platonism as alibi)); cf., with caution, Jenkyns (1980: 150–2).
[55] J. A. Symonds (1873: 403 = 1920: 557) (emphases added).
[56] J. A. Symonds (1878b: i. 20) (emphases added) and p. 5 of the undated pamphlet *Genius
Amoris*, a poem that also presents the statuesque image of 'Love, the athlete'. 'As to my cycle,
I determined in August to suppress these poems; and now the deed is done' (1984: 201).
[57] Interpreting Pater's writings as double-coded, 'appeal[ing] to an audience divided
(along various boundaries) into initiates and outsiders', is a familiar trope of Victorian
studies, as noted by J. E. Adams (1995: 151).

ethically committed interpretation of Hellenism therefore differs from Pater's in one important aspect. The Greece of Pater's essays is forever in tension between the opposing forces of Dorian and Ionian racial characters. The Dorians were virile and austere; the Ionians, mystical and sensuous, and perhaps a little louche. Throughout its history, Dorian Apollo vied in the Greek nature with Ionian Dionysus; vigour, with artistry; doers of deeds, with dreamers of dreams; Europe, with Asia; order and discipline, with speculative free association. 'Severe simplification' faced off against 'languid Ionian voluptuousness'—the different styles of column capital said it all.[58] Effectively Pater gave ancient Greece its own scaled-down version of the habitual polarities already in play between Hellenism and Hebraism, East and West.

Symonds was certainly alive to the ambiguities Pater was pointing out, and in particular to his new and characteristically whimsical gloss on Müller's Dorianism. Pater propounded a new characterization of the Spartans as manly aesthetes: pure-minded connoisseurs of the nude male body. Naturally, he touted Plato as his authority for the historical truth that it was the austere Dorians, not the Ionians, who 'first shook off the false Asiatic shame, and stripped off their clothing for purposes of exercise and training in the *gymnasium*; and it was part of the Dorian or European influence to assert the value in art of the unveiled and healthy human form'. The 'shame' of 'Winckelmann' and the 'sin' of 'The Genius of the Greeks' are now defined as Eastern, and against (Western) nature: an eye for the male nude is a badge of masculine virtue.[59]

Symonds will co-opt Müller's homophile warrior elite, and Pater's veiled equation of desire for the male body with sound discernment of truth in art, but the Hellas of *Studies* is primarily a land of 'sweetness and light' in the culturally dominant style of early Arnold—in Paterian terms, Apollonian, with Dionysiac irrationality emerging only in moments of ritual atavism.[60] Symonds was personally no admirer of Arnold's

---

[58] Pater (1895a: 252–62); for a worked-through example, see p. 217, on why Homer's Troy—in Pater's interpretation a city of Eastern Greeks racially characterized by 'an element of languid Ionian voluptuousness', and 'proportionally weaker on the practical or moral side'—was unable to sustain its war against Peloponnesians fired with 'the austere, more strictly European influence of the Dorian Apollo'. Severe simplification: p. 253. Pater's advocacy of putting the psychic underpinnings of Greek myth to work in care of the self (Dellamora 1990: 173) invites comparisons with his contemporary, Nietzsche. For useful discussion see Potts (1999).

[59] Pater (1895a: 262). Locating ascetic self-mastery in a keen eye for the male nude subverts the overarching nineteenth-century literary project that inscribed manliness into the project of literary creation by aligning it with the pose of 'charismatic self-mastery' and autarky that defined the idea of the Victorian gentleman (J. E. Adams 1995: 2, 5).

[60] Evangelista (2009a: 132–3). Arnold was later to backtrack on the Hellas popularized by *Culture and Anarchy* (and had never really got comfortable with his own Hellenism–

thought—as a young Fellow at Magdalen he had reviled one of his essays as 'abominably bumptious, swaggering, & illiberal' in private correspondence, and his opinion did not noticeably mellow with the years—but fashionable Arnoldianism was the language in which Greece in reception could talk to power and expect a hearing.[61] Its ubiquity in public discourse of Hellenism lends *Studies* a comforting familiarity, keeping non-specialist readers onside while Symonds deploys his carefully paced subtext in support of the radical thesis that here, just the once, he risks propounding all but explicitly. To be psychically whole and ethically clean one must only be a good human animal, 'reconciled' to the truth of one's own Nature—a Nature that is taken to include, at a fundamental level, what we would call sexual orientation.

4. BEATING THE CURVE: *STUDIES*, PASTORAL, AND EPIGRAM

It began with a boy: Norman Moor, a sixth-former at Clifton in the late 1860s, on whom Symonds developed a crush. As a pretext for being around the place, he offered a series of lectures, choosing as his theme the Greek poets, and the rest was history.[62] Not all of the *Studies* of the First Series began as lectures; some were Review articles in the *North British* and *Westminster*, and are identified as such at the outset, in a short preface that also flags up the influence of Müller as a signpost to the availability of subtext in what is to come.[63] What Symonds advertises

Hebraism polarity in the meantime: Jenkyns (1980: 91)) but by then the damage was done: Rajak (1999: 67–9). In the long term, and with important consequences for *Studies*, Symonds also chooses not to buy into Pater's polarity between Ionian and Dorian as two opposed styles of Greek homosexual eros (Orrells 2011a: 134–40, 159, on the latter's *Plato and Platonism*). Despite Orrells (2011a: 41), the correspondence seems to me to indicate only an early rhetorical phase (J. A. Symonds 1967–9: ii. 399) generating some poetic juvenilia, of which *Eudiades* is indicative.

[61] The essay was 'The bishop and the philosopher', the addressee, A. O. Rutson—and Symonds writes that he has also 'abuse[d] it heartily to' Jowett (J. A. Symonds 1967–9: i. 377). In a letter of 1867 he still finds Arnold's poetry unpleasantly 'frigid & affected' (i. 772). The Hellenism/Hebraism balancing act was taken genuinely seriously in the corridors of power—Gladstone was a True Believer: Lloyd-Jones (1982: 124). Arnoldian Platonism was a remarkably durable package, lingering in pockets of Oxford Classics into the early twentieth century: R. Symonds (2005).

[62] Grosskurth (1964: 128) on the lectures of 1868–9; Schultz (2004: 439); briefly, Orrells (2011a: 157).

[63] J. A. Symonds (1873: p. v); the correspondence gives rather more detail, broadening the picture (publication of 'The Greek Gnomic Poets' in the *Quarterly*: J. A. Symonds (1967–9: i. 838)) and documenting on how Review publication generated prompt and

here is a new kind of synoptic work, not yet comprehensive but certainly groundbreaking in 'apply[ing] to the Greek poets the same sort of criticism as that which modern classics receive'—aesthetic evaluation as works of literature, as opposed to the kind of historical and philological exegesis familiar from the authors of mid-century.[64]

As was the case with those earlier writers, the occasional character of Review journalism as a preliminary publication form is again reflected in the patchy and slightly eccentric coverage of the major chapters: no author starting a history of Greek poetry from scratch would choose to begin with Empedocles (Study 2). Book-ended by an introductory essay on periodization (Study 1) and the aforementioned essay on 'The Genius of Greek Art' (Study 12), the authors and topics covered in the First Series range chronologically from the archaic period to—with epigram (Study 11)—late antiquity:

1. The Periods of Greek Literature
2. Empedocles
3. The Gnomic Poets
4. The Satirists
5. The Lyric Poets
6. Pindar
7. Greek Tragedy and Euripides
8. Aristophanes
9. Ancient and Modern Tragedy
10. The Idyllists
11. The Anthology
12. The Genius of Greek Art

Comprehensiveness is at this stage not even dreamed of as an aim, and Symonds is still regarded with more than a hint of condescension as a gadfly essayist rather than a serious literary author—a perception that is underlined by the peculiar focus of some of his so-called chapters ('Greek Tragedy and Euripides', 'Ancient and Modern Tragedy').[65] Certainly in the late 1860s he was still writing on miscellaneous topics in European

---

critical peer feedback, which could then be factored into the book version (i. 783, 824, on the essay 'The Greek Idyllic Poets', retitled for *Studies* as 'The Idyllists'). For comparison, cf. ii. 920, on the composition of *Sketches in Italy and Greece*: 'Not quite half the essays are old.'

[64] J. A. Symonds (1873: pp. v–vi), acknowledging among his scholarly sources also Mure (see Ch. 2)—finally Mure gets an appreciative reader, if only as a repository of raw data.

[65] J. A. Symonds (1873: p. v). On Symonds as an author whose promise has heretofore 'been wasted on magazine articles', see Anon (1875: 378), who reasonably regards *Renaissance in Italy* as the first large-scale work conceived as such by Symonds, rather than cobbled together from journal pieces: 'Mr Symonds is well known to all students of the

and indeed American literature, developing the abiding interest in sub-text which would lead him to stalk Walt Whitman by mail; the Greek poets were just one among several interests.[66]

Symonds's schematization of the 'Periods of Greek Literature' (Study 1) builds on comfortably familiar antecedents, fine-tuning an existing three-stage model (pre-classical, classical, post-classical) by subdividing the pre- and post-classical into two distinct periods each:

1. Heroic
2. Archaic/Early Classical
3. Classical
4. Late Classical
5. Hellenistic, Roman, and Byzantine

In classic Winckelmanian style (and the inclusion of a final Study on 'Greek Art' flags up the debt), literary development runs in parallel with the political life of the Greek *Volk*. The 'brief but splendid' third age, in which the curve of culture reaches its peak and produces 'all [its] master-pieces', begins with the foundation of the Delian League in 477 and ends with the failure of the Sicilian Expedition in 413; the fourth age of waning creativity runs to the death of Alexander. The fifth age, the long tail of the Greek Genius in its extreme old age, occupies by far the greatest span of time, extending as it does from 323 BCE to 'the final extinction of classical civilization', an open-ended qualification that admits to the canon of Greek literature at least some of the poetry of Byzantium and could potentially end as late as 1453. (The vagueness of its terminus is probably deliberate; later in the chapter we get a hint of how to disambiguate it for ourselves when we are told that in Late Antiquity 'the spirit of Christianity proved fatal to the spirit of Greek art'.[67]) It is an age of decline and decay, producing 'nothing new . . . except the single, most idyllic flower of Idyllic poetry *and some few epigrams*'.[68]

The appeal here is to a Romantic ideal of literary originality, harnessed to the bell curve of cultural production but also granting token exemptions from it; pastoral and epigram, and *only* pastoral and epigram, express the still living Greek spirit of their age. We may observe in

---

current literature as the author of some of the pleasantest and most agreeable essays which have appeared in an age prolific of pleasant and agreeable essays.'

[66] J. A. Symonds (1967–9: i. 824) (Whitman).

[67] J. A. Symonds (1873: 35).

[68] J. A. Symonds (1873: 3–5, quoted at 4–5) (emphasis added). With the exception of the 'Heroic, or Prehistoric, or Legendary' first age, Symonds does not name his five periods, so I supply here my own approximations.

passing that, together with Plato, epigram and pastoral had long been part of Symonds's personal toolkit of homosexual self-fashioning. The *Memoirs* indicate that, even before coming up to Oxford, he was writing these genres and their tropes into the aetiology of his (actually not terribly Hellenic) desires for men and boys alike, often quoting them in Greek to keep his secret safe from prying eyes, and he continued the trick in his correspondence with intimate friends; its visual difference made it a shared code that helped define their network while soundproofing it against chance eavesdroppers.[69] There is nothing surprising about this: simply put, these were the tools available.

The 'single, most idyllic flower' of Hellenistic pastoral thus demands our immediate attention. It immediately precedes Symonds's account of epigram—and thus sets up particular readerly expectations for it; and it stands as an important moment in the author's self-revelation as a prophet of Hellenic eros. The name of Theocritus in particular (and 'single' cues up his predominance in Symonds's narrative) was one to conjure with in the later nineteenth century, standing in subcultural discourse as a rhetorical marker of gay identity in a way that bore scant relation to the majority content of his text; this is dangerous ground, and Symonds knows as much when he chooses to walk it.[70] What we find in the tenth chapter of *Studies* is an account informed by critical engagement with key German thinkers, building through homo-erotically tinged evocations of the Vatican Museum's greatest hits of Greek sculpture ('godlike youths'—Winckelmann is the elephant in the room for those in the know) towards an imaginative channelling of Müller's few pages on Dorian pederasty.[71]

The hit is brief, less than two pages in all, yet devastating. 'Not merely abominable in the eyes of men but also unpardonable at the bar of divine justice'—not homosexuality but witchcraft, the theme of the second Idyll,

---

[69] J. A. Symonds (1984: 99–100). In the early correspondence: e.g. J. A. Symonds (1967–9: i. 694), to Dakyns. On how use of Greek as a shared cryptogram defined Symonds's epistolary friendship circle as 'insiders', see Schultz (2004: 440). For a parallel to Symonds's use of Greek as a secret diary code, see entertainingly Waquet (2001: 244) on the diary of Cardinal Newman, kept entirely in Latin to safeguard confidential information from inquisitive domestic staff, whose social background excluded the possibility that they would be able to read it.

[70] Jenkyns (1980: 290–2): 'whenever the name of Theocritus crops up in later Victorian literature, or any reference to Sicily, homosexuality is seldom far to seek' (p. 290). Aldrich (1993: 20–3) takes the Victorians' presentist fantasies at face value and egregiously misreads Theocritus' text in translation.

[71] J. A. Symonds (1873: 304 (Ahrens on the authorship of the *Lament for Bion*), p. 306 (Schlegel), pp. 314–16 (art criticism, including passing reference to a sculpture that 'might be Hylas, or Uranian Eros, or Hymenaeus...' (p. 315))).

as perceived through the 'superstitious and fetichistic [*sic*] conception' of bigoted medieval religiosity. And then an immediate transition to a topic entirely opposite in tone, 'Doric chivalry'—an influential formulation within subculture—from 'the heroic age of Greece... The thirteenth Idyll is especially remarkable for the exquisite finish of its style and also for the light it throws on the mutual relations of knight and squire in early Greek warfare.'[72] The story of Herakles' love for Hylas 'is well known', we are told; this is the first most readers will have heard of it, but Symonds's rhetorical *praeteritio* gives us all the detail we need, while cueing up the real lesson: the institutionalization of the erastēs–erōmenos relationship as a pedagogic ideal, historically attested as culturally central, sanctioned by the conventional morality of its time, and with verifiably beneficial consequences for the state:

And in this respect Heracles was the Eponym and patron of an [sc., chivalric] order which existed throughout Dorian Hellas. This order, protected by religious tradition and public favour, produced the Cretan lovers, the Lacedaemonian 'hearers' and 'inspirers', the Theban immortals who lay with faces turned so stanchly [*sic*] to their foes that vice seemed incompatible with so much valour. Achilles was another Eponym of this order.

Responding opportunely to Müller, this evocation of the Sacred Band lays in ideological firewood ahead of time by pandering to the contemporary patriotric cliché of the plucky servant of Empire.[73] Naturally Symonds name-drops the *Phaedrus* here, as textual evidence of a golden age in which the erastēs/erōmenos relation was acknowledged as an everyday reality, morally indifferent if not positively virtuous—'simple, natural, and human'.[74] However, this golden age is only secondarily and by rule-bound emulation the Greece of known history and admired culture. Herakles is a demigod, only half human, and Symonds's Theocritus wistfully locates the apogee of 'Dorian chivalry' in the heroic prehistory of the Homeric age, framed by myth and as distant from the Classical as King Arthur from our own age.[75]

---

[72] J. A. Symonds (1873: 328 = 1920: 489–90), also the source of the passage on Heracles and Achilles cited below; on the appropriation of 'chivalry' as a Uranian–homophile buzzword in the run-up to the 1890s, see briefly Dellamora (1990: 157).

[73] Dowling (1994: 75, 79); briefly, Bristow (1995: 131) on how homophile authors queue up to push this button in post-1885 texts. More broadly, the summary of background at Marchand (1996: p. xvii) helps us understand how Symonds picked friendly voices across a broad continuum of nineteenth-century German Philhellenisms.

[74] Natural and human: J. A. Symonds (1873: 330); *Phaedrus*: p. 328.

[75] Herakles as superhuman: J. A. Symonds (1873: 330); Arthuriana frame the discussion at p. 328 (Tennyson's *Idylls of the King*—Tennyson reappears in a reception-themed coda at

In any case, and following Müller (whose influence weighs as heavily on the as yet unpublished *Greek Ethics*), Herakles and his peers propound their lesson in martial erotodidaxis only to one-half of the Greek nation, the Dorian, which during the periods of peak cultural achievement is conspicuously silent in poetry as in prose, and which was relegated to a strictly marginal supporting role in Victorian British Hellenism; the Dorians were assimilated to the Scots, whether as comic relief or in strictly local recuperations.[76] Inspiring as it may be in its full-blooded primitivism, this prehistoric Hellas, red in tooth and claw, offers not the slightest prospect of recuperation in the here and now: it is incompatible with humane culture.[77] It has vanished forever, leaving only a proud memory. (*Eudiades*: 'The men of whom I speak were strong and pure ... And the whole earth mourned at their funeral.')

5. 'THE MOST VALUABLE RELIC': POETS IN A NEW LANDSCAPE

From the point of view of a keen contemporary reader, Symonds had an excellent pretext for getting involved with Greek epigram: filial pietas. The senior John Addington Symonds, MD, had been a man of influence (vice-president of the BMA) and a published author on sense perception, mental health, and the physiology of sleep and dreaming. He was also an aficionado of the Greek Anthology whose 'epitaph on Protē' was still being singled out for praise nearly half a century after his death as the only translation in English to rank alongside Cory's famous 'Heraclitus' ('They told me, Heraclitus, they told me you were dead ... ').[78]

Symonds's earliest forays as a book-author were two volumes of his father's *Reminiscences* and *Poems*, produced to mark his passing in the year of his death (1871), taking Protē out for one more spin; and when he came to write his essay on the Anthology, it was to his father as well as to the collections of Burges and Wellesley that he would express his grateful

the chapter's end, pp. 339–430) and p. 330 (the exploits of Castor and Polydeuces compared 'with those of Tristram and Lancelot').

[76] Jenkyns (1980: 167–8) surveys the topic succinctly and with his usual panache.

[77] Herakles and his blood-spattered peers are 'purely Dorian ... brawny, fearless, of huge appetite ... Polydeuces, a notable bruiser; Castor, a skilled horseman and a man of blood' (J. A. Symonds 1873: 330).

[78] Baring (1913: 250). Symonds's background uncannily echoes that of Robert Bland, another son of an eminent physician.

indebtedness as the source of many of his translations (Protē is there, of course, along with many others).[79] But he already had a long personal history with epigram, a history kept secret from his father and the world: through citation of selected poems, he explored his long unrealized desires for intimate male companionship. At Harrow, a schoolfriend had poked gentle fun at him for picking the nickname 'Simonides'.[80]

In his last year at the school, devastated by his unrealizable passion for the chorister Willie Dyer, he 'devoured Greek literature'—Plato first and foremost, of course, and then 'I compared these [dialogues] with the *Clouds* of Aristophanes and the erotic dialogues of Lucian and Plutarch. I explored Theognis and the *Anthology*; learned Theocritus by heart...'.[81] Alongside pastoral, epigram in the original Greek became in Symonds's hands a private code, an invisible ink in which he could sketch out the parameters of his impossible desire as it took shape in his mind. At Clifton in November 1868 Dakyns had him to dinner at the College with three boys from the sixth form; this was the occasion on which he met Norman Moor, the desire to see more of whom induced Symonds to compose the Clifton College lectures that became the first of the *Studies*: 'I find the beginning of an epigram by Straton used as motto for this dinner party in my notes: "Καὶ μισθοὺς αἰτεῖτε, διδάσκαλοι; ὡς ἀχάριστοι."' At the same time, he was taking up a friend's suggestion by writing *Eudiades*.[82] The next spring, his diary puzzles out the gradations of an aesthetic conscience, with that poem firmly in mind: 'Next comes the personal work of art, in which we dream and know it is a dream, and pour our yearnings and our passions into the dream, and give it form in words, trying to realize a vision of what we desire: "εἰδώλοις κάλλευς κωφὰ χλιαινομένη".'[83] The first of these quoted lines, an incipit from the saucy Strato (AP 12.219.1), is no more than a wittily appropriate tag for the occasion (schoolmasters surrounded by pretty boys are ingrates for expecting tuition fees as well as kisses; Strato would happily pay good money to be in their position). The second is Meleagrian, and cuts deeper: it invokes through its original context a woeful self-characterization as the δύσερως ψυχή, the soul unhappy in love (AP 12.125.8). Simultaneously, Symonds was trying on a Meleagrian persona

[79] Symonds Sr (1871a, b); J. A. Symonds (1873: 345–6n.; Protē: p. 356).

[80] 'Simonides' ('"Monny"'): J. A. Symonds (1984: 61).

[81] J. A. Symonds (1984: 106).

[82] J. A. Symonds (1984: 195); cf., raiding Theocritean pastoral, pp. 105 and 193.

[83] J. A. Symonds (1984: 199). After hours of touching and kissing in bed in January 1870, a year after their first meeting and surely under the influence of Strato's Boyish Muse, Symonds writes in a frenzy of the 'nectar' of Norman's 'opened lips like flower petals' (1984: 209).

in an original composition in Greek sent to Norman shortly after a gift of flowers. The lovesick poet had sent the boy a bouquet of violets that he here reimagines as a 'garland' (στέφανος), an apt gift to the godlike youth who in ancient times would have been the toast of the symposium; its blooms smelled sweet, but Norman's is sweeter still. Or does Symonds affect to have sent a 'Garland', a chaplet of wooing verses, in emulation of Meleager's ancient precedent (AP 12.257, the sphragis of his Garland)?:

13 February.
ἴων πέπομφα στέφανον εὐωδέστατον
ἔαρος ἀπαρχήν, σοὶ μὲν εὐωδεστέρῳ.[84]

In the 1870s, finally out from under his father's thumb and creatively unleashed, he found in epigram the ideal genre to mark the latter's passing but also to find his own voice.[85] Placed by its lateness at the end of the First Series's chronological scheme, Symonds's chapter on the Anthology—by far the largest in the collection—reads as its climax.[86]

It begins:

The Anthology may from some points of view be regarded as the most valuable relic of antique literature which we possess. Composed of several thousand short poems... it is coextensive with the whole current of Greek history, from the splendid period of the Persian War to the decadence of Christianized Byzantium. Many subjects of interest in Greek life, which would otherwise have had to be laboriously illustrated from the historians or the comic poets are here fully and melodiously set forth. If we might compare the study of Greek Literature to a journey in some splendid mountain region, then we might say with propriety that from the sparkling summits where Aeschylus and Sophocles and Pindar sit enthroned, we turn in our less strenuous moods to gather the meadow flowers of Meleager, Palladas, Callimachus. Placing them between the leaves of the book of our memory, we possess an everlasting treasure of sweet thoughts, which will

---

[84] J. A. Symonds (1984: 197). The other precedent in the Mousa Paidikē for sending an Anthology as a love gift is AP 12.189, if read with a yearning eye.

[85] On how Symonds blossoms as a writer and critic in the years immediately following his father's death, see Schultz (2004: 394–5, 446). It may be significant that almost all the Symonds Sr versions in *Studies* are epitaphs, as if to draw a line under his legacy: to the famous Protē, cf., e.g., the epitaphic 360 (Orpheus), 363 (Diogenes), 367 (unnamed). All the same, the modern scholarship is perhaps too eager to buy into the image of Symonds *père* as a forbidding Victorian patriarch; his son remembered him fondly as always meaning for the best, and a sympathetic confidant once his university-age son opened up to him: J. A. Symonds (1984: 82, 116) ('an intimate friend').

[86] Fifty-seven pages; the next longest is forty-nine (Study 7, on Greek tragedy); 'The Anthology' is more than half as long again as the average of the literary Studies, thirty-six pages.

serve in after-days to remind us of those scenes of Olympian majesty through which we travelled.[87]

'Laborious illustration' may well be a dig at Wilhelm Becker's didactic novel *Charicles, or Illustrations of the Private Life of the Ancient Greeks, with Notes and Excursuses*, available in English translation since 1846 and continuously in print until around the century's end; its turgid and heavily footnoted narrative draws exhaustively on the very sources Symonds singles out as arduous and unyielding (historians, comic poets) when trying to reconstruct daily life in the private and domestic sphere. Epigram is presented as being much better for the purpose. In opening up the prospect of a Greek literature that delivers domestic intimacy, Symonds knowingly plays to the Victorian fondness for understanding the personalities of great men—and, thus, the history they make—through notionally minor household incidents and anecdotes.[88]

In the high literature of the Greeks, says Symonds, 'political or religious accidents' often obscure this common ground of sympathy. Tragedy's gods and kings get in the way; but epigram puts us directly in touch with the lived experience of relatively ordinary and often anonymous Greeks. As he writes in the chapter's conclusion:

after listening to the choice raptures of triumphant public art, we turn aside to hear the private utterances, the harmoniously modulated whispers of a multitude of Greek poets telling us their inmost thoughts and feelings...Over very many of the sweetest and the strongest of the epigrams is written the pathetic word ἀδέσποτον—'without a master'.[89]

This is studied misdirection on Symonds's part: *Charicles* leant on these sources and excluded (genuine) epigram because it was attempting to re-create the Athens of the early fourth century, prior to the emergence of epigram as a literary genre in the Hellenistic era. By keeping epigram's lateness out of the frame, Symonds safeguards it from allegations of degeneracy and maintains its usefulness as a tool for unpacking the quotidian complexities of 'antique' (that is, implicitly *classical*) Greek life. Becker's *Charicles* ('laboriously illustrated') may henceforth be retired as a sourcebook on Athenian domestic manners in favour of the Anthology. All Greek life is here, which is, of course, to say all human life, especially our own:

---

[87] J. A. Symonds (1873: 341–2 = 1920: 499).

[88] 'The Victorians Boswellized the past wholesale; the more one reverenced the ancients, the more exciting it was to find that one had something in common with them' (Jenkyns 1980: 81).

[89] J. A. Symonds (1873: 396–7).

The slight effusions of these minor poets are ever nearer to our hearts than the master-pieces of the noblest Greek literature. They treat with touching limpidity and sweetness of the joys and fears and hopes and sorrows that are common to all humanity. They introduce us to the actual life of a bygone civilization, stripped of its political or religious accidents, and tell us that the Greeks of Athens or of Sidon thought and felt exactly as we feel. Even the Graffiti of Pompeii have scarcely more power to reconstruct the past and summon as in dreams the voices and the forms of long-since buried men.[90]

To 'summon as in dreams': Symonds hints here at the Greek Anthology as a unique route into double consciousness. Even for the non-Hellenist, this dream-Hellas is given erotic charge by the culturally loaded invocation of louche Pompeii; by the ghostly physicality of male 'forms' summoned into the visual field; perhaps even by the invitation into intimacy itself (identification with 'ordinary' and thus non-exemplary ancient lives could swiftly bypass Boswellism's self-improvement agenda in favour of you-are-there soft pornography).[91] The evaluative context reassuringly gestures towards the Apollonian Hellenism of Arnold ('limpidity and sweetness' mirror-images 'sweetness and light'), but with a new insistence that the Hellenic ideal is more than mere abstraction: it can be mapped onto the facts of ancient life as experienced by the ordinary people who inhabited it.

The evidence for this is, precisely, the Greek Anthology. As 'minor' verse with a liminal relation to the ancient poetic canon, it mediates between the Classic and ordinary humanity and underscores the dignity of both.[92] Human experience is revealed through the Anthology to be common to all eras at its emotional core, as is human behaviour ('the actual life'). Actions and desires are natural to the species (a comforting trope that Bulwer-Lytton's Pompeiian bestseller went all out to sell to its readership); morality and taboo, on the other hand, are contingent products of culture.[93] The universe is not hardwired with normative absolutes, which the 'right' culture can know; instead morality is a set of

---

[90] J. A. Symonds (1873: 342 = 1920: 499–500).

[91] Montserrat (1998: 175) compellingly illustrates this with examples from the rhetoric that accompanied exhibitions of Greco-Egyptian mummy portraits. On Pompeiian finds as modern objects of erotic fascination, see Fisher and Langlands (2011); on how travel narrative cast the city's ancient inhabitants as ghostly presences, and burnished the aura of Pompeii as a site where the boundary between the worlds of the living and the dead was felt to be thin, see Bridges (2011: 94–7), part of her explanation of the narrative dynamic of Bulwer-Lytton's novel.

[92] ' "Minor" is a space at once in and out of recent categories of the canonical and the non-canonical' (Najarian 2003: 571).

[93] Bridges (2011: 100–2) nicely picks apart the narrative interventions in which Bulwer-Lytton reassures his gentle reader of the timelessness of 'the human passions and the human heart'.

more or less arbitrary conventions ('accidents') that apply in a particular time and place, historically and culturally conditioned by the institutions of social power. ('Superstitious and fetichistic conventions' ...)

Like the graffiti of Pompeii, epigram is the unmediated word on the ancient street, miraculously preserved. The Anthology is less high Poesy than a medley of the Greek nation's popular songs and lyrics, responding to the lives and concerns of the common man: 'this precious Golden Treasury of fugitive pieces.'[94] It therefore gives direct access to the experiences of people just like Symonds's readers; unassuming private persons, as well as the famous and great.

There is also the implicit assurance that what we find will be natural and wholesome: Symonds's characterization of the Anthology unmistakably alludes to the title of Francis Turner Palgrave's *Golden Treasury of English Songs and Lyrics*, first published in 1861 and an instant success, which was subsequently revised and enlarged in numerous editions by Palgrave and others. Palgrave's dedication (to the Poet Laureate, Alfred Tennyson) offered the *Golden Treasury* as 'a book which, I hope, may be found by many a lifelong fountain of innocent and exalted pleasure'.[95] Symonds is thus insisting that the Anthology is every bit as innocent. Meleager at least is also as exalted as any Romantic poet in Palgrave—'a spirit of the subtlest and the sweetest, a heart of the tenderest, and a genius of the purest that has been ever granted to an elegist of earthly love'.[96]

Epigram thus enables a new, socially inclusive perspective on literary posterity and a radically participatory re-conception of Canon. In the closing sentences of his essay, Symonds asserts that epigram-composition and inclusion in the Anthology has granted even to the humblest contributor a poetic immortality as assured and justified as that of Pindar or Sophocles; indeed, he says, the opinions of these ancient readers about the 'great' authors guarantee the essential integrity of the Greek literary canon we read today.[97] As the evocation of Pompeii underlines, this is

[94] J. A. Symonds (1873: 342).

[95] Palgrave (1861: n.p.). J. A. Symonds's description (1873: 342) of the *Anthology* as a 'Golden Treasury' supplies Lothian (1920) with his title, incidentally indicating just how pervasively Symonds's rhetoric shaped subsequent epigram-discourse, even when it rejected his preferred subtext.

[96] J. A. Symonds (1873: 374).

[97] Symonds ends the chapter with praise of the Anthology's many anonymous poems, insisting again that the collection's greatest strength is its reportage of 'private utterances', which convey the emotional and experiential reality of each writer. 'Hail to you, dead poets, unnamed, but dear to the Muses! Surely with Pindar and with Anacreon... the bed of flowers is already spread for you in those "black-petalled hollows of Pieria" where Ion bade farewell to Euripides' (J. A. Symonds 1873: 396–7). The last is a reference back to Ion's

very much the Alma-Tadema fantasy package. Like the antique house-hold knick-knacks that round out the visual field of the artist's paintings and authenticate his ancient world, the humble and humane epigram brings us home to the scenes of a genuine ancient private life in which we find our own feelings mirrored, regardless of any difference in social norms between then and now.

It is through this 'low' genre, not the 'high', archaic and classical genres of lyric and tragedy, that a contemporary and socially more diverse British readership may now legitimately focus its culturally mandated imagina-tive identification with the spirit of ancient Greece. It is with epigrams, not passages from tragedy or lyric, that we are urged systematically to populate our personal encyclopaedias of Greek thoughts, feelings, and actions—'the book of our memory', which we carry with us through our lives to keep reminding us of where 'we' come from and who 'we' are (Symonds's use of the inclusive first-person plural is seductive).

These unprecedented claims fly in the face of the inherited mid-century consensus, and effectively articulate a whole new way of interacting with the past—but rich figuration makes them seem like statements of the obvious. The 'book of our memory' is the lifelong souvenir of a tour through a vividly realized literary landscape of a singular type, with Symonds by strong implication offering his own services as guide. Word-paintings of landscape and flora were his speciality as a travel writer, and nineteenth-century Britain's mental picture of the terrain of Greece already owed far more to an imaginative reading of its literary texts than to any form of autopsy.[98] Here, however, the literature *is* the landscape: the Winckelmann curve of Greek cultural production is extruded into a three-dimensional terrain. The peak achievements of the 'high' genres are now actual peaks of stone, snow-capped 'sparkling

epitaph for Euripides (at 1873: 361), translated in a footnote: 'Dead though thou art, yet know thy fame shall be | Like Homer's green through all eternity.' Underwriting the canon's continuity and integrity: (1873: 365–6).

[98] Symonds as landscape artist in words, with a particularly strong sense of colour and light: (1874, 1884). On the terrain of Greece as an imaginative function of literary reception in the earlier nineteenth century, see Güthenke (2008). Symonds himself was later to go further than most towards a geographically real Greece, all the while betraying how literary education conditioned travellers in the nineteenth century to experience ancient sites through the prism of literature, ancient and/or modern (Ross 2009 makes good points about Romantic Hellen-ism's visually intense 'Greek' landscapes of literary memory). Moored off Sicily, 'we are tossing about on the very spot under Mount Eryx in the bay of Drepanum where Aeneas instituted the games for Anchises'; on a single overnight stay in Athens, 'the nightingales in the garden of the Academy sing as sweetly as they did to Sophocles or Plato' (Symonds 1967–9: iii. 291, 303, and cf. 298–9). Indeed, a love of the literature was the only conceivable reason for wanting to visit Greece: Constantine (1989: 11–12).

summits' in a 'splendid mountain region' that evokes by association the Romantic tropes of Sublimity. Symonds's readership will immediately have identified this picture-postcard scene as Alpine.[99]

Not too many years later, Symonds the travel writer will reinforce and subtly repurpose this associative word-picture when he explicitly characterizes the valleys of the actual Alps as a Theocritean 'Arcadia', strewn with flowers that are made to evoke his pastoral verse—and that bring us back once more to epigram as the book of memory.[100] When we are 'deafened by the noise of great cities', 'when our life is most commonplace, when we are ill or weary in city streets, *we can remember* the clouds upon the mountains we have seen, the sound of innumerable waterfalls, and the scent of countless flowers.'[101]

In real life as in meta-literary hallucination, the peaks are background scenery: one goes to the Alps not to climb them but to look at them, and the best view is to be had from the valleys, an Alpine paradise that delights each of the senses. In *Sketches*, the high Alps are Greek; in *Studies*, 'high' Greeks are Alps.

Placing epigram in the picturesque valleys below these peaks assimilates the poems of the Anthology to a distinct flora, the flowers of an Alpine 'meadow'.[102] This updates the flower imagery of Meleager in terms familiar to a contemporary audience, restoring to the poets their strong (because culture-specific) sense of visual identity *as* flowers, while still maintaining a whiff of the exotic. At the same time, a strong implicit contrast is established. To see this, we must briefly engage with the detail of Meleager's literary-critical flower hunt. I quote Paton's translation:

Many lilies of Anyte he inwove, and many of Moero, of Sappho few flowers, but they are roses; narcissus too, heavy with the clear song of Melanippides and a young branch of the vine of Simonides; and therewith he wove in the sweet-scented lovely iris of Nossis, the wax for whose writing-tablets Love himself melted; and with it marjoram from fragrant Rhianus, and Erinna's sweet crocus, maiden-hued, the hyacinth of Alcaeus...

---

[99] I write 'picture-postcard' advisedly; on the Alps as a destination for nineteenth-century British tourists, never more so than in Symonds's day, see Fleming (2000: 107–11, 324–5, 329–30).

[100] J. A. Symonds (1879: 280), and cf. p. 286: 'This indeed is the true pastoral life which poets have described—a happy summer holiday among the flowers.' Note, too, that the publisher issued *Sketches in Italy and Greece* in a binding that closely complemented that of *Studies*; the volumes sat happily together on the shelf, encouraging cross-readings and speculative association.

[101] J. A. Symonds (1873: 279–80) (emphasis added); 'great cities' (p. 278).

[102] Although this is in the first instance a smart tactical move, as the argument will show, when Symonds relocated to Davos a few years later he became a bona fide enthusiast of Alpine flora: J. A. Symonds (1967–9: i. 649–50).

he added the wild field-flowers of Posidippus and Hedylus, and the anemones of Sicelides [Theocritus] ... and the fair-tressed lotus of Chaeremon mingled with Phaedimus' phlox, and Antagoras' sweetly-turning oxeye, and Theodoridas' newly flowered thyme that loveth wine, and the blossom of Phanias' bean and the newly written buds of many others, and with all these the still early white violets of his own Muse.

The blooms of Meleager's verse preface are gathered from lowland locations, unsurprisingly so, as these are also the kinds of site in which pre-industrial human economic activity is typically present: the beach (Euphemus' spurge), the field (Bacchylides' corn and Polyclitus' corn-flower), orchard (apple and pomegranate), kitchen garden (bean), and woods (pine, poplar, and wild pear). The meadow, explicitly stated as an origin for just one poet (the celery blooms of Parthenis), is implicit as a wider backdrop for the iris, crocus, hyacinth, and others. This virtual backdrop may also suggest a shared narratological topography: the lowland meadows are the classic erotic location of, for instance, Moschus' epyllion, *Europa*.

Relocating the Anthology's meadow to a mountain valley distances epigram from this watery space of female desire, which Symonds instead transposes to his chapter on Sappho and archaic lyric. Ionian or even super-Ionian in their passionate intensity but (*contra* Pater) in no sense Asiatic, his Sappho and her literary circle blossom in a women-only Lesbos stocked with 'exquisite gardens, where the rose [Sappho's flower in Meleager's list] and hyacinth spread perfume; river-beds ablaze with the oleander and wild pomegranate ... In such scenes as these the Lesbian poets lived, and thought of Love.' Torrid yet chaste, Sappho and her circle of female intimates (themselves conceived as fellow poets) are presented as the irreproducible product of unique historical and geo-graphical circumstances. This purple passage explicitly attributes the gushes of lyric passion to the lifelong immersion of Sappho and her circle in a lush island paradise of hidden coves and plashing fountains— that is to say, a landscape troped as physically feminine.[103]

Moving epigram to the Alpine foothills also makes the genre 'high' enough to count as Classic in a useful sense. Gently strolling or reclining

---

[103] J. A. Symonds (1873: 128–9 = 1920: 192–3). Super-Ionian, but definitely not Eastern: (1873: 129); a brief blaze of passionate innocence: (1873: 127–8). Symonds's Sappho enjoyed a strange afterlife, notoriously being quoted verbatim and at considerable length by Denys Page in *Sappho and Alcaeus* (1955: 19–23) in lieu of any real view of his own; in the Epilogue to her *Fictions of Sappho*, DeJean (1989a: 304–5) picks apart the egregious oddness of what a contemporary reviewer already identified as a failure of nerve (J. A. Davidson, *CR* 7 (1957), 19–23, at 23). For a true sense of Sappho's effect in her characteristic metre, the intrigued reader is discreetly steered towards naughty Swinburne's 'Sapphics' in a footnote at (1873: 131).

at ease in this flower meadow, the tourist in the Greek literary landscape may enjoy the view to the summits while engaging in less 'strenuous' recreation than those hardy souls who attempt to climb them. At holiday's end, each visitor departs for the lowlands of the everyday bearing a hand-picked posy of the poets' blooms, pressed 'between the leaves of the book' as a perpetual keepsake of his or her tour in the Hellenic memory-scape—epigrams are after all short and easy to memorize, as generations of schoolboys had known, making them the ideal textual prop for recuperative escapes into double consciousness. MacGregor's dried flowers were bad, symptoms of bad literary housekeeping (see Chapter 2); Symonds's pressed flowers are good, preserving epigram and thereby perpetuating cultural memory.

As he directs our attention towards this dazzling synoptic view, Symonds is discreetly shifting marker posts to reallocate the broader general terrain that he programmatically outlined in his introductory Study on periodization. Although its five phases are still recognized, Greek cultural history is now a single current, running from the Persian Wars right through Late Antiquity, and its racial decadence fully comes in only with Byzantine Christianity. Indeed, epigram's essential lateness and long tail now become positive virtues, positioning it as a unique document for social and domestic life across all the seasons of the expanded Hellenic *saeculum*: a tree with 'leaves and buds and blossoms and fruitage of the Greek spirit on its boughs at once'.[104] Within this revised and enlarged version of the nation's lifespan, the Greeks of Athens and of Sidon are spoken of in the same breath as though calling them both 'Greek' (and expecting to be able to relate ourselves to both on that basis) were unexceptionable—a radical suggestion, slipped in in passing as if there were nothing more natural in the world. Hellenistic cosmopolitanism is now no longer being glossed as racial doom, but as an extension of the Greek spirit. The proof of this is the sole and unique genre that brings these geographically and temporally far-flung Greeks together in sympathy with each other, and thereafter with us: epigram itself.

6. ALPINE CONNOTATIONS 1: THE NORTH FACE OF AESCHYLUS

On the tops of the mountains, among the Alps, feeling myself alone and near to God, I have sent the passion of my spirit upward. But not an echo answers me . . .

[104] J. A. Symonds (1873: 342).

the Greeks...who had not yet been taught the isolation of their souls, c[oul]d not have loved the Alps.[105]

Symonds's audience needs no prompting to tour the high places of Greek literature, but why should they avoid the peaks themselves? Underlying the rhetorical showpiece with which Symonds begins his chapter on epigram is a web of associations from contemporary culture that, taken together, parse his recommendation of the genre as a salutary prescription for health and a necessary plea for sanity.

Symonds was co-opting a richly evocative, ethically and emotionally resonant terrain. The Alps already enjoyed a special place in the imagination of the contemporary readership of *Sketches* and *Studies*. From the 1850s onwards, in parallel with the rise of health tourism to the Alpine valleys, an equation of physical ascent with spiritual uplift had inspired generations of daring British Alpinists to conquer the remaining unclimbed peaks. The new mass media turned them into national heroes. Their conquests were viewed as patriotic and character-forming sporting endeavours; additionally, forging onwards and upwards towards a snow-capped summit neatly embodied and illustrated the contemporary social ideal of progress.[106] Founded in 1857, the Alpine Club excelled in bringing members' exploits to the attention of a broad reading public. Alpinism became overnight the defining sport of, in the revealing words of a Maga contributor, 'hundreds of *high*-spirited Britons...with *high* tastes and sympathies'.[107] Courage, perseverance, intelligence, spirit— these buzzwords defined a literally up-and-coming British generation against the wider degeneracy of the industrialized Western workforce, huddling in its insanitary slums.

Symonds's own evocation of the Genius of the Greeks is now inevitably read in terms of sexual subtext,[108] but also aligns the Greek ideal with the British mountaineering hero of the 1850s and 1860s. Quoted earlier, this passage bears revisiting with new emphases:

The *pride and strength* of adolescence are his—*audacity and endurance*, swift passions and exquisite sensibilities, the alternations of sublime repose and boyish noise, *grace, pliancy, and stubbornness and power*, love of all fair things and splendours of the world, *the frank enjoyment of the open air*, free merriment, *and melancholy well beloved*...

In an essay first published three years after the first series of *Studies*, Pater teases out this imagery to conjure up a Greece whose surviving literature

---

[105] J. A. Symonds (1967–9: i. 732, 648).   [106] Fleming (2000: 169–70).
[107] Quoted at Fleming (2000: 175–6) (emphases added).
[108] As e.g. at Holliday (2000: 88–9).

and art expressed 'men's sense and experience of their own bodily qualities—*swiftness, energy, power of concentrating sight and hand and foot on a momentary physical act*'.[109] Pater's fine-tuned version of Symonds's limber pagan outdoorsman comes very close here to explicit enrolment in the Alpine Club. But in a British Victorian context this crag-hopping Alcibiades, launching himself across the abyss towards the next handhold, had particularly good cause to feel a twinge of pleasurable grief—'melancholy well beloved'. The use of classical culture as a *memento mori* is well documented and studied, and Symonds elsewhere attributes to Alpine solitude a similar power to inspire pleasurably solemn reflection,[110] but his phrasing carried additional and specific force for a contemporary readership.

'Do nothing in haste; look well to each step; and from the beginning think what may be the end.' These are the closing words of Edward Whymper's bestselling 1871 memoir, *Scrambles Amongst the Alps* (p. 408)—written six years after, and in part to justify his decisions during, a technically successful first ascent of the Matterhorn in which several of his party had perished, including a 19-year-old English Lord. The British press had turned the Matterhorn disaster into a moral panic. Suddenly mountaineering was no longer straightforwardly admirable. It served no good end, and could even be morally dangerous. The social order was at stake whenever its young aristocrats pressed heedlessly into the death zone:

Why is the best blood of England to waste itself in scaling hitherto inaccessible peaks, in staining the eternal snows and reaching the unfathomable abyss never to return? . . . Well, this is magnificent. But is it life? Is it duty? Is it common sense? Is it allowable? Is it not wrong?[111]

Six years on, a review in the *Standard* of *Scrambles Amongst the Alps* criticized Whymper for feeding 'the depraved taste, which ought to be checked rather than cultivated, for doughty deeds in Alpine climbing'; the book was 'morally deteriorating, ministering to an unhealthy craving for excitement'.[112]

The mixed press for Alpinism was all the more resonant in the 1870s because so many more British visitors were now arriving there every year; Thomas Cook had been running Alpine package tours since 1863, and by now the market was established. Most simply took in the scenery and enjoyed the healthy air, but there was always a handful of daredevils, and in the decade from 1866 to 1876 there was at least one death every

---

[109] Pater (1901: 36) (emphases added).   [110] J. A. Symonds (1879: 279).
[111] *The Times* editorial, 27 July 1865, found through Fleming (2000: 291).
[112] Quoted at Fleming (2000: 294).

year. In 1870 a party of eleven tourists died in a blizzard on Mont Blanc.[113] Increased tourism not only increased the rate of British fatalities, it made them more publicly visible, more newsworthy. Even the Queen took notice, writing to Gladstone to see if anything she could say might put an end to the steady procession of unnecessary deaths.

To hail the canon authors of Greek literature as ice- and snow-clad 'sparkling summits', at just the time when attempts by British amateur climbers on major Alpine peaks were attracting unprecedented moral criticism and becoming identified as symptomatic of an un-British taste for sensation, must then be seen as a double-edged compliment. Contemporary print discourse of Alpine catastrophe informs Symonds's praise of mountains, literary as well as material, in their capacity as a ravishing view rather than as a set of climbing challenges. For the visitor of middling means and ambitions, the valleys offer enjoyment and recreation without mortal or social danger. Looking up at Aeschylus from the vantage-point of the Anthology's sunny Alpine meadow is better for us, and for society, than trying to read him.

7. THE ANTHOLOGY MEETS ITS PUBLIC

Meleager had a soul that inclined to all beautiful and tender things.[114]

The large majority of Symonds's readers in the 1870s will have come to this 'most valuable relic' with few preconceptions, and with little or no grasp of the genre's ancient historical and cultural contexts. The last general histories of Greek literature lay a generation in the past, and had in any case never mentioned epigram (see Chapter 2); Burges's slipshod Bohn had offered only a desultory preface of four-and-a-half pages, of which only three (pp. iii–v) had talked about the genre at all, and then mostly by parroting Bland; and Merivale's Collections of 1833, which had reproduced Bland's preface entire, had never been reprinted. A privileged elite still knew a little of the Anthology's text through school selections, but only as a basis for language drills. There was thus no publicly accepted story about the genre and how it related to ancient Greece, and Symonds was free to spin pretty much any narrative he wanted.

What is more, this story might now reach a larger readership than had been possible before. The retail price of each Series of Studies was

---

[113] My source for all this detail is again the invaluable Fleming (2000: 296).
[114] J. A. Symonds (1873: 377).

10s. 6d.—still a good chunk of money, but no dearer than other new books of the 1870s and considerably more affordable than the 15s. of *Polyglotta* two decades earlier. Although realistically he might have more immediate uses for the money, a jobbing carpenter could easily earn that in two days; a professional, much sooner (10s. 6d. was a plausible price for a hat).[115]

Following his two-page sales pitch, sampled above, Symonds begins his substantive account of epigram by narrating the complete history of the Anthology, from its early Hellenistic roots in collections of verse inscriptions right through to the rediscovery and subsequent fortunes of the Palatine MS of Cephalas. No writer in English had offered this necessary contextualization since Robert Bland in 1806, who had been the very first to tell epigram's story, and who half-buried a partly sound outline in eccentric digression.[116] Symonds's new history of the Anthology is a very different animal: clear, methodical, concise, and to the point,[117] it is meticulous in its scholarship but also a ripping yarn. It hooks the novice reader while enriching the understanding of the expert:

But about 200 B.C. one Polemon made a general collection of the authentic epigrams to be found upon the public buildings of the Greek cities. After him Alcetas copied the dedicatory verses at Delphi. Similar collections are ascribed to Mnestor and Apellas Ponticus...

So far, the collectors of epigrams had devoted themselves to historical monuments; and of their work, in any separate form at least, no trace exists. But Meleager of Gadara (B.C. 60) conceived the notion of arranging in alphabetical order a selection of lyric and erotic poetry, which he dedicated to his friend Diocles...[118]

Particularly gripping is the section on the reception history of the Palatine manuscript, which packs in a lot of painstakingly gleaned insider gossip:

A glance at this treasure assured the young scholar —for Saumaise was then aged only twenty-two—that he had made one of the most important discoveries which

---

[115] In the period 1871–3, a craftsman in the building trade could expect to earn between 5s. 4d. and 6s. for ten hours' work. The data are tabulated in a classic article by Phelps Brown and Hopkins (1955: 197–9). The retail purchasing power of the working-class consumer increases steadily from the 1820s through the rest of the century: Phelps Brown and Hopkins (1956: 302; data, p. 306). The hat of the Mad Hatter in Lewis Carroll's *Alice's Adventures in Wonderland* (1865) is labelled '10s. 6d.'.

[116] Bland (1806: pp. xii–xxxvii).

[117] Really very concise, at only just over three pages in generously spaced octavo (J. A. Symonds 1873: 342–6). Symonds packs a great deal of (by the standards of his time) very accurate information into this brief space.

[118] This and the immediately following passage are from J. A. Symonds (1873: 345).

remained within the reach of modern students. He spent years in preparing a critical edition of its text; but all his work was thrown away; for the Leyden publishers to whom he applied refused to publish the Greek without a Latin version, and death overtook him before he had completed the requisite labour...Isaac Voss, the rival of Saumaise, induced one Lucas Langermann to undertake a journey to Rome, in order that he might make a faithful transcript of the MS. and publish it to the annoyance of the great French scholar. But Saumaise dying in 1653, the work, undertaken from motives of jealousy, was suspended.

It is simply a masterpiece of its genre, and I would warmly recommend it to an interested student today; there are a couple of errors, and the modern scholarship (Cameron 1993) has added one or two intriguing twists, but no better short introductory account has been written.

With this genre history, Symonds at the outset establishes his own authority to speak for Greek epigram—and thus, through epigram, for ordinary ancient Greeks who are just like ourselves but for the 'accident' of when and where they were born. He also makes their story authentically Classic, up to a point—a point far in advance of any previous drawing of the line between Classical Greece and what came after. By doing so, and in slippery contravention of the nominally conventional scheme of periodization that he had outlined in his first chapter, he makes the Greeks of the Anthology—or *some* of them, at least—legitimately paradigmatic as standards for living in the present. At the very outset of Symonds's genre history, its inherent 'lateness' as a phenomenon of the Hellenistic, Imperial, Late Antique, and Byzantine eras is rhetorically finessed:

[Meleager] called this compilation by the name of στέφανος, each of the forty-six poets whom he admitted into his book being represented by a flower. Philip of Thessalonica in the time of Trajan, following his example, incorporated into the garland of Meleager those epigrams which had acquired celebrity in the interval. About the same time or a little later, Straton of Sardis made a special anthology of poems on one class of subjects, which is known as the μοῦσα παιδικὴ, and into which, besides ninety-eight of his own epigrams, he admitted many of the compositions of Meleager, Philip, and other predecessors. *These collections belong to the classical period of Greek literature.* But the Anthology, as we understand it, had not yet come into existence. It remained for Agathias, *a Byzantine Greek of the age of Justinian*, to undertake a comprehensive compilation from all the previous collections...[119]

---

[119] J. A. Symonds (1873: 343–4) (emphases added). With more than a century of scholarly hindsight one may easily spot a couple of basic mistakes here regarding what Philip and Strato actually did, but that is by the by.

Shockingly if we pause to think about it—and the trick is that, carried along by the excellent storytelling, most readers will not—not only late-Hellenistic Meleager but also Roman-era Philip and even Strato (second century CE) are now parsed as Classical Greek authors, and thus potentially recuperable as teachers for modernity. Agathias (sixth century), however, inhabits an entirely separate thought-world: 'Byzantine'; any poet of this dismal late era by definition has nothing to say to us in the present. But Meleager does, and so, amazingly, does Strato; more on this shortly.

Immediately following the genre history, and again with impeccable appearances of sober (yet stylistically delicious) exegesis, Symonds usefully leads his reader through the Anthology's overall structure. This is a service that no previous writer in English on the Anthology had undertaken to perform, in some cases through a paucity of resources. Bland had, of course, worked from Jacobs's first edition of 1794–8, which still followed Brunck's rearrangement of 1772–3 by author, and in doing so he had somehow acquired the mistaken impression that Brunck's labour had effectively reconstituted the 'lost' Greek Anthology from numerous scattered *disiecta membra*. His preface therefore showed no interest in explaining the original structure of Cephalas' Anthology, a work he presumed to be knowable only at second-hand through the German scholar's Herculean efforts in sifting the miscellaneous manuscripts of Europe. Bland simply did not realize that Brunck's edition was based on autopsy of a single manuscript, the Palatine MS, which he believed had yet to be edited and which he did not know had any direct relation to Cephalas—all this in a section added in 1813, the same year that the first volume of Jacobs's second edition, *ad fidem codicis olim Palatini edita*, was to prove him hopelessly wrong.[120]

Symonds's account of the structure of the Anthology is thus a highly necessary intervention, and again addresses a majority readership with little or no background knowledge or accompanying preconceptions. It continues the scholarly yet lively mode of the genre history, and summarizes the sixteen books of the Anthology from start to finish in a brisk one-and-a-half pages, while also helping the reader who knows some epigram-translations from the Reviews or *Polyglotta* to find his or her

---

[120] Bland's Brunck worked from 'various MSS. in almost all the great public libraries of Europe' and 'the great dictionary of Suidas', but Bland himself has learned of 'A splendid MS. known by the name of the Vatican, and now in the Imperial library at Paris, [which] seems to have been untouched by' Brunck and Jacobs alike—this is, of course, the Palatine MS, which they had both used, did Bland but know it (and Merivale (1833: p. xlii) reproduces the mistake of 1813 verbatim).

feet (Symonds explains that most of what they have been reading is from the epideictic AP 9), foreshadowing the exclusion from critical consideration of book 8 ('dismal' because 'post-pagan'—that is, Byzantine), and tactfully clarifying that the archaic lyric poets beloved of Bland have no real place in the Anthology proper. This is immediately followed by the real meat of the chapter: forty-eight pages of literary survey that sample individual poems to give a flavour of the Anthology's categories, moving through them in the order presented by Cephalas.[121]

An important omission, however, sets up Symonds's literary-critical narrative for bold ideological revisionism. Symonds very reasonably sets aside from his literary survey the Anthology's very miscellaneous and largely non-epigrammatic front end, books 1 through 4, and thus begins his critical account with...the dedicatory poems of book 6. Here and there is slipped in a suspect love-offering: 'In the epigrams before us we read how hunters hung their nets to Pan, and fishermen their gear to Poseidon...Meleager yields the lamp of his love-hours to Venus...Theocritus writes inscriptions for Uranian Aphrodite in the house of his friend Amphicles.'[122] Faithfully if very briefly reported in his summary account of the Anthology's structure, the heterosexually erotic book 5 has slipped through one of the cracks that articulate his own structural scheme.

Sepulchral epigram (AP 7) receives a long critical appreciation (pp. 351–66), playing to its conventional popularity as a model for translation and sentimental imitation but indulging in none of the sententious religiosity so prominent in MacGregor; then briefly the protreptic epigrams (AP 10), principally those of Palladas (pp. 366–70); and the skoptic and sympotic poems of that mixed bag, AP 11 (pp. 370–3), which we learn displays the Greek genius sullied by the crudity of its conquerors:

Lucillius, a Greek Martial of the age of Nero, is both best and most prolific in this kind of composition. But of all the sections of the Anthology this is certainly the least valuable. The true superiority of Greek to Latin literature is that it is far more a work of pure beauty, of unmixed poetry. In Lucillius the Hellenic muse has deigned for once to assume the Roman toga, and to show that if she chose, she could rival the hoarse-throated satirists of the empire on their own ground. But she has abandoned her lofty eminence, and descended to a lower level.[123]

[121] J. A. Symonds (1873: 346–7) (description of Anthology's arrangement); pp. 347–95 (literary survey of individual books in sequence).

[122] J. A. Symonds (1873: 349–50).

[123] J. A. Symonds (1873: 373).

The riddles of AP 14 are dismissed in the same breath and for the same reasons as not truly Greek; that they could have been written anywhere by anyone disqualifies them from 'true beauty', which is the preserve of Greeks alone.

Our thoughts immediately now turn to love, which by contrast is very Greek indeed.

8. STYLES OF EROS: MELEAGER, STRATO, RUFINUS

Of all the amatory poets of the Anthology, by far the noblest is Meleager. He was a native of Gadara in Palestine ... It is curious to think of this town, which from our childhood we have connected with the miracle of the demoniac and the swine, as a Syrian Athens, the birthplace of the most mellifluous of erotic songsters. Meleager's date is half a century or thereabouts before the Christian era. He therefore was ignorant of the work and the words of the One who made the insignificant place of his origin world-famous.

('Nor has he ever felt sin'...) This poet of cosmopolitan humanity and pure Greek Genius reveals the unchanging truth of love and desire:

This triple salutation [AP 7.419, the poet's epitaph for himself], coming from a son of Gadara and Tyre and Ceos, brings us close to the *pure humanity* which distinguished Meleager. Modern men, judging him by the standard of Christian morality, may feel justified in flinging a stone at the poet who celebrated his Muiscos and his Diocles, his Heliodora and his Zenophila, in too voluptuous verse. But those who are content to criticise a pagan by his own rule of right and wrong, will admit that Meleager had a spirit of the subtlest and the sweetest, a heart of the tenderest, and *a genius of the purest* that has ever been granted to an elegist of earthly love. While reading his verse, it is impossible to avoid laying down the book and pausing to exclaim: How modern is the phrase, how true the passion, how unique the style![124]

'His Muiscos and his Diocles, his Heliodora and his Zenophila': the heterosexual erotics of AP 5 suddenly re-enter the epigram-narrative of *Studies*, but at their first exampled appearance they are intermingled,

[124] J. A. Symonds (1873: 373–4) (emphases added). He begins (p. 373) by reminding us that the events at Gadara in the New Testament need to be kept mentally separate from Meleager's story. The trilingual greetings written into the poet's pseudo(?)-inscriptional epitaph are Syrian ('Salam!'), Phoenician ('Naidios!'—corrupt?), and of course the Greek ('Khaire!'), in which he composes the poem; for discussion. see Menahem Luz's article (1988), 'Salam, Meleager!'.

ethically interchangeable, and in all applicable senses of a piece with the homosexual AP 12. Both kinds of love are natural to human culture, then and now: '*How modern* is the phrase, *how true* the passion...!'. And how unique the style: Meleager's consummate 'purity' as an artist underwrites alike the truth-value, the moral cleanness, and the natural goodness of the desires he expresses. The style is the man, and the style defies any and all criticism. The poet's voice, 'mute a score of centuries' until revived by Symonds's hagiography, 'yet rings clear and vivid in our ears; because the man was a real poet, feeling intensely, expressing forcibly and beautifully, *steeping his style in the fountain of tender sentiment which is eternal*...All is simple, lively, fresh with *joyous experience* in his verse.'[125] This joyous experience embraces boys and girls interchangeably. (There is a certain amount of misrepresentation here, albeit in what most twenty-first-century readers of the present volume—not all—will consider a good cause; there is much more Meleager in AP 5 than in AP 12.) A telling juxtaposition follows: a hetero-erotic-*cum*-funerary elegy on Clearista, snatched in her youth by Hades to be his bride, and an epigram that 'recalls the song to Ageanax in Theocritus' 7th Idyll'. The two poems are presented in Greek, with translations appended in footnotes. The first is a paternal contribution, 'J. A. Symonds, M.D.':[126]

> Poor Clearisté loosed her virgin zone
> Not for her wedding, but for Acheron...

The second, immediately juxtaposing it on the page, is by Symonds junior:

> Fair blows the breeze: the seamen loose the sail:—
> O men that know not love, your favouring gale
> Steals half my soul, Andragathos, from me!...

Taken together, and each reinforcing the other, the heterosexual and homosexual poems establish Meleager's poetic purity, 'though many more examples might have been borrowed from his epigrams...on the mosquitoes who tormented Zenophila, on Antiochus, who might have been Erôs if Erôs had worn the boy's petasos and chlamys'. (Tellingly, however, of these two instances offered for consideration as paradigms, the boy is alive; the girl is dead.) Meleager's love for beauty in nature proves the natural beauty of his love; his epigrams are finely cut poetic gems (see Appendix) that attest to his consummate technical (and thus

---

[125] J. A. Symonds (1873: 374).   [126] J. A. Symonds (1873: 375).

highly masculine) command of his genre, but they are also roses in their purity. He is the supreme poet of Eros, and Eros is a beautiful boy *sans merci*; he is the supreme weaver of poetic garlands, and some of the flowers in his wreath are handsome youths. The truest artist gathers garlands of flowers and boys alike: 'Most exquisite are the lines in which he describes his garland of the Greek poets and assigns to each some favourite of the garden or the field, and again those other couplets which compare the boys of Tyre to a bouquet culled by Love for Aphrodite.'[127] The allusion is to AP 12.256, in which the poet sings of how Eros has woven for the Cyprian a παγκαρπόν... στέφανον, a wreath containing every kind of blossom, out of παίδων ἄνθος (ll. 1–2), the sexual bloom of boys. The poem playfully mirrors the language of the Garland's famous verse preface: 'into it he wove sweet Diodorus, and Asclepiades's sweet-smelling white violet; and on it he threaded Heraclitus...' (ll. 3–5); a Theron, too, is part of this meta-pederastic boy-garland, which may well be where Symonds found the name to use in his private poetry.

Only the sly reader, however, will pick up on any of this. Instead the surface message is that Meleager's erotic verse is uplifting, Apollonian, Arnoldian: it is no accident that the very first sentence of Symonds's encomium extols his 'limpidity', and the last his 'sweetness', in a closural gambit that (we are told) additionally aligns the poet with the single Greek epigram already to have achieved household-name status, Cory's famous translation of Callimachus. Earlier in the essay, Symonds has quoted the entire poem under the pretext of introducing his discussion of sepulchral epigram, calling Cory's version 'exquisite', so the allusion is sure to hit home even if the explicit echo is not consciously spotted; to add further spice for fellow-connoisseurs of elite homophile verse, Symonds there introduced Cory as 'the author of *Ionica*', a red flag for those in the know.[128]

Immediately following, and 'next in artistic excellence to Meleager among the amatory poets', we meet a rather different kind of lover–poet: Strato, whose lateness in relation to Meleager is immediately and unfussily established. But there is not much more that Symonds can tell us, at

---

[127] J. A. Symonds (1873: 376–8). Crystalline Meleager: (p. 374).
[128] Limpidity his 'first great merit' (J. A. Symonds 1873: 374); 'the sweetness and the splendour of the rose, the rapture and full-throated melody of the nightingale' (p. 378). Cf. from Cory's 'Heraclitus': 'Still are your pleasant voices, your nightingales, awake'. Poem quoted in full at (1873: 355). Symonds was given his copy of *Ionica* as an undergraduate at Balliol by Prof. John Conington, an early and sympathetic sounding-board for his ideas about his sexuality (J. A. Symonds 1984: 109–11). Cory's little book pops up again at p. 319.

least, not directly. His description of what Strato is, or rather of what he is not, is tantalizingly short at a single paragraph:

> But there are few readers who, even for the sake of his pure and perfect language, will be prepared to put up with the immodesty of his subject-matter. Straton is not so delicate and subtle in style as Meleager: but he has a masculine vigour and *netteté* of phrase peculiar to himself. It is not possible to quote many of his epigrams. He suffers the neglect which necessarily obscures those men of genius who misuse their powers...[129]

Symonds's teaser establishes Strato as a lover–poet in a 'pure' mode but impure in expression. Whatever the nature of his error may be, however, his manliness is incontrovertible. The terms in which this virile identity is expressed—physical toughness and clear, clipped, unfussy speech—gesture generically towards established public perceptions of Sparta (additionally evoking for those in the know the spectre of German-derived homophile Dorianism). Whatever else he may be—and the mention of a poem on Ganymede gives an immediate clue—this Strato is no effeminate.

But what is Strato, exactly? Symonds has been trailing hints for a while, indeed, since the outset of *Studies*. There is clearly something of the night about him:

> It is the fashion among a certain class of modern critics to rave about the art of Decadence, to praise the hectic hues of consumption and even the strange livors of corruption, more than the roses and the lilies of health. Let them peruse the epigrams of Meleager and of Straton. Of beauty in decay sufficient splendours may be found there.[130]

Bound by the context of Symonds's introductory narration, in which a largely conventional chronological scheme is being set out, this tantalizing adumbration of depraved beauty flags up the two authors as a matched pair. Its Meleager is inescapably 'late' and, as a consequence, alluringly sick (on which topic, more in a moment). As we have seen, that initial sketch is later comprehensively and pointedly overwritten by the rosily healthy Meleager of Symonds's own eleventh chapter, and clearly now also by the rude good health of Strato as well. According to this literary-critical account, both these poets now count as Classical and are not late after all, albeit that Meleager is more Classical ('purer') than Strato; they retain their 'beauty', but the threat of 'decay' has somehow been sidestepped, redirected elsewhere. As Classics, both are poets of

---

[129] J. A. Symonds (1873: 378), and cf. the introductory remarks at p. 347, again saying without saying: Strato's AP 12 'exhibits...the morality of ancient Hellas under the aspect which has least attraction for modern readers'.

[130] J. A. Symonds (1873: 33).

authentic and pure desire.[131] Symonds here has his cake and eats it too: epigram is granted a unique exemption from the Winckelmanian logic of the macrocosmic bell curve of Greek literary-cultural development, while at the same time enacting it faithfully in microcosm within its own generic micro-history.

This chronological sleight of hand enables him to tease out significant distinctions between Meleager, Strato, and other erotic poets of the Anthology. First, though, a figure familiar to Oxonian Hellenes hints strongly at the implicit grounds for literary-critical judgement: 'To mention all the poets of the amatory chapters [sic] would be impossible. Their name is legion. Even Plato the divine, by right of this epigram to Aster... And of this to Agathon... takes rank in the erotic cycle.[132] Be they devilish ('legion'), angelic ('divine'), or somewhere in between, the Anthology offers countless affirming prototypes for modern love in a Hellenic mode. 'Plato the divine' certifies that these are genuine works of the philosophic Plato we all know and admire, a view that modern epigram studies has disavowed but that was then orthodox; as an Anthology poet the philosopher was conventionally distinguished from a second Plato, taken to be a Hellenistic namesake.[133] At the other end of the scale from Plato are the major Hellenistic epigrammatists Philodemus and Antipater, mentioned immediately after him only to be dismissed as true 'poets of the amatory chapters'—the last a double-coded term whose very poor applicability to the Anthology's structure immediately cues up for those in the know the image of Dorian chivalry (the 'chapter' as a spiritually affiliated order of knights). Philodemus' heterosexual verses 'belong to that class of literature'—clearly a lower class—'which finds its illustration in the Gabinetto Segreto of the Neapolitan Museum', and their failure suggests that he should have stuck to the comic themes at which a single poem suggests he would have excelled; Antipater really only shines as a literary critic. At heart, neither is really an erotic epigrammatist at all.[134]

The distinction we are being asked to draw is between genuine love, and 'love' as a literary exercise. Symonds has already insisted upon just such a distinction to help us mentally subdivide the Anthology's books of

---

[131] That we are meant to think this way of Strato is reinforced through juxtaposition and contrast in Symonds's immediately following discussion of Callimachus, in quality 'a third with Meleager and Straton', whose style is let down by 'a frigidity of good scholarship which only at intervals warms into the fire of passionate poetry'—effectively he is 'later' than Strato in his bookish artificiality (J. A. Symonds 1873: 379).

[132] J. A. Symonds (1873: 379–80).

[133] On the enduring fiction of Plato the epigrammatist, see briefly Page (1981: 125–6); short contextualizing discussion at Livingstone and Nisbet (2010: 125).

[134] J. A. Symonds (1873: 380–1).

dedications (AP 6) and epitaphs (AP 7) into two kinds of poem: those that respond directly to real-life situations, and those that are merely 'epideiktic or rhetorical'. Tender Meleager, of course, is a poet of genuine and rhetorically unforced epitaphs, as is Callimachus (this is where Cory's 'Heraclitus' takes the stage) and of course the divine Plato. There is never any doubt which poems and which emotions are real, and which fake: the attuned reader simply knows.[135]

Emotional authenticity also underwrites Classical periodicity, and vice versa. Real feeling and frank expression belong to the health and strength of Greece's full life, while rhetorical simulation reveals the post-Classical latecomer; epigram's eventual expiry in extreme old age is accompanied by 'the thin lamentable wail of the dessicated rhetorician', an emotional husk cut off from lived experience and capable of expressing no emotion beyond querulous self-pity.[136] In Symonds's discussion of erotic epigram these paired binaries—early and late, Classic and non-Classic, authentic and artificial emotion and experience—come to fruition. Plato, Meleager, Strato: these are the poets of genuine human Eros. Philodemus, Antipater: their love did read by rote and could not spell.

Still worse are the post-Classical poets: that is to say, post-Strato. The passage bears quoting at length:

> Another group of amatory poets must be mentioned. Agathias, Macedonius, and Paulus Silentarius, Greeks of Byzantium about the age of Justinian, together with Rufinus, whose date is not yet certain, yield the very last fruits of the Greek genius, after it had been corrupted by the lusts of Rome and the effeminacy of the East. Very pale and hectic are the hues which give a sort of sickly beauty to their style. Their epigrams vary between querulous lamentations over old age and death, and highly coloured pictures of self-satisfied sensuality...
>
> a man need be neither a prude nor a Puritan to turn with sadness and with loathing from these last autumnal blossoms on the tree of Greek beauty. The brothel and the grave are all that is left for Rufinus and his contemporaries. Over the one hangs the black shadow of death; the other is tenanted by ghosts of carnal joy...[137]

We have been told at the outset that 'even the Graffiti of Pompeii have scarcely more power to reconstruct the past and summon as in dreams the voices and the forms of long-since buried men': here, however, Pompeii is invoked not as the Alma-Tadema-esque dressing-up box of bourgeois escapism but squarely in its capacity as the secular Gomorrah

---

[135] 'Really epideictic or rhetorical' and Cory's 'Heraclitus' (J. A. Symonds 1873: 351); Plato's private and public epitaphs (pp. 352–3); the sepulchral 'ring of truth' (p. 354).
[136] J. A. Symonds (1873: 370).   [137] J. A. Symonds (1873: 381–2).

of the West. At once 'brothel' and 'grave', this Pompeii is forever frozen at the exact moment when an outraged Nature exacted punishment for its sins of the flesh: the revellers' guilt and foreboding merge with the ash cloud of Vesuvius to hang above it as a figurative-*cum*-literal 'black shadow of death'.[138]

Agathias, Macedonius, Paulus the Silentiary: these are familiar names to the student of epigram's uses in Anglophone culture, and their deprecation in *Studies* marks a decisive critical break with the reduced Anthology of the linguistically focused pedagogic tradition (see Chapter 2). All three are prominent in the school collections raided by Burges. Paul has an unbroken run of many pages in Edwards's *Selection*; Agathias in particular has greater presence than Meleager in the Westminster and Eton *Selections*; Meleager has a slight edge over him in *Polyglotta*, but not by much.[139] Rufinus' date is here flagged as uncertain, but as the paragraph continues his lateness firms up. *Studies* thus affirms the ultra-late Rufinus of recent wisdom against the earlier dating suggested by Bland's arrangement, in which Rufinus was early and Strato very late indeed; effectively Symonds takes over Bland's implicit narrative of the genre's end-game (one in which Agathias, Paul, and Macedonius get generous coverage) but swaps the two poets around.[140] These Byzantine perverts mark the death of Greek literature and the Greek spirit. Paul's desires are unspeakably vile:

> Rufinus is a kind of second Straton in the firmness of his touch, the cynicism of his impudicity.... Of Paulus Silentarius I do not care to allude to more than the poem in which he describes the joy of two lovers (i. 106). What Ariosto and Boiardo have dwelt on in some of their most brilliant episodes, what Giorgione has painted in the eye of the shepherd who envies the kiss given by Rachel to Jacob, is

---

[138] Readers familiar with Symonds's homophile poetry would recognize in his Pompeii a characteristic motif. At (1875: 75), in the closing panel of a triptych entitled 'three Visions of Imperial Rome', the captured god of Uranian Love berates the Romans as a 'Nation of harlots!'. The 'Pompeii' of the same sequence is a 'foul' den of whoring. 'Large-breasted women born to murder shame' solicit custom under the lewd gaze of the Pandemic 'vulgar Venus' (p. 71), where the brothel bed is 'Piled up into a broad voluptuous mound | Upon that pyre of lust that burns away' (p. 72). This Pompeii is already its own funeral pyre; the eruption of Vesuvius just makes it official. That said, only a tiny handful of readers *were* familiar with these poems. On the nineteenth-century trope of Pompeii as a 'living grave', see the thoughtful chapter by Hales (2011).

[139] See Ch. 2. The Westminster and Eton collections supply two poems by Macedonius, three by Rufinus, five by Paul, five by Meleager, and eight by Agathias; Meleager gets eighteen poems in *Polyglotta* and Agathias fifteen.

[140] Bland places Rufinus just after Nicarchus and Ammianus, a fairly reasonable guess, and devotes three pages to him (1806: 65–7). Agathias, Paul, and Macedonius in Bland (1806: 71–8), immediately followed by Strato at p. 79, a single poem and very nearly the last by a named author; anonymous epigrams commence on the following page.

here compressed into eighteen lines of great literary beauty. But a man need be neither a prude nor a Puritan ... [etc.][141]

Rufinus is only 'a *kind* of second Straton'—audaciously physical, yes, but (unlike Strato) cut off by Roman contagion from the authentic Greek spirit and thus out of sympathy with healthy human nature. Because his 'sensuality' (a keyword that instantly flags up Oriental unmanliness) finds no healthy object through the role of philosophic lover but aims only at gratifying appetite, it is socially unproductive—non-Uranian love is really just a form of masturbation ('self-satisfied'). This makes it the proper target of Victorian moral condemnation—indeed, moral panic.[142] He and his fellow Byzantines (Rufinus is now re-parsed as their 'contemporary') write a more or less literally rotten and mongrel poetry ('corrupted by the lusts of Rome') that can evoke only disgust in the modern reader. To underpin his sermon, Symonds immediately gives us ten lines of Milton's classically allusive *Comus: A Mask*, on the inward rotting of the soul under the spell of lusts of the flesh, binding it to the defiled body even after death: 'Such are those thick and gloomy shadows damp | Oft seen in charnel-vaults and sepulchres, Lingering, and sitting by a new-made grave, | As loth to leave the body that it loved ...'.

The domains of sex and of death are now coterminous: 'the brothel and the grave' blur together in a morbid double consciousness of Gothically inflected Decadence, where poetic composition is indistinguishable from necrotic decomposition. (Read the love poems of Agathias after this description and you are in for a surprise; they are perfectly nice.) These voices of the late Empire are not poet–lovers, but necrophile pornographers. Unlike Strato, a rough wooer who followed his own nature (though not in the wisest way), *they have felt sin*. No wonder they are pale; but why are their hues 'hectic'?

9: ALPINE CONTEXTS 2: 'THE SOUL GROWS CLOTTED BY CONTAGION'

Man, who is all things *in the plain*, is nothing here .... Nature ... [is] here the face of God & not the slave of man ... God here hath

---

[141] J. A. Symonds (1873: 381–2). One reason he may be keen to steer his readers away from Rufinus in particular is that the poet characterizes same-sex desire as a youthful phase, which a grown man leaves behind in pursuit of girls, AP 5.19.

[142] From the extensive modern literature on Victorian demonization of masturbation, one might single out Lesley Hall (1992); in passing, Bristow (1991: 41, 71) is interesting on the way this filtered into the boys'-own stories aimed at the likeliest offenders.

not grown old: He is as young as on the first day: & the Alps are a
symbol of the self creating, self enjoying Universe wh[ich] lives for
its own end.[143]

Over the brothel of Rufinus and his Byzantine Christian 'contemporaries',
'corrupted by the lusts of Rome... hangs the black shadow of death'. We
have noted that Roman Pompeii lurks here, the excavated City of the Plain
notorious for its plethora of brothels (real or supposed) and conclusively
punished for its sexual sins by an insulted Nature. This melodramatic
reception of the ancient city operates in dialogue with contemporary
discourse of hygiene in the metropolis, in an era when public health was
inescapably political; pundits pinpointed the teeming slums as the site of
imminent British racial collapse, specifically contrasting the vile bodies of
urban poor to the perfection exemplified for the ages by the ancient Greek
physique onto which classical art offered a window through time.[144] From
the 1850s onward, therefore, interventionist legislation sought to regulate
the sexual behaviour of the proletariat for the health of the British race.
Control of the spread of venereal disease through codification-led social
engineering, most famously or infamously the Contagious Diseases Acts
of 1864 and 1866, was put on a par with regimes of epidemic avoidance
through investment in infrastructure.[145] Optimism on the prospects for
improvement in the combined fields of public hygiene and morality
through legal sanction peaked in the early 1870s, just when Symonds
was putting *Studies* together for publication.[146]

In parallel with control of sexual expression, State censorship of sexual
content in media was increasingly figured as part and parcel of the same
public health agenda. Prosecutions over obscene materials were discursively parsed as keeping poison out of the hands of the urban population,
just as legislation and medical activism strove to keep literal poisons out of
their daily bread. A Lords debate on the Poisons Bill of 1857 makes it clear
how deeply this figurative association was taking root: pornography was
described by the Lord Chief Justice on that occasion as not merely a poison
'more deadly than prussic acid, strychnine, or arsenic', but as 'pestilential'.

The rhetoric of plague is significant: pornography had taken quick
advantage of the latest print technologies to go mass market as the

---

[143] J. A. Symonds (1967-9: i. 648), to Dakyns (emphasis added).
[144] Challis (2010: 115-17) is illuminating.
[145] Typically of laws enacted to appease moral panic, these Acts were bad legislation.
A feminist, rights-based campaign to repeal them gathered traction in the early 1880s,
paying off in 1886: Mort (2000: 67).
[146] Mort (2000: 54-7).

ubiquitous and quintessential medium of urban modernity.[147] Like prussic acid, strychnine, and arsenic, porn was a product of chemical industry—the availability of cheap literature generally (even if not actually obscene) was seen as a worrying metropolitan infestation.[148] When Symonds tells us he 'do[es] not care to allude' to the detailed content of the post-Stratonian epigrammatists, he relegates their erotica to the modern category of pornography as a danger to public health in the big city. That Paul expresses this poison in lines of 'great literary beauty' makes him all the more reprehensible, tying him to the rhetorical-*cum*-literary topos of the Dangerous Book (long established, but gaining new weight and urgency in a mechanized world).[149]

'The brothel and the grave' construes Rufinus and his peers as syphilitic; 'pale and hectic', as tubercular ('hectic fever'). We will give some thought to the second of these momentarily. A third urban disease ran alongside these two in contemporary medical thought: homosexuality. Classifying homosexuality as a characteristic disorder of the metropolis aligned it with TB and syphilis, and thus with regimes of epidemic avoidance. The association between the metropolis and homosexual subculture was explicitly factored into the medical profession's construction of sexology as a public health concern: sexual deviance was seen as emerging out of and expressing racial degeneracy and neurological disorder, and the public press parlayed this medical discourse into veiled moral panic.[150]

Already by the 1870s, and discursively as well as in practice, homosexual identity in Britain was indelibly associated with London in its aspect of metropolitan alienation—a sea of anonymous individuals, and of urges indulged with no questions asked. This equation of homosexuality with an urban 'scene' was taken as a starting datum by the early sexologists.[151]

[147] Nead (2000: 149–51, quoted at 150). On nineteenth-century media concerns over potentially deadly practices of adulteration of food staples in urban mass-manufacture, see accessibly Wilson (2008).

[148] Nead (2000: 155).

[149] Nice summary of the main issues at Aliaga-Buchenau (2004: 125). The topos would of course help define literary Decadence in the *fin de siècle*: Dowling (1980: 28). The consistently interesting McDermott (2008: 26–8) pushes the idea further to include Symonds's narrative of his own encounter with 'the book that makes one gay', in his case the *Phaedrus* and secondarily Whitman's *Leaves of Grass*.

[150] Cook (2003a: 74, 78–9).

[151] City by city, the articulation of a self-consciously edgy experience of 'sites of narrative' within an alternate, liminal urban topography of pleasure and danger ('gay city') continues to underlie self-fashioning within subculture: Leap (2010: 190–2), with further bibliography. For an anthropologically rich description of actual urban gay experience in the period, including Symonds's own, see Kaplan (1999), and see again Cook (2003a: 74, 78–9). Symonds's own visceral distaste for the aggressive sexual culture of the metropolis: Cook (2003a: 130).

Although the Decadent movement of the 1890s was later to appropriate and amplify this rhetorical association, flaunting its louche metropolitanism in publications such as *The Yellow Book*, Symonds was not alone in his time in finding it unhelpful, since it confined homosexual identity within a site now defined by hygienic panic over life-limiting and debilitating infections, and submitted it to the epidemicists' ideology of the need to police sexual morality—hardly a reformer's charter.[152]

Panic over urban contagion was at the heart of this nexus of ideas. TB, too, was the classic metropolitan public-health problem of the century: while its culling of famous poets and artists lent it grim glamour and even made it a badge of sensitivity of soul, its reality was a peculiarly nasty and protracted death sentence, and the inadequately sanitized big city was where it ran amuck.[153] By the time of *Studies*, though, a new treatment that claimed miraculous results was all the rage: altitude, and specifically the Alps. Medical science already knew that dry air arrested the symptomatic progression, and Alpine resorts were now making big money as spa towns; residents of their hotels and clinics benefited from thin air (which was seen as placing less of a burden on raddled lungs) as well as dry. Going high was at least a life-extender, and was billed as a lifesaver—not merely a palliative therapy, but an actual cure. And the centre of this whole healthcare industry? Symonds's beloved Davos.[154]

10. CONCLUSION: ONWARD AND UPWARD

Nature again is greater here than man, & we forget our pains & passions for a while.[155]

I believe the subtext here is rapidly becoming, er, text.[156]

---

[152] Indeed, the very idea of a morally non-prescriptive sexology was typed as 'German and therefore suspect' (Cook 2003a: 76, quoting a pithy *sententia* from Forster's *Maurice*). Victorian homosexual subculture 'couldn't live with London, couldn't live without it' (Cook 2003b: 33–4). On sin-city posturing in 1890s Decadence, see Potolsky (2007) (good in passing on cosmopolitanism, subculture, and urban entrepreneurialism) and M. W. Turner (2005: 139).

[153] On the unhelpful myths that build up around socially emblematic diseases, with the TB–syphilis binary as an exemplar, see polemically and brilliantly Sontag (1978).

[154] The story is concisely, informatively, and enjoyably told by Fleming (2000: 325–9). Note too the cosmic 'childhood' ascribed to the Alpine heights in Symonds's letter to Dakyns, quoted at the head of the previous section, mirroring the standard Victorian figuration of ancient Greece as the 'childhood' of civilization, on which see Jenkyns (1980: 168–70).

[155] J. A. Symonds (1967–9: i. 651), again to Dakyns.

[156] *Buffy the Vampire Slayer* 2.11, 'Ted' (1997): Rupert Giles to Buffy.

Placing the supposedly Classical authors of the Anthology (everyone up to and including Strato, minus the AP 5 crowd) in an Alpine valley thus has pressing contemporary relevance. The post-Classical Rufinus and his 'contemporaries' are left behind in the diseased metropolis of Pandemic eros—Rome, Paris, London, they are all the same because Pandemic lust can be found in every big city at any period in history. Symonds's rhetorical sketch of this dystopia buys into and even amplifies the contemporary rhetoric of social and moral consternation: it is Pompeii reborn, the melodramatically sinful and doomed Roman city of the plain. The poets who dwell there are syphilitically 'corrupted by the lusts of Rome'; they cough out 'hectic' contagion. 'Hectic fever' was used synonymously with tuberculosis, but was also habitually cited as a symptom of syphilis, an extraordinarily nasty way to go. Syphilis was the time-bomb Muse; popular myth linked it to 'feverish' mental activity (spasms of crazed poetry as its characteristic lesions devoured the brain) and fast burnout. The literary outpourings of this descent into brute animalism could never claim Classic status.[157] With the imagery of venereal disease standing in for heterosexual desire, its poetry is implicitly classed as Pandemic—there is nothing essentially Greek about it at all.

Epigram up to and including Strato, meanwhile, is truly Greek: it escapes the dingy city, moving onwards and upwards into a high and sunny nature-idyll filled with Hellenic light. (And here we may recall Wilde's later declaration of faith in court: 'It may be a malady, but, if so, it appears only to attack the *highest* natures.') Here, landscape and identity reinforce and guarantee each other's authenticity: explaining the characteristic serenity of the Greeks with regard to the perfection of their natural environment was a gift of German Romantic Hellenism, and Symonds was an eloquent exponent of this fantasy of sunlit Greek hills and shores as the nurturing cradle of all that was best in our own civilization. In this secular Schlegelian Eden, human nature expressed itself in physical Beauty because Sin had not yet imprisoned it and alienated it from the body.[158]

Now Symonds materializes the fantasy as a landscape accessible to the person of moderate means, and refashions that landscape as a site for fashioning a newly ennobled, natural, and healthy homosexual identity. The diseased metropolis is the home of a sickening, Roman, and ultra-Pandemic Eros, which is now specifically equated with the compulsory heterosexuality of the Byzantine love-poets; the high Alpine valley is the scene of a healthy, Greek, and Uranian Eros. This idyllic scene finds its

---

[157] Sontag (1978: 23).   [158] Jenkyns (1980: 42–3); F. M. Turner (1981: 178).

ideal expression in the 'pure' Meleager, who rises figuratively and now quasi-geographically *above* bodily sexual compulsions (and with the benefit of historic retrospect we might at this point factor in the startling realization that at the time he wrote *Studies* the bold apologist for gay Eros was himself yet to go much beyond kissing and snuggles in his sexual explorations with other men); but Strato too, although he initially seems to be framed as Meleager's Pandemic Other (his problem is that he loves boys the way a straight man loves girls), earns entry to this paradise by merit of his 'clean' style and rude vigour. Unmistakably these are Dorian traits, as the nineteenth century understood them; they place implicit emphasis on his North European cultural alignment, and they make him perfectly at home in Symonds's Alpine haven, because, if there was one thing the Victorians knew for certain about the Dorians, it was that they were mountain men.[159]

In the greater scheme of things, and compared to the disgusting Rufinus and his ilk, it now looks very much as if Strato is not Pandemic after all, or not exactly. Symonds does not see advantage in pinning down just what he is, in case that frightens the horses; there is clearly some fudging going on, and, just as with Meleager, some judiciously timed backtracking—the 'livors of corruption' that Symonds's introduction flagged up as Stratonian now attach to the heterosexual poets instead. Rufinus may desire as earthily as does Strato, but he exists in a different moral world because the object of that desire is post- and un-Classical. Indeed, in Symonds's summation of Strato's 'clear pure style' at chapter's end, the defining voice of AP 12 is revealed to be closer in spirit to a poet at the other end of epigram's chronological scale: Simonides, flagged up as a stylistic paragon early in the chapter to remind us of substantial treatment much further back in the book (Study 5), where he is discussed in the company of the Lyric Poets. This patriotic and archaic forebear was 'the voice of Hellas ... always pure and exquisitely polished', and a tender nature-poet to boot; and his force of spirit made him an honorary Dorian, just like Strato.[160] Uranian (or Uranian enough) by virtue of his virile Hellenism, Strato loves boys because he is authentically Greek; he is authentically Greek because he loves boys.

---

[159] On the Victorian cliché of Dorian 'highlanders', see entertainingly Jenkyns (1980: 167–8).

[160] J. A. Symonds (1873: 396); 'the silver language of great Simonides' recalled to the reader's mind at p. 348. The Simonides of *Studies* has his own Eastern Other in the sensually 'luxuriant' Bacchylides: J. A. Symonds (1873: 146–52, quoted at p. 149). The youthful Symonds identified with Simonides.

Much of the persuasive power of Symonds's account lies in his ability to work selectively with the grain of hand-me-down opinion.[161] In his chapter on epigram, he has propounded the conventional bell curve of culture—while also tacitly exempting the whole genre from its logically obvious place in the Winckelmanian scheme of Greek culture's rise, peak, and decline. He has paid homage to Merivale's aim of 'exhibiting a more correct and classical representation of the original Anthology, by a more abundant infusion of the best specimens...and placing the authors themselves in chronological order of succession'.[162] Certainly he has achieved the last of these for erotic epigram—and arrived at a sequence that plays to his preferred subtext, thanks to some tacit reordering of individual voices; and he has 'exhibited...the best specimens' of a 'more correct and classical' Anthology, with the proviso that Classical now goes as far as Strato (and no further), while also endorsing Merivale's very useful adherence to the common wisdom that Classical is always best.

It is because of this that the climactic literary chapter of *Studies* manages to get away with implying a schematization much more radical than that expressed in the still unpublished subcultural pamphlet of *Greek Ethics*—and along with it an agenda for reform in the here and now; the lingering suggestion is that all 'Greek' love is good. It is Rufinus and his kind who are effeminate, their desires for soft female flesh that reek of Eastern Otherness. Contrastingly, quotation of Milton's classic English masque (itself set in an Arcadian-pastoral scene) aligns Classical male desire for other men with 'Saintly chastity', and frames the desired male body as the 'unpolluted temple of the mind'. Milton's scene of the ghost of the dead sensualist clinging to his tomb is itself, of course, straight out of the *Phaedo*, a nineteenth-century favourite among Plato's dialogues—and Jowett's new translation of Plato had drawn attention to this connection, quoting the very same passage as a home-grown parallel to *Phaedo* 80. Simply by quoting Milton paraphrasing Plato, then, Symonds is able to cue up the Uranian–Pandemic polarity.[163]

Reconceived and vividly brought to life as an accessible and inclusive Alpine-pastoral Utopia of clean air and ravishing prospects, Symonds's Anthology recuperates gay male desire as a cultural good—indeed, as a

---

[161] Ironically, it is through a face-value reading of Symonds's subtle and purposeful recycling of tropes that Jenkyns (1980: 172–3) mockingly singles him out as emblematic of an era of British classical studies wholly deficient in 'originality of mind'.

[162] Merivale (1833: pp. vii–viii).

[163] The *Phaedo* as Plato's artistic masterwork: Browne (1851–3: i. 454), quoting this very image.

national ideal. His bold and seemingly authoritative new historical and
literary-critical account of epigram sets out to redeem homosexuality
from its medicalization in public discourse as a newly diagnosed symptom of racial degeneracy and save it for culture, relocating it into a vividly
realized Utopian space at the heart of Britain's imaginative engagement
with ancient Greece, and thereby grounding recent subcultural memory
in an invented tradition that brilliantly recycles mainstream tropes.

Symonds's chapter on epigram pries open the faultline in Victorian
Britain's ideology of Hellenism, with Meleager and Strato emerging in
dynamic tension as mutually validating prototypes for fashioning new
identities in the present. Coming out as Uranian, even in the heart of the
city, one comes home to this dream-Hellas and to knowledge of one's
true and natural self, eternal and—what else?—Platonic.[164]

[164] Evangelista (2006: 231) inspires this last.

4

'The True *Liber Amoris* at Last'

This visionary isle, and the life to be led there by the fugitives from a
dull and undiscerning world...[1]

After maddening hold-ups at the printer's, not much helped by the
author himself having been out of the country for most of the time, the
First Series of *Studies* came out in June 1873. Arriving back in England
that autumn, Symonds was surprised to find that his lovely Crown
octavo volume had made him a minor celebrity. His views on Greek
poetry were solicited as authoritative by notable scholars and other
authorities, and elite word-of-mouth on the book opened the door to a
glittering social scene in London.[2] Despite his privately confessed view
that the First Series had been amateurish and self-indulgent, Symonds
was emboldened to think big:

My book of studies of Greek Poets has so far succeeded that I think it may be
worth while to bring out a second series, embracing Homer, Hesiod, Aeschylus,
Sophocles, and the minor comic fragments. If I live to do this, at some future time
the two series might be combined into a complete survey of Greek Poetry.[3]

It was to be many years before the second part of this plan came to
fruition, but the first was straightforwardly achieved: the essays of the
Second Series (1876) plugged the gaps identified in this letter to Sidgwick

---

[1] J. A. Symonds (1878a: 139), on the Uranian utopia of Shelley's 'Epipsychidion'; cf. the
'Elysium of Greek Lovers' of the private poetry.

[2] Publication pains: J. A. Symonds (1967–9: ii. 276, 304, cf. 300); Symonds as new
authority: ii. 317–18; feted in London: ii. 333; feeling the pressure to up his game so as
not to disappoint his new fan base: ii. 318.

[3] J. A. Symonds (1967–9: ii. 313), October 1873. Self-recrimination for the florid style of
Studies: ii. 318, to Dakyns. As a prose stylist Symonds was consistently his own fiercest
critic, as, e.g., at ii. 333, the year after the First Series, and he consciously worked to improve
his style; cf. ii. 819. Grosskurth (1964: 164) sees Symonds's early hopes for schoolbook
status as hopeless naivety on his part, but in the long term it came true; see pp. 205–6 and
329–30.

and more besides. Again some started life as Review articles, a method Symonds kept coming back to in this early phase of his career as a book-author.[4] Despite this miscellaneous genesis, the combined result is a literary survey unprecedented in its breadth as well as innovative in its method and aims. As published it is also a very disordered one, but the Preface to the Second Series explicitly sets out how to read across and between the two volumes in a chronologically coherent sequence: 'Those who care to read the two series together will find the order of the Studies to be as follows: 1. The Periods of Greek Literature; 2. Mythology; 3. Achilles; 4. The Women of Homer…'. This enabled each reader to create a comprehensive 'virtual' history of Greek poetry through active collaboration in the production of meaning (see Table 4.1).[5]

Both in 1873 and on the appearance of the sequel in 1876, the initial critical response was very supportive indeed. Noting its appearance, the *Examiner* of 14 June 1873 was brief but emphatic. Symonds had scored a hit in uncovering the relevance and vitality of Greek thought in the modern world: 'Mr Symonds's essays on the *Greek Poets* contain every subject that can be included in the art of poetry as expressed by the Greeks, and every Greek idea that is still powerful in art.'[6] Its full review, a few months down the line, was a little more qualified—perhaps some of the descriptions of landscape could have been cut, and could ancient Greece really have been as full of sweetness and light as Symonds seemed to presume?—but hardly less enthusiastic: 'we know few books that are more delightful reading from beginning to end.' Symonds's determination to take classical studies out of the grammar ghetto and into the mainstream of literary criticism won their admiration, although they thought the job was probably too large to pull off with just one book.[7] Fortunately Symonds already had his follow-up volume in mind. Meanwhile, his publishers were doing an excellent job of advertising the First Series in the quality papers.

---

[4] Composition of Second Series: J. A. Symonds (1967–9: ii. 379); the origin of the new Studies in journalism is acknowledged frankly in the preface (1876: p. v). Cf. his *Sketches in Italy and Greece* of 1874; 'Not quite half the essays are old' (ii. 920). On his essays in the *Westminster Review* of 1871–4, with details of what appears when, see ii. 482–3.

[5] J. A. Symonds (1876: pp. v–vi). Anon. (1876: 385) holds this feature up to scrutiny, but at least one reader followed the instructions: Oscar Wilde, who pencilled little '1's and '2's above the above-quoted text in his personal copy of Symonds (1876) to remind himself in which Series each Study appeared.

[6] Anon. (1873a).

[7] Anon. (1873b: 1). Symonds won the *Examiner* over completely with *Studies*; the following year (3455: 5, Saturday, 18 April 1874) they declared the excellence of *Sketches in Italy and Greece* a foregone conclusion given its authorship.

Table 4.1. Interleaving the two Series

First Series	Second Series
The Periods of Greek Literature	
	Mythology
	Achilles
	The Women of Homer
	Hesiod
	Parmenides
Empedocles	
The Gnomic Poets	
The Satirists	
The Lyric Poets	
Pindar	
	Aeschylus
	Sophocles
Greek Tragedy and Euripides	
	The Fragments of Aeschylus, Sophocles, Euripides
	The Fragments of the Lost Tragic Poets
Ancient and Modern Tragedy	
Aristophanes	
	The Comic Fragments
	Herondas
The Idyllists	
The Anthology	
	Hero and Leander
The Genius of Greek Art	
	Conclusion

Three years later, the quality weekly *John Bull*, a middle-class literary newspaper known for its uncompromising conservatism, praised the Second Series handsomely, thereby testifying to Symonds's finely tuned ability to slip his subtext past at least some of society's self-appointed guardians (he often ran versions by his friends first to be on the safe side).[8] The only substantial complaint raised in its review was that the

---

[8] Anon. (1876). 'The answer, probably, is that some people heard same-sex passion loud and clear, whereas others could not conceive of it' (Sinfield 1994b: 8). Even for work intended primarily for circulation within subculture, Symonds was always keen to get a sympathetic second opinion (contemporary subcultural production would call this a 'beta reader') to check his subtext was pitched at the right level—not too obvious, but still unmistakably 'there' for a subcultural reading, as at e.g. A. J. Symonds (1878b ii: 208, 210,

closing essay, on the relevance of Greek ethics in an age of science, was insufficiently Christian in its outlook and too sceptical for comfort— Symonds was a tireless enthusiast for the latest scientific thinking and already latching onto the radical ideological–discursive potential of the evolutionary model.[9] In time, too, Symonds's figurative landscape of epigram's Alpine meadows seems to have struck a chord with at least one translator. Andrew Lang's *Grass of Parnassus* (1888) offered several versions from the Anthology alongside original works. Out of modesty, his own poetic landscape sacrifices height, but the relative elevations are still recognizable: 'It may be as well to repeat in prose, what has already been said in verse, that Grass of Parnassus, the pretty Autumn flower, grows in the marshes at the foot of the Muses' hill, and other hills, not at the top by any means.'[10] Within a few years (1880) the two Series were republished as a matched pair in the United States, 'in partly piratical way'—the typical backhanded New York compliment to a title's critical and commercial success in the British market.[11]

Sooner than that, though—a scant year after the appearance of the First Series—an old bastion of British Conservatism had roused itself at the perceived threat of Symonds's queer epigrammatic Genius.

1. EPIGRAM FOR QUEEN AND COUNTRY: LORD CHARLES NEAVES, *THE GREEK ANTHOLOGY* (1874)

Planudes has been somewhat harshly assailed as not merely desti-tute of taste, but as having expurgated lines and even stanzas in the

and 255) (friends' feedback on First Series drafts). At (iii: 282–3), written to Dakyns in March 1873, he asks whether he needs to tone down parts of 'The Genius of Greek Art' so as not to set conservative alarm bells ringing. On the readership addressed by *John Bull* ('Quite a good literary paper'), see concisely Ellegård (1971: 6), noting that it also became some-thing of a High Church and Tory clerical organ. An anonymous write-up of the Second Series in the *Spectator* of 29 July 1876 was generous for unstated reasons of family interest; the *Cambridge Bibliography of English Literature*, iv. *1800–1900* outs the author as Sy-monds's brother-in-law, Edward Strachey. His son was the *Spectator*'s editor when the third edition came out in 1893; unsurprisingly that too got a good review (19 August).

[9] J. A. Symonds (1920: 584–5). Because the Second Series is now an extremely rare book, and is held in very few libraries, I refer to its essays through their republication in the third edition.

[10] Lang (1888: p. vii).

[11] J. A. Symonds (1967–9: iii. 737); the date is 1879.

original poems, and either omitted them altogether or replaced
them with phraseology of his own. We are not willing, however, to
cancel or much diminish the debt which we undoubtedly owe him;
and there are not a few epigrams suppressed by him which have
since come to light, and which had better never have been published
or never written.

Edited by the Reverend William Lucas Collins, *Ancient Classics for
English Readers* was one of a new breed of cheap, uniformly bound serial
handbooks in morally uplifting topics, among which the canon authors
and genres of Greek and Roman literature claimed a self-evident place.[12]
Its mission statement was explicitly to bring the great books to a readership that would never know the credentialed status traditionally endowed
by a classical education: the working class. Priced at a mere two shillings
and sixpence and rolling out to a bimonthly schedule, these slim uniform
volumes brought the prospect of book ownership to a mass public
who could otherwise only hope to access literary culture through public
libraries and Mechanics' Institutes (the latter a market already being
tapped by progressively minded lecturers looking to make some
pocket money on the side, who found that undemanding anecdotes on
the great men of Greco-Roman letters went over a treat). The first two
volumes, on Homer's *Iliad* and *Odyssey*, were lavishly praised in the
press. The 'merely English reader' would find himself, or indeed herself,
quickly equipped with a knowledge 'sufficient for all ordinary practical
purposes', from literary appreciation (both of translations and of an
indigenous literature steeped in classical allusion) to career advancement.
The religious press weighed in as well, underwriting the series'
social credentials, safe morality, and unexceptionable good taste, and
furnishing the endpapers of subsequent volumes with a rich repertoire
of puff-quotes:[13]

as good as a novel we might say, that being a common expression, were it not that
they are very much better than most novels... the unlearned reader follows and
comprehends without the labour of a weary study. (*St Paul's Magazine*)

---

[12] Oliphant (1897: 401), the firm's authorized chronicler, relates the conception and
naming of the series. On the ambit of the imprint and of a rival series from Macmillan, see
concisely Vance (2007: 95–6).

[13] On the Mechanics' Institutes as resources for limited working-class participation in
literate culture, see Altick (1957: 188–212); on ad hoc university 'outreach' to the Institutes,
see Hurst (2006: 27–30). 'Merely English': Swayne (1870: 6), quoting the Edinburgh
Courant; 'practical purposes' (1870: 2), from the Civil Service Gazette; the longer quotations
are from (1870: 3), which also quotes rave reviews from the *Literary Churchman* and *Tablet*.
The readers of *St Paul's* knew all about novels; the editor of this short-lived shilling monthly
was Anthony Trollope.

I fancy that the Odyssey is more to the taste of our sex than is the 'battle-breathing' Iliad; but a knowledge of ancient classics is gained by the perusal of these books—for which we women ought ever to be grateful—and a taste is inspired ... (*The Young Englishwoman*)

English readers of all classes now have an opportunity, which they should not neglect, of acquiring an acquaintance with the great writers of antiquity—super-ficial it may be when we compare it with that which a classical education would confer, but at the same time sufficient to enable them better to appreciate the numerous translations which issue from the press, and which for want of some such previous acquaintance lose half their charm and interest. (*John Bull*)

It was also anticipated that schoolboys would benefit from the oppor-tunity to learn the literary value and social relevance of the Greek and Latin texts they studied at school on a purely linguistic basis.

It will be argued here that a politically conservative fear of *Studies* being read in these unschooled interpretative spaces, where potential existed for collective and social reading outside the control of traditional elites and their system of values, lay behind the publication in 1874 in *Ancient Classics for English Readers* of a small book on the Greek Anthology by Lord Charles Neaves, an elderly and ailing patriarch of Scottish law (the 'Lord' is a courtesy title that came with being appointed judge of the Court of Session in 1853) and theologian.[14] The case for dialogue is strong even as an argument from coincidence—to wait forty years (following Mer-ivale 1833, the substantive introduction to which was, of course, even older) for a substantive discussion of the Greek Anthology, only for two to come along at once, strains credulity—but specific correspondences also emerge under scrutiny. One such is Neaves's spirited defence of Planudes, quoted at the onset of this section: the immediately obvious 'harsh assailer' of Planudes is, of course, Symonds, just the previous year.

That Symonds is the target will be clear to anyone who has read *Studies*, but Neaves does not mention him here, and hardly ever does. He does not leave his name out of epigram's story entirely (that would be too obvious) but, as we will see, painstakingly rules out from consider-ation all the problematic views of his immediate predecessor.[15] He does not *deny* those views, because that would entail naming them—an act

---

[14] Also a prolific critic in *Blackwood's* and elsewhere, Neaves (1800–76) was one of the great Scotsmen of his day; in 1872–4 he had served as Rector of St Andrews: Reilly (2000: 336). Helpful for context is Morwood (2012), sampling the rhetoric and practice of censorship of Greek and Latin authors in editions and commentaries intended for use in schools.

[15] Token citation of Symonds as a translator: Neaves (1874: 74); the famous 'Protē' of Symonds Senior is conspicuously snubbed at p. 62.

that would grant them discursive reality in the world view of readerships deemed by Neaves's conservative circle to be vulnerable to radical ideas and dangerously liable to act on them in socially unacceptable ways. Rather than explicitly condemn the perceived threat, he relies on a classic 1870s conservative strategy of containment: significant silence and discursive stonewalling. The subtextual and 'coded' texture of dissident discourse intrinsically relies on semiotic room for manœuvre, and this indeterminacy can never be conclusively owned by any one agenda; the tools of subversion and containment are one and the same.[16]

'The Anthology' was the literary capstone of Symonds's First Series of 1873; Neaves's *Greek Anthology* of 1874 is volume twenty of twenty under the *Ancient Classics* imprint. The parallel appears very neat in retrospect, but we should not read too much design into it. It is not known whether there was ever a grand design for the *Ancient Classics*; Collins and his publisher later claimed that twenty volumes had always been the plan, but they may simply have decided to call a halt at a conveniently round number, and within a few years a collector's edition was on sale with twenty-eight (the new additions filled some very obvious gaps in coverage to which reviewers had called attention).[17] In all likelihood the series was to a large extent cobbled together in a more or less opportunistic fashion, based on the availability and willingness of friendly authors from one month to the next.[18] If there ever had been an overarching master plan for the *Ancient Classics*, it is vanishingly unlikely that the Greek Anthology was its intended grand finale; either way, the series was evidently derailed to take hasty account of Symonds's Uranian heresy.

These imponderables need not detain us: our focus may instead gravitate to how the experience of the reader, who is also an agent in culture, is being policed. The overall tone of the *Ancient Classics* imprint is germane insofar as, by its nature as a collectible part-work with an educational ambit, it shapes expectations and explicitly guides its reader's cultural formation incrementally through iteration: each volume after the first is ideally read as the latest instalment in its series, building on lessons already conveyed. The tenor, as we have already seen, is paternalistic. The *St Andrews Gazette* promoted the early volumes as morally safe

---

[16] Sinfield (1994b: 6–7).

[17] Anon. (1874a) looks back critically on the series and identifies serious omissions in its coverage of the ancient historians in particular. The collector's edition was much more expensive than the individual volumes, at £3 10s., in a choice of leather or vellum binding.

[18] Cf. John Henderson (2007: 144) on the Oxford Reds, an apparently planned and designed series of commentaries on core Latin texts that behind the scenes was 'an organic story of happenstance rather than systematic prosecution of a formular strategy'.

reading matter for schoolboys, 'affording far better mental nourishment than the . . . sea-stories, sensational tales, and other unwholesome yellow-covered trash' that they were presumed to be consuming otherwise; meanwhile, the emphasis in the *Somerset County Gazette* was that the lower orders would be receiving the 'right' version of the past for their social station ('a cheap yet *reliable* guide').[19]

A dip into publication background makes this paternalism unsurprising: *Ancient Classics* is the pet project of Maga and its groupies. Somewhat against the facts, the old organ of Scots Toryism had long asserted its primacy in the field of epigram translation, often copied but never equalled:

> It must be amusing to many to see ever and anon in the Monthlies a translation, as it is called, of some poor solitary Greek epigram or another, shivering by itself at the bottom of a page, with a reference in a note at its foot to the place it is to be found in some erudite edition of the Anthology—the tiny turner having done no more than transmogrify an English version in Maga into a provincial dialect of the Cockney tongue. Maga has given them in dozens, scores, fifties, hundreds; pouring them out from her Cornucopia, till her path blushed with flowers.[20]

Neaves and Collins are both old Maga hands—the former under the smugly reticent *nom de plume* 'An Old Contributor to Maga'—and the series publisher is John Blackwood, younger brother of the William Blackwood who had founded *Blackwood's*. Since he took the business on when his brother died in 1834, he was now running both Maga (for three decades now) and *Ancient Classics*, which we must see as an arm of Maga ideology. Blackwood publications carried the family motto, *Per Vias Rectas* ('By Straight Roads'), over the armorial crest of the Edinburgh branch: the sun's rays, breaking through the dark cloud of ignorance to enlighten the common reader and steer him towards the 'right' knowledge for his station in life. There is no room in this reading strategy for dissident interpretations and searchers after subtext.

Briefly looking back to Neaves's justification of Planudes' moral and philological correctness—'a man of learning as well as of worth'—we find a fascinating touch of traditional Maga grudge-bearing in the way he

---

[19] Again, from the endpapers of Swayne (1870) (emphasis added).
[20] Anon. (1838: 254), a very eccentric contribution; 'Cockney' is, of course, Maga shorthand for the radical Romanticism of Shelley and Keats. Cf. Anon. (1836b: 803): 'Never, surely in this world, was there such a set of articles as that of ours on the Greek Anthology. You can form no idea of the "numbers without number numberless", of letters . . . that came flocking to us through the azure realms of air, each, like Noah's dove, with an olive branch between its wings.'

chooses to conclude his argument: 'it seems now to be proved that he was not the author of a foolish life of Aesop that was long ascribed to him.'[21] This otherwise baffling non sequitur must be motivated by the championing of the Planudes–Aesop connection by Maga's Liberal arch-nemesis, the *Edinburgh Review*, in its long-ago review of Bland over half a century earlier (see Chapter 1); for Maga, revenge is best served very cold indeed. At odd points in the book, too, old numbers of the Review are shamelessly plugged.[22]

By way of illustration of how *Ancient Classics* serviced political inter-ests we may take George Swayne's *Herodotus* volume, the third in the series (1870). Swayne's old Tory Royalist background made him a natural—and frequent—Maga contributor.[23] His is a Herodotus for Church and Empire. Working-class readers are told they should be most interested in the section where Herodotus does Egypt, for two reasons that should gladden the soul of any Briton. It throws light on Scripture; and it poses a geographical challenge—finding the source of the Nile—which British exploration is now taking up.[24] This latter was a topic dear to Swayne's heart; two years earlier he had edited an account by two British explorers of their search for this very goal, published (in a not entirely surprising coincidence) by William Blackwood and Sons.

While Swayne's colonial Herodotus pushes upriver for Queen and country, Neaves's Greek Anthology keeps the home fires burning. 'Com-mentators are not agreed as to the relation in which Meleager stood to some of the females to whom his verses were addressed, and in particular to Heliodora…We will believe that she was his wife.'[25] The *Blackwood's* Greece is a land of primitive piety (the dedicatory epigrams), love of country (select epitaphs), and happy domesticity. It is also insistently and exclusively heterosexual. Neaves chooses to end his introduction with extensive translation from a Latin ode to the Anthology, found in de Bosch's late-born edition of Planudes:[26]

[21] Neaves (1874: 5).
[22] As at Neaves (1874: 15 (Wilson's articles of 1833: 'the first serious attempt to exhibit the true character of the Greek epigram in English translation'—so much for Bland et al.), 23, 70, 138.
[23] Reilly (2000: 447). For some richly anecdotal family history from a local perspective, see http://www.pucklechurch.org/html/features_sept07.html#swayne (accessed February 2013). Swayne lived a life of serial sinecure-hopping on the lines noted in our first and second chapters: a former Fellow of Corpus Christi, Oxford (appointed its Dean in 1850), he had then taught at Harrow for a spell (1851–5) before holding down a couple of church posts.
[24] Swayne (1870: 40–1 (Moses), 45–6).
[25] Neaves (1874: 69).   [26] See Introduction, p. 17 n.37.

> The graceful Muse has here concisely sung
> The charms that woman sends from eye or tongue;
> What men have done she gives to understand,
> Whose zeal has saved or raised their native land.
> Cities, that in the dust long buried lie,
> Bear in their ancient seats their heads on high.
> Traces of shrines and temples seem to stand
> Heaped with large gifts from many a pious hand.
> The sad laments of friends now strike our ears:
>
> .   .   .   .   .
>
> Lessons of wisdom open to our view
> In all life's varied scenes of gay or gloomy hue.

'The charms that woman sends' looks back to the originally anonymous 1833 articles in which Maga had expressed its corporate approval of Merivale's final *Collections*. There we are told that translating Greek epigrams is like painting a portrait of a beautiful girl: in neither case should the desiring male 'translator' work in the presence of his model, but after gazing long on her and committing to memory

this or that feature of the face in which he feels to reside the chief power of enchantment... he translates the [poem] or paints the [face] so naturally, that you yield to the delusion, and believe that you are reading the very lines, or, better still, kissing the very lips of the original.[27]

The goal of translation is not to render what the poet said in so many words, but rather, what he surely *meant* to say—and the 'right' kind of translator–portraitist (and Merivale for one possesses this 'happy genius') instinctually knows what that was. Maga hands capitalized on this manifesto for on-message rewriting in several further articles over the next several years. William Hay was particularly tireless in his output, turning out over 100 pages of versions (1835, 1835–7), helping keep epigram more or less in the family as he did so (he was the tutor of John Blackwood, the founder's son). It was principally to the versions of 'North' and Hay that Neaves had recourse four decades later, fine-tuning their phrasing as he saw fit.[28]

Likewise, the patriotic 'zeal' of those great men who have 'saved or raised their native land' is straight out of the 1830s, a moment when, incredibly, Maga was actively promoting Greek epigram as a salve to the nation's ills

---

[27] Anon. (1833c: 868–9). Echoes here of the modern television comic character Swiss Toni, created by Charlie Higson and Bob Mortimer, who first appeared in the second series of the BBC show *The Smell of Reeves and Mortimer* (1995). For Toni, selling used cars, and much else besides, 'is like making love to a beautiful woman'.

[28] For publication details see Cook (1919: 363).

(as diagnosed from their editorial office) and even as a safeguard against the violent overthrow of the state by godless revolutionaries. Read aright, Greek epigram established British society's commonality with the spirit of antiquity in commemorating the glorious dead:

The Greeks were a glorious race. So are we. Our heroes are as theirs—so are our poets. Liberty! where had she ever nobler worship than in our fatherland?...And has not Albion had for ages, too, the dominion of the sea? Praise to her noble dead! Religion speaks from their tombs—Genius consecrates their monuments—a grateful Country, preserved by their valour, venerates their virtues—and Patriotism kindles at the thoughts of their everlasting fame. Peace to the souls of her heroes![29]

This extraordinary rant paints the saviours of Greece as Tory patriots—specifically, ancient Nelsons; the Anthology is to be prized as a treasury stocked with the inspiring epitaphs of great men, fit for emulation by coming generations of British heroes, as well as for the occasional light verse that shows these ancient statesmen in their lighter moments.[30] Five pages before this review began, Maga had wound up a substantial opinion piece on 'The State and Prospects of France' with harsh words on 'the fatal tendency of democratic power in France...tossed about by the passions of a jealous democracy, [France] is fast descending through years of suffering into centuries of servitude' (p. 110): while democracy ushers in tyranny and squalid anarchy (1832 had been a year of uprisings across the Channel), Liberty is the enduring legacy of King and Parliament.

Similarly, the initial instalment of Anthology-worship in Maga's immediately previous number had drawn peculiar attention to the power of Greek epigram to offer up to its contemplator 'meanings that *soothe or elevate*';[31] the specific political resonance of these two terms comes into focus in a sequential reading of the magazine when the immediately ensuing review article (of Archibald Allison's *The History of Europe during the French Revolution*, itself a product of the Blackwood publishing empire) warns that

We are at this hour threatened with a revolution in England. There was never a mine laid for the explosion of a citadel more palpably, than the materials of violent and total change are now laid under the whole fabric of the British constitution. Incessant appeals to popular excitement, furious stimulants to the natural passion of the populace for plunder, lying panegyrics of their merits, exaggerated pictures of their sufferings, *fiendish* calls for their revenge, a nobility libelled as tyrants, a church libelled as robbers, and a King libelled alternately as a royal encumbrance and a rebel leader, are the preparation. By whose hand the

---

[29] Anon. (1833d: 133).   [30] Anon. (1833d: 115), a blatantly bogus description.
[31] Anon. (1833c: 867) (emphasis added).

match is to be applied is another question... There are orators within the circuit of London... villains black to the core, outcasts from all character... who never cast a passing glance upon palace, church, or noble mansion, but with an instinctive admeasurement of it as an object of spoil or conflagration... nor will ever be satisfied... [short of the] vast, sanguinary, and final triumph of atheism and anarchy. (p. 889)

Furious stimulants, exaggerated pictures, *fiendish* calls (the emphasis is original): these are the socialist, secular and democratic irritants that are in desperate need of 'soothing', and against which the nation's true sons must rally, else the whole edifice of Church and State will be overthrown by the rapacious mob.

   Although 1833's moment of imminent conflagration may have passed, Neaves still has 'good' Anthology poets write in order to supply pretexts for sermonizing to a contemporary congregation. The working class should pile up its treasure in Heaven, not strive for self-betterment in this life: 'Whether life on the whole be a success or a failure, there can be no doubt that it is uncertain, both in its tenure and duration, and that at the best its enjoyments are fleeting and perishable. Hear, on this subject, a strain from our old friend Simonides...'. These poets offer a particular lesson to the kind of factory hand who might be buying *Ancient Classics for English Readers* or reading Symonds in a library copy. To toil without complaint is a Herculean virtue: 'The allusion to "sweat" as the outward token of generous exertion is frequent in the best Greek poets. Thus Hesiod, as translated by Elton...'.[32] Since the Anthology is a very unobliging source text on themes of Stoic endurance and the nobility of labour (to say nothing of deferring to the wisdom of one's social betters), Neaves steps outside it to round out this sermon: Hesiod is the first and most obviously congenial whistle-stop on an ethical mystery tour that in the space of a few pages takes in Archilochus, the *Georgics* of Vergil, and even Martial.[33] When a few years later the *Ancient Classics* are reissued for posterity in leather and marbled boards, with each volume now binding in a single cover a complementary pair of its humble cloth-backed predecessors—the *Iliad* with the *Odyssey*, Herodotus alongside Xenophon, Vergil with Horace, and so on—didactically serious Hesiod is the author with whom the newly moralized Anthology is quasi-naturally partnered.

   This Anthology, packed full of edifying homilies for our time, is a visitor from an alternate universe in which Strato's Mousa Paidikē

[32] Neaves (1874: 89, 91).
[33] Neaves (1874: 104–6), and cf. 189, strategically misreading the epigrams in question: 'The light and cheerful way in which poor men speak of their poverty is often pleasant.'

simply never happened.[34] To the extent possible without knowledge of the Christian dispensation, Neaves's ancient Greeks find their greatest fulfilment in the sacred bond of matrimony, just like his modern Britons—yet another indicator, were one needed, of the special relationship between the two races. This shared uxorial instinct also implicitly justifies modern British imperialism as a moral crusade against 'white slavery' and the institutional 'degradation' of women in the savage Orient. Epigram calls us to shoulder the white man's burden abroad, and at home to reverence the angel of the hearth:[35]

Notwithstanding the differences which exist in character and manners between the Greeks and ourselves, there could not fail to be a great community of feeling in the chief passions and affections of human nature. Both nations belong to one great and elevated family of the human race... Our languages have a great mutual affinity...

As regards the relation of the sexes, the great distinction arising from the presence or absence of polygamy is of itself enough to assimilate together those nations in which that source of female degradation does not exist. Faulty as Greek manners were, women were not treated as slaves or beasts of burden. The Greek matron was condemned to a certain seclusion, but she was held in respect; and in many cases, as we have already seen, the married life of the Greeks was one of affection and happiness.

'[A]s we have already seen' puts a brave face on some very thin pickings back in the Sepulchral chapter, but making this assertion up front lets Neaves off the hook in his trawl of AP 5. Instead of poems on courtships, proposals, and happy marriages (themes that AP 5 would be hard put to supply), we are instead offered a parade of rococo Venuses and of Cupids glossed as cherubs. 'The Greek amatory epigrams deal largely in mythological views': this decorously ornamental Love has little or nothing to do with bodily attraction.

The two great artificers of this socially polite mythic window-dressing are Meleager—and Rufinus, one of Symonds's two great villains, now recast as a poet much admired by posterity. He rivals Meleager's own amatory genius:

We give now an epigram by Rufinus referring to a garland sent to Rhodoclea, which may well match with Meleager's to Heliodora... We shall now add two more Love epigrams, by Rufinus, which exhibit considerable elegance...

---

[34] Neaves paraphrases Symonds's account of the history of the Anthology's prototype collections at (1874: 6–7), omitting only Strato's Boyish Muse; tit for tat, given that Symonds had missed out AP 5.

[35] The popular literature that made domestic heroes of Britain's imperial adventurers found particular resonance in dramatic accounts of their rescues of vulnerable subjects from locally institutionalized slavery, as at Anon. (1885: 49), complete with stock images of the happy moment of liberation ('Gordon discovering hidden slaves').

Here is another, also, we think, very beautiful. It is by some ascribed to Rufinus...[36]

He has come a long way in one year from 'the brothel and the grave'. Meleager himself is conceived as half-Oriental and thus not wholly to be trusted, even if as a collector he demonstrates an unerring eye for beauty: 'He was a Syrian ... His character seems to have been a remarkable one, not free from great faults, ardent in his passions, and acute in his susceptibilities.' When he writes heterosexual domestic verse, however, he rises to Rufinus' rank.

Neaves buys right into Symonds's new equation between early date, genuine occasionality, and authentic human feeling, only to turn it against his purposes.[37] In *Studies*, the bell curve of Greek literary culture had been daringly sidestepped to make Meleager 'early', within an unprecedented generic micro-history that extended the aura of the Classical far into the Roman era to squeeze in second-century Strato. Neaves takes Symonds's play and runs with it, stretching the definition of the Classic all the way to sixth-century Agathias, whom he pointedly singles out for praise in his capacity as the friend and collaborator of Symonds's other great villain, Paul the Silentiary. Agathias thus strips from an unmentioned Strato the title of last true Classical poet:

> It might be doubted if some of the latest of these writers deserved the name of Classical in the highest sense of the term. But Agathias, the last in the list, has so well caught the ancient spirit, that it would be harsh to exclude him. After his era the degeneracy of the literature became unmistakable.[38]

This 'ancient spirit' is now just like ours—the right kind of 'us': nineteenth-century Tories, and the lower orders who will do well to follow their lead.

2. SWELLING AND BURNS: DOCTORING
THE ANTHOLOGY

> The ideas and images suggested by the passions or strong affections
> of humanity are wonderfully alike in various forms of society and
> literature. *Nothing seems more natural ...*

---

[36] Neaves (1874: 89–90, 92).
[37] On the sepulchral epigrams: 'In general, the simpler and more natural the composition is, if it has genius at all, the more likely it is to be an ancient and original inscription.' This equation also underlies Neaves's clumsy misrepresentation of Meleager's *Garland* as a collection assembled through autopsy of inscriptions: (1874: 7).
[38] Neaves (1874: 7).

The Greek Anthology, *therefore, in its largest sense—swelled as it has been* by contributions from various sources—may now be considered as consisting, not merely of the collections of Cephalas and Planudes, but also of a large number of other short poems deserving the name of epigrams or epigraphs, found scattered about among the old Greek historians, biographers, and miscellaneous writers, and which it is likely that Meleager, Philippus, or Agathias, if we had them entire, would be found to have inserted in their collections, *or might reasonably have done so.*[39]

In keeping with the workings of this 'ancient spirit', the working-class readers of Maga's *Ancient Classics* are invited to find their socially appropriate 'nature' mirrored in a Greek Anthology where prescription trumps description: fairly explicitly it is now the sum total of the poems its contributory garland-weavers *ought* to have included, regardless of whether they actually did.[40] (From their roll call, of course, the name of Strato is elided.) This is a reactionary move after the strictly Cephalan Anthology of Symonds, recalling (while also taking care to disown) the miscellanies of Bland at the century's beginning.[41] At the same time, it brings the concerns of the Anthology poets so completely into line with an already old-fashioned sense of nineteenth-century decorum that, as read through Neaves, they now seem very quaint. Although stopping short of advertisement for outright abstinence (Maga was no friend of the Temperance cause), the poets of his Tory Anthology express a characteristic concern for moderation in the use of drink, and caution against over-indulgence in warm baths.[42] Pained sympathy is expressed for the plight of fallen women.[43] Through the lens of the Anthology, the Scottish senior magistrate who has seen all of human life from the bench confides his timeless wisdom on the essence of the weaker sex: 'The faults and foibles of women [spring] often so naturally from their innate wish to please.'

---

[39] Neaves (1874: 91, 13–14) (emphases added).

[40] Cf., yet more explicitly, Neaves (1874: 179–80) on his winnowed AP 11: 'We do not say that the Greek epigrammatist always abstained from making merry at mere bodily defects; but we shall avoid as much as possible those that have no other recommendation. The proper object of ridicule is surely Folly, and the proper object of satire, Vice.'

[41] Similarly recidivist is the category of 'Literary and Artistic' epigrams, conceived as Boswellian hero-worship along the lines pursued and exhausted at mid-century by Browne (1851-3) (see p. 80).

[42] Wine: Neaves (1874: 110–12). Maga's contributors habitually scorned the Temperance movement as an enemy of Tory Liberty (a man's house is his castle) and a hotbed of—what else?—'sedition': Burns (1861-4: 325–7). Women's magazines of the age warned that hot baths were dangerous—tepid was best: Beetham and Boardman (2001: 92).

[43] Neaves (1874: 49–51).

The gist of Neaves on Greek wives is that there was nothing wrong with them that a little exercise and fresh air would not have sorted out.[44]

Within this prescriptively modelled Anthology, gender identity and concomitant romantic (never explicitly sexual) object choice constitute natural and universal givens:

See how modern feelings are apt to run, as Christopher North says, 'into the same sort of amorous fancy' [as the feelings of Rufinus]. Romeo in Shakespeare breathes the wish—

'Oh that I were a glove upon that hand, That I might touch that cheek!'
Christopher also appropriately refers to Burns...

North's is one of two names the book repeatedly invokes as the century's great authorities on epigram; the other is that of Professor John Wilson, whose learned title the reader is never allowed to forget.[45] Wilson was indeed a bona fide Professor at Edinburgh, albeit as a political appointment rather than on strict scholarly merit, and in a subject other than Classics. A young man of good family, he had escaped financial ruin by becoming a hugely prolific writer for pay. From its foundation through to the mid-1830s, much of each issue of *Blackwood's* was written by him. He habitually used a pseudonym in his Maga work: 'Christopher North', and Wilson-'North' is now belatedly unmasked as the author of the anonymous articles of 1833. The Maga in-crowd is invited to share a joke that is very much on the series' intended readership of social outsiders: that Wilson and 'North' speak as if with one voice lends the 'individual' statements of these two experts an aura of objective authority.

And Robert Burns?

Burns, we should think, knew little or nothing of the Greek anthologists; yet see how he fell into their style, and instinctively adopted their spirit... [a further example follows]

Again, the exquisite 'Posie' of our Scottish bard equals and surpasses those garlands sent to their mistresses by Meleager and Rufinus, which we have above quoted. The truth is, that all these poets, Greek and British, had the same schoolmistress, Nature, who teaches her pupils a universal language.

---

[44] Neaves (1874: 47–50).

[45] Modern feelings run: Neaves (1874: 93). Adulation of Wilson at e.g. p. 85: 'We have already given several of Meleager's Sepulchral and Amatory epigrams; but it may now be convenient to add such others of his on the subject of Love as may best deserve our attention.... The first, which describes the advent of spring, is translated *by Professor Wilson himself*, in a flowing and spirited style' (emphasis added; I am particularly tickled by that 'himself').

Nature's 'universal language' exclusively dictates heterosexual reproduction within a lifelong monogamous union; it has no words for anything else.[46]

Neaves follows a pre-existing local party line: his Professor Wilson was known as a staunch (perhaps too staunch) advocate for Burns, defending the work of his beloved national bard 'with that headlong and dictatorial impetuosity which has done the Ayrshire ploughman no good with the critical of other nationalities'. Locally, however, he was far from alone in his views.[47] Invoking Burns asserted a local stake in a politically conservative nineteenth-century narrative of Britain's poetic tradition. In this timely ideological fiction, it is the providentially appointed task of the inspired poet—the 'bard', the organic voice of the racial Genius—to make plain to his nation the eternal and inviolable connection between human nature and the natural order of things.[48]

South of the border, meanwhile, the truth of the British public's relationship with Nature—a 'Nature' conceived as landscape—was held to have been made plainest by one eighteenth-century figure in particular: William Wordsworth. Read in retrospect through a conservative lens, his Lakeland reveries handily anticipated nineteenth-century schoolbooks in emphasizing the role of Nature as teacher and moral instructor; his particular flavour of the Romantic ideal set up nicely for Victorian lessons in 'the great Book of Nature' as proof of God's role as divine architect of the Creation.[49] In this revisionist history of Romanticism, Shelley is Wordsworth's 'womanish' Other—even to like his work was now taken as a sign of effeminacy.[50]

It must be conceded that Shelley had left his posthumous conservative critics plenty to work with. The poet had been an early aficionado of

[46] Neaves (1874: 934), and cf. 51–2 (Nature's universal will is 'a pure affection...terminating in wedlock').

[47] Gunnyon (1883: 27), likewise hailing Burns as Scotland's own Meleager while wishing that Wilson's clumsy advocacy would stop giving the English nay-sayers such an easy target. Gunnyon was also the author of a biography of the poet.

[48] Assertions of timelessness and (human or other) 'nature' are straight out of Ideology 101; I would additionally see the nineteenth-century reception of Wordsworth's nature-Romanticism as conveniently crystallizing a sense of the autonomy of the poetic realm, and thus of the 'true' poet's necessary disinvestment from and renunciation of a politically engaged voice, making Poesy safe for (in Sinfield's pungent formulation) 'the political economy, the market and empire' (1994b: 86; cf. 856).

[49] Marsden (1997: 5–6, 11–12); cf. Christie (2009: 2), on Wordsworth's recuperation in the service of 'an authorized or Tory version of literary history'.

[50] This critical dressing-down was eventually to feed into the early- to mid-twentieth-century formation of Literary Criticism as a 'manly' discipline: Sinfield (1994a: 33–4), and cf. Ch. 6 on epigram and the New Criticism.

Hellenism as the coded language of male homoerotic desire; he had translated Plato's *Symposium*, and riffed expertly on its text in his intertextually complex elegy for Keats's passing, 'Adonais', to vindicate his friend as the undeserving victim of hate-mongering in the Tory press, above all in Maga. When Shelley famously declared in his preface to *Hellas* (1822), written as a fundraiser for independence, that 'We are all Greeks' in 'our' cultural roots, the Greece he conjured up was a prototypical Radical opposition to unearned privilege and stagnant hierarchy.[51] The Cockney poets thus came to exemplify the wrong sort of 'we' from which Greece needed to be rescued by nineteenth-century social conservatism.[52] To cap it all, Symonds, a constant advocate of the poet, had now explicitly endorsed Shelley as a preferred interpreter of Greece in the introductory chapter of *Studies,* with particular reference to flower-language (Nature, but with the wrong owner!) as a critical-exegetic tool.[53] This had to be stopped, and Wordsworth had the answer.

The workings of the Greek character, as tending in these many ways to embody and perpetuate the national feeling of rude and sometimes, as it almost seems, of infantine piety, are nowhere better analysed and described than in those well-known passages in Wordsworth's 'Excursion' which it is unnecessary to quote ...

We proceed now to that class of inscriptions which may be called Sepulchral, and which are of universal use among nations. Wordsworth, in his 'Essay on Epitaphs', is anxious to prove the proposition of Weever in his 'Funeral Monuments', that the invention of such inscriptions proceeded from the presage or anticipation of immortality implanted in all men naturally ... There is much to support the views that Wordsworth urges upon the subject ...[54]

The Maga set had imagined Wordsworth as epigram's ideal respondent as early as 1833; now his seal of approval, expressed in 'those beautiful lines' (reverently quoted: 'One precious tender-hearted scroll | Of pure Simonides!'), is also the warrant necessary to authorize Simonides as in every sense a right-thinking bard for the Greek nation.[55] In a similar vein, Ruskin's disciple Richard Tyrwhitt (to whose attack on Symonds in

---

[51] Shelley (1822: pp. viii–ix).

[52] Homoerotic Hellenism in the Shelley circle: Lauritsen (2005). Translator of Plato: Everest (2007: 240–1). On 'Adonais', Keats, and the Tory Reviews, see Everest (2007: 237–9, 253).

[53] 'Yet we agree with Shelley' (J. A. Symonds 1873: 33, found through Jenkyns 1980: 296); his biography of the poet came out in 1878 and was well received. Symonds was buried within yards of his hero. Keats, another Symonds favourite, was likewise construed censoriously by the conservative critics as a sexually liminal figure: Najarian (2002), a subtle and fascinating read.

[54] Neaves (1874: 9, 57).   [55] Anon. (1833d: 134); Neaves (1874: 18).

1877 we shall shortly turn our attention) extolled the English tradition of landscape art as a 'perfectly Hellenic' schooling in 'natural beauty'; to find the true Greeks, the readers of these conservative critics were urged with all sincerity to bypass the *Charmides* and head for their own native Lake District. The truth of Hellenism lay close to home; to touch it, one had only to take a walk and sniff the air in the English countryside.[56]

Ramming the conservative agenda home, Neaves expropriates the Oxford Uranians' core homoerotic dichotomy of Pandemic and Heavenly Eros for the greater glory of matrimony:

> We shall have occasion to see that the Greeks had two Venuses whom they worshipped—one, the ordinary or Earthly, the other the Heavenly Venus. In like manner there were two Cupids corresponding to that distinction. There are epigrams in the Anthology referring specially to these several divinities.[57]

'Uranian' now means completely the opposite of what Symonds et al. had meant by it. The revered Plato is Uranian because his love embraces the spiritual aspect of heterosexual romance and courtship (we are left thinking that it must have been some other Plato who wrote the *Symposium* and *Phaedrus*).[58] So too is Theocritus redeemed from his modern subcultural degradation as the secret call sign of the self-styled Uranian sodomite. Neaves concludes his tour of the Amatory poets by quoting him in translation, pointedly titling the result 'On the HEAVENLY VENUS' (the emphatic majuscule is original) to set Symonds and his readers straight on the true meaning of Uranian Love:

> Venus, but not the Vulgar one, you view:
> Call her the Heavenly; 'tis her title due.
> Her image here Chrysogone, the chaste,
> Within the house of Amphicles has placed,
> With whom a happy married life she led,
> And many goodly children bore and bred.
> Each rolling year was better than the past,
> Flowing from thee, Divine One, first and last:
> For they who gratefully the gods adore,
> Still find their joys increasing more and more.[59]

---

[56] Tyrwhitt (1877: 560), part of a long prescriptive digression that finds the true Hellenic spirit of the modern age in public-school education and muscular Christianity (pp. 558–60).

[57] Neaves (1874: 82–3).

[58] 'This is also ascribed to Plato, and it is certain that when a young man he wrote several amatory poems: "My soul, love, on my lips, while kissing thee, | Fluttered and longed to flit across from me"' (Neaves 1874: 94).

[59] Neaves (1874: 96).

The dedicatory epigram here translated is AP 6.340, although, of course, Neaves does not give citation details; nor does he choose to observe that it is a variation on a literary theme found clustered earlier in the same book (AP 6.206–11). With the possible exception of 6.209, that clutch of poems is written to celebrate the fictive occasion of courtesans finding marriage matches that enable them to retire from their trade; their gift offerings are the tools of their profession, anklets, fans, and wine cups, and they wear stock names such as Bitinna and Philaenis. Neaves's translation is in any case loose, and is piously tweaked to distance 6.340 from its sister poems: 'happy', 'goodly', gratefully', and 'joys' are note-worthy expansions with no equivalent in the Greek.[60]

Ultimately we cannot say to what extent working-class readers were already engaging with Symonds's dangerous stories, and Neaves can have had no very clear idea himself.[61] What we can study is not who was actually reading *Studies*, but elite conservative fears of who *might* be, and of what kinds of inadmissible ideas they might be drawing from it. Symonds's socially Other readerships function here less as a finite collective than as a motivating topos.[62]

Intended to inoculate readers against Symonds's sexually dissident treatment of the Anthology, and with the considerable financial and organizational muscle of the Blackwood's empire backing up its bid to become epigram's version of record with non-elite readerships, Neaves's spoiling attack instead ended up drawing extra public attention to what it was meant to mask. The anonymous reviewer for *John Bull* showed no mercy. The series title is turned against the volume's contents:

We cannot think that Lord Neaves has been so successful as some of his collabor-ators [i.e., other authors in the *Ancient Classics* series]. He is dry and heavy, deficient in the animation of style which has lent so great a charm to some of the previous volumes . . . *We cannot but think that Mr J. A. Symonds would have been more successful in popularising the subject, and the charming chapter on the anthology in that author's 'Greek Poets' is, to our mind, better suited for 'English readers' than Lord Neaves' didactic volume, in which so many commonplaces are solemnly enunciated . . .* when he comes to the text he too often gives us versions which apparently he has himself tinkered up, and has by no means improved in

---

[60] Additionally, 'Each rolling year . . . flowing from thee' wilfully misconstrues ἐκ σέθεν ἀρχομένοις (AP 6.340.5), which must describe how Chrysogone and Amphicles began their relationship; a further elided link to the hetaira cycle?

[61] Cf. the early translators' chimerical mass market, pp. 73–4.

[62] Compare the ever-elusive Woozle of A. A. Milne's Pooh stories, which exists primar-ily and perhaps exclusively as a mirror of its pursuers' anxieties and *idées fixes*. The influence of Symonds on the working man has something of the Woozle about it; it does not inform on itself, but on its self-appointed hunters.

the process. Indeed, from the specimens thus presented, we should venture to doubt his ear for rhythm.[63]

An inveterate and explicit tinkerer with the many hand-me-down trans-lations included in his little book, Neaves was himself a published poet (naturally through the firm of William Blackwood and Sons); this last put-down publicly shames him as punishment for doing down a work that, oblivious to its subtext, *John Bull* was actively promoting.[64] This is not to say that *John Bull*'s understanding of Symonds on epigram was 'wrong'. Subtext there was in abundance for a subcultural readership to enjoy—the author was himself a habitual, even obsessive rooter-out of subtext in his own reading, identifying viscerally with fictional and real-life characters he unmasked as secret homosexuals, so he knew exactly how to give them their money's worth—but mainstream readers were clearly getting plenty of value from a straight reading of *Studies*, and its extensive publication history attests that they continued to do so in commercially attractive numbers.[65]

Indeed, that was the nub of the problem; what a few perverts might be getting up to in their own subcultural corner was neither here nor there, provided they kept it to themselves. The pointedness of Neaves's rhetoric indicates that, right from the start, the content of Symonds's chapter on epigram was being viewed as especially problematic and potentially socially dangerous; in his book for *Ancient Classics*, he is exorcising conservative dread that the common 'English reader' might be subliminally corrupted.[66]

---

[63] Anon. (1874a) (emphases added).

[64] On Neaves's book, which went through three editions, see briefly Reilly (2000: 335–6). Regardless of its reception, *Epigram* receives honourable mention in his *Times* obituary, 25 December 1876, p. 4. Symonds had already got away with a lot when first publishing various *Studies*-destined essays in the Reviews, and knew it: Schultz (2004: 782 n. 207).

[65] Symonds as subtext-hunter: Sweet (2001: 201), briefly; more substantially, McDer-mott (2008), who argues (p. 24) that for Symonds sexual identity and reading style were practically indistinguishable. Examples at, e.g., J. A. Symonds (1967–9: iii. 607), outing Michelangelo to Edmund Gosse ('I have wrestled with his "psyche" so that I seem absorbed in him'). At p. 381, pushing for a queer reading of Kipling's 'Soldiers Three', he writes: 'I mean to get more of this man's books—and perhaps to write to him [to seek disambigu-ation]. I cannot quite understand the Envoy. When first I read it I *felt* the Lover in it; and then I got confused because it seemed to be the artist in a mysteriously religious mood . . .'.

[66] An approximate parallel from more recent history is the American conservative-evangelical witch-hunt of the 1980s and 1990s over Satanic messages embedded at a subliminal level in classic rock and heavy metal records through the technique of reverse recording known as 'backmasking'. The big difference is that these supposed 'messages' largely existed only in the ear of the affronted evangelical listener; those that were not, were purposely inserted by mischievously minded musicians who found amusement in driving such listeners into paroxysms of righteous fury (a phenomenon known in Internet circles as 'trolling'). Also, of course, and unlike homosexual acts in Victorian Britain, even

In particular, his revisionist travesty of the 'two Venuses' demonstrates that conservative critics were already detecting in Symonds's Meleager and Strato a route map for the assertion that sexual dissidence could be a healthy identity.

Symonds himself remained Romantically fatalistic about the prospects of real social reform, but he had put the ideas out there to work whatever changes they could on individual readers, and for now he seemed to have got away with it.[67] This would shortly change.

3. TRUTH, BEAUTY, AND THE WORDSWORTHIAN WAY

In the last chapter I say that in the Apoxyomenos of Lysippus is written ὄλβιος ὅστις ἐρῶν γυμνάζεται ['Blessed is the man who, being in love, exercises at the gymnasium']. I think it is. *But might some malevolent critic hint what the ending of that couplet is?* You know: οἴκαδε γ᾽ἐλθών εὕδει σὺν καλῷ παιδὶ πανημέριος ['and, returning home, sleeps with a beautiful boy all day']. Would it be better to spoil the thought for the sake of propriety or substitute a [different Greek] phrase?...*I am particularly anxious, while not being too timid, yet not wantonly to offend.* Please therefore consider this when you read the proof.[68]

there are vices also which are not even named among us...[69]

The 'written' of the first quote is figurative; the statue (known only through copies) carries no inscription, but it beams out a subtext to the reader who knows the obscurer byways of the Greek literary canon: here, Theognis, *Elegies* 2.1335–6. On and off the page, Symonds inhabited a thought-world rich in hidden messages and layers of meaning. He was always aware of the potential for hostile readings by critics who might partially unpack his subtext as a spoiling tactic to de-authorize his narrative—although he was also aware that that any such critic would

worshipping Satan for real (not that this was actually happening in these instances) was not an indictable offence under criminal law. This particular panic over media effect is acutely picked apart by Brannon and Brock (1994); it finds its place within a wider pattern devastatingly reviewed and countered by Gauntlett (1998).

[67] Symonds's pessimism: Binkley (2000); Orrells (2011a: 163) refreshingly reads *Studies* as an exercise in Romantic angst.

[68] J. A. Symonds (1967–9: ii. 280–1), to Henry Dakyns.

[69] Tyrwhitt (1877: 566), concluding his essay with selective citation from Symonds's academic father-figure, Benjamin Jowett.

not be inclined to disambiguate the deviant content directly and explicitly in public print.[70] Unspeakability cut both ways.[71] He also knew that some things could safely be said *only* within subculture, in privately printed volumes circulated on a need-to-know basis, and that any leakage beyond subculture could have severe real-world consequences. For much the same reasons, he would later be at pains to keep his private life out of the public eye—once he actually acquired one worth hiding.[72]

He must have known that he was taking a risk in his treatment of epigram in *Studies*; we might read something into the apparent fact that, unlike his now-famous 'The Genius of Greek Art' ('that last chapter' in the excerpt quoted above), he did not solicit the sober advice of friends on this essay in draft. Sidgwick for one would surely have told him to tone it down for his own good.

The explicit attack came in March 1877, in a review article by Richard St John Tyrwhitt, a former Rector of the University Church of St Mary Magdalen. Tyrwhitt was an art critic, keen amateur artist, later a novelist, and an occasional poet, as well as a prolific publisher of his own sermons and tracts; his interest in art was primarily moral and religious, and this had made him a devotee of Ruskin, in whose favour he had gladly stepped aside from contention for the Slade Professorship in Fine Arts in 1869.[73] Ruskin argued for a religious conception of Beauty ('the beautiful as a gift of God') and for painting that embodied 'truth to nature', a truth that was moral as well as material—Turner the British Romantic landscapist possessed it, the Old Masters did not; and he deprecated the persistence of the Classical past in the present as a spur to dissolute sensuality, instead idealizing a Middle Ages conceived as an organic society whose natural cultural expression was the Gothic style in

---

[70] Schultz (2004: 446), commenting on the correspondence between Symonds and Sidgwick.

[71] Sinfield (1994b: 8) on 'indeterminacy' is useful as a point of departure here, and cf. Buckton (1998: 62–3).

[72] J. A. Symonds (1967–9: ii. 991), to Gosse; cf. ii. 544, to Dakyns on *Modern Ethics*. The risk of intimate affairs coming to light following the death of a correspondent to whom they had been confided: ii. 778, on Whitman. All this anxiety was to be proved sensibly cautious by the Wilde trials. Hyde (1972: 204) quotes Wilde in court: 'no one likes to have his private letters read.'

[73] Tyrwhitt was quite a good painter and a keen amateur photographer, a hobby that he shared with his friend Lewis Carroll; a handsome photographic portrait by Carroll survives. His collection of public lectures, *Christian Art and Symbolism* (1872), is introduced by Ruskin ('The writer of this book has long been my friend...I begged him to give these lectures', p. ix), and the men worked closely together in promoting a moralized attitude to art in Oxford; Tyrwhitt (1878) is indicative.

architecture.[74] Hemmed in by the pagan horde of Jowett's Platonists, with their dismaying conception of a Beauty crystallized in naked male youth, Tyrwhitt enthusiastically agreed: his 1881 *Greek and Gothic* is Ruskin-by-numbers, and his novel of the previous year, *Hugh Heron*, is an Anglican Tory beat-down of Paterian aesthetic Hellenism.[75]

At stake in 1877 was a second Chair, that of Poetry. The post was undemanding in its duties but an excellent soapbox for its holder's views on literature, art, and wider social issues, and Symonds and Pater were both up for it, each keen to be the next Matthew Arnold.[76] Tyrwhitt's spoiling essay, 'The Greek Spirit in Modern Literature', appeared in the *Contemporary Review*, a religiously serious upmarket monthly based in Oxford and which was even then being cleansed by its religiously conservative owner of a recent Liberal drift in commissioning policies.[77] Explosive in its implications and its impact, it openly denounced the ruinous consequences for sexual morality when unchecked Arnoldian Hellenism met Oxford's godless modern cult of Plato: 'it is well known that *Greek love of nature* and beauty *went frequently against nature* [sic].' A footnote later on the page, denouncing Symonds's advocacy of Whitman, helps clarify the underlying thought: 'What we say is that in their social relations the Greeks were not at one with nature, *using that term as it is used in the Epistle to the Romans, chap. 1.*' Tyrwhitt was not the only alert churchman to find in Symonds's advocacy of 'nature' a disturbing prescription to embrace a morally feral existence.[78]

Aesthetic Platonism could even spell Britain's fall into anarchy, if recent French experience was anything to go by—shades here of Maga's rants of the 1830s, which we encountered first in Chapter 2, and more recently with regard to Neaves's old-school counterblasts;

---

[74] One would never guess from Ruskin's dualist scheme that Turner also handled classical themes. Religious conception of Beauty, Ruskin (1903–12: iv. 47); moral-*cum*-material truth to nature: iii. 104; the Classical style 'an architecture invented, as it seems, to make . . . sybarites of its inhabitants' (xi. 227).

[75] His 1882 *The Natural Theology of Natural Beauty* likewise declares its author as a card-carrying Ruskinite. *Hugh Heron, Ch. Ch.: An Oxford Novel* is much discussed in the scholarship, with particular reference to its anti-intellectual tone and the crashing muscular Christianity of its hero: Proctor (1957: 120–3) is sympathetic. Stray (2004: 4) introduces and republishes the text.

[76] Dowling (1994: 91).

[77] Brake (2004: 123) on Strahan's ousting of Knowles; under his Liberal-agnostic editorial regime Matthew Arnold himself had placed pieces with the journal. The *Contemporary Review* is still in publication, based in Oxford.

[78] Tyrwhitt (1877: 557) (emphases added), and cf. the sermon by E. C. Lefroy reported at Mader (2005: 391–2).

this was not just a matter of what two men might get up to in bed.[79] Naming names and pulling no punches, the essay destroyed the hopes of both men. The essay has been much discussed in the scholarly literature on Symonds and on Victorian sexual dissidence more widely, and I do not propose to dwell on its particular charges and insinuations.[80]

The named target is *Studies*; the version cited, the First Series in its first edition. (The second had been published the previous year, but Tyrwhitt could not yet have seen the Second Series of 1877, which was probably just as well.) Although the later Arnold and by implication Pater are notionally in the frame, the lion's share of the essay's polemic animus is directed squarely and explicitly towards Symonds, for his perversion of Arnoldian doctrine.[81] Critics have related this both to his close brush with potential sexual scandal with a chorister a few years earlier (Tyrwhitt must have been aware of the gossip), and to the culminating essay of the First Series of *Studies*, 'The Genius of Greek Art'. Judged by the passages he singles out for explicit condemnation, Tyrwhitt took particular exception to this essay, and secondarily to that on Aristophanes.[82]

Had Tyrwhitt even read the essay on epigram? He never explicitly mentions the genre, and a general vagueness regarding content suggests that he did not know *Studies* well at first hand; indeed, he may well have been primarily following up on problem passages identified by others and ignoring context (a classic media-panic behaviour). What initially looks to be a strong hint that he is targeting the Uranian Anthology—a strikingly phrased condemnation of 'Mr Symonds' *iostephanous* account' (p. 563) (emphasis added)—turns out to be a red herring, born of misattribution. Instead of alluding to Meleager, the reference is to a notorious skit of 1853, *The Oxford Ars Poetica, or, How to Write a Newdigate*, on just how bad a poem has to be before it stands a chance of winning:

> O! For some bold, sonorous Billingsgate,
> Such nauseous trash in fitting terms to rate;

---

[79] 'Hellenism . . . is made a standard of the artistic wing of the great army of atheism . . . . We believe some attempt was made by Hebert and Chaumette to realize it in the Parisian churches during the first Revolution' (Tyrwhitt 1877: 560).

[80] e.g. (among many): Frank M. Turner (1981: 32); Blanshard (2010: 144–5); Dawson (2007: 194), with interesting things to say on how Tyrwhitt (as at, e.g., 1877: 558, 562) yokes anti-Platonism to an anti-science agenda as part of his attack on agnosticism; da Silva (2006: 211), a nice summation; Brake (2004: 123–4). The essay itself is usefully quoted at some length by Schultz (2004: 374–5); nature going 'against nature' is Tyrwhitt (1877: 557).

[81] Pater's literary output is condemned by association with the wicked late Renaissance: Tyrwhitt (1877: 554–5); on homosexual appropriations of Renaissance style in the later nineteenth century, see Ivory (2009).

[82] The page references given in his footnotes make this plain at Tyrwhitt (1877: 557).

> Some cabman's copious rhetoric, to abuse
> This *iostephanous* and tawdry muse,
> This cheap, loud style—this meretricious taste
> Which will sport diamonds, if they're only paste!...

Since Symonds had gone on to win the Newdigate in 1860, this is a cutting comment on his purple style; for the classically adept, it also pins the blame for his Greek follies not on a literary genre but squarely on a city, Athens.[83]

Tyrwhitt aside, *Studies* got off lightly. By the end of the year its author's failing health had forced his permanent relocation to Davos, with no prospect of coming down from his Uranian flower-meadow for more than temporary excursions; Symonds had been removed from play. People were still reading him, and sometimes rewriting him—Frank Jevons's cheap and cheerful *History of Greek Literature* of 1886 is shot through with small steals—but the phase of assimilation had passed surprisingly smoothly.[84] The threat level of *Studies* was also easing. The Second Series had not made nearly as much of an impression as its predecessor, and the second edition of both series (1877/9) created very little splash—copies of all three are now extremely rare. Symonds's incautious Greek Genius had had the luck to fall in a lull between episodes of homophobic repression, there had been no great scandal, and the whole unpleasant affair seemed to have gone away. Histories of Greek Poetry reverted to a mid-century narrative pattern, with epigram marginal to the picture at best: poetry proper once again ended at Euripides, or at latest the Hellenistic Idyllists.[85]

Symonds had indeed succeeded in placing Greek epigram before the eye of the reading public, but the translations of selected poems that now began to appear did *not* perpetuate his Uranian Anthology; it was as if he had never written. Ten years after *Studies* wound down, a pocket-sized

---

[83] Gow and Page (1965: ii. 591) quote 'iostephanous and tawdry muse' as Swinburne's verdict on Meleager; I have no idea where they got this, but I presume it goes back a while. The author is one George Murray of Magdalen College, and the targets of the poem are Newdigate winners of the earlier nineteenth century—here, Thomas Claughton, winner in 1829 with a poem on Arctic exploration. LSJ ἰοστέφανος notes its frequent use as an epithet of Athens.

[84] Jevons's evocation of a Matterhorn-like Aeschylus is Symonds-by-numbers: 'grand, severe, and not infrequently hard...[his characters] drawn in majestic outline...are commanding or terrible...' (1886: 775); cf. J. A. Symonds (1920: 238), from the Second Series: 'His outlines are huge; his figures are colossal'.

[85] Jevons (1886) (subtitle: 'From the Earliest Period to the Death of Demosthenes') may stand as a fair example. Drawing on a body of research by Jeffrey Weeks, Dellamora (1990: 296) identifies the major moral panics as falling in the 1860s, 1880s, and, of course, around the 1895 Wilde trial. Jevons (1886) is an example of a post-*Studies* 'History of Greek Literature' on familiar, pre-Symonds lines.

collection put together for the Canterbury Poets series by 'Graham R.' Tomson (actually Rosamund, Mrs Graham R. Tomson, publishing under her husband's name) samples recent or recent-ish volumes by Andrew Lang (1888) and Richard Garnett (1869, a fascinating attempt) and interweaves older and newer strands; Bland, Merivale, Wellesley, and Goldwin Smith are here, but also friends in the here and now.[86] Tomson buys wholeheartedly into Symonds's critical language of epigram-connoisseurship, his disdain for Planudes ('the monkish changeling of Byzantium'), and his conception of the Anthology as a document of universal humanity; she praises Meleager extravagantly as a soulful balladeer and keen-eyed lover of beauty in Nature; even her illustrative examples of his genius are carried over from *Studies*.[87]

At the same time, everything after Meleager is disdained as the 'worthless growths of the later decadence'—so that is Strato out of the window. Even Meleager's Hellenistic Greece is biologically and spiritually contaminated by 'the transfusion of Asiatic blood', instilling 'effeminate and corrupt luxury'—Meleager can only pioneer Romantic love because his Eastern birth makes him a dreamy mystic, and Greece reads his epigrams because it is no longer manly enough to read Homer.[88] And the use of Symonds's examples is rigorously selective: although youthful follies are hinted at in passing (p. xxi), the objects of Meleager's true desire are now presented as exclusively women.

The collection is not at all hostile to Symonds in his capacity as a translator—several of his versions are used and (a nice touch) one of his father's. Nor, for those in the know, is its editorial policy at all homophobic or backwards-looking. Tomson was decidedly avant-garde in her poetry, in the company she kept, and in her scandalously complicated personal life; she was later to publish in the *Yellow Book* alongside Beardsley and Sickert, and modern subtext-hunters sift her poems for tokens of lesbian

---

[86] Lang's *Grass of Parnassus* was long-lived; it returns in Ch. 6. Cook (1919: 369) has a tasty note on Lang's 'Little Garland', pointing out an H. Rider Haggard connection. As a woman breaking into a traditionally male occupation, Tomson was a person of interest to the feminist press: see Anon. (1889a and b) (the latter under the heading 'Women in the News').

[87] Tomson (1889: pp. xiv, xx) (epigrams as types of previous stone); p. xviiii (Planudes); Meleager as Romantic troubadour, p. xxii. Meleager and Nature: pp. xxix–xxx, responding to J. A. Symonds (1873: 377–8). The Anthology 'one of the most entirely human' of books, p. xxxviii, but a human universality tweaked towards *memento mori*, p. xxxix. The examples of Heliodora and Zenophila: pp. xxvii–xxix, cf. J. A. Symonds (1873: 374–6).

[88] Oriental degeneracy and 'voluptuous effeminacy' of the Hellenistic age, Tomson (1889: pp. xxv–vii), gushingly. (Tomson is a fan of euthanizing the elderly as well as eugenics, p. xxxi.) Post-classical Greece lacked the moral constitution to read Homer: pp. xxv–vi.

desire.[89] Rubbing alongside versions by respectable scholar-translators (Lang, Ernest Myers, Lewis Campbell) we find many from the *Chrysanthema* (1878) of William Money Hardinge, nicknamed at Oxford 'the Balliol Bugger', with whom Pater had had a fling; others are by Symonds's friend Edmund Gosse; and for the first and last time in our story a female translator, Miss Alma Strettell, is credited by name (and extensively—over forty poems are hers).[90] There are a handful, too, by Symonds's idol Shelley, the bane of the Maga crowd.[91] The book is not part of a backlash, as such; but it does sideline the views expressed in *Studies*, for everyone's safety and peace of mind.

Alphabetically arranged as if specifically to irritate him, the collection comes front-loaded with a sizeable helping of Symonds's detested Agathias (pp. 1–14). Paul the Silentiary and Rufinus are decently represented; there is no Strato. It is as if *Studies* and the fuss with Tyrwhitt never happened.

4. SAME TEXT, DIFFERENT BOOK: THE EDITIONS OF *STUDIES*

And the Greek voice sings in accord with so few souls now.[92]

> I seek thee yet, and yet shall seek,
> Though faint mine eyes, my spirit weak
>   With prayers unspoken.
> Meanwhile, best of friends, do thou ...
>
>   Forget me never![93]

The second edition of *Studies* started no fires, but it lit a slow-burning fuse. Additional material was slipped in, not least regarding the Anthology. The

---

[89] Lesbian desire in Tomson's verse: Hughes (2005: 115). Tomson in the *Yellow Book*: 'Vespertilia', *Yellow Book*, 4 (January 1895), 49–52. This was a vintage issue; its roll call included Garnett, Kenneth Grahame, Richard le Gallienne (on whom, more shortly), and Edith ('E.') Nesbit.

[90] On Hardinge and Pater, see Inman (1991). Like J. A. Symonds (in 1860) and subsequently Wilde (in 1878), Hardinge won the Newdigate Prize, with his poem, 'Troy', of 1876. *Chrysanthema* was published first as an article in a British journal, pirated in the USA for Mosher's *Bibelot*, and finally reissued as a slender bound volume in 1911—again by Mosher. Like Tomson, Strettell (a collector of Romanian folk song) would later have her work published in the *Yellow Book* (1896).

[91] Shelley in Tomson (1889: 41, 220, 229).

[92] J. A. Symonds (1967–9: iii. 537), writing to Dakyns from Davos in early January 1891.

[93] J. A. Symonds (1920: 510).

'free paraphrase' quoted immediately above, a version of AP 7.346, is an early sign that the essay is raising its game; notionally epitaphic, it speaks eloquently to its author's sexually and textually liminal *amour de l'impossible*. As the revised essay hits its stride, its main effect is to raise the profile of Uranian Meleager and particularly of Strato. As before, the second edition regrets that it was 'not possible to quote many' of the latter's epigrams, but what in the first edition was a passing citation of AP 12.8 (as 'ii.396'; the referencing throughout is to the Didot edition of 1864–72) becomes in 1877 an original paraphrase in six stanzas—thirty-six lines for the original's eight.

The conception of male Beauty here is explicitly pederastic, and the bedroom scene of the closing stanza lends itself readily to being interpreted as unabashedly sexual ('a better joy'). Highlighted here for the connoisseur is the figurative–semantic slippage that queers the Anthology through Strato's Boyish Muse: epigrams are flowers, picked and woven by the 'anthologist', but flowers are also lovers' code for pretty boys. The two languages of appreciation—one literary, one sensuous—are coterminous. Writers, and readers, can slip from one to the other at will, letting themselves be guided by context, imagery, or their own desires.

What is more, the first-person narration teases with the promise of a modern-day *épigramme à clef*. The very first day puts us in a dreamy antique Athens that is experienced in the here and now of 'To-day':

> To-day, when dawn was dim, I went
> Before the garland-weaver's stall,
> And saw a boy whose beauty sent,
> Like stars of autumn when they fall,
> An arrow swift of fire that left
> Glory upon the gloom it cleft.
>
> Roses he wove to make a wreath,
> And roses were his cheeks and lips.
> And faintly flushed the flowers beneath
> The roses of his finger-tips;
> He saw me stand in mute amaze,
> And rosy blushes met my gaze...
>
> Roses and wreaths with shy pretence,
> As for a bridal feast, I bought;
> And veiling all love's vehemence
> In languor, bade the flowers be brought
> To deck my chamber by the boy
> Who brings therewith a better joy.

Symonds's expansion comes close to making explicit the equation between the flower-garland and the 'flower' of the boy's sexual charms and favours, but not only does the desired youth feel no sin, his sense of socially correct behaviour—the virtuous *aidōs* signified by his blushes—is not violated by a less than ideally Uranian wooing; he gives his 'sweet symbol of assent' (stanza 5, line 6), and the narrator's erotic pursuit culminates in a pleasure reported as straightforwardly 'better' than conjugal.

Further on, we get more Meleager than before—versions given their first public hearing, if we believe Symonds's account elsewhere, to Swiss mountaineering comrades in a snow-storm:

> I'll join Love's rout! Let thunder break,
> 　Let lightning blast me by the way!
> Invulnerable Love shall shake
> 　His aegis o'er my head to-day.[94]

The discussion of the erotic Anthology moves on in the essay's revised form from dismal Rufinus to an entirely new encomium of Meleager—a counter-Neavesian Meleager, whose truthfulness to the world of Nature now explicitly underwrites the 'purity' of his 'passion'—and ultimately to Strato.[95] Presented explicitly as Symonds's last word on erotic epigram, we find 'an Envoy, slightly altered in the English translation from Straton's original':[96]

> It may be in the years to come
> That men who love shall think of me
> And reading o'er these verses see
> How love was my life's martyrdom.
>
> Love-songs I write for him and her,
> Now this, now that, as love dictates;
> One birthday gift alone the Fates
> gave me, to be Love's scrivener.

Strato's original is AP 12.258, and there is nothing 'slight' about Symonds's alterations; but Tyrwhitt was using the older edition of the First Series, so he never saw them, and no one else was really paying attention, at least not yet.[97]

---

[94] J. A. Symonds (1920: 528–30). The anecdote is in his essay 'Winter nights at Davos', at Symonds and Symonds (1892: 351–3).

[95] Rufinus: J. A. Symonds (1920: 727–8); Meleager's love for Nature proves his 'passionate love and... purity of heart' (p. 525); this is the Wordsworth topos of the *Maga* opposition turned on its head.

[96] J. A. Symonds (1920: 531).

[97] The Greek text runs: Ἡ τάχα τις μετόπισθε κλύων ἐμὰ παίγνια ταῦτα,| πάντας ἐμοὺς δόξει τοὺς ἐν ἔρωτι πόνους· | ἄλλα δ᾽ ἐγὼν ἄλλοισιν ἀεὶ φιλόπαισι χαράσσω | γράμματ᾽, ἐπεί τις ἐμοι τοῦτ᾽ ἐνέδωκε θεός. For a more literal translation, see Livingstone and Nisbet (2010: 147 n. 21), or, of course, the Loeb. By mistake, Grundy (1913: pp. lxii–iii) quotes Symonds's

By the time Symonds came to consider a third edition of *Studies*, emblematic prototypes from a long-ago Uranian idyll had slipped a long way down his list of priorities. He was still occasionally writing on the Greeks and Greek love, within what was by now his characteristic mode of publication of essays in Reviews (for honoraria that were not always immediately forthcoming) with a view to selective republication in book form. His 1890 essay for the *Contemporary Review*, for instance, 'The Platonic and Dantesque ideals of love', subsequently reappeared in *In the Key of Blue and Other Prose Essays* (1893), and the author's correspondence documents its transition; that same year he poured energy into a translation of Moschus' *Lament for Bion*, which two decades earlier (First Series) he had swooned over as an inspiration to Shelley's *Adonais*.[98] He was always happy to slip a little Hellenic colour into essays on other subjects when a case could be made for relevance—as when he compared a favoured Swiss athlete to ancient images of Achilles, a figure steeped in modern Uranian longing—and had a lively interest in beefcake photography under the pretext of classicism.[99]

Nonetheless, in the course of his 1880s self-exile in continental Europe he grew increasingly disillusioned with Platonic puff, if not necessarily with Hellas *per se*. This led to a public self-dissociation from mystical eros in an essay of 1890.[100] The Labouchère Amendment was injury heaped on insult, the law needed to be changed, and Hellenism was an insufficiently direct means of applying pressure.[101] Instead Symonds, already an outspoken science groupie in the First Series of *Studies*, reoriented himself towards the liberating potential of new paradigms. Moving from Plato to Ulrichs was a natural progression in his thought,

translation approvingly as by Meleager, under the impression that it reports on his 'beautiful love-poems'. On Grundy and his Oxonian *Ancient Gems in Modern Settings*, see now briefly Bowie (2012: 19–21).

[98] J. A. Symonds (1967–9: iii. 476–7, 499, 544); the varied provenance of *In the Key of Blue* is handily tabulated at 701. Moschus and *Adonais*: J. A. Symonds (1873: 333–40).

[99] Important letters on this at J. A. Symonds (1967–9: iii. 682–3, 699); Evangelista (2009b) delivers the goods; Stevenson (1998) is revealing on classically themed nudes as semi-admissible gay porn, as is Bryan E. Burns (2008a), and cf. for context Wyke (1997). Achilles as gay fantasy icon in Symonds: Bristow (1995: 130); Bann (2000) on Symonds's post-Shelley Antinous provides a usefully full comparative study, and is complemented by Bryan E. Burns (2008b). Antinous' enduring status as a gay pin-up is the subject of an excellent article by the novelist Sarah Waters (1995).

[100] Dowling (1994: 128).

[101] Symonds felt the injustice of the Amendment deeply, even from Davos: Dowling (1994: 127). Grosskurth (1964: 282–3) conveniently summarizes, mapping the shift in his focus as a writer from historical allegory towards head-on engagement.

and after the Oxford Hellenism boom of the 1860s and early 1870s evolutionary and psychological science were the next big bandwagons to jump on. That he sometimes had difficulty keeping his amateur science and his Greek poetics apart (his oddball speculations on semen resound with Homeric *menos*, or manly spunk) goes to show how deeply the former was becoming ingrained in his personal mythology as well as in his sexual politics.[102]

Symonds had been following developments in sexology and thought he was seeing progress. In the 1860s and 1870s it had been the enemy against which classical Greek parallels needed to be mustered, but 'my elaborate polemic [in 'Greek Ethics'] against Krafft-Ebing is hardly required now'; the new evolutionary paradigm of Wallace and Darwin in particular seemed to promise a counter-argument to the medicalization of gay identity as a pathology symptomatic of a race in decline.[103] In fixating on evolution as an explanatory panacea he was very much of his time—Darwinism was in this sense the new Winckelmania of the British public sphere[104]—but Symonds saw in it a scientific basis for authenticating dissident self-fashioning. There was no originary Eden, no fall of humanity from grace into a state of sin, but instead continual improvement of the life of the species as it developed towards the full and authentic self-realization. 'God' was the name for the best part of our nature, not an extraneous legislator: 'the whole Universe is literally in perpetual *Becoming* ... all things in the universe exist in process ... the right way toward living and thinking in the whole.' As a popularizer of science, however, Symonds was out of his depth, and these essays were cruelly rebuffed by contemporary reviewers.[105]

Symonds's methods of composition were now as anachronistic as his brand of Classics was a period piece. The newspaper press was now the pulpit of choice for the crusading man of letters, but he distrusted the commercialism he saw in its style of journalism.[106] From 1890, flattened by the damning reviews of his new *Essays Speculative and Suggestive*, Symonds professed to be winding down his own literary work and

---

[102] 'I have no doubt myself that the absorption of semen implies a real modification of the physique of the person who absorbs it, & that, in these homosexual relations, this constitutes an important basis for subsequent conditions—both spiritual & corporeal' (J. A. Symonds 1967–9: iii. 798; cf. p. 810).

[103] J. A. Symonds (1967–9: iii. 813).

[104] On Sidgwick's scepticism regarding the utility of Darwinism as a one-size-fits-all explanatory narrative, see briefly Collini (1992: 338).

[105] J. A. Symonds (1907: 5 (emphasis in original), 7); and cf., e.g., p. 11 (body and spirit are part of that cosmos that science is setting out to explain). Note that this is a third edition; for all the sniffy reviews, the collection aged well, perhaps getting a shot in the arm from the author's untimely death.

[106] J. A. Symonds (1967–9: iii. 565).

withdrawing from the public eye in favour of nurturing young talent. When he did get sucked back in, it was the Michelangelo biography that dominated, but at a more gentle pace than before. The old-school man of letters was consciously winding down his career.[107]

Writing to friends in 1892, Symonds envisaged the third edition of *Studies* as a simple reprint once the publisher had shifted his remaining stock of the second edition of the Second Series (still occupying warehouse space thirteen years after publication; Smith, Elder had clearly been far too optimistic in estimating its appeal). He was keen to revise its content at least a little, but other projects took priority, and that plan was quickly abandoned; by January 1893 he was reporting it to Gosse as no more than a reprint of the second edition.[108] Of course, this was not the whole story—the contents were at last reordered, so that what had been the separate chronological sequences of the two original series now offered a single, two-volume timeline—but the individual essays themselves remained all but untouched, with one seemingly minor exception (the addition of translations for key terms) to which we will turn at the start of our next section. On 19 March, with the published book in his hands at Clifton Hill House, he wrote to Dakyns calling it 'a young man's effort. Yet I do not think much would have been gained by rewriting the whole. It has a note of its own, a way of feeling & seeing things which seems to me fresh, & which maturer criticism sometimes lacks.'[109] On 19 April he was dead in Rome of tuberculosis, and inevitably this coloured the reception of the newly integrated *Studies* in the public sphere. Symonds was recalled as a much loved author and public personality; snatched away before his time, he was sadly missed.[110] To pass judgement on his final publication was also to write an obituary in which no ill could be spoken of the dead, no matter what one thought privately. Richard Jebb's favourable mention of *Studies* at the annual prize-giving of Mason Science College (later to become the University of Birmingham) in October of that year is a case in point; it was surely given through gritted teeth, given what Symonds had done to his beloved Sophocles.[111] An anonymous notice in the *American Journal of Philology*

---

[107] J. A. Symonds (1967–9: iii. 491, 502, 506). Michelangelo as endnote: (pp. 545, 558).

[108] J. A. Symonds (1967–9: iii. 683, 750, 804); for critical discussion, see Grosskurth (1964: 310).

[109] J. A. Symonds (1967–9: iii. 828).

[110] For Symonds the public speaker, evidently much in demand, see, e.g., J. A. Symonds (1967–9: ii. 412, 447–9).

[111] Reported in *The Times* of 10 October 1893: 4. The Second Series turned Sophocles into a nude pin-up, 'exceedingly beautiful and well-formed...According to Athenian custom, he appeared on this occasion naked, crowned, and holding in his hand a lyre'

of 1893 welcomed the re-edition of *Studies* with fond indulgence as a charming blast from the past, generously commending its author on his scholarly achievements and relishing the 'fine enthusiasm' of his youthful endeavour. We have run across 'enthusiasm' as a term of containment before (see Chapter 2), but the Americans probably meant it sincerely in its modern sense: they liked his perkiness. It helped, too, that *Studies* had had such mixed origins; the inclusion of worked-up lectures alongside journal articles played to the mass culture of self-improvement that had grown on the back of the newly upscaled and prioritized teaching ambit of the universities, and lent its author democratic authority as a public educative voice.[112]

Keyed to the critical register of contemporary discourse on the Roman satirists, an anonymous reviewer now casts the young Symonds of Jowett's Oxford in the role of earnest and overwrought moralist, in polarized contrast to the languidly amoral Pater. The style is the man, and the style is forever young and full of life—testament to the vital spirit of its author, whose chronic invalidism grants him the liminal authority of the classical prophet:[113]

Mr Pater's style has been pronounced to be a style of 'perfectly finished beauty, and full of exquisite restraint', but old-fashioned readers will miss in him what Persius missed in the *décadents* of his time, the throb that runs through the 'lushness' of Mr Symonds' fervid periods, the youthful sincerity with which one can never be angry. It is well, therefore, that Mr Symonds was not tempted to spoil his book by recasting it, it is well that he did not rob these early studies of the charm of youthfulness by lessening the glow and toning down the color. Of course, it is harder, very much harder, for an oldster to read Mr Symonds' *Studies* now than it was a generation ago. Neither the stream of time nor the reader has stood still, but whoever has to deal with Greek poetry will find his advantage in consulting the new edition... A wonderful amount of high and noble enjoyment did this invalid scholar snatch, day by day, for himself and for others, out of the jaws of death...[114]

<hr />

(J. A. Symonds 1920: 275–6). On Jebb's devotion to a morally stainless Sophocles, see entertainingly and acutely Stray (2007a).

[112] Collini (1991: 225–6) on the two types of source for book-material. 'Making one's role as a teacher central to one's identity [by building a book from lectures as well as or instead of essays from periodicals]... could involve adopting a different tone and argumentative horizon from those who spoke primarily from the periodical page rather than the lectern' (p. 226).

[113] On 'the invalid' as licensed outsider in the nineteenth-century *imaginaire*, see Frawley (2004).

[114] Anon. (1893a: 261).

Depending on who is reading, 'high and noble enjoyment' may either disallow or ennoble the pursuit of sexually dissident subtext; Basil Gildersleeve's journal will surely have intended the former, if indeed its contributors were alive to the issue at all. Symonds derives posthumous advantage here through being contrasted to Pater, whose stock had fallen both in Britain and in the USA; Gildersleeve himself in a near-contemporary review wrote him off as a sloppy and verbose recycler of commonplaces, and at home he was jeered at for peddling warmed-over views from forty years before.[115] As we have seen, Symonds's own views were not a million miles from Pater's and (as expressed in Studies at least) deliberately less radical in some important aspects; unlike Pater, though, he had had the grace to die young(ish) and leave a good-looking text.

And America was a whole different context within which that text might be received. While a few small-press connoisseurs there knew Symonds through publishers' lists as a Romantic Aesthete latterly rubbing shoulders with Decadents thanks to Mosher's piracies, the mass market cared nothing about London salons and Oxford gossip. This was a different social world. Symonds was read straight here, and the re-edited Studies was very much enjoyed as a reliable and accessible handbook to the Greek poets. American reviewers had always liked his sensitivity of thought—and even his prose style—and now he could do no wrong.[116] The newly founded School Review of 1893 (later to become the American Journal of Education) admiringly notes the appearance of the third edition, lavishing particular praise on its 'altogether entertaining' chapter on epigram. Posthumously, Symonds's charm offensive was working better than ever:

These volumes are 'Studies' in the most ideal sense of the word, and as such have high educational value. As an English introduction to the Greek poets it would be difficult to compare anything else with them. As a whole, the work gains in this third edition by a rearrangement which has brought the parts into better chronological order and by some important additions, especially in the way of translation. Otherwise the 'Studies' remain substantially what they were in the second edition.

The merit of the work appears quite as conspicuous in the handling of minor topics as in that of larger ones, as, for example, the comic poets, comic fragments, and the new chapter on Herondas and the Idyllists; while the twenty-third chapter on 'The Anthology', with its translations, is, from a popular point of view, perhaps

---

[115] Campbell (1893); Gildersleeve (1894).

[116] See, e.g., Anon. (1880), on the American imprint of the first edition by Harper & Brothers of New York: 'not only instructive and suggestive criticism, but a glow of feeling which cannot fail to kindle [the reader's own] appreciative sense of artistic excellence'; on the third edition, see Anon. (1893c).

the most altogether entertaining chapter of the entire work, a rare collection of quotable epigrams and verses.[117]

Three years later, again in the *School Review*, an American educator can unproblematically cite the third edition as one of 'the most essential books for a high school classical library', alongside Jebb's of 1893—and this in an era when classical pedagogy in US schools was at its most prescriptively moralistic.[118] For this market, going by the print discourse, the subtext in *Studies* simply was not there—although who knows what particular individuals were finding as they turned the pages.

Ten years on from publication, a further *School Review* article on the pedagogic value of classroom debates presupposes *Studies* as a fixture of any school library:

Give a boy about to enter college the question, 'Which was the greater writer, Homer or Virgil?' and would not he know more about the poetic power of these men than he had gained from all the linguistic study of his texts? It might even be that from the reading of Sellar's book on Virgil, or Symonds's book on the Greek poets, he would first really appreciate the fact that Homer and Virgil were poets.[119]

With American educators seemingly content to remain oblivious to its subtext, the author's long-dead ambition that *Studies* might one day be promoted as a school textbook had now come true, twenty years on and a long way from home.

5. WILDE TIMES: *STUDIES* AND THE *FIN DE SIÈCLE*

Oscar Wilde sent me his novelette, 'The Picture of Dorian Gray' . . .
If the British public will stand this, they can stand anything.[120]

(Symonds to Horatio Forbes Brown, July 1890)

---

[117] Anon. (1893b: 511–12) (emphases added).

[118] Meader (1896). There is rich irony in Symonds's work being cited in the same breath as Jebb's; see pp. 203, 231–5. American school editions of 'problem' classical texts in the 1890s and 1910s routinely censured classical vice and asserted the editors' moral obligation to expurgate; see, e.g., Westcott (1894: pp. iv–vi) and Post (1908: pp. xxvii–xxviii). For an overview of American censorship of books for the young and an analysis of the sociopolitical context in which it grew, see respectively Perrin (1992: 162–84) and Beisel (1997: 53–75).

[119] Churchill (1903: 279). Back home, too, Symonds's insistence on literary appreciation was surely a comfort to classical educators beleaguered by increasing technical specialization, be it in hardcore philology or dirt archaeology; disciplinary modernization was already being scare-stereotyped in the 1880s as the death of Classics's broad, public-educative mandate of instilling Romantic sympathy with the peak cultural achievements of Hellas: Marchand (1996: 115).

[120] J. A. Symonds (1967–9: iii. 477).

It seemed to my rapt senses that this frock-coated young god, with
the classic profile and the dark curls curving from the impeccable
silk 'tile' that surmounted them as curve the acanthus leaves of a
Corinthian capital, could be none other than Anacreon's self in
modern shape.[121]

(Oliver Herford recalls first catching sight of the Aesthetic poet
Richard le Gallienne in 1892 outside the Café Royal in Regent Street,
favourite haunt of Wilde and Beardsley)

Back in the UK, the cultural mood was making Symonds's newly re-
energized Uranian Meleager 'harder, very much harder' for traditionally
minded critics to stomach. The 'important additions, especially in the
way of translation' identified by the *School Review* in the new edition of
1893 were largely illusory—the only real expansions had come in the
obscure second edition of the late 1870s, which the Americans clearly
had not seen, and the third edition merely reprinted these. Nonetheless,
there were new 'translations' of a kind, and their size and extent—merely
a word or two, dotted here and there in the text—belied their importance. For the first time, *Studies* anticipated and was made fully accessible
to a readership who knew no Greek at all.

Writers of the late nineteenth century often expected the English
common reader to be able to make out a word or two of Greek script by
him- if not herself, or at least to play along and guess the meaning
from context when isolated Grecisms were slipped in to raise the tone (as
Chris Stray has pointed out, the frequency with which period bestsellers
require a salting of Greek typeface comes as a surprise to the twentieth-
or twenty-first-century reader).[122] Symonds's essay on epigram still does
not, for instance, give the English for the isolated terms ἐπιδεικτικά or
ἀναθηματικά, because to transliterate them is at once to have in one's hands
the scholarly terms appropriate to the topic. Just to be sure, the context fills
in for any blanks in the reader's Greek-derived English vocabulary and
knowledge of ancient cultures: 'ἐπιγράμματα ἀναθηματικά, the record of
the public and private votive-offerings in Hellas'—but essentially this is
business as usual.[123] At the same time, longer passages of continuous Greek
(or even just English written in Greek script) could be presumed to be
impenetrable to the inexpert and thus to offer safe hiding-places for sinful

---

[121] Introduction (n.p.) to Le Gallienne (1922).

[122] Stray (1998a: 81), on George Eliot, and cf. Haynes (2003: 34–6).

[123] J. A. Symonds (1920: 503), unchanged from (1873: 347–8). 'Anathematic' was
particularly worth glossing, since the English word is also used to mean 'of or relating to
anathema', hence 'reprehensible'.

knowledge—increasingly safe, perhaps, as classical learning began to lose its High Victorian ubiquity and unquestioned cultural centrality.[124] In the light of this differentiation (short = notionally accessible, long = putatively inaccessible), we can see Symonds's third edition making a clean break with the past in how it presents its Greek. All longer phrases, and all poems, are now translated, as at the outset are two potentially unfamiliar terms. Subtext was now text, briefly but breathtakingly:

[Meleager] called this compilation by the name of στέφανος, or wreath... About the same time [as Philip] or a little later, Straton of Sardis made a special collection of poems on one class of subjects, which is known as the μοῦσα παιδική (*poems on boy-love*)...[125]

Viewed in medical and legal terms, the years leading up to the third edition had notionally been bad ones for the cause of homosexuality, and allusions to same-sex desire in the public sphere continued to be shrouded in deniability and double-coding—a tendency from which *Studies* here momentarily deviates.[126] Ambiguity delivered its own special pleasures, though, and homophile authors of the early 1890s worked it hard; what is read in retrospect as an inevitable reckoning (the Wilde trials of 1895), no one saw coming. The public, it seemed, really *would* 'stand this': Decadent culture became a literary sensation.[127] Symonds was thrilled to detect ubiquitous and heavy Uranian subtext in novels by Wilde and his continental European contemporaries, and, although he was always a wishful reader, one would hardly call him wrong: 'What a number of Urnings are being portrayed in novels now! "Dorian Gray",

---

[124] A newsworthy example at the time of writing was the rediscovered notebook (subsequently printed for very limited scientific circulation) of Dr George Murray Levick, a medically trained Navy volunteer on Scott's *Terra Nova* expedition of 1910–12, who made the first sustained study of the Adélie Penguin; he can bring himself to record the unspeakable sexual habits of the male only in Greek transliteration: see Russell, Sladen, and Ainley (2012).

[125] J. A. Symonds (1920: 500) (emphasis added); the basic text is the same as at (1873: 343), but the addition of translation makes all the difference.

[126] Cook (2003a: 76–7), on the medical Establishment's hostile response to Kraft-Ebing's *Psychopathia Sexualis* in 1892, is germane to *Studies*' publication context; a few years down the line and the other side of the Wilde trials, Ellis's *Sexual Inversion* (to which Symonds was a major contributor) was to be hit even harder. But we should not over-egg the (negligible) impact of medical discourse on homosexuality in the public sphere; even in the technical literature, references to any and all sexual behaviours were routinely buried in long footnotes and other non-obvious places: Crozier (2001).

[127] See evocatively Dellamora (1990: 209), identifying 1894 as the 'high-water mark' of gay Victorian cultural creativity, and, colourfully, Kaplan (2005). While Symonds despised the Labouchère Amendment as an iniquitous and incompetent piece of lawmaking, he did not see it as a serious threat, and clearly he was not alone in this: J. A. Symonds (1967–9: iii. 792).

"Un Raté", "Monsieur Venus", this "Footsteps of Fate". I stumble on them casually, & find the same note.'[128] Thrilled by 'Greek' homophile content in *The Artist* of November 1891, Symonds was agog to discover the real-life identity of its author, who hid behind the less than subtle pseudonym 'Harmodius'. He was confident that someone in his friendship network would either know or be able to find out—Uranian Hellenism was pretty much an open secret among the Bohemian set.[129]

Symonds's own *Studies*, and indeed his chapter on the Anthology, were being read and cited approvingly by this daring new generation. We know that Wilde took especial interest in those passages in *Studies* that proclaimed the naturalness of same-sex desire and the glory of heroic male pairings 'that passed the love of women'.[130] He and his fellow Decadents subsequently built on and flaunted the queer associations of Symonds's flower-discourse, retrospectively making the Anthology's roses and lilies readable as luxuriant *fleurs du mal*, and expanding too on Symonds's more identifiably personal terminology in which epigrams were compared to precious stones.[131] In the new century's first decade, the poet and former *Yellow Book* contributor Richard le Gallienne was to make 'Love's scrivener' his literary touchstone. His American contemporary Oliver Herford paints a vivid picture of the young poet in his Regent Street glory, basking in literary London's adulation of his decadent new prose sensation, *The Book-Bills of Narcissus* (1892).[132] Since then he had put safe distance between himself and his *fin de siècle* associates. His prose works repeatedly cast back to Symonds's adaptation of Strato AP 12.258 into an *apologia pro vita sua*, quoted earlier. In *Little Conversations with the Sphinx*, allusively titled and framed as a kind of Socratic dialogue, 'Love's scrivener' becomes a position statement on the

---

[128] J. A. Symonds (1967–9: iii. 586, a letter of June 1891); the terms 'Urning' and 'Uranian' (the former popularized by the German homosexual-rights activist Karl Ulrichs) are used more or less interchangeably by British writers in this period. The authors of the notorious French Decadent novels *Monsieur Vénus* (1884) and *Un Raté* (1891) were both women, writing under the pseudonyms 'Rachilde' and 'Gyp' respectively. *Footsteps of Fate* (1890, original title *Noodlus*) was by a Dutchman, Louis Couperus; Oscar Wilde was a fan.

[129] J. A. Symonds (1967–9: iii. 627).

[130] In Wilde's personal copies of the First and Second Series, discussed later in this chapter, homoerotic passages are highlighted with a vertical stroke in the margin, as at, e.g., J. A. Symonds (1873: 8 (the text of which is quoted here); 1876: 35).

[131] Cruise (1999: 181); in passing, and typically mordant, Jenkyns (1980: 159): 'A taste for Greek vocabulary was a conspicuous feature of decadent sensibility, and words such as "sardonyx" and "asphodel" were freely employed by aesthetic individuals, who sometimes, one suspects, had very vague ideas about what the stone or flower looked like.' Symonds himself had been well aware of flower-discourse's radical susceptibility to double- and multiple-coding: (1967–9: i. 715 (a letter to his wife, 1867)).

[132] Quoted from Herford's admiring introduction (n.p.) to Le Gallienne (1922).

poetic profession of imaginative sympathy with all human experience (or, polymorphous promiscuity). The Sphinx speaks, and she of all people should know:

Do you remember those lines of Straton's in the Greek Anthology?

> 'Love-songs I write for him and her,
> Now this, now that, as Love dictates;
> One birthday gift alone the Fates
> Gave me, to be Love's scrivener.'

Of course, this is not the whole truth about the artist, but it is a good deal of it. In a sense the artist is the most unselfish of human beings, for his whole life is living for, and feeling for, others. The more lives and the more various he can live, the greater the number and the diversity of his feelings, the greater his art.[133]

Long afterward, Le Gallienne came back to and re-created Symonds's Strato in his own explicitly bisexual love poetry, albeit in a strictly limited print run; his 1922 collection from the Catskill Mountains of New York State, *A Jongleur Strayed*, begins movingly with a verse dedication 'To the Love of André and Gwen', signed off with 'After Strato':

> If after times
> Should pay the least attention to these rhymes
> I bid them learn
> 'Tis not my own heart here...
> *But like a scrivener in the market-place,*
> *I sit and write for lovers, him or her...*[134]

Wilde himself had been an enthusiastic early adopter of *Studies*, luxuriating in its prose style and dangerous ideas as an Oxford undergraduate. The First Series had appeared the year before he came up to Magdalen (1874), so was still a talking point. He carried a copy everywhere with him, enthusiastically annotating its margins with his personal reflections, and entries in his commonplace book and a surviving notebook from his Magdalen days round out a picture of attentive engagement. Of course, he was also perfectly capable of engaging directly with the same texts as Symonds, texts towards which his apprenticeship with Mahaffy in Dublin had already pointed him.[135] Wilde's flaunting of *Studies* was no

---

[133] Le Gallienne (1910: 34–5, and cf. p. 17), again quoting Strato-as-Symonds: 'The image is a good one. Yes, the poet is a scrivener of life.'

[134] Le Gallienne (1922: n.p.) (emphasis added); the edition was limited to 1,500 copies.

[135] The editors' index to Wilde (1989) is helpful in identifying moments of interaction with Symonds's text, principally *Studies* but also in passing the biography of Shelley; and with Plato including the model of eros outlined in the *Symposium* (1989: 121; cf. p. 115).

mere pose; his contemporaries at Oxford were to recall him as a terrific-ally good classicist. He was recognized at the time as outstanding in his year, an 'admirable and sensitive classical scholar'; indeed, this is how the dedicatory inscription to his anonymously endowed funerary monument in Père Lachaise would have the world remember him to this day.[136] The *fons et origo* of this lifelong classical habit was *Studies*. Wilde rushed to acquire a copy of the Second Series (1876) as soon as it came out; its marginalia testify to his growing confidence as an original critic, arguing the toss with Symonds over Müller on mythology and picking him up on some missed evidence on the character of Helen.[137] Having in mind to write a review and/or original essay that never materialized, he took the new Second Series away with him in August 1876 to the far west of Ireland, to the family's hunting lodge in Connemara—surely one of the best places in the world to get 'deep' into an important book, as he reports doing in a surviving letter. The manuscript of his draft survives, hastily written on the whole but carefully worked through in just those passages where he respectfully takes issue with Symonds's views; the ambitious young stylist was anxious to make a good impression on the important role model with whom he was to maintain an amicable epistolary correspondence in later years, when the pair surely knew each other face to face (both were elected to the Council of the newly formed Society for the Promotion of Hellenic Studies in 1879, only a year or so after Wilde finished his degree).[138]

---

[136] Admirable and sensitive: Mikhail (1979: i. 5); Mendelsohn (2010) wistfully imagines what might have been, had he stayed in academia. The epitaph, incised on the obverse of Epstein's noble monument and neglected by most visitors, singles out the award of the Berkeley Gold Medal for Greek in Wilde's last year at Dublin (1874) and his double First at Oxford (1876/8) as well as his victory in the Newdigate competition.

[137] Wilde in Connemara: Wilde (2000: 31). The MS draft of his review-*cum*-essay and his annotated copies of the First and Second Series survive, and I thank the Morgan Library of New York for enabling me to consult them. Mendelsohn (2010) alerted me to this; as noted by him, Wilde's inscription on the title page confirms that he purchased the Second Series immediately on its publication. Heckling over Helen: marginalia to J. A. Symonds (1876: 73, and cf. p. 91).

[138] e.g. on the twenty-fifth page of the MS Wilde first wrote 'Mr Symonds' essay on Helen is written with great beauty of thought and language. But very strangely he has omitted all mention of the beautiful panegyric [etc]'. He then crossed through 'is written with' and substituted in ink 'shows', before finally plumping for 'is marked with'. There are similar changes on pp. 31–2, and at p. 18 Wilde left a 6cm gap after 'But Mr Symonds is probably right in saying that it is a true parable'; clearly he intended to come back and say more. The MS has now been edited with a useful introduction (from which I borrow the SPHS nugget) by Thomas Wright and Donald Mead (Wilde 2008). In their notes on the text (95 n. 1) the editors observe that Wilde 'was almost certainly familiar with all of Symonds's writings, and reviewed at least four of them', and give nice background detail on the literary

The influence was profound. When Wilde toured Greece with his by now slightly disreputable old tutor Mahaffy, 'the scholar who taught me how to love Greek things'—Greek love, perhaps, included—his letters home (1877) revealed an experience of Mediterranean life and landscape fundamentally coloured by the fervid visualizations of *Studies*. It was from Symonds's *Studies* and Pater's *Renaissance* that Wilde patched together his own early take on Aestheticism—and *Studies* came first by several crucially formative years, fostering the adolescent ambition to become the Euripides of his culturally 'late' age.[139] Long-lasting habits of thought and mental furniture might be traced all the way back to the First Series. Looking back in penitence on his 'pagan' days in the few years he had left after his release from prison, Wilde (as recalled with perhaps some embroidery by his loyal friend Frank Harris) claimed to have experienced a Greek double-consciousness very like that modelled by Symonds's dreamy Genius of Greek Art, but in retrospect rather more tiresome: 'In my Pagan days the sea was always full of Tritons blowing conchs, and other unpleasant things. Now it is quite different.'[140]

In the essays for magazines with which he courted his public, Wilde cultivated the image of a Hellenizing modernist or modernizing Hellenist, as, for instance, on his pro-feminist efforts to promote Greek drapery as the future of womenswear. After Oxford he had drifted away from Symonds's particular brand of Arnoldian Hellenism in favour of the Greece of Pater, whose Dionysiac paradoxes were perhaps more obviously conducive to Wilde's own style of avant-garde flaunting and scandalizing respectability; a series of sniffy reviews made sure his public knew he no longer viewed Greece as unmixed sweetness and light.[141]

---

friendship. They also have helpful things to say on Symonds as an early stylistic influence on Wilde (pp. 19–20).

[139] On Wilde's aestheticism in this context, see Evangelista (2009a: 134); on the Greek tour with Mahaffy, see Ross (2009) and enjoyably Grech (2011); things Greek, Elmann (1988: 26). A Hellas 'full of idyllic loveliness and richness of colour' (Wilde 2000: 44). Mahaffy's *Greek Social Life from Homer to Menander* (1874), the proofs of which the young Oscar had helped him check, was the first book in English frankly to admit that the Greeks practiced homosexual relations; the offending passage was pulled from subsequent editions. Pater's *Renaissance* was published in Wilde's final undergraduate term. Much more could and should be said on Wilde's Euripidean self-fashioning; see (e.g., and for starters) (1989: 113, 119–20, 132), and his marginalia to J. A. Symonds (1873: 198–211)—e.g., his marginal emphasis to Euripides' 'audience greedy of intellectual subtleties, of pathetic situations, of splendid oratory, of clever reasoning—an audience more appreciative of the striking than [the true]' (pp. 200–1).

[140] Harris (1916: ii. 378). Orrells (2011a: 187–8) treats Harris as a friendly source but one overly inclined to bend the facts for the sake of a better anecdote.

[141] Evangelista (2009a: 143–4).

Nonetheless, his most infamous characterization is suffused with motifs from *Studies* (and even his drift towards Pater is a Symonds-esque move).[142] Viewed as a Greek lover, the eponymous anti-hero of *The Picture of Dorian Gray* (1890/1) is an alluring contradiction, indeed, a Paterian paradox made flesh. His name declares a virile European identity, invoking (surely through Symonds) the martial pederasty of Müller's *Die Dorier*, but his body is troped as Eastern in its languid sensuality. As described by his portraitist Basil Hallward in a passage cut from the revised edition of 1891, he is Paris, Adonis, Antinous, Narcissus:

He has stood as Paris in dainty armour, and as Adonis with huntsman's cloak and polished boar-spear. Crowned with heavy lotus-blossoms, he has sat on the prow of Adrian's barge, looking into the green, turbid Nile. He has leaned over the still pool of some Greek woodland, and seen in the water's silent silver the wonder of his own beauty.[143]

Dorian Gray emerges from this metaphoric priamel as Symonds's eternally youthful (and yet, with this choice of comparators, also eternally doomed) Genius of Greek Art, inflected through the studied ambivalence of Pater's Dionysus-cult as a bittersweet icon of erotic self-immolation, and mystically reincarnated into the present day through Decadent commitment to sensual appetite; there is something of the Syrian epigrammatist about him.[144] In the context of the early 1890s, this languid physique is a normative challenge to the elite masculine body and to the social order for which that body is an ethically legible sign.[145] Wilde was lastingly swayed by Symonds's position on Greek art; to the end he proclaimed the superior beauty of the slender male *kouros*, and protested that it was only the 'sinful sex-instinct' of the ordinary man that prevented him from 'worshipping the higher form of beauty'.[146]

---

[142] When Wilde mirrors Symonds in declaring Pater the only critic whose opinion counts for him (Hyde 1962: 109), he is surely being consciously allusive.

[143] Wilde (2005: 12); cf. the trimmed 1891 version in the same volume, p. 176.

[144] Cf. with characteristic acuteness Evangelista (2006: 240), on how the novella 'The Portrait of Mr W. H.' riffs on Jowett's beloved Plato (a feature also, of course, of *Dorian*): Wilde's use of classical colour is 'fundamentally a form of intertextuality that negotiates the transmission of homoeroticism through history'.

[145] With aristocratic hierarchy supplanted by middle-class values, and as a brake on 'excessive' social mobility, 'conservative commentators increasingly represent the gentleman as an organic ideal, rooted above all in an innate, physiological sensibility. The gentleman's status thus derives from, and is made visible in, his body' (Adams 1995: 152, and cf. 3–5, 153).

[146] Frank Harris (1916: ii. 461).

6. MELEAGER TAKES THE STAND

> A patriot put in prison for loving his country loves his country, and
> a poet put in prison for loving boys loves boys. To have altered my
> life would have been to have admitted that Uranian love is ignoble.
> I hold it to be noble—more noble than other forms.[147]
>
> (A letter from Paris to Wilde's great friend Robert Ross,
> February 1898)
>
> Wilde's evocation of Plato and Greek philosophy signals not some
> unproblematic triumph of modernity over the dead past but...a
> moment in those ceaseless recombinations of cultural materials in
> which the new or contemporary or modern most often comes to
> birth through some transmutation, under the pressures of history
> and ideology, of the old or ancient or even the archaic.[148]

The legal misadventures and ultimate conviction of Oscar Wilde in 1895
put Uranian and Pandemic eros in the dock. What had previously been a
vaguely coalescing set of notions was suddenly concretized as a known
entity within the public sphere: 'homosexuality' had arrived with a bang,
with Wilde emerging as victim zero of the Labouchère amendment in
popular awareness. A whole lifestyle was no sooner identified than
subjected to trial by media, and the prime exhibit of the prosecution
was the newly detected lifestyle's supporting package of associated
'Greek' cultural production: the conservative press cried out for legal
sanction against the 'worse than Eleusinian mysteries' of a 'Decadent'
subculture (the press's label, not its own) of which Wilde was now the
sinister 'high priest'.[149] The phrasing here is telling: 'Decadence' is
equated to and rooted in perverse readings of Greek classical heritage
by an outlaw elite, whose secretive nocturnal rites are by strong implication endangering the social order by travestying traditional gender politics.[150] Lurking behind this, and discursively all but inseparable from it,

---

[147] Wilde (2000: 1019).

[148] Dowling (1994: 4); on self-fashioning and the materials of history, see influentially
Greenblatt (1980).

[149] Thornton (1980), quoted at p. 16, an example taken from the high-end, conservative-
imperialist *National Observer*. 'In the cultural moment before the Wilde disaster there was
no implication of an impending doom, only the gradual emergence into visibility of a new
system of values and attitudes, associated with a variety of movements in art and society,
having in common their relation to the inchoate counterdiscourse of "homosexuality"'
(Dowling 1994: 132), and cf. (1994: 2). Wilde as victim zero: Bristow (1995: 2).

[150] By no means a groundless suspicion: to destabilize masculinity at this cultural
moment (first-wave feminism, the New Woman question) is also to throw male privilege
into question: Dellamora (1990: 196). Simon Goldhill has useful things to say on 'Decadence' and critical disquiet over how the male body should be represented, as e.g. at (2002:

was perhaps also the more strictly party-political agenda that by the close of the 1880s Aestheticism was already established as the firm friend of the radical Left.[151] A panic-stirring media quickly coached its public to read the hidden signs of inversion in Decadent prose and verse: subtext and double-coding were abruptly brought out of the closet.[152]

This is a pivotal cultural moment in the emergence of modern identities: the terms and categories of private experience and public discourse alike are being subjected to aggressive cross-examination.[153] Into this turbulent mixture Wilde interjects a culturally residual formation. Despite his earlier disavowals of Symonds's old-school Arnoldian figuration, it is essentially to the ancient Greece of Studies that he reverts when he needs to peddle a stain-free Hellas in court.[154] The passage is very famous:

'The love that dares not speak its name' in this century is such a great affection of an elder for a younger man as there was between David and Jonathan, such as Plato made the very basis of his philosophy, and such as you find in the sonnets of Michelangelo and Shakespeare. It is that deep spiritual affection that is as pure as

138), on reviews of Strauss's 'neurotic' Elektra. Even viewed simply as a style, Decadence relied on a good working knowledge of classical authors in the original Latin and Greek, extending beyond the basic 'school' authors, and familiarity with traditional elite (but now more widely shared) translation culture, in order to identify Greek and Latin authors 'of the Decadence' and find ways of applying them as stylistic models in English: this socially privileged skill set is implicit in the apologetics of Arthur Symons, quoted at Thornton (1980: 17).

[151] See Livesey (2007: 6–10, 20–1), including on the Aesthetic underpinnings of William Morris's socialism; Williams (1976: 28); and cf. briefly Cook (2003a: 76) on the legibility of the pastoral Utopias of Symonds et al. as socialist reform templates in the context of Fabianism, finding concrete expression a few years later in the Garden City movement. A generation later, J. W. Mackail (discussed more fully in the next chapter) is still inviting his audiences to share his abhorrence at how dissident representations of classical texts 'can distort to strange and perilous misuses such things as the psychology of Euripides [surely a dig at Verrall], the passion of Sappho or the communism of Plato'; together with atheism, asexual and political Otherness are the constituent parts of one and the same incendiary time bomb.

[152] Dellamora (1990: 219).

[153] Hariman's three propositions (1990: 18) are germane: 'First, popular trials constitute a major genre of public discourse; second, the function of this genre is primarily to adjudicate discourses; and third, the genre fulfils this function by applying specific generic constraints to more diffuse public debates . . . an additional suggestion follows as well, which is that the trials and the laws themselves are more profoundly rhetorical and less autonomously legal than supposed by either rhetorical or legal scholars.'

[154] It is of minor interest to note that in Reading Gaol he turns to Symonds for comfort reading; he has his Introduction to the Study of Dante (1872) in his cell, along with two works of Pater, and looks forward to re-reading Italian Byways (1883) when he gets out: Wilde (2000: 673 n. 3, 792). Symonds's prose corpus becomes his 'Hellas', his dream country of psychic escape. I am indebted to Diana Spencer for this last point.

it is perfect. It dictates and pervades great works of art, like those of Shakespeare and Michelangelo, and those two letters of mine, such as they are. It is in this century misunderstood, so much misunderstood that it may be described as 'the love that dares not speak its name', and on that account of it I am placed where I am now. It is beautiful, it is fine, it is the noblest form of affection. There is nothing unnatural about it. It is intellectual, and it repeatedly exists between an older and a younger man, when the older man has intellect, and the younger man has all the joy, hope and glamour of life before him. That it should be so, the world does not understand. The world mocks at it, and sometimes puts one in the pillory for it.[155]

Wilde's defence—and the gallery applauded him for articulating it in these fine words—is that he is a pure Uranian pederast: a Platonic lover of the school of Jowett, declaring a love that echoes through the history of artistic genius (Symonds had written influentially on Michelangelo).[156] Athenian rather than Dorian (Wilde would be a fine one to preach 'fire and valour'), this 'noblest form of affection' is the unselfish love of the ideal erastēs for his blushing erōmenos, notionally sublimated into an intercourse of pure intellect but with a subtextual nod towards bodily fulfilment: 'it is beautiful, it is fine' evokes the Athenian conceit of the *kaloskagathos*, the 'It' boy in whom physical and moral perfection come together. Nor was this mere empty sophistry: he genuinely seems to have bought his own rhetoric, if not at the time then certainly in later life.[157] At the same time, Wilde is poisoning the well of subtext for everyone else by spelling out how the nineteenth century compels his kind to 'speak their name' obliquely through double-coding.

The sublimated homophile Hellenism of Jowett's Platonic-Arnoldian Oxford is thereby thrust suddenly into renewed currency in the public sphere—and the 'book of the trial', the only readily available treatment of Uranian fellowship, is Symonds's *Studies of the Greek Poets*, freshly tidied for its third outing (1893) and still the standard work on Greek

---

[155] Hyde (1968: 201).

[156] Merely to say 'Renaissance' could flag up for interested parties a personal stake in gay history: Fisher (2008). Wilde may have been fooling himself as much as his audience with his performance as the ideal Platonic lover; in a compromising letter written to Bosie of January 1893 and presented as evidence at the trial two years later, he hails the young man (by then 22 years old) as Hyacinthus reborn and swoons for a semi-chaste 'madness of kisses' (Hyde 1972: 101).

[157] Dorian pluck and grit were not part of Wilde's personal Hellenic self-conception. Urged by the ever-loyal Frank Harris to blow the whistle on the warden's regime of torment at Reading Gaol, he sadly replied: 'I could not, I dare not, I have not Dante's strength, nor his bitterness; I am a Greek born out of due time' (Harris 1916: ii. 148). In the late 1890s he was still indignantly defending the lasting value of Uranian erotic pedagogy—'Frank, what a silly question!' (Harris 1916: ii. 465).

poetry.[158] In collective memory, Wilde's verses—'the love that dares not speak its name'—become the outward sign of his hidden homosexual identity, a secret open to be read if one had known what to look for. While his behaviour before and during the second and third trials is more that of a half-cocked Socrates,[159] it is in his capacity as a persecuted *poet*—not a dramatist, novelist, or essayist—that he hones his post-trial image as a sinless Uranian, in the letter to Ross that introduces this section.

Then again, we might have expected the 'poet put in prison' line; it was, after all, the poetry that had helped put him there, not the novels or the plays.[160] Had he really caught his Uranian enthusiasm from Symonds's chapter on epigram? If anything, the marginalia to his personal copy of the First Series suggest he largely skipped it, at least on his first read-through as a young student; the copy is rich in annotations on Plato and especially on drama, but the one marginal emphasis in 'The Anthology' is not even about epigram at all.[161] While the mature Wilde enjoyed Andrew Lang's selection in *Grass of Parnassus*, and has a character allude to the Anthology in familiar terms in his dialogue 'The Critic as Artist' (1891), there is every reason to think that Wilde the undergraduate read this part of *Studies* carelessly and missed its significance.

The obvious influence is instead the chapter 'The Genius of Greek Art', which in Wilde's copy is heavily annotated. Writing to Bosie from prison, he is still insisting (if only now to himself and his sounding-boards; no one else will pretend to believe him) that the fatal 'Hyacinth' letter that had done so much to doom his cause in the court of public opinion was merely 'a letter of fantastic literary conceits . . . It can only be read by those who have read the *Symposium* of Plato, or caught the spirit of a certain grave mood made beautiful for us in Greek marbles . . .'. These haunting statues are a major motif of Symonds's concluding chapter on art (1873: 405–8), where they cue up praise of Plato's *Phaedrus* (p. 409) and 'the Erôs of Agathon' (p. 410). And, of course, 'Hyacinth' is there too, in the fatefully loaded question: 'And where, if not here [the Bay of Naples], shall we meet with Hylas and Hyacinth, with Ganymede and Hymenaeus, in the flesh?' Wilde had found answers

[158] *Studies* as a standard work of reference: Frank M. Turner (1981: 100).
[159] See briefly Hyde (1972) on his distracted refusal-*cum*-failure to countenance self-exile before the second trial—'Wilde was given every opportunity to leave the country if he so desired' (p. 9)—and his firm refusal to jump bail prior to the verdict being decided in the third trial (pp. 224–5).
[160] For its place in the cross-examination of the fateful third trial, see Hyde (1972: 198–201).
[161] Instead Wilde highlights a remark attributed to Kant (J. A. Symonds 1873: 385).

closer to home and at last been caught out. He now wistfully reimagines his own record of Uranian writing as nothing more than a gracious literary calling-card. In this fantasy, Hellenism remains an exclusive Oxbridge boys' club, untouched by time and social change—a world away from rendezvous with streetwise London rent-boys in taverns and houses of ill repute.[162]

At the heart of Wilde's Uranian utopia, then, we find a fatal combination of Platonic eros and Symonds's lush art criticism; the Meleager of the 'Anthology' chapter has no part in its creation. And yet Oscar the poet, preaching Greek love from the witness stand, was to exercise a dramatic influence on how Greek epigram was subsequently received. Given the author's carefully crafted persona as the sharp-eyed scrivener of social foibles and comic misunderstandings, it is perversely fitting that his shadow loomed over the Anthology of the early twentieth century only because the receiving culture had put two and two together and made five. Wilde made a show of his endorsement of all things *Greek*—and he was famed for his facility in *epigram*.

However, this is 'epigram' in a sense with which the poems of the Anthology have almost nothing to do. The 'epigrams' for which Wilde was famed are instead his pointed and condensed *bons mots*, of the kind that the orators of Rome termed a *sententia*. In Wilde's hands, the sententious epigram tended to showcase his urbane wit and his brilliant facility in wicked paradox; 'epigram' now became a widely recognized marker of the amoral smart set. Early-ish in the new century, the scatty Jane Thropplestance of Saki's short story 'Louise' was to declare, thinking herself very clever:

'Laura Kettleway was going on about [the Salvation Army] in the lift of the Dover Street Tube the other day, saying what a lot of good work they did, and what a loss it would have been if they'd never existed. "If they had never existed", I said, "Granville Barker would have been certain to have invented something that looked exactly like them." If you say things like that, quite loud, in a Tube lift, they always sound like epigrams.'[163]

In *The Green Carnation,* a sensationally notorious *roman à clef* published in 1894 and used prejudicially against Wilde in the trials the year

---

[162] 'The sort of letter I would, in a happy if wilful moment, have written to any graceful young man of either university who had sent me a poem of his own devising' (Wilde 2000: 702); 'either university' is a beautifully revealing touch. Hylas and Hyacinth: J. A. Symonds (1873: 403), a passage we have visited before.
[163] Published posthumously in the short-story collection *The Toys of Peace* (1919); the author died on active service in France in 1916. Unsurprisingly, his own works court the aficionado of coded homosexual subtext.

after (rather in the way Aristophanes' comedies were held against Socrates), the anonymous author—actually Robert Hichens, an insider in the Wilde circle—gave a thrilled and outraged public what purported to be a fly-on-the-wall view of the Decadent social scene. The novel's louche anti-hero is a thinly disguised 'Esmé Amarinth'; his be-Greeked name screams Wilde, while also incidentally pointing back to Alfred Butler's durable selection from the Anthology, *Amaranth and Asphodel* (1881). 'Mr Amarinth's epigrams had been especially voluble during the garden scene': this is epigram squarely in its sense of pithy apophthegm.[164] So persuasively did *The Green Carnation* conjure up the atmosphere of the Wildean milieu that Wilde felt compelled to write to the *Pall Mall Gazette* (1 October 1894) to rebut the presumption that he had written it himself in a blaze of self-publicity.

The Amarinth–Wilde of *The Green Carnation* is already unmistakably a disciple of *Studies of the Greek Poets* in his views on Greek art and scientific morality:

How I hate that word 'natural'... To me it means all that is middle-class, all that is of the essence of jingoism, all that is colourless, and without form, and void. It might be a beautiful word, but it is the most debased coin in the currency of language... A boy is unnatural if he prefers looking at pictures to playing cricket, or dreaming over the white naked beauty of a Greek statue to a game of football under Rugby rules. If our virtues are not cut on a pattern, they are unnatural. If our vices are not according to rule, they are unnatural. We must be good naturally. We must sin naturally. We must live naturally, and die naturally.[165]

People-watching at a garden party, Madame Valtesi asks: 'It must be very trying socially to be so clever. So Lord Reggie is actually serious?' ('Lord Reggie' is the novel's pseudonym for Bosie.) Amarinth replies with his typical sardonic wit, again with Symonds as the obvious intertext: 'I hope he is never that. He will marry, as he sins, prettily, with the gaiety of a young Greek god.'[166] 'And as to his epigrams, they are in every one's mouth'; 'I was born epigrammatic, and my dying remark will be a paradox.'[167] The fateful conjunction and commixture of 'Greek' and

---

[164] Hichens (1894: 16), and compare, for instance, among many available examples: 'Reggie was very frank. When he could not be witty, he often told the naked truth; and truth, without any clothes on, frequently passes for epigram. It is daring, and so it seems clever' (Hichens 1894: 3); 'I would rather be able to talk in epigrams, and hear Society repeating what I said, than be the greatest author or artist that ever lived' (p. 8).

[165] Hichens (1894: 125–6).

[166] Hichens (1894: 148), and for 'young Greek god', cf. p. 123.

[167] Hichens (1894: 40, 26).

'epigram' in Wilde's flamboyant literary–performative persona, and in how he was being reported and represented within the public sphere, masked the prosaic and underwhelming truth that Wilde himself had missed the significance of Symonds's 'Anthology' (at least at first reading), and had not himself engaged with Greek epigram in any serious way. In any case, Symonds's revolutionary subtext had already been all too obvious to the essay's more careful readers; the hasty response of Neaves on behalf of the conservative interests served by Maga makes that very clear indeed, nearly two decades before the trials gave Uranian Love its unwelcome publicity boost.

Outside the walls of Reading Gaol, therefore, a counter-attack on epigrammatic Decadence was already well under way, and will be the subject of our next chapter. First, though, one important new context for the *fin de siècle* reception of *Studies* (alongside and in dialogue with Wilde) remains to be factored in: the work of Friedrich Nietzsche, prophet of the epiphany of the Übermensch.

7. BEYOND GOOD AND EVIL?

Symonds had missed Nietzsche first time around by accident of timing, and appears never to have felt he had lost out. The German publication of the breakthrough work *Das Geburt der Tragödie* (1872) came too late to feed into his ideas for the first series of *Studies*; the philosopher he was enthusing about in his correspondence that year was Marcus Aurelius, and most of the material for the book had in any case been sitting around for a while.[168] *Das Geburt* turned out to have mined roughly the same seam of Greek maenadic irrationality as had Pater, and at roughly the same time; of the two, however, it was with Pater and only Pater that Symonds was intellectually occupied, and ten years later he can briskly pooh-pooh the foolishness of 'philosophical Nihilism' without pointing outside the parochial context of the Reviews.[169]

---

[168] Symonds (1967–9: ii. 235–6), written July 1872; the book is pitched to George Smith of Smith, Elder in December of that year (pp. 254–5), and by January 1873 (pp. 268–9) he was ready to move on to other projects. Writing in 1882 to advise the younger writer Horatio Forbes Brown, he advises that any and all drafts and miscellanea should go into a 'desolation box' to be raided for future publications; he comments wryly that his own ('vast and well-filled') has generated several publications, of which *Studies* was one (pp. 786–7). I have found no mention of Nietzsche in the correspondence from this middle period of his life—but it is voluminous, and the editors' index is no help.

[169] J. A. Symonds (1967–9: ii. 273–6, 279); Nihilism: p. 818.

The vital work for the reception of *Studies* in its second crucial phase, though, is Nietzsche's novel-*cum*-philosophical rant *Also Sprach Zarathustra*, first published in German as a part-work in the early 1880s (1883–5) and not translated into English until 1896, when Alexander Tille presented the *Collected Works*. After years of neglect by the British, Nietzsche's had become a name to conjure with in the early 1890s, the subject of daring articles in the *Savoy*; now that he could be read in translation, he suddenly became a talking point.[170] As successive volumes of Tille's translation appeared, they were reviewed (again for the *Savoy*) by none other than Symonds's old collaborator Havelock Ellis, but the German's ideas were now getting much wider publicity. The Superman was in the air, or in the miasma that percolated from the Symbolist intelligentsia whose perspective reached overseas to contemporary radical thought as the by now deceased Symonds's could not.[171] What now seems incredible, but should not, is that Oscar Wilde was now avidly adopted across Europe as a Nietzschean poster boy. By the late 1890s, an *enfant terrible* of Russian Existentialism could complain that the international Oscar-cult was diluting and vulgarizing the Nietzsche of the philosophers into a pop-culture cliché:

The opinion that Wilde can be justified and elevated into an ideal by the philosophy of Nietzsche can be heard everywhere. Moreover, all kinds of people, tempted by Wilde's amusements, now consider it their duty to go about their business in the conviction that they are the precursors of the *Übermensch* and, therefore, the best workers in the field of human progress.[172]

The recuperation of Saint Oscar as a (sub-)Nietzschean talking point actually made a lot of sense. The *Übermensch* was not yet seen as the ideological prop of military authoritarianism and national chauvinism, a role to which he was in any case ill suited, but instead was embraced by the Anarchist and Internationalist avant-garde; only retrospect makes it ironic that in his native Germany Nietzsche was for many years the darling of the liberal Left.[173] What was more, he had predicted that the

---

[170] Nietzsche's late Victorian and Edwardian reception in England is surveyed by Thatcher (1970). Intoxication with Nietzsche's musical idol Wagner was also part of the package for the *Savoy* crowd: Sutton (2002) is enlightening.

[171] Stokes (1979: 152); Fletcher (1979a: 199). A good concise appraisal of the 'cult' of Nietzsche in Late Victorian England is at Taxidou (1998: 23–6).

[172] Bershtein (2010: 292), translating a novel of 1898 by Lev Shestov, *Dobro i zlo v uchenii Grafa Tolstogo i F. Nitsshe*.

[173] Taylor (1990); it is hard to picture Nietzsche's 'Superior Human' as a card-carrying member of any political party apparatus.

Übermensch would spread joy by his or her presence, effortlessly transcending the slave morality of the Judaeo-Christian inheritance and instantiating a new phase of superior human (indeed, post-human) identity and experience. Viewed through lilac-tinted spectacles as a martyr for progress brutalized by the repressive apparatus of the state in its capacity as moral policeman—crucified, in effect, for his society's sins of self-repression—Wilde could easily seem like a harbinger of this radiant entity.[174] That the merely real Oscar Wilde had in the meantime renounced his pagan ways was by the by.

In the years following 1896, then, for anyone whose head was buzzing with these audacious new ideas, and with lingering effect, the obvious reading of Symonds's 'Genius of the Greeks' *must* have been a Nietzschean one. As humans to the dumb beasts, so the *Übermensch* to contemporary humanity; beyond good and evil, he or she will exhibit a will to power unfettered by the slave morality of his or her lessers. Let us revisit the crucial passage with these emphases in mind:

Like a young man newly come from the wrestling-ground, anointed, chapleted, and very calm, the Genius of the Greeks appears before us. Upon his soul there is no burden of the world's pain; *the whole creation that groaneth and travaileth together, has touched him with no sense of anguish; nor has he yet felt sin. The pride and the strength of adolescence are his*—audacity and endurance, swift passions and exquisite sensibilities, the alternations of sublime repose and boyish noise, grace, pliancy, *and stubbornness and power,* love of all fair things and splendours of the world, the frank enjoyment of the open air, free merriment, and melancholy well beloved. Of these adolescent qualities of *this clear and stainless personality, this conscience whole and pure and reconciled to Nature,* what survives among us now? *The imagination must be strained to the uttermost before we can begin to sympathize with such a being.*[175]

'Frank enjoyment' had in the meantime been outed by *The Green Carnation*, in which 'frank' consistently marks out and draws attention to the dissident desires of its central pairing; and 'boyish' was also now indelibly coloured by Lord Reggie's effeminacy and prideful petulance.[176]

One may add that a proto-Nietzschean interpretation of 'sin' is *not at all* what Symonds is likely to have had in mind when he wrote this passage. While I take no issue with the literary–critical consensus that views authorial 'intention' as a chimera, a systematic reading of the

---

[174] Forth (1993).   [175] J. A. Symonds (1873: 399 = 1920: 554–5).
[176] 'Frank' as codeword: pp. 2–3 (several times), 71, 107, 206. Reggie is consistently 'boyish' in his sulky moods: see pp. 65, 114 ('a nature that seemed boyish to softness'), 129, 207.

private poetry reveals that for the early Symonds 'sin' was a codeword, and that its meaning in relation to homoerotic desire was always very tightly defined. Committing the further literary–critical fashion crime of reading-in from the known biography, we may then remind ourselves that the Symonds of the 1860s and early 1870s had not yet dared to know full sexual intimacy with the objects of his desire, an experience that when he at last came to it he would be amazed to find spiritually healing.[177] In the years of the *Studies*' gestation he remained filled with shame at what he felt to be the baseness of his sexual urges—urges that he did his best to sublimate into the semi-chaste 'Uranian' yearning, touching, and kissing for which his vision of ancient Platonic love provided the convenient exemplar.

Insofar as one can pin it down—and he did his best not to think about it too closely—'sin' in this context means genital contact leading to orgasm. The very idea of this drove the younger Symonds to spasms of religious self-hate; Platonism provided the terminology to dignify same-sex desire, but by following Plato in his conception of the tripartite soul he only worsened a conventionally pious and deeply felt fear of the psychic danger that lay in wait when carnal appetite reared its head.[178] The companion poems make it clear that 'no shame oppressed' our old friends Melanthias and Eudiades because they did not go all the way. The relationship threatens to become destructive only when the older lover is struck by the Pandemic desire for sexual satisfaction, probably through penetration, alluded to in the privately printed verse as 'some painful thing... the pleasure none may touch and live | Thenceforth unashamed' or as 'the unutterable thing'.[179] Symonds's ego-narrator berates the 'Relentless' Eros that drives his Melanthias to the brink:

---

[177] 'Throughout the whole of my malady and my discourses on it, I had omitted the word "love". That was because I judged my own sort of love to be sin. But when, in the stage of indifference, I became careless about sinning, then, and not until then, I discovered love, the keystone of all the rest of my less tortured life' (J. A. Symonds 1984: 176). Although he there identifies 1868 as the year in which he 'worked this part of my life problem out', he was still channeling his urges into the 'safety valve' of verse until 'some time after 1875' (p. 189).

[178] As, e.g., at J. A. Symonds (1967-9: i. 678) (November 1866), in which, stung by a letter of criticism from Sidgwick, he begs Dakyns to burn the 'Cretan Idyll' and other homosexual verses in his possession: 'I repent in dust & ashes of their unholiness, and until I hear from your lips that they are burned I rest not crying Miserere. Do not disobey me. They remain engraved on my mind & in Paradise we will repeat them when Sin is no more that hath set so sad a separation between the parts of our Souls.'

[179] These instances are quoted from J. A. Symonds 1878b i: 25 and 40; cf. i: 24, 42 ('sin'), ii: 52 ('selfless' abstention). And cf. the subtext-begging formulation at p. 5 of the undated pamphlet *Genius Amoris Amari Visio*, printed privately by Arrowsmith of Bristol: 'Whose flesh ne'er yet hath felt the *sting* of sin' (emphasis added).

> Will you, blind god and pitiless, be fain
> To change for loss their great and golden gain?

But Eudiades' virtuous submission inspires repentance, and the lovers achieve eternal fame by sublimating their natural sexual drive:

> Lo! If men like these
> Peopled their world with selfless deeds and gave
> Their longing for a sacrifice to save
> Bright honour...[180]

This means that even the reading proposed in Chapter 3—a reading in tune with today's scholarly consensus on Symonds as a sly homosexual apologist, and (I would like to think) respectful of the text as it stands—is one that the writer perhaps never 'intended', and conceivably never anticipated from the reviewers and reading public (a slightly separate issue). Of course, an author may knowingly use the same phraseology to communicate different meanings on different occasions and with different audiences in mind; or may recombine cherished tropes in previously untried combinations and end up persuading himself of something surprising. We come to new realizations by moving old ideas around and seeing how they might fit together in new ways, and in the case of *Studies* there is a good case to be made for thinking that Symonds had done just that: reconciling authentic expression of desire to sinless 'Nature' was a real breakthrough, and one that probably helped its author along in his personal journey towards self-knowledge and -realization.

Nonetheless, that he knowingly scripted the Genius of the Greeks as the harbinger of a brave new sexual reality seems to me quite unlikely. Privately, in the early years at least, he did *not* think that his paradise of Greek Love could ever again be achieved in reality; indeed, its imaginative power over him lay in its tantalizing and ghostlike otherworldliness, provoking 'double consciousness' as a purely imaginative liberation of the socially imprisoned self. When he writes to his wife that 'no one is happy who has not a deep firm faith in some ideal far beyond this world...superior to the apparent meanness, ugliness, evil discord of the present dispensation', it is impossible to say if he means the Heaven of Christianity or the Elysium of Greek Lovers—probably both.[181]

But, of course, next to no one *had* read the correspondence or the poetry, so it did not matter. Instead the first and third editions unfolded

---

[180] *Tales of Ancient Greece I*, p. 26.
[181] The tone of the letter is mostly religious, but the conclusion reached partway through is that 'a robust vice, an energetic state of sinning...is better than the condition of negation' (J. A. Symonds 1967–9: i. 722–3, and cf. 631).

their surface and subtextual meanings in dialogue with their respective reading publics. The first of these audiences was perhaps not so very large (1873/6), but was already being cued up by Neaves and Tyrwhitt to read between the lines of *Studies* (especially on epigram!) for a hidden agenda of sexual revolution; the second, much broader, was self-consciously eyeing up the event horizon of the *fin de siècle* (1893). The meanings of the evolving text also developed in dialogue with whatever other texts were part of the culture's big conversation. In the 1890s this meant Wilde and the Decadents, but also Nietzsche—initially by report, later also at first hand; with Symonds still cooling in his grave, and for any reader with even the most superficial and hand-me-down notion of Nietzschean thought, *Studies* now unmistakably alluded to *Zarathustra*. Wistful regret (*l'amour de l'impossible*, a Symondsian buzz phrase Wilde loved to play with) becomes the willing into existence of a new kind of human being.[182] Strain that imagination!

---

[182] Once again (as on 'double consciousness', see Ch. 3) Symonds's line of thought seems to anticipate Foucault as read at Orrells (2011a: 270), 'making the self a conscious project but also an endlessly impossible one'.

Part III

'The Book of Greek Life'

5

Responses to Symonds

'The Wilde trial had done its work', [Edward] Carpenter wrote, 'and silence must henceforth reign on sex-subjects.' However, it was a Wilde-shaped silence.[1]

> Our master, Meleager, he who framed
> The first Anthology and daintiest,
> Mated each minstrel with a flower, and named
> For each the blossom that beseemed him best.
> 'Twas then as now; garlands were somewhat rare,
> Candidates many...[2]

The Wilde years were a very good time to join a public library. The commercial circulating libraries of W. H. Smith and Mudie already serviced the middle class, but free municipal libraries (for which Ewart's Act of 1850 had laid the groundwork) were suddenly springing up everywhere to accommodate a much broader demographic, many assisted by grants from local benefactors. The years 1892–6 saw the fastest expansion of the public library system prior to the twentieth century. The overwhelming majority of these new users were working class, and many of them young; William Forster's Elementary Education Act of 1870 and the follow-up Act of 1880 had begun to bear fruit, mass-manufacturing the literate and numerate factory hands who were to inhabit the Liberal vision of Britain's technocratic future and be stake-holders in its polity. A whole new kind of reader was thereby admitted

---

[1] Sinfield (1994b: 124), quoting Carpenter's *My Days and Dreams, Being Autobiographical Notes* (1916).

[2] Garnett (1869: 50), one of the numerous original and frequently metapoetic compositions (cf., e.g., 1869: 1) by means of which the author–translator of *Idylls and Epigrams* assumes the role of a new Meleager for the later nineteenth century. Garnett was recognized as a fair English epigrammatist in the tradition of Alexander Pope; he is anthologized in Francis and Vera Mendell's *The Week-End Book*, and thus stayed continuously in print from 1922 all the way through to 1955.

into the public sphere, albeit in a strictly circumscribed manner and with very limited opportunities for active intervention in its discourse.[3] For those who wanted not merely to read but to reread and (like Symonds and Wilde) to scribble in the margins, books were in any case getting cheaper year on year; a new term had come in from the States, the 'best-seller', bringing in its wake four-figure advances for popular novelists.[4]

Reading the magazines of the later nineteenth century, modern scholarship finds its eye drawn to an increasingly explicit assertion of the civic role of the critic in dictating to working-class readers what they should be reading in their limited leisure time, so as to mould their character appropriately for their social role; and also increasing contestation as to who counts as the proper expert to be offering this literary prescription.[5] In this altered and rhetorically charged context of the 1890s, the mere presence of the third edition *as a handbook* (and potentially a school textbook) carried the danger of implying, to a much larger readership than ever before, that Symonds's view was the current state of the question in Classical literary studies. There was no hard and fast divide in nineteenth-century discourse between general non-fiction, school textbook, and specialist monograph; depending on who was reading it and in what context, one and the same book could be simultaneously a utilitarian handbook and an intellectually hard-hitting intervention in the public sphere, through the debates it stimulated in the press.[6] Even prior to this, *Studies* had been viewed as a threat to politically and socially conservative interests, as witnessed by the early efforts at damage control by (in particular) Neaves, but the liberal–progressive case for containing its subtextual dissidence was at least as strong.[7]

In the aftermath of its author's death, the *pietas* of family and friendship network was also a motive, to say nothing of safeguarding the reputations of the living. In this chapter we will see the critics of the backlash attempting to rehabilitate the Greek Anthology from Symonds's Uranian yearnings, excerpting with drastic selectivity in order to tell a comforting story to the public; but this is no more and no less than what the author's friend Horatio Brown's thoroughly disingenuous *Biography* of 1895 (itself a collaborative project with major

---

[3] Waller (2006: 41–51), citing official data, a work of compendious learning. 'By 1885 about 25 per cent of England's population was covered by a public library; by 1914, 62 per cent' (p. 50). My point about working-class readerships and the public sphere is from Mays (1995: 182). The Act of 1880 made elementary education compulsory; further Acts of 1891 and 1893 paid for school fees and raised the leaving age from 10 to 11.

[4] On how the 'best-seller' (an American neologism of 1889) came to the British market, see again Waller (2006: 668–9).

[5] Mays (1995: 169, 180).   [6] Kennedy (2001: 13).   [7] Schultz (2004: 457).

input from Sidgwick et al.) is doing to Symonds's own *Memoirs* around the same time.[8]

Broadly speaking, what we see in the critics of the backlash is an attempt to redefine the transmitted Greek Anthology as no true 'Anthology' at all, no Garland of chosen flowers—and semantically one must concede a large part of their point, given the sense in which 'Anthology' is commonly used in English. The Greek Anthology of the Byzantines is instead portrayed as a fat and jumbled corpus of mediocre overall quality, a mega-text that no actual reader outside of a research library would ever read from start to finish (and again the point is essentially valid). From it, however, and often from supplementary material as well, a 'real' Greek *Anthology* might be recuperated through the reintroduction of a unifying editorial principle and voice of the kind that had by this account made Meleager's collection a true Garland. The task that awaited the decisive modern editor was to whittle down the inherited corpus into a healthy size and attractive shape, returning it to Meleagrian slimness, and thus to real-world applicability.[9]

1. 'INTO A PURER AIR': JEBB'S GROWTH AND INFLUENCE (1893)

The Greeks were a physically beautiful race, with great quickness and fineness of perception, which made them feel at once when anything was exaggerated or absurd, or, as we say, in bad taste.... [they possessed] the instinct of drawing the line, as it were, at the right place.[10]

Those who find the ugly meanings in beautiful things are corrupt without being charming. This is a fault.

(Wilde, from the preface to *Dorian Gray* (1890/1))

All the way back in 1877, the year of Symonds's Second Series, Richard Claverhouse Jebb, of enduring Sophoclean fame, had been busy protecting the lower orders from dangerous ideas about ancient Greece, heading off the Aesthetic threat by turning the much-talked-up Greek sense of

---

[8] On Symonds's posthumous reputation management, see Heidt (2003).

[9] Kuipers (2003: 51, 57) is quite handy to think with on this, and on the inescapably pedagogic connotations of the very word 'Anthology' in a modern context. In all likelihood the actual lost Garland of Meleager was not nearly as slender as the critics of the backlash presumed; Cameron (1993) puts it at around 1,000 epigrams, a considerable bulk.

[10] Jebb (1877: 7).

Beauty into thoroughly Victorian propriety and decorum (as here, where in effect he re-parses the Delphic oracle's 'nothing in excess' as 'not before the servants'). Jebb had long been committed to countering popular treatments of classical authors for a non-elite readership when their argument tended in directions he considered morally and socially harmful.[11] His inexpensive little handbook on *Greek Literature*, quoted immediately above, is a case in point; it demonstrably responds to and by strong implication rebuts specific formulations made a few years earlier by Symonds—and in his chapter on the Anthology, to boot.[12] Jebb deflects attention from Symonds's dangerous ideas by addressing epigram cursorily but in an authoritative tone; in a mere half-page, he radically abridges 'the whole range of human interests' to exclude interests unbecoming an ancient Greek: 'Love, art, mourning for the dead, the whole range of human interests and sympathies, lend leaves to this garland of Greek song.'[13] This martial or sepulchral wreath of leaves (a 'garland' but with no lovers' flowers) comes late in the story of Greek literature, in the era of Decadence; the linguistic, aesthetic, and moral peak is of course the fifth-century Athens of Jebb's beloved Sophocles.[14] The conventionally Winckelmanian scheme is hammered home in providentialist terms that pointedly negate Symonds's praise of the Anthology as a botanical prodigy, 'a tree which bears the leaves and buds and blossoms and fruitage of the Greek spirit on its boughs at once'. Natural seasonality is the only way to greatness:

Natural Growth of Greek Literature.—The best literature of Greece was not artificial, but grew naturally out of Greek life. As the year brings violets before roses and ripens one fruit earlier than another, so the golden time of the Greek genius has its seasons, in which first one kind of growth, and then another, blossoms, flowers and fades...The process of development went step by step with the development of their mental and social life. Each great branch of the Greek race, as its natural turn came, did that special part in the work which it was fittest to do.[15]

By the 1890s Jebb was already a relic of another era, one of the last of the grand old men of gentlemanly scholarship. He was a solid scholar,

---

[11] Stray (2007a: 82).

[12] To Jebb's reading of Greek character here, cf. Stray's very astute observation (1997: 369) that Jebb's Sophocles is a 'classical sublimation' of his Christianity.

[13] Jebb (1877: 160).

[14] Jebb (1877: 10–13), establishing Attic as a golden mean 'between the too enervated Ionic and the somewhat harsh Doric' (p. 12), terms that are simultaneously linguistic, cultural, racial, and body types.

[15] Jebb (1877: 10), by strong implication rebutting Symonds (1873: 342).

particularly on Sophoclean style, but his mighty reputation was even at the time seen by some who knew him to rest more on good taste and decorum than critical acumen; and he was increasingly a flogger of dead horses, as in the debate over compulsory Greek.[16] Committed as he was to getting the 'right' version of Hellenism to non-elite audiences, he came across as paternalistic and unrealistically narrow in his ideas of how the academy should approach classical outreach; in a letter to *The Times* of 7 November 1893, pressing for state funding of the University Extension scheme of lecture courses leading to an examination (a precursor of the modern Open University), he specifies that the lectures must be delivered by 'the best men' (p. 13). The best men, saying the best things about the best texts; there is no room in this picture for dissident or even plural readings.[17]

Still, this ageing philosopher-king could pack in the crowds. *The Growth and Influence of Greek Poetry* works up an 1892 lecture series at Johns Hopkins, edited highlights of which had a second outing the next year at a public lecture in the Egyptian Hall of London's Mansion House, reported in *The Times* of 13 March. While cutting heavily to fit the quart of a whole lecture series into the pint pot of a one-off talk, this London performance retained Jebb's crucial moral points *verbatim*:

in the province of religion and morals Hellenism alone is not sufficient... Yet there is no inherent conflict between true Hellenism and spiritualized Hebraism, such Hebraism as has passed into Christianity...

There has, indeed, been some poetry in which the direct imitation of Greek form has been associated with unhealthy tendencies; there have been transient vagaries of modern fashion which have seemed to assume that Hellenism is found, as has been neatly said, in eccentricity tinged with vice. But the distinctive quality of the best Greek poetry and art, that by which it has lived and will live, is the faculty of rising from the earth into a clearer air... The best Greek work in every kind is essentially pure...[18]

Jebb immediately assured his audience that Plato's *Phaedrus*— Symonds's own *liber amoris*—in fact offers no support for these unspecified

---

[16] Stray (2007: 1–2); Brink (1986: 143–7). In a letter to *The Times* of 28 October 1891, helping his cause not one little bit, he asserts University privilege over reform-committee meddling.

[17] Jebb viewed major editions as a patriotic project (Stray 2007a: 95)—one suspects not merely for obvious reasons of national prestige but also because philological purification will, in his *imaginaire*, spontaneously generate 'pure' thoughts and lives.

[18] *The Times*, 13 March 1892: 4, substantially repeated at Jebb (1893: 280). Note the approving citation of Butcher (1893: 1): 'we shall also see how greatly they misread the mind of Greece who think to become Hellenic by means of eccentricity tinged with vice'.

'unhealthy' readings. The never-named sexual aberrations for which modern Decadence finds a pretext in a warped Platonism can have nothing to do with the true, pure, and 'best' Hellas, for which Plato is momentarily made to stand in. Jebb hints at conceding that in antiquity itself some forms of topical smut may have been necessary elements in the cultural mix from which emerged the eternally sublime masterpieces; given his particular reputation as a critic, he probably expects his public to read into this remark a polarity between Aristophanic comedy and his beloved Sophoclean tragedy. The lasting achievements of the Greek genius, 'rising from the earth into a clearer air', appear in this passage as beautiful blooms growing all the taller for the unmentionable manure around their roots. The would-be modern Aristophanes, on the other hand, lacks even this redeeming feature. The master of Old Comedy had a dirty mouth (as so often, dirt here functions as a synonym for obscenity), but one can be dirty and yet healthy, and dirt can nurture life; the deviants of the *fin de siècle* are merely diseased.

To bypass the problem of modern textual dissidence, Jebb rewinds the Hellenism–Hellenism binary a generation and more, steering his reader towards the prelapsarian sexual innocence of Arnold's original formulation before it was defiled by Symonds (and compare here the strategy of Tyrwhitt).[19] Jebb's equation of Hellenism with height is particularly worthy of attention as both a symptom of and reaction against Symondsism. The salutary Alpine epigram-scape of *Studies* is clearly in the semantic frame here, but its careful distinction between the immorally deadly peaks and the life-giving valleys is pointedly elided: in the published version of the lectures Jebb urges upon his readers the clean air of Greek poetry's 'high places' *and* its 'summits' as rest cures for the exhausted casualties of modernity. Homer and Aeschylus are once more peaks to be bagged by Britain's intrepid young Alpinists of the spirit, who thus follow in the footsteps of a race of Hellenes already conceived counterfactually as keen ancient mountaineers—the very conception against which Symonds had reacted in forming his new literary topography.[20] Cleanliness and clarity on the heights are rhetorically

---

[19] Tyrwhitt (1877: 560).
[20] Jebb (1893: 284); rugged mountains inculcated 'a sturdy spirit of freedom' (p. 34). A wildly popular mid-century treatment, George Grote's *History of Greece* (first two volumes 1846), had already pegged the Greeks as inveterate crag-hoppers (ii. 301), with a national character formed accordingly. The motif is picked up by Tyrwhitt in his attack on Symonds: 'we possess in some measure the genuinely Hellenic quality of love of external nature, of the beauty of mountains and torrents' (1877: 563); and cf., e.g., Jevons (1886: 485) on flat, dull Boeotia as the exception that proves the rule.

opposed to insanitary dirt (the impure 'earth') down below; only the pure can ascend to the gleaming heights.

Jebb was not the only one playing this game in 1893: Samuel Butcher's second edition of his hack-work *Some Aspects of the Greek Genius* (the very title of which nods lazily to Symonds's homoerotic racial phantom) quotes extra-selectively from Homer to turn his epics into a bracing hike: 'Yet there are probably many of us (need we be ashamed to confess it?) who turn back with fresh delight... to Homer's simpler world, where... "Every peak appears, and the tall headlands and glades, and from heaven breaketh open the infinite air".'[21] The purity of height could also have imperial overtones, reminding readers of the role of the civilizing power in disciplining the Orient and steering it towards the Western path of progress (onward and upward). Butcher's introductory encomium on the distinctive quality of the Greek authors invites us to view them in contrast against their Near Eastern predecessors: 'we are henceforth in an upper and serener air, in which man's spiritual and intellectual freedom is assured'.[22]

When Jebb warns against culturally current representations of Hellas that present a distorted picture of 'eccentricity tinged with vice', the natural response for the twenty-first-century reader is to think of *Dorian Gray* and Beardsley's deliciously smutty illustrations to Aristophanes, and this is surely right as far as it goes—but it was Pater and Symonds, not Wilde, who had written from a position of discursive authority. Furthermore, of those two, it was Symonds whose stock was riding high, and whose influence was at the heart of Wilde's Hellenic posturing. What is more, his suggestive *Studies* were about to make their second and long-deferred curtain call. There is no reason to suppose Jebb knew this, but the timing of the two publications puts them into close and active dialogue in the public sphere regardless of what either of their authors might have had in mind.

By the year's close they had been joined by a third intervention that this time unmistakably set out to grapple with *Studies*. The Revd William Cowan's article 'The Greek Anthology and the Teachings of Holy Scripture' appeared in *Good Words*, a hugely popular illustrated monthly that for a mere sixpence kept lower middle class Evangelical households well stocked with safe Sunday reading matter.[23] Sandwiched between essays on Norwegian tourism and Britain's naval heritage, Cowan's version of the Anthology was guaranteed not to startle the flock, still less frighten

---

[21] Butcher (1893: 317), quoting *Iliad* 7.557–8.   [22] Butcher (1893: 5).

[23] On its tone and constituency, see briefly Ellegård (1971: 21–2).

the horses: 'not the least source of its interest and attractiveness lies in the partial and often half-obscured parallelism to the loftier teaching of the Holy Scripture, and especially of the New Testament, in many of the wise and pithy sayings of those heathen worthies'. The Holy Spirit had guided these virtuous pagans in their strivings after truth, did they but know it. Morally, Solon and Pindar were on the same page as King Solomon, as was Hesiod, again invoked as an unlikely epigrammatist; and Cowan assures us that Philemon, 'the gentle rival of Menander', could almost be St Paul when he preaches on the vanity of lavish sacrifice.[24] (To Philemon is attributed a single epigram in the Anthology, AP 9.450; the text translated by Cowan is not it; the habit of borrowing decorous *sententiae* from non-epigrammatic sources when glossing 'the Anthology' for non-adepts is, of course, one we have seen before.) In a separate contribution later in the same number of *Good Words*, Cowan supplied an assortment of translated epigrams that conveniently illustrated all the assertions the article had made: 'Callimachus weaves a chaplet of honour for the virtuous man ... [in] language similar to that which we have in the New Testament.'[25]

A thoroughly on-message review of *Growth and Influence* by John William Mackail, a figure with whom this chapter will transact much business, puts *Studies* more squarely in the cross-hairs than had Jebb himself. The 'scholar ... of the second order' must be a dig at Symonds's brief and inglorious academic career; 'any aspect of the Greek life and spirit' hints broadly at sexual morality without, of course, coming out and saying it. The 'inexact truth' is surely that the Greeks loved youths in anything other than a strictly Christo-Platonic sense:

it is in such popular treatments of the classics as these lectures supply that even more certainly than in commentaries or technical discussions the distinction is clear between the really fine scholar and the scholar who is only of the second order ... to put in intelligible language the exact truth about a Greek author, or about any aspect of the Greek life and spirit, is a work not merely of acquirement but of genius. There is perhaps no subject in the world where the inexact truth is so easy to reach ...[26]

Training the non-elite reader in how to *receive* Greek poetry in the present is, for Mackail's money, 'the most difficult part' of Jebb's task,

---

[24] Cowan (1893a: 403, 404).
[25] Cowan (1893b: 828). Reading classical pagan texts for half-grasped intimations of Christian truth was an established if minor tendency, of which Cocker (1870) is a good example.
[26] Mackail (1894: 257).

and he carries it off brilliantly.[27] The review approvingly quotes *Growth and Influence* verbatim and at length on how Greek poetry, read properly, is compatible with and complementary to modern Christian morality. Sexual conduct is clearly in Jebb's sights, and now Mackail's as well:

> So far from being adverse to those religious and ethical influences which are beyond the compass of its own gift to modern life, it [the 'highest' Greek poetry] is, rightly understood, in concord with them, inasmuch as it tends to elevate and to refine the human spirit by the contemplation of *beauty in its noblest and purest form* ...[28]

'Beauty' was to become a recurring refrain in the containment of epigram's homoeroticism. The term became notorious the following year when Wilde was cross-questioned regarding the preface to *Dorian Gray*, which has its cake and eats it on the admissibility of subtextual readings inside and outside subculture:

> Those who find the ugly meanings in beautiful things are corrupt without being charming. This is a fault.
> Those who find beautiful meanings in beautiful things are cultivated. For these there is hope.
> They are the elect to whom beautiful things mean only Beauty.
> There is no such thing as a moral or an immoral book.
> Books are well written, or badly written. That is all.[29]

When Mackail proposed his own purportedly definitive selection from the Anthology five years after the trials, he used 'Beauty' as a code for those poems he took (few in number, and with careful hedging-about) from Strato's AP 12, knowing that this would discredit them by association while remaining usefully non-specific; history had in the meantime passed judgement on Beauty in about the most literal way imaginable.

2. 'ALL THE BEST': MACKAIL'S SELECT EPIGRAMS

Those who love art the most also censor it the most.[30]

The highest office of history is to preserve ideals, as it is of poetry to create them. The value of this selection of minor poetry ... [is that]

---

[27] Mackail (1894: 259). [28] Mackail (1894: 260).

[29] On 'Beauty' as a Wildean term, see Cruise (1999).

[30] Dollimore (2001: 96), a chapter heading that indulges a self-consciously Wildean paradox.

it may be taken as an epitome, slightly sketched with a facile hand, of the book of Greek life.[31]

To assume the role of a Meleager is to embark on the forging of a canon, and, in the case of Greek literature in the late nineteenth century, to present a pattern for life as well as art. Even today, the compiler of the humblest school handbook of literature in excerption knows that his or her work participates in forming the culture's sense of what counts as the 'great books', in however small a way; even when writing with the classroom partly or wholly in mind, the anthologist ambitious to leave his or her mark in Literature may seize the opportunity to 'author' a coherent story through selection, arrangement, and paratext and thus to craft a literary tradition that conditions how the excerpted authors will be understood as a set, and not just during the reader's school or college years.[32]

In construing 'the Greek Anthology' for the 1890s, with all that its title implied, the stakes were far higher. Symonds had named a few names and offered some fine versions; his discursive miscellany of Meleagrian gems and pressed Alpine blooms had at long last become a school-library staple; but he had not proposed a comprehensive checklist of authors and works, or a step-by-step programme of structured reading. This deficit would now be remedied, to all intents and purposes conclusively.

The purpose of this book, as stated in the preface to the original edition, was to present, in such a form as would appeal to the lover of literature and not be ungrateful to the scholar, a collection of *all the best extant Greek epigrams.* Among the five hundred epigrams included in it—less than one in ten of the whole number extant—will be found, *according to the editor's best judgment, all which are of the first excellence in any style . . .*

It would be easy to agree on three-fourths of the matter to be included in such a scope. With regard to the remainder, perhaps hardly any two persons would be in exact accordance. . . . [in borderline cases] the decision has to be made on a balance of very slight considerations, and becomes in the last resort one of personal taste.[33]

Judged on grounds of party politics, the Fabian socialist and progressive educationalist John William Mackail seems an unlikely inheritor of the Maga mandate to protect Greek epigram from perverts. However, if we take into account his public position on the value of classical literature in education, the pieces of the puzzle fall into place:

---

[31] Mackail (1890: 88).   [32] Johnson (2004: 385); Schrift (2004: 192–3).
[33] Mackail (1906: p. vii).

What an attainable acquaintance with the Classics gives us is *the power* to appreciate and discriminate, to know the difference, *or rather to feel it with a sort of instinct*, between relevance and irrelevance, between accuracy and inaccuracy, between excellence and mediocrity. It gives us what we most need, in the intellectual and artistic no less than in the ethical and mechanical sphere, a standard.

To be classically educated was to enter upon a lifelong power trip, granting title to a professedly meritocratic *auctoritas* that reliably sorted good from bad, 'them' from 'us'. In particular, first-hand knowledge of classical Greek set a chap up for a life spent with his feet firmly planted on the ground; but with great power came great responsibility. This standard, and this instinct, were more necessary than ever before if the increasingly technological civilization of Britain and her colonies was to retain its global lead in humane culture—that ineffable quality of being better than everyone else that justified the Empire.[34] The borderline between excellence and irrelevance needed to be policed, as rigorously as that between civilization and the savage. Judged by the 'instinct' of the trained critic, not even every work of the transmitted ancient canon was truly worthy of the Classic tag. Many were 'of no particular value': the literatures of post-classical Greece and post-Augustan Rome represented a post-classical society on the wane; 'the stream of time has brought down large quantities of rubbish as well as the gold', and it was the task of the critic to pan for nuggets in the broad and silty river.[35]

Mackail was a socialist up to a point and no further; we have already met him warning of the dangers of un-policed readings of 'the Communism of Plato', and he propounded the absolute yardstick of Classics as a bulwark against society's drift towards a Leftism of the lowest common denominator.[36] He was particularly concerned to keep improper interpretations out of the hands of audiences with no classical training, and kept himself busy on the lecture circuit warning them to pay no attention to the non-credentialed. Just as in 1833, the danger to society was extreme—a translation of Sappho or Plato in the wrong

---

[34] I quote Mackail (1925: 194); and cf. (1925: 40): 'It is an industrial community which has special need of a high civilization'. Firmly planted feet: (1925: 42); Greek as preparation for active citizenship: (1925: 89). 'To have attained this vision is to have overcome the world' (1925: 203), with echoes of Kipling's 1895 poem, 'If' ('Yours is the Earth and everything that's in it, | And—which is more—you'll be a Man, my son!').

[35] Mackail (1925: 12, 40).

[36] Mackail (1925: 199) (the Communism of Plato), 203: testing ourselves against the Classics 'stands between us and a tragedy, that the equality towards which the world is consciously tending may be a low and not a high equality.' And cf. (1925: 89–90), on Greek language study as a qualification for (indeed, a precondition of) active citizenship.

hands was an opium den, an illegal gin-still, or even an anarchist's cookbook: 'It may retain enough of its virtue to act, but to act, according to the circumstances, as an intoxicant, or a narcotic, or a high-explosive. Against this real danger, the touch of the Greek Classics themselves is the protection . . .'[37] The 'narcotic or high explosive' line had its first hearing in the author's Presidential Address to the 1923 annual conference of the Classical Association of England and Wales, and reached a wider audience still when his speech was published in *The Times*. Speaking to and for the party faithful of Classics UK, Mackail named the enemy more plainly: the careless translator, and the irresponsible exegete: 'As diluted or distorted . . . [by those] who attempt to popularise the unknown, Greek can become, as the case may be, a narcotic, or an intoxicant, or an explosive.'[38] Mackail's prior interest in epigram was minor, but of some years' standing; he had contributed in a small way to an initially anonymous collaboration of 1883 with two Balliol friends, *Love in Idleness*, which included decorous versions of love poems and laments for the dead out of Meleager and other Hellenistic epigrammatists. (The Anthology's third great exponent in English after Symonds and Mackail, William Roger Paton, was to come to his mighty labours on the Loeb edition of 1812 with similar past form in rendering epigram as the love of lads for lasses, sowing his wild oats with free renderings before submitting to the discipline of literal translation for his *magnum opus*.[39]) A Fellow of Balliol, he was taken seriously by poets as a critical friend (Housman counted on his judgement) and possessed a decisive instinct for textual emendations—perhaps too decisive; if his contemporaries were not uniformly persuaded of his philological soundness, they were certainly kinder in their judgements than was Mackail when the mood took him to castigate epigrammatic amateurs.[40]

---

[37] Mackail (1925: 203, 42).

[38] *The Times*, 9 April 1923: 9, reporting the conference from Bristol. Mackail came back to the formulation at least once more, in his *Essays in Humanism* (London: Longmans, Green, 1938), 51: clearly he was proud of it. On his CA address, see in passing Wrigley (2007: 58).

[39] Beeching, Mackail, and Nichols (1883). On the authorship and publication history of this book see invaluably Cook (1919: 368–9); and cf. p. 370, establishing that the Revd Beeching—a prolific author on Christian themes, and later Dean of Norwich—was the author of most of the Anthology versions of the 1883 work. Rice (1927: p. xii) suggests some of Mackail's efforts here were reused in his work of 1890, but this cannot be right: *Love in Idleness* was in verse, the translations of *Select Epigrams*, prose. Paton as love-epigrammatist, many years before his Loeb: Paton (1898), a sensitive literary verse translation a world apart from his necessarily pedestrian Loeb.

[40] Mackail as sounding-board for contemporary poets, including Housman: Lloyd-Jones (1982: 194), briefly. One side of their affectionate correspondence over the years may be followed up by recourse to the index to Housman (2007), heroically edited by Archie

In cutting the Anthology smartly down to size he found the ideal outlet for his zest for bold textual intervention. Poet X was in, poet Y was out; Mnasalcas was classically correct, Marcus Argentarius a deplorable mangler of the Greek language. The eye of Mackail saw all, knew all—a simple glance determined style, provenance, date, and above all, quality.[41] Meleager, Hellenistic collector-poet of the first Garland, was no longer the star; instead it was the classical master of inscriptional epitaphs, Simonides. In his hands epigram had at once found its fullest and most characteristic expression: 'In literature [the epigram as originally conceived] holds something of the same place as is held in art by an engraved gem.'[42] The comparison of poets to gemstones is of course a gambit straight out of Symonds, redeployed to reinstate as the genre's peak achievement the patriotic epitaphs of Simonides. This lapidary genius was a writer and cutter after Mackail's own heart, rejecting the linguistic indiscipline of lyric with 'instinctive certainty' in favour of 'brevity and high simplicity'; epigram in his hands achieved an immediate pinnacle of 'perfect taste and certainty in the use of language'. Finally someone had found the Anthology's own Wordsworth.[43]

Select Epigrams attracted international attention. The following is from a venerable liberal weekly, the *Nation*, published in Manhattan and at this point in its history primarily a literary review:

The Greek Anthology is a mass of heterogeneous material which may well dismay anything but the hardihood of scholars and editors like Jacobs and Dubner, or the professional student who mines it for antiquarian or philological lore. It has discouraged the enterprises of Prof. Mahaffy, for instance, who goes so far as to say that 'no study seems to him more wearisome and profitless than the Anthology.' The Anthology, as it stands, is not a selection, in any proper sense—it is simply a vast reservoir, with some subdivision, into which about 4,000 little poems have been thrown that bear a certain mechanical resemblance in brevity

---

Burnett. As a textual editor (as at Mackail 1892), he was reckoned sloppy—see Headlam (1892). His talent as a literary critic of ancient texts, however, was well enough regarded (Postgate 1896)—not a judgement that would last long into the new century, as we shall see. Witheringly harsh criticism of contemporaries' efforts at construing and improving the text of AP: Mackail (1896).

[41] Mackail (1892: 193). Reading Rufinus's date off his style, very late this time around: (1906: 21) (a view not voiced in the 1st edn).

[42] Mackail (1890: 4).

[43] Mackail (1926: 135, 13), and cf. p. 133, 'the greatest of the Greek epigrammatists'. Simonidean Wordsworth, or Wordsworthian Simonides—no sissy Shelleys here: (1926: 125, 137). The critical practice of reading the Anthology through a Wordsworthian filter, originally a habit of Maga (see Ch. 4), had never really gone away; cf. Cook (1919: 368), commenting on Headlam (1907).

and in metre. So far from being a 'garland of flowers', a metaphor which was applied legitimately to the earliest selection by Meleager, it is a garden run to weeds, in which the weeds predominate with varying degrees of worthlessness and noisomeness. But the flowers are there; it would be the greatest mistake to despair in the search, and to miss the exquisite bouquet which Mr Mackail has culled from the wilderness . . .

Mr Mackail's is the only serious attempt in English to do for the Anthology what Mr Matthew Arnold did for Wordsworth.[44]

Mackail's is the true Anthology of the Greeks; the 'Greek Anthology' from which he gleans it is merely real. The comparison to Arnold's selection from Wordsworth (1879; much reprinted) deftly steers the *Nation*'s reader towards recollection of its famous preface, an essay in which Arnold had predicated his case for recuperating the Lakeland poet as a worthy successor to Shakespeare and Milton on a thorough winnowing of his work. Wordsworth is truly great only when the Muse takes him, and the sympathetic posthumous editor does him a great service by clearing away the second-rate and allowing genius to shine through. In cleansing the Greek Anthology as Arnold had the Wordsworthian corpus in his *Selected Poems* of 1879, Mackail has recuperated and renewed this ancient text for the English literary tradition.

The underlying metaphor is again horticultural. Wordsworth's best and truest poetry is a specimen plant (a tree, or a splendid rose?) that Arnold had freed of the encroaching weeds (also incidentally, but *only* incidentally, written by him) which threatened to choke it:

To exhibit this body of Wordsworth's best work, to clear away obstructions from around it, and to let it speak for itself, is what every lover of Wordsworth should desire. Until this has been done, Wordsworth, whom we, to whom he is dear, all of us know and feel to be so great a poet, has not had a fair chance before the world.

Clearing away the dross reveals the proud stem of poetic Genius; letting this stand tall makes a statement about national character on the global stage.[45] And what did 'the world' want from its poetry? Morality, which made the English tradition the greatest in the world:

---

[44] Anon. (1892: 304); particularly nice to see Wilde's old tutor Mahaffy getting a mention, and his quoted comment perhaps reacts off Wilde's enthusiasm for *Studies*.

[45] Arnold (1903: 140) (the Second Series of *Essays in Criticism*, first collected in 1888); in the 1920s Mussolini will speak in tellingly similar terms when he calls for the medieval dross to be cleared from Rome's historic centre, exposing and stringing together the monuments of Imperial Rome as a backdrop and pretext for Fascism's own extraterritorial ambitions; for context, see, e.g., Stone (1999), 'A flexible Rome'.

Voltaire was right in thinking that the energetic and profound treatment of moral ideas, in this large sense, is what distinguishes the English poetry . . . It is important, therefore, to hold fast to this: that poetry is at bottom a criticism of life; that the greatness of a poet lies in his powerful and beautiful application of ideas to life—to the question: How to live.[46]

Once again (see p. 180) translating the Greek Anthology is compared to portrait-work from memory, conjuring up an image of the beloved that is all the more true in its sympathetic essence for being an idealized abstraction: 'If, in composing his sketch, [Mackail] has omitted some ugly spots and dark lines entirely, he has every reason of decency to justify him, and perhaps even of truthfulness.'[47] Sin is an ugly business; flowers are beautiful; the true Anthology must therefore be without sin. In culling a pristine Garland from the tangled 'wilderness' of the inherited text, Mackail has restored the Anthology to its 'proper' self.

'[A] garden run to weeds'—this is the long-established language of the self-righteous censor, crossing over with a trope in British epigram-work that goes all the way back to Bland's Preface of 1806. By figuring epigrams as types of flowers in imitation of Meleager, nineteenth-century connoisseurs of the *Anthology* unwittingly laid it wide open to expurgation; the text contained but a few blooms of true and natural feeling, and these could spread their petals only once the weeds that threatened to stifle them had been cleared away.[48]

3. GATHERING IN THE WHEAT

Another parable put he forth unto them, saying, The kingdom of heaven is likened unto a man which sowed good seed in his field:
But while men slept, his enemy came and sowed tares among the wheat, and went his way.

But when the blade was sprung up, and brought forth fruit, then appeared the tares also.

So the servants of the householder came and said unto him, Sir, didst not thou sow good seed in thy field? from whence then hath it tares?

---

[46] Arnold (1903: 143).   [47] Anon. (1892: 304).
[48] On the figurative language of 'weeding' texts, see Perrin (1992: 63) and cf. p. 200, with relevance to the immediately following passage (separating the wheat-crop from the poisonous tares). The self-identification of the modern Anthologists as 'gardeners' (a peculiarly English pastime) is touched on at Livingstone and Nisbet (2010: 159).

He said unto them, An enemy hath done this. The servants said unto him, Wilt thou then that we go and gather them up?

But he said, Nay; lest while ye gather up the tares, ye root up also the wheat with them.

Let both grow together until the harvest: and in the time of harvest I will say to the reapers, Gather ye together first the tares, and bind them in bundles to burn them: but gather the wheat into my barn.

The King James version of Matthew 13.24–30 is the Gospel passage prescribed for the fifth Sunday after the Epiphany in the Book of Common Prayer, the standard prayer book of the Church of England from 1662 (in its present form) to the late twentieth century. As its Collect makes clear, the fifth Sunday is all about separating the wheat from the chaff in redemption's endgame, good Anglican Protestants from hell-bound Others; the sixth Sunday rams the message home ('And every man that hath this hope in himself purifieth himself, even as he is pure ... He that committeth sin is of the devil'). Tares and wheat, wheat and chaff: this is the language of state-endorsed religion, of textual censorship, of the right ordering of the Protestant polity, and of the British as a national, colonial, and postcolonial language community over the last several hundred years (the Book of Common Prayer and the King James permeate our use of English as thoroughly as does Shakespeare).

'As the philosophers might say, "literature" and "weed" are *functional* rather than *ontological* terms: they tell us about what we do, not about the fixed being of things.'[49] Mackail's neo-Simonidean enthusiasm for winnowing and purifying the Classics rested on a conviction that language expressed the character of the *Volk*—the modern nation state, understood as a distinct ethnic grouping and blood legacy from which cultural heritage was inseparable. This scenario informs the 1890s panic over Decadent literary production, Wilde's included: racial and literary degeneration were two parts of the same system, and interacted directly.[50]

To cleanse the text was potentially to redeem the race, and it is in this context that we should read his call for a full British edition-with-commentary of the Anthology, racing the leaner effort of the Germans to claim the last slice of philological Empire. He appealed to national pride to promote the preparation of a proper national edition to match and if possible outdo Stadtmüller's in-progress Teubners: 'it is hardly to the credit of English scholarship that it still awaits accomplishment.'

---

[49] Eagleton (1983: 9) (emphases in original).   [50] Mackail (1925: 1–2).

Alas, this call to arms, repeated from one edition to the next, was to be heeded by only the most off-kilter of Albion's paladins.[51]

Indeed, Mackail's take on the Anthology was always explicitly about Empire, our own and the Romans' both (not that it was always easy in late-nineteenth-century discourse to tell the two apart), part of a distinctive brand of Classics in which colonial administration, development, and policing loomed large.[52] Its characteristic elegiac couplets were, he advertised,

> a metre which could refuse nothing, which could rise to the occasion and sink with it, and be equally suited to the epitaph of a hero or the verses accompanying a birthday present, a light jest or a profound moral idea, the sigh of a lover or the lament over a perished Empire.[53]

Fixing the form and dictating the meaning of the text through edition and commentary would also somehow head off the dissident and countercultural interpretations against which Mackail was an important spokesperson. There would be no *fin de siècle* meltdown of racial virtue; unlike that of the Romans, this Empire was not for perishing. Accordingly, Mackail's Simonides was a Hellene through and through—a veritable Sophocles by blood and circumstance. Born on Ceos, an island 'only divided by a few miles of sea from Sunium' and thus practically within the Athenian cultural sphere, he had spent his life free from the miasma of Asiatic influence and had breathed 'the thin clear air of Greece' (thin presumably because culturally 'high') all his days; in his hands, epigram reached a peak of Attic rigour. An Anthology reconceptualized around his gold standard preserved the purity of the ancient racial spirit as a rallying-point for the English-speaking world of the present day.[54]

---

[51] Mackail (1906: p. ix). Stadtmüller is not a threat at the time of the 1st edn (1890), so there is no call to arms. By the 2nd edn the German is two up going into half time, but it is a game of two halves, and all to play for (1906: p. ix). His call is answered, as far as I am aware, only by the extremely eccentric Lumb (1920), an assistant master at Merchant Tailors' School. Dismissing the Teubner effort as 'usually beneath contempt' (p. v), Lumb embarks on a programme of wholesale emendations as dogmatic (e.g. 'The true reading is' (pp. 2, 5, 14, 18, 20, etc.), 'The true text is' (p. 7), 'The author wrote' (pp. 9, 10 (x 2), 11)) as they are improbable—the reader quickly learns to dread the formula 'may/should we (not) read ...?' (*passim*). One for cognoscenti. Mackail is still flogging his hobby-horse in the 3rd edn of 1912—Stadtmüller is dead, the field is open (p. xi).

[52] Classics and 'imperial studies' (Mackail 1925: 211–31). The value of Classics to a 'white Australia', keeping the colony culturally as well as ethnically up to the standard of the breed: (1925: 50); for important context, see Challis (2010: 110).

[53] Mackail (1906: 6).

[54] Mackail (1926: 121–2, cf. 133). The phrasing echoes Pater (1895a: 138), on what is missed when we study Greek art in our modern museum galleries: 'the clear Greek skies, the

The Meleager of this newly winnowed Anthology was a poetry critic of sound editorial instinct, and to that extent a worthy prototype for Mackail's own critically sure value judgements: in matching each author of the Garland to his or her particular flower in his famous verse prologue he had shown unerring taste; but his original Garland had been lost beyond recall in the Anthology's mass, and his critical and aesthetic acumen had not always been matched by the moral good sense that an anthologist needed if he was to 'create an ideal'.[55] It was not his fault; he was the biological and cultural product of his historical moment, the close of the Hellenistic period, 'where the Greek spirit was touched by Oriental passion'.[56]

The Oriental fantasy of Syria as a den of supine mysticism and steamy sensuality was nothing new in the historiography of the classical world— it is there already in Gibbon, a century before—but in the epigram-discourse of the British *fin de siècle* it takes a distinctively racialist turn.[57] Meleager is now a Syrian first and foremost, a Hellene second. His epigrams

sound the whole lyre of passion. Meleager was born in a Syrian town and educated at Tyre in the last days of the Seleucid empire; and though he writes Greek with complete mastery, it becomes in his hands almost a new language, full of dreams, at once more languid and more passionate... In Meleager, the touch of Asiatic blood creates a new type, delicate, exotic, fantastic... The atmosphere is loaded with a steam of perfumes.[58]

Mackail clearly has his sights set on Decadent cultural production in his own 1890s—the passage has more to do with Beardsley ('delicate, exotic, fantastic') and Wilde ('languid and passionate') than with a first-century epigram-collector—and his careful ring-fencing of Meleager's admissible range of sentiment must have *Studies* as its ultimate target. Meleager's more carnal AP 5 poems are disallowed as belonging to the wrong end of a dichotomy that readers of Symonds will immediately recognize. Now even hetero-erotics are implicitly divisible into Pandemic and Uranian:

---

poetical Greek life.' Simonides of a piece with Sophocles: 1925: 48. Attic 'brevity and high simplicity', 1926: 135.

[55] '[T]he light and sure touch of a critic who is also a poet himself': Mackail (ed.) (1890: 15).

[56] Mackail (1890: 33).

[57] Roman Syria kept from self-betterment by 'slothful effeminacy': Gibbon (1993.1: 45). On how late nineteenth-century Classics bought into pseudo-scientific racialist theory to re-imagine the ancient Greeks as a Master Race within a Northern European rather than a Mediterranean family tree, see now the important discussion by Debbie Challis (2010).

[58] Mackail (1890: 33–4).

'Some of Meleager's epigrams are direct and simple, even to coarseness; but in all the best and most characteristic there is this difference from purely Greek work, that love has become a religion; the spirit of the East has touched them.' To the extent that Meleager is admissibly erotic at all, he is Eastern; not so much a Classic as a prototype of the Medieval troubadour.[59] 'For a moment Meleager can be piercingly simple; and then the fantastic mood comes over him again, and emotion dissolves in a mist of metaphors'—a criticism we might at this point consider levelling at Mackail rather than his late-Hellenistic target, and it would not be many years before a self-consciously modernist twentieth-century academy came round to just this way of thinking ('at the end of the chapter on Homer, the reader asks himself, "What has it all been about?— [William] Morris, or Hugo, or early French tapestry?"'). As academic writing, Mackail's critical style as an essayist on ancient authors went out of date very quickly. By the early 1910s he was being written off as a mere historical curiosity—a Romantic dinosaur and poet manqué; a decade later, patronizingly indulged as a beloved grandfather figure to the modern discipline.[60]

This last fond verdict is American; Mackail's old-school critical declamations were going down a storm with the public there. 'Mackail's *Latin Literature*, his *Lectures on Greek Poetry*, and his translations from the *Greek Anthology*, have created an appetite. Any book that bears the name Mackail is sure to command respectful attention in America'; and we recall the *Nation*'s rave review of his *Select Epigrams* on their first appearance in 1892.[61] They did very well with the public at home too. Viewed as exercises in scholarship, his classical exegeses were easily and quickly dismissed, but their strong authorial voice helped them become an unusually long-lived international brand within the sphere of Anglophone public print. Beyond the small world of university criticism, and over a span of time that extended to decades, his version of the Anthology thus went from strength to strength. His self-advertisement as an

---

[59] Mackail (1906: 36).

[60] Mist of metaphors: Mackail (1890: 35). Early French tapestry: 'He approaches Greek poetry as a Romantic of the old school, and only as a Romantic; poetry for him is romantic poetry... His eyes are the eyes of William Morris, and we believe the book will have value as a record of that poet's point of view... But one cannot help feeling that much that is here said in florid prose would have been better condensed into sonnet form' (Anon. 1911: 327), reviewing his *Lectures on Greek Poetry* (1910). In a nice irony, Mackail, scourge of the Uranians, now finds himself pigeonholed as an 'enthusiast' (Anon. 1911: 327) every bit as much as did Symonds two decades earlier. De Witt (1923: 198) affectionately paints him as the American academy's favourite old coot, whom it would be bad manners to upset with cavilling criticisms.

[61] Smiley (1926: 638).

editor of heroic mettle inspired something of a literary cult of personality over the next several decades:[62] 'The handy little volume containing the Greek text of Mr Mackail's *Select Epigrams from the Greek Anthology* was at that time my constant companion...Mr Mackail's selection is so admirably done as to leave but few gleanings of equal value to those he has chosen.'[63] There were now *two* standard treatments of the Anthology: Symonds's original essay in *Studies*, still going strong after twenty-odd years, and Mackail's *Select Epigrams*, which acquired immediate classic status.[64]

4. MACKAIL'S GOSPEL: THE NEW BOOK OF LIFE

Of particular influence was Mackail's new organizational scheme. We saw at the beginning of Chapter 2 that the question of structure had seemed to offer no easy solution. The 1806 compendium of Merivale and Bland had presented a notionally chronological scheme that to all intents and purposes offered miscellany in a familiar eighteenth-century mode, but their 1813 revision had been savaged for a scheme partially modelled on the Anthology's own, with what Merivale subsequently conceded to have been a 'pretty copious infusion...of irrelevant matter':

1. Amatory
2. Convivial
3. Moral (elegiac, gnomic)
4. Extracts from drama
5. Funeral and monumental
   1. private
   2. historic personages and poets
6. Descriptive
   1. on statues and pictures
7. Dedicatory
8. Satirical and Humorous
9. Riddles

---

[62] 'The five hundred epigrams included in it—less than one in ten of the whole number extant'—these are heroic odds, few against many, and the editor who can marshal them under his 'best judgment' must have something of the Leonidas about him.

[63] Leaf (1922: 7).

[64] A reviewer of the second edition (Anon. 1906: 215): 'This book is so well known, has now so assured a place among works of fine scholarship, that the new edition needs no detailed review.'

This scheme retained some Anthology categories in more or less their original guise (e.g., AP 5 = 'Amatory', AP 6 = 'Dedicatory'); split up others (AP 11 divided into 'Convivial' and 'Satirical and Humorous', and AP 7's content parcelled out under two subheadings); and, of course, brought in substantial material from outside. No one had liked it and for his last try in 1833 Merivale had reverted to a chronological scheme—a safe choice, but where was the fun in that? Where for that matter was the performance of editorial virtuosity, and the ethical lesson? MacGregor in 1864 had settled for a subset of AP categories, with the results we saw in Chapter 2; Tomson in 1889 had arranged alphabetically by ancient author, resulting in a sizeable stack of 'Anonymous' being sandwiched between Anacreon and the Antipaters; and Garnett in 1869 had offered simple miscellany, as had Lang in his 'Little Garland' of 1888. These last two assortments were nicely put together, and artful juxtaposition made them pleasant enough to dip into, but it really looked as if the structure question was going nowhere; after nearly a century the Anthology was back at square one.

'This is not a natural division, and is not satisfactory in its results': Mackail now offered a bold new programme that briskly whipped the existing AP categories into a poetically and morally modern shape. That the new-and-improved Anthology falls into twelve parts, a number both classically epic and with strong Judaeo-Christian significance, is surely no accident—Mackail was both a noted Vergilian and subsequently a re-teller of Bible stories for the young:[65]

1. Love
2. Prayers and Dedications
3. Epitaphs
4. Literature and Art
5. Religion
6. Nature
7. The Family
8. Beauty
9. Fate and Change
10. The Human Comedy
11. Death
12. Life

[65] Cephalan scheme 'not a natural division', Mackail (1890: 29). His retellings of stories from the Old and New Testaments for children, *Biblia Innocentium* (2 vols), are charming; the first volume was published in 1892 by William Morris's Kelmscott Press.

The Cephalan Anthology's superannuated scheme could now be permanently retired. Mackail's rationale repays in close reading the attention it calls to itself: 'by a new and somewhat more detailed division, an attempt has been made *to give a closer unity to each section* [sc. than in their AP prototypes], *and to make the whole of them illustrate progressively the aspect of the ancient world.*'[66] The winnowed and rearranged Anthology-according-to-Mackail is pitched as a unified literary work. For the first time since Meleager wove the primal Garland from which it grew, the Anthology is finally a proper poetry book again; and its categories of poems, *when read sequentially* ('progressively') *in the order presented by the editor–translator*, tell the true story of Greek cultural production in its relation to life as it was lived by the ancient Greeks. Independently of the poems selected and arranged for inclusion under them—although, of course, these individual choices are important too—Mackail's thematic headings tell their own story. Indeed, he bills them as not sections but 'chapters', like the chapters of a novel. Mackail's definitive selection—and by implication no other, not even the lost Garland of Meleager—is 'the book of Greek life' in pocketable form, a claim made by its author in the quotation with which we opened the preceding section.[67] The 'book' rhetoric recalls the Worsdworthians' 'Book of Nature' (see p. 187), and it is the essential nature of Greek racial character that Mackail promises to unveil for us through this thematically articulated sequential story. Contemporary popular media now use a tellingly near-identical phrasing as shorthand for the successful charting of the entire human genetic sequence by the Human Genome Project: 'the book of life' is the shared DNA that makes us all human, which may often predict our individual strengths and susceptibilities, and which our species can now read, interpret, and annotate.

At the same time, this racial character is further parsed and its message made personal as the coherent life story of a paradigmatic Hellenic Everyman—shades of Symonds's 'the Genius of the Greeks' made flesh. Mackail's chapters denote not merely a novel-like narrative, but specifically a *Bildungsroman* in which personal and racial development stand in for one another. Love, Prayers and Dedications, Epitaphs, and the rest—

---

[66] Mackail (1890: 29) (emphasis added); in the 2nd edn (1906: 31) 'the ancient world' is replaced by a more precise formulation, 'Greek art and life'.

[67] Mackail notes that Meleager's choice of alphabetization by incipit has no merit beyond 'the uncommon variety it must give to the reader'—it tells no story, is not a 'Book' in that sense at all. (Like all the critics of his time Mackail is faithfully reporting an erroneous tradition regarding Meleager. It was not him but his successor, Philip, who alphabetized; see now Cameron (1993: 20–6), conclusively).

these are the things that matter in the individual Greek life, as much as in the life of the Greek race. The tale they impart begins with a flourish of worldly joys and pride of talent (Mackail's chapters 1–4), but then achieves moral seriousness and accepts mature responsibility (chapters 5–7).

'Beauty' is a fleeting mid-life crisis, sandwiched between 'The Family' (chapter 7—at least one's social duty has been safely fulfilled) and the more sombre concerns of later life (his chapters 9–12): Fate, the vicissitudes of human existence, Death, and finally 'Life'—which means more Death (Death's inevitability as a lifelong sermon-text). The introduction to *Select Epigrams* is relentlessly morbid—epigram's principal value now lies in its being the genre best suited to telling us how to die:

Behind the flutes and flowers change comes and the shadow of fate stands waiting...For over all Greek life there lay a shadow...[in treating death], if anywhere, the Greek genius had its fullest scope and most decisive triumph; and here it is that we come upon the epigram in its inmost essence and utmost perfection.[68]

As glossed in the book's very extensive introduction, an individual category may stand as a sentimental education in and of itself. The sixth chapter thus presents the Greek evolution (as read by Mackail) in attitudes to Nature as explicitly analogous to, and functionally interchangeable with, the phases of a young person's awakening into aesthetic and finally moral self-realization. Reading through his selection on the Family (his chapter 7), we are unsubtly steered to recognize our own social world mirrored in this never-ending cycle of married domesticity and the passing generations. Mackail's introduction vividly evokes a series of nostalgic snapshots of the organic and autarkic society that always lies just round history's corner—and Symonds's Uranian Aphrodite is now hailed as the traditional guarantor of its rhythms of life. The rightly ordered household under its god-fearing paterfamilias; the thrifty and contented smallholder; the girl at her loom, ripening like a rose—a rose that in no sense resembles a pretty boy but will instead spread wide petals of female sexual readiness, on a distinctly Austen-esque marriage day:[69]

We see the house of the good man, an abiding rest from the labours of a busy life, bountiful to all, masters and servants [*sic*—not slaves], who dwell under its

[68] Mackail (1890: 61, 64). The proportion of the introduction devoted to Fate and Death is simply huge: notionally (1890: 61–78), but really also pp. 79–84 (at least).

[69] Indeed, Austen was wittily meta-fictional about it: 'We are all hastening together to perfect felicity', she assures her readers towards the end of *Northanger Abbey* (1817, but written 1798–9). The passage quoted here is Mackail (1890: 52–4) (emphases added).

shelter, and extending a large hospitality to the friend and the stranger. One generation after another grows up in it under all gracious influences; *a special providence, under the symbolic forms of Cypris Urania or Artemis the Giver of Light, holds the house in keeping,* and each new year brings increased blessing from the gods of the household in recompense of piety and duty. Many dedications bring vividly before us the humbler life of the country cottager, no man's servant or master, happy in the daily labour over his little plot of land, his cornfield and vineyard and coppice; of the fowler with his boys in the woods, the forester and the beekeeper, the fisherman in his thatched hut on the beach . . .

A shadow passes over the picture in the complaint of a girl sitting indoors, full of dim thoughts, while the boys go out to their games and enjoy unhindered the colour and movement of the streets. But this is the melancholy of youth, the shadow of the brightness that passes before the maiden's eyes as she sits, sunk in daydreams, over her loom; it passes away again in the portrait of the girl growing up with the sweet eyes of her mother, *the budding rose that will soon unfold its heart of flame; and once more the bride renders thanks for perfect felicity to the gods who have given her 'a stainless youth and the lover whom she desired.'*

'Cypris Urania' perhaps looks back to Neaves's majuscule insistence on the matrimonial character of the Anthology's HEAVENLY VENUS.[70] Of course, this lush tableau is largely fabulation: in the section immediately following, the author's phrasing ('*Scattered over the sections* of the Anthology *are a number of epigrams* touching on this life') tacitly admits the fib. The Anthology does not tell this story at all, or had not before Mackail got his hands on it; but the white lie serves a higher truth, the identity of the 'right' Greek life with our own.[71]

Mackail's chapters are not, therefore, meant to be understood as mere categories of poems; we are expected to recognize in them the categories of universal human experience, as documented by the ancient race adopted by nineteenth-century Britain as its principal aspirational paradigm of life and thought. All human life—all admissible human life—is here: 'a light jest or a profound moral idea, the sigh of a lover or the lament over a perished Empire,' Mackail's checklist of human activity here closely echoes that of Jebb nearly twenty years earlier ('Love, art, mourning for the dead'), but now delivers the structural logic that backs up Jebb's old equation of these on-message behaviours and emotions with 'the whole range of human interests and sympathies'. Mackail's

[70] Mackail had surely looked into Neaves; at Nisbet (2012b: 92 n. 48) I suggest that his 'Literature and Art' chapter consciously echoes and endorses Neaves's category of 'Literary and Artistic' (1874: 16).
[71] The good man's house, a passing shadow, and a stainless youth: Mackail (1890: 39–40). The 'scattered' Greek family album: Mackail (1890: 38) (emphases added).

chapters are tick-boxes for the formation of personal subjectivity and social identity.

5. THE WHOLE LYRE OF PASSION? MACKAIL AND GREEK LOVE

Writing against the grain of Symonds's dangerous intervention, Mackail allocates space in this 'whole range' to an all-but-explicit discussion that will contain and shut down the Uranian pederasty of his predecessor's Meleager. At the level of structure, we saw Greek love pigeonholed as a passing phase—an anomaly in the life of the individual and the culture; at the level of discourse, the strategy is rather more supple and polysemic. An initial brief mention makes it look as if Mackail will write it out of the picture by pointedly saying a particular and instantly connotative variety of nothing—Strato's Mousa Paidikē (the title naturally presented in the decent obscurity of a transliterated dead language) is 'a new Anthology of epigrams dealing with this special subject'—but it later turns out he has plenty to say in setting up reader expectations for his poems from 'Beauty'.[72]

Partly this is straightforward condemnation, a verdict that establishes his own moral credentials and further affirms the virile exactness and actively redemptive spirit of his own editorial selectivity. Muscular Hebraism beats down a pseudo-Hellenism infected by the effeminate East:

[Homosexual content] fills so large a part of the Anthology that it can hardly be passed over without notice. The few epigrams selected from the Anthology of Strato and included in this collection under the heading of Beauty *are not of course* a representative selection. Of the great mass of those epigrams no selection is possible or desirable. They belong to that side of Greek life which is akin to the Oriental world, and remote and even revolting to the western mind. On this subject the common moral sense of civilised mankind has pronounced a judgment which requires no justification as it allows of no appeal.[73]

Mackail writes here like a hanging judge, but the discussion that this verdict cues up is more miscellaneous, hedging the death sentence and finding avenues of special pleading. Mackail provokes his reader to consider that figuring Eros as a boy, familiar as the trope is to us through Renaissance art and so on, is actually weird if you stop and think about it in modern terms; its omnipresence in Europe's Greek cultural heritage

---

[72] Mackail (1890: 18).   [73] Mackail (1890: 38), emphasis added.

reflects a historically specific ancient cross-fertilization between polite social convention and the gymnastic culture of the body beautiful. Human nature was the same for them as for us, then, but the social construction of sexual and gendered identity made homoerotic desire *understandable in context*, no matter how 'revolting' it may be to us now. 'To all this there must be added a fact of no less importance in historical Greece, the seclusion of women. Not that this ever existed in the Oriental sense'—but even in a Westernized variant the invisibility of the female body in social space had its own effect.[74]

In an intriguingly left-field follow-up we are encouraged to try out a previously unexplored Christian parallel. In figuring out how and why Greek art and literature fashioned the adolescent male as an ideal of beauty transcending mere flesh, medieval art's invention of the angel is good to think with, says Mackail—the Greeks' 'cult of beauty'

was the issue of their attempt, imperfect indeed at best and at worst disastrous, to reunite the fragments of this human ideal. *In much of this poetry too we are in the world of pastoral; for pastoral, it must be remembered, does not profess to represent an actual world*...A truer picture of Greek life is happily given us in those epigrams which deal with...the life of the simple human relations from day to day *within the circle of the family.*[75]

Theocritus's *Idylls*, a favoured code-text of nineteenth-century Urnings, are mere pretty pictures—they have nothing to do with real life, which *naturally* finds its eternal realization in the family home of good fathers and budding daughters. Thoughts of these latter are also in play when, in passing, Mackail explains away and excuses certain AP 12 poems as mistakenly included there by virtue of the masculine appearance of some diminutive female proper names; from among the book's toyboys he is able to rescue a few misplaced tomboys for the cause of femininity.[76]

Mackail's other major strategy is to play for time, tweaking curves to get the result he wants. Ostensibly he is far too modern to fall for the old art-historical myth of pre-shaped rise, peak, and decline: in an account indebted to Symonds's labours, we learn that epigram is an 'art, practised with...infinite grace by Greek artists of almost every age between Solon and Justinian'.[77] Nonetheless, the Winckelmann curve is a line of thought familiar to his readers as part of hand-me-down

---

[74] Mackail (1890: 36–7).   [75] Mackail (1890: 40).   [76] Mackail (1890: 19).
[77] Mackail (1895: 194–5), the context being a discussion of how Martial's insistence on cheap and often sordid punchlines warped the meaning of 'epigram' in the classical tradition. Cf. Mackail's sensible account of textual transmission, which agrees with and builds on that of Symonds, e.g. in his narration of the relation of the Cephalan and Planudean Anthologies and in his appraisal of the latter (1890: 22) as 'made carelessly

common sense, and his timeline of quality plays to that awareness. Thus with Philip in the Roman era we are invited to see 'the decline of the art from its first exquisiteness'; late-antique Agathias is a love-poet of 'unrelenting tediousness'.[78] Although the genre does not now decline and fall in Winckelmanian style, the living soul has gone out of it by the end, leaving a mere formal perfection—albeit that this stylistic continuity attests vividly to the 'extraordinary vitality of [a] Greek genius' rooted in the 'great' generation of Simonides (all calculated digs at Symonds's legacy).[79] To rub salt in the wound, Paul the Silentiary and his circle are appraised generously as formally successful latecomers: love-poets by rote, admittedly, but 'graceful enough' on their own terms.[80]

But, in this great 'chain of poems',[81] running uninterrupted from the dawn of written history to the European vernacular era, there is one wobble into bad taste at a moment of weakness in national character: the Roman Empire of the first and second centuries CE; 'in any collection of Greek epigrammatic poetry these authors naturally sink to their own place.'[82] Strato is the particular target here, albeit with some discreet misdirection as to what 'Strato' might stand for. The Strato of *Select Epigrams* is primarily to be noted not as an erotic poet but as a probable literary fraud, and a very poor one at that (the reader learns that he is the real author of a supposed colophon to Meleager's Garland, 'a stupid and clumsy forgery...not worth quoting').[83] In a major publication a few years later, the much-reprinted *Latin Literature*, Mackail embroiders further, retraining Strato as an AP 11 poet—a satirist inspired by Martial. There is no hint here that he ever wrote or compiled poems on that 'special subject' at all. Strato is now excluded not so much for sodomitical sin as for sheer lack of merit: like his skoptic colleagues Lucillius and

---

and, it would seem, hurriedly...Not only so, but he mutilated the text freely, and made sweeping conjectural restorations where it was imperfect'; cf. to this Symonds (1873: 344).

[78] Mackail (1890: 17, 19).

[79] Formal perfection: Mackail (1890: 35–6). The ever-living Greek genius: (1908: p. vi), in a two-page preface that boils down the argument for the Greekless reader. The last poets and 'their great models': (1906: 38).

[80] Mackail (1890: 66).

[81] Mackail (1906: 8), embroidering on a topos already present in the first edition (1890: 7, 'essential unity and continuous life...golden bridge').

[82] Mackail (1895: 195), and cf. 194–5: 'The art...was just at this period sunk to a low ebb.'

[83] Mackail (1890: 15); retained in subsequent editions. The reference must be to Meleager (or by this account ps.-Meleager) AP 12.256, in which the poet playfully weaves a garland of pretty boy-flowers for Aphrodite; see Ch. 3, pp. 139–40.

Nicarchus, he 'naturally sink[s] to [his] own place' in any assortment of epigrams, and his stock must be all the lower in Mackail's own elevated selection.[84]

6. EPIGRAMS AND EMPIRE: MACKAIL'S LEGACY

England and Egypt! How strange it seems that these two countries should in any way be connected! How wonderful that one should now so powerfully influence the other!... The one, though cold in climate, wanting in sunshine, is inhabited by a race of hardy and active men, who have however to turn the very disadvantages under which they labour to advantages; to spread themselves over all the world, and to fill the whole earth with the fame of their deeds. The other is placed under a burning sun, which produces either the terrible sterility of the desert or the rank luxuriance of the mois-tened valley. It is inhabited by a race of princes, oppressors, and their miserable serfs.[85]

Greek 'leisure' is sometimes spoken of slightingly as if it were the luxury of the rich or the dilettanti, an easy sauntering through life and avoidance of painful effort. But in truth it is not the opposite of activity, but a special form of activity, the strenuous exercise of the intellectual or artistic faculties. It is no state of blissful indolence, which is the ideal of some Orientals... It is work, genuine work.[86]

What Mackail leaves for his successors, in sum, is a workable canon of Greek epigram, set in a morally logical sequence; a well-formed Greek text with commentary, ideally formed as an intermediary source for future translators; and his own tasteful and sufficiently accurate English rendering, to serve as a pattern for emulation. He also bequeathes a usefully broad and supple set of explanations for the contents of the Anthology—an Anthology that for the coming decades will effectively be synonymous with his *Select Epigrams*. Our closing chapter will track Mackail's enduring influence into the 1920s, but his work won hearts and minds right from the start.

---

[84] The imperial Greek poets: Mackail (1895: 195).

[85] Anon. (1885: 1–2), inaugurating a volume of boys'-own Empire stories cashing in on the death of 'Chinese' Gordon at Khartoum. Egypt, of course, had been briefly a Napoleonic possession, gloriously knocked out of the enemy's grasp by Nelson's victory at the Nile, so there is definite national one-upmanship going on here; I thank Diana Spencer for pointing this angle out to me.

[86] Butcher (1893: 241).

A year after *Select Epigrams* (1891), Edinburgh's Professor of Greek, the noted Aristotelianist Samuel Butcher, brought out a new literary–cultural appraisal of the Greek Genius that introduced the epigrams of the Anthology in its fourth chapter, 'The Melancholy of the Greeks'. Two years on (1893), his second edition ditched the conventional terminus of Aristotle for a new concluding chapter, 'The Dawn of Romanticism in Greek Poetry', which climaxed with a substantial discussion of the Anthology. As its woeful title indicates, the 1891 chapter was already heavily indebted to Mackail's project: Butcher's Anthology is presented as a pointillist study in pagan fatalism. After the great age of Simonides, whose epigrams shone as white as the marble funerary monuments they adorned, a Decadent ennui ('satiety', p. 173) marks the weakening of the racial Genius under Alexander and then Rome:

A word remains to be said about those exquisite gems of verse which are contained in the Greek Anthology. Many moods are there reflected. The lines are sometimes bright and playful, sometimes pathetic, sometimes cynical, always graceful. But the motto which is written on the pages as a whole is the same as that of the book of Ecclesiastes, 'Vanity of Vanities'—ματαιότης ματαιοτήτων— and the dominant note of sadness deepens the farther we follow the poems into Roman times. 'All is laughter, all is ashes, all is nothingness'...

The minds of nobler temper in the Anthology suffer from something akin to the modern 'Weltschmerz', a feeling in which the mystery of life and the sense of the infinite mingle with personal weariness or satiety. Such poets console themselves by singing in charming verse of graves and ruin; of the fallen grandeur of ancient cities...'...All else is fearfulness and pain'.[87]

'Weariness of living' maps onto literary lateness; this Mackail-derived Anthology is the index of racial history, within the overarching frame of a cultural encomium that explicitly sets up the classical Greeks as the self-created forebears of Western technological civilization, progressive imperialism, and benign hegemony over an Orient typed as simultaneously, lazy, dreamy, savage, and fanatical. The only difference between Butcher's Hellas and the British Liberal–imperial package of his time was the complementary dose of Hebraism that inoculated the Victorians against 'late' despair and decline—a comfort the Greeks were never able to know.[88] 'All is laughter...' and 'All else is fearfulness...' are standard

---

[87] Butcher (1893: 170—'All is laughter' is his rendering of the first line of AP 10.124, cited in a footnote—and pp. 172–3; post-classical world-weariness replacing 'the same stately and reserved pathos which is depicted on Attic tombstones' (pp. 174–5)).

[88] Butcher (1893: 33–6, 40–1, 44–6); and cf. p. 254, on colonial regimes of knowledge; cf. usefully Montserrat (1998a), on Orientalizing typologies and cliché in the mass-cultural packaging of mummy portraits in the same period.

homiletic pieties on the spiritually reassuring insignificance of the earthly self; the ultimate sources of the former are Job 30.19 ('dust and dust') and Ecclesiastes 7.6 ('For as the crackling of thorns under a pot, so is the laughter of the fool: this also is vanity'), but edging Rome into the picture freights it with additional narrative drama as a miniaturist encapsulation of *The Last Days of Pompeii*, the paradigmatic fable of pagan self-indulgence punished by a vengeful Nature.

The chapter added for Butcher's 1893 edition ramps up the colonial subtext: Meleager's half-breed ethnicity cuts him off from the racial wellspring of classical good form ('antique simplicity') and plunges him into the heady atmosphere of the souk. All of this is straight out of *Select Epigrams*, as we have seen, and its author is explicitly hailed as the Anthology's translator of record.[89] More particularly, 'The Dawn of Romanticism' sets out to endorse Mackail's new road map of an Anthology predicated on the love of family and countryside: 'In these, the fairest lyrics of expiring antiquity, there is a touch of intenser feeling in the appreciation of nature than can be discovered in any previous period of Greek literature ... A romantic touch now glorifies the common things of the home.'[90]

A decade on, Britain's imperial legate in Egypt was heaping praise on Mackail's Greek selection and English translation and bidding for his own small slice of epigrammatic glory. Mackail's was the text, and the scheme of organization into chapters ('Love', 'Dedication', and the rest)—even the individual titles assigned by Mackail to his chosen poems were largely taken over wholesale:

As to the difficulty of translation, I cannot do better than quote from a letter of Mr Mackail's. 'What I think one always feels', Mr Mackail wrote to me, 'about translations from the Greek at the present day, is the extraordinary difficulty of retaining what (for want of a better word) may be called the dignity of the

---

[89] Butcher (1893: 307–8); Mackail-worship: p. 305. A tellingly close parallel in the construction of the liminal Greek 'gone native' in nineteenth-century popular art-critical rhetoric is anatomized by Montserrat (1998a), on the binary taxonomy of mummy-portraits as public attractions; see particularly his analysis at pp. 163, 165, and 169 of how this stream of commentary constructs the borderline-Greek ancient body of 'Eastern' portrait-types as the exotic site of uncomfortable dualities (desire/disgust, gay/straight; cf. for our purposes Hellenism/Hebraism, Uranian/Pandemic); and cf. p. 162, on how 'Western' versus 'Eastern' desires are rhetorically mapped onto 'Western' versus 'Eastern' bodies. On how these scopic regimes and taxonomies are structured by the ideology of colonialism, Montserrat (1998: 171–2) is merely suggestive; Mirzoeff (1999: 129–61) is for my money unsurpassed as a vivid introduction to the issues, and older work by Marcel Mauss (1935) on *les techniques du corps* remains invaluable on the use and regulation of the body as a culture-bound phenomenon.

[90] Butcher (1893: 305, 311).

original, which is as marked a quality of Greek writing as its inimitable ease. It always remained, even when used by weak hands for trivial purposes, the language of Homer and Simonides...'[91]

'Lord Cromer... would, I think, pardon me for quoting him as one in whom the Greek lucidity of intelligence is combined with the Roman faculty of constructive administration': Evelyn Baring, First Earl of Cromer, was the hard-headed colonial prefect of an Egypt that officially ran its own affairs but whose native rulers answered solely to him, with an army of occupation at his back to secure the Suez Canal as Britain's sea route to India.[92] This system of puppet government, the 'Veiled Protectorate', was Baring's own invention, and under it he ruled Egypt for a quarter of a century. In off-duty moments he tinkered up his versions from Mackail, publishing *Paraphrases and Translations from the Greek* while still in office (1903); he returned to England only in 1907 on the pretext of advancing years (to a £50,000 golden handshake and the Albert Medal).[93] His resignation was a major media event. A *Times* editorial of 12 April hailed 'a great administrative career that must rank among the highest in our history as a governing race... To Englishmen, and in a large measure to all the world, his name had become synonymous with modern Egypt.'

A monstrous Id to Mackail's progressive Ego, Baring talked modernization but was content to let big business and the old political elite permanently scar the nation state whose early development he oversaw, taking Liberal laissez-faire to callous extremes.[94] He self-consciously conceived his role

[91] Baring (1903: p. vi); he thanks him for constructive criticism at p. vii, and cf. praise of Mackail at Baring (1913: 327). That his selection was dependent on Mackail's was noted and not faulted by his reviewer for *CR*, James Gow (1906: 62), who praises the 'manly wit' of his best efforts.

[92] Mackail (1925: 12). Mackail was a sucker for aristocratic mystique; cf. (1926: 97).

[93] Intriguingly, Baring was not the first to translate from the Anthology into English while in Egypt: writing at Alexandria in July 1880, A. J. Butler (1922: p. xviii) enthused: 'After two thousand years to render a Greek song about the Nile while sailing down the same river, a song about Memphis or the Pyramids in sight of their ruins and remains... is perhaps a pleasure everyone will not appreciate.' Quite unlike Baring, the liberally inclined Butler finds many clues to the Greek spirit in modern Arab life: pp. xviii–xix. On the circumstances of Baring's retirement, see concisely Reisz (2010: 212). Nor was he to be the last; we may compare Montagu Butler, a globe-trotting old Harrovian (what else?), quoted in 1914 at Stray (1992: 6). The Egyptian connection is carried as far as 1931 by Robert Furness, on whom a little will be said in the Conclusion.

[94] Abul-Magd (2010: 695–709); Russell (2001: 51), with further bibliography, dissects his cynical restriction of educational opportunities to keep government service jobs in the hands of the collaborating elite—a policy about which he lied brazenly once back in civilian life: Baring (1913: 159–60). Two of the pieces collected in Baring (1913) are from that bastion of Liberalism, the *Edinburgh Review*.

as proconsular in the ancient style, writing repeatedly on imperial Rome as the appropriate historic template for colonial administration, and peppering his work-related conversation with classical mottoes; his engagement with epigram in Egypt asks to be seen within this pattern:

> I have endeavoured to avoid the use of ornate language...I beg any one who may do me the honour of glancing at this little volume to bear in mind that it is not the work of a scholar, or even of a very minor poet, but that of a Government official who, during the leisure moments of a somewhat busy life, has dabbled a little in Greek literature, and has occasionally amused himself by making versions—which is not the same thing as writing poetry.[95]

'Versions' excuses the occasional lapse into modern drag—which in turn takes the imperial mission as read. Cromer prefixes each with the Greek original, and the opening lines of his first selection (a 'Prelude', drawn from Posidippus) assert his credentials in glossing it—the glory of Greece has trickled down to a like spirit:

> Let the jar of Athens drip,
>   Drench the feast as though with dew,
> Here let each the wine-cup sip,
>   Boon companions, blithe and true...[96]

With Baring and his *aides de camp* established as true heirs of the classic Greek vintage, the very next poem adds sparkle to the expatriate symposium:

> Sweet in the sultry dog-days 'tis to drain
> Thy sparkling vintage, O divine champagne!...

—perhaps Bollinger, which a Royal Warrant of 1884 had made the official fizz of the British Empire; the pop of its cork carried administrators and entrepreneurs through many a sweltering 'dog-day' in the tropics.[97] The explanatory note expressly invokes as pretext the white man's burden.

---

[95] Baring (1903: pp. vi–vii), winding up the preface. Rome as template: Baring (1913: 17–23, 35, etc.); striking proconsular poses: D. M. Reid (1996: 2). Use of classical tags in his dealings with his staff: Marlowe (1970: 234). Suggestively, Reid (1996: 8) reads Cromer's keenness on epigram as part of his self-conception as a Roman proconsul *manqué*; this works very well within an Egyptian context in particular—see, on the Memnon epigrams, Bowie (1990: 61–6).

[96] Baring (1903: 5).

[97] Stocqueler (1857: 72) presents an amusing stereotype of the British rubber-planter in India coming to town at the end of the growing season and immediately sending out for the best champagne: for sure, didn't the fate of the next season depend entirely on the pop of the first bottle opened on the first day of manufacturing?'

Then as now, it is his allotted duty to impose order on the indolent and savage East:

I feel that some apology is necessary for this obvious anachronism. Mr Harold Perry points out to me that in what Macaulay (*Works*, vi. p. 614) calls Warren Hastings' 'pleasing imitation' of *Otium Divos rogat in patenti*, 'slow Mahrattas' and 'hardier Sikhs' are made to do service for Horace's warlike Thracians and 'quiver-graced' Medes. I do not mind erring in such illustrious company, and, have, therefore, ventured to make Asclepiades vaunt the merits of champagne.[98]

Nature had made the subject races inferior; by turns indolent ('slow') and fanatical, and constitutionally incapable of governing themselves, they needed to be ruled by the West for their own good, and the deaths of a few peasants from hunger were a small price to pay for the advance of free-market capitalism.[99] A few years down the line, Baring would take the Presidency of the Classical Association of England and Wales in a new direction by using it as a public platform to advocate for classical studies as the best preparation for the modern administrator in the East. This was a theme on which he had already held forth when lording it over the British School at Athens, the year after his return from Egypt: while a Roman capacity for administrative rigour was of course a necessary precondition, only the Hellenic *megalopsuchia* and *sōphrosunē* inculcated by a classical education (or in his own case won through assiduous self-application as an autodidact) could properly equip Britain's ephebes for the disinterested Guardianship of a world-spanning Empire. This Platonic sentiment was Baring's own take on a colonial classicism that was already institutionally embedded, and had been for half a century.[100]

[98] Baring (1903: 6).
[99] Baring is consistent in justifying his policy in these terms: see, e.g., Baring (1908: ii. 154–5, 566–9 (Egyptians incapable of governing themselves), 139 (Islam a religion of violent fanaticism against nonbelievers)). Baring is more nuanced but still singles out 'the withering hand of Islam' (1913: 347; cf. 286) as the main bar to progress in overseas colonies.
[100] Baring's CA presidential address ('Ancient and Modern Imperialism'), reported in *The Times* of 12 January 1910, p. 4, drew from Rome the historic lesson that success was all about securing the acquiescence of the 'subject races'; it was later worked up for publication as a book. In its early years the CA tended to recruit big guns of Empire as its Presidents when it could get them: Hooker (2003: 184) cites Cromer as an important example, and observes that the now traditional model of the discursive Presidential Address at the Conference began with him. Reisz (2010: 211–17) offers a fuller discussion. Address to BSA reported in *The Times* of 28 October 1908, p. 4. R. Symonds (1986: 186) concisely informs on how in 1854 the Committee on the Examination of Candidates for the Indian Civil Service, chaired by Gladstone and including among its members Jowett, made 'skill in Latin verses' a requisite of success; Vasunia (2013) shows to what uses these skills were put

Following Mackail, Cromer downplays the poems of AP 12; under his category of 'Beauty' he gives just one, a conspicuously de-sexed version from Rhianus. The poet's κοῦρε, 'boy', becomes 'dear heart'; ἡλίκος χάρις, the physical loveliness of an adolescent male at the peak of his desirability, dissolves into 'all the attributes of love'.[101] The love of man for woman looms large, as the book's first category (here as elsewhere following Mackail's scheme) and by far its largest; and the connection between heterosexual desire and Nature (a Nature conceived as Western and even specifically British) is further reinforced by a climactic shift in mode to pastoral miscellany. There are shades of old Merivale from the start in Baring's Latinized and Anglicized pet names (Pyrrha becomes 'Katie', Zenophila 'Zoe'), and the formal similarity is strikingly extended by the way the book ends—the twelve categories of epigrams canonized by Mackail are followed by bucolic selections from Theocritus and Moschus.[102] The former is not the gay-friendly poet beloved of Symonds and the Uranians, but a chronicler of heterosexual longing, ladylike pursuits, and (with Baring's own title for *Idyll* 3) 'Rustic Courtship':

> Ah! Lovely Amaryllis, thy sweet eye
> No longer gleams inviting from the cave.
> Am I ill-favoured? Thou hast seen me nigh,
> Or dost thou hate me—I that am thy slave?[103]

Epigram is now the voice of socially sanctioned romance in a bucolic never-never land. The yoking of the Anthology's love-poems to the organic rhythms of a Nature conceived as conservative scenography— hedge and grove, swains and wenches—will be a major theme of our next chapter. But this love at home carries a military aura; the section ends with epigrams titled 'Love's Masterdom' and 'Love the Conqueror'. Cromer then moves swiftly through a solitary example of dedicatory epigram ('To Aphrodite, by Lais'—attributed pointedly to a counter-Uranian Plato, p. 43) to an epitaphic section front-loaded with patriotic sacrifice against the Persian menace (pp. 47–51); the green mother country is the nurse of heroes who 'proudly cried, | "I spurn your Asian tribute"' and of those who yet await her call to arms (pp. 48–9).

---

on the ground. On Baring's interactions with British Egyptology and papyrology, see Fearn (2010: 160–1 (Grenfell and Hunt), 173–4 (Budge)), an eye-opening account.

[101] Baring (1903: 109).

[102] Katie and Zoe: Baring (1903: 8, 14). Baring's attitude to women's natural capacity and station in life was of a piece with his paternalistic contempt for his native Egyptians; he was a prominent campaigner against Suffrage.

[103] Baring (1903: 192).

One further precedent is set, and it is a significant one. Cromer declares frankly at the outset that he did not learn classical Greek at school: instead he learned to get by in the modern language while soldiering as a young man in Corfu and worked backwards from there, continuing his interest into later years, 'though after a very desultory fashion'. The versions he presents are very much those of an amateur—to leaf through them is to see misconstructions leap off the page—although that did not disqualify him being called on in later years to review in the area of epigram.[104] The genre's merit is now that it is the verse-form of the active man, with better things to do than bury his head in a book. Its impatience is muscular, vigorous, outdoorsy, and resolutely English-pastoral:

> As over Hesiod's page I pore,
>   Comes tripping in my lovely Katie.
> I fling the book upon the floor,
>   And cry, 'O Hesiod, how I hate ye!'[105]

...and off he trots, the reader presumes, to make more little soldiers for Empire. That same year, and in a similarly pastoral vein, the composer Edward Elgar published five unaccompanied part-songs for male choirs, setting translations by the usual suspects of the post-*Studies* era (Strettell, Garnett, Lang, Gosse, Hardinge) to four-part tenor and bass harmonies, again conjuring a romantic pastoral scene:

> After many a dusty mile,
> Wand'rer, linger here a while;
> Stretch your limbs in this long grass...
> It is Pan that counsels you.[106]

Pan will return, in our closing chapter.

7. LOST BOYS: 'OSWALD' AND RODD

My As.D.C. [aides de camp] have to listen politely when I quote verse to them—that is a privilege of a Commander-in-Chief; my

---

[104] Very desultory: Baring (1903: pp. v–vi n). Baring (1913: 226–36), reprinting a review of Grundy (1913) from the *Spectator*, 10 May 1913.

[105] Baring (1903: 8), 'Love and the Scholar', loosely rendering Marcus Argentarius.

[106] Elgar (1903: 8–14); lyrics by Symonds's deceitful friend, Edmund Gosse, from an anonymous original.

wife and daughters have quietly but firmly cured me of the habit as far as they are concerned.[107]

Before the facts of Nature we have to preserve a certain humility and reverence; nor rush in with our preconceived and obstinate assumptions.[108]

Was epigram now for hearties or aesthetes? Acclaimed on its first appearance as an instant classic, Mackail's patriotic selection was bedding in nicely as a school text and instilling Simonides in the national consciousness.[109] Nonetheless, the Uranian camp had not renounced its claim. In 1902, the year before *Paraphrases and Translations*, the eccentric social reformer and rights activist Edward Carpenter's *Iolaus: An Anthology of Friendship* had quoted extensively and approvingly from *Studies*—and even from the previously more or less obscure *Problem in Greek Ethics*. Carpenter had been one of the seven recipients of the copies distributed under strictest confidence by Symonds in his lifetime. His particular interest lay in Symonds's account of Plato, and more in the latter's capacity as a theorist of manly Eros than as an ersatz epigrammatist; nonetheless, *Iolaus* saw 'Plato' and Meleager trotted out one more time as a Uranian-epigrammatic double act, with Symonds cited as the authority of record on matters Anthological. Carpenter's work typically sailed under the same flag of convenience as had Symonds's explicitly subcultural treatises—notionally at least his books were printed for limited circulation for the usual 'medical men...judges and the like', and this was at times a legally as well as a rhetorically necessary fiction—but in fact they went into numerous editions and reprints, a sign of the still expanding popular book market.[110]

That same year, Frederick Rolfe—better known by his atavistic alias 'Baron Corvo'—had completed a lush and sweetly illustrated translation of all of Meleager. His starting-point had been a literal prose translation prepared by the painter Sholto Douglas, a cousin of Wilde's Bosie, who

---

[107] Wavell (1944: 16); his title picks up on Montaigne (p. 15), in turn picking up on Meleager and Philip. Although *Other Men's Flowers* is an anthology of English verse, it does include one version from Simonides, by our old friend Richard Garnett (p. 408).

[108] Carpenter (1912: 11).

[109] *Select Epigrams* as a set book in Edwardian public schools: Vandiver (2010: 43).

[110] I quote from Carpenter (1908: 10), which went into at least seven reprints; there were real occasions when publication was only legally permitted through a medical press with controlled circulation: Cook (2003a: 77). Cook is also good (pp. 76–7) on the consciously piquant effect created for the genre-aware reader by formulaic appeals to a medical Establishment that was itself simultaneously and loudly denying any interest in reading about such muck. On the popularity and several editions of *Iolaus*, known (he asserts) in the trade as 'The Buggers' Bible', see in passing but entertainingly d'Arch Smith (1978: p. xi).

had put up £500 of Oscar's bail money in 1895. The major section headings of Corvo's *Songs of Meleager* balanced 'Fair Women' and 'Love of Women' (AP 5) with 'Fair Children' and 'Love of Children' (AP 12); now him, now her, as love dictates. However, Douglas and Corvo fell out, the self-styled Baron went even madder, and the project stalled, seeing print only in a limited run some thirty-five years later.[111]

In the meantime, the Meleager of the Uranians was not idle. The year 1914 saw the appearance of a sanitized rearrangement of AP 12 by 'Sydney Oswald', a *nom de plume* of Sydney Lomer. A career Army officer (by then a captain in the Sherwood Foresters), Lomer was known for his handsome and compliant batman; in 1914, with his neat little red-bound volume fresh from the printers, he was off on seaside jaunts with the painter Philip Streatfield and a young, provocatively dragged-up Noel Coward. Soon he and the painter would be off together to active service, where Lomer quickly made a name for himself as a war poet, riffing patriotically on the Horatian theme that we now associate with his disillusioned contemporary, Wilfred Owen: *Dulce et decorum est.*[112] In the meantime his privately printed *The Greek Anthology: Epigrams from Anthologia Palatina XII* preached eloquently to the converted. Lomer arranged his AP 12 winnowings by author, starting with Strato, and bookending the collection with formally matched end-pieces of his own composition.

These paean-laments for Greek love in a cold climate both personalized and politicized the ancient content, and they bear quotation in full. The verse foreword (n.p.) channels Symonds's Uranian comradeship through Wilde's 'love that dare not speak its name', before concluding optimistically that the beauty of the anonymous beloved may work its magic and 'charm' the world from hatred to acceptance:

> To ——
> This little book to thee I dedicate,
> These ancient songs retold in halting rhyme,
> The Greeks who sang them in the ancient time
> When Eros reigned, guessed not the present fate

---

[111] Alphonse Symons's introduction to 'Corvo' (1937: pp. v–viii) is hugely informative; a renowned bibliographer, he had founded the First Edition Club (under which imprint *Songs of Meleager* at last saw the light of day) and wrote an astonishing biography of Corvo.

[112] The motoring holiday: Hoare (1995: 33–4). On Oswald the war poet, see Vandiver (2010: 397–8), discussing his 'Dulce et decorum est pro patria mori' (1915), a eulogy for three of his soldiers killed at Gallipoli, which was anthologized the next year in Galloway Kyle's first volume of his very popular *Soldier Poets* (on which see Vandiver 2010: 3–4). Vandiver hints at the possibility that Owen's 'Old Lie' is written in conscious counterpoint to it. Oswald's 'The Dead Soldier' and 'The Battlefield' were also contemporary favourites.

Of love sublime, mistrust and scornful hate.
O come my Sweet, and let us seek a clime
Where men be pure, and it shall be no crime
To call thee friend of friends and my soul's mate.

Here in this book I will not write thy name,
For in this sad world shall never know the might
Of our grand love; so let it hidden stay,
Graved in my heart; and though men deem it shame
That thou and I should love, the very sight
Of thy dear face shall charm their scorn away.

'Let us seek a clime' evokes both a long history of homophile love in Mediterranean exile and an imaginative escape into double consciousness through the literature of the classical past; now the Uranians have their own translation of the one text that can take them there.

The verse afterword (1914: 95) ups the political ante by appealing to London's homosexuals to wear their Platonic idealism on their sleeves. Lomer's subcultural readership is addressed as a collective that can hold to a party line; its members are urged to draw from the unexpurgated text a lesson in self-censorship of thought and deed, with a view to winning social acceptance. The re-coding of Uranism as heroic friendship consciously echoes Müller, through Symonds, through Carpenter—*Iolaus* had made a big deal of the Theban Band, as of Athens's revered Tyrannicides:

Readers, who in my written pages find
True love amid the dross, hold not aloof,
But join with me, and speak in love's behoof,
That not the strength of hate and scorn combined
Can friends divide; and thus with equal mind
We'll worship Beauty, heedless of reproof,
In purity and calm, until the woof
Of hate be changed to garb by love designed.

Yea all, who worship at the shrine of Youth,
I bid you live pure lives, so shall no breath
Of slander from a sinful world ascend
To dim the mirror of your love; in truth
E'en as the Theban Band strove on till death,
So be ye comrades faithful to the end.

Or had Lomer got the Theban Band straight out of Symonds's *Problem in Greek Ethics*, perhaps by way of a bootleg copy? Either way it will have appealed to his soldierly sensibility, and it is hard now not to read these lines without sensing the gathering storm. 'True love amid the dross', however, is very much more in the line of the censors' rhetoric of flowers amid the wilderness; and the parsing of homophile Eros as loving devotion to 'Beauty' is straight out of Mackail, whom indeed Lomer thanks at the outset in his preface (n.p.) for granting permission to use certain poem titles from *Select Epigrams*.

This is a striking revelation, for Mackail can hardly have been ignorant of what 'Oswald' was about. It would be easy to divide the *dramatis personae* of epigram's reception in this era into heroes and villains, but this would be to apply the Cultural Materialist model of subversion and containment far too simplistically, indeed melodramatically. As we will see again at the close of Chapter 6, authors could talk a very different game depending on their likely readership or audience on each occasion. Mackail himself had been involved in his younger days in a collective small-press poetry book, the anonymous *Love in Idleness*.[113] The legend of the titular flower is that Eros gave it the power to make a person fall in love at first sight, however romantically unlikely or socially unacceptable the object of that infatuation might be; poetry-lovers will have recognized it from its use as a plot device in Shakespeare's *A Midsummer Night's Dream* and *The Taming of the Shrew*.

The power of the mystic pansy gave *Love in Idleness* its pretext for some very strongly homoerotic material. Mackail's contribution was, one may guess, confined to the book's decorous selection of heteroerotic and dedicatory epigrams by Meleager and others (1883: 157–76) and/or miscellaneous Greek excerpts (pp. 177–82), but one would be hard pushed to prove it; the collective character of the enterprise implicates him in the whole of the text, the bulk of which is original verse. Here we meet yearning Uranism (as e.g. at pp. 62–4), an encomium of Hylas (pp. 59–61), and much more besides. Art is often the pretext, just as it had been for the author of *Studies*; Symonds had found rich seams of subtext in the art of the Renaissance as well as of the Greeks, and the contributors to *Love in Idleness* extend this pattern to take in the Pre-Raphaelites too. The following responds notionally to the *Birth of Venus* by Botticelli:

> The same, yet not the same: to this new birth
> The world has travailed for a thousand years,
> And a changed Venus dawns on a changed earth
> From out a sea of whose waves are salt with tears;
> And this our Love, since Greece lives not again,
> If she give every joy gives too all pain.

---

[113] Beeching, Mackail, and Nichols (1883). D'Arch Smith (1978), by way of whom I came to *Love in Idleness*, reports a sumptuous limited print run of 100 copies (n.p.).

This, to a drawing by Burne Jones:

> I saw how Love was leading on a way
> Beset with stones and thorns that grew thereby...

And this, to one by da Vinci in Venice:

> O virginal soft mouth of girl or boy,
> Mysterious lips which praise not or reprove,
> Will you not say one word to bring us joy?
> Will you not speak, and tell us, 'I am love'?...[114]

The rise of the small presses made it much easier than before to find homes for marginal perspectives such as these, and for naughty boys to publish and yet escape public censure. 'Sydney Oswald' did not only survive the war, retiring in 1919 as a lieutenant-colonel; his war poetry earned him an OBE. He had translated Strato's *Musa Puerilis* and got clean away with it. Some printers and translators chose to specialize in racy stuff for the self-identified connoisseur.

One such was the American poet, bibliophile, and soft pornographer Mitchell Starrett Buck. Working frequently in partnership with the small Philadelphia bookseller–printer Nicholas L. Brown, and always in limited print runs, Buck translated Lucian's *Dialogues of Courtesans*, the Latin *Priapeia*, and Pierre Louÿs's pseudo-classical *Songs of Bilitis*, a work that he also closely imitated in several kiss-and-tell compositions of his own, all written from a fictitious first-person female perspective: *Syrinx: Pastels of Hellas* (1914), reissued with added lesbianism in 1916 as *Ephemera: Greek Prose Poems*; *The Songs of Phryne* (1917); and the illustrated *Rose of Corinth* (1929). In between these exercises in soft-focus titillation came a book its author could boast was the first complete and unexpurgated translation of AP 5, *The Greek Anthology (Palatine MS): The Amatory Epigrams* (1916). The Loeb for AP 5 came out that same year, but Buck's claim had some truth to it regardless; Paton hid sex terms behind euphemism and fell back on the decent obscurity of Latin for the worst bits, a practice not without precedent in notionally complete translations of erotic epigram.[115]

---

[114] Beeching, Mackail, and Nichols (1883: 148, 149; cf. e.g. 41–2, 76–7; 32 and 81 (Vergil-tinged homoerotica); 85).

[115] e.g. at Paton (1916–18: i. 144–7) all but the first two lines of Rufinus AP 5.35 and most of AP 5.36 go straight into Latin, as does all of Gallus AP 5.49 at (1916–18: i. 152–3) and two poems by Dioscorides at (1916–18: i. 154–7). On Latin in Paton's version of AP 12, see now Lawton (2012: 189–91). The near-contemporary Loeb of Martial by Walter Ker (1919–20) ducked the problem by simply not translating 'obscene' poems, leaving them easy to find—one just flicks through looking for the blanks, and an older translation for the

In all other ways, Buck's working method left much to be desired; rather than looking directly to the Greek, he worked from an existing French translation, itself based on the obsolete text of Jacobs (1813–17).[116] Late in the day, he discovered that some of his French originals were a long way from the Greek and quickly threw together a stapled appendix of the worst offenders, freshly retranslated into English direct from the more current edition by Dübner (1864). It was no great labour to slip one of these into the back of every copy before it shipped; only 750 were bound, 'intended for private circulation only'.[117] His version was not really even all that frank, for all his editorial bragging. Paton dully renders βινεῖν (Cillactor AP 5.29.1, 'to fuck') as 'fruition', which at least is lexically in the ballpark; from his *soi-disant* unexpurgated rival we get merely 'A kiss'. Buck teased his readers for decades with the promise of a world of pagan sensuality, but never really delivered.[118]

Another translator that year was determined to stamp out any suggestion of the fires of youthful enthusiasm. He was James Rennell Rodd, who as a young man at Oxford had been devoted to Wilde; he had won the Newdigate two years after his friend and had dedicated a privately printed poetry book to him, *Songs in the South*, the very title of which whispers to the cognoscenti of 'Greek' sensuality in a permissive Mediterranean idyll. Oscar's personal advance copy survives in the British Library, with title-page dedication in the donor's own hand (the recipient naturally had the volume plushly rebound):

Al tuo martirio cupida e feroce, Questa turba cui parli accorrerà; Ti verranno a veder sulla tua croce Tutti, e nessuna ti campiagnerà. Rennell to Oscar July 1880.

Rodd takes these lines from *Postuma* (1877), a work by Olindo Guerrini (1845–1916), who purported to present the posthumously gathered *Canzoniere* of one 'Lorenzo Stecchetti'; the title of this particular poem (p. 73) is 'Ad un poeta'. Stecchetti is a fictional mask for Guerrini, and this poem in particular could have been written expressly for Wilde. It

---

Bohn series went into Italian instead; see briefly Livingstone and Nisbet (2010: 113) and again Lawton (2012: 191–3).

[116] Buck (1916: 11).

[117] Imprimatur from the facing title page; my battered copy is stamped by hand as number 12.

[118] Paton (1916–18: i. 142–3); Buck (1916: 27). The bold rhetoric of the latter's preface ('flowers of that clean sensual delight', p. 9) is amplified by a Dedication (p. 13) to 'Aphrodite Multiform', trailing unabashed sex romps; no such luck. Although not named, the Philadelphia printer of *The Amatory Epigrams* is surely Nicholas L. Brown, who in 1916 was just starting out; Buck thus helped set the tone for a catalogue that was soon to become known for its concentration on soft erotica under a classical pretext.

concludes with wry metapoetics—unadorned candour is all very well as an ideal, but this world is made for the artful liars:

> La verità non è di questo mondo,
> È un imbecille chi non sa mentir!

The year after the official publication of *Songs in the South* (1881), though, Oscar repaid his young friend's devotion with embarrassment. During his American tour he took it on himself to arrange an American republication of Rodd's volume under a peculiar new title, *Rose Leaf and Apple Leaf* (1882). Bound in a colourful, Beardsley-esque design that left no doubt that it was meant to be read as a Decadent text, the repackaged *Songs* were now introduced (pp. 11–28) by a substantial essay of Wilde's own composition. This is the infamous 'L'Envoi', an extensive manifesto for a criticism freed from morality. Wilde proclaimed his friend as a champion of these radical new Oxford Hellenes:

Among the many young men in England who are seeking along with me to continue and to perfect the English renaissance—*jeunes guerriers du drapeau romantique*, as Gautier would have called us—there is none whose love of art is more flawless and fervent, whose artistic sense is more subtle and more delicate—none, indeed, who is dearer to myself—than the young poet whose verses I have brought with me to America...

Now, this increased sense of the absolutely satisfying value of beautiful work-manship, this recognition of the primary importance of the sensuous element in art, this love of art for art's sake, is the point in which we of the younger school have made a departure from the teaching of Mr Ruskin,—a departure definite and different and decisive...it was he who by the magic of his presence and the music of his lips taught us at Oxford that enthusiasm for beauty which is the secret of Hellenism...[but] we are no longer with him; for the keystone to his aesthetic system is ethical, always. He would judge a picture by the amount of noble moral ideas it expresses...

—as opposed to the loveliness of its boys (with friends like these...). Was Rodd a homosexual poet? Opinions differ, but, whatever his own sexual identity and choices may have been, Wilde's 'L'Envoi' ran up the flag of Greek boy-love for the fans, hailing Rodd as a pastoral vignettist of a Theocritean bent.[119] Rodd reacted strongly against this unwelcome publicity. The *New York Tribune* of 25 November 1882 reports: 'Mr Rennell Rodd...has altered his faith. He now disdains any connection with the aesthetic school, and lets it be known that he had nothing to do

---

[119] We encountered the use of 'Theocritus' as an instantly recognizable alias for homosexual themes in Ch.3, p. 36.

with the amazing dress in which his verses occurred. He intends to publish a new volume.' That new volume was a long time coming. The very next year (1883), Rodd entered the diplomatic service. After a succession of minor embassy postings, he spent eight years under, of all people, Cromer in Egypt (1894–1902); from 1897 he was *Sir* Rennell Rodd, and he ended his days as a Baron. When he came to compile his own little epigram-book he was enjoying a long stint (1908–19) as Britain's Ambassador to Italy. His volume of translations into verse, arranged by the dates of their ancient authors, wears its ideological colours on its spine: *Love, Worship and Death* (1916/19) is Mackail-by-numbers:

These little flowers of song reveal, as does no other phase of that great [Greek] literature, a personal outlook on life, kindly, direct and simple, the tenderness which characterised family relations, the reciprocal affection of master and slave, sympathy with the domestic animals, a generous sense of the obligations of friendship, a gentle piety and a close intimacy with the nature gods … [in Greece] even still to-day, more than anywhere else in the world, the correlation of our life with nature may be felt instinctively … [120]

Like his former boss, Rodd has voyaged to Hellas and returned to tell the tale written in its coastline and mountains: in the organic social scene of conservative nostalgia lies humanity's timeless and immutable nature. (From behind 'the reciprocal affection of master and slave' peeks out Cromer the stern proconsul.) In Rodd we find another name-dropping friend of Mackail—many of his verses bear 'M' numbers so we may compare them with the master's prose versions—and a hard-working colonial executive who extols epigram's virtue as a salve in troubled times, just as had Cromer some years before. This time around, the poets of the Anthology comfort the Ambassador to a nation fighting a hard campaign against the Austrians in the North. [121]

Rodd has come a long way from his Oxford salad days, and is at pains to let us know it. For those who have a little of the back-story outlined above, his handling of Strato is piquant; he translates a single poem, 'The Kiss' (1919: 67), but makes its named addressee Moeris a 'she'. The name is masculine; the Greek-less reader is not to know that, but to the Greek scholar the travesty is piquant and may even invite a biographical

---

[120] Rodd (1919: pp. vii–viii); cf. p. vi, the sympathies that 'are eternal and essential in the heart of man'.

[121] Rodd (1919: pp. xi–xii (Mackail a personal friend and a virtuoso translator)), and cf. the Mackailian stylistic chronology at pp. xiii–xiv; p. vi ('consoling reflection'), p. xiv ('my sole and grateful distraction during a period of ceaseless work and intense anxiety in the tragic years, 1914–16').

reading (Rodd's youthful follies redemptively re-sexed?). Earlier, Meleager's sexual ambivalence has been veiled in euphemism: ἐν πυρὶ παίδων | βαλλόμενος ('tossed in the fire of boys') becomes 'youth's consuming fire'. Rodd's introductory gloss on the Syrian poet makes a point of toeing the Mackail line, delivering an ethnically suspect Ionian Greek seduced by the 'suggestive and exotic fascination' of the East and gone native—clearly a poet who needs to be governed for his own good.[122]

Rodd ends his Anthology with a poem we have met before, the anonymous AP 9.40, and in a version that is silently derivative of Wellesley's of 1849—he too, of course, had used it as a closing gambit:

The End of the Comedy

> Fortune and Hope, a long adieu!
>   My ship is safe in port.
> With me is nothing left to do,
>   Make other lives your sport.[123]

Where Wellesley had signed off with visible relief on a taxing international collaboration, Rodd's coda invites a rereading in terms of his separation from Wilde and what came after; having once skirted the reefs and shoals of youthful enthusiasm, he is now a pillar of the Establishment. *Rose Leaf and Apple Leaf* happened a busy lifetime ago; Oscar's unquiet ghost is exorcized.

Or is it?

The Anthology in Evolution

> [We must expect that] as in any other class of human being, there will be among these too, good and bad, high and low, worthy and unworthy—some perhaps exhibiting through their double temperament *a rare and beautiful flower of humanity, others a perverse and tangled ruin.*[124]

This is Carpenter again, writing in 1912; his socialist homoerotics turn the emergence of the homosexual into not merely a Kuhnian paradigm shift but quite literally a new phase in the biological progress of our

---

[122] Rodd (1919: 49); explaining Meleager after Mackail: p. xi.
[123] Rodd (1919: 82); in the expanded and rearranged edition of 1919 this coda is followed by an appendix on the women poets of (or mentioned in) the Anthology. Incidentally, Neaves ends with this same poem (1874: 210), in a particularly poor version; it too is derivative of Wellesley's.
[124] Carpenter (1912: 10–11) (emphasis added).

species. Social liberalization is firmly and explicitly on the agenda: the causes of homosexual liberation and democracy are one and the same. Symonds and Pater (and their precedessors Winckelmann and Goethe) are now explicitly hailed as culture heroes who laid the groundwork to a better future for everyone by 'reconstructing Greek life and ideals', a provocatively open-ended formulation.[125] Homosexuality as presented in *The Intermediate Sex* is an evolutionary adaptation: humanity's biologically inherited sex and gender categories are mutating under environmental pressure. Caught up as we are in the middle of this evolution, we cannot yet see why the change is occurring, but Darwinian logic dictates that this mutation *must* be for the good: if it were not advantageous to individual and/or species survival, it would not be happening. Writing not just for subculture but with the bold hope of changing the culture at large, Carpenter (the advocate of sandals for men) persistently preaches society's need to re-parse its relationship with the body; properly used, the body becomes an organic mechanism of escape into a brighter tomorrow. Carpenter's message did not fall on deaf ears; the Socialist movement in particular was receptive. In the aftermath of the Wilde trials, as literary culture suddenly got cold feet about masculine affection, he had carried the homophile standard practically alone and been isolated as an eccentric, but, as the twentieth century bedded in, his views earned a much more sympathetic and public hearing.[126]

Here we see Carpenter profess that there will be 'good' and 'bad' homosexuals because they are people just like anyone else—to borrow the title of a more recent assimilationist tract, 'virtually normal'. The distinction between 'high' and 'low' types echoes the Uranian–Pandemic dichotomy that underlay *Studies*, and that was dramatically enacted in the contrasting personae of Plato/Meleager and Strato; now, ten years on from *Iolaus*, he is also able to point readers towards a proper, nonclandestine publication of *Greek Ethics*, albeit in German.[127] Thus far, Carpenter's introductory remarks have not deployed any proprietary

[125] Uranian democracy: (Carpenter 1912: 70), expanding on Symonds's advocacy of Whitman. 'Reconstructing' (p. 103) is nicely ambiguous: forensic analysis, experiential re-enactment, or a bit of both?
[126] Dellamora (1990: 209) notes how the Wilde trials mark a sudden watershed after which it was no longer possible to praise romantic bonds between men and be part of mainstream culture. Livesey (2007: 112–13) is excellent; for the big picture of Carpenter's career and reception in the 1910s–20s, see Weeks (1990: 76, 135), the classic modern study.
[127] And compare Carpenter's take (1912: 83–4) on the manly chivalry of the Greeks, which is lifted straight out of Symonds's *Greek Ethics*. In a long and eloquent disquisition he rhetorically opposes it to the coarse sensuality and 'gutter' morality of public-school homosexual experimentation, by clear implication Pandemic as it is all about the satisfaction of sexual appetite with no concern for character (pp. 85–93); a recognizably Uranian

homophile terminology, but he will go on to use 'Uranian' and 'Urning' interchangeably, taking advantage of their near-homophony to blur together German sexological pseudoscience and Oxford Classical idealism.[128]

Why not 'homosexual'? The notional justification is philological prissiness, and in this Carpenter echoes Symonds; he rejects the sexological descriptor as 'a bastard word', part Greek, part Latin, appropriately enough in a learned footnote.[129] Symonds had been reluctant to buy into the new terminology, at least in print and in the posterity-courting *Memoirs*—although it occurs frequently in the later correspondence. To avoid it was not yet to commit blatant archaism; 'homosexual' did not become the preferred term overnight, and its eventual predominance was by no means foreordained.[130] Etymological pedantry was, then, a convenient pretext. Right then writers could choose between two entirely separate discourses to explain same-sex desire: an idealizing Platonism damaged by the fall of Wilde, but perhaps not irredeemably discredited; and a sexology that pathologized homosexual desire, and that itself was seen as socially beyond the pale. Freud's work on human sexuality was not translated into English until 1910, and even then was very slow to gain exposure and credence; if they wanted to win same-sex desire a public hearing, writers such as Carpenter had to work with what they had already got.[131]

Carpenter's solution is bold. He takes the very different perspectives of early Symonds (the Oxford Uranian) and late Symonds (the enthusiast of evolutionary theory) and declares them reconciled. The 'higher' Greek love is spiritual, just as before, but the explanatory framework is not Platonic idealism but Darwinian science. Plato, Theocritus, and the Anthology lurk between the lines of this slanted narrative of human evolution:

Though these gradations of human type [in terms of object of sexual desire] *have always, and among all people, been more or less known and recognised*, yet their frequency today, or even the concentration of attention upon them, may be the

---

'ideal attachment' (p. 91) is the baby thrown out with the bathwater when schoolmasters crack down on this. Touting the German translation: p. 65.

[128] Carpenter (1912: 13).

[129] Carpenter (1912: 38); on Symonds's etymological distaste for 'homosexual', see Schultz (2004: 782 n. 216).

[130] Bristow (1995: ii. 132). In a letter of 1891 to Dakyns, Symonds remarks on how Ulrichs has abandoned his own contribution to the terminology, 'Urning'—'How odd!' (Symonds 1967–9: iii. 548).

[131] Cook (2003a: 77); Livesey (2007: 110) is excellent on Carpenter as a creative re-forger of dominant tropes for dissident ends.

indication of some important change actually in progress. We do NOT know, in fact, what possible evolutions are to come, or what new forms, of permanent place and value, are being already slowly differentiated from the surrounding mass of humanity... at the present time certain new types of human kind may be emerging, which will have an important part to play in the societies of the future...[132]

Presaging the superpowered mutants of Marvel's *X-Men* universe, the homosexual is a new kind of human—an adaptive mutation to meet the changing circumstances and needs of the species; even if we cannot yet see exactly where they fit in, the logic and necessity of their emergence will become clearer in the long run. Symonds's Greek forerunners demonstrate the truth of homosexuality's gradual emergence as a fact of human biology, and the historic failure of their particular form of Uranism to achieve long-term traction correlates this: their evolutionary moment had not yet fully arrived. Carpenter will shortly explain that his Urnings have 'a special work to do as reconcilers and interpreters of the two sexes to one another'—the better kind (Symonds's Uranians) are part of the pro-feminist project to which he is explicitly committed ('It is probable that the superior Urnings will become, in affairs of the heart, to a large extent the teachers of future society'). There is also scope for female Urnings, a major departure from the drift of *Studies* and *Greek Ethics*: indeed, Carpenter wraps up his argument by quoting in full a letter from a female American correspondent.[133] Far away on the hilltop of Colonus, Karl Otfried Müller is spinning in his grave; we have come a long way from the Dorian hyper-masculinity that his keen reader Symonds parsed into 'fire and valour'.[134]

Scratch the surface, though, and the package is classic Symonds. Although Pandemic eros is rhetorically played down in Carpenter's apologetics—he much prefers to focus on Uranian 'comradeship', eulogized in a register that owes much to Whitman—the phrasing ('high and low, worthy and unworthy') makes it crystal-clear to the classically-*cum*-subculturally aware reader that Symonds's distinction is still very much in play. What is more, it is revealed early on that even the 'lower' Urnings, are not '*as a rule*... so sensual as the average normal man'

---

[132] Carpenter (1912: 11).

[133] Carpenter (1912: 167). On Symonds's fudging of ancient lesbianism, see briefly Orrells (2011a: 180–1).

[134] Orrells (2011a: 141) comments usefully on how great a departure this is from the old Winckelmann–Pater template of pederasty glossed as art appreciation. On German constructions of butch Dorianism, DeJean (1989b) is illuminating.

(1912: 13);[135] we must recall here Symonds's Strato, who for all his faults was always one up on 'the brothel and the grave' haunted by Paulus Silentarius and his fellow poets of AP 5.

Recalled, too, is the backlash rhetoric of necessary pruning. As we saw earlier in this chapter, the expurgators of the post-*Studies* Anthology had inherited a rich figurative language for the characterization and justification of literary censorship regardless of the origin and genre of the text under consideration—a language that, through a uniquely convenient overlap with the ancient flower-language of epigram connoisseurship, immediately fell into place as the self-evidently 'right' mode of curating its text. By common consent, to expurgate was to be a good gardener: turfing out the plants that were unproductive, ugly, or poisonous revealed the work as it should always have been, wholesome and orderly. When applied to the Anthology, that tangled and overgrown semi-Classic, this commonplace took on new clarity and colour. There *had* been an original design, hand-picked by Meleager, and it was demonstrably nothing like what met the eye today . . . but those original blooms were still there somewhere, buried (as in the *Nation*'s review quoted earlier) amid the briars and rubble of the garden's Late Antique and Byzantine decay.

In an audacious twist, Carpenter subverts the rhetoric of the post-*Studies* backlash for a homophile agenda that builds directly on Symonds's own.[136] Homosexuality itself is now the garden in which weeds and flowers jostle for space, because all human life can be found there—some of its members 'exhibiting . . . a rare and beautiful flower of humanity, others a perverse and tangled ruin'.

No wonder Sir Richard Livingstone had his work cut out for him that year:

It is the same with Hellenism [as with Christianity]. To understand its genius, we must look, not at the men in whom some faint tincture of it was mixed with alien and indifferent things, but at those in whom it was most fully realized, at its 'saints'; and in these, must fix our eyes, not on their weakness but on their

---

[135] Carpenter (1912: 13).

[136] Carpenter is a master of this kind of transgressive appropriation; cf. (1912: 12), mapping the emergence of homosexual identity onto the cherished early history of the very Church that condemns it: 'It seems almost a law of Nature that new and important movements should be misunderstood and vilified—even though afterwards they may be widely approved or admitted to honour . . . the early Christians, in the eyes of Romans, were chiefly known as the perpetrators of obscure rites and crimes in the darkness of the catacombs.' Long before Kuhn, Carpenter was talking a good game on paradigm shifts, while also carving himself a nice niche as a prophet neglected in his own lifetime.

strength; not on what they were but on what they were tending to be, in the expressive Greek phrase, ὃ ἐδύναντο εἶναι, their meaning.[137]

A decade on, Livingstone gives 'the ordinary educated reader'—and grammar-school boys who have never felt the benefit of Greek rigour[138]—an Anthology carefully tailored to Rodd's themes of Love, Worship, and Death. Theocritus is paired with the epigrammatists under his aspect as a virile nature-poet who anticipates—who else?— Wordsworth; next, epigram's lapidary origins set up the reader of *The Pageant of Greece* for a tripartite division into 'Love Poems', Epitaphs, and Dedications. Rounded off with a few 'Humorous Epigrams' to leaven the lesson, these, of course, are Rodd's trifecta of Love, Worship, and Death.[139] Taken together, Cromer and Rodd had set a trend for reading the Anthology as simultaneously bucolic and epitaphic. In a chapter entitled 'The Last Greek Peasant' from her 1911 book *Outdoor Life in Greek and Roman Poets*, the Contessa Evelyn Martinengo-Cesaresco pairs Theocritus and the epigrammatists as joint chroniclers of wholesome country life in Greece's extreme old age, when the spectre of death hung even over Arcadia: 'The *Anthology* is a true book of Pity and Death.'[140]

Of Livingstone's 'Love Poems', all of which are, of course, heterosexual, one is by Plato—a Plato presented with never a hint that the attribution is known to be spurious—and four by Meleager; of these latter, three are in Rodd's translation, and one in Garnett's. Livingstone looks back to a prelapsarian Anthology, before Symonds set it on the wrong track. His preferred translators are Merivale, Cory (of that perennial favourite, 'They told me, Heraclitus'), and the generation of *Anthologia Polyglotta*—with a little space set aside for Rodd's old boss Cromer; he casts Planudes as no shabby censor, but the capstone of the Anthology tradition.[141]

[137] Livingstone (1912: 19–20). On his idealist-rationalist brand of classical studies, see Turner (1981: 35–6) and in more detail R. Symonds (2005).

[138] Livingstone 1923a: p. v.

[139] Theocritus: Livingstone (1923a: 367–94); as poet of nature: p. 369 (and a morally serious one—prototype of Milton, 370); as hetero-eroticist: pp. 370–80. Livingstone's four categories: pp. 386–7, 387–90, 391–2, 393–4; emphasis on epitaphs and dedications as the original and definitive categories: p. 384. Shout-outs to Rodd, Garnett, and Grundy: p. viii; keeping the comic relief for near the end is a trait picked up from Neaves's *Greek Anthology* of a half-century before (1874: 179–96).

[140] Martinengo-Cesaresco (1911: 59–78, quoted at p. 66); her description of the Anthology as a 'precious collection' of 'gems' (p. 64) recalls the terminology of Symonds.

[141] Planudes: Livingstone (1923a: 385); Goldwin Smith, Wellesley et al., plus Cromer: p. 393.

Livingstone wants to wind back the clock, but he is working against an association between epigram and sexual dissidence that by now (no matter how illusory its basis) has taken definite shape in the literary sphere. In death, Symonds had become the patron of a new movement of homosexual poets, dubbed in retrospect the 'Uranians' in recognition of his formative influence; pamphlet by small-press pamphlet, the sexual underground was having its say, in fey verse and sometimes explicit manifestos as well.[142] Even Mackail's negative rhetoric of Eastern contagion would soon enough turn out to be capable of being ironically repurposed as a chat-up line, as when T. E. Lawrence met Robert Graves at Oxford in 1920:

Lawrence's eyes immediately held me . . . [They] flickered up and down as though making an inventory of clothes and limbs . . . He went on to speak of Meleager, and the other Syrian–Greek contributors to the Greek Anthology, whose poems he intended to publish in English translation. I joined in the conversation and mentioned a morning-star image which Meleager once used in rather an un-Greek way. Lawrence turned to me. 'You must be Graves the poet? I read a book of yours in Egypt in 1917, and thought it pretty good.'[143]

We take our leave of the Edwardians with the era's greatest if most eccentric detective. In G. K. Chesterton's short story 'The Strange Crime of John Boulnois' (1913), the worldly-wise Father Brown acquits the titular character of having committed a flamboyant murder: 'Please do not think I mean that Boulnois could not be so wicked . . . [but] If Boulnois killed anyone he'd do it quietly and heavily, as he'd do any other doubtful thing—take a tenth glass of port, or read a loose Greek poet.'[144] With the *fin de siècle* blurring from living memory into cultural myth, the ghost of Wilde casts over the wickeder parts of the Anthology a

---

[142] Mader (2005) supplies rich detail and analysis; the basic dynamic is already identified at D'Arch Smith (1978: 11–12). Besides Carpenter, we may point to Edward Percy Warren, the wealthy Bostonian Oxonophile who endowed a distinctly Socratic Praelectorship at Corpus Christi College with the proviso that the appointee should be on call at any hour for the philosophic counselling of his young charges, and should never teach women. As 'A. L. Raile', he followed up his several slim volumes of verse (1903–13) with a substantial prose manifesto, *The Defence of Uranian Love*, begun after the war and eventually published privately in three volumes in 1928. R. Symonds (1995) has the full story.

[143] Graves (2000: 28); Phil Burton introduced me to this wonderful episode. The allusion is to Meleager AP 12.114, ironically one of the misplaced heterosexual poems. In emphasizing the erotic power of Lawrence's gaze, Graves's account of the meeting alludes (probably consciously) to a favourite topos of Meleager's pederastic verse, as at, e.g., AP 12.92, 101, 106, 109. Lawrence never finished his translation of Meleager, but slipped 'the immoral Greek–Syrian' into *Seven Pillars of Wisdom* under the pretext of a mission to Um Keis, the ancient Gadara.

[144] Quoted from the *Penguin Complete Father Brown* (Harmondsworth, 1981), 300–1.

pallid aura of over-sweet lubricity. Its forbidden poems have become *fleurs du mal*—poison blooms, to dally with which is to court addiction. We may remember here that it was always the *little* pamphlets and magazines of the Decadent set that attracted the most indignant moral clamour; Strato at least now implicitly joins their number as a miniaturist of evil.[145] Nor is the strange evolution of the Anthology by any means over.

---

[145] Fletcher (1979a).

6

Reed and Girdle: The Anthology in the 1920s

> Here in the orchard's breezy nook
> I Hermes stand;
> And from the cross-roads overlook
> The plashing strand.
> Here to the wayfarer forspent
> Repose I bring;
> A plashing spring.[1]

The lure of the Greek *Anthology* continues to claim its victims.[2]

We pick up the Anthology's story at the start of the 1920s, when a reviewer could look out on the contemporary poetic scene and see the numbers of 'lovers, and readers, of the *Anthology*...increasing...Fresh efforts at translation are constantly being made.'[3] The inspiration for this epigrammatic renaissance was none other than the *Select Epigrams* of Mackail. First published in 1890, this evergreen mini-anthology had gone from strength to strength through two further editions, most recently in 1911. Time and use had lent even more authority to the critical commonplace that Mackail's garland of 500 flowers was the definitive selection for the modern age—all the best poems, and none but the best. Walter Leaf, whose *Little Poems from the Greek* (1922) supplies this chapter's opening quotation, declares that the large majority of his translations were done from Mackail's text during the war years; since then he has had the chance to read the entire Anthology in Paton's

---

[1] Leaf (1922: 29), translating Anyte.

[2] Harrower (1924: 174).

[3] 'J. G. L.' (1922: 42). The market was certainly ripe for more versions; A. J. Butler's old *Amaranth and Asphodel*, obscure in its 1881 first imprint (most of which was lost in a warehouse fire), was reissued in an expanded form in 1922 and quickly found an American publisher as well (Houghton Mifflin, 1923).

five Loeb volumes, 'but the additions hence made are not many in proportion; Mr Mackail's selection is so admirably done as to leave but few gleanings of equal value to those he has chosen.'

Leaf is far from alone; from the 1890s through to the early 1920s, it is standard practice for translators to affirm the authority of *Select Epigrams* in their prefatory matter, their choice of epigrams, and even their systems of citation and indexing. Even with the Loeb in place, offering a complete text and all-but-complete translation, 'M' (for Mackail) continues to overwrite 'AP' as the definitive source for the Anthology in the modern world.[4] As with Mayor in British Juvenal studies, invoking the sacred name of Mackail affirmed the pedigreed naturalization of the Anthology as a fixture of the 'native' literary tradition through which the national character found clear and definitive public expression.[5]

Select Epigrams owed much of its continuing cultural centrality to its diversity of formats: its English translation and Greek text, minus any scholarly apparatus, had been spun off as two separate and much smaller books. Durably and attractively bound in green boards with a decorative spine (or for an extra shilling in leather), these slim octavo volumes were priced and sized for the common reader's pocket. Thus *Select Epigrams* remained the constant recourse of scholars and hobbyists alike, as it had been since its first appearance all those years ago; it was a work without which not even the most modest classical library could be called complete, but, if we believe a word of what the translators were saying, its most important work was done out of doors.[6]

It was just as I completed the usual scholastic training of our Universities, that Mr Mackail's lesser volume of Selections came into my hands; and for some years it was my custom in leisure times to carry these little poems about with me, not in my pockets only, but in my head and heart...[7]

The handy little volume containing the Greek text of Mr Mackail's *Select Epigrams from the Greek Anthology* was [during the war] my constant companion; and a large proportion of the work of love was done in the 'daily bread' trains which conveyed me between my country home and my office in the City.[8]

---

[4] Leaf (1922: 7); cf., in practically the same words, Benson (1922: p. viii); for further examples, see briefly Livingstone and Nisbet (2010: 155–6).

[5] Nisbet (2012a: 492–4).

[6] 'J. G. L.' (1922: 43), Agar (1923); overnight, a standard work for libraries: Tucker (1892).

[7] Lothian (1920: n.p.).

[8] Leaf (1922: 7), rhetorically echoing Cromer on epigram-tinkering as 'a relief from more pressing occupations and anxieties'.

Right from the start of the war, Simonides's patriotic epitaphs for the fallen at Thermopylae and Plataea were the principal models for British poetry of civic and individual commemoration for the glorious dead. As Elizabeth Vandiver has shown, this was not just any Simonides—it was the Simonides of *Select Epigrams*. A Simonidean tradition was already flourishing in the public poetry that had celebrated Britain's nineteenth-century Crimean and Boer war dead, fed by influential versions in the Reviews, but the fairly literal ubiquity of Mackail's pocketable volumes made his favourite epitaph-poet into a definitive point of reference for militarists and cynics alike, whether at the Front or back home.[9]

It is against this heavy reliance on the patriotic–commemorative aspect of *Select Epigrams* between 1914 and 1919 that we must place the choices made by translators in the decade that followed, for what we find is a clear shift of emphasis away from the epitaphic nexus of civic pride and private grief. The post-war Anthology of the published translations refocuses instead around the topics of untroubled peace; specifically, it is refashioned as a very particular kind of bucolic scene.

Mackail himself had gauged the Cephalan Anthology for Nature-sentiment and found plenty of it to confound the sceptics; cautioning his readers not to read backward into the poets' characteristic Greek restraint the fervid gush associated with Romanticism's wilder landscapes, he instead singled out epigram's intense evocations of the pastoral impulse:

The music of Pan, at which the rustle of the oak-wood ceases and the waterfall from the cliff is silent and the faint bleating of the sheep dies away, is the expression in an ancient language of the spirit of Nature, fixed and embodied by the enchanting touch of art.[10]

His post-war acolytes take this vivid and quasi-mystical endorsement as their point of departure, latching onto Mackail's own mini-Anthology as the boon companion of the outdoorsman. In 1920s, Alexander Lothian writes evocatively of dipping into his little Greek text (the 'lesser volume') while tramping in the high places of his native Scotland. For Leaf, to slip the smaller Mackail into his pocket is to carry a piece of the English countryside into town with him ('Here to the wayfarer forspent | Repose I bring'), or even—albeit from peacetime retrospect—into the

---

[9] Vandiver (2010: 334–63) is the indispensable discussion here, and cf. pp. 384–5. Influence of Thermopylae epitaph: pp. 335–46; Plataea epitaph: pp. 346–52. Kipling echoing Simonides: pp. 15–20. Thermopylae as de-historicized motif of self-sacrificial courage: pp. 170–8.

[10] Mackail (1890: 52–7), quoted at p. 55, where naturally Wordsworth is invoked as arbiter.

trenches of the new warfare, fought with machines and practised on an industrial scale.

Leaf's evocation of the *Select Epigrams* in an urban context sets itself off nicely against an older meditation by his erstwhile collaborator on Homer, Andrew Lang, an old epigram hand (we first encountered his 1888 collection *Grass of Parnassus* in Chapter 4):

> Last night, within the stifling train,
>   Lit by the foggy lamp o'erhead,
>   Sick of the sad Last News, I read
> Verse of that joyous child of Spain,
> Who dwelt when Rome was waxing cold,
>   Within the Roman din and smoke...
>
> So from thy city prison broke,
>   Martial, thy wail for life misspent,
> And so, through London's noise and smoke
>   My heart replies to the lament...

The smog-bound and weary London commuter of Lang's 'Martial in Town', sickened by the modern industrial metropolis, turns from his late-edition newspaper (the apocalyptically tinged 'sad Last News') and finds meagre consolation in contemplating an ancient Rome that was already much the same: 'stifling...foggy...waxing cold...thy city prison'.[11] The 'Town' of the title does double duty for both, and the 'Roman din and smoke' of the second stanza (six lines into the poem) is mirrored six lines from the end by 'London's noise and smoke'. For the career Hellenist peeking warily over the disciplinary fence at life in the *Urbs*, the thud of the steam-hammer and the hubbub of the insanitary crowd resound through ancient and modern urban dystopias alike. Lang's sentimentally penitent Martial 'wail[s] for' a 'life misspent' as a wholesaler of epigrammatic smut in the Big Smoke, and pines for the long-abandoned landscape of his provincial youth. At the poem's heart, a deceptively tweaked version of Martial 5.20 pre-empts and classically patterns Lang's own sentimental longing for a bucolic childhood, which lingers in his memory as a watery green idyll—the poem's final line sighs for 'The streams that circle Fernilea!'—but to which distance and duty preclude his return.[12] A generation later, and turning from Latin

---

[11] I cite the text of his third edition (the most commonly available): Lang (1892: 21–2).

[12] Lang is not an honest broker: Martial in 5.20 seeks summer shade not 'by field and well' in the company of family, but strolling at ease with a wealthy patron in the shade of the capital city's grand colonnades, enjoying the civilized amenities that make life worthwhile: *campus, porticus, umbra, Virgo, thermae* (5.20.9). He yearns to exchange, not town for country, but business (the duties of a *cliens*, 5.20.5–7) for subsidized leisure. Lang translates

epigram to Greek, his colleague finds a warmer solace: the Anthology is a pocketable slice of England's green heaven.

This is not the only direction in which the Anthology could have gone in the post-war era, had Simonides not been fully committed elsewhere. Already in the 1910s, the modernist poetic movement that titled itself Imagism found in the Anthology a rich resource of classical concision and directness that its members counterpoised to (what they chose to see or represent as) the stiffness of late Victorianism and the gush of Romanticism. Writing to Harriet Monroe to recommend she publish three poems by H.D. in her newly founded magazine *Poetry*, Ezra Pound bragged:

This is the sort of American stuff that I can show here in Paris without its being ridiculed. Objective—no slither; direct—no excessive use of adjectives; no metaphors that won't permit examination. It's straight talk, straight as the Greek![13]

Pound had been playing around with the Anthology since 1916, the year of Paton's first volume, although with characteristic perversity his preferred source had been an obscure sixteenth-century translation into Latin; but he only ever translated ten poems from it. It was more important to him as a figure of speech, stalking horse, and loose totemic inspiration than as a detailed model for imitation; all kinds of local traditions of folk verse turned out to be like Pound's idea of Greek epigram if one looked at them with Pound's eye.[14]

Ezra Pound aside, the Anthology of the Imagists was *Select Epigrams*. It is not going too far to say that Mackail's lapidary selection became a key text of the movement, perhaps the key text. The rhetoric of his introduction, which packaged the Anthology as the unmediated transcription ('straight talk') of humble and healthy Greek life, was swallowed wholesale—as it still is, in some of the criticism of the movement—and his spare, un-prettified prose versions of the Greek

---

campus (5.20.9) as 'field'—accurate up to a point, but deliberately misleading in this context; taken with the other terms in Martial's list it must mean the Campus Martius.

[13] Pound (1971: 11), a line much quoted in the scholarly literature, as e.g. at the highly recommended Ayers (2004: 2).

[14] On H.D. and the epigrams of the Anthology, see now Tarlo (2012), delivering a pithy anecdote (p. 242) in which we find H.D. waxing ecstatic over Meleager in his post-Mackailian persona as a *plein-air* lover of country lasses. Riikonen (2008) gives an excellent account of Pound's dealings with the Anthology; on the specific points raised here, see pp. 183–5, 192. Did you know that Virginia Woolf gave Paton's first Loeb a rave review in *TLS*? Riikonen did (p. 184). He also points out (pp. 191–2) that a later translator from the Anthology, Dudley Fitts (1938, and cf. 1941, 1957), founds his work on Pound's principles. Fitts reappears in our Conclusion.

inspired the Imagists to feats of adjective-stripped laconism.[15] But as a rule these poets are not translators; Imagism as a movement fizzled out in 1917, the contributors to its anthologistic manifestos going their separate ways; and when in the 1920s we see a book with 'Greek Anthology' in its title, it invariably pursues neither the battling Simonides of Mackail nor the stripped-down Simonideanism of the modernist poetic movement he helped inspire. Instead it delivers a pastoral Anthology, a lovers' plesaunce—and implicitly a rehabilitation of the non-Simonidean Anthology from association with Wilde and his circle.

1. ET IN ARCADIA...

Here mantled is the country
    In pale-green rich array,
And showing all the beauty
    Of fair and fruitful spray.

Here, too, beneath the cypress,
    With sombre shadow thick,
The mother hen is calling
    Her callow brood, the chick.

The siskin shrill is chirping...

To farmstead Nymphs and shaggy Pan
Theodotus the husbandman...

Say, little Faun, does this thy pipe unbidden
    Make secret music in thy listening ear?
Say, dost thou bend to trace the sweet notes hidden,—
    Unearthly sounds, which mortals may not hear?[16]

Leaf's commitment to a chronological scheme precludes any kind of structurally embedded meta-narrative, but unsurprisingly his selection is biased towards *memento mori* and pastoral; Theocritus does well here (Leaf 1922: 40–2). The pairing of the Anthology with a straightened-out and strictly bucolic Theocritus had of course been a significant structuring

---

[15] Imagist laconism: Ayers (2004: 4, 7); 'This tiny volume... is itself almost a model for the Imagist anthologies' (p. 3). Simon (2010), useful for bibliography, takes Mackail's family tableaux at face value, and then some. *Select Epigrams* as H.D.'s 'bible': Gregory (1997: 169), an important treatment.

[16] Woodward (1924: 34), translating very loosely Agathias AP 5.292; Leaf (1922: 29); Benson (1922: 28).

gambit in Baring's *Paraphrases and Translations* (1903), and, the year
after *Little Poems*, Livingstone (1923a) was to preach the exact same
sermon to the Greekless masses.

Sympathy with animal life and 'the nature gods', already a major
ideological plank of the ancient Greek hetero-domestic package asserted
by Rodd's counter-Uranian palinode, *Love, Worship and Death*, merges
in the Anthology of the 1920s into the curious Edwardian cult of Pan.[17]
Leaf is no exception, favouring also Dionysus in the jollified rustic form
of a 'Bacchus' accompanied by Satyrs and 'saucy wench[es]' straight out
of a chocolate-box vision of Merrie England.[18] The Pan of contemporary
literary culture may flaunt a fey aesthetic, but his fertile heterosexuality is
never in question:

> The songs that I have gathered here
> With all their radiance crystal-clear,
> Their silvery gleam, their ruby glow,
> Were sung by singers long ago...
>
> So, though I veil in formal dress
> Their inner ancient loveliness,
> Yet they, in duller robe attired,
> May be more soberly desired.[19]

The language of connoisseurship here—epigrams as precious gems—
derives ultimately from Symonds (Appendix), but is placed in the service
of an anti-Decadent translation agenda: *sober* and lawfully procreative
desire replaces the intoxication and enthusiasm of the Wildean *fin de
siècle*. Clearing his throat to sound *The Reed of Pan* (1922), the book's
author—A. C. Benson, the closeted Master of Magdalene College, Cambridge—bows low to Cory's decorously grief-stricken 'Heraclitus' as a
yardstick of modern epigram-work, just as would Livingstone the
following year. The newly assigned titles of his poems advertise an
assortment massively front-loaded with pastoral scenes of dalliance
between lads and lasses—and bookended at its close with cautionary
thoughts of the grave that is our common end:[20]

---

[17] I quote Rodd at (1919: p. vii).
[18] Leaf (1922: 23, 29, 37, 41 (twice), 42, 54, 57, 69, 74 (Pan); 39, 46, 55, etc. (Bacchus); 34 (wench)).
[19] Benson (1922: p. xvii).
[20] Benson (1922: p. vii). A verse coda, responding to the verse preface quoted above, rams home the *lacrimae rerum*: 'And yet a song is as a screen | For saddest thoughts that brood unseen' (p. 238). The brother of the novelist E. F. Benson, he also wrote speculative fiction.

Subtlety is not on the menu. Limned by Dryad-haunted brooks, this extended country picnic (largely out of Mackail but with extra helpings of nymphs and shepherds) borders the eternal public-school scene of chastened youth in poem XVII, 'Playing Fields':

> I guard the pleasant fields of play
> Which nestle by the mountain-side.
> The boys upon my altar set
> Fresh hyacinth blooms, and garlands twined
> Of marjoram and violet,
> And what beseems the virgin mind.[22]

Naturally this is disingenuous; in Nicias's original, four lines to Benson's eight, the 'Playing Fields' are a city gymnasium, and the voiced inscription adorns a statue of Hermes, its traditional guardian. 'And what beseems the virgin mind' responds to nothing in the Greek, which indeed singles out the gymnasium as a site of erotic longing (ἐρατοῦ γυμνασίου). Nicias has his boys offer up the same plants, but twines his garlands of

---

[21] Benson (1922: p. ix), and one could go on and on (Echo, The Pursuit, Al Fresco, A Pastoral, etc, etc): p. xvi.

[22] Benson (1922: 17), translating poem 188 of the Planudean Appendix; Mackail as fount of all good things p. viii.

violets alone—violets that match their donors' first fresh bloom of beauty (θαλεροὺς ... ἴων στεφάνους). By interlacing his wreaths with sharp-smelling marjoram, the herb from which is woven the garland of Hymenaeus in Catullus's wedding-song (61.7), Benson avoids too close an echo of 'iostephanous' Symonds.[23]

Then again, we have been warned: too exact a correspondence to the Greek, or even too scholarly a knowledge of the language, can actually count against the fidelity of the modern version to the sentiment that underlay the original. Common-sense paraphrase, says Benson, has the merit of rendering what the ancient author had surely *meant* to say, rather than getting bogged down in the detail of what he or occasionally she had in fact said.[24] Although still greater liberties are taken elsewhere—much could be written on, for instance, a version of Strato 12.234, which turns the proud καλός into a 'disdainful maid', and there are recurring tips of the hat to Rodd's revisionist *Love, Worship and Death*—the pastoral scene repays our continued attention.[25] Benson's *Anthology* follows that of Rodd in more than merely its displays of counter-Uranian duplicity: his timeless Shire idyll is the seedbed of Empire, and the playing-fields of home prepare the public-school sporting hero for his career as an Augustan *uir pietate grauis* who will calm the insurgent mob just as Vergil's Neptune calmed the raging seas off Carthage.[26]

England's wheeling seasons—summer (ll. 12–24), autumn, and winter (ll. 25–33)—cue up a springtime meant for sailing forth ll. (34–41); and reverent recollection of home's green nature-gods sustains the venture, whether the far-off destination be the *ur*-pastoral scene of Theocritus'

---

[23] It is mildly satisfying to note *en passant* a connection between the two: Benson was the nephew of that wise old owl, and constant friend to Symonds, Henry Sidgwick.

[24] Benson (1922: p. viii). The following year, Livingstone's popular anthology of Greek literature in translation, *The Pageant of Greece* (1923a), puts Rodd's own translations of the Heliodore poems front and centre when it represents epigram as the genre of love (pp. 386–7), death (pp. 387–90), and worship (pp. 390–2); a spoonful of 'humorous' epigrams helps the medicine go down (pp. 393–4).

[25] Strato: Benson (1922: 176), also bowdlerizing the original's scatological second line—dung becomes 'dust': p. 159. (Strato is also implicitly a heterosexual love-poet at, e.g., p. 185.) The καλός is the sexually desirable It boy of classical Athenian pederastic discourse; each youth's acme of desirability was fleeting, with the consequence that vases that carry a 'καλός-name' can often be dated very precisely. Following in Rodd's footsteps: p. 159 (the Moeris poem, again from a Stratonian original and following Rodd's re-sexing of Moeris as 'she'), p. 175 (Hesiod and Pyrrha).

[26] The tag is assigned by Benson to his poem CCXXIII; it is adapted closely from V. *Aen.* 1.153, where it is part of perhaps the poem's most famous simile; its use as a commonplace in English encomia might repay further study.

Sicily or the 'Afric sands' on which Rome first contended for overseas Empire:

> Calm is the sea, a purple plain;
> No tempest frets the whitening wave;
> Landward no more the billows strain,
>
> .   .   .   .   .
>
> Now, trusty mariners, arise,
> Renew the old adventurous quest!
> Whether to Afric sands ye ply,
> Or rock-fringed bays of Sicily.[27]

A tireless essayist and short-story writer as well as a poet, and widely read in his own time, Benson is today remembered for composing the lyrics to Edward VII's coronation ode, *Land of Hope and Glory* (1902)—the latter to a tune by a fellow epigram-tinkerer, Edward Elgar. 'Wider still and wider shall thy bounds be set': ode and epigram alike call on the British to renew their fathers' spirit of enterprise and sacrifice for the glory of global Empire, the 'old adventurous quest'.

2. HATING DAN CUPID: AN ANTHOLOGY FOR ROUTLEDGE

The Girdle of Aphrodite: The Complete Love Poems of the Palatine Anthology was worked up by Frederic Adam Wright (1923) for publication in the Broadway Translations. Well presented and accessibly priced at 7*s.* 6*d.* per volume, this uniform imprint of foreign literary classics in English translation brought critical and commercial success to its publisher, George Routledge & Sons; its customers got a lot for their money, and the series was regarded as having real literary significance. Wright was one of Routledge's stable of regular authors: in the years 1923–4 alone he turned out three classical Broadway Translations and revised a fourth, as well as writing a handbook on *Feminism in Greek Literature from Homer to Aristotle* (1923), which blamed the fall of Greece on its men's inability to relate to their wives.[28]

---

[27] Benson (1922: 34); cf. p. 36 (the green, green fields of home), p. 37 ('I trust in God, and not in man').

[28] Knapp (1926) reviews the imprint as a whole. A prolific writer on Greek and Latin classics, including Late Antique material, Wright went on to prepare the new edition (1946) of Lemprière's Classical Dictionary, again for Routledge.

The *Girdle* wears its agenda on its title page: for the readers of the Broadway version, 'Complete Love Poems' will mean AP 5. No other form of love exists, or not any more, heavens be praised. The translator pauses briefly to reassure us:

Book XII, Strato's 'Musa Puerilis', deals with *an aberration from which the modern world happily has escaped: some of Meleager's most graceful poems have been included by mistake*, and give the book a certain value.[29]

Whatever the ancient error may have been (and the avoidance of specificity is by now a familiar trope), it is now extinct; in any case, Meleager can never himself have committed it, and any of his poems that we may find in AP 12 are assuredly the victims of a filing error. Wright's insistence on a blameless Meleager, whose pure emotions place him at the pinnacle of his genre, will repay our further attention. The other feature of note in Wright's title is his particular emphasis on the *Palatine* Anthology, a point that his introduction amplifies, following a pattern first set by Symonds. The Planudean redaction is 'a very blurred and imperfect copy of the original' by Cephalas:

He selects those epigrams which we could willingly forgo, he omits those which seem to us the most desirable. Often he fails to do what he ought to have done, by gross carelessness in transcription; while he does what he ought not to have done, by rash alterations and expurgations of the text.[30]

In this self-consciously modern formulation, predicated on a view of poetry as authentic emotion striving to be free—which we are told is what makes Meleager the greatest love-poet ever to live, feel, and write—censorship is always what someone else is doing. Planudes 'allowed his moral preoccupations to interfere with his critical judgment'; happily, however, twentieth-century literary criticism is an objective science, fearless and frank.[31] Which makes it all the odder when we start hitting poems by Rufinus—Wright's translations can fall far short of what the common reader has come to expect from a Broadway Translation:

> *Membrum trium vidi; nam monstravere puellae,*
> *spectarem ut clunes posteriusque decus.*
> *Prima quidem nituit sulcis signata rotundis...*

[29] Wright (1923: p. xii) (emphasis added).
[30] Wright (1923: p. viii).
[31] Wright (1923: p. xv (great poetry = true emotion, the rest is mere *vers de société*)), and cf. p. xix, on Meleager's unrivalled authenticity and directness of feeling; p. viii (moral judgement).

In all, a round half-dozen versions render the ruder bits of Rufinus, Gallus, Dioscorides, and Marcus Argentarius in Latin's decent obscurity; Meleager, of course, is too tender a poet to need this service.[32]

Wright was an author in a hurry, and his versions from AP 5 hang together awkwardly; the reader of the *Girdle* is bounced from Fies!, Tweres, Thees, and Enows to obtrusive slang that jarred even at the time:

> I hate Dan Cupid; he is cruel found
> And ever aims his shafts my heart to wound...
>
> Her father, he was Battling Fred,
> Her mother Slap-dash Moll...
>
> I had a fair neighbour, Miss Nelly her name...

If a girl is kissable, she is 'Kate'.[33] Miss Nelly might have been at home in the early miscellanies of Bland and Merivale; likewise Meleager's Helio-dora, in two versions whose titles recast her with borderline racism as an 'Irish Rose', Helydore, the 'Dark-Eyed Colleen': 'She's a fairy who puts | E'en the fairies to shame.'[34] In one of his versions from Rufinus, too, Wright throws a cute glance at his ultimate forebears—the 'French Privateer' enjoys one last inglorious pleasure cruise around the harbour, in the guise of two ladies of the night:

> The Frenchy and the Privateer
> Each night you'll see upon the pier,
> Or else patrolling in the town
> Gulping poor silly youngsters down.
> Beware these pirate-craft, my friends;
> Such skirmishes have bitter ends.[35]

Because it is superior hack-work, hastily thrown together to hitch a ride on a hot trend, *The Girdle of Aphrodite* bears careful consideration—not for the small literary merit of its translations, but precisely because it is careless in papering over the contradictions that have come to underlie epigram-work in English since the 1870s. The confused, neither-fish-nor-fowl literary tone of the *Girdle* is echoed in the volume's mixed

---

[32] Wright (1923: 35 (quoted here), 36, 49, 54–5, 116). In his companion volume, he presumes some schoolboy Latin in his reader: 1924: 102, cf. 106, 110.

[33] Wright (1923: 10 (butchering Alcaeus AP 5.10)), and cf. pp. 93, 'Dan Bacchus'; 71; 75; and cf., e.g., p. 243, 'pretty Nelly'. There are many other examples just as bad if not worse: e.g., pp. 184, 186. Kiss me, Kate: pp. 245, 271. Reviewing the *Girdle*, Harrower (1924: 174) lives up to his name: 'the theory of modern equivalents is pushed absurdly, indeed offensively, far in things like "Slap-dash Moll", "At Mrs Brown's to tea"'—the latter is at Wright (1923: 269) and deserves what it gets.

[34] Wright (1923: 149 (quoted), 158).

[35] Wright (1923: 44).

messages on Meleager: a figure of the East, or sometimes of the West; of true passion, or then again of passing fancy. The confusion sets in right from the verse preface, facing the title page. From the dedication of the volume to a male addressee cast as a fellow love-poet (Harold Cox), this heady concoction sets the physical charms of Wright's own Roman-elegiac mistress ('My Delia') above all the sensual inducements of the exotic Orient. The *Girdle* is a Tibullan Anthology—an anti-Rubáiyát:

> O pluck no more the rose
> In Persian gardens gay,
> Nor scarlet lotus choose
> By lakes of far Cathay.
> My Delia's lips more fragrant are
> Than all the flowers of Alcazar.
>
> O seek no more the land
> Where ancient jewels gleam,
> Green jade of Samarkand,
> Red rubies from Pereem.
> My Delia's eyes more brightly shine
> Than any stone in Indian mine.[36]

So much for Meleager, the star of the book, and so much indeed for Greek epigram's flowers and gems. It is in Wright's self-contradictory bricolage of found materials—Syrian Meleager gushes 'sensuous perfume', and Strato displays 'cynical effrontery'—that his value lies for the purpose of our enquiry: he cannot take the time or care to keep his story straight.[37]

A follow-up volume the next year—*The Poets of the Greek Anthology*—excavates deeper into the faultline. This descriptive handbook presents potted biographies for a selection of authors, with sample translations. Naturally Meleager gets the biggest slice of the pie, more than all the 'Greeks of the Empire' put together. On these latter, Wright peddles an uneasy blend of Mackail (the Imperial era as a temporary dip in quality before the Byzantine resurgence) and Symonds (the same era as the irreversible fall of a literature coarsened and enfeebled by Roman intrusions)—or then again perhaps it was the fault of the immoral East. Since his grasp of Late Antique history derives primarily from Charles

---

[36] Meleager 'too much the victim of his own wayward and perverse fancies' to be a true lover, because too easily swayed by physical beauty (Wright 1923: p. xxx); sensuous perfume, and more in the same vein: p. xxix. Pluck no more: p. ii.

[37] 'The cynical effrontery of Strato' (Wright 1924: p. x), closely echoing Symonds's 'the cynicism of his impudicity'.

Kingsley's *Hypatia*, dressed up with a little Gibbon for form's sake, this lack of clarity may be excused.[38]

Kingsley's unsubtle paean to racially virtuous Anglo-Saxon virility (proto-Protestant, to be redeemed for Christ at some convenient later date) over and above the effete clerisy of the Catholic South additionally informs, and informs on, Wright's expanded rhetoric of censorship. The kind of expurgation that comes easily to religious extremists will by definition be unnatural, because their fear and hatred of women is as much against nature as was that of their historic prototypes, the boy-lovers of ancient Greece: 'The taste that could endure Strato and Rufinus at their worst refused to [Nossis] even a very modest licence, and the asceticism of the Early Christians proved as unfavourable to women as had the perversions of classical Greece.'[39]

This is Wright the pro-feminist talking, in the context of his substantial chapter on the Women Poets of the Anthology, but it is also a wishful open letter to the past asking it to get its priorities straight, in every applicable sense. Unlike the Late Antique book-burners, Wright's modernity *cannot* 'endure' Strato and Rufinus—if it must translate them at all, it puts them into Latin or assiduously misconstrues. The boy-lovers of Strato's closural AP 12.194 are now simply 'lovers', natural denizens of AP 5; conversely, however, and only a page away, his unnameable vice (and the repeated title of *Musa Puerilis* keeps it decorously deniable) is what brought the Empire down: never again.[40]

Meleager is a special case. The *Girdle* had declared him the greatest of the Anthology's poets, and there is no back-sliding here—'no one comes near to equalling him' as a chronicler of romantic love, nor does his acumen as a critic find any rival in the field of literary appreciation before the coming of the modern scientific age.[41] He is a schoolbook Catullus without the messy inconvenience of the Latin poet's adultery. According to the *Girdle*, however, and (as we saw) following the Mackail line, some

---

[38] 'Coarse' Greco-Roman epigrams: Wright (1924: 192), an evaluative term straight out of Symonds, and cf. p. 178 on the senility of Rome's subject races, 'either cringing or coarse'. Strato's faults are Asian: pp. 194–5. The fourth and fifth centuries reduced to Hypatia's story, into which the life and poetry of Palladas is speculatively embedded—someone has been reading too much Kingsley: pp. 215–17, and cf. pp. 96–7 on early monastic asceticism. Wright is shaky on literary history generally; Sappho is believed in without irony as an epigrammatist: pp. 79–80.

[39] Wright (1924: 96–7).

[40] AP 12.258: Wright (1924: 194). Lots of pronoun-dodging at, e.g., pp. 195–6; dodgy versions, pp. 197–8 (translating AP 12.248 and 12.177). 'The compiler of the *Musa Puerilis* is one of the least estimable of poets and ... reveals only too plainly the anarchy of morals which preceded the anarchy of government in the third century AD.' (p. 193).

[41] Wright (1924: 148).

few poems of his had ended up in AP 12 through a clerical mistake—Meleager was purely a poet of heterosexual amours; a year later, the story is tellingly different. The Meleager of 1924 *did* have feelings for young men—but only in his own callow youth:

> But while he was still a student at Gadara...Meleager had probably written the first draft of 'The Poems of Youthful Love', celebrating the beauty of his university comrades. A second volume published at Tyre and consisting of poems addressed to his various mistresses, notably to Zenophila and Heliodora, records the love adventures of his manhood.[42]

Meleager's boy-poems thus have nothing to do with AP 12, Strato, or the *Musa Puerilis*—three names that Wright is careful to keep at a remove from this discussion of his prize poet—and instead belong to a period of juvenilia; to hold them, a new and separate poetry book is accordingly run up from whole cloth, title and all.[43] In floating the idea of two separate Meleagrian collections Wright is at least following an old model—Bland had spun a similar tale, a century and more before—but he expands upon it in six pages of pure fantasy, derived from the sure knowledge that the work is the man, and that true poetry transcribes lived experience and feeling. In this extended fictional biography, poems celebrating boy-love can only have been written *by* a boy, coming up to Varsity in a Gadara glossed as a minor ancient Oxford, and swept up in the heady excitement of Freshers' Week:

> he celebrates those *passionate attachments*, so common among the Greeks, where alone they could find expression for the *youthful* desire for romance, which their customs diverted from its natural channel, the love of young man and maid. Of his own and his comrades' *friendships* Meleager sings...In his emotions Meleager shows all the extravagance of youth; each new comrade is the most graceful, the most charming, *the most delightful friend* that ever poet possessed...But these fiery attachments soon burned themselves out...

> These young students were always coming and going from Gadara, and each fresh arrival and departure gives the opportunity for a poem.[44]

Oxonian Uranism, retrojected here into first-century Roman Syria, is the distraction of nature from its sure purpose—and only ever a passing phase. What is more, these boyish crushes went no further than chaste

---

[42] Wright (1924: 121).

[43] Indeed, elsewhere Wright (1924: 193) returns to the *Girdle*'s theme that Meleagrian content slips into AP 12 by 'a somewhat ludicrous mistake', once again amplifying Mackail on how easily the diminutives of feminine names may be mistaken for boys.

[44] Wright (1924: 128–9, 131) (emphases added). Gadara as Oxford (and Tyre as Liverpool!): pp. 126, 134.

admiration: Meleager loved his fellow-pupils as he had loved his mother, a love expressed in both cases through innocent nature rambles in a gender- and age-appropriate landscape.[45]

Meleager the fulfilled man, conversely, is his true and natural self, a distracted lover of many 'mistresses' in a bustling port city (one sees him in a floppy shirt, dashing off sonnets). As a pure poet, recording his Eastern amours with Greek precision—and we may detect in Wright's fabulation a late and garbled echo of that old Arnoldian chestnut, Hellenism versus Hebraism—he uniquely embodies the heterosexualized Uranian ideal:

> though he is passionate and even sensuous, *he is never coarse* . . . A comparison with any other of the love poems of the 'Anthology', with his compatriot Philodemus, *with Rufinus,* or with Agathias, will reveal the essential delicacy of Meleager's art. He is free alike from brutality, pedantry, and triviality—the three besetting sins of our collection; and considering the mechanical [!] perfections of the Palatine MS., it is safe to regard with the greatest suspicion the few poems there attributed to him which fall below his usual level.[46]

The Meleager of Symonds's *Studies* (where Rufinus was of course his abject Other) has grown up and grown into the proper object of his affections. Now he learns, falteringly, to see beyond the surface 'beauty' of the city's courtesans[47]—the term is one worth reclaiming from the Boyish Muse for the cause of 'natural' passions—and meets the love of his life, Heliodora:

> To Heliodora, Meleager remained faithful to the end. 'Open my heart', he cries, 'and you will find my Heliodora's name' . . . We have the history of their passion in some twenty short poems, as various as love itself. Sometimes the poet is oppressed by the fervency of his desires, but more often he is as blithe and merry as an Irish song writer.[48]

Ah, Helydore, that dark-eyed Colleen. But then she dies; heartbroken, her lover leaves Tyre's 'riotous splendour' for the seclusion of Cos, where, 'surrounded by a quiet folk whose main trade was the tending of their vines, and the making of those soft, transparent fabrics that women loved

---

[45] Meleager and his mother: Wright (1924: 124), a vividly imagined scene. 'His comrades now took his mother's place and with them he climbed the hills', etc—whereas his nature-outings with his mother had stuck to Gadara's flowery meadows: p. 126.

[46] Wright (1924: 135–6) (emphases added). Catalogue of mistresses: p. 136. Eastern fervour from his mother's side ('quite probably . . . a Jewess'), Greek rigour from his father, p. 124—the latter a no-nonsense businessman whose fortune Meleager spends like water: p. 123. Gadara of the Decapolis as a Helleno-Hebraic melting pot: pp. 124–5.

[47] Wright (1924: 135).   [48] Wright (1924: 138).

to wear, the poet gradually recovered from the grief of Heliodora's death, and wrote for her tomb the record of his sorrow'.[49]

3. THE ANTHOLOGY AND THE NEW CRITICS

'The methods of [Meleager's literary] criticism are not ours, for they are imaginative rather than scientific.' Coming as it does after twenty-plus pages of hallucinatory cod-biographical gush, this remark may seem a bit rich, but important issues are at stake for Wright. Meleager is a poet for posterity and for the British literary tradition in particular—a role model for manly Elizabethans.[50]

That Shakespeare's generation should be invoked is no surprise, for they are the declared autochthonous domain of Eng. Lit., a discipline that in the 1920s was beginning to find its feet and arguing hard to differentiate itself both from its unspectacular early decades and from its senior neighbours in the literary Humanities. Tying those academic Others to a deprecated 'literary appreciation', and marking out the junior discipline's science-friendliness, was a plank of New Criticism's rhetoric of corporate self-fashioning. Marketing and policing literary criticism as a 'science' made it sound so much more *manly* (and more forward looking, more egalitarian) than what was happening over the fence in Modern Languages, or in Classics—proper redbrick stuff for the modern university that was going places in the world. So too did the New Criticism's reconception of the literary text as a complex network of 'tensions' requiring 'resolution'; lit. crit. took on the brisk tone of phys. ed.[51]

The New Critics aspired to democratize and demystify the business of literary criticism so that non-elite participants could try their hand: their tone was technocratic, and they emphatically rejected the biographical method of interpretation as the tool of a bygone social order.

---

[49] Wright (1924: 139–40).

[50] Wright (1924: 148 (method), 137 (Elizabethan Meleager)).

[51] Sinfield (1994a: 34), provocatively but with some justice: 'If it was soppy, girls' stuff, you couldn't plausibly offer it as an academic discipline. This, I suggest, was the abiding factor in the maneuverings of literary criticism in the first half of this century.' The classic polemic account is Eagleton (1983: 30–53). Eagleton is particularly interesting (and suggests additional reading) on Eng. Lit.'s self-fashioning against the methods of classical philology—a dispassionate 'science' by its own account, but one tainted in the post-war era by its German pedigree: pp. 29–30. Distaste for Hunnish philology surely underlies Lothian's remark (1920: n.p) that 'I profess myself no very scientific student of the Anthology'.

Nonetheless, beneath the surface, their muscle-flexing literary modernism was firmly rooted in an idealizing Romantic vision of the poet's
corpus as *Bindungsroman* that derived ultimately from Goethe, and in
traditional Victorian conservatism. As we have seen from the outset,
there was nothing new in rhetorically playing off Wordsworth, the Tory
farmer's favourite, against the rabble-rousing Cockneys of English verse.
The Leavisite emphasis, though, was very particularly and narrowly on
Wordsworth as a *masculine* poet—a distinction that rather stretches the
text, but that was of a piece with Eng. Lit.'s straightening-out of Shakespeare's sonnets and its savaging of Symonds's Muse, the posthumously
outed Walt Whitman. Again we might identify this hunger for an
authentic masculinity, rooted organically in blood and soil, as deeply
nostalgic, with all the propensity for ideological closure that that term
entails.[52]

Though worn lightly, Wright's New Critical sympathies are unmistakable. In taking the poems to be psychological documents, a close reading
of which will reveal the inner life of the man and thereby teach a broader
societal lesson, he follows I. A. Richards, the Cambridge mentor of
Empson and Leavis and a fellow-traveller in the reclamation of Poesy
for a psychologically well-adjusted 'natural' masculinity. Alan Sinfield
pithily chronicles the efforts of the Leavisites to draw a line under English
poetry's sissy Romantics, Keats and Shelley, whose aficionados were
warned off in no uncertain terms: the 'emotional discipline' and 'matur-
ing reflection' of Wordsworth were now the order of the day. Mackail, of
course, had got there first, and found the Anthology's Wordsworth in the
lapidary austerity of Simonides. Now Wright re-glosses Syrian Meleager
as the 'right' kind of Easterner, uniquely moulded by his Hebraic mater-
nal and Hellenic paternal influences to grow beyond 'the extravagance
of youth' into the first chronicler of the full range of healthy modern
feeling.[53]

The modern critic informed by the new psychology can probe beneath
the surface incident to diagnose the passions of the author's soul; and the
manly critic at once recognizes in his author a kindred spirit. Writing a
few years earlier, Paton had already cut to the heart of Meleager's

---

[52] As observed by Sinfield (1994a: 34–5), and cf. p. 11: 'Quite a lot [of textual meaning]
may be sacrificed to dispel the specter of bardic queerness.' Eagleton (1983: 36–7 and 47) is
suggestive on New Criticism as a project of nostalgic recuperation. Symonds's own style, of
course, fell from favour in the early years of the century as too florid, too frothy, too *gay*,
although no one was going to come out and say as much: Booth (2000: 154–5).

[53] Wright (1924: 129, 135, 137 (in the Heliodora cycle 'we hear at last the accents of real
love')).

pederastic verse and found no emotional reality behind the formal tropes. 'Coarseness' looks back to the old distinction between Uranian and Pandemic, to be sure—and we recall that Strato and Rufinus are 'coarse' in Wright as well—but with a new sense of the text as a map to the psychic hinterland of its author:[54]

'It is noteworthy that among the most beautiful of [Meleager's] poems [in AP 12] are just some of those I have mentioned addressed to girls and included by mistake here. In the rest, if I err not, we miss the distinguishing note of passion, which his other love-poems so often have. The elements of his imagery of love are all here—Love and His mother, burning arrows and stormy seas—but somewhat devoid of soul and at times disfigured by a coarseness foreign to his gentle spirit. These [homosexual] attachments were in his case *rather a matter of fashion than of passion*.'[55]

Passion, or fashion? The critic of virile discrimination (and erstwhile translator of AP 5) simply knows; he can tell them apart at a glance, and anyone who cannot is suspect, on the page and between the sheets ('if I err not, we miss' invites assent and will not take 'no' for an answer). The love of man for maid is the real thing, and expresses the healthily developed psyche without which literary greatness is inconceivable. Anything else is either sick, or a mere rote exercise that panders to a passing cultural trend and packs in no genuine feeling. Either way, it is not Literature. As a chronicler of natural desire, Meleager is timeless and sublime; when he panders to the passing craze that is Greek boy-love, he stumbles into the Pandemic gutter. Indeed, these soulless moments may unmask a literary fake; any 'coarseness' in the transmitted text of Meleager may now be rejected not so much for its immorality as for its lack of fit with his psychological profile.[56]

Viewed in this light, the New Criticism of which Wright is a part is not merely an extended gesture of disciplinary re-foundation. In some of its byways at least, and decidedly so in *Poets of the Greek Anthology*, it is a counter-Uranian project.

---

[54] Leavis (1936: 216); Sinfield (1994a: 34) goes to town on this. On Richards, see with more than typical acerbity Eagleton (1983: 44–6). 'Coarse' Strato and Rufinus in Wright (1924: 192).

[55] Paton (1916–18.4: 281) (emphasis added).

[56] Wright (1924: 136), 'it is safe to regard . . .'—safe because scientifically sound. Cf. usefully Sinfield (1994a: 10–11), on the relentless heterosexism of twentieth-century Shakespeare studies, with good examples of the rhetorical wiggling employed to excuse and disallow the Bard's homoerotic content. This is not the last we will hear of 'fashion' by any means.

4. 'NEARER PAN'S GREAT SOUL': WALLACE RICE'S *PAGAN PICTURES* (1927)

PAN PIPES

Pan is sounding His pipes. Be still,
Thou rustling wood on the craggy hill,
    Thou bleating flock and bellowing herd,
    Melodious thrush and mating bird,
And pleasantly murmuring spring and rill!

        .   .   .   .   .

From many a reedy length the thrill
Hath caught the heart of the vale, until
    Yonder the dancing dryads ungird
    And here, every limb by the melody stirred,
The satyrs tread, as with many a trill
    Pan is sounding His pipes.

                (*Plato the Younger*) [*sic*, and naturally
                                with no further details]

This facing title page inaugurates *Pagan Pictures*, a free (very free) translation from the Anthology and the lyric poets, 'Variously Augmented by
Modern Instances'—which is to say original compositions by the author's
own hand, in his best approximation of 'the ancient Grecian manner of
thought'.[57] The thought in question is decidedly Puckish. At the twee 'trill'
of Pan's pipes on May-Day, Nature becomes fecund; the woodland goddesses slip off their robes, and the priapic, demi-human satyrs creep
forwards, '*every* limb...stirred' (saucy!), for an implicit and immediate
sequel of earthy and unashamed rutting *sur l'herbe*.[58] Pseudo-Plato has
fallen far from his Uranian peak under Symonds and Wilde. The message
is obtrusively programmatic, and, in case we miss the point, Wallace Rice
quickly follows up with a long and detailed personal meditation upon a
classically styled modern mistress, 'Dedication to Rhodonia':

            Worshipping loveliness
            How have I not adored
            High beauty's jewelled hoard
            Within your spirit stored

----

[57] Rice (1927: p. ii (facing title), p. iii (title page), p. xvi).
[58] Cf., e.g., Rice (1927: 2), 'Dryads in May', yet a third programmatic proem in verse:
'"Let us find some lad astray, | With a heart for anything", | Saith the Dryad of the fair May-
Day'; and p. 3, 'Pan in Arcady': 'And every nymph in Arcady, Each sturdy satyr, too...'
Modern courting couples are to follow the Arcadian lesson (p. 45, 'Love's Meeting'): 'With
lads and maidens the thickets thro' | We had played and danced as the hours flew by; | And
lo! in the dusk there were only you | And Love and I.'

Body and mind to bless?

. . . . .

Your breasts so virginal,
Scarce reddening at their tips,
With tender curves and small—
What lovely fairness slips
To them from wakening heart and lips!

There are twenty stanzas of this creepy stuff, ending with a dedication to the beloved's inner and outer beauty, her 'soul' and 'breast', which have inspired the translations and original verses alike:

And whensoe'er was fitter origin
Far from our laughless world of sin
For pictures in a pagan nook?

Modernity's 'laughless world of sin' loosely echoes the old Genius of the Greeks from *Studies*, Symonds's figure of prelapsarian Eros—'nor has he ever felt sin'—and Rice's Introduction will in fact go on to cement the link by rhapsodizing on Hellenic 'grace and charm, restraint and beauty, buoyancy and sinlessness' in terms that ape Symonds practically word for word.[59] But all this is now mere background shading; the figure at the centre of the scene is the emotionally matured and psychologically balanced heterosexual female, deemed healthy and whole only insofar as she is ready and open for her lover. Like any field worth ploughing, women's bodies and desires have their seasons, and Pan is the arbiter of their fruition:

There now the woman's soul
That was a girl's arises, sings
Miraculously clear and whole...

The blossoming of your mind in May
Thro' passionate April showers
Delicate hours
That sped their ripening way
To June's delicious day...

She cast about for fitting mate
And great Pan made me fortunate.

The theme is constant, and many such instances could be cited.[60] At the volume's close as at its onset, Pan is explicitly the partner of Eros in hetero-erotodidaxis, ironically in Sapphics:

---

[59] Rice (1927: pp. v, vi, viii, xvi).
[60] Rice (1927: pp. vii, 144), and cf., e.g., p. 14, 'Pan and the Virgin': 'Why should not Pan detest the virgin | Who to herself denies the urge in | The springtide...So Eros broods

> Still in the moonrays, secret in the coppice,
> Young men and maidens blest of Cytherea,
> Wounded by Eros, have their merry playtime,
>   Pan e'er their prompter.

Pan is the broker of youthful heterosexual liaisons that are as natural in their instinctual cycle as the seasons themselves—spring comes, and the young sap rises.[61]

Rice's volume was never going to be a best-seller; issued through a minor though not insignificant New York publishing house, it was conceived as a limited print run of 1,600 copies, of which 100 were reserved as personal gifts.[62] One wonders how many such gifts were to young women, and how many threw them back in the old lecher's face. The girls cannot help it, the goat-god rules their gonads:

> Women are not as men
> But nearer Pan's great soul...
>
> The child that each would bear
>   Leaves them like children too,
> Intent to give and share
>   As Pan would have them do.[63]

This little ditty is attributed to an obscure Greek epigrammatist, 'Xenos Palaestes'. By this point in the volume even the half-canny reader of *Pagan Pictures* will have come to recognize the name as the author's own quasi-Hellenic and indeed metapoetic *nom de plume*—as their translator, he is the stranger or guest-friend (*xenos*) who grapples strenuously (*palaestēs*) with his virile ancient hosts. At times this wrestling takes the form of active dialogue and one-upmanship, as at 1927: 19

---

within her burning, | Assured some day she will be learning | That when it comes the proper season...'; or p. 148, in the author's cycle of 'Didactics': ''Twas on a day in sunny spring | With songs of birds and bourgeoning bloom | That first our hearts began to sing; | She came to meet her joyous doom | As autumn's gold and crimson loom...'.

[61] Pan's prompting: Rice (1927: 192) ('Beauty Invincible'); heterosexual seasonality: pp. 144, 148. Both these latter stanzas fall under the translator's own miscellany, tellingly entitled 'Didactics'.

[62] Aside from its Modern Library imprint of European reprints, Boni and Liveright was never a big success, and Horace Liveright (an alcoholic skirt-chaser) was by 1927 well on his way to running it into the ground; but in its early years it had been an important publisher of the avant-garde with a willingness to take risks on new authors, among them Ernest Hemingway, William Faulkner, and Dorothy Parker. Eliot's *The Waste Land* had its first publication in book form through Boni and Liveright, immediately after its first magazine appearance in November 1922.

[63] Rice (1927: 84).

bouncing off Theophanes on the theme of (what else?) breasts and their correct handling.[64]

Multiple influences rub along here, half assimilated at best. A watered-down, sub-Arnoldian 'Hellenism' and 'Hebraism' are now refigured as the twin streams of ancient heterosexual love poetry—the *Anthology* and the Song of Solomon.[65] Symonds too is thrown to the mat. Roses are now no longer pretty boys, their physical charms, and the poems they inspire; now they embody the blooming summer of Woman's erotic maturation. The Uranian flower meadow is aggressively repurposed as the flowering body of the female beloved: 'For Young my Love is a paradise | Of fervent flowers held high and warm', with 'high' suggesting pert girlish bosoms. A coy young virgin is pressed to comply with the ego-narrator's sexual demands; if she refuses, Pan will 'teach her unpluckt roses moulder', a *carpe diem* motif familiar from the pederastic verses of AP 12. Nipples in Rice are always especially roseate ('Suckled by rosebuds').[66]

That Wallace Rice was now nearing the end of a long and very public career in authorship and media management—he had been born all the way back in 1859, so could have read *Studies* hot off the press in his own teens—makes this soft-core leering all the seamier. Read through modern retrospect, Pan's pagan Anthology is a Mills and Boon romance gone terribly wrong, all the more so for its quasi-Hellenic drapery:

> Her yearning rose made smooth and moist
> Could, full rejoicing, be rejoiced.[67]

A more admissible comparator might be Lawrence, whose *Lady Chatterley's Lover* was published the following year.

With the unavoidable exception of Paton's Loeb, Rice purports to have read no translator or re-weaver of the Anthology more recent than Pott and Grundy (both 1913); his annotated Bibliography (pp. xix–xxiii) is heavily weighted towards nineteenth-century staples, and is even nostalgic for the mouldering 1820s tail end of the Planudean editions, although

---

[64] A fixation of Rice's; cf., e.g., (1927: 14), again from 'Pan and the Virgin': 'She knows not that upon her nipple | Eros can find delicious tipple...'. More than we wanted to know regarding his own erogenous zones: p. 147.

[65] Rice (1927: p. x), and cf. Wright (1924: 135) (Song of Songs).

[66] Rice (1927: 165, 174), and cf., e.g., pp. 14, 151 ('Our maidens, like the flowers'). Nipples are roses: pp. 117 (quoted), 173, 190 ('Breast brought to fulness or their buds to flower'), etc.

[67] Rice (1927: 149), a particularly horribly achieved passage, although cf. also the dreadful p. 146, 'Like storm waves rising on the shore | Her maidenhood began to fill | With gusty passion...'. Rice may or may not know that the rose is used figuratively for the vagina and labia in Old Comedy (Jeffrey Henderson 1991: 135, citing in particular *Lysistrata*).

Planudes himself is execrated in counter-Symondsian terms as the dogmatic and 'narrow' censor of *straight* sex (Mackail's account of him is now the go-to source).[68] All the same, the emphases of *Pagan Pictures* are decidedly *du jour*. In faithful adherence to the road map laid out three years previously in Wright's discursive *Poets of the Greek Anthology*, the erotic career of Rice's Meleager moves sequentially through early dalliances with liberated city girls to an all-but-conjugal completion. The intensity of youthful infatuation—'Xenophila, one draft | And thou my soul has quaft [sic]'—reveals itself as a healthy sowing of wild oats, interspersed as it is with other loves—Timo, Ilias. Freshly arrived in the big city, young Meleager has a roving eye, in Rice just as in Wright.[69]

Only when he meets Heliodora does the consummate love-poet find his fit object, in art as in life. From initial boozy high spirits ('To Heliodora fill the cup') and jejune bragging ('I prophesy the lovely tale | Of Heliodora shall not fail'), Rice's Meleager falls fast and hard in love, gladly becomes Cupid's fool, lays his heart at his beloved's feet...and then loses her, and with her everything:

HELIODORA DEAD

Love's last sorry gift,
Tears, I give thee, ill in shedding,
All that's left me now to give thee,
Heliodora...

If Rice's Meleager does not then complete the pattern by finding solace from his grief in the arms of a pert adolescent, as did Wright's with his sweet Phanion, the book's imminent end (a mere ten pages remain) could be cited as pretext—or perhaps the theme cut too close to the bone. Either way, the Anthology of *Pagan Pictures* lingers in the brothel and indefinitely defers the grave.[70]

5. 'THE GREAT ROLLING STONE OF GREECE': SHANE LESLIE'S *GREEK ANTHOLOGY* (1929)

All these strands come together in the *Greek Anthology* of Shane Leslie, which contends with Peter Jay's Penguin Classic (1973) as perhaps the

---

[68] Mackail (1927: p. xix).   [69] Rice (1927: 48, 95 (Xenophila), 90 (Timo and Ilias)).
[70] Rice (1927: 100 x 2 (fill the cup), 112 (passion aflame), implicitly 117, 151, 157, 181 ('Heliodora Dead')); p. 130 is an isolated indiscretion with Xenophila (once more for old times' sake?) but the overall pattern is crystal-clear. Phanion, 'a young girl' (Wright 1924: 141–3).

most publicly visible version of the twentieth century. A Baronet of the Protestant Ascendancy (with an American mother) who converted to Catholicism and advocated Irish Home Rule, Sir John Randolph (later 'Shane') Leslie lost a promising political career to bad timing and subsequently made his home in London as an eccentric man of letters; he was a published poet and a prolific writer on miscellaneous (but especially ecclesiastical) topics, and a frequent reviewer.[71] Contemporary reviews of his own work dismissed him as a superficial recycler of commonplaces, and his hack history of the Anthology bears out this characterization. From the outset, the roots of an older age are showing:

> Many a silver pitcher has been lowered by many a purple cord into these gathered fountains of Hellas, and this attempt will not be the last to dredge that ancient but sweet-smelling deep. This collection is for the many, the '*polloi*', who know no Greek nor why they are so called, but would as gladly fathom the content and sample the savour of the Anthology as a periphrase of Dante or synopsis of the Rubáiyát or reading of the Song of Songs... The Epigrams read distantly from our civilisation, but a little modern dress brings some of them deliciously home.[72]

This sentimental mash-up ranges freely across the decades. The Aesthetics' purple gush cues up the old theme of the dignity and duty of the translator for the working man (1830s–70s); 'a little modern dress' looks back all the way to Bland and Merivale (1800s–30s), just as had Wright's recent *Girdle of Aphrodite*; and the ghost of Omar Khayyam conjures Syrian Meleager amid a steam of perfumes (1890s–1900s), an exotic Easterner redeemed by his Hebraic sincerity and directness (1920s). In this passage and indeed at other moments of metaphoric excess, the Old Testament is the touchstone of Leslie's rhetorical imagination: the 'silver pitcher' looks to be a garbled echo of Ecclesiastes 12:6–7 ('Or ever the silver cord be loosed, or the golden bowl be broken, or the pitcher be broken at the fountain...'), with additional inflection from Louisa May Alcott's *Silver Pitchers* (1876), in which three girls dedicate themselves to the cause of Temperance and choose the pitcher as their emblem; the purple cord is the Israelites' constantly worn reminder to keep the Commandments and shun worldly temptation (Numbers 15.38–9).

---

[71] A good recent biography by Otto Rauchbauer (2009), *Shane Leslie: Magnificent Failure* (Dublin: Lilliput Press), gives a sympathetic account of his literary career and explores the contradictions he embodied.

[72] Leslie (1929: 9).

After all these years the strongest single influence is still explicitly Mackail, whose airy conceits do not outlive Leslie's keen attempt to make them concrete and particular:

With Simonides the Greek Epigram reached an immediate height, to which it never reascended, but the decadence of Alexandria and Constantinople was strewn with the intellectual and the ingenious. The nearest parallels to Simonides in English have been Tennyson's Epitaph on Sir John Franklin, Wordsworth's cry for Lucy, Walt Whitman's stanza on President Lincoln. Housman's Army of Mercenaries…and Kipling's Sleepy Sentry are Greek epigrams in other manners.[73]

It is no surprise to meet Wordsworth again here, in the company of the early classical epigrammatist singled out by Mackail as his ancient correspondent. The rebranding en passant of Whitman, Symonds's idol of man-love, as America's Simonides is a piquant touch; the remaining exemplars of the Genius of the Greek Anthology in the modern age are defenders and extenders of British imperial influence (Leslie had agitated for Home Rule but always saw himself as a loyal subject of the Crown). Once again, as often in times of old, the health of the nation state must rest on sound morals and bodies—bodies that must be held ready for sacrifice in the cause.

Leslie the religious convert singles out by name not merely Mackail, a wise old owl of epigram studies, but also Neaves on the virtues of Planudes as expurgator:

In making a single volume of selections, hundreds have been omitted as dull or indecent or repetitious. Many daring and unmoral epigrams have been retained with a goodly balance from Christianized Hellenism. In dealing with the Erotic, a frank cleavage has been made between the natural and unnatural. It is too late in time to explain why the Greeks attributed so much romance to the love described in Scripture as passing the love of women. Many a flashing line and winged word cover legitimate hero-worship or joyous admiration for youth in the Anthology, but the section entitled 'Stratonis lusus puerilis' cannot be accounted blameless. Too many epigrams therein had better been tied to a millstone and dropped into the sea—'Better never published or never written', said the sage Lord Neaves in his summary of the Anthology. A certain number, however, can be salvaged for modern readers by the accident that they were originally inspired by passion for women, who, like some modern actresses, had taken the names of boys.[74]

[73] Leslie (1929: 10).
[74] Leslie (1929: 11), loosely quoting Neaves (1874: 5). Disappointingly, the dates of the examples given by the OED (the earliest being 1946) do not encourage reading a subtext of jutting bosoms into 'frank cleavage'. A later work by Leslie (addressed in this chapter's conclusion) clarifies that 'actresses' is meant to be read as a euphemism: the diminutive

Pagan Greece might have been sexually racy—they knew no better—but a judicious admixture of epigrams from later antiquity keeps the modern selection in good health; if the balance is right, a little slap and tickle does no harm (at least to the adult reader for whom the book is intended). Leslie's phrasing recalls the elaborate apologetics of Jebb in the 1890s ('there is no inherent conflict between true Hellenism and spiritualized Hebraism, such Hebraism as has passed into Christianity'). Multiple narratives jostle for priority: early is good (Simonides) and late is bad, but at the same time late is good (Christian) and early is bad (pagan); sexual content is dangerously exciting ('daring and immoral'), but also tedious ('dull or indecent or repetitious').[75] As with Wright, it is all a bit of a mess—and thus usefully revealing of the tensions that continue to underlie the project of Anthology for the common reader, singled out early on as 'the man in the street'.[76]

At the heart of this confusion is a version of Oxford's old distinction between Uranian and Pandemic love. The love of men for boys is biblically excused (David and Jonathan) when encountered in its sublime form, an excuse that also confines its proper expression to distant antiquity—the past is a foreign country, and they did things differently there—but when it falls short of idealism and touches the body with Pandemic lust, the translator is duty-bound to retreat into the Latin of the learned professions.

BOOK THE TWELFTH . . . The apples of Sodom are generally omitted in Greek studies, but such of their dead blossoms as survive in the Anthology turn to dust in modern taste . . . No doubt it was often too strong to be anything but Platonic. Its weaker side was gross.[77]

The distinction between Pandemic and Uranian is the grit around which layers of later commentary accrue, in exaggerated or garbled form— Neaves's cult of Planudes, Mackail's tomboys. At the same time, the forbidden desire at its heart defies modern understanding, so Leslie's

---

female names of AP 12 'happened to be the semi-masculine names coquettes have always enjoyed assuming' (1932: 10).

[75] He had said similar things, though more emphatically, in a vitriolic review of Joyce's *Ulysses* (in the *Dublin Review* of September 1922: 112–19) which is much excerpted in the literature on that author; Joyce was obscene (enough so that the Church ought to add his book to the *Index Expurgatorius*), but somehow also so dull and list-like as not to be worth looking at anyway.

[76] Leslie (1929: 11).

[77] Leslie (1929: 27). Described by Josephus (4.8.4), 'apples of Sodom' became a quasi-Biblical figure of speech; if Leslie has one proximate source it is probably Milton's *Paradise Lost* (10.520–8).

readers are advised not even to try. 'It is too late in time to explain'—and never mind that the job has already been done more or less scientifically, by Symonds and before him by the Germans. Leslie's readers need not labour to comprehend that which they must in any case condemn in accordance with biblical teaching. The millstone business invokes Matthew 18.6—anyone who leads a Christian child into sin deserves to sleep with the fishes—and 'turn to dust in modern taste' unmistakably recalls Isaiah 44.20–1:

> He feedeth on ashes: a deceived heart hath turned him aside, that he cannot deliver his soul, nor say, Is there not a lie in my right hand?
>
> Remember these, O Jacob and Israel; for thou art my servant: I have formed thee; thou art my servant: O Israel, thou shalt not be forgotten of me.

In sinning against the God-given order of things, the Uranian Anthologists had worshipped at the feet of a false idol—and here one cannot but think of Symonds's statuesque and seductive Genius of the Greeks, perhaps with added shades of Dorian Gray—and spiritually self-destructed. In fashioning his capstone to the 1920s Anthology tradition, Leslie counters all this by bringing to a climax the national project of assimilating Greek epigram to a nostalgic vision of Nature (the twee archaism of 'goodly' speaks volumes) from which 'the unnatural' is semantically excluded. Leslie claims that his particular flavour of Nature is predicated less on field and wood—in passing he concedes the frailty of the notion of the Greeks as country-lovers in the sense imagined by Lothian, Wright, and others, while still insisting on their sentimentality for animals—than on the 'timeless' truths of human nature, the 'I have formed thee'.[78] The Greeks of the Anthology hold up the mirror of common sense, which (it hardly needs saying) never changes; their wit and wisdom illuminate 'situations which recur with the centuries'; their ironic eye misses nothing.[79]

Above all, the Anthology in Leslie's hands bottles the lightning of compulsory heterosexuality—the 'fierceness of the true Venereal flame'—and makes of it a template for the ages. Meleager is the one poet who does most to make this possible:

> In this Book Meleager makes good his claim to be the supreme love poet of Greece. His passionate utterances steam like bonfires of wine-scented incense. His extravagant reproaches and despairs ring sincerely under covering of that

---

[78] The Greeks 'only rarely…showed a sense of Nature' (Leslie 1929: 22); pity for animals 'creeps through the Anthology' (p. 24).

[79] Leslie (1929: 24–5). Irony and detail: pp. 19, 25.

heroic hexameter [*sic*], which to Mackail can equally convey 'the sigh of a lover or the lament over a perished Empire'...

Meleager's compliments to the divine sex are the richest and his lamentations are the most human in the Anthology.[80]

When Leslie reinstalls his vision of Woman on her old Victorian pedestal, his phrasing—'the divine sex'—speaks unmistakably to the true (heterosexual) nature of the Heavenly Venus, Symonds's old Uranian Aphrodite, and to Meleager's destined role as its champion. Rufinus, we are told, comes a close second, and even Paul the Silentiary 'had a touch worthy of great love'—not for him the brothel and the grave assigned by *Studies*.[81] But only Meleager—the heterosexual Meleager—is truly sublime. When he writes for AP 12, one can immediately tell that his heart is not in it, unlike that of vile but authentic Strato. The rhetoric echoes Paton, on fashion versus passion, and the life story is straight out of Wright. The young poet-about-town puts aside the flitting and 'fashionable' infatuations of his university days as soon as he discovers women, and then falls head over heels for his Helydore. Her glance captures his soul as if it were a songbird:

Boys pass quickly through their youth and fall in love with other boys themselves. As Meleager says: 'Here is a new marvel I see. Fire is afire and burnt by flame.' Strato's verses are crudely naked under their skill, while Meleager's are those of a Laureate writing to a set theme. He aims more at his own pretty effect than at the prettiness of the boys... it is a woman's eyes that inspire his wonderful outcry to his limed and struggling soul... The pursuit of boys [henceforth] seems to him a mockery...[82]

Although Wright's elaborate fantasies of Meleager's youthful nature-hikes do not make it into Leslie's account, this is still (and despite his token protestations about the Greeks and Nature) very much an Anthology for the active rambler. Expurgation is now explicitly yoked to manliness, and to manly pursuits, as Leslie declares himself a Planudes *redivivus* for the modern age:

Lascaris printed the *editio princeps* in Florence from the Planudean as a work of art with the statement that Planudes 'had less arranged than mutilated and castrated the book by subtracting the more lascivious epigrams to his own glory but that his merit in so doing must be left to others to judge'. However, the omission of the purely lascivious does not entail a castrated book, and the

---

[80] Leslie (1929: 14).   [81] Leslie (1929: 14, 15 (Paul)).
[82] Leslie (1929: 28). Acknowledgement of Paton's edition as his working text: p. 12, and cf. Wolfe (1927a: 7; 1927b: p. iv).

present collection makes a stronger appeal to the masculine than to the effeminate, for this collection is not to garnish a scholar's study or to make a grammarian's holiday, but for the man in the street, the woman at home, the country
gentleman, the traveller, the mourner and the cynic, the preacher and the lover,
the moralist and the poet, the journalist and the *littérateur*.[83]

All human life is here—again, all that is fit to print—in a 'masculine'
volume for men and women alike, each in their proper place ('the
street... at home') in the established order of things, and inhabiting a
timeless idyll where the proper hierarchies (the church, the squire) and
organic rhythms of life remain magically undisturbed. (Again we might
find this piquant in the light of the rogue Baronet's political sympathies.)
The rigorous selectivity of the decisive translator—a role conceived in the
long shadow of Mackail's proconsular virtuosity—takes concrete form in
a book whose essential and unassailable ballsiness is rhetorically
opposed, not to femininity, the wholesome and necessary complement
to the eternal masculine principle, but to the corporeally and morally
bankrupt 'effeminacy' of those who sit and think too much in the
unmanly seclusion of mere academia.

Leslie signs off on his grandly titled Prolegomenon with a passage of
purple to rival and outdo anything on the wilder shores of Mackail:

Such is the great rolling stone of Greece, which gathered not only moss down
the ages but withered rose-leaves and crushed wisps of asphodel and amaranth
and thyme. There is no beginning nor end to the Greek Anthology. It may be
read by those who run or by the sedentary scholar... It is a brittle mass, for at
the touch it scatters into a thousand crystals, lenses and fragments of broken or
coloured glass... The riches of the Anthology are encyclopaedic. The Greek
tapestry is woven by a thousand deft fingers down the centuries... Christian
and pagan intermingle as though the old tradition were too beautiful to suffer
destruction at the hands of the new God. Here lies in Epigram and Epitaph, in
poesy and in cunning, in pathos and humour all that the Greek mind cared to
crystallise concerning life and love, sport and art, Nature and Philosophy.
Herein was stored flower and fungus, wreath and rubbish, hive besides hive,
and honeycomb within honeycomb. The dull and the didactic were joined to
the sentimental and the divine. The thoughts and themes of Hellas passed
through their Pagan sieve and under the Christian winnowing-fan, to be ground
between the millstones of Hexameter and Pentameter like fine grain worthy of
the lips of the gods.

The constancy of the passions and the transiency of human emotions remain
marvellously reflected in its pages... All the vices, all the virtues, all the arts are

---

[83] Leslie (1929: 12).

represented and descend side by side. The scrap-heap of Greece survives in a scrap-book. If there is a Bible portraying the Greeks as the Old Testament portrays the Jews, it lies less in the Homeric Canon than in the Greek Anthology.[84]

Leslie's parting shot thus singles out the Anthology as a Mackailian 'book of Greek life', a pointillist racial portrait from which the modern translator crafts his own redemptive epitome. And Leslie's own, neo-Planudean 'Anthology' is the real rolling stone here, accumulating layers of withered literary appreciation as it bumps its way from one unlikely metaphor to the next—one moment a grenade of paste baubles (wretched echo of Symonds's gem-language), the next a tapestry, encyclopaedia, beehive, dump, or scrapbook...or all of them at once. Butler's title (1881/1922) echoes in 'asphodel and amaranth'; behind 'wreath and rubbish' lies Mackail's bullish introductory matter ('large quantities of rubbish as well as the gold') as well as the adulatory rhetoric of his reception (the decisive modern Anthologist who salvages a 'garden run to weeds'). This mystified Anthology can never be met head-on, only glimpsed through a haze of figuration and miscellaneous cant; to give a sober or rounded account of it would be the act of an academic, which is to say, an 'effeminate'—out of touch with lived experience and gendered identity alike.[85]

6. PROLEPSIS: MELEAGER AND THE CULT OF THE AMATEUR

The Greek Anthology is no garden of chosen flowers. In it we find to our surprise that Greek may be wooden, vague, inexpressive. It is a garden full of roses, of waste ground, of rubbish heaps confused together. But it began as a flower garden, with the Wreath which Meleager made...[86]

---

[84] Leslie (1929: 30–1).

[85] Cf., e.g., Wolfe (1927b: p. iv) (emphasis added), trivializing the academic project: 'There is no space here, nor have I the learning to follow the professors in the discussion of the actual sources of much of the Anthology. Here is a rich and unexhausted playground *for the scholiast*. My interest was to find good Greek poems...'. Wolfe's pamphlet, which collects versions from the English literary tradition, is front-loaded (p. 9) with epigrams that underwrite the Englishness and sexual regularity of the Anthology: 'A Shakespearean Sonnet' from Marianus Scholasticus, all nymphs and shepherds, immediately followed by lashings of heterosexual Plato and Meleager (pp. 9–11).

[86] Lothian (1920: n.p. ('Introduction')).

'Surprise' is important here; it would not do to seem to know too much. Amateurism is now a necessary qualification for epigram-work. 'I know what the Greek means', attests a translator of a later age, as if even that is in doubt.[87] Rather sooner, in a delightful verse selection inspired by Leslie's dangled silver pitcher, the 'translator' John Irvine will admit in his preface with disarming candour that he knows no Greek at all.[88] His working method is not declared; most likely he has just worked up some poetic equivalents from poems found in Paton's prose Loeb. What is important is not philology, but a lived connection to the land. Irvine's dedication is to Richard Rowley, 'who found Helicon in the goodly lands of Mourne', and his preface signs off with the seasonally grounded 'Spring 1943': the buds of the Anthology are coming into bloom.[89]

The unscientific translation, made far from dictionaries and commentaries (and in Irvine's case without even knowing the text), is all the more authentic a human document for being in touch with the rhythms and roots of a life lived out of doors. The new Anthologists brag of their unscholar-like credentials and the organic immediacy of their process: 'I have rarely troubled to go behind [Mackail's] notes'; '[I make] no pretense to scholarship myself... much joy and a little learning have gone to the making of these pages'. Wallace Rice of *Pagan Pictures* advertises that his versions have been worked up 'as time availed' over a period of more than forty years, in the interstices of a life lived to the full as befits a man of the world.[90]

Irvine's slender collection is illustrated by the Belfast woodcut artist Leslie Owen Baxter; it thus perpetuates the minor trend of illustrated 'Anthologies' kicked off posthumously by Corvo (1937), and subsequently to be continued in Jacques Le Clercq's exquisitely made, limited-run *Love Poems from the Greek Anthology* of 1955.[91] The uses

[87] Rexroth (1962: n.p.), ironically given that much of the content of his so-called Greek Anthology was never in Greek to begin with; I address this in a forthcoming publication.

[88] Irvine (1943: 9), in a work disarmingly subtitled 'Poems from the Greek Anthology *Attempted* in English Verse' (emphasis added).

[89] Irvine (1943: 5, 9); looking back to the nineteenth century we might compare Andrew Lang's titular paean (1892: 79) to the 'Grass of Parnassus', revealed to be the heather of his beloved Galloway Hills. These flowers of song, humbly proffered, are also 'jewels from the treasury of Hellenic song' (Irvine 1943: 9)—Symonds's rhetoric of the 1870s still re-echoes after all these years. 'Richard Rowley' was the literary pseudonym of the Belfast industrialist Richard Valentine Williams, author of the one-act play *Apollo in Mourne* (1926), which was reprinted in his short story collection *Tales of Mourne* (1937).

[90] Lothian (1920: n.p.); Rice (1927: pp. xvi–xvii).

[91] Le Clercq's volume was brought out by the Peter Pauper Press, a small fine-art imprint run by Peter and Edna Beilenson; affordable at the time, its books are now coveted by collectors. At around the same time (the exact date is not known), they also brought out

of illustration in print translations and stories from the classics would, I think, repay investigation; an introductory survey would be a good beginning. On an anecdotal basis one might note that scenes of human figures tend to accompany versions of ancient authors who are perceived as 'light' or minor, and ancient works that are considered sexually titillating or risqué. Lucian frequently qualifies, typically in editions produced by small 'art' presses for a limited release; some readers will know Charles Cullen's 1920s illustrations for the delightful, kiss-and-tell *Dialogues of Courtesans*. That the Greek Anthology now begins to go the illustrated route is indicative of how far the translators of the 1920s had pushed it towards what we might term a Lucianic gloss. Refracted through AP 5 under the sign of Meleager, the Greek Anthology may now be indulgently passed off as a charming and innocuous erotic relish for the connoisseur.

However, this soft-focus slap and tickle is not merely by and for the gentleman scholar in his oak-panelled study: the practice of Anthology is no longer the exclusive preserve of a traditional elite. With the rise of the small presses, anyone can be some kind of published author—which had always been one of the great appeals of epigram in antiquity too. Just as the books of the Palatine Anthology echo with classical and late antique Adespota, so too in the early decades of the twentieth century do miscellaneous amateurs try their hand. In the cracks between the best-sellers (and crashing duds) of the major publishers examined in this chapter we find for the first time quieter voices. Of course, there had been privately printed pamphlets before, passed hand to hand within subculture when the subject matter was inadmissible to mainstream print— 'Sydney Oswald' comes to mind, scribbling his Puerile Muse under a pseudonym to preserve his career and reputation—but now the middle classes have their turn.

'The Greek epigram as it appears in Mr Mackail's pages, and in a lesser degree in what follows... In its intimacy and directness... is like the snap-shots of our amateur photographers.'[92] Admittedly the writer of these words was no man on the Clapham omnibus—he is the eminent Quaker jurist Sir Edward Fry, introducing a collection of 100 Mackail-sourced favourites tinkered up around the family hearth with Lady

---

a lovely slipcased run of Mackail's prose translations of his *Select Epigrams*. Peter had previously founded an imprint, 'At the Sign of the Blue-Behinded Ape', which specialized in smut. Of course, Corvo's was not the very first illustrated Anthology; that dubious honour belongs to de Bosch and van Lennep (1795–1822).

[92] Fry (1915: p. viii).

Mariabella and Miss Agnes[93]—but he was onto something all the same; hobby photography was becoming ever cheaper and socially more omni-present as the years rolled by. Kodak had been selling inexpensive cameras since the 1880s, the dollar Box Brownie of 1900 had sold in the hundreds of thousands, and from 1912 onwards the Vest Pocket models let amateurs carry their hobby with them wherever they went, whether on a country ramble or into the wartime trenches; the pleasure of artistic composition was now democratized. The Frys translated first and foremost for friends and family, and their ethos of home-crafting is presented as all the more classically authentic because it is in contact with epigram's ancient spirit of immediacy, its personal touch. Mackail is the Kodak of modern Anthology, its enabling genius of affordable and durable technology that anyone can pick up and use with no need for a technical background.

Making no pretense to scholarship myself...

I profess myself no very scientific student of the Anthology... Of about half these versions [chosen by Mackail] I have in this book made a Garland, after the ancient fashion, picking a flower here, another there, and setting them against each other as seemed to me fitting; adding also a few things, curious or charac-teristic, which took my fancy.[94]

Here we are with Alexander Lothian once more, the hill-walking gradu-ate ('no very scientific student') of an ancient Scottish university who loved 'in leisure times to carry [Mackail's Greek *editio minor*] about with me, not in my pockets only, but in my head and heart'. That modern and living heart is in turn inspired to sing its own Greek song, to usher in its ancient counterparts:

> 'You give me Spring;' cried She
>
> .   .   .   .   .
>
> Euterpe, since they brought to you the long
> unbroken centuries of Grecian song,
> after another thousand years, I bring
> these English echoes, and, though faltering,
> will you, because I dare not, offer these
> to Meleager and Simonides.

---

[93] Born into Bristol's eponymous chocolate dynasty, Sir Edward Fry was knighted (rather against his family's religious convictions) in 1877 for his services to the judiciary. He was by now long retired, having picked up additional honours including the G.C.B. (1907) attested on the title page of his foray into Anthology. His publisher, Letchworth's Garden City Press, was a Quaker firm in a model community founded on Quaker ideals. Most of his other publications are in botany.

[94] Rice (1927: p. xvi); Lothian (1920: n.p. ('Advertisement')).

> You, who served the wayward Muse,
> Pondering till the lamps were low,
> And saw the paling of the stars,
> In groves of Hellas long ago...[95]

Irvine titles his effort 'THE GARLAND'—a twentieth-century translator confidently channelling the spirit of Meleager. Wolfe, more modestly, calls his programmatic ode an 'Invocation': the latter-day Cephalas gazes back with longing and trepidation towards the Mackailian wellsprings of Simonides and Meleager.[96] He does well to be cautious. Whatever these latter-day Anthologists are up to, they are *not* making Garlands 'after the ancient fashion', whimsically 'picking a flower here, a flower there' as the spirit moves them—because that is not how Meleager, Cephalas, or their several Imperial and Late Antique intermediaries went about their orderly business as they populated their functionally structured and more or less conventional schemes, filing epigrams alphabetically or by topic. Putting it plainly, these ancient Anthologists *were* scientific students of Anthology; in affecting an Arts-and-Crafts ethos, their self-declared modern counterparts are being quite un-Meleagrian.

The pattern nonetheless sticks for posterity within the English tradition of translating the 'Greek Anthology'. The hearth and heath are now the key scenes of modern epigram-work, and the don's study is a poor substitute for these paradigmatic locations of vigorous masculinity and family devotion, the very values that connect 'us' with 'them' across the intervening centuries. In the face of this timeless gut sympathy—a proposition proved by the very existence and nature of the Anthology itself—the truest translator is the least scholarly. Indeed, the trained and credentialed classicist with his or her up-to-date editions and commentaries is the reader least qualified to feel and transmit the vital spark of the original poems.

This ideology proved to have sticking power. The hearty halloo of the questing amateur was to resound through decades of the Anthology in English translation:

---

[95] Lothian (1920: n.p.); Wolfe (1927a: 11); Irvine (1943: 11).

[96] More strictly speaking an Agathias if we go by his list of categories (Wolfe 1927a: 9), but 'after another thousand years' bids for Cephalan status. The very title of Wolfe's delightful follow-up volume of 1930, *Homage to Meleager*, affirms the Hellenistic love-poet as the decade's talismanic Anthology author; the book's largest category (1930: 5–47, of 129 pages in all) is Love Poems of a strictly heterosexual sort, playfully prefaced with a 'Proem' out of Strato (the sexually non-specific AP 12.2) as a little treat for those few who are in the know.

the following versions were hammered out, with the aid of 'cribs', precisely in the same spirit as that in which a small boy makes his drawings or his poetry—namely, for his own private pleasure, to amuse an idle hour, and with no intention that they shall ever meet any more critical eye than, say, that of 'Mother'.

I have not really undertaken translation at all—translation, that is to say, as it is understood in the schools. I have simply tried to restate in my own idiom what the Greek verses have meant to me.

It is with great reluctance that I give this book to the press ... As translations, these poems make no pretense of scholarship ... Many of the translations came to me as I turned the Greek poem over in my head, with no text at all ... In a few cases, what might seem to the pedant to be mistranslations are deliberate *jeux d'esprit*.[97]

The hearties of modern Anthology will brook no criticism from mere nitpicking academics. The scholar who identifies errors and misconceptions in their work exposes himself as a pale bookworm, a grammar-grinding relic to whom Meleager's zesty appetites are unfamiliar ground—less than a man, and thus unfit for the task of explaining epigram and Greece to a modern public.

7. CONCLUSION: THE HIGHGATE CAROLLER; LESLIE'S EVIL TWIN

> Seek not in these leaves of mine
> Priam at the altar-shrine:
> Look not for Medea's woes,
> Nor for Niobe's ill throes;
>
> .   .   .   .   .
>
> But the blitheful Graces three,
> And sweet Eros ye shall see,
> Blent with Bacchus; and, I wot,
> Serious looks become them not.[98]

Thus the Revd George Ratcliffe Woodward of St Augustine's in Highgate—a fair classicist, and as an old Harrovian no stranger to epigram-work—inaugurates his little book of *Love-Epigrams from the Greek*

---

[97] Reid (1943: 10); Fitts (1957: 12–13), in introductory matter ironically titled a 'Commentary'; Rexroth (1962: n.p. ('Foreword')).
[98] Woodward (1924: 3).

Anthology (1924).[99] Woodward is not a household name, but his original compositions are well-loved national favourites marking the turning seasons of the Anglican year: 'This Joyful Eastertide', 'Ding Dong Merrily on High', 'Past Three O'Clock'. In the year of 'Seek not in these leaves of mine' (1924) he co-edited (with Charles Wood) the *Cambridge Carol-Book*; he was a great collector of the things, and that year his contributions to carol-lore were recognized with the honorary doctorate in music from Lambeth, of which he cannot help bragging on his title page ('Mus. Doc., Formerly Scholar of Gonville & Caius College, Cambridge'). Small wonder then perhaps that he was also drawn to epigram, that consummate literary collectible.

In numerous little books—many of which appeared in a flurry in 1931—the retired Reverend ran through what by now were the classic, indeed the jaded, themes of the century's translated Anthology: Rodd's enduring triumvirate of Love, Worship, and Death.[100] These were little books indeed: *133 Love-Epigrams* is the longest, at 92 pages including errata; counting blank endpapers, most are in the region of 10 to 20 pages. Hand cut from hand-made paper and simply sewn between covers of thin brown card, the pages are tiny (9.5 cm by 13 cm). The print runs were similarly minuscule, which today makes the books themselves minor collectibles. There were 120 copies of each, with the exception of the last, *Tales of Sea-Sorrow*; that one time, Woodward pushed the boat out and printed 136, each numbered neatly in his small clear hand. All were run off privately at the same address: 48 West Hill, Highgate Village.

Unsurprisingly given his lifelong vocation (and one of his poem titles—'Hims Ancient and Hers Modern'—puns on the title of the standard Anglican hymnal), Woodward's selection of love poems tends

[99] With Harold Mattingly, Woodward translated St John Damascene's *Barlaam and Ioasaph* for the Loeb series; with a new introduction, it remains in print today.

[100] Besides *Love-Epigrams*, I am aware of the following titles: *Domestica: Being Greek Epigrams Turned into English* (1925); *Greek Anthology: Beauty-Epigrams* (1926), presumably picking up on Mackail's euphemism for cherry-picked content from AP 12; *Tart and Homely Gibes or Greek Epigrammatists* (1928); *Greek Epigrams on and by Famous Poets and Musicians* (1929); *Epigrams on Sappho and Other Famous Greek Lyric Poetesses* (1931); *Greek Epigrams on Timon, Diogenes & Others* (1931); *Five and Forty Examples of the Epigram Sepulchral* (1931); *Greek Epigrams Religious and Dedicatory* (2 parts) (1931); *Tales of Sea-Sorrow* (1931). Woodward was by now an elderly man (1848–1934) and his mode is consciously old-fashioned, as the opening quotation indicates, with many a hither, 'neath, and prithee; for clarity's sake I spare my readers his predilection for rendering 's' as an Olde-Worlde 'f' ('Lefbian laffes, to and fro | Twirl the light fantaftic toe: | There appoint a feemly dance.').

towards the conservative.[101] Eros is subordinated to the seasons of human life: 'Once I loved: and who hath not?', but giddy calf-love is a youthful phase and with maturity comes a wiser self-control. The translator gives this common sense a distinctly Anglo-Saxon cast, which indicates that the torrid pagan Eros of the Greeks can never really be naturalized in this sceptred isle. 'Shun this bow-man as your foe-man'; any former Boy Scout must at this point recall that campfire favourite, the Woad Ode.[102]

It is brazen cheek, therefore, that his opening poem (quoted above) is a version of Strato 12.2—albeit that the Greek original makes for a suitably programmatic beginning, and comes conveniently free of any gender specificity. (Six years later, Humbert Wolfe would use the same tactic and the very same poem to inaugurate his *Homage to Meleager*; see p. 318.) In fact Woodward will turn out to raid the Boyish Muse startlingly often: at times implicitly under the Mackailian pretext that behind masculine-sounding diminutives lurk the names of girls (Meleager's Phanion becomes 'Fanny'); just the once re-sexing a pronoun to redeem the text for natural desire), but typically not needing to, whether because of non-specificity in the very carefully chosen originals (or because ancient editors misfiled the poem to begin with).[103]

The predominant author of Woodward's AP 12 is Meleager; through selective citation the translator makes him over in the image of his 1920s *alter ego*, the paradigmatically tender and sincere lover of women in God's green acre, an image that endured in public awareness for decades to come.[104] Nonetheless, he states his sources honestly and in plain view (albeit with some creeping errors of poem-numbering). There is not an 'M'-number in sight; it is all 'AP', which is by no means a necessary choice even at this date, and anyone can go look up what that means— more or less (there is still no introductory treatment that will give them

---

[101] 'Hims' Ancient: Woodward (1924: 21), headlining an old heterosexual Anthology favourite, 9.161, in which Marcus Argentarius casts aside Hesiod's *Works and Days* to spend time with his girl Pyrrha instead; see discussion, p. 263 and p. 289 n. 25.

[102] Woodward (1924: 15, 57). For 'foeman', this time with a distinctly Imperial–colonial drift, cf. Lang (1892: 72) ('Advance, Australia', subtitled 'On the Offer of Help from the Australians after the Fall of Khartoum'). 'Woad's the stuff to show men. | Woad to scare your foemen': the song, by William Hope-Jones to the tune of 'Men of Harlech', was published in 1921 in *The Hackney Scout Songbook* and remains a favourite among Britons of a hearty stamp.

[103] Echoing Mackail: Woodward (1924: 54); 'Fanny': p. 68; re-sexing, pp. 14–15; non-specificity, pp. 16, 26, 50–1, 58–9, 62, 68; ancient misfiling, p. 50 (Meleager on Heliodora), p. 66.

[104] My copy of Le Clercq (1955) bears the handwritten inscription, 'For my wife Peggy on the first anniversary of our life together.'

all the gory details). Woodward's little pamphlets are an early and obscure indication that, in the quiet backwaters of suburbia if not in the main channel of the big presses, the backlash against Symonds's Uranian Anthology is on the ebb.

By design, this chapter has blended and mediated between loud and quiet voices, bestsellers and modest pamphlets; none came more modest than Woodward's. We end with a similarly extreme contrast that illustrates the range of responses available even to one and the same translator, depending on the type of publication and the audience(s) it might reach. We have seen that Shane Leslie's (1929) cold contempt for Strato's *Musa Puerilis* exercised a particular concern to redeem Meleager from homosexual contagion for the common reader (he was after all translating for Routledge, a mass-market publisher); threats of drowning were darkly hinted at, with biblical authority never more than an overheated metaphor away. For the uncommon reader, though, and in a limited run of a thousand hand-numbered copies on hand-made paper, Leslie (a first cousin of Winston Churchill) was happy to translate zestily the whole of AP 12—albeit from behind the safety of a suggestively Eastern Greek pseudonym, 'Ion Ionicos' (1932).[105]

Like Corvo's *Songs of Meleager*, Leslie's version was prettied up with illustrations, and the mere fact of illustration told its own story to canny shoppers who relished ancient smut. The Belgian writer–artist Jean de Bosschère, known for his work on the erotic ancient classics (as well as some period Victorian naughties: Wilde, Baudelaire) for London's small presses, furnished *Strato's Boyish Muse* with its Beardsley-esque line drawings. The purchasers of the first 400 copies also got four of his exquisite etchings, tipped in between numbered pages and going much further than the line drawings in sexual suggestiveness.[106]

Like the fact of illustration, and again tipping the wink for readers who know their way around the subculture's literature, Leslie's *nom de plume* already seems to declare his volume's theme—more, to declare its particular flavour. 'Ion Ionicos' points back to William Cory's *Ionica* of 1858, a word-of-mouth hit that profoundly moved Symonds at Oxford.[107] The choice conveys a strong hint on what we might expect to be the volume's preferred flavour of masculine Eros: Eastern Greek and therefore soft and yearning, a far fry from Symonds's own personally unlikely visions of Northern Dorian fire.

---

[105] I came to this lovely and vanishingly rare book by way of d'Arch Smith (1978: p. ix).

[106] The copy held by the rare books room of Cambridge University Library is numbered '360' and is well worth asking to see.

[107] Orrells (2011a: 159–61) is worth a look on the Johnson–Symonds connection.

Is this then Leslie's private sissy-homosexual self, poking out in a terribly discreet limited edition from behind the public mask of hearty contempt for sexual deviance? Probably not; it is hard to say; the answer might not be terribly interesting in any case, but Leslie's habitual mish-mash of hand-me-down rhetoric makes it next to impossible to determine what he is saying about ancient sexualities, still less modern ones. His introduction flip-flops six times in seven pages, for instance, on the old question of whether Greek boy-love was a matter of passion or fashion; homosexuality is responsible for almost all progress in the Arts, its persecutors are the stock villains of history, and (a point straight out of *Studies*) Achilles's love for Patroclus was the great exemplar for all Greece, but homosexuality 'may be frankly stated'—by some but perhaps not all, maybe for Leslie and his reader, maybe not—'as a possible cause as well as a certain symptom' of the decline and fall of Greece and Rome alike.[108] It is all rather a muddle, just like the introductory matter of his big Routledge volume, with which indeed it shares some turns of rhetoric.[109]

Leslie is, however, emphatic on two clear points. The first is that 'any serious student of antiquity has the right to' get to grips with this material, and indeed needs to; without the key of the *Mousa Paidikē* one cannot 'estimate properly all the social forces of those two great civilisations', Greece and Rome. If you turn a blind eye to Greek love you cannot call yourself a competent classicist.[110] The second is that Strato's book is not in fact liable to harm the modern reader, even the non-specialist. Although the Boyish Muse may be primarily of interest 'as a medical or moral exhibit' (and here Leslie echoes the oldest pretext for printing sex stuff), the 'general reader' too has every right to know about it. This is the *modern* world, and common sense has replaced Victorian

---

[108] Passion versus fashion: Leslie (1932: 5–11); great artists and puritanical oppressors, p. 5 ('as at the hands of the Inquisition in Spain'); 'The *Iliad* shows signs of later expurgation' to hide the erastēs–erōmenos relationship between Achilles and his 'Squire': p. 78 n. 27 (the theme is flagged up in the introduction, p. 7); and cf. p. 10, where Leslie professes two completely different positions on Meleager's bisexuality in one and the same paragraph. Decline and fall due to 'this particular form of decadence' in the eyes of 'those, who enjoy making sweeping lines of historical survey' (p. 6)—Leslie is careful not to come down off the fence on whether he believes this or not.

[109] 'These attachments were (to judge by the literature) either harmless and educative or pitifully sensual', (Leslie 1932: 6); cf. (1929: 27), cited earlier in this chapter. In the years between his Routledge volume and *Strato's Boyish Muse* Leslie would seem to have (re-?) read *Studies*; there is now talk of Roman 'coarseness' that closely echoes Symonds on Lucillius, and Strato has moments of 'unredeemable frankness' that challenge the translator (1932: 5 and 11, 9).

[110] Leslie (1932: 6–).

narrow-mindedness and shockability.[111] Reading homosexual epigrams in translation does not deprave or corrupt, and the public has a right to do so and to judge for themselves—something easier to say, we might cynically note, in a limited luxury edition and under a pseudonym than in the mass-market translation (1927) that aimed actually to address that public.[112]

And for once a title tells the truth: for the first time, the Boyish Muse genuinely is 'translated wholly into English'. Leslie is clearly writing with Paton's Loeb at his elbow (no harm in that), but stands fairly well on his own two feet as a linguist where Paton veers, as he not infrequently does, into either Latin or abject obfuscation. His introduction has warned us that he will hedge a little where bodily terms become too explicit in the original, but he gets the general sense across just fine:

Boyish nature falls into three forms, Diodorus. Learn their names. The virgin shape is called *lalou*. The swelling adolescent is called *coco* and the youthfulness, that dances to the touch, call a lizard. You know what to call it in perfection.

Philocles, if the Desires love thee and Persuasion, whose breath is incense, and the Graces, who gather the flowers of beauty, mayest thou have Diodorus in thy arms and may sweet Dorotheus stand and sing to thee and may Callicrates lie on thy knee and Dio melt, hold and warm thy passions [*sic*] aim and Uliades bring them to a head, while Philo kisses thee sweetly and Theron chatters and Eudemus you press under your [*sic*] tunic. For, if God allowed thee all these delights, blessed man, what a mixed dish of boys you would serve!

(On 'mixed dish of boys', an endnote offers, more in salacious hope than in scholarly earnest: 'Literally "a Roman salad of boys." Perhaps = Roman orgy.'[113])

Taken as a pair, the carolling Reverend of Highgate and the rhetorically mixed dish of 'Ion Ionicos' show which way the wind is blowing; the post-Symonds backlash is at last beginning to recede. In another twenty-five or thirty years it will be possible to refer to AP 12 playfully and without frightening the horses, at least to a smallish and self-selecting audience of discerning lovers of smut, and in terms that remain coy; Le Clercq's introduction of 1955 pokes amateur fun at the female-diminutives party

---

[111] Leslie (1932: 5 ('medical or moral exhibit'), 7–8).
[112] Leslie (1932: 6).
[113] Leslie 1932: 14, translating Strato AP 12.6, and 34, translating Strato AP 12.95. When originally printed, Paton's Loeb went into Latin for four lines of the latter; later in its publication history (I presume the revision of 1971), this was quietly altered to translate the poem in full. Picturing the scene in my head, I think it should be 'his tunic', not 'your tunic'. The endnote: 77 n. 13. Apicius gives several variant recipes for a salad which layers multiple ingredients, the *sala cattaba*, 4.1.1–3.

line peddled by Mackail and Paton, mischievously observing that 'a mere bowing acquaintance with sodomy and linguistics might suggest that female diminutives are often substituted for male praenomens among the gentry of the Urning persuasion.'[114] In the meantime, one may wonder what Woodward thought he was about: aggressive reclamation, *sotto voce* acknowledgement, or perhaps a little bit of both? As for Leslie, dipping ceaselessly as a matter of first recourse into the kitty of received notions, who knows what was on his mind? As characters in the long drama of Greek epigram in its modern reception, though, their place in its patterns of rhetorical iteration and circumlocution comes into focus. It is simply not the case that epigram in reception tells a story of straightforward heroes and villains, or of private yearnings behind public masks; the genre is a cork bobbing on powerful and murky currents, on its way to a destination these writers could not see. Any more than we can.

[114] Le Clercq (1955: n.p.).

Conclusion

> Three years, I finally concluded, might suffice for the venture. Three
> years, under some vine-wreathed arbour, with the necessary books
> at one's elbow, and one's soul at ease...Such a thing, it is obvious,
> should be a holiday performance, written *con amore* and not
> otherwise; in reverential, playfully-erudite fashion...Three years,
> I kept on saying to myself—where shall they be found?
>
> I shall not find them.[1]

Thus Norman Douglas, author of the utterly charming *Birds and Beasts
of the Greek Anthology* (1928), sums up how he came to write his late
and level-headed intervention in the Anthology's post-war nature cult.[2]
The better part of a century later, in an era of publish-or-perish, his
words ring all the truer. Often the genre's scholars as well as its translators
must squeeze epigram in between more obviously serious or urgent business; that being said, we have seen time and again that pressure of one or
another kind (of time, of influence, of ideology) is precisely what lays bare
the contradictions and tensions that underlie the sunny conformity of the
genre's public front. Long after Symonds goes to his grave in leafy Testaccio,
tentacles of subtext rise to grapple with the unwary or merely uncommitted
translator—and trip up even the most assiduous of scholars.

This short concluding chapter pursues three distinct but intercon-
nected tasks. First, and most substantially, we cast forward from the time
frame of the six main chapters (1805–1929) to revisit the Anthology
in translations of the 1930s and later. Dipping into the text's fortunes in
the years following the Mackailian ascendancy, we see how rapidly an
apparently robust consensus can go out of style; the old counter-Uranian
rhetoric is now itself a 'garden run to weeds', a vast edifice in ruin.

Second, and continuing the drift of this chapter's narrative towards the
present day, we briefly home in on some piquant moments in the recent

---

[1] Douglas (1928: 9–10).   [2] See Ch. 6.

history of scholarship on epigram—moments at which, with the critic's keen critical eye directed elsewhere, glimmers of the old rhetorics seize the chance to poke through into present discourse.

Third, and finally, we engage speculatively with the postmodern afterlives of Uranian and counter-Uranian Anthology as legacy documents in a global digital archive. This third part rounds off with brief closing remarks that relate the book's findings to some larger concerns of research and pedagogy.

What happened to Meleager *then*, and what will happen to him *now* (is he still more a talking point than a text)? Where *next* for the Anthology, and for the generations of modern acolytes whose antics have inspired this book? What might its story imply for how we do Classics and Humanities *now*, in an age of sound-biting and excerption? These are the questions that Wilde's Meleager continues to inspire, and that this chapter will attempt to address.

1. PAN'S AFTERMATH: THE ANTHOLOGY IN LATER TRANSLATIONS

i. 'Goodbye, Vile Canting Puritan': The return of Strato

> Melanthias stooped, and took one hand in his,
> And stroking those soft tresses murmured low
> Such little words as all true lovers know.
> Nor need my tale to teach them...
> Thus by the Love-God's shrine, beneath the trees,
> Fragrant with summer, musical with bees,
> While in the boughs the loud cicada sang,
> And through the fields glad boyish laughter rang,
> These lovers vowed unspoken vows and blent
> Their throbbing souls in love's accomplishment.

> (from *Eudiades*, printed privately in 1878)

> I have written a lot of bad poetry & dreamed many excellent dreams.

> (postscript to a letter to Henry Dakyns,
> Davos, 15 February 1878)[3]

---

[3] *Eudiades* is among the poems sampled by the excellent John Addington Symonds pages http://rictornorton.co.uk/symonds (accessed 14 April 2013); its original publication context is the vanishingly rare Symonds (1878b: i. 1–33, quoted at 19–20). In the Pierpont

Symonds's excellent dreams were not quashed by the critics of the backlash. A mere two years after Leslie's selection for Ernest Benn, the rival firm of Jonathan Cape came out with a volume of *Translations from the Greek Anthology* by Robert Allason Furness (1931). Yet again, the translator was an old Egypt hand; as an Inspector in the Alexandria Police he had been awarded the Order of the Nile, Fourth Class, back in 1917,[4] an honour to which in later life he added a CMG, CBE, OBE, and more besides. Furness had recently (1929) joined the staff of the High Commissioner of Egypt—the august official whose powers Evelyn Baring had formerly exercised under the more explicitly Roman Imperial title of 'Consul-General'—and his translator's introduction of 1931 places the Anthology within a presumptive colonial framework with the passing observation that Syria and Egypt supplied some of its authors (both, of course, had been Roman provinces and were in Furness's time possessions of France and Britain respectively).

For all that, this servant of Empire's autumn years has moved the game on. The 'admirable' Mackail is politely nodded to, but no more, as a handy source of biographical nuggets; one of the book's posthumous dedicatees is Walter Headlam, who had called it as he saw it in critiquing Mackail's philology for the *Classical Review* all the way back in 1890.[5] Likewise, there is a faint trace, and no more than a trace, of habits of composition that were old hat even when Symonds took to them: Furness thanks the editor of the *Athenaeum* and *Nation and Athenaeum* for his permission to reproduce a 'few' versions first aired in their pages (1931: 11). And then it is on with the show, in a volume arranged alphabetically by author—and giving an unapologetically homosexual first-person voice to Strato, a poet acknowledged openly at the outset as the author and collector of pederastic verse:

> Passing just now upon my way
> The garland-weaver's stall,
> I spied a boy, with flower and spray
> Twining a coronal;
>
> And stabbed, I stopped; and standing by
> The boy, soft in his ear

Morgan Library volume in which this and Symonds (1878b: ii) are bound together, a pencil note on the flyleaf by Edmund Gosse explains that 'very few copies were printed privately, by Arrowsmith of Bristol. J.A.S. destroyed the greater part of even these small editions, and some may be considered almost unique.' The letter is at Symonds (1967–9: ii. 528).

[4] My source for this tidbit is the *Edinburgh Gazette* of 10 August 1917, at 1607.
[5] The Anthology's Levantine poets: Furness (1931: 8); Mackail: p. 10; Headlam: p. 15.

> I whispered, 'I should like to buy
> Your circlet: is it dear?'...
>
> I caught aflame when Theudis first
> Among the boys outshone
> As though upon the stars there burst
> The newly risen sun...[6]

References to each poem's location in the Anthology are given precisely, and Strato is praised as a 'neat and elegant writer'—a characterization that must ultimately recall the Strato of Symonds's *Studies*, whose clean style had underwritten the presumption that, whatever his morals were, they were definitely pure Greek. In his conspicuous lack of panic over Strato's sexuality Furness seems to echo the casualness of Douglas a few years earlier, for whom sexual object-choice is a matter of personal taste and no one else's business; but he goes further in letting Strato speak frankly of his desires.[7] In describing Meleager, Furness briefly raids the dressing-up box of Mackailian cliché ('inventive, fanciful...rather soft and over-sweet'), but goes on to deliver a poet unproblematically balanced between hetero- and homoerotic passions, both translated with equal gusto and charm—a Meleager just like that of Symonds, in other words, but now delineated explicitly rather than through hints and asides. The translator's scheme of citation points past Mackail to the Anthology's own arrangement, knowledge of which had, of course, been available for the past fifteen years even to those who knew no Greek thanks to Paton's Loebs:

> Your kiss is birdlime and your gaze
> Is fire, Timarion:
> A look from you, and love's ablaze;
> A touch—escape is none.
> (V.96)
>
> Whene'er I look on Thero's face
> My eyes the universe embrace:
> The universe when I survey,
> Naught's to be seen, if he's away.
> (XII.60)[8]

---

[6] These examples are taken from Furness (1931: 182–3); the nature of the 'Musa Puerilis' is explained concisely and without embarrassment at p. 10.

[7] Neat and elegant Strato: Furness (1931: 227). Douglas (1928: 23) alludes indulgently to when 'Strato, on a certain disreputable occasion, compares himself to a wolf', and cf. p. 35, 'Rufinus, alluding to his sudden and almost incredible change of taste in matters erotical...'.

[8] Furness (1931: 103, 117); syrupy Meleager: p. 220.

It is surely no coincidence that Furness's final version from Strato opens with the line: 'Good-bye, vile canting Puritan, good-bye!' (AP 12.237, at 1931: 184). The old cue-cards ('limpidity' and soft Eastern exuberance) may still be there, but they underlie a new sexual politics, dissociated from the Victorian and Edwardian reception back-story that generated them; and all this only two years after Leslie.

ii. Ghost Flowers: Translating and explaining the Anthology in the later twentieth century

'Men, it has been well said, think in herds; it will be seen that they go mad in herds, while they only recover their senses slowly, and one by one.'[9] Notwithstanding the wind of change blowing through Furness's Anthology of 1931, the stock ideas and figures of speech of epigram's Victorian and Edwardian heyday were to prove remarkably tenacious in the genre's longer twentieth-century reception.

'In the middle of the Suez crisis I found it the most comforting thing in the world to translate Catullus; the tedium of a railway journey I have often used to render an epigram from the Greek Anthology.'[10] With these words of conventional wisdom, delivered to the Classical Association in his Presidential Address of 1961, Lord Hailsham (who had served as First Lord of the Admiralty under Anthony Eden) takes epigram's Anglo-Egyptian connection into the incipiently post-colonial aftermath of a Second World War; the incidents of history aside, however, he could as easily have been writing a half-century before. Indeed, what epigram's post-war afterlife reveals is the extraordinary potency of cliché; the intimate interconnection between, on the one hand, figurative language, and, on the other, the reflex habits of thought and mental pigeonholing that that language encodes and perpetuates. In these later echoes as before, summary evaluation of the poets of the Anthology is geared to the much larger critical–ethical project of putting the Greeks to work in the here and now.

Here is Gilbert Highet some years earlier, summing up the legacy of Greek epigram (and thus under pressure of space) as a minor motif in the vast concerto that is Classical Tradition: 'There was also the Greek

---

[9] I quote Charles Mackay's preface to the 1852 edition of his salutary classic, *Extraordinary Popular Delusions and the Madness of Crowds*.

[10] I owe this particular morsel to Schofield (2003: 196); it closely and pointedly echoes a sentiment we have already seen rehearsed at Leaf (1922: 7) (see p. 282) and of course Baring (1903: pp. vi–vii), discussed at p. 260.

Anthology, an enormous collection of epigrams and short lyrics on every conceivable subject, from almost every period of Greek literature. *It contains a vast quantity of trash, some skilful journeyman work, and a surprising number of real gems: small, but diamonds.*[11] Elsewhere in his *magnum opus*, Highet pontificates against late-nineteenth-century European Decadents in terms straight out of Mackail's defence of Sappho's pure art—and of the counter-discourse to Symonds's Platonic Uranism. Dismissing Pierre Louÿs's Lesbian lyric imposture, *The Songs of Bilitis* (1894), he declares that its 'crucial faults' are

> that oriental passions and extravagances are attributed to the self-disciplined Greeks, and that a homosexual lust is represented as the moving force of Sappho's art... *Evidently what Louÿs and his readers wanted was not the clear water of Ilissus, beside which Socrates talked to young Phaedrus of passion and the mastery of reason, but a draught from the turbid Nile.*[12]

A conservatively framed 'Greek love' is here carefully distanced from the lush sexuality of the half-Greeks of the Roman Decadence. The phrasing points towards Wilde's Dorian Gray in his aspect as Antinous *rediuiuus*, as encountered in Chapter 4—'Crowned with heavy lotus-blossoms, he has sat on the prow of Adrian's barge, looking into the green, turbid Nile'—in order to dissociate the true Greek eros from *fin de siècle* Decadence. This higher love is identified precisely as the philosophic eros of Symonds's beloved *Phaedrus*, read here as a sermon in chastened sublimation; the battle against 'The Genius of Greek Art' is still being fought.

A couple of years later, Frank Lucas's *Greek Poetry for Everyman* (1951) beats the same war drum: modern intellectuals are 'eccentrics and neurotics, decadents and suicides', distracted from plain common sense and healthy morals by the savage creeds of primitive races. The idea is an extreme development of one already found forty years before, in Livingstone's championing of an idealized Greek literature as an immunization programme against 'the morbid pathology and the charming affectations of modern literature'; but it is given the specific inflection of the Anthology's post-Mackailian cult of the healthy amateur.[13] Symonds's beloved Shelley is one of the culprits Lucas singles out by name, while the more threateningly *outré* Wilde is invoked only through coy and censorious

---

[11] Highet (1949: 229) (emphases added, here and in subsequent passage).
[12] Highet (1949: 458–9). Mackail's defence of Sappho, decorously explaining away those 'ambiguities of expression which malice or prurience may distort' without ever saying what those distortions might be: (1926: 93–5).
[13] Livingstone (1912: 168), discussed at F. Turner (1981: 34).

allusion, just as he had been in Livingstone's day—*The Green Carnation* is, of course, the title of the kiss-and-tell bestseller of 1894 (see Chapter 4):

[The Greeks] did not crave blue wine—red was enough; *they did not cultivate green carnations* ... There are human beings so anaemic that they need drink or drugs to feel alive; there are others so alive that, *like Wordsworth, they can find intoxication in a mountain burn*. There is no need to romanticize the Greeks in the style of Lord Leighton: the truth is remarkable enough. These men ... were much nearer to the primitive than we; but they were much farther from the madhouse.[14]

Lucas's Greeks are a nation of seafarers and hardy mountaineers (1951: p. xxvi), exactly like those of Butcher sixty years before, and his admissible epigrammatists are immediately hailed as embodying 'the *limpid purity* of *bright spring-water leaping beside a hot and stony track*'.[15] The qualities of this highland stream have come trickling down to Lucas's generation from Matthew Arnold's long-ago 'sweetness and light'—and we recall Meleager's crystalline 'limpidity' in Symonds's essay on the Anthology, albeit that there Strato vied with him for 'purity' of style. Lucas himself had spent plenty of time hands-on with the text of the Anthology—his exquisite illustrated *Greek Anthology* for the little Golden Cockerel Press (1937) had cued up an OUP *Greek Garland* with wider reach (1939)—but one would not know it from the hand-me-down nature of his remarks here. Old tropes jostle and merge: those intensely vital and clean-living individuals who 'find intoxication in a mountain *burn*' inhabit a familiar, Wordsworthian-Tory 'Book of Nature', but also tilt their walking-sticks towards the Scottishing and ramblerization of epigram enacted by Lang and Lothian. Lucas includes a single, sympotic, epigram of Strato from outside the Boyish Muse (AP 11.19). His selection from Meleager, meanwhile, is heteroerotic and at last funerary: yet again, and surely not for the last time, Clearista unfastens 'her knot of maidenhood' for Death.[16]

If Symonds-esque sentiments on the Anthology continued to echo into the later twentieth century and even beyond, it was surely in part because *Studies* long remained embedded as a school-library fixture—indeed, it was specifically endorsed as preparatory reading for the university-bound sixth-former. Already in the 1920s, Symonds was being

---

[14] Lucas (1951: p. xxix), an extraordinary passage; the 'jaded restlessness' of 'our intellectuals', who in their folly 'have genuflected before Negro mumbo-jumbos', is held to blame for both World Wars. (Emphases are added.)

[15] Lucas (1951: p. xxx) (emphasis added).

[16] Sympotic Strato: Lucas (1951: 363); Meleager: pp. 39 51–3; Clearista as bride of Death: p. 352.

recommended as an authority on Greek poetry in Gilbert Norwood's little handbook *The Writers of Greece*.[17] More influentially, John Arbuthnot Nairn's long-lived *Classical Hand-List* of 1931, a standard reference work, stipulates four modern works as the standard secondary reading on Greek literature in verse: Jebb's *Growth and Influence*, Mackail's *Lectures*, the newcomer Gilbert Murray's *Classical Tradition in Poetry* (1927)—and, finally, the third edition of *Studies*, in the newly repaginated and very popular single-volume imprint of 1920. Symonds was still on board in the *Hand-List*'s second edition of 1939, in an expanded list of standard reading: ten books in all. The new names include Murray's protégé Maurice Bowra and Wilamowitz, whose *Kleine Schriften* are recommended in the original German, surely for the keen student only. The Clifton College lectures and periodical essays of *Studies* are now keeping some very elevated and austere academic company indeed; being recommended in the same breath as Wilamowitz had to convey cachet. Astonishingly, Nairn's was still pointing the classical tyro in Symonds's direction in its third and final edition of 1953—and handbooks for teachers in Classics and Ancient History continued to direct schools towards Nairn's well into the 1970s.

Symonds's Late Victorian/Edwardian Nemesis lingered as well. Dudley Fitts's little book of translations from the Anthology for Faber (1957), rehashing a preface he had written for a limited-issue prototype of 1938, still cites eagerly by 'M'-number where an AP reference is not available, and hails the *Select Epigrams* of Mackail as 'a *liber aureus*, unsurpassed of its kind'. His readers are urged to seek out and inwardly digest an introduction that even after sixty years they may regard as the definitive statement of epigram-lore.[18] Fitts's Latinate allusion (*liber aureus*) is, of course, to the famed *Libro d'Oro*, in which all the nobility of Renaissance Venice was enrolled; by implication, then, Mackail has confirmed the lineage and worth of each of his 500 ancient poems, inscribing them with unquestionable authority as the aristocracy of their genre. Any poem excluded from the list is not worth knowing: it has failed to make the grade socially. Eighty-some years after Symonds gushed over the

---

[17] Norwood (1925: 123).

[18] Fitts (1938) was printed in 500 numbered and slipcased copies by New Directions, a Connecticut press specializing in avant-garde authors, as part of its 'Poet of the Month' series; see Ch. 6, pp. 285–6, for the Imagist connection here. There was a follow-up volume in 1941. Fitts is probably better known for his collaborations with his former pupil, Robert Fitzgerald, on translations of Greek tragedy. Faber had already dipped its toe in Greek Anthology with Reid (1943).

Anthology, his all-comers' Golden Treasury of ancient folk verse has been firmly set aside in favour of a Golden Book. Indeed, Mackail's masterpiece of canon-formation is so self-evidently definitive that the Faber translator has not bothered to read anything published since: his Meleager still exudes 'half-Oriental luxuriance', and his Imperial Greeks churn out 'tedious doggerel' in classic Mackailian style; acknowledgements of Leslie and Paton are nugatory.[19]

'Finally', Fitts remarks, 'for the student who must have the entire *Anthology* [the Cephalan rabble, so to speak; *hoi polloi*] there are five volumes of the Loeb Classical Library'—and we may at this point recall that their translator, Paton, had done his best to dissuade even his most studious of readers from trying to read them from cover to cover (see pp. 35–6); but this merely real Anthology could never match up to Mackail's genius for nosing out what is earliest and best. The choicer Hellenistic poets have real merit for Fitts, Callimachus in particular, as does Plato (a Plato still not explicitly 'pseudo-'), but the stale poetasting of 'the Imperial riffraff' puts the genre in its coffin; Meleager himself, a lyricist of the souk, must be treated with caution.[20] All of this of course is very familiar ground; so too is Fitts's authorial sign-off, on the outdoorsy authenticity of the modern epigram-worker's process, which we encountered proleptically in Chapter 6 ('I have not really undertaken translation at all—translation, that is to say, as it is understood in the schools . . . ').[21]

That these views of the 1890s–1920s are still being peddled in the late 1950s is straightforwardly explained: Fitts is re-warming a 1930s plate that was already a *réchauffé* of mixed leftovers. We may be rather more surprised to find the same conventional pieties cropping up afresh in a translation of the late 1960s. After the classical gold of Simonides and Plato—Andrew Sinclair's preferred scheme of arrangement is chronological—come the 'silver' Alexandrians, of whom Callimachus alone deserves really serious attention, and after them the iron coarseness of Imperial Greek court jesters such as Lucillius; the love of Greek men for youths was a local and transitory fashion, not a natural expression of desire at all; and finally, 'the themes of the Anthology are universal, love and life and death' (should that not be love, *worship*, and death?). And this in a selection that bills itself as edgy and provocative, jolting a

[19] Fitts (1957: 5 (M-numbers), 11); name-checking Leslie and Paton: p. 14.
[20] Callimachus and Plato: Fitts (1957: 11); on Paton's attempt to dissuade his own hypothetical *lector studiosus* from reading the whole Anthology, see Nisbet (2012b: 75–7) and briefly, of course, this book's Introduction.
[21] Fitts (1957: 13).

complacent modernity with object-lessons from a defamiliarized and thrillingly alien Hellenic past.[22]

When Peter Jay introduces his Penguin translation of 1973, it is to Mackail's 500 poems of eighty years before—the most recent 'useful selection' in circulation, we are told (in what is surely a put-down of Shane Leslie's Routledge volume of 1929)—that he looks back in homage. For the precedent of marshalling a collaborative attempt at an Anthology in verse, he looks further back still—all the way to Bland and Merivale. 'I have attempted to fill this gap by providing versions of *all the poems of living interest—to wrest them from the disorganized mass* of the sixteen books which form the Greek Anthology': again the surviving text is a ruined garden run to weeds and rubble, from which the flowers of timeless human feeling and experience may yet be gathered in by the discerning eye and decisive hand.[23] Again the arrangement is chronological, by period; of these, only the first can be called 'Greek', and reaches its terminus in the fourth-century Athens of a more or less genuinely epigrammatic Plato.[24]

This is a Plato with nothing of the Uranian about him; homosexuality is a fad of the Decadence, an attention-seeking fashion, then as now: 'Strato has, if anything, *too much that is modishly "contemporary" in his favour. There is nothing that can be done about this.* The reader must acclimatize himself as best he can to the different sorts of effort required of him to enter into the poems' lost occasions.' The apologetic rhetoric of readerly adjustment is par for the course in Penguin Classics of a certain age (Walter Hamilton's *Symposium* (1951) goes all out to placate the affronted common reader, presumed to be a virile Anglo-Saxon contemptuous of sissy queers). Strato's love poems for boys are explained as technical exercises in a fashionable theme, nothing more; the poet's lack of authentic feeling even earns him backhanded credit for stylistic virtuosity, 'an adept and witty writer of light, mildly pornographic verse, using the Alexandrian erotic conventions'.[25] When at last they

---

[22] Sinclair (1967: 14 (silver and gold), 16 (just a phase), 17 (universal themes), 20 (those radical Greeks)). Cf. Skelton (1971: p. xvii): 'It is, of course, well known that it was, at various times and in various places in the long post-classical period, fashionable to compose verses in favour of beautiful boys, and many of these epigrams have an air of flirtatious delicacy which makes one suspect their origins to lie more in fantasy than fact.'

[23] Jay (1973: 9) (emphasis added). His roster of modern translators includes Tony Harrison and Christopher Logue.

[24] Jay's Plato (1973: 44) is 'traditionally supposed to have written poetry...I include here only the best attested poems.'.

[25] Jay (1973: 25, 270). Again cf. Skelton (1971: p. xvii, quoted at n. 20), on boy-love as a fashion of 'the long post-classical period'.

are translated for the general reading public, their translator's boast echoes those of Lothian and Rice in the 1920s, and others since (see Chapter 6): 'I am no textual scholar but a poet who knows which texts make sense.'[26]

2. HOW TO BURY A POET, SPEAKING FIGURATIVELY

What do these schoolbooks and handbooks have to do with academia? The simple answer is that scholars come up through commentaries and translations, even cribs; from time to time we have all leaned on a Loeb. Specialization, too, nudges us to rely on the discipline's *communis opinio* as the backdrop to our particular and frequently very narrow lines of enquiry. Nairn's *Classical Hand-List* directed the tyro to general reading on a wealth of topics, but must also have been handy as an 'Enquire within upon Everything' for the more experienced hand; sometimes a quick answer (these days more likely out of the *Oxford Classical Dictionary*) will do just fine. But it is the nature of *communis opinio* always to work around what went before; traces of the old remain residually and near-invisibly embedded in what seems a modern whole.

The scholars whose work on epigram I most admire are not immune to Mackailian moments (and I am sure I have committed the odd Mackailism of my own). Ewen Bowie's work on the sophists and poets has put epigram at the heart of the academic study of Greek literary culture in the Roman Empire. It was he who called for the academic rehabilitation of Strato, and the call was answered, keeping the academic study of the poet in pace with the admission of his Boyish Muse into the public sphere.[27] Nonetheless, Bowie's own artful and bloodless Strato 'writes exclusively about boys. The reasons could be literary: Rufinus had come close to exhausting the available moves in poetry about girls, so Strato turns his pen to the obvious alternative. But another factor surely operates too...'. That factor is that his *floruit* is by modern consensus placed under Hadrian, a lover of all things Greek and of one Bithynian

---

[26] Hine (2001: p. xx).
[27] Bowie's Strato (1990: 57) is 'a good [poet]...as deserving of a modern edition as Rufinus', for whom Denys Page did the honours in 1978. His call has been answered twice that I know of, though not yet in English. Daryl Hine (2001) anticipates an un-affronted popular market for his own zesty translation of AP 12.

Greek youth in particular. Bowie's Strato is not so much writing homosexual desire as developing a literary treatment so as to court the
patronage of a known connoisseur; that is to say, his poems reflect
fashion, not passion.[28]

Alan Cameron is the Anthology's great modern myth-buster whose
work on textual transmission underpins our field. Called upon to put the
topic in a nutshell for a non-specialist market, he explains in his article
on 'Anthology' for the *Oxford Classical Dictionary* that: 'The Greek
Anthology is one of the great books of European literature, *a garden
containing the flowers and weeds of fifteen hundred years of Greek poetry*,
from the most humdrum doggerel to the purest poetry...' (emphasis
added). The phrasing has survived revision and is still there in the
current (fourth) edition. Because we come to new realizations by moving
old ideas around, none of us is immune to the residual momentum of the
baggage we trail: the half-forgotten figurative connections and the buried
habits of thought; the moss on the great rolling stone; the madness of
herds. When Denys Page came to write the introduction to the final
monument of modern scholarship he had co-edited with Andrew Gow,
the great *The Greek Anthology: The Garland of Philip* (1968), he found he
had nothing in particular to say about what epigram had been *for* in the
ancient world: Frank Lucas had put it all better than he ever could, so he
tipped in a lengthy quotation from *Greek Poetry for Everyman* in lieu of a
paraphrase. For readers who wanted more, he set homework—sixty
pages of Mackail in full flow: 'See also Mackail *Select Epigrams from
the Greek Anthology* (1911) 32–90.'[29]

A rich legacy of figurative embroidery has certainly done the Anthology no favours over the years as a literary text in Anglophone scholarship. With the signal exceptions of Gow and Page, Mackail's patriotic
call to arms against the German philological foeman (see Chapter 5)
has been roundly ignored. Meleager's own fortunes may be taken as
emblematic of this steady academic marginalization. For two centuries
and more *the* name to conjure with in epigram-discourse, this most
important of late Hellenistic epigrammatists and pioneer of Anthology
spent the nineteenth and twentieth centuries as little more *than* a
name; in 2013 he at last gets his own critical edition with commentary

---

[28] Bowie (1990: 57); earlier on the page he has called Strato 'ready with both wit and
passion', but his remarks on literary game-playing seem to reclassify 'passion' in this
instance as a subcategory of wit, best understood as a product of market forces.

[29] Gow and Page (1968: I, pp. xxxv–vi); Mackail is recommended in the footnote at
p. xxxv; by beginning at p. 32 the reader skips his introductory remarks on the definition of
epigram, issues of arrangement, and the history of the Anthology.

thanks to the labours of Kathryn Gutzwiller, a scholar long renowned for cutting through the pretty rhetoric to the blunt fact of what can actually be known. Rescued from his pedestal of hand-me-down mystification, he will probably turn out to be a pretty good poet. But where is all the scholarship on him? Where has Meleager *been* for the last hundred and more years, as a teaching text and a topic for articles and dissertations?

3. GREEK GENIUS ON DEMAND: POSTMODERN ANTHOLOGY

> The email, telling a friend we're not too bad considering
> the state of the world, crosses the Atlantic
> with the touch of a key. The leaves of an evergreen blow
> like a shoal of emerald fish returning to the same place.[30]

I started researching Greek epigram in reception because it was what I could afford. Round the corner from the Department in Glasgow is, among several others in the vicinity, the second-hand bookshop Voltaire and Rousseau; its everything-for-a-pound lobby is where mouldering Victoriana go to die, indiscriminately shelved among old religious tracts and horrid cookbooks in a veritable elephant's graveyard of print. It was there that I first encountered Symonds's *Studies*—once so famous, now all but forgotten—and later Neaves, and more besides, gradually amassing for myself a private hoard of obscure nineteenth-century Anthology. The character of Glasgow's second-hand bookshops is peculiar to its *genius loci*; a life history of high culture and heavy industry, pay-day hedonism and Presbyterian thrift, has given the city a set of attitudes to education and the written word that is not quite like what you find anywhere else. So I have Glasgow to thank for giving me a steer as no other place could have at the time, at least not for pocket-money prices.

Seven years or so later, the scene is very different: the Anthology of our forebears has gone global. Had I but known it, Symonds had sneaked a head start already, in Honolulu of all places, re-issued in a 2002 facsimile (which remains in print) by the University Press of the Pacific; but this was merely a taster of what was to come. A trawl on Amazon turns up Mackail in an electronic facsimile by AMA Publications, a specialist company founded as recently as 2011 to package out-of-copyright

---

[30] Delanty (2012: 3), attributed to the make-believe poet 'Grigorographos'.

content for the online retailer's Kindle tablet, alongside e-editions of Symonds by BiblioBazaar, an entrepreneurial forerunner to AMA. BiblioBazaar and its sibling BiblioLife are part of BiblioLabs, which Amazon has snapped up as an in-house packager of out-of-copyright content for ebooks. In this way Mackail, Symonds, and their peers have become deeply integrated into the systems of the planet's largest Internet retailer. (But they may also be had for free from archive.org and www.gutenberg. org, Internet repositories of public-domain text that year on year edge closer to comprehensive coverage.)

Another arm of the BiblioLabs operation, the exotically named Nabu Press, does the same thing with books on paper as does BiblioBazaar with ebooks. Nabu is a major player in the fluid and diverse new sector of the 'traditional' print book market opened up by the startling economic possibilities of current digital printing and scanning technologies. The overheads are now so low that a single copy of a book can be run off from a digital file to order and shipped to anywhere in the world, be it from the States or New Delhi (where Nabu's rival Pranava Books does a roaring trade), and still make money from a modest cover price—the online shopper can pick up *Select Epigrams* or either volume of *Studies* for £20 or so. The profit from a print run of one is small, to be sure; but if a company has a catalogue of thousands of such files, all chosen on the calculation that they will be wanted every now and then, all those small sums add up over time to something big. Nabu will need to watch its margins, though; already it is being undercut by up-and-coming competitors. Forgotten Books will sell you its own admittedly grotty scan of *Select Epigrams* for half of what Nabu is asking.[31]

It is impossible to say who is reading these new–old books, where, and in what kinds of numbers; the imponderables are roughly akin to those we identified in sizing up the teensy-tiny print runs of the carolling Reverend Woodward or 'Ion Ionicos' (see Chapter 6), but now rolled out on a global scale and with no end in sight. Give it another few years and it is conceivable that more people alive today will have read Mackail and Symonds on epigram than ever read them first time around, all those years ago. The same could even happen to Bland and Merivale and Wellesley and Neaves and Garnett and Pott and Rodd and Buck and Butler and Tomson and Burges, to MacGregor of wretched memory

---

[31] On BiblioLabs' business model, one so successful that it now ships hundreds of thousands of books a year, see usefully Albanese (2010); Bradley et al. (2011) survey the (then) state of the digital and print-on-demand sector and review the scholarship. Other digital-economy margin publishers issuing Anthology-related reprints include Hardpress and Read.

and even poor Lumb, and to others besides, on whom this book has not touched; right now it seems an unlikely scenario, but they are all just a OneClick purchase away, and increasingly they are readable for free as e-texts.[32]

When Shane Leslie called the Anthology 'the great rolling stone of Greece' he was right, if not perhaps for the right reasons: it is the stickiest and most pliable of ancient texts (indeed it both is and is not an 'ancient text' in the first place), accruing layer upon layer of moss as it rolls down the decades since its reclamation as a source for versioning and interpretation at the cusp of the seventeenth and eighteenth centuries.[33] We have seen how, over the course of the nineteenth and earlier twentieth centuries, this cumulative detritus of cross-cultural explanation spread its mossy tendrils and wove together into a shape determined more by its own patterns of growth than by the ancient stone at its heart; indeed, by the century's turn most of the players were agreeing that this stone was better forgotten in favour of a redacted text by one of their own (see Chapters 5–6).

In the intervening years, what was secondary literature has become a new kind of primary text, susceptible and deserving of being read by classicists under the sign of reception study; but each text really makes sense only as a voice within the cantata (see pp. 9, 30–1). I hope to have shown how, for a century and more, this work-in-progress was forever rewriting itself, adding new voice parts to re-inflect dissident notes and bring them willy-nilly into harmony with the ideological drift of the whole; endlessly elaborating and reiterating so as to drown out those who refused to sing from the right score; perhaps not always succeeding as well as they would have liked.

---

[32] What, for instance, of Lilla Cabot Perry, the American Impressionist painter and occasional poet, whose *From the Garden of Hellas* (1891) was her sole foray into translation from Greek? Or William Gunnyon, with his *A Century of Translations from the Greek Anthology* (1883)—a 'century' not of years but of one hundred versions, like a cricket score? Purportedly written 'solely as a literary solace' (p. 5), they first appeared in the Reviews and reflect a distinctly Scottish conception of Anthology—Gunnyon had already edited the complete poetical works of that Wordsworth of the North, Burns (1875). And what of James Granville Legge, who rooted his *Echoes from the Greek Anthology* (1919) in Mackail's selection but could never forget the transgressive 'thrill' of reading Symonds's panegyric of Meleager as an undergraduate in that 'glowing chapter' of *Studies* (p. 5), and who mostly turned his verses 'on top of a municipal tram, or in railway carriages on tedious war-time journeys' (p. 7)? Legge knew Wilde and his circle, and later became the first Professor of Chinese at Oxford. All these stories and more could have fed into this book had it been longer, and their pursuit would surely reward the curious reader.
[33] Here as in the Introduction I lean, of course, on the ideas of Julia Gaisser, this time applying them in a more conventional way.

What will the e-reader-equipped customers of 2020 or 2030 (if tablets, Kindles, et al. are still the thing) make of these strange ancient voices, brought back to life from the dusty tomb—and of the Greek poems they translate and discuss? Time alone will tell. From Narva to Nabu, it has been a long, strange ride, and it is not over yet (in 2012 the Irish poet and translator Greg Delanty 'unearthed' a *Greek Anthology Book XVIII* to supplement the sixteen of the standard texts, window-dressed with a perhaps tongue-in-cheek sub-scholarly preface).[34] What we have seen so far—the story this book has tried to tell—is a genre that is continually being reinvented and rediscovered, creatively forgotten and remembered for culture, in ways that may continue to make it a useful weather-gauge for how Classics is intersecting with the public sphere as well as how it thrashes out its internal controversies.

The genealogy of the Anthology's afterlife in modernity offers useful pointers for academia in postmodernity, constantly turning over as it does key questions of the social relevance of philological hermeneutics and how we reconstruct (or simply construct) the past from the materials that come to hand, materials whose back-story we may not always see. But with at least as much urgency, and with ever-increasing timeliness, the whole of our story speaks also to anthology *beyond* the Anthology—that is, to the means on which the Humanities increasingly rely to perpetuate themselves as a cultural formation and as a site of socially privileged knowledge. The field of anthology studies is still in the process of articulating and constituting itself,[35] but what it is facing up to address is an international culture of pedagogy in which the anthology format is becoming ever more indispensable, leaving the uncut text in its dust. As a true cautionary tale, the story of the Uranians and counter-Uranians (and of the strange paths taken since and sampled in this chapter) deserves to be factored in, and to be returned to repeatedly as a touchstone, as academic cultures work through the cognitive, ethical, and pedagogic issues that arise from anthologization. The winnowing, filtering, chunking, and sound-biting of literary heritage puts the anthologist on a par with the translator as a gatekeeper to cultural capital—and, from time to time, a guardian of dangerous knowledge. With so much at stake, there is no neutral mediation.

How do we practice Classics, on what pretext, and for whose benefit? What do we elide when we Anthologize; which voices do we silence, and which ventriloquize? These are the questions raised by epigram's strange modern back-story, and they deserve not to go away.

---

[34] Delanty (2012).   [35] Notable thus far is Di Leo (2004).

ENVOI

Meanwhile, in the shadow of an ancient Polynesian idol: .

At his base, in his shadow, looking as if under his protection, lay two human beings, naked, clasped in each other's arms, and fast asleep. One could scarcely pity his vigil, had it been marked sometimes through the years by such an incident as this. The thing had been conducted just as the birds conduct their love affairs. *An affair absolutely natural, absolutely blameless, and without sin.*

It was a marriage according to Nature, without feast or guests, consummated with accidental cynicism under the shadow of a religion a thousand years dead.

(from *The Blue Lagoon* (1908) by Henry de Vere Stacpoole,
a keen Hellenist and former hanger-on of the
Yellow Book crowd; emphasis added)

APPENDIX

Symonds and the Language of Gems

Touched on in passing in the discussion of Symonds's *Studies* (Ch. 3) is his fondness for figuring Greek epigrams as types of precious stone. The *locus classicus* is his description of Meleager:

The first great merit of Meleager as a poet is limpidity. A crystal is not more transparent than his style; but the crystal to which we compare it must be coloured with the softest flush of beryl or of amethyst.

But there is at least one further instance, in which the image is unpacked a little further:

Among the epigrams which seem to have been composed in the same spirit as those exquisite little *capricci* engraved by Greek artists upon gems, few are more exquisite than the three following [citing three pastoral vignettes]...[1]

A couple of pages later, we learn that

cups engraved with figures in relief of Tantalus or Love, seals inscribed with Phoebus or Medusa, *gems and intaglios of all kinds* furnish matter for other epigrams. The following couplet on a Bacchus engraved in amethyst turns upon an untranslatable play of words...[2]

Wrapping up the chapter, Symonds foregrounds the importance in his scheme of connoisseurship of the exact aesthetic equivalence between epigrams and carved gems. Each occupies the same rank and achieves the same effects within their respective realms of verse literature and plastic art. The passage merits quotation at slightly greater length to illustrate the rhetorical sleight of hand by which flowers and gems are made interchangeable as symbols in Anthology:

The very riches of *this flower-garden of little poems* are an obstacle to its due appreciation. Each epigram in itself is perfect, and ought to be carefully and lovingly studied [a principle which his successors will go out of their way to repudiate]. But it is difficult for the critic to deal in a single chapter with *upwards of four thousands of these precious gems*. There are many points of view which, with adequate space and opportunity, might have been taken for the better illustration of the epigrams. Their connection with the later literature of Greece, especially with the rhetoricians...*their still more intimate aesthetic harmony with the engraved stones and minor bas-reliefs, which bear exactly the same relation to Greek sculpture as the epigrams to the more*

---

[1] Symonds (1920: 522 (Meleager), 536 (*capricci*)).
[2] Symonds (1920: 538) (emphasis added).

august forms of Greek poetry; the lives of their authors; the historical events to which they not infrequently allude—all these are topics for elaborate dissertation.[3]

To classify Greek epigrams as types of precious stone was a striking departure. To be sure, back in 1809 Byron had hailed Merivale and Bland as the intrepid miners who had brought to the surface 'those gems too long withheld from modern sight'—but the terminology of the translators themselves was strictly floral, after the manner of Meleager (Ch. 1), and the mid-century Anthologists followed suit (Ch. 2), so his decision to invoke gemstones is a refreshing change.

What is more, Symonds's innovation had lasting influence. As we have seen, the option to swap between two distinct but complementary figurative languages of epigram-collection wins some favour with his successors: Walter Leaf and Shane Leslie are among those who find advantage in shuttling between the flower album and the gem cabinet, between images of unforced spontaneity and artful polish. A more public acknowledgement comes in the title of Grundy's Oxford miscellany of 1913, *Ancient Gems in Modern Settings*; much of Grundy's rhetoric is out of Symonds, so we may safely presume that this is homage.[4] Looking (far) beyond the Anthology, the connoisseur of bad verse may even imagine that the title chosen by Scotland's legendary William McGonagall (he of 'The Tay Bridge Disaster' fame) for the one book of his poems published in his lifetime—*Poetic Gems* (1890–1)—owes something to the influence of Symonds's First Series.

In asserting a clear metaphoric equivalency between epigrams and engraved gemstones, moreover, Symonds tapped into an authentic ancient vein of sentiment: in one major Hellenistic poet at least, the modern scholarship very reasonably detects a sustained programme of metapoetic play upon the similarities between two art-forms united by a spirit of miniaturism.[5] *Symonds was right.*

Symonds did not know this. The Hellenistic poet in question is Posidippus, if indeed (as the modern consensus holds) the 'Milan Posidippus' papyrus is the substantial remnant of a book authored and arranged by him; its category of subtle poems on precious stones, the 'Lithika', is without real precedent in what we had of epigram before the 1990s. In the declamatory and ekphrastic vastness of AP 9 (827 poems in all) I count eight that are about gems; that is all, and the art holdings of the Planudean Appendix add nothing further. Eight poems in upwards of four thousand—'gems and intaglios of all kinds' is a dramatic overstatement.

Symonds was making it up. Why? What did the beryl and amethyst mean to him? The colour of the amethyst picks up the bouquet of violets that Symonds once sent to a young Norman Moor, and about which he wrote a Meleager-inspired epigram (Ch. 3), but only a large leap of faith would turn this into the

---

[3] Symonds (1920: 540) (emphasis added).

[4] As, e.g., at Grundy (1913: p. lxiv), plundering Symonds for a de-fanged take on the Greek aesthetic conscience. Grundy's fat little book ranges across the rich back catalogue of epigram in English translation, all the way from Bland to Baring, while ignoring the Maga set; details at pp. vii–xi.

[5] On the 'Lithika', see Hunter (2004).

discovery of a homosexual code-word;[6] and beryl is more often than not blue or bluish-green, which suggests very little. The classical Greek etymology of the amethyst is that it prevents intoxication, which the optimistic reader might take as a subtle point about the elevated nature of Meleager's eros, but beryl carries no such story in its name.

In post-classical European culture, gems have long constituted a 'language' in which particular stones carry agreed sentimental or religious meanings, but these are ever-changing. One particularly intriguing possibility is suggested by the old French practice, widely popular in Britain in the earlier part of the nineteenth century, of wearing gems acrostically—a romantic motto could be spelled out by gems in sequence, set in a ring or threaded on a bracelet. The lover's name or a message was read off the first letters of the gems: Malachite, Amethyst, Ruby, Iris, and Emerald spelled out 'Marie'.[7] Beryl and Amethyst, 'B.A.', *could* thus point towards one of the great passions of Symonds's life, the Bristol Cathedral chorister, Albert Brooke, with whom he was miserably besotted between 1861 and 1865. This 'ever-recurrent, ever-repressed longing' was very nearly his ruin, in his later estimation, plunging him into a 'close unwelcome labyrinth of tyrannous desires and morbid thoughts' in which he wandered, tormented by sexual dreams and waking fantasies upon which he dared not act.[8] In that case, though, why not 'A.B.'?

The real explanation is probably more mundane; Symonds was a habitual water-colourist in his prose. His lush evocations of landscape and vegetation won him great popularity as a travel writer, as, for instance, in *New Italian Sketches* (1884). Note the palette:

On them our eyes rest lovingly; imagination wanders for a moment through those mossy glades, where cyclamens are growing now, and primroses in spring will peep amid anemones from rustling foliage strewn by winter's winds...

Yet the sea-lover may justify his preference by appealing to the beauty of empurpled shadows, toned by amethyst or opal or shining with violet light, reflected from the clouds that cross and find in those dark shields a mirror.

He liked the colours; he liked the sound the words made. Is this all? Still, he was right.

---

[6] Just once at AP 12.112 (Anon.), a purple cord is used to lead the ensnared *erastēs*—if only Shane Leslie (1929: 9, see Ch. 6) had known this!, or perhaps he did and was being arch—and it has the look of a novel spin on a pre-existing cliché; further, the haughty boys of 12.185 wear purple-edged robes.

[7] For an entertaining and informative discussion, see Kane (2011).

[8] Symonds (1984: 123, 127). The beryl does seem to have had some kind of personal symbolic meaning for Symonds in relation to his passion for Brooke, as expressed in the private poetry (quoted at 1984: 123), but by definition this intertext would remain inaccessible to all but a tiny handful of his readers.

References

1. Editions

de Bosch, Jeronimo, and van Lennep, David Jacob (1795–1822) (eds). *Anthologia Graeca cum versione Latina Hugonis Grotii*. 4 vols. Utrecht: Wild and Altheer.

Brunck, Richard Franz Philipp (1772–6) (ed.). *Analecta veterum poetarum Graecorum*. 3 vols. Strasbourg: I. G. Bauer.

Dübner, Johann Friedrich, and Cougny, Edouard (1864–90) (eds). *Epigrammatum Anthologia Palatina: cum Planudeis et appendice nova epigrammatum veterum ex libris et marmoribus ductorum*. 3 vols. Paris: Didot.

Gow, Andrew S. F., and Page, Denys L. (1965) (eds). *The Greek Anthology: Hellenistic Epigrams*. 2 vols. Cambridge: Cambridge University Press.

Gow, Andrew S. F., and Page, Denys L. (1968) (eds). *The Greek Anthology: The Garland of Philip*. 2 vols. Cambridge: Cambridge University Press.

Jacobs, Friedrich (1794–8) (ed.). *Anthologia Graeca sive poetarum Graecorum lusus. Ex Recensione Brunkii*. 5 vols. Leipzig: Dyck.

Jacobs, Friedrich (1813–17) (ed.). *Anthologia Graeca ad fidem codicis olim Palatini edita*. 3 vols. Leipzig: Dyck.

Page, Denys Lionel (1978) (ed.). *The Epigrams of Rufinus: Edited, with an Introduction and Commentary*. Cambridge: Cambridge University Press.

Page, Denys Lionel (1981) (ed.). *Further Greek Epigrams: Epigrams before AD 50 from the Greek Anthology and Other Sources, Not Included in Hellenistic Epigrams or The Garland of Philip*. Cambridge: Cambridge University Press.

Paton, William Roger (1916–18) (ed. and trans.). *The Greek Anthology: With an English Translation*. 5 vols. London: Heinemann.

Stadtmüller, Hugo (ed.) (1894–1906) (ed.). *Anthologia Graeca epigrammatum Palatina cum Planudea*. 3 vols. Leipzig: Teubner.

2. Translations, works of period (pre-1950) scholarship, and other primary texts

Adams, John (1791). *Elegant Tales, Histories, and Epistles of a Moral Tendency: On Love, Friendship, Matrimony, Conjugal Felicity, Jealousy, Constancy, Magnanimity, Cheerfulness, and Other Important Subjects*. London: G. Kearsley.

Agar, T. L. (1923). 'Notes on the Greek Anthology', *CQ* 17/2: 82–6.

Allison, (Sir) Robert Andrew (1921). *Translations into English Verse, Mainly from the Greek Anthology.* London: A. L. Humphreys.

Anon. (1667). *Anthologia Deutera. Sive Græcorum epigrammatum florilegium novum. Cum aliis veterum poematis, &c. In usum scholae Westmonasteriensis.* London: Elizabeth Redmayne.

Anon. (1699). *Epigrammatum Delectus, ex omnibus, tum Veteribus tum Recentioribus, Poetis accurate decerptus. Cum Dissertatione De Vera Pulchritudine et adumbrata, in qua, ex certis Principiis Rejectionis et Selectionis Epigrammatam causae redduntur. Adjectae sunt elegantes Sententiae, ex antiquis Poetis parce, sed serviore judicio, selectæ. Cum brevioribus Sententiis ac Proverbiis, ex Auctoribus Graecis et Latinis. Quibus hac Quinta Editione subjungitur. Alterius Delectus Specimen, ex nuperis maxime Poetis ab Electoribus praetermissis; in usum Scholae Etonensis.* London: S. Smith and B. Walford.

Anon. (1724). *Ἀνθολογία, sive Epigrammatum Graecorum ex Ἀνθολογία edita, MS. Bodleiana, aliisque autoribus delectus in usum scholae Westmonasteriensis.* Oxford: Clarendon Press.

Anon. (1791). *A Selection of Greek Epigrams or Inscriptions from Brunck's Anthologia: To Which is Annexed a Translation in English Verse, with Notes. For the Use of Winchester School.* Oxford: J. Cooke.

Anon. (1793). Review of Johann Gottfried Herder, *Zerstraute Blättern: Vierte Sammlung* (Gotha: C. W. Ettinger, 1792), *Critical Review, or Annals of Literature*, 7: 506–10.

Anon. (1804). 'Memoir of Gottfried Herder', *Monthly Magazine and British Register*, 18: 133–4.

Anon. (1807). Review of Bland (1806), *Edinburgh Review*, 8: 319–31.

Anon. (1813). Review of Bland (1813), *Monthly Review or Literary Journal, Enlarged*, 78: 204–49.

Anon. (1826). Review of Bland (1813), *Museum Criticum*, 1: 262–73.

Anon. (1833a). Review of Merivale (1833), *Athenaeum*, 271–322: 226–7.

Anon. (1833b). 'Epigrams from the Anthology', *Athenaeum*, 271–322: 56, 199, 301, 517, 589, 741, 753, 815.

Anon. (1833c). 'The Greek Anthology. No. I', *Blackwood's Edinburgh Magazine*, 33: 865–88.

Anon. (1833d). 'The Greek Anthology. No. II', *Blackwood's Edinburgh Magazine*, 34: 115–40.

Anon. (1833e). Review of Merivale (1833), *London Literary Gazette and Journal of Belles Lettres, Arts, Sciences, Etc.*, 845: 193–4.

Anon. (1833f). Review of Merivale (1833), *Gentleman's Magazine*, 153: 536–8.

Anon. (1836a). 'Ecclesiastical Intelligence', *John Bull*, 837: 488.

Anon. (1836b). 'The Epigrams of Theocritus', *Blackwood's Edinburgh Magazine*, 40: 803–11.

Anon. (1838). 'Loss of our Golden Key', *Blackwood's Edinburgh Magazine*, 43: 248–57.

Anon. (1850a). Review of Wellesley (1849), *Christian Remembrancer*, 19: 429–44.

Anon. (1850b). Review of Mure (1850), *Edinburgh Review*, 92: 398–435.

Anon. (1853). Obituary of Charles Abraham Elton, *Gentleman's Magazine*, 40: 88–9.

Anon. (1855). Review notice of MacGregor (1855), *Leader*, 333: 763–4.

Anon. (1857a). Review notice of MacGregor (1857), *Leader*, 393: 956.

Anon. (1857b). Review notice of MacGregor (1857), *John Bull and Britannia*, 1914: 523.

Anon. (1857c). Review of Mure (1857), *Westminster Review*, 68–9: 313–15.

Anon. (1857d). Review of Mure (1857), *Saturday Review of Politics, Literature, Science, and Art*, 4: 134–5.

Anon. (1864a). 'Greek Anthology' [review of Macgregor (1864)], *New Monthly Magazine*, 132: 445–8.

Anon. (1864b). Review of Macgregor (1864), *London Review of Politics, Society, Literature, Art, and Science*, 9: 643–4.

Anon. (1865a). Review of Macgregor (1864), *Museum and English Journal of Education*, 1: 384–6.

Anon. (1865b). Review of Macgregor (1864), *Westminster Review*, 83–4: 300.

Anon. (1865c). 'Epigrams' [review article], *London Quarterly Review*, 117: 204–49.

Anon. (1866). Obituary of Henry Wellesley, *Gentleman's Magazine*, 220: 440.

Anon. (1871). Review of Benjamin Jowett, *The Dialogues of Plato* (4 vols; Oxford: Oxford University Press, 1871), *The Times* (Wednesday, 12 April): 7.

Anon. (1873a). Review notice of Symonds (1873), *Examiner*, 3411 (Saturday, 14 June): 8.

Anon. (1873b). Review of Symonds (1873), *Examiner*, 3429 (Saturday, 18 October): 1–2.

Anon. (1874a). Review of Neaves (1874), *John Bull*, 2793: 417.

Anon. (1874b). 'Speech Day at Harrow School', *John Bull*, 2795: 446.

Anon. (1875). Review of Symonds (1875), *John Bull*, 2843: 178.

Anon. (1876). Review of Symonds (1876), *John Bull*, 2896: 385.

Anon. (1880). Review of the American edition of Symonds (1873/6), *Lippincott's Magazine*, 25: 263.

Anon. (1885). *Pictorial Records of the English in Egypt, with a Full and Descriptive Life of General Gordon, the Hero of Khartoum. Together with Graphic Narratives of the Lives and Adventures of Lord Wolseley, Stewart, Burnaby, Horatio Nelson, Abercromby, Sidney Smith, Sir John Moore, Bruce, and other World-famous Heroes* (London: James Sangster).

Anon. (1889a). Review notice of Tomson (1889), *Ladies Monthly Magazine, Le Monde Élégant, or the World of Fashion, etc.*, 790: 162.

Anon. (1889b). 'Current News about Women', *Women's Penny Paper*, 50: 2.

Anon. (1892). Review of Mackail (1890), *The Nation*, 55.1425 (October): 304–5.

Anon. (1893a). 'Brief Mention', *AJP* 14/2: 258–62.

Anon. (1893b). Critical notice of Symonds (1893), *School Review*, 1/8: 511–12.

Anon. (1893c). Review of Symonds 1893, *Book Reviews: A Monthly Journal Devoted to New and Current Publications*, 1/3: 68; 1/5: 117.

Anon. (1906). Critical notice of Mackail (1905), *CR* 21/7: 215.

Arnold, Matthew (1869). *Culture and Anarchy: An Essay in Political and Social Criticism*. London: Smith, Elder.

Arnold, Matthew (1903). *Essays in Criticism: Second Series*. London and New York: Macmillan.

Baring, Evelyn (Earl of Cromer) (1903). *Paraphrases and Translations from the Greek*. London: Macmillan.

Baring, Evelyn (Earl of Cromer) (1908). *Modern Egypt*. 2 vols. London: Macmillan.

Baring, Evelyn (Earl of Cromer) (1911). Critical notice of Mackail 1910, *JHS* 31: 327.

Baring, Evelyn (Earl of Cromer) (1913). *Political and Literary Essays, 1908–1913*. London: Macmillan.

Barnard, Francis Pierrepoint (1922). *A Fardel of Epigrams, Done into English*. London: Oxford University Press.

Becker, Wilhelm Adolf, trans. Revd Frederick Metcalfe (1854). *Charicles, or Illustrations of the Private Life of the Ancient Greeks*. London: John Parker.

Beeching, Henry Charles, Mackail, John William, and Nichols, John Bowyer Buchanan (1883). *Love in Idleness: A Volume of Poems*. London: Kegan Paul.

Benecke, Edward Felix Mendelssohn (1896). *Antimachus of Colophon and the Position of Women in Greek Poetry: A Fragment, Printed for the Use of Scholars*. London: Swan Sonnenschein.

Benson, Arthur Christopher (1922). *The Reed of Pan: English Renderings of Greek Epigrams and Lyrics*. London: John Murray.

Bland, Robert (1806). With John Herman Merivale and Francis Hodgson, published anonymously. *Translations Chiefly from the Greek Anthology: With Tales and Miscellaneous Poems*. London: Richard Phillips.

Bland, Robert (1813). With John Herman Merivale. *Collections from the Greek Anthology and from the Pastoral, Elegiac, and Dramatic Poets of Greece. By the Rev. Robert Bland and Others*. London: John Murray.

Bland, Robert, and Merivale, John Herman, writing as 'Narva' (1805–6). 'Epigrams, Fragments, and Fugitive Pieces from the Greek', *Monthly Magazine and British Register*, 19: 136–8, 215–18, 338–42, 456–9, 541–5; 20: 20–4, 123–6, 211–15, 311–19, 401–5, 508–11; 21: 17–22, 109–11.

Browne, Robert William (1851–3). *A History of Classical Literature*. 2 vols. London: Richard Bentley.

Buck, Mitchells Starrett (1916). *The Greek Anthology (Palatine MS): The Amatory Epigrams*. Privately printed.

Burges, George (1852). *The Greek Anthology, as Selected for the Use of Westminster, Eton and other Public Schools. Literally Translated into English Prose, Chiefly by George Burges, A.M., Trinity College, Cambridge, to which are Added Metrical Versions by Bland, Merivale, and Others*. London: George Bell and Sons.

Burns, James Dawson, Revd (1861–4). *The Temperance Dictionary*. 34 fascicles. London: Job Cauldwell.

Burton, Margaret (1937). With Arundell James Kennedy Esdaile, *Famous Libraries of the World: Their History, Collections, and Administrations*. London: Grafton.

Butcher, S. H. (1893). *Some Aspects of the Greek Genius*. 2nd edn. London and New York: Macmillan.

Butler, Alfred Joshua (1881). *Amaranth and Asphodel: Songs from the Greek Anthology*. London: Kegan Paul.

Butler, Alfred Joshua (1922). *Amaranth and Asphodel: Poems from the Greek Anthology. Done into English Verse*. Oxford: Basil Blackwell.

Butler, Eliza M. (1935). *The Tyranny of Greece over Germany*. London: Cambridge University Press.

Byron, (Lord) George Gordon (1973–82). *Byron's Letters and Journals*, ed. Leslie A. Marchand. 12 vols. Cambridge, MA: Harvard University Press.

Campbell, Lewis (1893). Review of Walter Pater, *Plato and Platonism* (1893), *Classical Review* 7/6: 263–6.

Carpenter, Edward (1902). *Iolaus: An Anthology of Friendship*. London: Swan Sonnenschein.

Carpenter, Edward (1912). *The Intermediate Sex: A Study of Some Transitional Types of Men and Women*. 3rd edn. London: Swan Sonnenschein, Manchester: S. Clarke. (1st edn, 1908.)

Chatterton, Thomas (1770). 'Narva and Mored: An African Eclogue', *London Magazine*, 31 (May 1770): 268–9.

Church, Richard William (1891). *The Oxford Movement: Twelve Years, 1833–45*. London: Macmillan.

Churchill, George B. (1903). 'Public-Speaking Work in the Secondary School', *School Review*, 11/4: 269–87.

Cobb, George Henry (1908). *Poems from the Greek Anthology: Attempted in English Verse*. London: Simpkin, Marshall.

Cocker, Benjamin Franklin (1870). *Christianity and Greek Philosophy, or The Relation between Spontaneous and Reflective Thought in Greece and the Positive Teaching of Christ and his Apostles*. New York: Harper.

Cook, (Sir) Edward Tyas (1919). *More Literary Recreations*. London: Macmillan.

Cook, Edward Tyas, and Wedderburn, Alexander (1903–12) (eds). *The Works of John Ruskin*. 39 vols. London: George Allen.

'Corvo, Frederich (Baron)', pseud. of Frederick William Rolfe, with Sholto Douglas (1937). *The Songs of Meleager: Made into English with Designs*. London: Chiswick Press.

Cowan, William (1893a). 'The Greek Anthology and the Teachings of Holy Scripture', *Good Words*, 34: 403–5.

Cowan, William (1893b). 'Some Ancient and Modern Epigrams', *Good Words*, 34: 827–9.

Cracroft, Bernard (1865). Review of Macgregor (1864), *Spectator*, 38: 301–2. Reprinted in an expanded form at Cracroft (1868): 79–86.

Cracroft, Bernard (1868). *Essays, Political and Miscellaneous: Reprinted from Various Sources. Volume II*. London: Trübner.

Cramer, (Revd) John Anthony (1841). *The Second Book of the Travels of Nicander Nucius of Corcyra: Edited from the Original Greek MS in the Bodleian Library, with an English Translation*. London: Camden Society.

Cruickshank, Alfred Hamilton (1908). *Fair Copies: English Poems by Various Authors, with Latin Versions*. Oxford: Basil Blackwell.

Delanty, Greg (2012). *The Greek Anthology Book XVII*. Manchester: Carcanet.

De Witt, Norman W. (1923). Review of Mackail (1922), *Classical Weekly*, 16/25: 198–9.

Dickinson, Goldsworthy Lowes (1896). *The Greek View of Life*. London: Methuen.

Dodd, (Revd) Henry Philip (1870) (ed.). *The Epigrammatists: A Selection from the Epigrammatic Literature of Ancient, Mediaeval, and Modern Times. With Notes, Observations, Illustrations, and an Introduction*. London: Bell and Daldy.

Douglas, Norman (1928). *Birds and Beasts of the Greek Anthology*. London: Chapman and Hall.

Edwards, John (1825). *Epigrammata e purioribus Græcæ anthologiæ fontibus hausit. Annotationibus Jacobsii, de Bosch et aliorum instruxit, suas subinde notulas et tabulam scriptorum chronologicam adjunxit*. London: George Whittaker.

Elgar, Edward (1903). *From the Greek Anthology: Five Unaccompanied Part-Songs for TTBB*. London: Novello.

Ellis, Havelock, and Symonds, John Addington (1897). *Studies in the Psychology of Sex*, i: *Sexual Inversion*. London: Wilson and Macmillan.

Elton, (Sir) Charles Abraham (1814). *Specimens of the Classic Poets, in a Chronological Series from Homer to Tryphiodorus: Translated into English*

Verse, and Illustrated with Biographical and Critical Notices. 3 vols. London: Robert Baldwin.

Farnaby, Thomas (1453). *He tes anthologias anthologia. Florilegium epigrammatum graecorum, eorumque latino versu a variis redditorum.* London: E. Tyler and R. Holt.

Fitts, Dudley (1938). *One Hundred Poems from the Palatine Anthology.* Norfolk, CT: New Directions.

Fitts, Dudley (1941). *More Poems from the Palatine Anthology: In English Paraphrase.* Norfolk, CT: New Directions.

Fitts, Dudley (1957). *From the Greek Anthology: Poems in English Paraphrase.* London: Faber and Faber.

Furness, Robert Allason (1931). *Translations from the Greek Anthology.* London and Toronto: Jonathan Cape.

Fry, (Sir) Edward, with (Lady) Mariabella Fry and Agnes Fry (1915). *A Century of Greek Epigrams: Done into English Verse.* Letchworth: Letchworth City Garden Press, 'Printed for Private Circulation'.

Garnett, Richard (1869). *Idylls and Epigrams: Chiefly from the Greek Anthology.* London: Macmillan.

Garnett, Richard (1892). *A Chaplet from the Greek Anthology.* London: T. Fisher Unwin.

Gibbon, Edward (1993). *The Decline and Fall of the Roman Empire.* 6 vols. New York, London, and Toronto: Alfred A. Knopf.

Gildersleeve, Basil L. (1894). Review of Walter Pater, *Plato and Platonism,* and Ferdinand Horn, *Platonstudien, American Journal of Philology,* 15/1: 89–94.

Gow, James (1906). 'Burghclere's and Cromer's Classical Translations', *Classical Review,* 20/1: 62–3.

Graves, Robert (2000). *Goodbye to All That.* London: Penguin.

Greenwood, (Sir) George (1908). *The Shakespeare Problem Restated.* London: John Lane; Chiswick: Chiswick Press.

Greenwood, (Sir) George (1937). *The Shakespeare Problem Restated.* Condensed edn. London: John Lane; Chiswick: Chiswick Press.

Grundy, George Beardoe (1913). *Ancient Gems in Modern Settings: Being Versions of the Greek Anthology in English Rhyme by Various Writers.* Oxford: B. H. Blackwell.

Gunnyon, William (1883). *A Century of Translations from the Greek Anthology.* Kilmarnock: Dunlop & Drennan.

Hardinge, William M. (1878). 'Chrysanthema Gathered from the Greek Anthology', *Nineteenth Century,* 4 (November): 869–88; republished (1903) as *The Bibelot,* 9/1–2 (January–February).

Hardinge, William M. (1911). *Chrysanthema Gathered from the Greek Anthology.* Portland, ME: Thomas S. Mosher.

Harris, Frank (1916). *Oscar Wilde: His Life and Confessions*. 2 vols. New York: privately printed.

Harris, Frank (1919). *Contemporary Portraits: Second Series*. New York: privately printed.

Harrower, John (1924). 'Some Translations' (Review), *CR* 38/7–8: 172–5.

Hay, William (1835). 'A Few More Greek Epigrams, Translated', *Blackwood's Edinburgh Magazine*, 38: 142–1, 192–5.

Hay, William (1935–7). 'Translations from the Greek Anthology', *Blackwood's Edinburgh Magazine*, 38: 401–5, 642–6; 39: 128–30, 404–6, 551–4, 576–600, 793–7; 40: 274–7, 557–60; 41: 236–40, 622–81.

Headlam, Walter George (1890) (ed.). *Fifty Poems of Meleager, with a Translation*. London: Macmillan.

Headlam, Walter George (1892). Review of Mackail (1890), *CR* 6/6: 269–71.

Headlam, Walter George (1907) (ed.). *A Book of Greek Verse*. Cambridge: Cambridge University Press.

Hichens, Robert (1894). *The Green Carnation*. New York: D. Appleton.

Highet, Gilbert (1949). *The Classical Tradition: Greek and Roman Influences on Western Literature*. New York and London: Oxford University Press.

Hine, Daryl (2001). *Puerilities: Erotic Epigrams of the Greek Anthology*. Princeton: Princeton University Press.

Hodgson, (Revd) Francis (1878). *Memoir of the Rev. Francis Hodgson, B. D., Scholar, Poet, and Divine: with Numerous Letters from Lord Byron and Others*, ed. (Baron) George Gordon Byron. 2 vols. London: Macmillan.

Housman, Alfred Edward, (2007). *The Letters of A. E. Housman*, ed. Archie Burnett. Oxford: Oxford University Press.

Hutton, James (1935). *The Greek Anthology in Italy to the Year 1800*. Ithaca, NY: Cornell University Press.

Hutton, James (1946). *The Greek Anthology in France and in the Latin Writers of the Netherlands to the Year 1800*. Ithaca, NY: Cornell University Press.

Hyde, Montgomery (1948) (ed.). *The Trials of Oscar Wilde: Regina (Wilde) V. Queensberry, Regina V. Wilde and Taylor. Edited, with an Introduction*. London: William Hodge.

'Ionicos, Ion', see Leslie, Shane.

Irvine, John (1943). *The Fountain of Hellas: Poems from the Greek Anthology, Attempted in English Verse*, illustrated by Leslie Owen Baxter. Belfast: Derrick MacCord.

Jay, Peter (1973). *The Greek Anthology and Other Ancient Epigrams: A Selection in Modern Verse Translations, Edited with an Introduction*. Harmondsworth: Penguin.

Jebb, Richard Claverhouse (1877). *Greek Literature*. London: Macmillan.

Jebb, Richard Claverhouse (1893). *The Growth and Influence of Classical Greek Poetry: Lectures Delivered in 1892 on the Percy Turnbull Memorial*

Foundation in the Johns Hopkins University. London and New York: Macmillan.

Jevons, Frank Byron (1886). *A History of Greek Literature: From the Earliest Period to the Death of Demosthenes*. London: Charles Griffin.

Johnson, Thomas (1699). *Novus Graecorum epigrammatum & poematon delectus cum nova versione et notis. In usum scholae Etonensis*. 2nd edn. London: S. Smith and B. Walford. (1st edn, 1694.)

Johnson, Thomas (1712). *Novus Graecorum epigrammatum & poematon delectus. Cum nova versione et notis*. London: William Innis.

Kennedy, Benjamin Hall, and Riddell, James (1850) (eds). *Sabrinae Corolla in Hortulis Regiae Scholae Salopiensis contextuerunt tres viri, floribus legendis*. London: publisher unknown.

Knapp, Charles (1926). Series review of the Broadway Translations, *Classical Weekly*, 19/24: 195–8.

'L., J. G.' (1922). Review of Lumb 1920, *CR* 36.1–2: 42–3.

Lamb, Charles, and Lamb, Mary Anne (1978). *The Letters*, iii. *1809–1817*, ed. Edwin W. Marrs. Ithaca, NY: Cornell University Press.

Lancelot, Claude (1659). *Epigrammatum Delectus ex omnibus tum veteribus tum recentioribus Poetis . . . decerptus*. Paris: Savreux.

Lang, Andrew (1888). *Grass of Parnassus: Rhymes Old and New*. London: Longmans, Green.

Lang, Andrew (1892). *Grass of Parnassus: Rhymes Old and New. New Edition*. London: Longmans, Green.

Leavis, Frank R. (1936). *Revaluation: Tradition and Development in English Poetry*. London: Chatto & Windus.

Le Clercq, Jacques (1955). *Love Poems from the Greek Anthology*. Mount Vernon, NY: Peter Pauper Press.

Le Gallienne, Richard (1907). *Little Dinners with the Sphinx, and Other Prose Fancies*. New York: Moffat, Yard.

Le Gallienne, Richard (1910). *Attitudes and Avowals, with some Retrospective Reviews*. New York and London: John Lane.

Le Gallienne Richard (1922). *A Jongleur Strayed: Verses on Love and Other Matters Sacred and Profane*. Garden City, NY: Doubleday, Page.

Leaf, Walter (1922). *Little Poems from the Greek*. London: Grant Richards.

Leslie, Shane (1929). *The Greek Anthology: Selected and Translated with a Prolegomenon*. London: Ernest Benn.

Leslie, Shane, as 'Ion Ionicos' (1932). *Strato's Boyish Muse: Now First Translated Wholly into English*. London: Fortune Press.

Livingstone, (Sir) Richard W. (1912). *The Greek Genius and its Meaning to Us*. Oxford: Clarendon Press.

Livingstone, (Sir) Richard W. (1923a). *The Pageant of Greece*. Oxford: Clarendon Press.

Livingstone, (Sir) Richard W. (1923b). Review of Mackail (1923), *Classical Review*, 37/5–6: 116–17.

Livingstone, (Sir) Richard W. (1923c) (ed.). *The Pageant of Greece*. Oxford: Clarendon Press.

Lomer, Sydney: see 'Oswald'.

Lothian, Alexander (1920). *The Golden Treasury of the Greeks*. Oxford: Basil Blackwell.

Lucas, Frank Laurence (1937). *The Golden Cockerel Greek Anthology: A Selection of the Poems. Edited, with Translation into English Verse and an Introduction.* London: Golden Cockerel Press.

Lucas, Frank Laurence (1939). *A Greek Garland: A Selection from the Palatine Anthology. The Greek Text with Translations into English Verse.* Oxford: Oxford University Press.

Lucas, Frank Laurence (1951). *Greek Poetry for Everyman*. London: J. M. Dent.

Lumb, T. W. (1920). *Notes on the Greek Anthology*. London: Rivingtons.

Lydiat, Simon (1696). *Stachyologia. = Spicilegium: quod maxime conducat ad puerorum nutriendum ingenia. Sive, nova quorundam Græcorum epigrammatum collectio, versione Latina, et necessariis notis explicata. Cum indice cum verborum tum rerum. In usum scholæ Felstediensis, Com. Essexiæ.* London: H. Bonwick.

MacGregor, Robert Guthrie (1854). *Indian Leisure: Petrarch (Translations in Verse). On the Character of Othello, Agamemnon, The Henriad, Anthology.* London: Smith, Elder.

MacGregor, Robert Guthrie (1855). *Specimens of Greek Anthology. Translated.* Privately printed.

MacGregor, Robert Guthrie (1857). *Epitaphs from the Greek.* Translated by Major Robert Guthrie MacGregor of the Bengal Retired List. London: Nissen and Parker.

MacGregor, Robert Guthrie (1864). *Greek Anthology, with Notes Critical and Explanatory, Translated.* London: Nissen and Parker.

Mackail, John William (1890) (ed.). *Select Epigrams from the Greek Anthology: Edited with Revised Text, Translation, Introduction and Notes.* London: Longmans, Green.

Mackail, John William (1892). 'Notes on the Greek Anthology', *Classical Review*, 6/5: 192–3.

Mackail, John William (1894). Review of Jebb (1893), *Classical Review*, 8/6: 257–60.

Mackail, John William (1895). *Latin Literature.* London: John Murray.

Mackail, John William (1896). Review of James Spencer Pomeroy (6th Viscount Harberton) (1895), Meleager, and the Other Poets of Jacobs' Anthology: From Plato to Leon. Alex. together with the Fragment of Hermesianax, and a Selection from the Adespota, *CR* 10/5: 261.

Mackail, John William (1906) (ed.). *Select Epigrams from the Greek Anthology: Edited with Revised Text, Translation, Introduction and Notes*. London: Longmans, Green.

Mackail, John William (1907) (ed.). *Select Epigrams from the Greek Anthology: Edited*. London: Longmans, Green.

Mackail, John William (1908) (ed.). *Select Epigrams from the Greek Anthology: Translated*. London: Longmans, Green.

Mackail, John William (1910). *Lectures on Greek Poetry*. London: Longmans, Green.

Mackail, John William (1911) (ed.). *Select Epigrams from the Greek Anthology: Edited with Revised Text, Translation, Introduction and Notes*. Third Edition (London: Longmans, Green).

Mackail, John William (1922). *Virgil and his Meaning to the World of Today*. Boston: Marshall Jones.

Mackail, John William (1925). *Classical Studies*. London: John Murray.

Mackail, John William (1926). *Lectures on Greek Poetry*. London: Longmans, Green.

Mahaffy, (Revd) John Pentland (1880). *A History of Classical Greek Literature*. 2 vols. London: Longmans, Green.

Martinengo-Cesaresco, (Contessa) Evelyn L. H. C. (1911). *The Outdoor Life in Greek and Roman Poets, and Kindred Studies*. London: Macmillan.

Maxwell Lyte, Henry Churchill (Sir) (1875). *A History of Eton College, 1440–1875*. London: Macmillan.

Meader, Clarence L. (1896). 'The Most Essential Books for a High School Classical Library', *School Review*, 4/3: 149–57.

Merivale, John Herman (1833) (ed.). *Collections from the Greek Anthology: By the Late Rev. Robert Bland, and Others. A New Edition: Comprising the Fragments of Early Lyric Poetry, with Specimens of All the Poets Included in Meleager's Garland*. London: Longman and John Murray.

Michie, James (1990). *Poems from the Greek Anthology*. London: Folio.

Miscellaneous (1833). Correspondence on epigram by multiple authors, *Edinburgh Review*, 34: 415–27.

Müller, Karl Otried (1830). *History and Antiquities of the Doric Race*, trans. (Sir) George Cornewall Lewis (original Die Dorier). 2 vols. London: John Murray. (Rev. and enlarged edn, 1839.)

Mure, (Col.) William (1850–7). *A Critical History of the Language and Literature of Antient [sic] Greece*. 5 vols. London: Longman, Brown, Green, and Longmans.

Murray, Gilbert (1897). *A History of Ancient Greek Literature*. London: Heinemann.

Neaves, (Lord) Charles (1874). *The Greek Anthology*. Edinburgh and London: William Blackwood and Sons.

'North, Christopher' (1833a). 'The Greek Anthology. No. I' [review of Merivale (1833); author named as 'Wilson' at *The Athenaeum*, 271–322 (1833): 516], *Blackwood's Edinburgh Magazine*, 33: 865–88.

'North, Christopher' (1833b). 'The Greek Anthology. No. II', *Blackwood's Edinburgh Magazine*, 33: 115–40.

'North, Christopher' (1833c). 'The Greek Anthology. No. III', *Blackwood's Edinburgh Magazine*, 33: 258–84.

'North, Christopher' (1833d). 'The Greek Anthology. No. IV', *Blackwood's Edinburgh Magazine*, 33: 373–415.

'North, Christopher' (1833e). 'The Greek Anthology. No. V', *Blackwood's Edinburgh Magazine*, 33: 961–98.

Norwood, Gilbert (1925). *The Writers of Greece*. London: Oxford University Press and Humphrey Milford.

Oliphant, Margaret (1897). *Annals of a Publishing House: William Blackwood and his Sons: Their Magazine and Friends*. 2nd edn. 2 vols. Edinburgh: William Blackwood and Sons.

'Oswald', Sydney, pseud. of Sydney Lomer (1914). *The Greek Anthology: Epigrams from Anthologia Palatina XII*. Privately printed.

Pater, Walter (1873). *Studies in the History of the Renaissance*. London: Macmillan.

Pater, Walter (1877). *The Renaissance: Studies in Art and Poetry* (2nd edn of *Studies in the History of the Renaissance*). London: Macmillan.

Pater, Walter (1895a). *Greek Studies*, ed. C. L. Shadwell. London: Macmillan

Pater, Walter (1895b). *Miscellaneous Studies: A Series of Essays*, ed. C. L. Shadwell. London: Macmillan.

Pater, Walter (1896). *Essays from the 'Guardian'*, ed. Anon. (Shadwell?). Privately printed.

Pater, Walter (1901). *Greek Studies*, ed. C. L. Shadwell. 2nd edn. London: Macmillan.

Paton, William Roger (1898). *Anthologiae Graecae Erotica: The Love Epigrams or Book V of the Palatine Anthology. Edited, and Partly Rendered into English Verse*. London: David Nutt.

Paton, William Roger (1912). *The Greek Anth*ology. 5 vols. Cambridge, MA: Harvard University Press; London: Heinemann).

Post, Edwin (1908) (ed.). *Selected Epigrams of Martial: Edited, with Introduction and Notes*. Boston: Ginn.

Postgate, John Percival (1896). Review of Mackail (1895), *Classical Review*, 10/5: 259–61.

Pound, Ezra (1971). *The Selected Letters of Ezra Pound, 1907–1941*, ed. Douglas Duncan Paige. New edn. New York: New Directions.

Reid, Forrest (1943). *Poems from the Greek Anthology: Translated*. London: Faber and Faber.

Repp, RÞorleifur Guðmundsson (1864). *Epigrömm, snúin og eptir stæld á íslenzku eptir griska textanum í Dr. Wellesley's Anthologia polyglotta.* Kaupmannahöfń: S. L. Möller.

Rexroth, Kenneth (1962). *Poems from the Greek Anthology: Translated, with a Foreword.* Ann Arbor: University of Michigan Press.

Rexroth, Kenneth (1967). 'The Greek Anthology', *Saturday Review,* 29 July: 21.

Rexroth, Kenneth (1969). *Classics Revisited.* New York: Avon.

Rice, Wallace deGroot Cecil (1927). *Pagan Pictures: Freely Translated and Fully Expanded from the Anthology and the Greek Lyrical Poets, Variously Augmented by Modern Instances.* Chicago: Boni and Liveright.

Rodd, (Sir) James Rennell (1881). *Songs in the South.* London: David Bogue.

Rodd, (Sir) James Rennell (1882). *Rose Leaf and Apple Leaf.* Philadelphia: J. M. Stoddart.

Rodd, (Sir) James Rennell (1916). *Love, Worship and Death: Some Renderings from the Greek Anthology.* London: Edward Arnold.

Rodd, (Sir) James Rennell (1919). *Love, Worship and Death: Some Renderings from the Greek Anthology.* Enlarged edn. London: Edward Arnold.

Rodd, (Sir) James Rennell (1923-5). *Social and Diplomatic Memories.* 3 vols. London: Edward Arnold.

Rolleston, J. D. (1914). 'The Medical Aspects of the Greek Anthology', *Proceedings of the Royal Society of Medicine: Section of the History of Medicine,* 7: 3-13.

Rouse, William Henry Denham (1899). *An Echo of Greek Song.* London: J. M. Dent.

Ruskin, John (1870). *Lectures on Art, Delivered before the University of Oxford in Hilary Term, 1870.* Oxford: Clarendon Press.

Ruskin, John (1903-12). *The Works of John Ruskin,* ed. (Sir) Edward Tyas Cook and Alexander D. Wedderburn. 39 vols. London and New York: Longmans, Green.

Shelley, Percy Bysshe (1822). *Hellas: A Lyrical Drama.* London: Charles and James Ollier.

Sinclair, Andrew (1967). *Selections from the Greek Anthology: Translated.* London: Weidenfeld and Nicolson.

Skelton, Robin (1971). *Two Hundred Poems from the Greek Anthology.* London: Methuen.

Smiley, Charles N. (1926). Review of Mackail (1925), *Classical Journal,* 21/8: 638-9.

Soutar, George (1939). *Nature in Greek Poetry.* London: Humphrey Milford and Oxford University Press.

Stephens, Edward Bell (1837). *The Basque Provinces: Their Political State, Scenery, and Inhabitants; with Adventures Among the Carlists and Christinos.* 2 vols. London: Whittaker.

Stockwood, John (1597). *Progymnasma Scholasticum. Hoc est, Epigrammatum Græcorum, ex anthologia selectorum ab He. Stephano, duplicique ejusdem interpretatione explicatorum praxis grammatica, ordine facili & perspicuo, omnia quae in his occurrunt alicuius momenti & difficultatis vocabula explanans, & enodans, ad magnum tam docentium quam discentium emolumentum & levamen. Opera & industria Iohannis Stockvvoodi, scholae Tunbridgiensis olim ludimagistri. Græca praeterea sunt omnia per lineas interlineares Latinis expressa typis, ad faciliorem eorundem lectionem, in studiosae juventutis gratiam.* London: Adam Islip.

Stocqueler, Joachim H. (1857). *India: Its History, Climate, Productions. With a Full Account of the Origin, Progress, and Development of the Bengal Mutiny, and Suggestions as to the Future Government of India.* London: G. Routledge.

Sutherland, Alistair, and Anderson, Patrick (1963) (eds). *Eros: An Anthology of Male Friendship.* New York: Citadel Press.

Swayne, George Carless (1870). *Herodotus.* Edinburgh and London: William Blackwood and Sons.

Symonds, John Addington (1873). *Studies of the Greek Poets* [First Series]. London: Black.

Symonds, John Addington (1874). *Sketches in Italy and Greece.* London: Smith, Elder.

Symonds, John Addington (1875). *Lyra Viginti Chordarum.* Privately printed.

Symonds, John Addington (1875–86). *Renaissance in Italy.* 6 vols. London: Smith, Elder.

Symonds, John Addington (1876). *Studies of the Greek Poets.* Second Series. London: Black.

Symonds, John Addington (1877). *Studies of the Greek Poets.* First Series. Second Edition. London: Black.

Symonds, John Addington (1878a). *Shelley.* London: Macmillan.

Symonds, John Addington (1878b). *Tales of Ancient Greece*, 2 volumes, publisher and place of publication unknown.

Symonds, John Addington (1879). *Studies of the Greek Poets.* Second Series. Second Edition. London: Black.

Symonds, John Addington (1883). *A Problem in Greek Ethics.* Privately printed.

Symonds, John Addington (1884). *New Italian Sketches* (Leipzig: Tauschnitz).

Symonds, John Addington (1890). *Essays Speculative and Suggestive.* London: Chapman and Hall.

Symonds, John Addington (1891). *A Problem in Modern Ethics.* Privately printed.

Symonds, John Addington (1893). *The Life of Michelangelo Buonarotti.* 2 vols. London: J. C. Nimmo.

Symonds, John Addington (1907). *Essays Speculative and Suggestive.* 3rd edn. London: Chapman and Hall.

Symonds, John Addington (1920). *Studies of the Greek Poets.* Third Edition. London: Black.

Symonds, John Addington (1967–9). *The Letters of John Addington Symonds,* ed. Herbert M. Schueller and Robert L. Peters. 3 vols. Detroit: Wayne State University Press.

Symonds, John Addington (1984). *The Memoirs of John Addington Symonds: Edited and Introduced,* ed. Phyllis Grosskurth. London: Hutchinson.

Symonds, John Addington, and Symonds, Margaret (1892). *Our Life in the Swiss Highlands.* London and Edinburgh: Adam and Charles Black.

Symonds, John Addington, Sr (1871a). *Miscellanies, by J. A. S.: Selected and Edited, with an Introductory Memoir by his Son,* ed. John Addington Symonds. London: Macmillan.

Symonds, John Addington, Sr (1871b). *Verses.* Privately printed.

Talfourd, (Sir) Thomas Noon, Blomfield, Charles James, et al. (1850). *History of Greek Literature.* 2nd edn. London: J. J. Griffin and Glasgow: R. Griffin.

Tarbell, Frank Bigelow (1896). *A History of Greek Art: With an Introductory Chapter on Art in Egypt and Mesopotamia.* Meadville, PA: Flood and Vincent.

Tillyard, Eustace Mandeville Wetenhall (1948). *The Elizabethan World Picture.* London: Chatto and Windus.

Tomson, 'Graham R.' (1889). Pseud. of Rosamund Tomson, *Selections from the Greek Anthology: Edited.* London, Felling-on-Tyne, New York, and Melbourne: Walter Scott.

Tredrey, Frank D. (1954). *The House of Blackwood, 1804–1954: The History of a Publishing Firm.* Edinburgh and London: William Blackwood and Sons.

Tucker, Thomas George (1892). 'Adversaria on the Greek Anthology', *Classical Review,* 6/3: 86–7.

Tyrwhitt, Richard St John (1874). *The Art Teaching of the Primitive Church: With an Index of Subjects, Historical and Emblematic, Etc.* London: Christian Knowledge Society.

Tyrwhitt, Richard St John (1877). 'The Greek Spirit in Modern Literature', *Contemporary Review,* 298 (March): 552–66.

Tyrwhitt, Richard St John (1878). *An Address Delivered to the Oxford School of Science and Art, at the Distribution of Prizes, 19 October 1878.* Oxford?: publisher unknown.

Tyrwhitt, Richard St John (1880). *Hugh Heron, Ch. Ch.: An Oxford Novel.* London: Strahan.

Valpy, Richard (1860). *Delectus Sententiarum Graecarum,* rev. John Tahourdin White. London: Longman, Green, Longman, and Roberts.

Wavell, (Viscount) Archibald Percival (1944). *Other Men's Flowers: An Anthology of Poetry.* London: Jonathan Cape and the Book Society.

Wellesley, Henry (1849) (ed.). *Anthologia Polyglotta: A Selection of Versions in Various Languages, Chiefly from the Greek Anthology.* London: John Murray and Oxford: J. H. Parker.

Wells, Herbert George (1910). *The New Macchiavelli.* New York: Duffield.

Westcott, J. H. (1894) (ed.). *One Hundred and Twenty Epigrams of Martial.* Boston: Allyn and Bacon.

Whymper, Edward (1871). *Scrambles amongst the Alps in the Years 1860–1869.* London: John Murray.

Wilde, Oscar (1913). *Charmides and Other Poems.* 2nd edn. London: Methuen.

Wilde, Oscar (1989). *Oscar Wilde's Oxford Notebooks: A Portrait of a Mind in the Making,* ed. Philip E. Smith II and Michael S. Helfand. New York: Oxford University Press.

Wilde, Oscar (2000). *The Complete Letters of Oscar Wilde,* ed. Merlin Holland and Rupert Hart-Davis. New York: Henry Holt.

Wilde, Oscar (2005). *The Complete Works of Oscar Wilde,* iii. *The Picture of Dorian Gray: The 1890 and 1891 Texts,* ed. Joseph Bristow. Oxford: Oxford University Press.

Wilde, Oscar (2008). *The Women of Homer,* ed. Thomas Wright and Donald Mead. London: Oscar Wilde Society.

Williams, Howard (1888). *Lucian's Dialogues: Namely, the Dialogues of the Gods, of the Sea-Gods, and of the Dead; Zeus the Tragedian, the Ferry-boat, etc. Translated with Notes and a Preliminary Memoir.* London: George Bell.

Wolfe, Humbert (1927a). *Others Abide: Translations in Verse from the Greek Anthology.* London: Ernest Benn.

Wolfe, Humbert (1927brex) (ed.). *Poems from the Greek.* London: Ernest Benn.

Wolfe, Humbert (1930). *Homage to Meleager.* New York: Fountain Press.

Woodward, (Revd) George Ratcliffe (1924). *Greek Anthology: 133 Love-Epigrams in English Verse.* Privately printed.

Woodward, (Revd) George Ratcliffe (1931). *Tales of Sea-Sorrow from the Greek Anthology.* Privately printed.

Wright, Frederic Adam (1923). *The Girdle of Aphrodite: The Complete Love-Poems of the Palatine Anthology.* London: George Routledge; New York: E. P. Dutton.

Wright, Frederic Adam (1924). *The Poets of the Greek Anthology: Translated, with Biographical and Critical Prefaces.* London: George Routledge; New York: E. P. Dutton.

3. Modern Scholarship

Abelove, Henry (1995). 'The Queering of Lesbian/Gay History', *Radical History,* 62: 44–57.

Abul-Magd, Zeinab (2010). 'Rebellion in the Time of Cholera: Failed Empire, Unfinished Nation in Egypt, 1840–1920', *Journal of World History,* 21/4: 691–719.

Acosta-Hughes, Benjamin (2010). *Arion's Lyre: Archaic Lyric into Hellenistic Poetry*. Princeton: Princeton University Press.

Acosta-Hughes, B., Kosmetatou, E., and Baumbach, M. (2004) (eds). *Labored in Papyrus Leaves. Perspectives on an Epigram Collection Attributed to Posidippus (P.Mil.Vogl. VIII 309)*. Washington: Harvard University Press.

Adams, James Eli (1995). *Dandies and Desert Saints: Styles of Victorian Masculinity*. Ithaca, NY, and London: Cornell University Press.

Albanese, Andrew (2010). 'Bibliobazaar: How a Company Produces 272, 930 Books a Year', *Publisher's* Weekly, 15 April 2010 <http://www.publishersweekly.com/pw/by-topic/industry-news/publisher-news/article/42850-bibliobazaar-how-a-company-produces-272-930-books-a-year.html> (accessed 6 March 2013).

Aldrich, Robert (1993). *The Seduction of the Mediterranean: Writing, Art and Homosexual Fantasy*. London: Routledge.

Aliaga-Buchenau, Ana Isabel (2004). *The 'Dangerous' Potential of Reading: Readers and the Negotiation of Power in Nineteenth-Century Narratives*. New York and London: Routledge.

Althusser, Louis (1971). *Lenin and Philosophy, and Other Essays*, trans. Ben Brewster. London: New Left Books.

Altick, Richard D. (1957). *The English Common Reader*. Chicago and London: University of Chicago Press.

Anderson, Benedict (2006). *Imagined Communities*. Rev. edn. London and New York: Verso.

Armstrong, Richard H. (2005). *A Compulsion for Antiquity: Freud and the Ancient World*. Ithaca, NY: Cornell University Press.

Ashton, Rosemary (1980). *The German Idea: Four English Writers and the Reception of German Thought*. Cambridge: Cambridge University Press.

Assmann, Jan (2006). *Religion and Cultural Memory: Ten Studies*, trans. Rodney Livingstone. Stanford: Stanford University Press.

Ayers, David (2004). *Modernism: a Short Introduction*. Malden, MA, and Oxford: Blackwell.

Bal, Mieke, Crewe, Jonathan, and Spitzer, Leo (1999) (eds). *Acts of Memory: Cultural Recall in the Present*. Hanover, NH: University Press of New England.

Bann, Stephen (2000). 'Versions of Antinous: Symonds between Shelley and Yourcenar', in Pemble (2000b), 136–53.

Barker, Stephen (1996) (ed.). *Excavations and their Objects: Freud's Collections of Antiquities*. Binghampton, NY: State University of New York.

Barrow, Rosemary (2003). *Lawrence Alma-Tadema*. Oxford: Phaidon.

Barrow, Rosemary (2007). *The Use of Classical Art and Literature by Victorian Painters 1869–1912: Creating Continuity with the Traditions of High Art*. Lewiston, NY: Edwin Mellen Press.

Bassnett, Susan (1998). 'The Translation Turn in Cultural Studies', in Susan Bassnett and André Lefevere (eds), *Constructing Cultures. Essays on Literary Translation*. Clevedon: Multilingual Matters, 123–40.

Baudrillard, Jean (1994). 'The System of Collecting', in John Elsner and Roger Cardinal (eds), *The Cultures of Collecting*. London: Reaktion, 7–24.

Beard, Mary (2001). 'Learning to Pick the Easy Plums: The Invention of Ancient History in Nineteenth-Century Classics', in Smith and Stray (2001), 89–106.

Beard, Mary, and Henderson, John (2001). *Classical Art from Greece to Rome*. Oxford: Oxford University Press.

Beetham, Margaret, and Boardman, Kay (2001) (eds). *Victorian Women's Magazines: An Anthology*. Manchester: Manchester University Press.

Beisel, Nicola (1997). *Imperiled Innocents: Anthony Comstock and Family Reproduction in Victorian America*. Princeton: Princeton University Press.

Benedict, Barbara M. (2003). 'The Paradox of the Anthology: Collecting and *différence* in Eighteenth-Century Britain', *New Literary History*, 34/2: 231–56.

Bermingham, Ann, and Brewer, John (1995) (eds). *The Consumption of Culture, 1600–1800*. London and New York: Routledge.

Bershtein, Evgenii (2010). 'Next to Christ: Oscar Wilde in Russian Modernism', in Stefano Evangelista (ed.), *The Reception of Oscar Wilde in Europe*. London and New York: Continuum, 285–300.

Biddiss, Michael (1999). 'The Invention of Modern Olympic Tradition', in Wyke and Biddiss (1999b), 125–43.

Bing, Peter, and Bruss, Jon Steffen (2007) (eds). *Brill's Companion to Hellenistic Epigram*. Leiden: Brill.

Binkley, Sam (2000). 'The Romantic Sexology of John Addington Symonds', *Journal of Homosexuality*, 40/1: 79–103.

Bishop, Philip R. (1998). *Thomas Bird Mosher: Pirate Prince of Publishers*. New Castle, DE: Oak Knoll Press.

Blanshard, Alastair (2010). *Sex: Vice and Love from Antiquity to Modernity*. Chichester and Malden, MA: Wiley-Blackwell.

Boime, Albert (2004). *Art in an Age of Counter-Revolution, 1815–1858*. Chicago: University of Chicago Press.

Booth, Howard J. (2000). '"A certain disarray of faculties": Surpassing the Modernist Reception of Symonds', in Pemble (2000b), 154–69.

Booth, Howard J. (2002). 'Same-Sex Desire, Ethics and Double-Mindedness: The Correspondence of Henry Graham Dakyns, Henry Sidgwick and John Addington Symonds', *Journal of European Studies*, 32: 283–301.

Bowen, James (1989). 'Education, Ideology and the Ruling Class: Hellenism and English Public Schools in the Nineteenth Century', in Clarke (1989), 161–86.

Bowie, Ewen (1990). 'Greek Poetry in the Antonine Age', in Donald A. Russell (ed.), *Antonine Literature*. Oxford: Oxford University Press, 53–90.

Bowie, Ewen (2012). 'Unnatural Selection: Expurgation of Greek Melic, Elegiac and Iambic Poetry', in Harrison and Stray (2012), 9–24.

Bradley, Jana, Fulton, Bruce, Helm, Marlene, and Pittner, Katherine A. (2011). 'Non-Traditional Book Publishing', *First Monday*, 16/8, 22 July 2011 <http://firstmonday.org/htbin/cgiwrap/bin/ojs/index.php/fm/article/view/3353> (accessed 6 March 2013).

Bradley, Mark (2010a). 'Introduction', in Bradley (2010c), 1–25.

Bradley, Mark (2010b). 'Tacitus' Agricola and the Conquest of Britain: Representations of Empire in Victorian and Edwardian England', in Bradley (2010c), 123–57.

Bradley, Mark (2010c) (ed.). *Classics and Imperialism in the British Empire*. Oxford: Oxford University Press.

Brake, Laurel (1995). 'The "wicked *Westminster*," the *Fortnightly*, and Walter Pater's *Renaissance*', in Jordan and Patten (1995), 289–305.

Brake, Laurel (2004). '"The profession of letters": Walter Pater and Greek Studies', in Kate Campbell (ed.), *Journalism, Literature and Modernity: From Hazlitt to Modernism*. Edinburgh: Edinburgh University Press, 121–40.

Brake, Laurel (2005). 'Introduction: Encountering The Press', in Brake and Codell (2005), 1–7.

Brake, Laurel, and Codell, Julie F. (2005). *Encounters in the Victorian Press: Editors, Authors, Readers*. Houndmills and New York: Palgrave Macmillan.

Brannon, Laura A., and Brock, Timothy C. (1994). 'The Subliminal Persuasion Controversy: Reality, Enduring Fable, and Polonius's Weasel', in Sharon Shavitt and Timothy C. Brock (eds), *Persuasion: Psychological Insights and Perspectives*. Needham Heights, MA: Allyn & Bacon, 279–93.

Bray, Alan (1990). 'Homosexuality and the Signs of Male Friendship in Elizabethan England', *History Workshop*, 29: 1–19.

Bridges, Meilee D. (2011). 'Objects of Affection: Necromantic Pathos in Bulwer-Lytton's City of the Dead', in Hales and Paul (2011), 90–104.

Brink, Charles O. (1986). *English Classical Scholarship: Historical Reflections on Bentley, Porson, and Housman*. Cambridge: Clarke.

Bristow, Joseph (1991). *Empire Boys: Adventures in a Man's World*. London: HarperCollins.

Bristow, Joseph (1995). *Effeminate England: Homoerotic Writing after 1885*. Buckingham: Open University Press.

Brock, Michael G. (2000). 'A Plastic Structure', in Michael G. Brock and Mark C. Curthoys (eds), *The History of the University of Oxford*, vii. *Nineteenth-Century Oxford, Part 2*. Oxford: Oxford University Press, 3–66.

Brown, R. D. (1956). 'Suetonius, Symonds, and Gibbon in *The Picture of Dorian Gray*', *Modern Language Notes*, 71/4: 264.

Bruss, Jon Steffen (2005). 'Hidden Presences: Monuments, Gravesites, and Corpses in Greek Funerary Epigram', *Hellenistica Groningana*, 10. Leuven: Peeters.

Buckton, Oliver S. (1998). *Secret Selves: Confession and Same-Sex Desire in Victorian Autobiography*. Chapel Hill, NC: University of North Carolina Press.

Burnikel, Walter (1980). *Untersuchungen zur Struktur des Witzepigramms bei Lukillios und Martial*. Wiesbaden: Steiner.

Burns, Bryan E. (2008a). 'Classicizing Bodies: Male Photography', in Hardwick and Stray (2008), 440–51.

Burns, Bryan E. (2008b). 'Sculpting Antinous', *Helios*, 35/2: 121–42.

Caesar, Adrian (1993). *Taking It Like a Man: Suffering, Sexuality and the War Poets. Brooke, Sassoon, Owen, Graves*. Manchester and New York: Manchester University Press.

Cameron, Alan (1982). 'Strato and Rufinus', *Classical Quarterly*, 32/1: 162–73.

Cameron, Alan (1993). *The Greek Anthology from Meleager to Planudes*. Oxford: Oxford University Press.

Cameron, Alan (1995). *Callimachus and his Critics*. Harvard: Princeton University Press.

Cameron, Alan (1996). 'Anthology', in Simon Hornblower and Antony Spawforth (eds), *The Oxford Classical Dictionary*. Oxford: Oxford University Press, 101–2.

Challis, Debbie (2010). '"The ablest race": The Ancient Greeks in Victorian Racial Theory', in Bradley (2010c), 94–120.

Christie, William (2009). *The Edinburgh Review in the Literary Culture of Romantic Britain: Mammoth and Megalonyx*. London: Pickering and Chatto.

Clarke, Graeme W. (1989) (ed.). *Rediscovering Hellenism: The Hellenic Inheritance and the English Imagination*. Cambridge: Cambridge University Press.

Cohen, Stanley (1972). *Folk Devils and Moral Panics: The Creation of the Mods and Rockers*. London: MacGibbon and Kee.

Collini, Stefan (1991). *Public Moralists: Political Thought and Intellectual Life in Britain, 1850–1930*. Oxford: Clarendon Press.

Collini, Stefan (1992). 'The Ordinary Experience of Everyday Life: Sidgwick's Politics and the Method of Reflective Analysis', in Schultz (1992), 333–67.

Conley, Cary H. (1927). *The First English Translators of the Classics*. New Haven: Yale University Press.

Constantine, David (1989). 'The Question of Authenticity in Some Early Accounts of Greece', in Clarke (1989), 1–22.

Cook, Matt (2003a). *London and the Culture of Homosexuality, 1885–1914*. Cambridge: Cambridge University Press.

Cook, Matt (2003b). '"A new city of friends": London and Homosexuality in the 1890s', *History Workshop Journal*, 56: 33–58.

Cordasco, Francesco (1951). *The Bohn Libraries: A History and Checklist.* New York: Burt Franklin.

Crosby, Christina (1991). *The Ends of History: Victorians and the 'Woman Question'.* London and New York: Routledge.

Crozier, Ivan Dalley (2001). 'The Medical Construction of Homosexuality and its Relation to the Law in Nineteenth-Century England', *Medical History*, 45: 61–82.

Cruise, Colin (1999). 'Versions of the Annunciation: Wilde's Aestheticism and the Message of Beauty', in Prettejohn (1999), 167–87.

Curtis, Gregory (2005). *Disarmed: The Story of the Venus de Milo.* Stroud: Sutton.

da Silva, Stephen (2006). 'Papa, Postcards, Perfume, Phallic Keys: James, Symonds, and Late-Victorian Fictions of Homosexuality', in David Garrett Izzo and Daniel T. O'Hara (eds), *Henry James against the Aesthetic Movement: Essays on the Middle and Late Fiction.* Jefferson, NC: McFarland, 201–28.

Danson, Lawrence (1991). 'Oscar Wilde, W.H., and the Unspoken Name of Love', *ELH* 58/4: 979–1000.

d'Arch Smith, Timothy (1978). 'An Appreciation', in Edward M. Slocum, *Men and Boys: An Anthology.* New York: Coltsfoot Press, n.p.

Darnton, Robert (2001). 'First Steps towards a History of Reading', in James L. Machor and Philip Goldstein (eds), *Reception Study: From Literary Theory to Cultural Studies.* New York and London: Routledge, 160–79.

Das, Santanu (2002). '"Kiss me, Hardy": Intimacy, Gender, and Gesture in World War I Trench Literature', *Modernism/modernity*, 9/1: 51–74.

Davis, Whitney (1996). Review of Aldrich (1993), *Journal of the History of Sexuality*, 6/4: 618–21.

Davis, Whitney (1999). 'The Image in the Middle: John Addington Symonds and Homoerotic Art Criticism', in Prettejohn (1999), 188–217.

Davis, Whitney (2000). 'Symonds and Visual Impressionability', in Pemble (2000b), 62–80.

Dawson, Gowan (2007). *Darwin, Literature and Victorian Respectability.* Cambridge: Cambridge University Press.

DeJean, Joan (1989a). *Fictions of Sappho, 1546–1937.* Chicago: University of Chicago Press.

DeJean, Joan (1989b). 'Sex and Philology: Sappho and the Rise of German Nationalism', *Representations*, 27: 148–71.

Dellamora, Richard (1990). *Masculine Desire: The Sexual Politics of Victorian Aestheticism.* Chapel Hill, NC, and London: University of North Carolina Press.

Di Leo, Jeffery R. (2004) (ed.). *On Anthologies: Politics and Pedagogy.* Lincoln, NE: University of Nebraska Press.

Dollimore, Jonathan (1991). *Sexual Dissidence: Augustine to Wilde, Freud to Foucault.* Oxford: Clarendon Press.

Dollimore, Jonathan (2001). *Sex, Literature and Censorship.* Cambridge: Polity.

Dollimore, Jonathan, and Sinfield, Alan (1994) (eds). *Political Shakespeare: Essays in Cultural Materialism.* 2nd edn. Manchester: Manchester University Press.

Donoghue, Frank (1995). 'Colonizing Readers: Review Criticism and the Formation of a Reading Public', in Bermingham and Brewer (1995), 54–74.

Dorman, Susann (1979). 'Hypatia and Callista: The Initial Skirmish between Kingsley and Newman', *Nineteenth-Century Fiction*, 34/2: 173–93.

Dover, Kenneth J. (1979). 'Expurgation of Greek Literature', in Willem den Boer (ed.), *Les Études Classiques aux XIXe et XXe Siècles: Leur place dans l'histoire des idées.* Entretiens Hardt 26. Vandoeuvres and Geneva: Fondation Hardt, 55–89.

Dowling, Linda (1980). 'Imposture and Absence in Wilde's "The Portrait of Mr W.H."', *Victorian* Newsletter, 58: 26–9.

Dowling, Linda (1989). 'Ruskin's Pied Beauty and the Constitution of a Homosexual "Code"', *Victorian Newsletter*, 75: 1–8.

Dowling, Linda (1994). *Hellenism and Homosexuality in Victorian Oxford.* Ithaca, NY, and London: Cornell University Press.

Draper, John W. (1921). 'The Theory of Translation in the Eighteenth Century', *Neophilologus*, 6: 241–54.

DuBois, Page (2001). *Trojan Horses: Saving the Classics from Conservatives.* New York: New York University Press.

Eagleton, Terry (1983). *Literary Theory: An Introduction.* Oxford: Basil Blackwell.

Easterling, Pat (2005). '"The speaking page": Reading Sophocles with Jebb', in Christopher Stray (ed.), *The Owl of Minerva: The Cambridge Praelections of 1906. Reassessments of Richard Jebb, James Adam, Walter Headlam, Henry Jackson, William Ridgeway, and Arthur Verrall. Proceedings of the Cambridge Philological Society*, Suppl. 28: 25–46.

Edwards, Catharine (1999) (ed.). *Roman Presences: Representations of Rome in European Culture, 1789–1945.* Cambridge: Cambridge University Press.

Ellegård, Alvar (1971). 'The Readership of the Periodical Press in mid-Victorian Britain: II. Directory', *Victorian Periodicals Newsletter*, 13: 3–22.

Elmann, Richard (1988). *Oscar Wilde.* New York: Vintage Books.

Evangelista, Stefano (2006). '"Lovers and philosophers at once": Aesthetic Platonism in the Victorian *fin de siècle*', *Yearbook of English Studies*, 36/2: 230–44.

Evangelista, Stefano (2009a). *British Aestheticism and Ancient Greece: Hellenism, Reception, Gods in Exil.* Houndmills: Palgrave Macmillan.

Evangelista, Stefano (2009b). 'Aesthetic Encounters: The Erotic Visions of John Addington Symonds and Wilhelm von Gloeden', in Luisa Calè and Patrizia di Bello (eds), *Illustrations, Optics and Objects in Nineteenth-Century Literary and Visual Cultures.* Houndmills: Palgrave Macmillan, 87–104.

Everest, Kelvin (2007). 'Shelley's Adonais and John Keats', *Essays in Criticism*, 57/3: 237–64.

Fantuzzi, Marco, and Hunter, Richard (2005). *Tradition and Innovation in Hellenistic Poetry.* Cambridge: Cambridge University Press.

Fearn, David (2010). 'Imperialist Fragmentation and the Discovery of Bacchylides', in Bradley (2010c), 158–85.

Fish, Stanley (1980). *Is There a Text in this Class?* Cambridge, MA: Harvard University Press.

Fisher, Kate, and Langlands, Rebecca (2011). 'The Censorship Myth and the Secret Museum', in Hales and Paul (2011), 301–15.

Fisher, Will (2008). 'The Sexual Politics of Victorian Historiographical Writing about the "Renaissance"', *GLQ: A Journal of Lesbian and Gay Studies*, 14/1: 41–67.

Fisher, Will (2009). 'A Hundred Years of Queering the Renaissance', in Vin Nardizzi, Stephen Guy-Bray, and Will Stockton (eds), *Queer Renaissance Historiography: Backward Gaze.* Farnham and Burlington, VT: Ashgate, 13–40.

Fiske, Shanyn (2008). *Heretical Hellenisms: Women Writers, Ancient Greece, and the Victorian Popular Imagination.* Athens, OH: Ohio University Press.

Fitzgerald, William (2007). *Martial: The World of the Epigram.* Chicago: Chicago University Press.

Flaig, Egon (2003). 'Towards "Rassenhygiene": Wilamowitz and the German New Right', in Ingo Gildenhard and Martin Ruehl (eds), *Out of Arcadia: Classics and Politics in Germany in the Age of Burkhardt, Nietzsche and Wilamowitz.* London: Institute of Classical Studies, 105–27.

Fleming, Fergus (2000). *Killing Dragons: The Conquest of the Alps.* London: Granta.

Fletcher, Ian (1979a). 'Decadence and the Little Magazines', in Fletcher (1979b), 173–202.

Fletcher, Ian (1979b) (ed.). *Decadence and the 1990s.* New York: Holmes and Meier.

Fletcher, Ian, and Bradbury, Malcolm (1979). 'Preface', in Fletcher (1979b), 7–13.

Forrester, John (1994). '"Mille e tre": Freud and collecting', in John Elsner and Roger Cardinal (eds), *The Cultures of Collecting.* London: Reaktion Books, 224–51.

Forth, Christopher (1993). 'Nietzsche, Decadence, and Regeneration in France, 1891–95', *Journal of the History of Ideas*, 54/1: 97–117.

Frawley, Maria H. (2004). *Invalidism and Identity in Nineteenth-Century Britain.* Chicago: University of Chicago Press.

Frost, William (1955). *Dryden and the Art of Translation.* New Haven: Yale University Press.

Gaisser, Julia Haig (2002). 'The Reception of Classical Texts in the Renaissance', in Allen J. Grieco, Michael Rocke, and Fiorella Superbi Giofreddi (eds), *The Italian Renaissance in the Twentieth Century.* Florence: Leo S. Olschki, 387–400.

Gallagher, Catharine, and Laqueur, Thomas (1987). 'Introduction', in Catharine Gallagher and Thomas Laqueur (eds), *The Making of the Modern Body: Sexuality and Society in the Nineteenth Century.* Berkeley and Los Angeles, and London: University of California Press, pp. vii–xv.

Gauntlett, David (1998). 'Ten Things Wrong with the "Effects Model"', in Roger Dickinson, Ramaswani Harindranath, and Olga Linné (eds), *Approaches to Audiences: A Reader.* London: Arnold, 10–24.

Goff, Barbara (2005a). 'Introduction', in Goff (2005b), 1–24.

Goff, Barbara (2005b) (ed.). *Classics and Colonialism.* London: Duckworth.

Goldhill, Simon (2002). *Who Needs Greek? Contests in the Cultural History of Hellenism.* Cambridge: Cambridge University Press..

Goldhill, Simon (2010). Review of Evangelista (2009a), *Victorian Studies*, 52/3: 474–6.

Goldhill, Simon (2011). *Victorian Culture and Classical Antiquity: Art, Opera, Fiction, and the Proclamation of Modernity.* Princeton: Princeton University Press.

Goldstein, Robert Justin (1992). 'A Land of Relative Freedom: Censorship of the Press and the Arts in the Nineteenth Century (1815–1914)', in Paul Hyland and Neil Sammells (eds), *Writing and Censorship in Britain.* London, 125–40.

Gordon, Jan B. (1979). '"Decadent Spaces": Notes for a Phenomenology of the *fin de siècle*', in Fletcher (1979b), 31–58.

Graff, Gerald (1997). 'Commentary: Agonistics: Eight Controversial Propositions on Controversy', *Transactions of the American Philological Association*, 127: 389–93.

Grafton, Anthony (1994). Defenders of the Text: The Traditions of Scholarship in an Age of Science, 1450–1800. Cambridge, MA: Harvard University Press.

Gray, Jonathan, Sandvoss, Cornell, and Harrington, C. Lee (2007). 'Introduction: Why Study Fans?', in Jonathan Gray, Cornell Sandvoss, and C. Lee Harrington (eds), *Fandoms: Identities and Communities in an Mediated World.* New York and London: New York University Press, 1–16.

Grech, Leanne (2011). 'From Popery to Paganism: Oscar Wilde in Greece', in Anne Mackay (ed.), *ASCS 32 Select Proceedings* <http://www.ascs.org.au/news/ascs32/Grech.pdf> accessed 1 May 2013.

Green, Peter (1998). *Classical Bearings: Interpreting Ancient History and Culture*. Berkeley and Los Angeles: University of California Press.

Greenblatt, Stephen (1980). *Renaissance Self-Fashioning from More to Shakespeare*. Chicago: University of Chicago Press.

Greenblatt, Stephen (1994). 'Invisible Bullets: Renaissance Authority and its Subversion, *Henry IV* and *Henry V*', in Dollimore and Sinfield (1994), 18–47.

Gregory, Eileen (1997). *H.D. and Hellenism: Classic Lines*. Cambridge: Cambridge University Press.

Gross, John J. (1992). *The Rise and Fall of the Man of Letters: Aspects of English Literary Life since 1800*. New edn. Chicago: Ivan R. Dee.

Grosskurth, Phyllis (1963). 'Swinburne and Symonds: An Uneasy Literary Relationship', *Review of English Studies*, 14/55: 257–68.

Grosskurth, Phyllis (1964). *John Addington Symonds: A Biography*. London: Longmans, Green.

Güthenke, Constanze Magdalene (2008). *Placing Modern Greece. The Dynamics of Romantic Hellenism, 1770–1850*. Oxford: Oxford University Press.

Gutzwiller, Kathryn (1998). *Poetic Garlands: Hellenistic Epigrams in Context*. Berkeley and Los Angeles: University of California Press.

Gutzwiller, Kathryn (2005) (ed.). *The New Posidippus: A Hellenistic Poetry Book*. Oxford: Oxford University Press.

Gutzwiller, Kathryn (ed.) (forthcoming). *The Epigrams of Meleager*. Oxford: Oxford University Press.

Habermas, Jürgen (1988). *The Structural Transformation of the Public Sphere: An Inquiry into a Category of Bourgeois Society*. Cambridge, MA: Harvard University Press.

Hagerman, Christopher A. (2009). 'In the Footsteps of the "Macedonian Conqueror": Alexander the Great and British India', *International Journal of the Classical Tradition*, 16/3–4: 344–92.

Halbwachs, Maurice (1992). *On Collective Memory*, trans. and ed. Lewis A. Coser. Chicago: University of Chicago Press.

Hales, Shelley (2011). 'Cities of the Dead', in Hales and Paul (2011), 153–70.

Hales, Shelley, and Paul, Joanna (2011) (eds). *Pompeii in the Public Imagination from its Rediscovery to Today*. Oxford: Oxford University Press.

Hall, Edith (1997). 'Talfourd's Ancient Greeks in the Theatre of Reform', *IJCT* 3/3: 283–307.

Hall, Edith (2008). 'Putting the Class into Classical Reception', in Hardwick and Stray (2008), 386–97.

Hall, Lesley A. (1992). 'Forbidden by God, Despised by Men: Masturbation, Medical Warnings, Moral Panic, and Manhood in Great Britain, 1850–1950', *Journal of the History of Sexuality*, 2: 365–87.

Hallett, Judith, and van Nortwick, Thomas (1997) (eds). *Compromising Traditions: The Personal Voice in Classical Scholarship*. London and New York: Routledge.

Halperin, David M. (2002). *How to Do the History of Homosexuality*. Chicago and London: Chicago University Press.

Harder, M. A., Regtuit, R. F., and Wakker, G. C. (eds.) (2002) (eds). *Hellenistic Epigrams*. Hellenistica Groningana 6. Leuven: Peeters.

Hardwick, Lorna (2000). *Translating Words, Translating Cultures*. London: Duckworth.

Hardwick, Lorna (2003). *Reception Studies*. Greece and Rome New Surveys 33. Oxford: Oxford University Press.

Hardwick, Lorna, and Stray, Christopher (2008) (eds). *A Companion to Classical Receptions*. Malden, MA, and Oxford: Wiley-Blackwell.

Hariman, Robert (1990). 'Performing the Law: Popular Trials and Social Knowledge', in Robert Hariman (ed.), *Popular Trials: Rhetoric, Mass Media, and the Law*. Tuscaloosa, AL: University of Alabama Press, 17–30.

Harris, Judith (2007). *Pompeii Awakened: A Story of Rediscovery*. London and New York: I. B. Tauris.

Harrison, Stephen (2011). 'Bulwer-Lytton's *The Last Days of Pompeii*: Re-creating the City', in Hales and Paul (2011), 75–89.

Harrison, Stephen, and Stray, Christopher (2012) (eds), *Expurgating the Classics: Editing out in Latin and Greek*. Bristol: Bristol Classical Press.

Hayes, Julie Candler (2009). *Translation, Subjectivity, and Culture in France and England, 1600–1800*. Palo Alto, CA: Stanford University Press.

Haynes, Kenneth (2003). *English Literature and Ancient Languages*. Oxford: Oxford University Press.

Haynes, Kenneth (2006). 'Introduction', in Peter Francis and Kenneth Haynes (eds), *The Oxford History of Literary Translation in English*, iv. *1790–1900*. Oxford: Oxford University Press, 155–67.

Haynes, Kenneth (2007). 'The Modern Reception of Greek Epigram', in Bing and Bruss (2007), 566–83.

Haywood, Ian (2004). *The Revolution in Popular Literature: Print, Politics and the People, 1790–1860*. Cambridge: Cambridge University Press.

Heacox, Thomas L. (2004). '"Idealized through Greece": Hellenism and Homoeroticism in Works by Wilde, Symonds, Mann, and Forster', *Sexuality and Culture*, 8/2: 52–79.

Heidt, Sarah J. (2003). '"Let JAS words stand": Publishing John Addington Symonds's Desires', *Victorian Studies*, 46.1: 7–31.

Henderson, John (2007). 'The "Euripides Red" Story: Best-Laid Plans at OUP', in Stray (2007c), 143–75.

References   371

Henderson, Jeffrey (1991). *The Maculate Muse: Obscene Language in Attic Comedy.* 2nd edn. New York: Oxford University Press.

Hills, Matt (2002). *Fan Cultures.* Abingdon and New York: Routledge.

Hingley, Richard (2000). *Roman Officers and English Gentlemen: The Imperial Origins of Roman Archaeology.* London: Routledge.

Hingley, Richard (2001) (ed.). 'Images of Rome: Perceptions of Ancient Rome in Europe and the United States in the Modern Age', *Journal of Roman Archaeology,* suppl. 44.

Hirsch, Marjorie Wing (2007). *Romantic Lieder and the Search for Lost Paradise.* Cambridge: Cambridge University Press.

Hoare, Philip (1995). *Noel Coward: A Biography.* Chicago: University of Chicago Press.

Hobsbawm, Eric (1983). 'Mass-Producing Traditions: Europe, 1870–1914', in Hobsbawm and Ranger (1983), 263–307.

Hobsbawm, Eric, and Ranger, Terence (1983) (eds). *The Invention of Tradition.* Cambridge: Cambridge University Press.

Holliday, Peter J. (2000). 'Symonds and the Model of Ancient Greece', in Pemble (2000b), 81–101.

Hollis, A. S. (1997). 'A Fragmentary Addiction', in Most (1997a), 111–23.

Holzberg, Niklas (2002). *Martial und das antike Epigramm.* Darmstadt: Wissenschaftliche Buchgesellschaft.

Hooker, Philip (2003). 'The Presidents', in in Christopher Stray (ed.), *The Classical Association: The First Century, 1903–2003.* Oxford: Oxford University Press. 183–90.

Hopkins, David (2008). 'On Anthologies', *Cambridge Quarterly,* 27/3: 285–305.

Huet, Valerie (1999). 'Napoleon I: A New Augustus?', in Catharine Edwards (1999), 53–69.

Hughes, Linda K. (2005). *Graham R.: Rosamund Marriott Watson, Woman of Letters.* Athens, OH: Ohio University Press.

Hunter, Richard (2004). 'Notes on the Lithika of Posidippus', in Acosta-Hughes, Kosmetatou, and Baumbach (2004), 94–104.

Hurst, Isobel (2006). *Victorian Women Writers and the Classics: The Feminine of Homer.* Oxford: Oxford University Press.

Hyde, Hartford Montgomery (1972). *The Trials of Oscar Wilde.* 2nd edn. New York: Dover.

Inman, Billie Andrew (1991). 'Estrangement and Connection: Walter Pater, Benjamin Jowett, and William M. Hardinge', in Laurel Brake and Ian Small (eds), *Pater in the 1990s.* London: ELT Press, 1–20.

Irwin, Terence H. (1992). 'Eminent Victorians and Greek Ethics: Sidgwick, Green, and Aristotle', in Schultz (1992), 279–310.

Iser, Wolfgang (1978). *The Act of Reading: A Theory of Aesthetic Response.* Baltimore and London: Johns Hopkins University Press.

Iser, Wolfgang (1987). *Walter Pater: The Aesthetic Moment*, trans. David Henry Wilson. Cambridge: Cambridge University Press.

Ivory, Yvonne (2009). *The Homosexual Revival of Renaissance Style, 1850–1930*. Houndmills: Palgrave Macmillan.

Jauss, Hans Robert (1982). *Towards an Aesthetic of Reception*, trans. Timothy Bahti. Brighton: Harvester.

Jenkins, Henry (1992). *Textual Poachers: Television Fans and Participatory Culture*. New York: Routledge.

Jenkins, Henry (2006). *Fans, Bloggers, and Gamers: Exploring Participatory Culture*. New York and London: New York University Press.

Jenkins, Keith (1995). *On 'What is History?': From Carr and Elton to Rorty and White*. London: Routledge.

Jenkins, Thomas E. (2005). 'An American "Classic": Hillman and Cullen's Mimes of the Courtesans', *Arethusa*, 38: 387–414.

Jenkyns, Richard (1980). *The Victorians and Ancient Greece*. Cambridge, MA: Harvard University Press.

Johnson, Barbara (2004). 'Headnotes', in Di Leo (2004), 384–94.

Jordan, John O. (1995). 'Introduction: Publishing History as Hypertext', in Jordan and Patten (1995), 1–18.

Jordan, John O., and Patten, Robert L. (1995) (eds). *Literature in the Marketplace: Nineteenth-Century British Publishing and Reading Practices*. Cambridge: Cambridge University Press.

Kandl, John (2001). 'The Politics of Keats's Early Poetry', in Susan J. Watson (ed.), *The Cambridge Companion to Keats*. Cambridge: Cambridge University Press, 1–19.

Kane, Kathryn (2011). 'Alphabet of Gems: The Language of Stones during the Regency' <https://regencyredingote.wordpress.com/2011/01/07/alphabet-of-gems-the-language-of-stones-during-the-regency/> (accessed 1 May 2013).

Kaplan, Maurice B. (1999). 'Who's Afraid Of John Saul? Urban Culture and the Politics of Desire in Late Victorian London', *GLQ: A Journal of Lesbian and Gay Studies*, 5/3: 267–314.

Kaplan, Maurice B. (2005). *Sodom on the Thames: Sex, Love, and Scandal in Wilde Times*. Ithaca, NY: Cornell University Press.

Kaster, Robert A. (1997). 'Fruitful Disputes: Controversy and its Consequences in the (More or Less Recent) History of Classical Studies', *Transactions of the American Philological Society*, 127: 345–7.

Kemp, Jonathan (2000). 'A Problem in Gay Heroics: Symonds and *l'amour de l'impossible*', in Pemble (2000b.), 46–61.

Kennedy, Alison (2001). 'John Leitch, John Kenrick, History and Myth: The Textbook as a Signpost of Intellectual Change', *Paradigm*, 2/4: 13–22.

Klein, Lawrence E. (1995). 'Politeness for Plebes: Consumption and Social Identity in Early-Eighteenth-Century England', in Bermingham and Brewer (1995), 362–82.

Knoepflmacher, U. C., and Tennyson, G. B. (1977) (eds). *Nature and the Victorian Imagination*. Berkeley and Los Angeles, and London: University of California Press.

Kuipers, Christopher M. (2003). 'The Anthology/Corpus Dynamic: A Field History of the Canon', *College Literature*, 30/2: 51–71.

Kuipers, Christopher M. (2005). 'The Diachronic Canon: Two Possible Universals in the Evolution of Literary Anthologies', *Consciousness, Literature and the Arts*, 6/2.

Lathrop, Henry B. (1933). *Translations from the Classics into English from Caxton to Chapman 1477–1620*. University of Wisconsin Studies in Language and Literature 35. Madison: University of Wisconsin Press.

Lawton, Philip (2012). 'For the Gentleman and the Scholar: Sexual and Scatological References in the Loeb Classical Library', in Harrison and Stray (2012), 175–96.

Leap, William L. (2010). 'Homophobia as Moral Geography', Gender and Language 4/2: 187–220.

Leary, Tim J. (2012). 'Modifying Martial in Nineteenth-Century Britain', in Harrison and Stray (2012.), 127–42.

Lauritsen, John (2005). 'Hellenism and Homoeroticism in Shelley and his Circle', Journal of Homosexuality, 49: 357–76.

Lefkowitz, Mary L. (1981). *The Lives of the Greek Poets*. Baltimore: Johns Hopkins University Press.

Leitch, Vincent B. (2004). 'Ideology of Headnotes', in Di Leo (2004), 373–83.

Leoussi, Athena S. (1999). 'Nationalism and the Antique in Nineteenth-Century English and French Art', in Wyke and Biddiss (1999b), 79–105.

Levine, George (1977). 'High and Low: Ruskin and the Novelists', in Knoepflmacher and Tennyson (1977), 137–52.

Lianeri, Alexandra, and Zajko, Vanda (2008) (eds). *Translation and the Classic: Identity as Change in the History of Culture*. Oxford: Oxford University Press.

Littlewood, Ian (2001). *Sultry Climates: Travel and Sex since the Grand Tour*. London: John Murray.

Liversidge, Michael, and Edwards, Catharine (1996) (eds). *Imagining Rome: British Artists and Rome in the Nineteenth Century*. London: Merrell Holberton.

Livesey, Ruth (2007). *Socialism, Sex and the Culture of Aestheticism in Britain, 1880–1914*. Oxford: Oxford University Press.

Livingstone, Niall, and Nisbet, Gideon (2010). *Epigram*. Greece and Rome New Surveys 38. Cambridge: Cambridge University Press.

Lloyd-Jones, Hugh (1982). *Blood for the Ghosts: Classical Influences in the Nineteenth and Twentieth Centuries*. Baltimore: Johns Hopkins University Press.

Luz, Menahem (1988). 'Salam, Meleager!', *Studi Italiani di Filologia Classica*, 6: 222–31.

374 *References*

McDermott, Ryan Patrick (2008). 'The Gay Hermeneutic: Victorian Genealogies of Homosexuality and the Practice of Reading'. Ph.D. thesis, University of California, Berkeley.

Macfarlane, Robert (2003). *Mountains of the Mind: A History of a Fascination*. London: Granta.

McKenna, Neil (1995). 'Men Loving Men: Taxonomies of Male-to-Male Sexualities in the Developing World', *Perversions: The International Journal of Gay and Lesbian Studies*, 5: 54–101.

Mader, Donald H. (2005). 'The Greek Mirror: The Uranians and their Use of Greece', *Journal of Homosexuality*, 49/3–4: 377–420.

Majeed, Javed (1999). 'Comparativism and References to Rome in British Imperial Attitudes to India', in Edwards (ed.), 88–109.

Malamud, Margaret (2009). *Ancient Rome and Modern America*. Malden, MA, and Oxford: Blackwell.

Mantena, Rama (2010). 'Imperial Ideology and the Uses of Rome in Discourses on Britain's Indian Empire', in Bradley (2010c), 54–73.

Marchand, Susan L. (1996). *Down from Olympus: Archaeology and Philhellenism in Germany, 1750–1970*. Princeton: Princeton University Press.

Marlowe, John (1970). *Cromer in Egypt*. New York: Praeger.

Marsden, Bill (1997). 'Book of Nature and the Stuff of Epitaphs: Religion, Romanticism and Some Historical Connections in Environmental Education', *Paragraph*, 24: 4–15.

Martindale, Charles, and Thomas, Richard F. (2006) (eds). *Classics and the Uses of Reception*. Malden, MA, and Oxford: Blackwell.

Matthiesen, Francis O. (1931). *Translation, an Elizabethan Art*. Cambridge, MA: Harvard University Press.

Mauss, Marcel (1935). sshan Artioness.lhellenis, *Journal de psychologie normal et pathologique*, 32: 271 de

Mayer, D. (1994). *Playing out the Empire: Ben-Hur and Other Toga Plays and Films, 1883–1908: A Critical Anthology*. Oxford: Clarendon Press.

Mays, Kelly J. (1995). 'The Disease of Reading and Victorian Periodicals', in Jordan and Patten (1995), 165–94.

Mendelsohn, Daniel (2010). 'Oscar Wilde: Classics Scholar', *New York Review of Books*, 57/17, 11 November, 61–5.

Mikhail, E. H. (1979) (ed.). *Oscar Wilde: Interviews and Recollections*. 2 vols. New York: Barnes and Noble; London: Macmillan.

Mirzoeff, Nicholas (1999). *An Introduction to Visual Culture*. London and New York: Routledge.

Monsman, Gerald C. (1970). 'Old Mortality at Oxford', *Studies in Philology*, 67/3: 359–89.

Montserrat, Dominic (1998a). 'Unidentified Human Remains: Mummies and the Erotics of Biography', in Montserrat (1998b), 162–97.

Montserrat, Dominic (1998b) (ed.). *Changing Bodies, Changing Meanings: Studies on the Human Body in Antiquity.* London and New York: Routledge.

Moore, Dafydd (2004). *Ossian and Ossianism.* 4 vols. London: Routledge.

Morgan, Prys (1983). 'From a Death to a View: The Hunt for the Welsh Past in the Romantic Period', in Hobsbawm and Ranger (1983), 43–100.

Morley, Neville (2004). '"Unhistorical Greeks": Myth, History and the Uses of Antiquity', in Paul Bishop (ed.), *Nietzsche and Antiquity: His Reaction and Response to the Classical Tradition.* Rochester, NY, and Woodbridge: Camden House.

Morris, Mick (2007). '"Sneaking, foul-mouthed, scurrilous reptiles": The Battle of the Grammars, Edinburgh 1849–50', in Stray (2007c), 55–73.

Mort, Frank (2000). *Dangerous Sexualities: Medico-Moral Politics in England since 1830.* 2nd edn. London and New York: Routledge. (1 st edn, 1987.)

Morwood, James (2012). '"From out the Schoolboy's Vision": Expurgation and the Young Reader', in Harrison and Stray (2012), 163–73.

Most, Glenn W. (1997a) (ed.). *Collecting Fragments—Fragmente sammeln.* Göttingen: Vandenhoeck and Ruprecht.

Most, Glenn W. (1997b). 'One Hundred Years of Fractiousness: Disciplining Polemics in Nineteenth-Century German Classical Scholarship', *Transactions of the American Philological Association*, 127: 349–61.

Najarian, James (2002). *Victorian Keats: Manliness, Sexuality, and Desire.* Houndmills: Palgrave Macmillan.

Najarian, James (2003). 'Canonicity, Marginality, and the Celebration of the Minor', *Victorian Poetry*, 41/4: 570–4.

Nead, Linda (2000). *Victorian Babylon: People, Streets and Images in Nineteenth-Century London.* New Haven and London: Yale University Press.

Nelson, Cary (1996). 'Literature as Cultural Studies: "American" Poetry of the Spanish Civil War', in Cary Nelson and Dilip Parameshwar Gaonkar (eds), *Disciplinarity and Dissent in Cultural Studies.* New York and London: Routledge, 63–102.

Nisbet, Gideon (1997). Review of Hallett and van Nortwick (1997) <http://bmcr.brynmawr.edu/1997/97.07.02.html> (accessed 1 May 2013).

Nisbet, Gideon (2003). *Greek Epigram in the Roman Empire: Martial's Forgotten Rivals.* Oxford: Oxford University Press.

Nisbet, Gideon (2006). *Ancient Greece in Film and Popular Culture.* Expanded 2nd edn 2008. Exeter: Exeter Press.

Nisbet, Gideon (2012a). 'Imperial Satire Revoiced', in Susanna Braund and Josiah Osgood (eds), *A Companion to Persius and Juvenal.* Malden, MA, and Oxford:Wiley-Blackwell, 486–512.

Nisbet, Gideon (2012b). 'Flowers in the Wilderness: Greek Epigram in the Late Nineteenth and Early Twentieth Centuries', in Harrison and Stray (2012), 73–94.

Nora, Pierre (1984–92). *Les Lieux de mémoire*. 3 vols. Paris: Gallimard.

Orrells, Daniel (2011a). *Classical Culture and Modern Masculinity*. Oxford: Oxford University Press.

Orrells, Daniel (2011b). 'Rocks, Ghosts and Footprints: Freudian Archaeology', in Hales and Paul (2011), 185–98.

Page, Denys Lionel (1955). *Sappho and Alcaeus: An Introduction to the Study of Ancient Lesbian Poetry*. Oxford: Clarendon Press.

Parker, Jan, and Mathews, Timothy (2011) (eds). *Tradition, Translation, Trauma: The Classic and the Modern*. Oxford: Oxford University Press.

Pemble, John (2000a). 'Art, Disease and Mountains', in Pemble (2000b), 1–21.

Pemble, John (2000b) (ed.). *John Addington Symonds: Culture and the Demon Desire*. Houndmills: Macmillan.

Pemble, John (2005). Review of Schultz (2004), *Journal of the History of Sexuality*, 14/1: 224–32.

Perrin, Noel (1992). *Dr Bowdler's Legacy: A History of Expurgated Books in England and America*. Rev. edn. Boston: David R. Godine.

Peters, Robert L. (1962). 'Athens and Troy: Notes on John Addington Symonds' Aestheticism', *English Literature in Transition, 1880–1920*, 5/5: 14–26.

Phelps Brown, Ernest Henry, and Hopkins, Sheila V. (1955). 'Seven Centuries of Building Wages', *Economica*, 22/87: 195–206.

Phelps Brown, Ernest Henry, and Hopkins, Sheila V. (1956). 'Seven Centuries of the Price of Consumables, Compared with Builders' Wage Rates', *Economica*, 23/92: 296–314.

Phillips, Paul T. (2002). *The Controversialist: An Intellectual Life of Goldwin Smith*. Westport: Praeger, 2002.

Plummer, Kenneth (1995). *Telling Sexual Stories: Power, Change and Social Worlds*. London and New York: Psychology Press.

Porter, James I. (2006) (ed.). *Classical Pasts: the Classical Traditions of Greece and Rome*. Princeton: Princeton University Press.

Potolsky, Matthew (2007). 'The Decadent Counterpublic', *Romanticism and Victorianism on the Net*, 48 <http://www.erudit.org/revue/ravon/2007/v/n48/017444ar.html> (accessed 1 May 2013).

Pott, John Arthur (1919). *Love Songs and Epigrams from the Anthology*. London: Kegan Paul.

Potter, Liz (2004). 'British Philhellenism and the Historiography of Greece: A Case Study of George Finlay (1799–1875)', *Historical Review*, 1: 183–206.

Potts, Alex (1994). *Flesh and the Ideal: Winckelmann and the Origins of Art History*. New Haven and London: Yale University Press.

Potts, Alex (1999). 'Walter Pater's Unsettling of the Apollonian Ideal', in Wyke and Biddiss (199b), 107–24.

Potts, Alex (2000). 'Pungent Prophecies of Art: Symonds, Pater, and Michelangelo', in Pemble (2000b), 102–21.

Prettejohn, Elizabeth (1999) (ed.). *After the Pre-Raphaelites: Art and Aestheticism in Victorian England*. Manchester: Manchester University Press.

Prins, Yopie (1999). *Victorian Sappho*. Princeton: Princeton University Press.

Proctor, Mortimer Robinson (1957). *The English University Novel*. Berkeley and Los Angeles: University of California Press.

Rabinowitz, Nancy S. (2002). 'Introduction', in Nancy S. Rabinowitz and Lisa Auanger (eds), *Among Women: From the Homosocial to the Homoerotic in the Ancient World*. Austin: University of Texas Press.

Rajak, Tessa (1999). 'Jews and Greeks: The Invention and Exploitation of Polarities in the Nineteenth Century', in Wyke and Biddiss (1999b), 57–77.

Reid, Donald M. (1996). 'Cromer and the Classics: Imperialism, Nationalism and the Greco-Roman Past in Modern Egypt', *Middle Eastern Studies*, 32/1: 1–29.

Reilly, Catherine R. (2000). *Mid-Victorian Poetry, 1860–1879: An Annotated Biobibliography*. London and New York: Cassell.

Reinhold, Meyer (1984). *Classica Americana: The Greek and Roman Heritage in the United States*. Detroit: Wayne State University Press.

Reisz, Emma (2010). 'Classics, Race, and Edwardian Anxieties about Empire', in Bradley (2010c), 210–28.

Richards, Jeffrey (1987). '"Passing the love of women": Manly Love and Victorian Society', in J. A. Mangan and James Walvin (eds), *Manliness and Morality: Middle-Class Masculinity in Britain and America, 1800–1940*. Manchester: Manchester University Press, 108–24.

Riikonen, Hannu K. (2008). 'Ezra Pound and the Greek Anthology', *Quaderni di Palazzo Serra*, 15: 181–94.

Robert, Louis (1968). 'Les Épigrammes satiriques de Lucillius sur les athlètes. Parodie et réalités', in Albrecht Dihle (ed.), *L'Épigramme Grecque*. Entretiens Hardt 14. Geneva: Fondation Hardt, 181–291.

Roberts, Deborah H. (2008). 'Translation and the "Surreptitious Classic": Obscenity and Translatability', in Lianeri and Zajko (2008), 278–311.

Robertson, David (1977). 'Mid-Victorians amongst the Alps', in Knoepflmacher and Tennyson (1977), 113–36.

Rolley, Katrina (1992). 'The Treatment of Homosexuality and The Well of Loneliness', in Paul Hyland and Neil Sammells (eds) *Writing and Censorship in Britain*. London: Routledge, Chapman and Hall, 219–31.

Rose, Jonathan (1995). 'How Historians Study Reader Response: or, what did Jo Think of Bleak House?', in Jordan and Patten (1995), 195–212.

Rosenberg, Sheila (2005). 'Encounters in the Westminster Review: Dialogues on Marriage and Divorce', in Brake and Codell (2005), 119–37.

Ross, Iain (2008). 'The New Hellenism: Oscar Wilde and Ancient Greece'. D.Phil. thesis, University of Oxford.

Ross, Iain (2009). 'Oscar Wilde in Greece: Topography and the Hellenist Imagination', *IJCT* 16/2: 176–96.

Rota, Antony (1998). *Apart from the Text*. Pinner: Private Libraries Association; New Castle, DE: Oak Knoll Press.

Ruprecht, Louis A., Jr (1996). *Afterwords: Hellenism, Modernism, and the Myth of Decadence*. Albany, NY: State University of New York Press.

Russell, Douglas G. D., Sladen, William J. L., and Ainley, David G. (2012). 'Dr George Murray Levick (1876–1956): Unpublished Notes on the Sexual Habits of the Adélie Penguin', *Polar*, 48/4: 387–93.

Russell, Mona (2001). 'Competing, Overlapping, and Contradictory Agendas: Egyptian Education under British Occupation, 1882–1922', *Comparative Studies of South Asia, Africa and the Middle East*, 21/1–2: 50–60.

Sachs, Jonathan (2010). *Romantic Antiquity: Rome in the British Imagination, 1789–1832*. Oxford: Oxford University Press.

Said, Edward (1978). *Orientalism*. Harmondsworth: Penguin.

Sauder, Gerhard (2009). 'Herder's Poetic Works, his Translations, and his Views on Poetry', in Hans Adler and Wulf Köpke (eds), *A Companion to the Works of Johann Gottfried Herder*. Rochester, NY, and Woodbridge: Boydell & Brewer, 305–30.

Schaffner, Anna Katharina (2011). 'Fiction as Evidence: On the Uses of Literature in Nineteenth-Century Sexological Discourse', *Comparative Literature Studies*, 48/2: 165–99.

Schofield, Malcolm (2003). 'The Presidential Address', in Christopher Stray (ed.), *The Classical Association: The First Century, 1903–2003*. Oxford: Oxford University Press, 193–208.

Schrift, Alan D. (2004). 'Confessions of an Anthology Editor', in Di Leo (2004), 186–204.

Schuetz, Lawrence R. (1974). 'The Suppressed "Conclusion" to the Renaissance and Pater's Modern Image', *English Literature in Transition, 1880–1920*, 17: 251–9.

Schuetz, Lawrence R. (1976). 'Pater and the Suppressed "Conclusion" to the Renaissance: Comment and Reply', *English Literature in Transition, 1880–1920*, 19: 313–21.

Schultz, Bart (1992) (ed.). *Essays on Henry Sidgwick*. Cambridge: Cambridge University Press.

Schultz, Bart (2000). 'Truth and its Consequences: The Friendship of Symonds and Henry Sidgwick', in Pemble (2000b), 22–45.

Schultz, Bart (2004). *Henry Sidgwick: Eye of the Universe. An Intellectual Biography*. Cambridge: Cambridge University Press.

Seidensticker, Bernd, Staehli, Adrian, and Wessels, Antje (2012) (eds). *Poseidippos. Die neuen Epigramme. P. Mil. Vogl. 309*. Darmstadt: Wissenschaftliche Buchgesellschaft.

Simon, Lisa (2010). 'The Anthropologic Eye: H.D.'s Call for a New Poetics', *Journal for Cultural and Religious Theory*, 10/2: 14–34.

Sinfield, Alan (1994a). *Cultural Politics—Queer Reading*. London: Routledge; Philadelphia: University of Pennsylvania Press.

Sinfield, Alan (1994b). *The Wilde Century: Effeminacy, Oscar Wilde and the Queer Moment*. New York: Columbia University Press.

Smiles, Sam (1994). *The Image of Antiquity: Ancient Britain and the Romantic Imagination*. New Haven and London: Yale University Press.

Smith, Jonathan, and Stray, Christopher (2001) (eds). *Teaching and Learning in 19th-Century Cambridge*. Woodridge: Boydell Press.

Sontag, Susan (1978). *Illness as Metaphor*. New York: Farrar, Straus and Giroux.

Spencer, Diana (2010). *Roman Landscape: Culture and Identity*. Cambridge: Cambridge University Press.

Staiger, Janet (2005). *Media Reception Studies*. New York and London: New York University Press.

Stark, Susanne (1999). *'Behind Inverted Commas': Translation and Anglo-German Cultural Relations in the Nineteenth Century*. Clevedon: Multilingual Matters.

Stevenson, Jane (1998). 'Nacktleben', in Montserrat (1998b), 198–212.

Stokes, John (1979). 'The Legend of Duse', in Fletcher (1979b), 151–72.

Stone, Marla (1999). 'A Flexible Rome: Fascism and the Cult of *romanità*', in Catharine Edwards (1999), 205–20.

Stray, Christopher (1992). *The Living Word: W. H. D. Rouse and the Crisis of Classics in Edwardian England*. London: Bristol Classical Press.

Stray, Christopher (1997). ' "Thucydides or Grote?": Classical Disputes and Disputed Classics in Nineteenth-Century Cambridge', *Transactions of the American Philological Association*, 127: 363–71.

Stray, Christopher (1998a). *Classics Transformed: Schools, Universities, and Society in England, 1830–1960*. Oxford: Oxford University Press.

Stray, Christopher (1998b). 'Schoolboys and Gentlemen: Classical Pedagogy and Authority in the English Public School', in Yun Lee Too and Niall Livingstone (eds), *Pedagogy and Power: Rhetorics of Classical Learning*. Cambridge: Cambridge University Press, 29–46.

Stray, Christopher (2004) (ed.). *Victorian Novels of Oxbridge Life*. 5 vols. Bristol: Thoemmes Continuum.

Stray, Christopher (2007a). 'Jebb's Sophocles: An Edition and its Maker', in Stray (2007c), 77–96.

Stray, Christopher (2007b). 'Politics, Culture, and Scholarship: Classics in the Quarterly Review', in J. Cutmore (ed.), *Conservatism and the Quarterly Review*. London: Pickering and Chatto, 87–106, 233–8.

Stray, Christopher (2007c) (ed.). *Classical Books: Scholarship and Publishing in Britain since 1800*. BICS Supplement 101. London.

Sullivan, John P. (1991). *Martial: The Unexpected Classic*. Cambridge: Cambridge University Press.

Sutton, Emma (2002). *Aubrey Beardsley and British Wagnerism in the 1890s: The Imperfect Wagnerites*. Oxford: Oxford University Press.

Sweet, Matthew (2001). *Inventing the Victorians*. London: Faber and Faber.

Symonds, Richard (1986). *Oxford and Empire: The Last Lost Cause?* London: Macmillan.

Symonds, Richard (1995). 'Greece, Women and the Tunnel: E. P. Warren and his Corpus Connection', *Pelican Record*, 39/2: 12–21.

Symonds, Richard (2005). 'Plato with Everything: Sir Richard Livingstone and the Greek Genius', *Pelican Record*, 42/1: 57–68.

Tarán, Sonya Lida (1979). *The Art of Variation in the Hellenistic Epigram*. Leiden: Brill.

Tarlo, Harriet (2012). 'An Insurmountable Chasm? Re-Visiting, Re-Imagining and Re-Writing Classical Pastoral through the Modernist Poetry of H.D.', *Classical Receptions* Journal, 4/2: 235–60.

Taxidou, Olga (1998). *The Mask: A Periodical Performance by Edward Gordon Craig*. Amsterdam: Harwood Academic.

Taylor, Seth (1990). *Left-Wing Nietzscheans: The Politics of German Expressionism, 1910–1920*. Berlin and New York: de Gruyter.

Thatcher, David S. (1970). *Nietzsche in England, 1890–1914: The Growth of a Reputation*. Toronto: University of Toronto Press.

Thornton, R. K. R. (1980). '"Decadence" in Later Nineteenth-Century England', in Fletcher (1979b), 15–30.

Trevor-Roper, Hugh (1983). 'The Invention of Tradition: The Highland Tradition of Scotland', in Hobsbawm and Ranger (1983), 15–41.

Tueller, Michael A. (2008). *Look Who's Talking: Innovations in Voice and Identity in Hellenistic Epigram*. Leuven: Peeters.

Turner, Frank M. (1981). *The Greek Heritage in Victorian Britain*. New Haven: Yale University Press.

Turner, Frank M. (1989). 'Why the Greeks and not the Romans in Victorian Britain?', in Clarke (1989), 61–81.

Turner, Mark W. (2005). 'Urban Encounters and Visual Play in the Yellow Book', in Brake and Codell (2005), 38–60.

Vance, Norman (1985). *The Sinews of the Spirit: The Ideal of Christian Manliness in Victorian Literature and Religious Thought*. Cambridge: Cambridge University Press.

Vance, Norman (1997). *The Victorians and Ancient Rome*. Oxford: Blackwell.

Vance, Norman (1999). 'Decadence and the Subversion of Empire', in Catharine Edwards (1999), 110–24.

Vance, Norman (2007). 'Victorian', in Craig Kallendorf (ed.), *A Companion to the Classical Tradition*. Malden, MA, and Oxford: Wiley-Blackwell, 87–100.

Vandiver, Elizabeth (2010). *Stand in the Trench, Achilles: Classical Receptions in British Poetry of the Great War*. Oxford: Oxford University Press.

Vasunia, Phiroze (2005). 'Greater Rome and Greater Britain', in Goff (2005b), 38–64.

Vasunia, Phiroze (2013). *The Classics and Colofnial India*. Oxford: Oxford University Press.

Venables, Ian (2000). 'Appendix: Symonds' Peccant Poetry', in Pemble (2000b), 178–85.

Wagner, Rudolf (1997). 'Twice Removed from the Truth: Fragment Collection in 18th and 19th Century China', in Most (1997a), 34–52.

Waller, Philip (2006). *Writers, Readers, and Reputations: Literary Life in Britain 1870–1918*. Oxford: Oxford University Press.

Waquet, Françoise (2001). *Latin, or The Empire of a Sign: From the Sixteenth to the Twentieth Centuries*, trans. John Howe. London: Verso.

Waters, Michael (1998). *The Garden in Victorian Literature*. Aldershot: Scolar Press.

Waters, Sarah (1995). '"The Most Famous Fairy in History": Antinous and Homosexual Fantasy', *Journal of the History of Sexuality*, 6/2: 194–230.

Weeks, Jeffrey (1990). *Coming Out: Homosexual Politics in Britain from the Nineteenth Century to the Present*. Rev. edn. London and New York: Quartet Books.

White, Hayden (1973). *Metahistory: The Historical Imagination in Nineteenth Century Europe*. Baltimore: Johns Hopkins University Press.

Wiener, Joel H. (1988). *Papers for the Millions: The New Journalism in Britain, 1850 to 1914*. Westport, CT: Greenwood.

Williams, Raymond (1976). *Keywords*. Glasow: Fontana/Croom Helm.

Wilson, Bee (2008). *Swindled: From Poison Sweets to Counterfeit Coffee. The Dark History of the Food Cheats*. London: John Murray.

Winterer, Caroline (2002). *The Culture of Classicism: Ancient Greece and Rome in American Intellectual Life, 1780–1910*. Baltimore and London: Johns Hopkins University Press.

Wright, Thomas (2011). 'The Difficult Art of Prose', *Oxonian Review*, 16/2 <http://www.oxonianreview.org/wp/the-difficult-art-of-prose/> (accessed 1 May 2013).

Wrigley, Amanda (2007). 'Stages of Imagination: Greek Plays on BBC Radio', in Christopher Stray (ed.), *Remaking the Classics: Literature, Genre and Media in Britain, 1800–2000*. London: Duckworth, 57–74.

Wyke, Maria (1997). 'Herculean Muscle! The Classicizing Rhetoric of Bodybuilding', *Arion*, 4/3: 51–79.

Wyke, Maria, and Biddiss, Michael (1999a). 'Introduction: Using and Abusing Antiquity', in Wyke and Biddiss (1999b), 13–17.

Wyke, Maria, and Biddiss, Michael (1999b) (eds). *The Uses and Abuses of Antiquity*. New York: Peter Lang.

Zorzi, Rosella Mamoli (2000). 'Into Forbidden Territory: Symonds and Tiepolo', in Pemble (2000b), 122–35.

Index

Achilles and Patroclus 118n. 10, 137, 172, 201, 320
Aeschylus 46, 79, 140, 147, 150, 171, 196 n. 84, 234
Aestheticism 20, 96, 120, 212, 214–5, 231–2, 264, 305
Agathias 56, 102, 160–2, 184, 198, 255, 286 n. 16, 296: see also Anthology, Greek
Alcaeus 145, 292 n. 33
Alma-Tadema, Sir Lawrence 22–3, 144, 160
Alps and Alpinism 47, 116, 145–50, 165–9, 174, 196, 200, 234–5
amateur, cult of the 19, 64, 109–10, 112, 260, 263, 282, 310–16, 328, 333
Anacreon 107, 207, 249
Ancient Classics for English Readers 175–9
Anthologia Polyglotta: see Wellesley, Henry
anthologization 13–14, 31 n. 71, 34–5, 42, 72, 104–5, 286, 315, 324, 337
and canon formation 32, 42, 231, 238–9, 242, 246, 248, 256, 330–1, 338
Anthology, Greek 16–17, 21, 55–8, 231, 315, 336, 342
Anthology of Constantine Cephalas 15–18, 56, 59–60, 106, 151, 154–5, 185, 250, 254 n. 77, 291, 296, 318
Anthology of Diogenianus 15, 315
Anthology of Maximus Planudes 16–18, 52, 54, 60, 174–6, 178–9, 197, 254 n. 77, 277, 291, 303–4, 309, 311
Cycle of Agathias 49–50, 152–3, 315 n. 96
Garland of Meleager: see Meleager
Garland of Philip 49, 56, 152–3, 255
Antinous and Hadrian 201 n. 99, 213, 328, 333–4
Antipater 49, 57, 159–60, 249
Anyte 14, 55, 145
Archilochus 55, 102, 182
Aristophanes 80, 129, 139, 195, 219, 234–5, 303 n. 67
Arnold, Matthew, and Arnoldianism
as editor of Wordsworth 242
as poet 117 n. 7
Hellenism and Hebraism 3–5, 126–7, 132–3, 142, 194, 215–6, 233–4, 253–4, 257, 296, 298, 303, 305–7
'sweetness and light' 2, 21, 132–3, 157, 166, 172, 212, 215–16, 329

Asclepiades 48
Athenaeum 68 n. 87, 325
Aulus Gellius 64
Ausonius 44 n. 12, 83

Baring, Evelyn 138 n. 78, 258–63, 271, 277, 282 n. 8, 287, 325, 327 n. 10, 342
Baudelaire 120
Beardsley, Aubrey 197, 235, 246, 270, 319
'Beauty', as topos 75, 155, 158, 164, 166, 189, 193–4, 197, 199, 231–2, 237, 251, 253–4, 262, 266–7, 296, 301, 317 n. 100
Becker, Wilhelm: see *Charicles*
Benson, A. C. 282 n. 4, 287–90
Blackwood, John 178, 180
Blackwood's Edinburgh Magazine 41 n. 5, 61, 66–7, 103, 107–8, 148, 178–82, 185–8, 194, 238, 342 n. 4
Bland, Robert 39–44, 46–60, 63–4, 68–75, 77–8, 90, 94 n. 58, 97, 102, 138 n. 78, 150–1, 153–4, 161, 197, 243, 248, 292, 295, 305, 332, 336, 338, 342
Blomfield, Charles 61 n. 67, 79–80
Bowra, Maurice 82, 330
Brooke, Alfred 129–30, 343
Browne, Robert William 80
Brown, Horatio 220 n. 168, 230–1
Buck, Mitchell 268–9, 336
Burges, George 96–7, 100–4, 109–10, 112, 138, 150, 336
Burns, Robert 186–7, 337 n. 32
Butcher, Samuel 233 n. 18, 235, 257, 329
Butler, Alfred 219, 259 n. 93, 281 n. 3, 311, 336
Byron, Lord George Gordon 40, 59–60, 63, 67 n. 86, 68–9, 72, 75–6, 342

Callimachus 48, 79, 91 n. 46, 97 n. 65, 140, 159–60, 236, 331
Cambridge University 6, 19, 40, 63, 111 n. 111, 123, 218 n. 162
Carpenter, Edward 229, 264, 266, 272–6
Catullus 15, 289, 294, 327
censorship and expurgation 1, 16–17, 27, 51–4, 72–3, 163–4, 174–5, 183, 185, 206 n. 118, 212 n. 139, 237, 242–4, 252–3, 262, 266–7, 276–7, 291, 294, 304, 306, 307 n. 75, 309–10, 321, 336, 338